The Politics of the Presidency

The Politics of the Presidency

REVISED SEVENTH EDITION

Joseph A. Pika, *University of Delaware*

John Anthony Maltese, *University of Georgia*

CQ PRESS

A Division of SAGE
Washington, D.C.

CQ Press
2300 N Street, NW, Suite 800
Washington, DC 20037

Phone: 202-729-1900; toll-free, 1-866-4CQ-PRESS (1-866-427-7737)

Web: www.cqpress.com

Cover design: Malcolm McGaughy, McGaughy Design
Cover photos: *Top:* ASSOCIATED PRESS; *Bottom:* AP Images/Charles Dharapak
Composition: C&M Digitals (P) Ltd.

⊗ The paper used in this publication exceeds the requirements of the American National Standard for Information Sciences—Permanence of Paper for Printed Library Materials, ANSI Z39.48-1992.

Printed and bound in the United States of America

13   12   11   10   09   1   2   3   4   5

LIBRARY OF CONGRESS CATALOGING-IN-PUBLICATION DATA

Pika, Joseph August, 1947-
   The politics of the presidency / Joseph A. Pika, John Anthony Maltese. – Rev. 7th ed.
      p. cm.
   Includes bibliographical references and index.
   ISBN 978-0-87289-469-3 (pbk. : alk. paper) 1. Presidents–United States–Textbooks. I. Maltese, John Anthony. II. Title.

   JK516.P53 2010
   352.230973–dc22

                              2009023508

To Mary and Anna

Contents

Tables and Figures

FIGURES

Preface

Few if any presidents have entered office amidst the high levels of excitement and expectation that surrounded Barack Obama. As the nation's first president of color, Obama broke a barrier that had stood for more than two centuries. But he also confronted a remarkably challenging list of public problems. At the top of the list was the worst economic recession in more than half a century, and that was followed by two wars, a dysfunctional health care system, a rapidly warming planet, widespread public distrust of politics, and a Washington riven by partisan discord. The nation wondered, as it has with forty-three other individuals, whether this president would succeed.

After more than two centuries of change and development, the presidency stands not only as the nation's preeminent public office but also as its most problematic. Because presidents today are far more important for peace and prosperity than were their nineteenth-century counterparts, ensuring the selection of qualified candidates and enhancing the winner's effectiveness in office are major concerns of specialists and citizens alike. In the post–World War II period, however, few presidents have left office with a record of unqualified success. In fact, academic and media observers have labeled most presidents since Lyndon B. Johnson as "failures," although reputations sometimes improve with the passage of time.

Johnson enjoyed unparalleled success in getting his Great Society legislative program through Congress, but he could not extricate himself or the country from the Vietnam War. Richard Nixon managed to bring the war to an end and initiate new relationships with the Soviet Union and China, but Watergate cost him the confidence of the country. Gerald Ford and Jimmy Carter failed to convince voters that they could exercise effective leadership. Like Johnson, Ronald Reagan persuaded Congress to approve his program of economic reforms, but the budgetary consequences of those policies and his mishandling of the Iran-contra affair tarnished his reputation—a reputation that is improving as time goes by. George H. W. Bush and Bill Clinton were threatened by the same difficulties that beset Ford and Carter—a perception of ineffectiveness. Clinton also came to be viewed as possessing a severely flawed character, committing errors in his personal life that prompted an unsuccessful effort to have him removed from office. During his two terms, George W. Bush's public approval ratings went from the highest ever recorded to among the lowest, dragged down by the war in Iraq, the Hurricane Katrina disaster, and a meltdown of the nation's financial system that dominated his last months in office. Lost along the way was Bush's ambitious second-term agenda, which included Social Security reform, immigration reform, and rewriting the tax code, as well as his party's control of Congress. Given the inflated expectations of performance held by the public and political elites, it is reasonable to wonder if any modern president can be considered a success. It should be noted, however, that most of these failed chief executives contributed to the public's negative perception through their own actions.

Our focus in *The Politics of the Presidency* is on how presidents govern—the country and in Washington. The book views the presidency as essentially a political office; that is, the chief executive must govern more through skilled political leadership than through the assertion of constitutional prerogatives. We examine how effectiveness in office varies with the character, personality, and political style of the incumbent. Major developments in society, the U.S. political system, and the international arena also affect how well or how poorly a president performs in office. By examining this full range of influences, *The Politics of the Presidency* provides a comprehensive treatment of the nation's most important political office.

Part I begins with an analysis of the origins and development of the presidency and an examination of the changing conceptions of the office. It then explores the president's relations with the public in electoral politics and in the process of governing. Next, it looks at the kinds of people who have become president and how they interact with the office itself. Part II analyzes the president's relations with other government elites— members of Congress, the bureaucracy, and the judiciary. Part III focuses on how presidents formulate and implement domestic, economic, and national security policies. The book concludes with an analysis of Obama's first one hundred days in office.

This revised edition includes extensive discussions of George W. Bush's terms in office, the 2008 presidential election campaign, the first few months of the Obama administration, and the new president's personal history. Chapters have been thoroughly updated to provide coverage of the unitary executive, the Democrats' return to power in Congress, recent and anticipated Supreme Court appointments, the role of the vice president, struggles with Congress over Iraq funding, Obama's ambitious domestic agenda, and both the onset of and response to the economic recession that began in 2007. From the first Electoral College misfire in more than a century, to the terrorist attacks of 9/11 and the ensuing wars in Afghanistan and Iraq, the growing role of religion in politics, and Obama's electrifying victory, we cover the twists and turns of the past decade while incorporating findings from a wide range of scholarship. At the same time we have sought to retain a strong appreciation for historical development, starting with an exploration of the constitutional foundations of the presidency.

We wish to thank Philip Mundo and Thomas Langston as well as three reviewers—Suzanne Gold, Pennsylvania State University; Michael Mezey, DePaul University; and Charles Smith, Ohio State University—for their helpful comments on the revised sixth edition. Their reflections helped our own thinking, even if we did not always follow their advice.

We are grateful to Brenda Carter, Charisse Kiino, Allison McKay, and Sarah Fell of CQ Press for their encouragement and contributions to this edition. Carolyn Goldinger improved this edition with her fine copyediting. We also appreciate the research assistance provided over the years by Elizabeth Coggins, Mark Cutrona, Julia Kohen, Josh Templet, Brian Beedenbender, Rebecca Riley, and Amanda Rosenburg, as well as the clipping services contributed by Frank Langr. John Maltese accepts primary responsibility for chapters 1, 3, 7, and 11, and Joseph Pika does so for chapters 2, 4–6, and 8–10.

CHAPTER 1

The Changing Presidency

The White House—nerve center of the executive branch and home of its chief.

For most Americans the president is the focal point of public life. Almost every day, we see the president on television newscasts interpreting current events, meeting with foreign dignitaries, proposing policy, or grappling with national problems. This person appears to be in charge, and such recurrent images of an engaged leader are reassuring. But the reality of the presidency rests on a very different truth: presidents are seldom in command and usually must negotiate with others to achieve their goals. It is only by exercising adroit political skill in winning public and elite support and knowing how to use it that a president can succeed in office. This lesson has come to dominate scholarly accounts of the presidency, but it has not always been fully appreciated by either the public or the presidents themselves.

The Scope of Presidential Power

In some respects, modern presidents are stronger than ever before. At the beginning of the twentieth century presidents embraced new, expansive views of presidential power that by midcentury were accepted as normal. They used the power of the "bully pulpit" to shape public opinion. With the advent of radio and television, they became the leading voice in government. Congress added to the power of presidents by requiring them to submit annual federal budgets for congressional approval—an action that made presidents policy leaders in a way they had never been before. Staff support for presidents multiplied. And by leading the United States to victory in two world wars and playing for high stakes in the Cold War, presidents took center stage on the world scene.

And yet, since World War II, we have witnessed a string of "failed" or otherwise abbreviated presidencies. Of the ten presidents serving from 1945 through the end of the twentieth century, only three—Dwight D. Eisenhower, Ronald Reagan, and Bill Clinton—served out two full terms of office. Despite strong public support when they were thrust into the presidency, Harry S. Truman and Lyndon Baines Johnson left office repudiated by their party after they involved the country in controversial military conflicts abroad. Both were eligible to run for another term, but neither chose to do so. John F. Kennedy was assassinated before completing his first term. Richard Nixon resigned in disgrace two years after his landslide reelection. Nixon's vice president, Gerald R. Ford, failed to win the presidency in his own right after completing Nixon's term. Jimmy Carter lost his reelection bid after his public approval ratings plummeted to a record low of 21 percent because of the Iranian hostage crisis and runaway inflation. George H. W. Bush, whose approval rating skyrocketed to 89 percent during the Persian Gulf War, then confronted an economic recession and criticism of his domestic agenda and was not reelected. Even Reagan and Clinton were distracted by scandal in their second terms. Reagan faced congressional investigations and an independent counsel probe into the Iran-contra affair. Clinton was subjected to an independent counsel probe and became the first president since Andrew Johnson in 1868 to be impeached by the House of Representatives. Like Johnson, Clinton was acquitted by the Senate. Moreover, both Reagan and Clinton were constrained in their second terms by a Congress controlled by the opposition party.

George W. Bush found himself in a similar predicament in his second term. Democrats won control of both houses of Congress in the 2006 midterm elections. The Democratic victory paved the way for congressional investigations of alleged abuses by the administration and led to heightened oversight of the president's war strategy in Iraq. It also made it more difficult for the president to secure passage of his legislative proposals. Bush's job approval rating plummeted. By October 2008 his Gallup approval rating stood at 25 percent—down from a high of 90 percent in the aftermath of the September 11, 2001, terrorist attacks. Bush's last Gallup approval rating before he left office in January 2009 was 34 percent.[1] His experience reminds us that presidential power is not a fixed commodity. Formal powers mean little if presidents cannot convince others to follow their lead. As Richard Neustadt so succinctly put it: "Presidential power is the power to persuade."[2]

Dramatic changes in presidential fortunes are not new to American politics, nor are "failed" presidencies. Only about 20 percent of all U.S. presidents have served out two full terms. Through both success and failure, however, one might think that constitutional provisions would serve as a steady source of presidential power. But, as the following sections demonstrate, those provisions were not only the subject of great debate at the Constitutional Convention but also have been interpreted differently by presidents and others ever since. Quite simply, the scope of presidential power and the conceptions of the office have changed dramatically over the years.

Inventing the Presidency

Those who invented the presidency in 1787 did not expect the office to become the nation's central political institution. In fact, Article II of the Constitution, which deals with the executive branch, is known for its brevity and lack of clarity, particularly in comparison with the carefully detailed description of the legislative branch in Article I. But within the presidency's vague constitutional description lay the seeds of a far more powerful position, one that has grown through elaboration of its explicit, **enumerated powers** as well as interpretation of its **implied** and **inherent powers.** Moreover, through the years Congress and the public have caused the range of responsibilities associated with the presidency to expand, particularly in response to changes in society and America's position in the world. What has developed since 1789 is the office that now stands at the center of American government and American politics. As Stephen Skowronek puts it, the president has become "the lightning rod of national politics."[3]

The office of the presidency gained stature and a set of precedents from its initial occupant, George Washington. During the nineteenth century, however, the office languished, so much so that Lord Bryce, the British chronicler of American government, felt compelled to explain in 1890 that because of the institution's weaknesses, great men do not become president. Government during this period centered on Congress and political parties, an American invention the founders did not anticipate. A few presidents—most notably Thomas Jefferson, Andrew Jackson, and Abraham Lincoln—seemed to foreshadow strong presidents of the future, but most receded quickly from history. How, then, did the presidency come to assume its

This is James Hoban's original architectural drawing of the White House from 1792. Like the building itself, the office of the presidency has changed over time.

exalted position? The answer is complex and involves a variety of factors. At one level, the original design of the office—its structure, mode of selection, and powers—continues to exercise important influence on its operation today. But the office has changed over time in response to the influence of its occupants, changing expectations in Congress and by the public, and the internal dynamics of institutional development.

Constitutional Design

The events leading to the American Revolution led the colonists to disparage anything resembling a monarch. Thomas Paine's enormously influential pamphlet, *Common Sense,* published in January 1776, sharply dismissed the institution of monarchy, calling it "the most prosperous invention the Devil ever set on foot for the promotion of idolatry."[4] Paine called for a new government that had no executive. Some 120,000 copies of *Common Sense* were sold in just the three months following its publication.[5] The pamphlet's rallying cry against monarchy and executive power had hit a nerve.

In the weeks leading up to the Declaration of Independence, the Continental Congress urged the colonies to adopt new constitutions in anticipation of statehood. The resulting state constitutions drafted in 1776 and 1777 "systematically emasculated the power of the governors."[6] Pennsylvania's constitution, drafted by

Benjamin Franklin, provided for a unicameral legislature but no chief executive at all. Those states that did create chief executives made them subordinate to the legislature. Most governors served one-year terms, were elected by the legislature, and had little or no appointment or veto powers.[7] Even where governors were not chosen by the legislature (such as in Massachusetts), their powers were checked by a privy council.[8] New York stood out as the exception to this practice of weak governors and strong legislatures.[9]

As a result, most state legislatures became all-powerful, which led to something of a backlash against strong legislatures by other participants and observers of the political process. For example, after serving as governor of Virginia for two years, Thomas Jefferson strongly criticized the concentration of power in the Virginia legislature. Although the Virginia Constitution explicitly called for the separation of the three branches, the executive and judicial branches were so dependent upon the legislative branch that their powers had been eviscerated. Although mindful of the fear of executive power, Jefferson wrote that his experience with the Virginia legislature had convinced him that "173 despots would surely be as oppressive as one."[10] If an unchecked executive could lead to tyranny, so too could an unchecked legislature. These experiences would inform the delegates to the Constitutional Convention in 1787 and make them more willing to accept a strong executive than they would have been immediately after the Revolution.

Experience with the Articles of Confederation also would inform the delegates. The articles were a compact among the thirteen states that the Continental Congress had endorsed in 1777 and the states had ratified by 1781. The articles not only avoided the creation of anything resembling a president but also failed even to create an independent executive branch. Over time, this omission proved problematic. Attempts to administer laws through ad hoc committees, councils, or conventions proved unsuccessful, and Congress found it necessary to create several permanent departments in 1781 (including treasury, foreign affairs, and war). Although Congress appointed eminent men such as Robert Livingston, John Jay, and Robert Morris to head them, the departments remained mere appendages of the legislature.[11] Because the articles also failed to create a federal judiciary, the resulting government revolved around a single legislative body. In their zeal to ward off monarchy, the writers of the articles ignored the principle of separation of powers. And because the states had not delegated much power to the national government under the new scheme, the Confederation Congress remained impotent. Indeed, the national government had so little power to control the states that the confederation seemed to be but a "cobweb."[12] Congress did not even have the authority to regulate commerce among the states. This flaw led to a dire situation in which states fought with each other for economic advantage. Protective tariffs and trade barriers became routine weapons used by one state against another. Trade was further complicated by the states' different currencies. Some states went so far as to pass legislation canceling their debts. With no federal judiciary to turn to, those affected by such legislation sometimes had no legal recourse. The resulting chaos became a driving force for the Constitutional Convention.

Riots and mob actions in various states, culminating in Shays's Rebellion in Massachusetts, also signaled the need for change. Shays's Rebellion—an uprising in 1786–1787 by more than two thousand farmers who faced foreclosures because of high property taxes and economic depression—underscored the chaos. Massachusetts had to rely on a volunteer army to stop the rebellion because Congress was powerless to act. This failure of Congress highlighted the need for a national government capable of maintaining public order and prompted several states to vote to send delegates to the proposed Constitutional Convention. Even more significant, it helped to legitimize the idea of a strong *executive.* As Forrest McDonald has written: "Shays' Rebellion stimulated many Americans, especially in New England, to talk openly of monarchy as a safer guardian of liberty and property than republican institutions could be, particularly in a country as large as the United States." [13]

The delegates to the Constitutional Convention came to Philadelphia with these problems in mind. They agreed that the power of the national government had to be increased, although they disagreed over *how* to increase it and how *much* to increase it. Virtually all agreed that the new constitution should impose some form of separation of powers with a distinct executive branch at the national level. But delegates disagreed fundamentally about what that executive branch should look like and just how strong it should be. Despite that disagreement, it is striking that just eleven years after the Declaration of Independence, support had grown for an executive (and even support for a *strong* executive) because of events at the state and the national levels. In short, the delegates brought to the task of designing an executive office two conflicting attitudes: a healthy skepticism for executive power and a new appreciation of its necessity.

Initial Convention Debates. James Madison, the thirty-six-year-old Virginian commonly credited as the chief architect of the Constitution, was the first delegate to arrive in Philadelphia. He was convinced that the national government had to be refashioned, especially to increase its power over the states, but he had given little thought to executive power. In a letter to George Washington two weeks earlier, Madison admitted that "a national Executive must . . . be provided" but confessed,

"I have scarcely ventured as yet to form my own opinion either of the manner in which it ought to be constituted or of the authorities with which it ought to be cloathed."[14]

The "Virginia Plan"—written mostly by Madison but introduced on the first working day of the convention by fellow Virginian Edmund Randolph—reflected this uncertainty. The plan called for an executive of unspecified size and tenure, selected by the legislature, and with unclear powers.[15] Indeed, the executive did not appear to be a matter of high importance to Randolph. His opening speech on May 29, 1787, included a lengthy analysis of the defects of the Articles of Confederation, but did not include the lack of an executive as one of them.[16]

When the convention began its executive branch deliberations on June 1, Randolph revealed his preference for a weak executive by arguing for a plural executive. More than a quarter of the delegates agreed.[17] Although we now take a single president for granted, the delegates debated whether there should be a singular or plural executive—one president or multiple presidents. Benjamin Franklin, for one, had long argued for a plural executive.[18] When his fellow delegate from Pennsylvania, James Wilson, moved that the executive should be singular, a "lengthy embarrassed silence ensued."[19] Franklin broke the silence by encouraging the delegates to express their views on the matter. The debate that followed was the first of many between those advocating a strong executive and those a weak one.

Roger Sherman, a delegate from Connecticut, took the most extreme position on a weak executive. He saw no need to give the executive an explicit grant of power in the Constitution. Sherman believed the executive should be completely subservient to the legislature: "nothing more than an institution for carrying the will of the Legislature into effect" and "appointed by and accountable to the Legislature only."[20] In addition, he argued that Congress should be able to change the size of the office at will. Wilson's motion for a singular executive—a first step toward creating a strong one—eventually won on June 4. But Sherman's suggestion for legislative appointment, something that Wilson and other proponents of a strong executive vigorously opposed, had won on June 2. On yet another issue, presidential veto power, the delegates steered a middle course. After voting for a single executive, the delegates gave the executive a qualified veto power, subject to an override by a two-thirds vote of the legislature.

These decisions, however, proved to be just the beginning of the debate over the position. On June 15 Paterson introduced the "New Jersey Plan," which proposed simply amending the existing Articles of Confederation rather than replacing them with a new constitution. The plan reintroduced the idea of a plural executive and said the executive should be elected by Congress for a single term.[21] Although the primary motivation of the New Jersey Plan was to protect the power of small states (the Virginia Plan apportioned representation in the national legislature according to population; the New Jersey Plan called for equal representation regardless of size), it is clear that those favoring the New Jersey Plan preferred a weak executive.

Since the first debates on executive power in early June, Gouverneur Morris, a delegate from Pennsylvania, had joined the convention. Morris, who had spent most of his life in New York, became, along with James Wilson, one of the most influential proponents of a strong executive. He stood out because of his appearance—he had a wooden leg as a result of a carriage accident and a crippled arm as a result of a scalding as a child—but, as Richard J. Ellis writes, "It was his rapier wit, infectious humor, and brilliant mind that set him apart and drew others."[22] On July 17 he began his offensive. Attempting to free the executive from its dependence on the legislature, Morris called for popular election by freeholders. Sherman vigorously objected, and Morris's motion was quickly defeated by a resounding margin. But the battle lines were drawn, and the debate over presidential selection was far from over.

Heated argument over presidential selection continued for the next week, but when the delegates finished talking on July 26, the plan for an executive that had been agreed upon in early June remained unchanged: legislative appointment of a single executive for one unrenewable seven-year term. Thereupon the delegates turned their resolutions over to a five-member Committee of Detail chaired by Wilson. Its task was to take the resolutions passed by the Committee of the Whole and turn them into a draft of the Constitution.

Committee Work and Final Action. One of the notable contributions of the Committee of Detail was its decision to use the word *president* to identify what the delegates had simply referred to as "the Executive." The committee rejected the word *governor,* suggested by John Rutledge of South Carolina, because of the negative connotations associated with the royal governors who had ruled the colonies. The committee chose *president* because it was an innocuous term. Derived from the Latin word *praesidere* ("to sit in front of or at the head of" and "to defend"), president had historically been used to denote passive guardianship rather than strong executive power. The presiding officer of Congress under the Articles of Confederation was called its president. George Washington, who performed a mostly ceremonial function at the Constitutional Convention, served as its president.[23] Arguably, this choice of a term helped to sugarcoat executive power and make it more palatable.

In its draft of the Constitution, the Committee of Detail followed the convention's wishes and gave the president relatively little power. That it gave the president a specific constitutional grant of power at all was, however, significant. The alternative would have been to follow Sherman's suggestion and allow

Congress to dictate presidential powers. The Committee of Detail followed the convention's recommendation for a single executive elected by Congress to one unrenewable term, subject to impeachment, and with a qualified veto power. The draft also gave the president the power to appoint executive officers, to grant pardons, and to receive ambassadors. But many powers traditionally associated with the prerogative of the executive—such as raising armies, making war, making treaties, appointing ambassadors, and coining money—were all withheld from the president and given to the legislative branch. [24]

Convention debate resumed on August 6. When the delegates took up the article dealing with the president, it was obvious that they remained dissatisfied. But they could not agree on how to improve things, and debate ended on August 31 with the powers of the president largely unchanged. At that point, the convention sent unresolved issues to the Committee on Postponed Matters. The committee, chaired by David Brearly of New Jersey, consisted of one member from each state (including Gouverneur Morris). It was in that committee that the final constitutional vision of the presidency took shape.

One of the committee's most significant accomplishments was its cobbling together of a compromise plan for presidential selection. Various proposals had been introduced either for popular election of the president or selection by an electoral body, but the delegates had always reverted back to selection by Congress. The Committee on Postponed Matters revisited this issue and offered a novel twist on James Wilson's suggestion. The committee proposed that a president—and a *vice president* (the first time this position had been recommended)—be chosen by an "Electoral College" consisting of electors from each of the states. Each state would be free to choose its electors (equaling that state's combined number of senators and representatives in the U.S. Congress) as its state legislature saw fit. Electors would meet and vote in their respective states. Each elector would have two votes, only one of which could be cast for a candidate from that elector's state. When the votes from all states' electors were counted, the candidate with the most votes would be elected president and the runner-up would be elected vice president. If no candidate received a majority in the Electoral College, the Senate would choose from among the five candidates who had received the most electoral votes. (The convention later changed this provision so that the House of Representatives, with each state delegation having an equal vote, would decide the outcome in such cases.)

The committee's proposed Electoral College seemed to resolve the problems that had stymied the convention. First, it placated both large and small states. Basing the number of electors on the combined number of a state's senators and representatives served as a compromise between equal and proportional allocation

George Washington presides over the signing of the Constitution by members of the Constitutional Convention in Philadelphia on September 17, 1787. This depiction of the event was painted by Howard Chandler Christy and hangs in the U.S. Capitol.

of electors. Large states could support the plan with the hope that they would dominate the Electoral College. At the same time, small states were pleased that each elector could cast only one vote for a home-state candidate. Small states were further assured that if the election were thrown to Congress, each state would have an equal vote. Second, the compromise plan satisfied proponents of an independent president and proponents of congressional selection of the president. Proponents of congressional selection argued that a presidential candidate would seldom get a majority of votes from the Electoral College. They believed that Congress would choose the president most of the time anyway, with the Electoral College acting simply as a nominating convention. Advocates of an independent president, on the other hand, saw the Electoral College as an explicit rejection of congressional selection and believed the electors would select the president.[25] Even on those occasions when a candidate did not get a majority, Congress was limited in its choice to the five candidates who had received the most votes in the

Electoral College.[26] This provision clearly limited Congress more than the original plan, in which congressional choice was unrestricted. Finally, the proposal for both a president and a vice president resolved concerns about succession if presidents did not complete their terms.

In addition to its plan for an Electoral College, the Committee on Postponed Matters made a few other significant decisions. It shortened the president's term from seven to four years and made the president eligible for reelection to an unlimited number of terms. And—of great importance to advocates of a strong executive—it gave the president a number of executive powers that the delegates had previously given to the Senate, including expanded appointment power and the power to make treaties. The resulting language was again a compromise. The president could **nominate** ambassadors and other public ministers, Supreme Court justices, and all other officers whose appointments were not otherwise provided for. Actual **appointment** would come only with the **"advice and consent"** of the Senate. And although the president could make treaties, they could be ratified only by a two-thirds vote of the Senate.[27]

The convention as a whole spent several days in early September scrutinizing the proposals of the Committee on Postponed Matters. The only major change came on September 6, when the convention gave the House of Representatives the power to choose the president if no candidate received a majority in the Electoral College. The change was the result of fear among the delegates that the Senate was becoming too powerful. When voting for president, each state delegation in the House would have one vote. This guaranteed that each state would have an equal vote (a counterbalance to the Electoral College itself, which gives large states an advantage).

On September 8 the delegates created a five-member Committee of Style, chaired by Morris, to write a final draft of the Constitution. This committee was responsible for the opening words of Article II: "The executive Power shall be vested in a President of the United States of America." As we shall see, the ambiguity of this sentence continues to be the subject of debate, and it stood in marked contrast to the opening words of Article I, which seemed to explicitly limit Congress's powers to those listed in the Constitution: "All legislative powers *herein granted* shall be vested in a Congress of the United States." Ironically, the **vesting clause** of Article II was accepted by the whole of the Constitutional Convention without any discussion of its specific language.[28] The constitutional language regarding the presidency resulted from compromise, but it was a compromise that ultimately favored the strong executive model more than the weak one (see Table 1-1). Credit usually goes to a small group of delegates, especially Wilson and Morris, who used their strategic positions within the convention's working committees to further their goal of a strong executive.

TABLE 1-1   Models of Executive Considered by the Constitutional Convention

Elements of executive	Weak-executive model	Strong-executive model	Decision by convention
Relation to Congress	To put into effect will of Congress	Powers independent of Congress	Powers independent of Congress but with checks and balances
Number of executives	Plural or single individual checked by council	Single individual with no council or only advisory one	Single individual with Senate advisory on some matters
Method of choosing	By Congress	By means other than congressional selection	Electoral college
Tenure	Limited term; not renewable	No limitation	Unlimited
Method of removal	By Congress during term of office	Only for definite, enumerated reasons after impeachment and conviction by judicial body or Congress	For treason, bribery, high crimes and misdemeanors, by impeachment by majority of House and conviction by two-thirds of Senate
Scope and source of powers	Limited powers delegated by Congress	Broad powers from Constitution, not subject to congressional interference	Broad powers delegated by Constitution
Appointment and foreign policy and war-making powers	None—province of Congress	Would appoint judicial and diplomatic officials and participate in foreign policy and war-making powers, including making of treaties	Appoints executive and judicial officials with consent of Senate; shares foreign policy and war-making powers with Congress; Senate must approve treaties negotiated by president
Veto	None	Veto over legislation passed by Congress, exercised alone or with judiciary	Qualified veto, may be overridden by two-thirds vote of House and Senate

SOURCE: Joseph E. Kallenbach, *The American Chief Executive: The Presidency and the Governorship* (New York: Harper and Row, 1966), chap. 2.

Interpreting Constitutional Language

The ambivalence over executive power exhibited by the convention became a permanent feature of American political culture. Like the delegates in 1787, Americans have had to confront the trade-off between tyranny and effectiveness—the one to be feared and the other to be prized. The anti-Federalists, who opposed ratification of the Constitution, frequently pointed to the risks inherent in a national executive, which some considered even more threatening than its British counterpart. As George Mason, a delegate from Virginia who ultimately refused to sign the Constitution, had argued: "We are not indeed constituting a British monarchy, but a more dangerous monarchy, an elective one."[29] But others— Alexander Hamilton, for example—saw the newly created presidency as essential to effective government, the source of energy, dispatch, and responsibility in the conduct of domestic and foreign affairs.[30]

This ambivalence has been reflected over the years in differing interpretations of constitutional language concerning presidential power. The vesting clause drafted by Morris and the Committee of Style—"The executive Power shall be vested in a President of the United States of America"—has proven to be, as presidential scholar Charles C. Thach Jr. put it in the 1920s, the "joker" in the game of presidential power.[31] Constitutional language limits both legislative and judicial power. Article I limits legislative powers to those "herein granted." Article III uses the phrase "the judicial power shall extend to," followed by an enumeration of those powers, which suggests the same sort of limitation of power as that in Article I. But Article II contains no such limit. Whether the omission was intentional is unclear because the full convention never debated the language. Thach, however, points to letters that Morris wrote in which he admitted how much impact small, seemingly inconsequential changes of phraseology could have on the meaning of constitutional clauses. Although Morris did not refer explicitly to presidential power in these letters, his advocacy of a strong executive is well known, and Thach suspects that Morris embraced the language of Article II with "full realization of its possibilities."[32] By failing to limit executive power to those "herein granted," Article II suggests that the scope of presidential power is not confined to the powers enumerated in the Constitution. Carried to its extreme, this view gives the president unlimited executive power. The ambiguity of the first sentence of Article II has led to three widely divergent theories of presidential power: the constitutional theory, the stewardship theory, and the prerogative theory.

Proponents of the **constitutional theory,** such as William Howard Taft, argue that presidential power is strictly limited. According to the constitutional theory, presidents have only those powers that are either enumerated in the Constitution or granted by Congress under its constitutional powers. As Taft put it in his book *Our Chief Magistrate and His Powers:*

The true view of the Executive function is, as I conceive it, that the President can exercise no power which cannot fairly and reasonably be traced to some specific grant of power or justly implied and included within such grant as proper and necessary to its exercise. Such specific grant must be either in the Federal Constitution or in an act of Congress passed in pursuance thereof. There is no undefined residuum of power that he can exercise because it seems to him to be in the public interest. . . . [Presidential power] must be justified and vindicated by affirmative constitutional or statutory provision, or it does not exist. [33]

In contrast, the **stewardship theory** holds that the president can do anything not explicitly *forbidden* by the Constitution or by laws passed by Congress under its constitutional powers. Theodore Roosevelt embraced this view as president and explained it in his *Autobiography:*

My view was that every Executive officer and above all every Executive officer in high position was a steward of the people bound actively and affirmatively to do all he could for the people. . . . I declined to adopt [the] view that what was imperatively necessary for the Nation could not be done by the President, unless he could find some specific authorization to do it. My belief was that it was not only his right but his duty to do anything that the needs of the Nation demanded unless such action was forbidden by the Constitution or by the laws. Under this interpretation of executive power I did and caused to be done many things not previously done by the President and the heads of the departments. I did not usurp power but I did greatly broaden the use of executive power. In other words, I acted for the common well being of all our people whenever and in whatever measure was necessary, unless prevented by direct constitutional or legislative prohibition. [34]

Taft, who had served as Roosevelt's secretary of war but later ran against him for president, took direct issue with the stewardship theory in his book:

My judgment is that the [stewardship theory], ascribing an undefined residuum of power to the President, is an unsafe doctrine and that it might lead under emergencies to results of an arbitrary character, doing irremediable injustice to private right. The mainspring of such a view is that the Executive is charged with responsibility for the welfare of all the people in a general way, that he is to play the part of a Universal Providence and set all things right, and that anything that in his judgment will help the people he ought to do, unless he is expressly forbidden not to do it. The wide field of action that this would give the Executive one can hardly limit. [35]

The **prerogative theory** is the most expansive of these three theories of presidential power. John Locke defined the concept of prerogative power in his *Second Treatise of Government* as the power "to act according to discretion for the public good, without the prescription of the law, *and sometimes even against it.*" [36] The prerogative theory not only allows presidents to do anything that is *not* forbidden but allows them to do things that *are* explicitly forbidden when in the national interest. Lincoln exercised such prerogative power at the outset of the Civil War. From the outbreak of hostilities at Fort Sumter, South Carolina, on April 12, 1861, to the convening of Congress in a special session on July 4, Lincoln stretched the executive's emergency powers further than ever before. This period has been described as a time of "constitutional dictatorship." [37] Lincoln unilaterally authorized a number of drastic actions. He called up the militia and volunteers, blockaded Southern ports, expanded the army and navy beyond the limits set by statute, pledged the credit of the United States without congressional authority to do so, closed the mails to "treasonous" correspondence, arrested persons suspected of disloyalty, and suspended the writ of habeas corpus in areas around the nation's capital. Admitting that most of these matters lay within the jurisdiction of Congress rather than the president, Lincoln asserted that they were done because of popular demand and public necessity and with the trust "that Congress would readily ratify them." But he deliberately chose not to call the national legislature into special session until he was ready to do so, and then he presented it with faits accomplis.

Although Lincoln's use of executive power was most freewheeling in the early days of hostilities, he continued to exercise firm control over the war until it ended. He controlled the mails and newspapers, confiscated property of people suspected of impeding the conduct of the war, and even tried civilians in military courts in areas where civilian courts were operating. To justify such actions, he appealed to military necessity, asserting that the Constitution's commander in chief clause (requiring command of the armed forces) and its take care clause (that the laws be faithfully executed) combined to create a "war power" for the president that was virtually unlimited. Lincoln's success in defending that position is demonstrated by the fact that neither Congress nor the courts placed any significant limits on his actions during the war.

A century later, Richard Nixon pointed to Lincoln's actions in an attempt to justify illegal covert actions he had taken as president. In fact, Nixon went so far as to claim that if a president chooses to do something illegal because he believes it to be in the national interest, it is—by definition—no longer illegal. As he explained in a televised interview with David Frost in 1977:

When the President does it, that means that it is not illegal. . . . If the President, for example, approves something because of the national security, or in this case because of a threat to internal peace and order of significant magnitude, then the President's decision in that instance is one that enables those who carry it out, to carry it out without violating the law. Otherwise they're in an impossible position. [38]

Following the September 11, 2001, terrorist attacks, President Bush also exercised prerogative powers. As part of the "war on terror" he authorized the detention of "enemy combatants" at Guantánamo Bay, Cuba. He argued that detainees could be held there indefinitely without charge, without access to a lawyer, and without regard to the laws of armed conflict, which many argued violates the Geneva

Conventions and basic due process rights. [39] He also authorized the CIA to establish secret prisons in several countries to detain and interrogate al Qaeda suspects, a possible violation of international law. [40] The president eventually admitted that "an alternative set of procedures" was used as part of the interrogation process at those prisons, but insisted that the procedures, though "tough," were lawful and did not constitute torture. [41] But behind the scenes, two deputy attorneys general in the Office of Legal Counsel had written memos that justified the use of torture against terror suspects and argued that international law should not interfere with the president's prerogative war power to use torture if necessary. [42]

Bush also used his war power domestically. Critics claimed that he violated the Foreign Intelligence Surveillance Act of 1978 when he authorized the use of domestic wiretaps without warrants. The nonpartisan Congressional Research Service found the wiretaps to be "inconsistent with the law." [43] The Bush administration, however, pointed to the use of emergency war power by Lincoln and other presidents as justification for the wiretaps and noted that the Authorization for Use of Military Force passed by Congress on September 14, 2001, implicitly gave approval for the president to take broad measures in response to the war on terror. [44]

In short, the ambiguity of the opening sentence of Article II, section 1, has allowed individual presidents to expand significantly the power of the office. As constitutional scholar Edward S. Corwin wrote in 1957, "Taken by and large, the history of the presidency is a history of aggrandizement." [45] By the 1970s Arthur Schlesinger Jr. had coined the phrase "the imperial presidency" to describe the office. [46]

Presidents have also relied on ambiguities in their specifically enumerated powers, in sections 2 and 3 of Article II, to further that aggrandizement. Together, the enumerated powers have created at least five presidential roles that have evolved and expanded over time.

Chief Administrator. This role for the president is more implicit than explicit as set forth in the Constitution. It rests on the executive power clause (Article II, section 1, paragraph 1) as well as passages dealing with the right to require opinions from the heads of government departments (Article II, section 2, paragraph 1) and the power to make personnel appointments subject to whatever approval Congress may require (Article II, section 2, paragraph 2). George W. Bush took the role of chief administrator very seriously. He actively embraced the concept of the **unitary executive**—a concept not widely discussed outside the conservative Federalist Society before Bush took office. [47] Supporters of the unitary executive argue that because the president alone possesses the executive power, the president must have absolute control over the executive branch and its administration, including the ability to control all subordinates and to veto or nullify their exercise of discretionary executive power. Moreover, the president must be able to fire any executive branch officials at will.[48] This view of the presidency holds that attempts by Congress to limit the president's removal power, even in the case of independent agencies, are improper, as are other oversight measures that interfere with executive branch functions.

If fully implemented, these ideas would be a major shift in the balance of power because traditionally Congress has jealously guarded its oversight powers, thereby denying the president anything approximating a monopoly of administrative power. Moreover, in 1935 the Supreme Court unanimously recognized Congress's power to limit the president's ability to fire officers who perform quasi-legislative or quasi-judicial functions in independent agencies within the executive branch.[49] In 1926 the Court had ruled that only purely executive officials performing purely executive functions can be fired by the president at will.[50] Given the large number of independent federal agencies, the Court's ruling places a significant limitation on the president's removal power.

Commander in Chief. This role is specifically enumerated in Article II, section 2, paragraph 1: "The President shall be Commander in Chief of the Army and Navy of the United States, and of the Militia of the several States, when called into the actual Service of the United States." But did this language merely confer a title on the president or imply wide-ranging powers in times of emergency? Lincoln believed the latter. From this germ of constitutional power has grown the enormous control that modern presidents exercise over a permanent military establishment and its deployment. The Constitution stipulates that the legislative and executive branches share the war power, but the pressure of events and the presidency's institutional advantages in taking decisive action have led Congress to give greater discretion to the executive. Nor was this delegation of power completely unexpected. Recognizing the need to repel attacks when Congress was not in session, the Constitutional Convention altered language describing the role of Congress in armed hostilities from "make" war to "declare" war (Article I, section 8, paragraph 11), thereby expanding the president's realm of discretionary action.[51] Over time, presidents have invoked the commander in chief clause to justify military expenditures without congressional authorization, emergency powers to suppress rebellion, the internment of American citizens of Japanese descent during World War II, the seizure of domestic steel mills during the undeclared armed conflict in Korea in the 1950s, and the use of warrantless wiretapping as part of the war on terror. [52]

Moreover, presidents have initiated the use of force far more frequently than they have awaited congressional authorization, and they have continued to wage war—sometimes for years—without a congressional declaration of war. They do so, as political scientist Richard Pious points out, by relying on "congressional resolutions of support, UN resolutions, NATO resolutions, congressional authorizations, and what they consider to be self-executing treaty provisions, relying on whatever is at hand." [53] John C. Yoo, a strong proponent of the unitary executive who served as deputy attorney general in the Bush administration's Office of Legal Counsel from 2001 to 2003, argued in a memo dated September 25, 2001, that "the Constitution vests the President with the plenary authority, as Commander in Chief and the sole organ of the Nation in its foreign relations, to use military force abroad—especially in response to grave national emergencies created by sudden unforeseen attacks on the people and territory of the United States." Yoo concluded that military actions in the wake of the September 11 attacks "need not be limited to those individuals, groups, or states that participated in the attacks on the World Trade Center and the Pentagon." He argued that Congress could not "place any limits on the President's determinations as to any terrorist threat, the amount of military force to be used in response, or the method, timing, and nature of the response. These decisions, under our Constitution, are for the President alone to make." [54] Pious has noted that some of the framers, such as Madison, came to an opposite conclusion. Madison "claimed that the Constitution assigned all war and foreign affairs powers to the legislature, with only such exceptions as were explicitly assigned by the Constitution to the executive." [55]

Chief Diplomat. When combined with the president's expanded war power, constitutional primacy in the conduct of foreign affairs establishes the office's claim to being the government's principal agent in the world, if not its "sole organ." Presidents are not only authorized to make treaties "by and with the Advice and Consent of the Senate" but also empowered to nominate ambassadors, subject to Senate approval (Article II, section 2, paragraph 2) and to receive diplomatic emissaries from abroad (Article II, section 3). Presidents have varied in how closely they collaborate with the Senate in making treaties, most waiting until after negotiations have been concluded before allowing any Senate participation. More significant, the conduct of foreign affairs has come to rely on **executive agreements** between heads of state in place of treaties. These agreements do not require Senate ratification, as treaties do, although many are given legislative approval by statute (as was NAFTA, the North American Free Trade Agreement, under President Clinton) or a joint resolution of Congress (as was SALT I, the first strategic arms limitation agreement with the Soviet Union, under President Nixon). Statutes and joint resolutions require only a simple majority, rather than the two-thirds approval necessary for Senate ratification of a treaty.[56] When given such legislative approval, they are referred to as "congressional-executive agreements."[57]

Chief Legislator. This feature of the job did not fully develop until the twentieth century. Before then, the president's role in legislation was essentially negative: the ability to veto. Today, however, the president's power to provide leadership for Congress rests primarily on the ability to shape the legislative agenda through active leadership. Congress fostered this development in 1921 when it passed legislation requiring the president to submit a budget for the whole of government. Constitutional language in Article II, section 3, merely obliged the president to give "the Congress Information of the State of the Union" and to recommend such other measures for its consideration as deemed "necessary and expedient." Legislative leadership is now considered a task for all presidents to fulfill, and they routinely develop detailed legislative agendas and present them to Congress and the nation.

Chief Magistrate. This area of presidential activity is perhaps the least clearly recognized, but it is one that George W. Bush expanded as part of his embrace of the unitary executive. It is based on the oath clause of Article II, section 1, paragraph 8, of the Constitution, directing the president to "preserve, protect and defend the Constitution of the United States," and the general charge in Article II, section 3, directing the president to "take Care that the Laws be faithfully executed." Proponents of a unitary executive argue that these clauses require coordinate construction. In other words, the president, along with the courts and Congress, has the power and the duty to interpret the Constitution to make sure that it is preserved and faithfully executed. President Bush's interpretation led to his controversial use of presidential signing statements when signing a bill into law. Presidents since James Monroe have issued them, but usually they were ceremonial in nature—designed to state why the president signed a law or to celebrate its passage. Occasionally, however, a president would use them to point out portions of a bill he thought were unconstitutional. In some rare instances, the president would say that he would not execute that provision. Other presidents, Clinton, for example, noted constitutional problems in their signing statements, but made it clear that they would enforce the provision until a court struck it down.[58] Starting with Reagan, signing statements were used more systematically—often to clarify how the president believed executive branch agencies should interpret ambiguous sections of the law. In 1986 the Justice Department added signing statements to the legislative history section of the U.S. Code.[59]

Bush, however, used signing statements routinely to state his intent *not* to enforce specific provisions of legislation. The American Bar Association Task Force on Presidential Signing Statements reported in August 2006 that Bush had challenged more than eight hundred specific provisions of legislation he signed. In a single signing statement accompanying the Consolidated Appropriations Act of 2005, Bush issued 116 specific objections relating to almost every part of the bill.[60] Bush's signing statements rejected encroachments on the unitary executive. For example, he rejected congressional oversight of Patriot Act authority to search homes secretly and to seize private papers. Although he signed the McCain amendment banning the use of torture by U.S. officials, Bush quietly indicated that he could disregard the law and use torture under his commander in chief powers when he deemed it necessary.[61] In short, Bush claimed the right to disobey laws that he had signed whenever he felt those laws conflicted with his interpretation of the Constitution without waiting for action by a court. His conception of the power of the chief magistrate went far beyond the normal executive branch role, but until 2006, most people—including members of Congress—were largely unaware of Bush's extensive use of signing statements.[62] On March 9, 2009, President Barack Obama instructed executive officials not to enforce any of President Bush's signing statements without first consulting with the attorney general, but he indicated that he would use signing statements under some circumstances.[63] In fact, he issued a signing statement just two days later in which he reserved the right to bypass dozens of provisions in the $410 billion spending bill that he was signing into law.[64]

President Bush interpreted all five presidential roles broadly. Law professor Jeffrey Rosen points out that the result was "the largest expansion of executive power since FDR."[65] Because the constitutional job description for presidents is permissive rather than confining, it aids such aggrandizement of presidential power.

Expansion of the Presidency

Students of the presidency commonly divide the office's development into two major periods: traditional and modern. In the traditional era, presidential power was relatively limited, and Congress was the primary policymaker. The modern era is typified by presidential dominance in the policymaking process and a significant expansion of the president's powers and resources. The presidency of Franklin D. Roosevelt was the turning point into the modern era. Political scientist Fred I. Greenstein argues that the modern presidency is distinguished by four features: (1) the president is expected to develop a legislative program and to persuade Congress to enact it; (2) presidents regularly engage in direct policymaking through actions not requiring congressional approval; (3) the presidential office has become an extensive bureaucracy designed to enable presidents to undertake points 1 and 2; and (4) presidents have come to symbolize the nation and to personify its government to such an extent that the public holds them primarily responsible for its condition and closely monitors their performance through intensive media coverage.[66]

A number of factors contributed to the expansion of the American presidency. These include actions by individual presidents, statutes enacted by Congress, the emergence of customs, and institutional development. We examine each of these factors in turn.

Expansion by Individual Presidents

Several early presidents, including George Washington, Thomas Jefferson, Andrew Jackson, and Abraham Lincoln, are often credited with providing their successors with an institutional legacy that left the office more powerful than before.[67] This assertion is true to a certain extent, but it was three twentieth-century presidents, Theodore Roosevelt, Woodrow Wilson, and FDR, who were largely responsible for expanding presidential power and creating the modern presidency.

Theodore Roosevelt. As president, Theodore Roosevelt helped the United States become a world power. Concerned over the rise of Japan as a threat to American interests in the Pacific, Roosevelt sought and obtained a major role in negotiating the Portsmouth treaty, which terminated the Russo-Japanese War of 1905. Closer to home he intervened in the affairs of neighbors to the south when he considered it vital to U.S. national interests, sending troops to the Dominican Republic and Cuba. Even more blatant was Roosevelt's part in fomenting the rebellion of Panama against Colombia so that the United States could acquire rights to build a canal. An avowed nationalist with the desire to expand U.S. influence in international affairs, Roosevelt ordered the navy to sail around the world as a symbolic demonstration of American military might. The image of U.S. naval ships sailing off the shores of other countries would serve as a potent reminder to those nations that the United States was now a major world power. When Congress balked at the expense, he countered that he had sufficient funds to get the navy there; if the lawmakers wanted the fleet back home, they would have to provide the money for the return trip.

Roosevelt also responded vigorously to the rapid industrialization of American life and its attendant evils. He had charges pressed against corporations that violated antitrust laws, and he pushed legislation through Congress that gave the Interstate Commerce Commission power to reduce railroad rates. When coal mine operators in Colorado refused to agree to arbitration of a dispute with their workers, Roosevelt threatened to have troops seize the mines and administer them as a receiver for the government. He was the first American chief executive to intervene in a labor dispute who did *not* take management's side. Roosevelt also championed major reclamation and conservation projects as well as meat inspection and pure food and drug laws.

Perhaps most important, Roosevelt did much to popularize the presidency after three decades of lackluster leaders. (Of the eight men who served between Lincoln and Roosevelt, only Grover Cleveland is considered at all significant.) A dynamic personality, an attractive family, and love of the public spotlight enabled Roosevelt "to put the presidency on the front page of every newspaper in America."[68] Considering himself the "steward of the people" and seeing the office as a "bully pulpit" from which the incumbent should set the tone of American life, Roosevelt was the first president to provide meeting rooms for members of the press and to hold informal news conferences to link the presidency with the people. His style of leadership depended upon extensive use of popular speech, a distinctive reinterpretation of statesmanship that ushered in the era of the "rhetorical presidency."[69] In keeping with his stewardship theory of presidential power, Roosevelt was also the first president to rely on broad discretionary authority in peacetime as well as in crisis.[70]

Woodrow Wilson. Although Theodore Roosevelt laid the groundwork for use of popular appeals during his presidency (1901–1909), it was Wilson (1913–1921) who linked inspirational rhetoric to a broad program of action in an effort to address domestic and foreign affairs. Jeffrey Tulis has argued that this effort rested on a systematic, ambitious reinterpretation of the president's role in the constitutional order.[71] A skilled public speaker, Wilson was the first president since John Adams to go before Congress in person to give his State of the Union message, a practice we now take for granted.[72] Like Jefferson, he was a powerful party chief who worked through congressional leaders and the Democratic caucus to influence legislation. He also did not hesitate to take his case to the people, casting himself as the interpreter as well as the representative of their interests.

During his first term in office, Wilson pushed through a vast program of economic reform that lowered tariffs, raised taxes on the wealthy, created a central banking system, regulated unfair trade practices, provided low-interest loans to farmers, and established an eight-hour day for railroad employees. When the United States became involved in World War I during his second term, Wilson went to Congress and obtained authority to control the economic as well as the military aspects of the war, rather than prosecuting it through unilateral executive action. This grant gave him the power to allocate food and fuel, license trade with the enemy, censor the mail, regulate the foreign language press of the country, and operate railroads, water transportation systems, and telegraph and telephone facilities. At the end of the war, he made a triumphant trip to Europe, where he assumed the leading role in the writing of the Versailles peace treaty.

Wilson also provided a lesson in how *not* to work with Congress: his adamant refusal to accept any reservations proposed by the Senate for the League of Nations Covenant of the Treaty of Versailles ensured that the United States would not participate. Wilson's archenemy, Sen. Henry Cabot Lodge, R-Mass., calculated that the president's intransigence and personal hatred of him was so intense that the president would reject all compromises proposed to the treaty. Lodge was right: Wilson said it "better a thousand times to go down fighting than to dip your colors to dishonorable compromise." A trip to win popular support for the League ended in failure and a physical breakdown when Wilson suffered a stroke. As a result, the country whose leader proposed the League of Nations ended up not belonging to the organization at all.

Franklin D. Roosevelt. Confronted by enormous domestic and international crises, FDR began a program of action and innovation unmatched by any chief executive in U.S. history. In most respects, his service is now used as a yardstick against which the performance of his successors is measured.[73] When Roosevelt came into office in March 1933, business failures were legion, 12 million people were unemployed, banks all over the country were closed or doing business under restrictions, and Americans had lost confidence in their leaders and themselves. Counseling the nation in his inaugural address—the first of four—that "the only thing we have to fear is fear itself," the new chief executive swung into action: a four-day bank holiday was declared, and an emergency banking bill was prepared within a day's time. During Roosevelt's first hundred days in office, the nation witnessed a social and economic revolution in the form of his New Deal. Congress adopted a series of far-reaching government programs insuring bank deposits, providing crop payments for farmers, establishing codes of fair competition for industry, granting labor the right to organize, providing relief and jobs for the unemployed, and creating the Tennessee Valley Authority, a government corporation, to develop that region. With these measures and others such as Social Security, public housing, and unemployment compensation, Roosevelt established the concept of the "positive state" in America—a government that has the obligation to take the lead in providing for the welfare of all the people.

Internationally, Roosevelt extended diplomatic recognition to the Soviet Union, embarked on the Good Neighbor policy toward South America, and pushed through the Reciprocal Trade Program, which lowered tariffs with other nations. In his second term, FDR began the slow and difficult task of preparing the nation for its eventual entry into World War II. He funneled aid to the Allies; traded fifty "over-age" destroyers to Britain for naval and air bases in the British West Indies, Newfoundland, and Bermuda; and obtained passage of the nation's first peacetime draft. After Pearl Harbor, in his own words, "Dr. New Deal" became "Dr. Win-the-War." He took over economic control of the war effort granted him by Congress and established the victorious strategy of concentrating on defeating Germany before Japan. While hostilities were still going on, he took the lead in setting up the United Nations, but died before he could see the organization established in 1945.

Roosevelt was an innovator whose actions reshaped the presidential office. He was not only an effective legislative leader but also a skilled administrator responsible for a thorough reorganization of the executive branch, including the creation of the Executive Office of the President (see chapter 6). Even more important, FDR was probably the most effective molder of public opinion the nation has ever known. He pioneered the use of "fireside chats" over radio to explain his actions to the people. In addition, he raised the presidential press conference to new heights as a tool of public persuasion. As a man who could take idealistic goals, reduce them to manageable and practical programs, and then sell them to Congress and the American people, Roosevelt has no peer.

Expansion through Statute

Congress is another major source of change in the presidency. Legislators have mandated activities that earlier presidents exercised on a discretionary basis or have formally delegated responsibility for activities that traditionally resided with Congress. One of the contemporary presidency's major responsibilities—serving as the nation's economic manager—is nowhere suggested in the Constitution.[74] Congress foisted this power on the president. In 1921 Congress passed the Budget and Accounting Act as part of an effort to increase the fiscal responsibility and efficiency of government. The act created the Bureau of the Budget in the Treasury Department and required the president to use the expert advice of the bureau to propose annual fiscal policy to the government. Quite simply, the legislation compelled the president to take an active role in domestic policy formulation. According to James Sundquist:

Before 1921, a president did not have to have a program for the whole of the government, and none did; after that date he was compelled by the Budget and Accounting Act to present a program for every department and every bureau, and to do it annually. Before 1921, a president did not have to propose a fiscal policy for the government, and many did not; after 1921, every chief executive had to have a fiscal policy, every year. That made the president a leader, a policy and program initiator, and a manager, whether he wished to be or not.[75]

Naturally, strong presidents exerted policy leadership before 1921, but nothing had compelled them to act. Likewise, it is wrong to assume that the Budget and Accounting Act automatically produced strong presidents. The first three affected by the act, Warren Harding, Calvin Coolidge, and Herbert Hoover, dutifully submitted proposals to Congress but seldom exerted strong leadership to secure enactment.[76] That pattern changed under FDR, who used the crisis of the Depression as a rallying cry for policy enactment.

Over time, Congress further expanded presidential power. It created the Executive Office of the President in 1939 as a source of expert advice to help presidents formulate policy. Congress also added to the president's economic responsibilities by passing the Employment Act of 1946. As Sundquist explains, the act "compels the president to maintain a continuous surveillance of the nation's economy, to report on the state of its health at least annually, and if there are signs of pathology— inflation, recession, stagnation—to recommend corrective action."[77] Despite giving the president new tasks, Congress did not surrender its traditional right to alter presidential proposals, thereby ensuring that tax rates and spending proposals would continue to be a mainstay of partisan politics as well as legislative-executive relations. (See chapter 9 for the politics of economic policymaking.)

Congress has taken comparable action in other areas as well. In 1947 Congress charged the president with coordinating national security policy—foreign policy, intelligence collection and evaluation, and defense policy—through the creation of the National Security Council (NSC). Truman resisted the newly created NSC as an intrusion on his powers and was slow to use it. In fact, no president can be *required* to use such a structure, but during the Cold War one president after another established administrative machinery designed to achieve the same goal of coordinating American foreign policy (see chapter 10).

During George W. Bush's administration, the Republican-controlled Congress sanctioned many of the actions Bush had already taken unilaterally under his war power. Prior to the Democrats' regaining control in the 2006 midterm elections, Congress passed the Military Commissions Act of 2006. As Richard Pious wrote, the act

authorized the military commissions initially promulgated by Bush's military order to try noncitizen detainees in the War on Terror; granted vast delegation of power to the president to determine their rules of procedure; delegated to the president the power to determine by executive order what interrogation techniques would be used on detainees (with the exception of a set of limited techniques defined to constitute torture that would be prohibited, such as sleep deprivation and waterboarding); allowed the president to "interpret the meaning and application" of international conventions involving treatment of prisoners; permitted information acquired through harsh interrogations (prior to passage of the Detainee Treatment Act of 2005) [which contains the McCain amendment] to be used in trials if the commission found the statements reliable and in the "interests of justice"; and stripped federal courts of pending habeas corpus petitions filed by detainees (as of October 2006 numbering 196).[78]

One of Barack Obama's first acts as president was to order a halt to the use of military commissions to try detainees at Guantánamo Bay.[79] He also signed an executive order directing the CIA to shut down the Guantánamo prison within a year.[80] And faced with an economic emergency unparalleled since the Great Depression, Obama asked Congress for legislation authorizing the executive branch to seize troubled financial institutions deemed by the Treasury secretary to be too important to fail.[81] This request reminds us that Congress can authorize presidents to act in areas wholly absent from the original constitutional design or encourage executives to devise new ways to exercise their traditional responsibilities.

Expansion through Custom and Practice

Across a wide range of presidential activities, "action based on usage may acquire legitimacy."[82] Nowhere in the Constitution does it say that presidents would serve as leaders of their party, but that task has been associated with the office since Thomas Jefferson first established his dominance of the Democratic-Republicans' congressional caucus. Enormous variation may be found in how presidents pursued such activities and in how successful they were. Some, like Jefferson, had a close relationship with their party, while other executives were virtually abandoned by their partisan allies (Rutherford B. Hayes). At other times, presidents sought, and seemed to derive, greater influence by appearing to serve "above" party (Eisenhower). If the political parties continue to weaken or have difficulty reasserting themselves as structures vital to democracy, this informal part of the president's job description could disappear.

A second example of precedent and custom can be found in Theodore Roosevelt's attempt to mediate a labor-management dispute. Earlier presidents had intervened on the side of company owners, but Roosevelt put his prestige on the line when he sought to resolve the anthracite coal strike of 1902, a struggle that had paralyzed a vital industry. Other presidents followed suit: Wilson intervened in eight major disputes, Harding in two, FDR in eleven, and Truman in three.[83] The response of one president to emergency conditions became an accepted precedent for his successors, if they wished to pursue it.

Institutional Sources of Change

The modern presidency cannot be considered a one-person job, a reality that has had significant consequences for the evolution of the office. To dispatch the many responsibilities placed at the president's door, the presidency has become a working collectivity. During FDR's first term, the average number of full-time White House staffers was forty-seven. By Nixon's second term, that number had grown to well over five hundred. The shift toward what has been called the "institutional presidency" is partly a result of changing customs and practice, but it is also something that was furthered by statute.

Congress spurred the increase in staff by creating the Executive Office of the President (EOP) in 1939 and then passing subsequent legislation to create additional staff units, such as the Council of Economic Advisers and the National Security Council, within that structure. At the same time, presidents unilaterally created their own specialized staff units. These include the Congressional Liaison Office (to help secure congressional passage of presidential initiatives), the Office of Communications (to help communicate the president's agenda to the public and to coordinate the flow of information from the many departments and agencies within the executive branch), and the Office of Public Liaison (to maintain support from interest groups). By some counts, the president's full-time executive staff under Nixon, including presidential advisers in the EOP, grew to more than five thousand. During FDR's first term, comparable executive staff (including groundskeepers and the White House police force) numbered only 103.[84]

Presidential Culture

Understanding the presidency's institutional development provides an important perspective on the functions of the office, but we also need to address a less concrete question: what does the presidency *mean* to Americans? The final section of this chapter focuses on the development of the office's emotional and psychological significance.

Despite the framers' ambivalence toward executive power, the office of president quickly acquired mythic dimensions when it was filled by the country's first true hero. George Washington, argues Seymour Martin Lipset, supplied the virtues of a charismatic leader who serves as "symbol of the new nation, its hero who embodies in his person its values and aspirations. But more than merely symbolizing the new nation, he legitimizes the state, the new secular government, by endowing it with his 'gift of grace,'" the near magical qualities such leaders supposedly possess.[85] A cult of personality grew up around Washington so that well into the nineteenth century citizens displayed his likeness in their homes, named their children after him, and paid him endless tributes.

In the process of contributing stability and identity to the new nation, Washington also endowed the presidential office with a special meaning that has become part of our collective heritage. Bruce Buchanan refers to this as **presidential culture**, "widely held meanings of the presidency, derived from selected episodes in the history of the institution and transmitted from one generation to the next by political socialization." Buchanan explains that families, teachers, and the media sustain this view of the presidency as an office with the ability to deliver the nation from danger as a result of its occupants' greatness. Somehow, it is widely believed, the institution "has the potential to make extraordinary events happen" and the incumbent "should be able to realize that potential."[86] Occupants of the position, then, are expected to live up to these levels of performance and are roundly criticized when they fall short.

Why have such unrealistic expectations taken hold? One reason is that we have glorified the memories of past presidents. The "great" presidents, particularly those who took decisive action and bold initiatives, and even some of the "not so great" are treated as folk heroes and enshrined in a national mythology—figures whose birthdays we celebrate, whose virtues we are urged to emulate, whose achievements we memorialize, and whose sex lives continue to interest us long after their deaths. Schoolchildren throughout America are regaled with stories of Washington and Lincoln every February. Every summer, thousands of vacationers make the pilgrimage to visit shrines located along the Potomac in Washington, D.C., or scattered throughout the nation in presidential libraries and museums. Historical and popular glorification, however, does not constitute the full story. The presidency has always been important in American civic life, but it may have assumed even greater proportions in the modern era, assisted by new technologies and resting on new conceptions of the office.

A number of political scientists have pointed to the importance of the presidency in meeting the emotional and psychological needs of the populace. In particular, it is argued that citizens have expressive needs for confidence, security, reassurance, and pride in citizenship.[87] In the view of Murray Edelman, citizens suffer from a "general sense of anxiety about the comprehensive function played in human affairs by chance, ignorance, and inability to comprehend, plan, and take responsibility for remote and complicated contingencies." The natural response is to seek emotional comfort through attachment to reassuring symbols, "and what symbol can be more reassuring than the incumbent of a high position who knows what to do and is willing to act, especially when others are bewildered and alone?"[88] We know that American children develop a highly idealized image of presidents that emphasizes both their power and their benevolence, a source of reassurance that may be transferred from childhood to adulthood.

Fred Greenstein suggests additional psychological needs that are met through the presidency. Citizens seeking to sort through the complexity of political life turn to presidents for cognitive assistance. Presidents personify the government and make it possible to become engaged by what would otherwise be an impersonal abstraction. By following the president's activities, citizens may also experience a sort of vicarious participation in public affairs, giving them a sense of power and control that ordinarily would be unavailable. As a symbol of stability, predictability, and national unity, the president soothes fears and enables us to proceed with our daily lives.[89]

This aspect of the presidential office has become particularly "potent as a symbol of the public welfare, built-in benevolence, and competence to lead."[90] Barbara Hinckley points out that "symbols evoke ideas the society wants to believe are true. . . . [They] can substitute for something that does not exist otherwise." In fact, Hinckley argues that because the Constitution failed to clarify the presidency's nature and responsibilities, symbols have become enormously significant: "The office is undefined; thus presidents become what people want them to be."[91] And the people want them to be many things. The list of desirable personal attributes is impressive, as Ray Price, an aide to Richard Nixon during the 1968 presidential campaign, pointed out in a memo to the staff:

People identify with a President in a way they do with no other public figure. Potential presidents are measured against an ideal that's a combination of leading man, God, father, hero, pope, king, with maybe just a touch of the avenging Furies thrown in. They want him to be larger than life, a living legend, and yet quintessentially human; someone to be held up to their children as a model; someone to be cherished by themselves as a revered member of the family, in somewhat the same way in which peasant families pray to the icon in the corner. Reverence goes where power is.[92]

The problem for candidates (and incumbents) is how to project an image that matches these public expectations. Theodore Lowi has argued that "the expectations of the masses have grown faster than the capacity of presidential government to meet them."[93] According to Lowi, modern presidents resort to illusions to cover failures and seek quick fixes for their flagging public support in foreign adventures. As we discuss in chapter 3, advances in the means of communication have increased the ability of presidents to do this. Such behavior—portrayed by Lowi as rooted in the presidential institution, not in individual presidents' personalities—is ultimately self-defeating because it inflates expectations and ensures public disappointment, which may help to explain the string of failed presidencies described at the beginning of this chapter.

Conclusion: The Changeable, Political Presidency

There can be little doubt that today's presidency is a far cry from the office designed by the Constitutional Convention. Responsibilities have grown enormously as have means to fulfill them. So have the mythic dimensions of the office. Unlike the office that was launched in 1789, today's presidency is firmly rooted in the national consciousness as the consequence of childhood socialization and a secular mythology whose idealized images are magnified with the passage of time. There is no way to determine whether the office of president means more to Americans today than it did two centuries ago in terms of the emotional and psychological needs it meets, but certainly it occupies a more central—some observers would argue excessive—place in the public consciousness.

The contemporary presidency is not a static construct, however. As this overview of institutional development demonstrates, Americans' perceptions of the office and what they want from it can and does change over time. All too often, observers of the presidency treat temporary conditions as if they were permanent—mistaking a snapshot for a portrait.

To summarize, the presidency is variable for several reasons. First, in no other public office do the personality, character, and political style of the incumbent make as much difference as they do in the presidency. As an institution, the presidency exhibits important continuities across administrations, but the entry of each new occupant has an undeniably pervasive effect on the position's operation. The presidency is also heavily influenced by changes outside the office and throughout the U.S. political system—whether in the formal political structure

(Congress, the executive branch, the courts), in the informal political institutions (political parties and interest groups), in society at large, in the mass media, or in conditions surrounding substantive issues, particularly national security and the economy. Because of their extensive responsibilities, presidents must contend with all of these influences. Furthermore, although the Constitution and historical precedents give structure to the office, the powers of the presidency are so vague that incumbents have tremendous latitude to shape the office to their particular desires.

The presidency is not only highly *changeable* but also essentially *political*. On occasion, especially in times of crisis, presidents rule by asserting their constitutional prerogatives, but usually they are forced to govern by political maneuvering—by trying to persuade the many participants in the political process. This is a very complex task. Not only must they perform on the public stage of mass politics, but also they must master the intricacies of elite politics, a game played among skilled insiders. In the following chapters, we first examine "public politics" (chapters 2, 3, and 4) and then turn to the skills that presidents bring to relations with other public elites (chapters 5, 6, and 7). These separate dimensions are linked in discussions of major policy areas (chapters 8, 9, and 10).

Suggested Readings

Corwin, Edward S. *The President: Office and Powers, 1789–1984,* 5th ed. New York: New York University Press, 1984.

Ellis, Richard J., ed. *Founding the American Presidency.* Lanham, Md.: Rowman and Littlefield, 1999.

Farrand, Max, ed. *The Records of the Federal Convention of 1787.* New Haven: Yale University Press, 1911.

Lowi, Theodore J. *The Personal President: Power Invested, Promise Unfulfilled.* Ithaca: Cornell University Press, 1985.

McDonald, Forrest. *The American Presidency: An Intellectual History.* Lawrence: University Press of Kansas, 1994.

Milkis, Sidney M., and Michael Nelson. *The American Presidency: Origins and Development, 1776–2007,* 5th ed. Washington, D.C.: CQ Press, 2007.

Nelson, Michael, ed. *The Presidency and the Political System,* 9th ed. Washington, D.C.: CQ Press, 2010.

Neustadt, Richard E. *Presidential Power: The Politics of Leadership.* New York: Wiley, 1960.

Rudalevige, Andrew. *The New Imperial Presidency: Renewing Presidential Power after Watergate.* Ann Arbor: University of Michigan Press, 2006.

Skowronek, Stephen. *The Politics Presidents Make: Leadership from John Adams to Bill Clinton,* Revised Edition. Cambridge: Harvard University Press, 1997.

Yoo, John. *The Powers of War and Peace: The Constitution and Foreign Affairs after 9/11.* Chicago: University of Chicago Press, 2006.

Notes

1. For a full overview of Bush's ratings as well as up-to-date polling data, see www.pollingreport.com.

2. Richard E. Neustadt, *Presidential Power: The Politics of Leadership* (New York: Wiley, 1960), 26.

3. Stephen Skowronek, *The Politics Presidents Make: Leadership from John Adams to George Bush* (Cambridge: Harvard University Press, 1993), 20.

4. Quoted in Forrest McDonald, *The American Presidency: An Intellectual History* (Lawrence: University Press of Kansas, 1994), 127.

5. McDonald, *The American Presidency*, 126.

6. Richard J. Ellis, ed., *Founding the American Presidency* (Lanham, Md.: Rowman and Littlefield, 1999), 1.

7. McDonald, *The American Presidency*, 132–133.

8. Richard M. Pious, *The American Presidency* (New York: Basic Books, 1979), 23.

9. Sidney M. Milkis and Michael Nelson, *The American Presidency: Origins and Development, 1776–1993*, 2nd ed. (Washington, D.C.: CQ Press, 1994), 5. One of the drafters of the New York Constitution, Gouverneur Morris, later influenced the creation of presidential power at the 1787 Constitutional Convention.

10. Thomas Jefferson, *Notes on the State of Virginia*, quoted in Ellis, *Founding the American Presidency*, 4.

11. Charles C. Thach Jr., *The Creation of the Presidency, 1775–1789: A Study in Constitutional History* (Baltimore: Johns Hopkins University Press, 1923), chap. 3.

12. Pious, *The American Presidency*, 22.

13. McDonald, *The American Presidency*, 151.

14. Quoted in Ellis, *Founding the American Presidency*, 6.

15. Milkis and Nelson, *The American Presidency*, 13–14.

16. McDonald, *The American Presidency*, 163.

17. Ibid., 164.

18. Ellis, *Founding the American Presidency*, 31–32.

19. McDonald, *The American Presidency*, 164; see also Max Farrand, ed., *The Records of the Federal Convention of 1787* (New Haven: Yale University Press, 1911), 1:65.

20. Farrand, *Records*, 1:65.

21. Ibid., 1:244.

22. Ellis, *Founding the American Presidency*, 13.

23. This paragraph is based on McDonald, *The American Presidency*, 157.

24. Ibid., 171.

25. Ellis, *Founding the American Presidency*, 112–113.

26. We use the term *Congress* loosely here. As we have pointed out, the original recommendation of the Committee on Postponed Matters called for the *Senate* alone to choose from among the top five presidential candidates. As finally ratified, the Constitution called for the *House* alone to choose from the top five candidates. After the ratification of the Twelfth Amendment in 1804, the Constitution called for the House to choose from among the top *three* presidential candidates.

27. This account of the Committee on Postponed Matters is drawn largely from McDonald, *The American Presidency*, 176–178; see also Milkis and Nelson, *The American Presidency*, 21–22.

28. Edward S. Corwin, *The President: Office and Powers*, 4th ed. (New York: New York University Press, 1957), 12.

29. Quoted in Michael Nelson, ed., *Guide to the Presidency*, 2nd ed. (Washington, D.C.: CQ Press, 1996),

30. Although this sort of hostility toward a strong executive was common among anti-Federalists, Herbert J. Storing has pointed out that there are greater differences of opinion among them than one might expect.

Some anti-Federalists continued to argue for a plural executive or an executive council, but others agreed that a unitary executive was necessary. Storing points out that among anti-Federalists there was even "a fair amount of sympathy for a strong (even, under some circumstances, a hereditary) executive to resist the aristocratic tendencies of the legislature; and some of the Anti-Federalists objected that the President would be too weak to stand up to the Senate and would become a mere tool of aristocratic domination." Herbert J. Storing, ed., *The Complete Anti-Federalist* (Chicago: University of Chicago Press, 1981), 1:49.

30. Alexander Hamilton, *Federalist* No. 70.

31. Thach, *The Creation of the Presidency,* 138.

32. Ibid., 139.

33. William Howard Taft, *Our Chief Magistrate and His Powers* (New York: Columbia University Press, 1916), 139–140.

34. Theodore Roosevelt, *Autobiography* (New York: Macmillan, 1913), 388–389.

35. Taft, *Our Chief Magistrate,* 144–145.

36. Quoted in Corwin, *The President,* 8 (emphasis added).

37. Clinton Rossiter, *Constitutional Dictatorship* (Princeton: Princeton University Press, 1948).

38. Interview with Richard Nixon by David Frost, televised May 19, 1977; quoted in Craig Ducat, *Constitutional Interpretation,* 7th ed. (Belmont, Calif.: West, 2000), 206.

39. Charles Babington, "Critics of Guantánamo Urge Hill to Intervene," *Washington Post,* June 16, 2005, A2.

40. Dana Priest, "CIA Holds Terror Suspects in Secret Prisons; Debate Is Growing Within Agency About Legality and Morality of Overseas System Set Up After 9/11," *Washington Post,* November 2, 2005, A1.

41. "Bush: CIA holds terror suspects in secret prisons," CNN.com, September 7, 2006.

42. Christopher S. Kelley, "Rethinking Presidential Power: The Unitary Executive and the George W. Bush Presidency" (paper presented at the annual meeting of the Midwest Political Science Association, Chicago, April 7–10, 2005), 25. The two memos are: Jay S. Bybee, "Memorandum for Alberto Gonzales, Re: Standards of Conduct for Interrogation under 18 U.S.C. Sections 2340-2340A," Office of Legal Counsel, August 1, 2002 (full text at www.washingtonpost.com/wp-srv/nation/documents/dojinterrogation memo20020801.pdf); and John Yoo, "Memorandum to The Honorable Alberto R. Gonzales," Office of Legal Counsel, August 1, 2001 (full text at http://news.findlaw.com/wp/docs/doj/bybee80102ltr.html).

43. Scott Shane, "Report Questions Legality of Briefings on Surveillance," *New York Times,* January 19, 2006, A19. The *New York Times* first reported the administration's use of domestic wiretaps in December 2005: James Risen and Eric Lichtblau, "Bush Lets U.S. Spy on Callers Without Courts," *New York Times,* December 15, 2005, A1.

44. Edward Epstein, "Wiretap defense invokes Lincoln, Roosevelt; Attorney general says they didn't get warrants, either," *San Francisco Chronicle,* January 25, 2006, A3.

45. Corwin, *The President,* 30.

46. Arthur M. Schlesinger Jr., *The Imperial Presidency,* 2nd ed. (Boston: Houghton Mifflin, 1989).

47. Kelley, "Rethinking Presidential Power."

48. Christopher S. Yoo, Steven G. Calabresi, and Anthony J. Colangelo, "The Unitary Executive in the Modern Era," *Iowa Law Review* 90 (January 2005): 606.

49. *Humphrey's Executor v. United States,* 295 U.S. 602 (1935).

50. *Myers v. United States,* 272 U.S. 52 (1926). In 1988 the Court ruled in *Morrison v. Olson,* 487 U.S. 654, that Congress could limit the power to remove an independent counsel, even though an independent counsel is a purely executive official performing a purely executive function. The lone dissenter was Justice Antonin Scalia.

51. McDonald, *The American Presidency,* 173–174.

52. Louis Fisher, *Constitutional Conflicts between Congress and the President,* 5th ed. (Lawrence: University Press of Kansas, 2007), chap. 9.

53. Richard M. Pious, "Inherent War and Executive Powers and Prerogative Politics," *Presidential Studies Quarterly* 37 (March 2007): 77.

54. John C. Yoo, "Memorandum Opinion for the Deputy Counsel to the President: The President's Constitutional Authority to Conduct Military Operations Against Terrorists and Nations Supporting Them," September 25, 2001. The full text of the memorandum is posted at the U.S. Department of Justice Web site at www.usdoj.gov/olc/warpowers925.htm. Yoo's book, *The Powers of War and Peace: The Constitution and Foreign Affairs After 9/11* (Chicago: University of Chicago Press, 2005), explicates this theory.

55. Pious, "Inherent War and Executive Powers," 70.

56. Fisher, *Constitutional Conflicts,* chap. 8.

57. For a defense of congressional-executive agreements, see John C. Yoo, "Laws as Treaties? The Constitutionality of Congressional-Executive Agreements," *Michigan Law Review* 99 (February 2001): 757. For a critique of congressional-executive agreements, including the argument that NAFTA is unconstitutional, see Laurence H. Tribe, "Taking Text and Structure Seriously: Reflections on Free-form Method in Constitutional Interpretation," *Harvard Law Review* 108 (April 1995): 1221.

58. American Bar Association Task Force on Presidential Signing Statements, "Report," August 2006, 7–14. The full text of the report is available at www.abanet.org/media/docs/signstatereport.pdf.

59. Kelley, "Rethinking Presidential Power," 27.

60. American Bar Association Task Force on Presidential Signing Statements, "Report," 14; Kelley, "Rethinking Presidential Power," 32. A single signing statement may contain multiple challenges. These figures relate to the number of specific challenges within signing statements rather than the total number of signing statements themselves.

61. American Bar Association Task Force on Presidential Signing Statements, "Report," 16.

62. Charlie Savage, "Bush challenges hundreds of laws, President cites powers of his office," *Boston Globe,* April 30, 2006, A1. Although this article is what brought public attention to Bush's use of signing statements, political scientist Christopher S. Kelley had already written a doctoral dissertation on the topic: Christopher S. Kelley, "The Unitary Executive and the Presidential Signing Statement (Ph.D. diss., Miami University, 2003).

63. Charlie Savage, "Obama Looks to Limit Impact of Tactic Bush Used to Sidestep New Laws," *New York Times,* March 10, 2009, A12.

64. Charlie Savage, "Obama Says He Can Ignore Some Parts of Spending Bill," *New York Times,* March 12, 2009, A18.

65. Jeffrey Rosen, "Bush's Leviathan State: Power of One," *New Republic,* July 24, 2006.

66. Fred Greenstein, "Change and Continuity in the Modern Presidency," in *The New American Political System,* ed. Anthony King (Washington, D.C.: American Enterprise Institute, 1978), 45–46.

67. See, for example, Corwin, *The President,* chap. 1.

68. Clinton Rossiter, *The American Presidency,* rev. ed. (New York: Harcourt, Brace, 1960), 102.

69. Jeffrey K. Tulis, *The Rhetorical Presidency* (Princeton: Princeton University Press, 1987), chap. 4.

70. Milkis and Nelson, *The American Presidency,* 208.

71. Tulis, *The Rhetorical Presidency,* chap. 5. Also see Jeffrey K. Tulis, "The Two Constitutional Presidencies," in *The Presidency and the Political System,* 6th ed., ed. Michael Nelson (Washington, D.C.: CQ Press, 2000).

72. Thomas Jefferson had discontinued the practice as an undesirable indication of monarchist tendencies.

73. William E. Leuchtenberg, *In the Shadow of FDR: From Harry Truman to Ronald Reagan,* rev. ed. (Ithaca: Cornell University Press, 1985).

74. James L. Sundquist uses the term *economic stabilizer,* and earlier Clinton Rossiter had used the term *Manager of Prosperity.* See Sundquist, *The Decline and Resurgence of Congress* (Washington, D.C.: Brookings, 1981), chap. 4.

75. Ibid., 39.

76. Ibid., 33.

77. Ibid., 66–67.

78. Pious, "Inherent War and Executive Powers," 78. Legal challenges to the act were filed almost immediately, and in *Boumediene v. Bush,* 553 U.S. — (2008) the U.S. Supreme Court ruled that detainees have the right to file habeas corpus petitions.

79. William Glaberson, "Obama Orders Halt to Prosecutions at Guantánamo," *New York Times,* January 21, 2009, online edition, http://www.nytimes.com/2009/01/22/washington/22gitmo.html?hp.

80. Mark Mazzetti and William Glaberson, "Obama Issues Directive to Shut Down Guantánamo," *New York Times,* January 21, 2009, online edition, http://www.nytimes.com/2009/01/22/us/politics/22gitmo.html.

81. Edmund L. Andrews and Eric Dash, "U.S. Seeks Expanded Power in Seizing Firms," *New York Times,* March 24, 2009, online edition, http://www.nytimes.com/2009/03/25/business/economy/25web-bailout.html?hpw.

82. Fisher, *Constitutional Conflicts,* 24.

83. Corwin, *The President,* 175–177.

84. Gary King and Lyn Ragsdale, eds., *The Elusive Executive: Discovering Statistical Patterns in the Presidency* (Washington, D.C.: CQ Press, 1988), Table 4-1, 205. The precise size of presidential staff, however, is hard to calculate. For a discussion of this and an overview of the debates over how to count presidential staff, see John Hart, *The Presidential Branch: From Washington to Clinton,* 2nd ed. (Chatham, N.J.: Chatham House, 1995), 43–45, 112–125.

85. Seymour Martin Lipset, *The First New Nation: The United States in Historical and Comparative Perspective* (New York: Norton, 1979), 18.

86. Bruce Buchanan, *The Citizen's Presidency: Standards of Choice and Judgment* (Washington, D.C.: CQ Press, 1987), 25, 28.

87. See especially Murray Edelman, *The Symbolic Uses of Politics* (Urbana: University of Illinois Press, 1964); and Fred I. Greenstein, "What the President Means to Americans: Presidential 'Choice' between Elections," in *Choosing the President,* ed. James David Barber (Englewood Cliffs, N.J.: Prentice Hall, 1974).

88. Edelman, *The Symbolic Uses of Politics,* 76–77.

89. Greenstein, "What the President Means to Americans," 142–147. It should be noted that in this essay Greenstein deemphasized the likelihood that children socialized to a positive feeling about the president as an authority figure would extend this reliance on an "unconscious symbolic surrogate of childhood authority figures" into adulthood.

90. Murray Edelman, "The Politics of Persuasion," in Barber, *Choosing the President,* 172.

91. Barbara Hinckley, *The Symbolic Presidency: How Presidents Portray Themselves* (New York: Routledge, 1990), 5, 8.

92. As cited in Michael Novak, *Choosing Our King: Powerful Symbols in Presidential Politics* (New York: Macmillan, 1974), 44.

93. Theodore J. Lowi, *The Personal President: Power Invested, Promise Unfulfilled* (Ithaca: Cornell University Press, 1985), xii.

CHAPTER 2

Election Politics

Before widespread air travel, candidates relied on whistle-stop tours conducted from a campaign train. Here, Harry Truman and his wife speak to a crowd in Philadelphia before his come-from-behind victory in the 1948 presidential election.

Because for most Americans the president is the focal point of public life, it follows that the presidential election is the country's pivotal political event. More citizens participate in this process than in any other aspect of civic life—a record 131.3 million in 2008—and their choices have enormous significance for the nation and, indeed, for the world. Historians break history into four-year blocks of time coinciding with presidential terms, and policymaking at the federal level follows the same rhythm. The election is also a unifying event, a collective celebration of democracy coming at the conclusion of an elaborate pageant replete with familiar rituals, colorful characters, and plot lines that capture attention despite their familiarity.

Today's selection process bears little resemblance to what the founders outlined in the Constitution. Most of the changes have been extraconstitutional; that is, they have resulted from the evolution of political parties, media practices, and citizen expectations rather than constitutional amendments. There has been almost constant tinkering with the rules governing presidential elections, with most changes producing greater democratization. Remnants of indirect democracy persist, including the means used to select delegates to the party nominating conventions and the Electoral College. The 2000 election, when George W. Bush won in the Electoral College but lost the popular vote, gave new life to the debate about election rules as the nation waited thirty-six days for the final tally from Florida. Bush's victory resulted from winning Florida's electoral votes by a mere 537 votes out of nearly 6 million ballots. During the prolonged period of uncertainty that followed election day, Americans relearned the arcane workings of the Electoral College and discovered the fallibility of voting methods and counting rules. In contrast, Bush's reelection victory in 2004 was clear cut, as was Barack Obama's in 2008.

At the conclusion of this chapter, we review recommendations for reform intended to improve system performance and provide for a greater degree of direct democracy. To appreciate the current selection process and suggestions for reform, it is necessary to first examine the major transformations in the nomination and general election phases of the process.

Evolution of the Selection Process

In 1789 and 1792 electing a president was simple. Each member of the Electoral College cast two votes, one of which had to be for a person outside the elector's state. Both times George Washington was elected by unanimous votes.[1] And both times John Adams received the second highest number of votes to become the vice president. In 1789 the process took three months: no one campaigned; electors were chosen on the first Wednesday of January; they met in their respective states to vote on the first Wednesday in February; and the votes were counted on April 6. In 1792 the procedure took even less time. The contrast with today's process could not be sharper: candidates now launch nomination campaigns up to two years before the general election, collectively spending hundreds of millions of dollars in pursuit of the office, and everyone expects to know the winner on election night.

Consensus support for Washington ensured smooth operation of the selection procedure during the first two elections: there was widespread confidence that the nation's wartime hero would govern in the interest of all the people. When political consensus eroded, elites developed a separate nomination procedure. Policy differences in Congress created the basis for an important institution not mentioned in the Constitution—the political party. By the early 1790s the Federalist Party had formed around the economic policies of Secretary of the Treasury Alexander Hamilton, and his supporters in Congress backed his programs.[2] Resigning as secretary of state in 1793, Thomas Jefferson joined James Madison, then serving in the House of Representatives, as a critic of Hamilton's policies, and they formed the rival Republican Party, which came to be known as the Democratic-Republican Party.[3] By the mid-1790s, cohesive pro- and anti-administration blocs had formed in Congress, and congressional candidates were labeled either Democratic-Republicans or Federalists.[4]

Political parties had an almost immediate impact on the Electoral College. Electors became party loyalists, whose discipline was apparent in 1800, when Jefferson, the Democratic-Republicans' candidate for president, and Aaron Burr, the party's candidate for vice president, tied in the Electoral College vote. Loyal to their party, the electors had cast their ballots for both candidates, but the Constitution had no provision for counting the ballots separately for president and vice president. Jefferson and Burr each received seventy-three votes to President Adams's sixty-five. The House of Representatives decided the election, where Jefferson won after thirty-six ballots. Hamilton broke the tie by throwing his support behind Jefferson, his longtime rival. Party loyalty, with infrequent exceptions, has prevailed in Electoral College balloting ever since. (The Twelfth Amendment to the Constitution, ratified in 1804, provided for separate presidential and vice-presidential balloting.)[5]

The rise of parties also altered presidential selection by creating a separate nomination stage: the parties had to devise a method for choosing their nominees. Influence over presidential selection shifted from the local notables who had served as electors to party elites. In 1796 the Federalists' leaders chose their candidate, John Adams, and the Democratic-Republicans relied on their party members in Congress, the **congressional caucus,** to nominate Jefferson. Four years later, the congressional caucus became the nominating mechanism for both parties, a practice that continued until 1824, when the system broke down.

A party's members of Congress, already assembled in the nation's capital and facing minimal transportation problems, selected a nominee. Because legislators were familiar with potential presidential candidates from all parts of the new country, they were the logical agents for choosing candidates for an office with a nationwide constituency. Caucuses provided peer review of candidates' credentials: essentially, a group of politicians assessed a fellow politician's skills, abilities, and political appeal. But the congressional caucus violated the constitutional principle of separation of powers by giving members of the legislative body a routine role in choosing the president rather than an emergency role, assumed only in the event of an Electoral College deadlock. The caucus also could not represent areas in which the party had lost the previous congressional election, a problem quickly encountered by the Federalists, whose support was dwindling. Moreover, interested and informed citizens who participated in grassroots party activities, especially campaigns, had no means to participate in congressional caucus deliberations.

The 1824 election brought an end to nomination by congressional caucus. First, the Democratic-Republicans in Congress insisted on nominating Secretary of the Treasury William Crawford, who had suffered a debilitating stroke. Then, in the general election, Andrew Jackson, nominated by the Tennessee legislature, won more popular votes and more electoral votes than any other candidate but failed to achieve a majority in the Electoral College. The election again was decided by the House, where John Quincy Adams emerged victorious after he agreed to make Henry Clay, another of the five contestants, secretary of state in return for his support. These shenanigans permanently discredited *King Caucus,* as its critics called it. Favorite sons nominated by state legislatures and state conventions dominated the 1828 campaign, but this method proved too decentralized to select a national official. A device was needed that would represent party elements throughout the country, tap the new participatory fervor, and facilitate the nomination of a candidate.

National Party Conventions

What developed was the **party nominating convention,** an assembly made truly national by including delegates from all the states. Rail transportation made such meetings feasible, and the expanding citizen participation in presidential elections made the change necessary. Influence over selection of the party nominee therefore shifted to state and local party leaders, particularly those able to commit large blocs of delegate votes to a candidate.

Two minor parties with no appreciable representation in Congress, the Anti-Masons and the National Republicans, led the way with conventions in 1831.[6] To rally support in 1832, the Democrats, under President Andrew Jackson (elected in 1828), also held a convention. Major political parties have nominated their presidential and vice-presidential candidates by holding national conventions ever since. National committees composed of state party leaders call the presidential nominating conventions into session to choose nominees and to adopt a platform of common policy positions.[7] Delegates are selected by states and allocated primarily on the basis of population.

Although today's conventions in some ways resemble those of the past, the nomination process has undergone drastic revision, especially since 1968, when Democrats introduced reforms that diminished the conventions' importance. Just as influence over selection of the party nominee shifted from Congress to party leaders, it has moved within the party from a small group of organization professionals to a broad base of activists and voters. The origins of this shift can be traced to the development of presidential primary elections that began early in the twentieth century. (Florida passed the first primary election law in 1901.)

Under the system that operated from roughly 1850 to 1950, party leaders from the largest states could bargain over presidential nominations. Most influential were those who controlled large blocs of delegates and would throw their support behind a candidate for the right price. These power brokers—hence the term **brokered conventions**—might seek a program commitment in the platform, a position in the president's cabinet, or other forms of federal patronage in return for support. To be successful, candidates had to curry favor with party and elected officials before and during the national convention. An effective campaign manager might tour the country selling the candidate's virtues and securing delegate commitments prior to the convention, but about half the conventions began with no sense of the likely outcome. Protracted bargaining and negotiation among powerful state and local party leaders were often the result. In 1924 the Democrats needed 103 ballots cast over seventeen days to nominate John W. Davis, an effort that must have seemed pointless later when he attracted only 29 percent of the popular vote. Nevertheless, the convention was a deliberative body that reached decisions on common policy positions as well as on nominees. Providing a way to accommodate the demands of major elements within the party established the base for a nationwide campaign.

In this respect, modern conventions are quite different. Not since 1952, when the Democrats needed three ballots to nominate Gov. Adlai Stevenson of Illinois for president, has it taken more than one ballot to determine either party's nominee.[8] Raucous floor battles over procedures and delegate credentials have given way to a stream of symbols and speakers whose appearances are carefully choreographed to appeal to a prime-time television audience. Conventions today serve as ratifying assemblies for a popular choice rather than deliberative bodies, and candidates with popular appeal have the advantage over those whose appeal is primarily with party leaders.

Although much of the convention's business is still conducted in backroom meetings, the most important business—choosing the presidential nominee— already has been decided through the grueling process used to select convention delegates. Compared with their forerunners, modern conventions conduct their business in a routine fashion, adhere to enforceable national party standards for delegate selection and demographic representation, and are more heavily influenced by rank-and-file party supporters than by party leaders.[9] These changes appeared gradually through a process often fraught with conflict that centered on the rules governing delegate selection.

Reform of the Selection Process

The pace of change accelerated when the Democratic Party adopted internal reforms after it lost the presidency in 1968. In addition to the actions already noted, rules adopted by a variety of actors—one hundred state political parties and fifty legislatures, the national political parties, and Congress—reformed the process, and they continue to modify it. Sometimes individuals turned to the courts to interpret provisions of these regulations and reconcile conflicts. In addition, the rules were adjusted so drastically and so often that, particularly in the Democratic Party, candidates and their supporters found it difficult to keep up.

Reform has been especially pervasive in the nomination process. Following their tumultuous convention in 1968, when Vietnam War protesters clashed with police in the streets of Chicago, the Democrats adopted a set of guidelines that reduced the influence of party leaders, encouraged participation by rank-and-file Democrats, and expanded convention representation of previously underrepresented groups, particularly women and African Americans. The result was a pronounced shift of influence within the party from *party professionals* toward *amateurs,* a term encompassing citizens who become engaged in the presidential contest because of a short-term concern such as an attractive candidate (candidate enthusiasts) or an especially important issue (issue enthusiasts).

States, seeking to conform to the party's new guidelines on participation, adopted the **primary** as the preferred means of selecting convention delegates. Primaries allow a party's registered voters—and, in some states, independents—to express a presidential preference that is translated into convention delegates. The **party caucus** is another way to select delegates. The caucus is a local meeting of registered party voters that often involves speeches and discussion about the candidates' merits. A caucus is more social, public, and time-consuming (often requiring two hours to complete) than a primary, in which voters make choices in the voting booth. The caucus method is also multistage: delegates from the local caucuses go to a county convention that selects delegates to a state convention that selects the national delegates. In 1968 only seventeen states chose delegates through primaries, the remainder using caucuses dominated by party leaders. In 2008, forty-one states held primaries, and the remaining caucuses provided for additional participation.[10] Because of these changes, nominations are more apt to reflect the voters' immediate concerns, nominees are unofficially chosen well before the convention, and the influence of party leaders is reduced. The cost of these changes is the loss of peer review—politicians evaluating the capability of fellow politicians. Moreover, the changes have enhanced the importance of the media. By operating as the principal source of information about the candidates and by emphasizing the "horse race"—who is ahead—the media have become enormously influential during the delegate selection process. Not everyone was satisfied with the general movement toward a more democratized selection process, as evidenced by several counterreforms that appeared during the 1980s.

The Contemporary Selection Process

Despite the seemingly perpetual flux that characterizes presidential elections, it is possible to identify four stages in the process: (1) defining the pool of eligible candidates; (2) nominating the parties' candidates at the national conventions following delegate selection in the primaries and caucuses; (3) waging the general election campaign, culminating in election day; and (4) validating results through the Electoral College.

No two presidential election cycles are identical, but the customary time line is relatively predictable (see Figure 2-1). Potential candidates maneuver for position during the one or two years preceding the election. Selection of convention delegates begins in January and February of the election year, with conventions typically scheduled first for the **out party,** the one seeking the White House.[11] In 2008 the Democrats met August 25–28 in Denver, and the Republicans September 1–4 in Minneapolis–St. Paul. Traditionally, the general election campaign begins on Labor Day and runs until election day, the first Tuesday after the first Monday in November, but modern campaigns really begin once the identity of major party nominees becomes clear. That date was much later in 2008 than in other recent elections because the contest between Senator Obama and Sen. Hillary Rodham Clinton was not decided until late June. Unlike in 2000, voters usually know the general election winner on election night, and the mid-December balloting by electors in their state capitals is automatic. Finally, the electors' ballots are officially tabulated the first week in January during a joint session of the U.S. Congress, presided over by the incumbent vice president. The duly elected president is inaugurated on January 20, a date set in the Twentieth Amendment.

FIGURE 2-1   The 2008 Presidential Contest Time Line

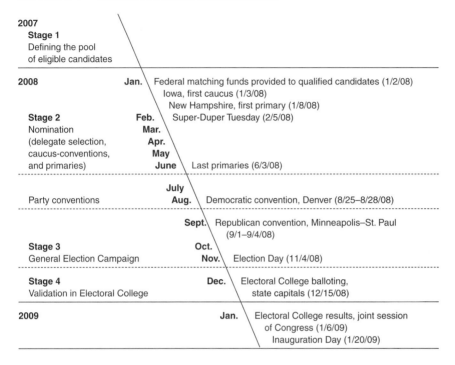

Defining the Pool of Eligibles

Who is eligible to serve as president? The formal rules relating to qualifications are minimal and have been remarkably stable over time. Individuals need to meet only three requirements set forth in Article II, section 1, of the Constitution. One must be a natural-born citizen, at least thirty-five years of age, and a resident of the United States for fourteen years or longer.[12] In 2008 approximately 130 million Americans met these constitutional requirements, but the pool of plausible candidates was far smaller.[13]

The informal requirements for the presidency are less easily satisfied. People who entertain presidential ambitions must have what is generally called **political availability,** the political experiences and personal characteristics that make them attractive to political activists and to the general voting public. Potential candidates accumulate these credentials through personal and career decisions made long before the election year, but there is no explicit checklist of qualifications for the presidency. One method to determine what particular political experiences and personal characteristics put an individual in line for a nomination is to look at past candidates. Even this approach poses some difficulties because the attitudes of political leaders and the public change over time.

Political Experience of Candidates

Who is nominated to run for president? Overwhelmingly, the answer is people with experience in one of a few civilian, elective, political offices. Nominees' backgrounds have changed very little since the second half of the nineteenth century.[14] Since 1932, with only two exceptions, major party nominees have been drawn from one of four positions: the presidency, the vice presidency, a state governorship, or a U.S. Senate seat. (See Appendix B.) Candidates with other backgrounds are seldom successful. In 2000, five aspirants who lacked experience in elected office unsuccessfully sought the Republican nomination. In 1992 H. Ross Perot, a billionaire businessman, sought election without a party nomination and did so again in 1996 as nominee of the Reform Party.

Presidents and Vice Presidents. Since 1932 the party controlling the presidency has turned to the presidency or vice presidency for candidates, and the out party has turned primarily to governors and then to senators. In only two of the twenty elections from 1932 to 2008 was the name of an incumbent president or vice president not on the ballot. Fourteen times, the incumbent president was renominated, and in four of the six instances when the incumbent president was either prohibited by the Twenty-second Amendment from running again (Dwight Eisenhower in 1960, Ronald Reagan in 1988, Bill Clinton in 2000, and George W. Bush in 2008) or declined to do so (Harry S. Truman in 1952 and Lyndon Baines Johnson in 1968), the incumbent vice president won his party's nomination. The exceptions occurred in 1952 and 2008. When Truman halted his reelection effort in 1952, Adlai Stevenson became the nominee rather than the vice president, seventy-five-year-old Alben Barkley. In 2008 the incumbent party also had an open competition for the presidential nomination because Vice President Dick Cheney chose not to pursue the office.

There are no guarantees that an incumbent president will be renominated, but it is enormously difficult for the party in power to remove these leaders from the national ticket. Incumbents have considerable advantages when it comes to winning the nomination, as demonstrated by Gerald Ford in 1976, Jimmy Carter in 1980, George H. W. Bush in 1992, and George W. Bush in 2004. Party leaders are reluctant to admit they made a mistake four years earlier; incumbents can direct federal programs toward politically important areas or make politically useful executive branch appointments; and presidents enjoy far greater name recognition and media exposure than others seeking the nomination. As a result, even unpopular presidents tend to be renominated. The Republicans chose Ford despite an energy crisis and slow economy; and the Democrats renominated Carter when both inflation and unemployment were high, Americans were being held hostage in Iran, and Soviet troops occupied Afghanistan; and George H. W. Bush was renominated in 1992 despite a weakening economy and charges that he broke a campaign pledge not to raise taxes. George W. Bush faced no challengers in 2004 and waltzed to the nomination despite job losses in the economy and controversy surrounding the justification for going to war in Iraq.

Incumbent vice presidents are more likely to win their party's nomination today than in the past.[15] Recent presidential candidates have chosen running mates who are arguably more capable than their predecessors, which makes these individuals more viable prospects for the presidency. Moreover, presidents now assign their vice presidents meaningful responsibilities, including political party activities (especially campaigning in off-year elections), liaison assignments with social groups, and diplomatic missions abroad. As the position's visibility and significance have increased, so have the political chances of its occupants improved.[16]

If it is an asset in securing the party's nomination, the vice presidency once seemed a liability in winning the general election. George H. W. Bush's victory in 1988 broke a 152-year-old record of losing campaigns. Richard Nixon and Hubert Humphrey lost as incumbent vice presidents in 1960 and 1968, and Al Gore suffered a similar fate in 2000, despite winning a popular vote plurality.

Senators and Governors. From 1932 through 2008 the party out of power nominated ten governors, six senators, two former vice presidents, one general (Eisenhower), and one businessman (Wendell Willkie). (See Table 2-1.) Both major parties have looked to governors as promising candidates, except for the period from 1960 to 1972, when Sens. John Kennedy (D-1960), Barry Goldwater (R-1964), and George McGovern (D-1972), and former vice president Nixon (R-1968), won the nomination. Governorships later regained prominence with the nomination of former governors Carter (D-1976) and Reagan (R-1980) and sitting governors Michael Dukakis (D-1988), Bill Clinton (D-1992), and George W. Bush (R-2000). Only four times in the past nine elections did the party out of power not turn to a governor: former vice president Walter Mondale was the Democratic nominee in 1984, Senate majority leader Robert Dole was the Republican nominee in 1996, Sen. John Kerry was the Democrats' standard bearer in 2004, and Senator Obama led the Democrats in 2008.

TABLE 2-1   Principal Experience of In- and Out-Party Candidates before Gaining
Nomination, 1932–2008

Election year	In party	Out party
1932	President (R)	Governor (D)
1936	President (D)	Governor (R)
1940	President (D)	Businessman (R)
1944	President (D)	Governor (R)
1948	President (D)	Governor (R)
1952	Governor (D)	General/educator (R)
1956	President (R)	Governor (former) (D)
1960	Vice president (R)	Senator (D)
1964	President (D)	Senator (R)
1968	Vice president (D)	Vice president (former) (R)
1972	President (R)	Senator (D)
1976	President (R)	Governor (former) (D)
1980	President (D)	Governor (former) (R)
1984	President (R)	Vice president (former) (D)
1988	Vice president (R)	Governor (D)
1992	President (R)	Governor (D)
1996	President (D)	Senator (R)
2000	Vice president (D)	Governor (R)
2004	President (R)	Senator (D)
2008	Senator (R)	Senator (D)

It is possible to argue that these patterns understate the importance of the Senate as a recruiting ground for president. Certainly, many senators have sought their parties' presidential nomination since the early 1950s. Senators share the political and media spotlight focused on the capital, enjoy the opportunity to address major public problems and develop a record in foreign affairs, and they usually can pursue the presidency without leaving the Senate. Nevertheless, only three times in American history have senators been elected directly to the White House (Warren Harding in 1920, Kennedy in 1960, and Obama in 2008).[17]

Instead of a stepping-stone to the presidency, the Senate has been a path to the vice presidency, which then gave its occupants the inside track either to assume the presidency through succession or to win nomination on their own. Vice Presidents Truman, Nixon, Johnson, Humphrey, Mondale, Quayle, and Gore served as senators immediately before assuming their executive posts. (Gerald Ford, who succeeded to the presidency when Nixon resigned in 1974, had moved into the vice presidency from the House of Representatives. Dick Cheney, elected vice president in 2000 and 2004, had served in the House before becoming secretary of defense and then a businessman.) Service in the Senate, therefore, has been an important source of experience for presidents since 1932, but almost all have gained seasoning in the vice presidency.

Until 2008, governors seemed to have a competitive advantage over senators. Bill Clinton and George W. Bush moved directly into the Oval Office from a governor's mansion. Two others—Carter and Reagan—were former governors who were free to devote themselves full time to the demanding task of winning the nomination, an opportunity not available to the senators who sought the presidency in those years. Governors can claim valuable executive experience in managing large-scale public enterprises and thousands of state government employees in contrast to a senator's essentially legislative duties and direction of a small personal staff. Moreover, the public's concern with foreign affairs declined after 1976 and was replaced by anxiety over the domestic economy, taxes, the budget, education, and health care. This shift in public attitudes was especially evident in 1992 and 2000, when Clinton and Bush benefited from the Cold War's reduced prominence during their successful election campaigns. With the terrorist attacks of September 11, 2001, public concerns once again shifted to national security, which may have given senators the advantage over governors in the nomination contest. At the outset of 2008, it seemed the war in Iraq would be the dominant issue, again giving senators prominence, but public attention shifted during the year to domestic issues, led by the economy. The Democratic candidates included four sitting senators (Biden, Clinton, Dodd, Obama), two former senators (Edwards, Gravel), one House member (Kucinich), one sitting governor (Richardson), and one former governor (Vilsack). Among Republican contestants were two sitting senators (Brownback, McCain), one former senator (F. Thompson), four former governors (Gilmore, Huckabee, Romney, T. Thompson), three sitting members of the House (Hunter, Paul, Tancredo), and one former mayor (Giuliani).

Personal Characteristics of Candidates

Although millions meet the formal requirements for president, far fewer meet the informal criteria that have guided past choices. Most constraining have been the limits imposed by social conventions on gender and race, constraints that the Democrats challenged in 2008. Until Obama's victory over Clinton for the nomination in 2008, only males of European heritage had been nominated for president by either of the two major parties, although several women and African Americans had waged national campaigns since 1972, and former representative Geraldine Ferraro of New York was the Democrats' 1984 nominee for vice president. In 2008 Bill

Richardson became the first Hispanic American to seek a major party's presidential nomination.

Presidential aspirants also have had to pass other "tests" based on personal characteristics, although these informal requirements have changed in the past five decades.[18] Until 1960 candidates had to meet unspoken demographic and religious requirements: that they hail from English ethnic stock and practice a Protestant religion. The successful candidacy of John Kennedy, a Roman Catholic, challenged the traditional preference for Protestants. The Democrats nominated Alfred Smith, a Catholic, in 1928, but he lost the general election. John Kerry's Catholicism was not an issue in 2004. The Republican senator Barry Goldwater was the first nominee from a partly Jewish background, and Sen. Joseph Lieberman, an Orthodox Jew, joined the Democratic ticket in 2000. Religion as an issue resurfaced in 2008 when Republican Mitt Romney became the first Mormon to try for the nomination, and Obama's critics alleged that he was a Muslim. Recent candidates have come from Irish, Norwegian, Greek, and Kenyan heritage, suggesting that the traditional preference for English stock has weakened.

Representing an idealized version of home and family life also seemed essential to winning nomination. These criteria have undergone modest change. Nelson Rockefeller's divorce in 1963 from his wife of more than thirty years and his rapid remarriage virtually ensured the failure of his campaign for the Republican nomination in 1964 and 1968. The marital status of several later candidates was an issue as well, but in 1980 Reagan became the first divorced and remarried president. Public attitudes about other moral and ethical questions may or may not become deciding factors. Gary Hart's widely reported extramarital affair ended his presidential hopes for 1988, even though he began the campaign as the clear front-runner. Bill Clinton's alleged extramarital relationships and drug use became issues in 1992, but allegations of prior drug use and an admission of alcohol abuse did not damage George W. Bush in 2000.

It appears, therefore, that several of the informal qualifications applied to the presidency have altered with the passage of time, probably because of changes in the nomination process itself as well as broader currents in U.S. society. One observer suggests that the proliferation of presidential primaries "provides a forum in which prejudices can be addressed openly,"[19] and the public is possibly becoming more tolerant. As demonstrated in 2008, as African Americans, women, and descendants of immigrants from Asia, Latin America, and eastern and southern Europe occupy governorships and seats in the U.S. Senate, they enhance their chances of becoming serious candidates for the presidency.

Crowded fields marked both the Republican and Democratic contests for the 2008 nomination. Republican candidates participating in this October 2007 Florida debate are, from left, Rep. Tom Tancredo, Rep. Ron Paul, former governor Mike Huckabee, former mayor Rudy Giuliani, former governor Mitt Romney, former senator Fred Thompson, Sen. John McCain, and Rep. Duncan Hunter. Republican Party of Florida chair Jim Greer stands between Romney and Thompson.

Competing for the Nomination

Once the pool of eligible candidates is established, the selection process begins. This phase has two major components: choosing delegates to the two parties' national conventions and selecting the nominees at the conventions. By far the more complicated of these steps, the selection of delegates, became the principal focus of party reform efforts after 1968 and continues to undergo change. Prior to the conventions, candidates crisscross the country to win delegates, who then attend the convention to select the party's nominee.

The first primary of 2008 was held in New Hampshire following the Iowa caucuses. Delegate selection extended into June, when a handful of states held primaries, the last of the party contests to choose delegates.[20] Through this complex process, the Republicans selected 2,517 delegates, and the Democrats 4,361. Consistent with post-1968 reforms, most delegates were chosen through primaries. A record number of Americans participated in primaries and caucuses, an estimated 58.75 million, up sharply from 2000 and 2004.[21]

In truth, the nomination contest begins much earlier than January of the election year. By starting their campaigns early, candidates seek to amass the financial backing, attract media attention, and generate the popular support necessary to ensure eventual victory. By the end of January 2007, all the Democratic candidates had either announced their candidacy or launched exploratory committees, and two Republicans, Rudolph Giuliani and Sen. John McCain, had announced their intention to run before Thanksgiving in 2006. Many candidates, then, had roughly one year to campaign before the first delegates were selected.

The Nomination Campaign

The nomination campaign is a winnowing process in which each of the two major parties eliminates from the pool of potential candidates all but the one who will represent the party in the general election. As political scientist Austin Ranney pointed out in 1974, the nomination phase of the campaign is more important than the election stage because "the parties' nominating processes eliminate far more presidential possibilities than do the voters' electing processes."[22] His observation was especially true in 2008 when both parties had crowded fields of hopefuls. In the past, nomination campaigns were relatively unstructured. Aspirants typically did not know how many opponents they would face or who they would be. The competition took place in weekly stages, with candidates hopscotching the nation in pursuit of votes and contributions. Conducting such a campaign was enormously difficult, especially for first-time candidates who had to organize a nationwide political effort, a chore that dwarfs the campaign required to win a Senate seat or governorship in even the largest states.

This competitive situation has changed. As more states moved their primaries to earlier spots in the schedule—a pattern called **front-loading**—the critical events take place during a very brief window near the beginning of the six-month process. Instead of having the opportunity to adjust strategy along the way, candidates need to establish campaign organizations in many states and to raise enormous sums of money early in the process. Many of the traditional uncertainties—for example, new candidates entering the competition—have become less likely, as early contests quickly trigger the departure of weaker candidates instead of creating opportunities for new entries.[23] In 2008 both parties were expected to choose 50 percent of their convention delegates by the end of the day on February 5, and more than three-quarters of all delegates by the first Tuesday in March.[24] But predictions for early nominations were proved wrong when the Democrats' contest extended into June.

Presidential hopefuls spend considerable time before January of the election year laying the campaign's groundwork. Decades ago, journalist Arthur Hadley called this period the "invisible primary," a testing ground for the would-be president to determine whether his or her candidacy is viable.[25] Candidates must assemble a staff to help raise money, develop campaign strategy, hone a message, and identify a larger group of people willing to do the advance work necessary to organize states for the primaries and caucuses. Candidates visit party organizations throughout the country, especially in the two traditional early states, Iowa and New Hampshire, to curry favor with activists and solicit endorsements.[26] Democrats authorized two states—Nevada and South Carolina—to join the early group of contests in 2008, but Florida and Michigan then demanded to be added as well. The resulting legal and political challenges complicated candidates' strategies. Competition takes on the trappings of a full-fledged campaign: candidates broadcast television ads, engage in debates, and seek to finish well in prenomination popularity contests known as straw polls.

Because media coverage provides name recognition and potentially positive publicity, developing a favorable relationship with reporters and commentators is crucial. Those hopefuls the media ignore because they do not regard them as serious contenders find it almost impossible to become viable candidates. Even the suggestion that some candidates are "top tier" and others "second tier," the terms widely used in 2008 to sort out the large fields, could adversely affect a candidacy. Most candidates' campaigns are scuttled, if not officially canceled, during the "invisible primary" stage.

Financing Nomination Campaigns

Candidates for the nomination must raise funds early. Reforms introduced for the 1976 election provided federal assistance: candidates can qualify to receive federal funds that match individual contributions of $250 or less if they can raise $100,000 in individual contributions, with at least $5,000 collected in twenty different states. By checking a box on their federal income tax forms, taxpayers authorize the government to set aside $3.00 of their tax payments for public financing of campaigns. The Federal Election Commission (FEC), a bipartisan body of six members nominated by the president and confirmed by the Senate, oversees the administration of the public financing provisions. But participation in this system dropped from 25.5 percent of all tax returns in 1976 to about 10 percent in 2006.[27] Candidates who accept public financing must also accept limitations on total expenditures and a cap on spending in individual states that is based on population. Many candidates prefer to avoid these limits. The 2004 election was the first in which both parties' nominees declined federal matching funds. In 2008 the leading candidates also declined these funds, making the system's future uncertain. Neither Obama nor Clinton used matching funds in 2008, and each raised totals that dwarfed those of previous candidates. Clinton raised nearly $250 million in her unsuccessful effort.[28]

By providing partial funding of nomination campaigns, congressional reformers in the 1970s sought to establish a system of broad-based citizen contributions, replacing the financial support of a small number of "fat cats," who previously bankrolled candidates.[29] But today, only weak candidates rely on matching funds. In 2008, six candidates qualified for $21.73 million in matching funds, down from $62.261 million in 2000 and $28.4 million in 2004.[30] The federal government also provided $16.3 million each to the Democratic and Republican Parties to finance their nominating conventions, but this amount was a small fraction of the total spending on the conventions. The Center for Responsive Politics estimated the Democrats spent an additional $59 million, and the Republicans, $60 million.[31]

Personal wealth sometimes plays a role in the prenomination stage. In 1996 Steve Forbes loaned his campaign $37.5 million, and another businessman, Maurice Taylor, spent $6.5 million of his own resources. Neither was ultimately successful, but Forbes dramatically influenced the Republican nomination process by outspending his rivals in Iowa, New Hampshire, and several other early contests. Even Bob Dole, who led all candidates in fund-raising that year, could not match such expenditures because he had to observe federal limits.[32] This experience partly shaped Bush's strategy in 2000. Anticipating that Forbes would pursue a similar tactic the second time around, Bush raised a record $94 million in private funds, double that of Forbes and McCain, his closest competitors; he therefore avoided the spending limits associated with public funding.[33] For 2004 the Bush campaign nearly tripled its earlier fund-raising total to $292.6 million. John Kerry declined matching funds and raised $253.9 million, nearly six times more than any previous Democrat, to keep pace with Howard Dean, his principal opponent, who also declined federal matching funds.[34] The major candidates in both parties' 2008 field declined public funds. Without spending limits they could compete more effectively during the nomination phase and launch a national campaign as soon as they secured sufficient delegates for a first-ballot nomination. Eleven Republicans collectively raised $656.3 million, and the twelve Democrats raised $1.15 billion. In both cases, most of the money came from individual contributions.

In the postreform era, most candidates solicit funds from large numbers of individuals through direct mail and now through the Web.[35] In theory, public funds would open the door for candidates who formerly could not afford to mount a nomination campaign because large contributors would not support them. Although public funds reduced financial disparities among candidates, their financial resources are still highly unequal, and in most election years, the field's leading fund-raiser won the nomination.[36] This did not happen in 2004; Howard Dean, the Democrats' champion fund-raiser heading into the election year, lost the nomination. In 2008 McCain was not the leading Republican fund-raiser before securing the nomination, but Obama was the unexpected leader in the Democratic field.

Superior financial resources enable candidates to compete in more of the early nomination contests, help them extend their fund-raising lead, make it possible to survive poor results (such as Bush's loss of New Hampshire in 2000), and make them stronger in later primaries. Failing to do well in early caucus and primary contests means more than losing delegates to opponents; it also means that contributions stop. Moreover, under the campaign finance law, federal matching funds must be cut off within thirty days if a candidate receives less than 10 percent of the votes in two consecutive primaries. Leading Republican candidates in 1995 worked aggressively to reach the target of $20 million in contributions by year's end, the consensus target among political consultants on what it would take to run a "serious" campaign.[37] Bush's record fund-raising in 2000 dramatically raised that threshold for 2004 when his campaign aimed for $200 million.[38] Those expectations rose even higher heading into 2008 with the goal of raising $100 million during 2007 and then continuing to raise money prior to the late summer conventions. Candidates who could not keep up the pace lost credibility with the media; for example, McCain's early fund-raising was disappointing, but he later rallied for a nomination victory.[39]

Approaching the 2004 election, candidates confronted a remarkably uncertain campaign finance picture. In March 2002 Congress adopted, and President Bush signed into law, the Bipartisan Campaign Reform Act of 2002 (BCRA), the final product of multiyear reform efforts by McCain; Sen. Russ Feingold, D-Wis.; and Reps. Christopher Shays, R-Conn., and Martin Meehan, D-Mass. Most of the reforms focus on congressional elections, but many observers believed (accurately as it turned out) that the changes would exacerbate, rather than solve, problems in financing presidential elections. The Campaign Finance Institute convened a blue-ribbon task force in July 2002 on financing presidential nominations.[40] Because the two major parties have front-loaded their nomination contests in the past few election cycles, candidates reached the spending limit and secured a majority of delegates early in the campaign, several months before the convention. Parties used soft money as a way to pay for the expected nominee's campaign during the period before the conventions, a practice the BCRA made illegal, although the provisions confronted a constitutional challenge. In *McConnell v. Federal Election Commission* (2003) the Supreme Court upheld the law. The law allows individuals to contribute more (initially increased to $2,000 from the previous $1,000 and raised to $2,300 for 2008).[41] It failed to increase the portion eligible for matching funds beyond the $250 limit in place since 1976.

The result is a public funding and primary system that creates strong incentives for candidates not to take public funds, precisely what happened in 2008. The new system favors very wealthy candidates or those who—like Bush in 2000 and 2004 and Clinton and Obama in 2008—can tap or establish networks of donors during the "invisible primary" before the Iowa and New Hampshire contests, raising enough money early to turn down public funding and sail through to the end. The calendar and funding system rules will also favor front-runners, making it hard for primary voters to give others a second look.[42]

Dynamics of the Contest

Candidates who begin the election year as leaders in the public opinion polls frequently go on to win nomination. This pattern prevailed from 1936 through 1968, was interrupted in four Democratic contests between 1972 and 1992, but returned in the 1990s.[43] In 1996 and 2000 early leaders won the nomination in both parties: Bill Clinton and Bob Dole in 1996, and Al Gore and George W. Bush in 2000. But 2004 showed that a leader in the polls (Dean) must guard against critical campaign mistakes, verbal slips, and the assumption that early popularity is permanent.

Before front-loading became so pronounced, candidates competed in as many locations as funds allowed. This was especially true for Democrats, whose rules call for proportional allocation of delegates: as long as candidates achieve at least 15 percent of the vote, they are awarded a share of delegates proportional to the vote share.[44] The earliest contests, the Iowa caucuses and New Hampshire primary, attract most of the major contenders because they are the first tests of rank-and-file voter sentiment. Iowa returned to prominence in 2008 after being overshadowed for many years by New Hampshire, where the delegate total is small but the winner receives immediate attention. Pat Buchanan was the surprise winner in 1996, with a slim 1 percent victory margin over Dole, and McCain defeated Bush in 2000 by the relatively wide margin of 48.5 to 30.4 percent. The small New Hampshire electorate enables candidates with more modest financial resources to conduct labor-intensive campaigns, as was the case for McCain.

A new twist in the 1988 campaign was the large number of primaries held on Tuesday, March 8, a day subsequently known as Super Tuesday. Twenty states selected delegates, sixteen through primaries and four through caucuses. In 1992 only eleven states participated in Super Tuesday, but the Democratic designers accomplished their goal of boosting the chances of a moderate candidate when Clinton won all six of the southern primaries and two caucuses, while Paul Tsongas, his principal rival, claimed victories in just two primaries and one caucus. George

H. W. Bush, who swept all sixteen of the 1988 Super Tuesday primaries, repeated this success in March 1992. Likewise, Dole won all seven Super Tuesday primaries in 1996. Super Tuesday was called "Titanic Tuesday" and "Mega Tuesday" in 2000 because the delegate total rose dramatically when New York and California joined the list of states holding primaries that day. In 2008 the list grew to twenty-two contests to choose delegates on February 5. Although Hillary Clinton had hoped to score a knock-out that day, when nearly 40 percent of all convention delegates were selected, she split the results with Obama. McCain, on the other hand, pulled away from Romney, his closest competitor.

Holding primaries early in the nomination process is a reversal from the past when late primaries could decide an election. Until 1996 California scheduled its primary on the final day of delegate selection, giving Golden State voters the chance to determine a party's nominee, as with Goldwater in 1964 and McGovern in 1972. After their loss in 1996, Republicans adopted rules that encouraged states to schedule their primaries later in 2000 by providing them with bonus delegates.[45] But the schedule was only slightly less front-loaded in 2000, and the contests were concluded earlier than ever before—March 9, when both McCain and former senator Bill Bradley, the number-two candidate in each party, discontinued their campaigns.

The two parties set a "window" for delegate selection, providing special exceptions for Iowa and New Hampshire, as well as for South Carolina and Nevada in 2008. In these relatively small states, candidates engage in "retail" politics, meeting with voters on a more personal basis than is possible in larger states, where candidates must rely on media advertising in practicing "wholesale" politics. States position themselves as early in the process as possible, and more states than ever want to hold their contests before March. In 2004, by the end of the first Tuesday in March, 58 percent of the Democratic convention delegates had been chosen. That figure rose to 84 percent by the same Tuesday in March 2008. The Democrats overcame a congested field in 2004 to unofficially select their nominee before the middle of March. Observers expected the same thing to happen in 2008, but Clinton and Obama were so evenly matched that the states scheduled later in the process—Pennsylvania, for one—played an unexpectedly important role. For a while, Democrats wondered whether the nomination campaign would continue until the convention decided on a nominee, a scenario that has not occurred since 1952. But **superdelegates,** Democratic elected and party officials who attend the convention by virtue of their positions, sided with Obama, whose delegate total exceeded Clinton's after all primaries and caucuses had been concluded. Republicans, even less accustomed to crowded candidate fields experienced an "open convention" in 1976 when Ford's victory over Ronald Reagan was not sealed until just before the delegates convened. The Republicans' big surprises in 2008 were the weakness of Giuliani ($40 million spent, zero delegates won) and the strength of Mike Huckabee, former governor of Arkansas.

State caucuses operate in the shadow of the primaries, although they remain important for candidates able to mobilize an intensely motivated group of supporters who can exert greater influence than in a primary. Until 2008 the Iowa caucuses, long the first-in-the-nation delegate selection contest, had diminished in importance as a launching pad for presidential contenders. McCain sidestepped Iowa altogether in 2000 to focus on New Hampshire, but Dean's 2004 defeat in Iowa signaled the decline of his candidacy. Obama's 2008 victory in Iowa triggered a surge of favorable media coverage, and his campaign targeted caucus contests more than Clinton's. Although the number of states holding caucuses can vary, the overall role of caucuses has been steadily declining.

Media Influence and Campaign Consultants

"For most of us, the combination of media coverage and media advertising *is* the campaign; few voters see the candidates in person or involve themselves directly in campaign events," wrote Marjorie Randon Hershey after the 2000 election.[46] Little has changed. As the nomination process has grown in complexity, the influence of the media also has grown. Candidates who must campaign in a score of states within two weeks, as they have done since 1992, necessarily rely on the media to communicate with large numbers of potential voters. Televised ads, network- and station-sponsored debates, prime-time news coverage, and the Internet are critical to candidates' efforts. Talk-show appearances have gained in importance: Republican Fred Thompson even chose to announce his candidacy on Jay Leno's late-night show in 2008.

The media tend to focus on the game aspects of the preelection-year maneuvering and the early contests. As candidates begin to emerge, journalists concentrate on the race for financial contributions, the reputations of professionals enlisted to work on a campaign, and speculations about the candidates' relative chances of success based on polls and nonbinding straw votes in various states. Once the delegate selection contests begin, the media focus on political tactics, strategy, and competitive position more than on the candidates' messages and issue stands, particularly in coverage of Iowa, New Hampshire, and the other early contests. In general, the media use a winner-take-all principle that, regardless of how narrow the victory or the number of popular votes involved, gives virtually all the publicity to the victorious candidate. In the 1976 Iowa caucuses, for example, Carter was declared the "clear winner" and described as leading the pack of contenders even though he received only about 14,000 votes, 28 percent of the 50,000 cast; he actually trailed the "uncommitted" group.[47] Gore defeated Bradley in the 2000 New Hampshire primary by a mere 49.7 to 45.6 percent, but Bradley's narrow loss was a less important story than Gore's victory.[48] Kerry salvaged his campaign with a first-place finish in Iowa in 2004, even though he led Edwards by only a modest number of votes. Sometimes, a surprise showing by a runner-up may garner the most attention: After winning just 16 percent of the votes to finish an unexpected second in the Iowa caucuses in 1984, Gary Hart got as much publicity as Walter Mondale, who captured three times as many votes.[49]

As the fate of presidential candidates has passed from a small group of party professionals to rank-and-file voters, media coverage and public opinion polls have grown in importance. The media help determine who the viable candidates are, label them first as likely or unlikely and then as winners or losers. The media influence the results of future contests as voters and contributors gravitate to the winners and desert the losers. Polls reflecting voters' presidential preferences are a fixture of media coverage. Favorable polls impress media representatives as well as political activists and many rank-and-file voters, leading to more victories for the poll leaders in both nonprimary and primary contests. The result of this reinforcement process is that by the time the delegates gather for their party's national convention, one candidate usually has enough delegates to receive the nomination.[50]

The National Convention

No part of the selection process has undergone more dramatic change than the nominating conventions. Long the province of party leaders, today's conventions are largely media extravaganzas choreographed to project images designed to reawaken party loyalty, appeal to contemporary public concerns, and project the most desirable aspects of the newly anointed presidential ticket. In short, the convention is important for two reasons. First, whatever may have happened during the long search for delegates, the actual nomination occurs at the convention. Second, a well-run convention can boost a candidate's chances in the general election while a convention in disarray can be damaging.

Nominating the Ticket

Since the early 1950s, conventions have offered little drama about the choice of the presidential nominee. In the thirty-two conventions held by the two major parties from 1948 through 2008, only two nominees—Thomas Dewey in 1948 and Adlai Stevenson in 1952—failed to win a majority of the convention votes on the first ballot. In all other cases, victory has gone to the candidate who arrived at the convention with the largest number of pledged delegates. Nevertheless, the state-by-state balloting remains a traditional feature of the process.

Selecting the vice-presidential nominee is the convention's final chore and the only chance to create any suspense. Although in theory the delegates make the choice, it has been a matter of political custom since 1940 to allow presidential nominees to pick their running mates after conferring with leaders whose judgment they trust. Parties traditionally attempt to balance the ticket—that is, broaden its appeal by selecting a person who differs in helpful ways from the presidential nominee. In 1980 George H. W. Bush's links to the eastern establishment and moderate wing of the Republican Party complemented the conservative, western Reagan. Ferraro balanced the 1984 Democratic ticket geographically and in other ways: the first woman to serve as a major party candidate in a presidential contest, she was also the first Italian American.

In 1988 Dan Quayle brought generational balance to the ticket, and the party's conservatives enthusiastically supported him. But the media raised questions about Quayle's service in the National Guard during the Vietnam War, and his modest academic performance, and his ability to perform as president should the need arise. Quayle remained on the Republican ticket in 1992 despite speculation about his replacement. Clinton violated political tradition by selecting Al Gore, a fellow southerner and baby boomer, but the choice was well received by the party faithful and probably helped Clinton erode Republican support in the South. For the 1996 election, Dole chose Jack Kemp, a one-time presidential candidate who was highly popular with Republican activists. In 2000 George W. Bush asked a fellow western conservative, Dick Cheney, to join the ticket. Cheney brought extensive Washington and White House experience to offset Bush's inexperience, and Bush kept Cheney on the ticket in 2004. In what the media described as a "bold" move, Gore added Lieberman to the 2000 ticket, breaking a long-existent barrier to having a practicing Jew on a national ticket. Lieberman's early criticism of Clinton's personal conduct helped Gore to further distance himself from the incumbent president. Kerry's choice of Edwards, a southerner, brought regional balance to the 2004 ticket and followed a more traditional pattern of asking the second-place finisher to join the ticket. Obama turned to Sen. Joseph Biden in 2008, an eastern liberal with extensive Washington experience and ties to several hotly contested states, including Pennsylvania. McCain sought to shake up the election with his selection of Sarah Palin, the governor of Alaska, who was popular with evangelical voters in the

Republican Party. Palin proved to be highly controversial, an asset at campaign rallies, but a liability in nationally broadcast interviews.

The final night of the convention is devoted to acceptance speeches. The presidential nominee tries to make peace with former competitors and to reunite party factions that have confronted one another during the long campaign and the hectic days of the convention. Major party figures usually come to the stage and pledge their support.

Conducting Party Business

Parties continue to write and adopt convention platforms, although participants acknowledge that winning presidential candidates may disavow planks with which they disagree. Because delegates, party leaders, and major groups affiliated with the party have strong feelings about some issues, the platform provides an opportunity to resolve differences and find a politically palatable position.[51] Civil rights and the Vietnam War once prompted major disagreements within the Democratic Party; civil rights, foreign policy, and abortion have been important bones of contention among Republicans.

Despite intraparty differences, conventions provide strong incentives for compromise, to bring back to the fold a disgruntled segment of the party that might otherwise offer only lukewarm support during the fall election or launch a third-party effort. To avoid such damage, almost every presidential candidate decides to provide major rivals and their supporters with concessions in the platform and a prime-time speaking opportunity during the convention. Occasionally, this tactic can backfire. At the Republican convention in 1992, Pat Buchanan was given an opportunity to address a national audience, but his address proved so controversial that he was not invited to speak four years later.

National nominating conventions have become so predictable that network television coverage has been dramatically reduced since 1996. To obtain the traditional "gavel to gavel" coverage that ushered in the television age, viewers must follow proceedings on cable news networks such as CNN and Fox News, or on the Internet. Parties may have become so adept at scripting these quadrennial gatherings that their very existence is jeopardized, despite suggestions on how conventions might be reconfigured to ensure their continuation.[52]

The General Election

With nominees unofficially selected by March (in most cases) and officially nominated in late summer, the nation moves into the general election period.

Candidates must develop new political appeals for this stage, primarily a contest between the nominees of the two major parties and, occasionally, an independent candidate. The campaign's audience increases greatly: more than twice as many people vote in the general election as participate in the nomination process. Candidates and staff must decide how they can win the support of these voters, appeal to people who identify with the other party, and woo partisans who backed losing candidates for the nomination. Time is a further complication because the nationwide phase of the presidential contest when most citizens become attentive is compressed into ten weeks, traditionally running from Labor Day to election day. Since 1996, however, the two eventual party nominees have begun campaigning as soon as the opponent is known, thereby extending the campaign into nearly a nine-month competition.

The general election phase differs from the nomination phase for two reasons: the way the Electoral College works and the distinctive provisions of the campaign finance laws. Compared with changes effected in the nomination stage, the constitutional requirements surrounding the president's election have been remarkably stable over time, while campaign finance laws have undergone significant change since 1972.

The Electoral College

Presidential candidates plan and carry out their general election strategies with one ultimate goal: winning a majority of the Electoral College votes cast by state electors. At first, electoral votes were determined by congressional districts. The winner of a popular vote plurality in each district would receive the associated electoral vote, with the statewide winner of the popular vote getting the two electoral votes representing senators. But legislatures soon began to adopt the "unit" or "general-ticket" rule, whereby all the state's electoral votes went to the candidate who received the plurality of the statewide popular vote. This rule benefited the state's majority party and maximized the state's influence in the election by permitting it to throw all its electoral votes to one candidate. By 1836 the unit system had replaced the district plan. Since then, two states have returned to the old plan: Maine in 1969, and Nebraska in 1992.

The final product is a strange method for choosing a chief executive. Although most Americans view the system as a popular election, it is not. When voters mark their ballots, the vote actually determines which slate of electors pledged to support the party's presidential candidate will vote. The electors are party loyalists, chosen in primaries, at party conventions, or by state party committees. In mid-December, the electors pledged to the winning candidate meet in their state capitals to cast ballots. (Twenty-seven states and the District of Columbia attempt by law to bind the electors to vote for the winner of the popular vote, but some question whether such laws are constitutional.)[53] The electoral votes are transmitted to Washington, D.C., and counted in early January. Next, the presiding officer of the Senate—the incumbent vice president—announces the outcome before a joint session of Congress. If, as usually happens, one candidate receives an absolute majority of the electoral votes, currently 270, the vice president officially declares that candidate president. Because the winner of the popular vote usually wins in the Electoral College as well, we call this final stage of the selection process the "validation" of the popular vote outcome. For candidates who win without a popular vote plurality, as George W. Bush did in 2000, the Electoral College may validate a victory but not necessarily provide legitimacy.

Financing the General Election

Mounting a nationwide campaign requires greater financial resources than winning the nomination. For the general election, public financing is provided to nominees of the major parties, and any party that won 25 percent or more of the popular vote in the last presidential election is considered a major party. In the 2004 presidential election, the federal government gave each major party candidate $74.62 million, up from $67.56 million in 2000.[54] John McCain received $84.1 million in 2008, but Obama declined public funding. Candidates of minor parties, those that won between 5 percent and 25 percent of the vote in the previous election, receive partial public financing and can raise private funds up to the major party limit. Candidates whose parties are just getting started or did not win at least 5 percent of the vote in the previous election receive no help, a major disadvantage. Perot sought no federal funds in 1992 but spent an estimated $63 million of his own money to mount a major campaign effort. In 1996, however, he accepted $29 million in federal funds and was limited to using only $50,000 of his own money in the general election. As the official Reform Party nominee in 2000, Buchanan received $12.6 million as a result of Perot's 8.4 percent share of the vote in 1996. But the party was ineligible for public funding in 2004 after Buchanan's poor showing of 0.43 percent. Candidates of parties that won less than 5 percent of the vote in the previous election can be partially reimbursed after the current election if they receive at least 5 percent of that vote. Ralph Nader of the Green Party came closest to this goal with a 2.7 percent share of the national vote in 2000, achieved with $3.3 million in private contributions, but he fell far short of those totals in 2004 (0.38 percent) and 2008 (0.56 percent).

Campaign expenditures other than those from public funding may be paid by two sources. Until adoption of the BCRA in 2002, there had been no limit on **independent campaign expenditures,** which are made by individuals or political committees that advocate the defeat or election of a presidential candidate but are not made in conjunction with a candidate's campaign. The new law prohibited corporations and labor unions from spending their treasury funds on television ads broadly construed as for or against candidates thirty days before a primary and sixty days before a general election.[55] In June 2007, however, the Supreme Court in *Federal Election Commission v. Wisconsin Right to Life* declared the provisions unconstitutional. For the 2008 campaign, only ads that clearly ask voters to support or oppose a specific candidate were prohibited, and sponsors had little difficulty avoiding that kind of specific language.[56] In addition, the BCRA placed new limits on fund-raising and spending by state and local party organizations. Until 1996 party organizations raised funds, commonly called **soft money,** that had largely been used for grassroots activities such as distributing campaign buttons, stickers, and yard signs; registering voters; and transporting voters to the polls. Spending from these sources has varied: between 1988 and 1992 independent expenditures declined from $10.1 million to about $4 million, while soft money expenditures remained steady at $42.5 million.[57] In 1996 the Democratic and Republican Parties enormously expanded their use of soft money to fund **issue advocacy** campaigns, media advertisements that do not expressly support or oppose a candidate but ostensibly educate the public about an issue or a candidate's position on an issue. The Democratic National Committee launched an aggressive series of such ads in mid-1995, designed to help Bill Clinton even before the nomination contests began. When Dole ran short of money in late spring 1996, the Republican National Committee stepped in with a similar campaign to help their expected standard-bearer. The two parties spent a combined total of more than $65 million in these efforts. In 2000 these activities grew even larger: the national parties spent more for television advertising in the presidential election than did the candidates, especially in the "battleground states."[58] In Florida, the key to Bush's victory, pro-Bush expenditures exceeded those for Gore by about $4 million.[59]

The BCRA "prohibits federal candidates and officeholders, and groups they control, from raising, directing or spending soft money" and sought to halt the activities triggered by Clinton's aggressive fund-raising in 1995–1996.[60] In the place of soft money, however, independent expenditures rose dramatically from $14.7 million in 2000 to $192.4 million in 2004 and to about $170 million in 2008. Both parties have been big spenders: the DNC spent $120 million in 2004 (much less in 2008) and the RNC $59 million in 2008.[61]

Until 2008 the system of public financing introduced in the 1976 election was viewed as a success: major party candidates no longer depended on wealthy contributors and other private sources to finance their campaigns; expenditures of the two major party candidates were limited and equalized, an advantage for Democrats who were historically outspent by their opponents.[62] The 1996 and 2000 experiences with soft money called into question the adequacy of regulations, triggering further reforms. But each presidential election set new records: the 2008 presidential election was the most expensive in history, with more than $1.6 billion raised and $1.3 billion spent.[63]

In 2008, for the first time since 1972, candidates and their advisers openly discussed the possibility of not taking public funds for the general election. Obama raised far more than the $84 million available through the FEC and, by refusing public funds, was able to spend as much as he wanted during the general election stage and continue raising money through the election. Once he accepted public funding, McCain could not accept private contributions for his campaign. Including all funds raised by these two candidates for both the nomination and general election stages, Obama outdid McCain by $741.7 million to $367.1 million. The RNC made up some of that difference by outspending the DNC $126.4 to $50.7 million, and McCain carefully budgeted his money so that he had nearly as much left going into the final weeks of the election as Obama, but the Democrat continued to bring in money.[64] Candidates seek contributions from well-to-do individual donors who may give up to $2,400 to the primary and another $2,400 to the general election campaign (this limit was raised from $2,300 following the 2008 elections). Moreover, parties can still raise and spend so-called "hard money" that under the BCRA guidelines can be used to help the presidential candidates. These developments are certain to trigger renewed calls for reform.

Targeting the Campaign

As in the nomination process, candidates must decide which states will be the focus of their efforts in the fall campaign. The most important consideration is the Electoral College: a candidate must win a majority—270—of the 538 electoral votes.[65] This fact places a premium on carrying the states with the most electoral votes (see Figure 2-2). In 2004 and 2008 the candidate winning the eleven largest states—California, Florida, Georgia, Illinois, Michigan, New Jersey, New York, North Carolina, Ohio, Pennsylvania, and Texas—could win the presidency while

FIGURE 2-2   State Size by Number of Electoral Votes, 2008

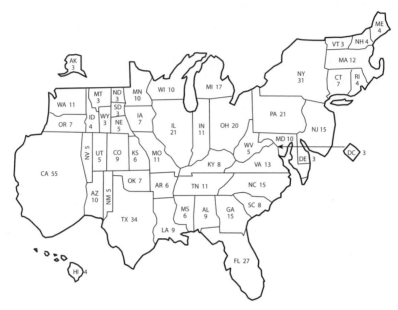

SOURCE: For more information on shifting state electoral vote totals over time see http://uselectionatlas.org/INFORMATION/index.php.

losing the thirty-nine other states and the District of Columbia. Naturally, candidates from both major parties concentrate their personal visits and spending on the most populous states.

Another element affecting candidates' decisions on where to campaign is competitiveness, the chance of winning a particular state. Are the party's candidates generally successful there, or do the results swing back and forth from one election to the next? Distinctly one-party states are likely to be slighted by the major party candidates as a waste of time and money, while swing states with large populations draw a good deal of attention.

In formulating campaign strategy, therefore, candidates and their advisers start with the electoral map as modified by calculations of probable success. The Electoral College creates fifty-one separate presidential contests—fifty states plus the District of Columbia—primarily following the winner-take-all principle; the goal is a popular vote victory, no matter how small the margin. The winner in a large state benefits from the unit or general-ticket system by getting all the state's electoral votes. In 2000 Bush won Florida by a margin of 537 votes of the 5.963 million legitimate ballots cast.[66] But he won all twenty-five of the state's electoral votes, which gave him

271 votes in the Electoral College.[67] Bush's victory in Florida was not final until a controversial 5–4 U.S. Supreme Court decision in *Bush v. Gore* (2000). This decision reversed the Florida Supreme Court's order for a statewide recount, which led to Gore's final concession on December 13. Gore had conceded on election night after early returns showed him trailing in Florida, but reversed field a few hours later when the totals changed. It took more than a month to resolve the Florida outcome as the nation followed the confusing process of recounts and court maneuvers. Although seven justices agreed that Florida did not have a clear, consistent standard to govern manual recounts, only five—all Republican appointees—believed that a deadline established in an obscure 1887 law that precluded recounts within six days of Electoral College balloting applied in this instance. Despite deep disagreement on the Court, the Florida recount was halted, and Bush emerged the victor.

Electoral votes were reapportioned for the 2004 presidential election, reflecting the results of the 2000 census and the reallocation of seats in the House of Representatives. States in the North, East, and Midwest lost seats, while those in the South and West gained.[68] The next reapportionment will take place after the 2010 census.

In formulating a strategy likely to produce victory, Democratic candidates have confronted a difficult strategic problem, most of it due to the historic realignment of the South in presidential politics. For many decades following the Civil War, southern voters were a bastion of solid Democratic support and critical to their candidates' success. Until 1992 no Democrat had ever won the White House without carrying a majority of southern states, but southern voters had not supported the party's nominee since 1976, when they helped to elect Jimmy Carter. Southern support evaporated in 1980, when only Georgia supported its favorite son. No southern state voted for the Democratic ticket in 1984 or 1988. The Solid South was a Republican stronghold until Clinton cut into the incumbent's support in 1992 by winning Arkansas, Georgia, Louisiana, and Tennessee. But unlike Carter, Clinton would have won in the Electoral College in 1992 and 1996 without southern support.[69]

The tables were turned in 2000. George W. Bush won the entire South, including Gore's home state of Tennessee and Clinton's of Arkansas. Together, eleven states switched columns from 1996, including Florida, New Hampshire, and West Virginia, a traditional Democratic stronghold. Gore could have won the election with either New Hampshire's four votes or Florida's twenty-five; many Gore voters believed that liberal Democrats supporting Ralph Nader in both states made that impossible. Bush supporters could also argue that votes for Buchanan may have denied Bush victories in New Mexico and Wisconsin and their sixteen electoral votes.[70]

For all the money spent in the 2004 campaign, the outcome changed from 2000 in only three states: Iowa and New Mexico moved from the Democrats' column to Bush, and New Hampshire from the Republicans' to Kerry. Once again, no southern state voted for the Democratic candidate, which meant the Kerry campaign had virtually no room for error in reaching 270. Even the twelve electoral votes from Iowa and New Mexico would not have been enough to secure victory. The election came down to Ohio's twenty electoral votes, and the nation waited anxiously to see if there would be a repeat of 2000—the loser of the popular vote winning in the Electoral College. In the end, Kerry lost Ohio by 118,599 votes out of 5,627,903 cast.

With his solid financial advantage, Obama pursued a fifty-state strategy while concentrating resources on the crucial target states. As a result, nine states shifted party columns from how they voted in 2004, including three in the South—Florida, North Carolina, and Virginia. In the West, Colorado, Nevada, and New Mexico shifted to the Democrats; and in the Midwest, Indiana, Iowa, and Ohio went Democratic. One electoral vote also shifted in Nebraska, the result of a congressional district supporting Obama while the rest of the state supported McCain. With broad popular support, Obama won in the Electoral College, 365–173, the largest margin of victory since Clinton in 1996. Among consensus battleground states, McCain won only in Missouri by a narrow margin of less than 4,000 votes.

Appealing for Public Support

Presidential campaigns spend millions of dollars and untold hours pursuing two goals: motivating people to cast a ballot and winning their support for a particular candidate. Several factors other than campaign appeals determine who votes and how they vote. Voters' choices depend on their long-term political predispositions, such as party loyalties and social group affiliations, and their reactions to short-term forces, such as the particular candidates and issues involved in specific elections. Candidates and their campaign professionals try to design appeals that activate these influences, attract support, and counter perceived weaknesses.

Because the audience is larger and the time is shorter during the general election period than during the nomination period, candidates use their resources primarily for mass-media appeals. Advertising expenditures have risen accordingly, with campaigns spending half their public funding on radio and television messages. Since 1952 television has been the chief source of campaign information for most

Americans and is now a more trusted source of information than radio or newspapers. Rather than being national in scope, however, advertising is targeted to selected markets in crucial Electoral College states, a pattern especially apparent in 2000 and 2004 when both campaigns focused on a defined list of battleground states. Obama's money advantage allowed him to challenge in many more states in 2008, even those considered long shots such as McCain's home state of Arizona.

Long-Term Influences. Students of elections have categorized influences on voter decisions as either long term or short term. Long-term influences include partisanship and group membership, while issues, candidate image, and campaign incidents are short term.

Partisan loyalty, although still important for a large part of the public, has become less significant as a determinant of election outcomes. Conditions have changed considerably since researchers studying presidential elections in the 1950s concluded that the single most important determinant of voting was the voter's **party identification**.[71] This general psychological attachment, shaped by family and social groups, tended to intensify with age. For the average person looking for guidance on how to vote amid the complexities of personalities, issues, and events of the 1950s, the party label of the candidates was the most important reference point. Partisanship was also fairly constant: about 45 percent of Americans in 1952 and 1956 said they thought of themselves as Democrats, and about 28 percent viewed themselves as Republicans, for a combined total of nearly three-fourths of the electorate. When asked to classify themselves further as "strong" or "weak" partisans, Republicans and Democrats both tended to divide equally between those two categories. Independents in 1952 and 1956 averaged about 23 percent of the electorate.

In the mid- to late 1960s, however, partisan affiliation in the United States began to change (see Table 2-2). Beginning with the 1968 election, the number of independents started to rise, primarily at the expense of the Democrats; by 1972 independents constituted one-third of the electorate. Even voters who stayed with the Democrats were more inclined than formerly to say they were weak, rather than strong, party members. This trend progressed one step further in 1988, when some polls found that independents outnumbered Democrats. Since 1968 more people also identify themselves as independents than as Republicans. The rise in the number of independents was notable among people who entered the electorate in 1964 or later. Voters who came of age since then are much more likely to be political independents than voters of earlier political generations were, a development that has been linked to the influence of Vietnam and Watergate and later to declining confidence in government.

TABLE 2-2 Party Identification, 1952–2004 (Percent)

Party	1952	1956	1960	1964	1968	1972	1976	1980	1984	1988	1992	1994	1996	1998	2000	2002	2004
Strong Democratic	22	21	20	27	20	15	15	18	17	17	18	15	18	19	19	17	17
Weak Democratic	25	23	25	25	25	26	25	23	20	18	18	19	19	18	15	17	16
Total	47	44	45	52	45	41	40	41	37	35	36	34	37	37	34	34	33
Strong Republican	14	15	16	11	10	10	9	9	12	14	11	16	12	10	12	14	16
Weak Republican	14	14	14	14	15	13	14	14	15	14	14	15	15	16	12	16	12
Total	27	29	30	25	25	23	23	23	25	28	25	31	27	26	24	30	28
Independent	23	23	23	23	30	34	37	34	34	36	38	35	35	36	40	36	39

SOURCE: Data drawn from The American National Election Studies, Center for Political Studies at the University of Michigan's Institute for Social Research; *The ANES Guide to Public Opinion and Electoral Behavior*, Table 2A.1, http://www.electionstudies.org/nesguide/toptable/tab2a_1.htm. Data for 2008 were not available for the revised edition.

NOTES: Responses to the question: "Generally speaking, do you usually think of yourself as a Republican, a Democrat, an Independent, or what?" Independents include voters labeled as "Independent Democrats" and "Independent Republicans," sometimes referred to as "leaners."

Total partisanship—the combined percentage of citizens declaring themselves Democrats or Republicans—fell to its lowest level between 1972 and 1976, rebounded slightly in the 1980s, and sank again to that level in 1992, with another modest uptick in 1996. The percentage of independents remained strong since the 1970s. By the 2004 election, 33 percent of the electorate were Democrats, 28 percent were Republicans, and 39 percent independents. Another 17 percent of independents "leaned" Democratic, and 12 percent "leaned" Republican.[72] In 2008 the Pew Research Center for the People & the Press found that on the eve of the election, Democrats outnumbered Republicans 38 percent to 28 percent, and 34 percent identified as independents. Among the latter, 13 percent leaned Democrat and 11 percent Republican.[73] Because partisanship remains an important factor for so many voters, campaigns seek support from their own identifiers by activating traditional loyalties, yet they also attempt to lure identifiers of the other party by blurring traditional themes, a tightrope act that can confuse the general public.

Social group membership is another potentially important influence on voting that candidates try to tap. Patterns of group support established during the New Deal have persisted during succeeding decades, although with decreasing vibrancy. In the 1940s Democrats received most of their support from southerners, union members, Catholics, and people with limited education, lower incomes, and a working-class background. Northerners, whites, Protestants, and people with more education, higher incomes, and a professional or business background supported Republican candidates. Table 2-3, which is based on Gallup polls, shows the support of various groups on the eve of presidential elections from 1952 through 2008. The support of many groups for their traditional party's candidates varied over that period. The most significant drop for the Democrats came in the southern white vote: in 1988 only one in three white votes went to Dukakis, and only 26 percent of white males supported him.[74] One group that significantly increased its support for its traditional party candidate over this period was nonwhites, whose support for Democrats strengthened between 1964 and 1988, returned to the 1952 level in 2000 and 2004, and reached near-historic levels in 2008.[75] Obama's victorious coalition in 2008 rested on strong support among women (56 percent), African Americans (95), Hispanics (67), and young voters. Exit polls showed Obama winning 69 percent of support from first-time voters and a similar percentage among the eighteen to twenty-nine-year-old voters (66 percent).[76] Obama lost among white voters (55 to 43), those sixty and older (51 to 47), Protestants (54 to 45), and rural voters (53 to 45). He garnered the votes of just 31 percent of southern whites, but his advantage in other categories was so great that the popular vote outcome—53 percent to

TABLE 2-3 Group Voting Patterns in Presidential Elections, Selected Years (Percent)

Year:	1952 (R)		1960 (D)		1964 (D)		1968 (R)			1976 (D)		1980 (R)			1988 (R)		1992 (D)			2000 (R)			2004 (R)		2008 (D)	
Group	Stevenson	Eisenhower	Kennedy	Nixon	Johnson	Gold-water	Humphrey	Nixon	Wallace	Carter	Ford	Carter	Reagan	Anderson	Dukakis	Bush, G.H.W.	Clinton	Bush, G.H.W.	Perot	Gore	Bush, G.W.	Nader	Kerry	Bush, G.W.	Obama	McCain
Sex																										
male	47	53	52	48	60	40	41	43	16	53	45	38	53	7	44	56	41	38	19	42	53	4	44	56	50	50
female	42	58	49	51	62	38	45	43	12	48	49	44	49	6	49	51	45	37	17	54	43	2	52	48	57	43
Race																										
white	43	57	49	51	59	41	38	47	15	47	52	36	56	7	41	59	39	41	20	42	55	3	43	57	45	55
nonwhite	79	21	68	32	94	6	85	12	3	85	15	86	10	2	82	18	77	11	7	90	8	1	90	10	90	10
Education																										
college	34	66	39	61	52	48	37	54	9	42	55	35	53	10	42	58	44	39	14	45	49	5	42	58	55	45
high school	45	55	52	48	62	38	42	43	15	54	46	43	51	5	46	54	43	37	12	46	44	4	54	46	47	53
grade school	52	48	55	45	66	34	52	33	15	58	42	54	42	3	55	45	43	35	15	NA	NA	NA	NA	NA	67	33
Occupation																										
professional, business	36	64	42	58	46	54	34	56	10	31	69	33	55	10	NA	NA	NA	NA	NA	NA	NA	NA	NA	NA	NA	NA
white collar	40	60	48	52	43	57	41	44	15	36	64	40	51	9	NA	NA	NA	NA	NA	NA	NA	NA	NA	NA	NA	NA
manual	55	45	60	40	71	29	50	41	15	58	41	46	54	5	NA	NA	NA	NA	NA	NA	NA	NA	NA	NA	NA	NA
Age																										
under 30	51	49	54	46	64	36	47	38	15	48	51	47	41	11	37	63	44	34	22	48	46	5	54	45	61	39
30–49	47	53	54	46	63	37	44	41	15	33	67	38	52	8	45	55	42	38	20	43	50	5	43	57	53	47
50 and older	39	61	46	54	59	41	41	47	12	36	64	41	54	4	49	51	46	37	11	46	46	3	47	53	51	49
Religion																										
Protestant	37	63	38	62	55	45	35	49	16	30	70	39	54	6	42	58	33	47	NA	42	62	NA	38	47	47	53
Catholic	56	44	78	22	76	24	59	33	8	48	52	46	47	6	51	49	45	35	NA	45	48	5	52	48	53	47
Region																										
East	45	55	53	47	68	32	50	43	7	42	58	43	47	9	51	49	47	33	15	52	38	6	58	42	57	43
Midwest	42	58	48	52	61	39	44	47	9	40	60	41	51	7	47	53	45	35	13	43	47	4	48	52	53	47
South	51	49	51	49	52	48	31	36	33	29	71	44	52	3	40	60	40	42	13	36	56	3	43	57	50	50
West	42	58	49	51	60	40	44	49	7	41	59	35	54	9	46	54	43	36	15	43	47	6	48	52	55	45
Members of labor union families	61	39	65	35	73	27	56	29	15	46	54	50	43	5	63	37	NA	NA	NA	NA	NA	—	67	33	64	36
National	45	55	50	50	61	39	43	43	14	38	62	41	51	7	46	54	44	37	14	43	47	5	49	51	53	46

SOURCE: Excerpted from *Gallup Report*, November 1988, 6, 7; *The Gallup Poll Monthly*, November 1992, 6, 7; *The Gallup Poll Monthly*, November 1992, 9; 1996 data provided by Gallup Organization from poll conducted November 3 to November 4, 1996; 2000 data released November 6, 2000, and posted on Web site, www.gallup.com. 2004 data appear in *The Gallup Poll Tuesday Briefing*, November 5, 2004, 42–44. 2008 data from Gallup.com http://proxy.nss.udel.edu:7410/ poll/112132/Election-Polls-Vote-Groups-2008.aspx.

NOTE: NA = Not available.

46 percent in his favor—was not in question. Obama's margin of victory over McCain was the tenth largest of the sixteen first-term victories in presidential elections since 1896, substantial but far short of a landslide.[77]

The weakening of party loyalties means candidates must target many groups. Organized labor, far from a monolithic entity, has been seriously divided in many elections, and both camps have openly courted ethnic groups. Moreover, new groups emerged over the past half-century as critical factors: women, fundamentalist Christians, young voters, and Hispanics have attracted particular attention. But because many American voters have lost their partisan anchor, short-term influences—candidates, issues, and events—and presidential performance are now more important to them.

Short-Term Influences. During presidential campaigns, the public focuses a great deal of attention on the candidates' personality and character traits. Each campaign organization therefore strives to create a composite image of its candidate's most attractive features. To do this sometimes means transforming liabilities into assets: age becomes mature judgment (Eisenhower); youth and inexperience become vigor (Kennedy). Alternatively, a candidate can direct attention to the opponent's personal liabilities, a move that has proved beneficial even though some voters see such an effort as dirty campaigning and beneath the dignity of the office.

The 1988 and 1992 campaigns provide good examples of how candidates try to shape each other's image. George H. W. Bush succeeded in creating a negative portrait of Michael Dukakis in 1988. Dukakis enjoyed a largely favorable image before the summer conventions, but Bush's pollsters discovered it was based on very little information.[78] Interviews conducted with small groups of Democrats who had supported Reagan in 1980 and 1984 shaped the Bush campaign's charges that the Democratic nominee was sympathetic to criminals, weak on defense, opposed to saying the pledge of allegiance in school, and a liberal who favored high taxes and big government.[79] Bush launched a similar effort against Clinton in 1992. First, he tried to portray Clinton as the failed governor of a crime-filled state with environmental problems and as an unpatriotic antiwar activist. In the final weeks of the campaign Bush focused on trust and taxes, but these negative tactics proved less successful against Clinton than they had against Dukakis for at least two reasons. Since 1988 observers have demanded more supporting evidence for campaign charges. Furthermore, unlike Dukakis, Clinton met all negative charges with broadcast rebuttals and attacks of his own that focused on Bush's role in the Iran-contra incident, his administration's pro-Iraq actions prior to the Persian Gulf War, and his violation of 1988 campaign promises.[80] In 2004 the George W. Bush campaign sought to brand Kerry as indecisive (a "flip-flopper") and liberal, charges that Kerry was slow in countering.

Voters look for many qualities in a president. In a 1992 exit poll that asked voters what qualities mattered most in deciding how they voted, Clinton led among voters concerned about the ability to bring about change, which candidate had the best plan for the nation, cared about people, and had the best vice-presidential candidate. Bush was preferred by voters concerned with experience, trustworthiness, and good judgment in a crisis.[81] In 1996 Dole won 84 percent of those mentioning honesty and trustworthiness, but Clinton won the support of those who mentioned caring, having a vision for the future, and being in touch with the 1990s.[82] In 2000 honesty was the trait mentioned most by voters (24 percent), and 80 percent of those who mentioned it voted for George W. Bush, also perceived as the stronger leader and more likeable. Gore was regarded as more experienced, better able to deal with complexity, and more caring about people.[83] In 2004 an ABC survey released just before election day found Bush was regarded as more honest and trustworthy (47 percent to 40 percent), the stronger leader (56 to 36), and clearer on the issues (57 to 34), while Kerry was slightly more likely to understand the problems of "people like you" (46 to 44).[84]

In 2008 most attention was focused on experience versus change: which candidate would bring the necessary experience to the job and be able to hit the ground running on "day one" as Hillary Clinton put it, as opposed to which would be an agent for change. As the year unfolded, change became a more powerful appeal than experience. Both Clinton, with eight years in the White House as first lady and eight years in the Senate, and John McCain, with four years in the U.S. House and twenty-two in the Senate, modified their campaigns to highlight their capacity to serve as change agents, an indication of how powerful was Obama's appeal for "change you can believe in." By election day, exit polls showed that 59 percent of voters thought McCain had the right experience to be president and 51 percent thought the same of Obama.[85] Obama's judgment was preferred over McCain's (57 to 49), and more people thought Obama was in touch with people like themselves (57 to 39). Among McCain's voters, nearly as many said that his leadership and personal qualities mattered most to them (49 to 48), while Obama's voters said that his issue positions (68 percent) mattered more than his personal qualities (30).

Issues are the other major short-term influence on voting behavior. University of Michigan researchers in the 1950s suggested that issues influence a voter's choice only if three conditions are present: the voter is aware that an issue or a number of issues exist, issues are of some personal concern to the voter, and the voter perceives that one party represents his or her position better than the other party does.[86] When the three conditions were applied to U.S. voters in the 1952 and 1956 presidential elections, researchers found that these criteria existed for relatively few voters—at most one-quarter to one-third. Another one-third of the respondents were unaware of *any* of the sixteen principal issues about which they were questioned. Even the two-thirds who were aware of one or more issues frequently had no personal concern about them. Finally, many of those who were aware and concerned about issues were unable to perceive differences between the two parties' positions. The analysts concluded that issues *potentially* determined the choice of, at the most, only one-third of the electorate. (The proportion who *actually* voted as they did because of issues could have been, and probably was, even less.)

Studies of political attitudes in the 1960s and 1970s found that the number and types of issues of which voters were aware had increased.[87] Voters during the Eisenhower years exhibited some interest in traditional domestic matters, such as welfare and labor-management relationships, and in a few foreign policy issues, such as the threat of communism and the danger of the atomic bomb. Beginning with the 1964 election, however, voters' interests broadened to include concerns such as civil rights and the Vietnam War. The war in particular remained an important consideration in the 1968 and 1972 contests and was joined by new matters—crime, disorder, and juvenile delinquency, which, along with race problems, are known as "social issues." Naturally, the issues that are salient vary from election to election. The economy and jobs led the list in 2000, followed by education, Social Security, taxes, world affairs, health care, and prescription drugs.[88] Candidates also differ in how clearly they articulate their positions and draw distinctions with their opponent. In 2000 voters were able to perceive significant issue differences between Bush and Gore, but neither candidate was consistently favored.[89] Greater issue clarity existed in the elections of 1984, 1992, 1996, and 2004.[90] Exit polls in 2004 revealed that Bush voters identified moral values and terrorism as their most important issues, while the economy and jobs, Iraq, and health care mattered most to Kerry voters.[91] Many commentators quickly concluded that abortion, gay marriage, and related issues important to the religious right had determined the outcome, but other surveys, posing different questions, suggested that the emphasis was on public safety issues—terrorism, Islamic extremism, and homeland security; foreign policy was second in importance, and the economy third.[92]

The economy dominated voter concerns in 2008; 63 percent of voters cited it as their most important concern, which was not surprising given the rapidly deteriorating conditions that set in during September 2008. Of those who were very worried about the economy, 59 percent favored Obama. In all, Obama was favored on four of the five most important issues mentioned by voters: economy (top concern of 63 percent), Iraq (10 percent), health care (9 percent), and energy (7 percent). McCain was favored only by those voters who mentioned terrorism (9 percent) where his advantage over Obama was 86 to 13. McCain was also favored by voters who supported offshore drilling for oil as a strategy to reduce gasoline prices, but fewer voters felt this way. Voters' feelings about George W. Bush weighed heavily against McCain. Seventy-one percent of the voters disapproved of the way Bush was performing as president, and 48 percent said McCain would continue Bush's policies.[93]

In 2004 Martin Wattenberg observed that today's presidential elections are heavily candidate-centered, but not in the way we normally think of them. Voters are casting ballots less on the basis of candidates' personal qualities than on candidate-centered issues, those that the nominee has chosen to stress during the campaign. Beginning in 1976, the percentage of positive comments made about the candidates (even the winners) has declined sharply from the 1952–1972 period, prompting Wattenberg to conclude that "the more people come to know about the candidates, the less they like them."[94] And in some instances—Reagan in 1980 and George W. Bush in 2000—the public made more unfavorable than favorable comments about the winner. Because issues are inherently controversial, as their importance for voters has risen, positive views of the candidates have declined. Moreover, the public today sees parties as projections of their nominee's issue stands, not as a separate entity with distinct issue positions. The result is a voting public highly focused on candidates, but on their issues as well as their personal qualities, an apt description of 2008.

Incumbency. Incumbency may be viewed as a candidate characteristic that also involves issues. Service in the job provides experience no one else can claim. Incumbency provides concrete advantages: an incumbent already has national campaign experience (true for all incumbents except Gerald Ford who had been appointed to the vice presidency), can obtain media coverage more easily, and has considerable discretion in allocating benefits.

Of the six incumbent presidents who ran for reelection between 1976 and 2004, only Reagan, Clinton, and George W. Bush succeeded, and of the past four incumbent vice presidents who sought the presidency, only George H. W. Bush was elected. The failure of Ford, Carter, and G. H. W. Bush to gain a second term demonstrates the *disadvantages* of incumbency, particularly if service in the presidency coincides with negative economic conditions such as a recession and high inflation or an unresolved foreign crisis for which a president is blamed, even if erroneously. In 2004 Democrats emphasized the problems in Iraq and a slow economic recovery, expecting them to diminish support for President Bush, but he escaped their effects by in turn emphasizing the war on terrorism and job creation. Experience in the job, then, is not a political plus if a sitting president's record is considered weak or national conditions seem to have deteriorated under the incumbent's stewardship. The president may be held accountable by voters who cast their ballots *retrospectively* rather than *prospectively;* in other words, these voters evaluate an administration's past performance rather than try to predict future performance.

Retrospective voting has been suggested as the major explanation for Carter's defeat in 1980 and Bush's in 1992. To illustrate the problem, many voters perceived Carter's failure to resolve the hostage crisis in Iran as a demonstration of national weakness; in contrast, when Reagan ran for reelection in 1984, restoring pride in America was a major campaign theme. Both elections found citizens voting retrospectively, first providing a negative and then a positive verdict. In the 1996 election, Clinton benefited from the conditions of peace and prosperity during his first term, but this record was not transferred to his chosen successor. Al Gore failed to highlight these accomplishments during the campaign as he tried to distance himself from Clinton to avoid association with the president's objectionable personal conduct. In doing so, he also distanced himself from the administration's achievements.[95] In 2004 "Bush generally won approval for his handling of the war on terrorism but was, on average, negatively evaluated for his handling of Iraq and foreign relations, generally."[96] Paul Abramson, John Aldrich, and David Rohde conclude that Kerry benefited slightly on prospective evaluations, but Bush did better on retrospective evaluations.

Personal incumbency was not a factor in 2008, but party incumbency was. For the first time since 1952, neither party's nominee was an incumbent president or vice president, but Democrats actively linked Bush's record to the Republican nominee even though the president made no campaign appearances with McCain.

Presidential Debates. Voters have the opportunity to assess the issue positions and personal characteristics of presidential and vice-presidential contenders during nationally televised debates. Debates, first staged in 1960, have been held each election year since 1976 and are the most widely watched campaign events. Candidates recognize the danger of making a mistake or committing an embarrassing gaffe on live television, a particular danger for incumbents. Ford misspoke in 1976 when he

The debates between Democratic senator John F. Kennedy and Republican vice president Richard Nixon in 1960 were the first to be televised. Kennedy benefited from his strong performance in the debates against his more politically experienced opponent. Today, candidates use this forum to challenge opponents' ideas and portray themselves as presidential and likeable.

suggested that the countries of Eastern Europe were not under Soviet domination; Reagan appeared to be confused and out of touch during his first debate with Mondale in 1984 but rallied in the second encounter. Challengers try to demonstrate their knowledge of issues and their presidential bearing to a nationwide audience. Kennedy in 1960, Reagan in 1980, and George W. Bush in 2000 seem to have benefited the most from debating a more experienced opponent, in part because they exceeded performance expectations and dispelled negative impressions. Most candidates prepare carefully prior to the meeting and follow a conservative game plan of reemphasizing themes already made prominent during the campaign. As a result, the exchanges often seem wooden rather than spontaneous, an impression heightened by the cautious rules the candidates insist upon. Kerry trailed Bush heading into the 2004 debates and needed a good showing to sustain his campaign. Post-debate polls and media commentary declared Kerry the decisive winner of the first debate; his calm delivery of pointed criticisms contrasted sharply with pained grimaces on the president's face. Kerry was accorded narrower victories in the second and third debates; these successes produced a tighter race but not a decisive turnaround. Post-debate polls showed that Obama was considered the winner in the three presidential debates held in 2008. Although McCain was more aggressive and effective in the final debate, his performance was widely viewed as being too little and too late to alter Obama's lead in the national polls.

The vice-presidential debate drew the largest audience in 2008. An estimated 69.9 million viewers tuned in to see the encounter between veteran Washington legislator Joe Biden and national neophyte Sarah Palin. Governor Palin had performed badly in several interviews with national news anchors, arousing speculation over whether she would self-destruct during this high-stakes encounter. The governor, however, held her own for most of the debate, using a folksy style that contrasted sharply with Biden, who occasionally lapsed into Washington-speak.

The Biden-Palin debate was the latest encounter in a series that dates back to 1976. Dan Quayle's performance was the focus of two vice-presidential debates. Much younger than Lloyd Bentsen, his 1988 opponent, Quayle was repeatedly asked what he would do if forced to assume the duties of president. When Quayle compared himself to former president John F. Kennedy, Bentsen pounced with withering directness: "Senator, I served with Jack Kennedy. I knew Jack Kennedy. Jack Kennedy was a friend of mine. Senator, you're no Jack Kennedy." Quayle never recovered.[97] In 1992 Quayle debated Democrat Al Gore and James Stockdale, Perot's running mate, who watched as his younger opponents struggled to dominate one another. Gore's encounter with Jack Kemp in 1996 previewed some of the problems he would experience in 2000. Gore was so focused on the campaign message that he appeared even more wooden than usual.

Televised debates enable even the least engaged citizen to develop an impression of the major party contenders. Candidates, however, have become quite adept at stagecraft, and the public may now expect more than just a polite exchange of policy challenges as candidates try to display assertiveness, empathy, humor, or "character."

Election Day

One of the ironies of presidential elections since 1960 is that although more citizens have acquired the right to vote, until 2004 a smaller proportion had exercised that right. As Table 2-4 indicates, the estimated number of people of voting age has more than doubled since 1932. After reaching a peak in 1960, however, the percentage of people who voted declined in the next five presidential elections. Despite a modest increase in 1984, only 50.1 percent went to the polls in 1988. This pattern was unexpectedly reversed in 1992, when 55.2 percent voted.[98] The resurgence proved short-lived, however; only 49.1 percent showed up in 1996, the lowest turnout since 1924. There was a modest uptick in 2000 to 51.3 percent, and a

TABLE 2-4   Participation of General Public in Presidential Elections, 1932–2008

Year	Estimated population of voting age (in millions)	Number of votes cast (in millions)	Number of votes as percentage of population of voting age
1932	75.8	39.7	52.4
1936	80.2	45.6	56.0
1940	84.7	49.9	58.9
1944	85.7	48.0	56.0
1948	95.6	48.8	51.1
1952	99.9	61.6	61.6
1956	104.5	62.0	59.3
1960	109.7	68.8	62.8
1964	114.1	70.6	61.9
1968	120.3	73.2	60.9
1972[a]	140.8	77.6	55.1
1976	152.3	81.6	53.6
1980	164.6	86.5	52.6
1984	174.5	92.7	53.1
1988	182.8	91.6	50.1
1992	189.0	104.4	55.2
1996	196.5	96.5	49.1
2000	205.8	105.4	51.2
2004	221.3	122.3	55.3
2008	230.9	131.3	56.8

SOURCE: U.S. Bureau of the Census, *Current Population Reports,* Series P–25, No. 1085 (Washington, D.C.: U.S. Government Printing Office, 1994). 1996, 2000, and 2004 data from Federal Election Commission Web site, www.fec.gov, and U.S. Census Bureau Web site, www.census.gov. 2008 data from United States Elections Project, http://elections.gmu.edu/Turnout2008G.html.

a. Beginning in 1972, persons eighteen to twenty years old were eligible to vote in all states.

startling increase in 2004, variously set at 55.3 percent based on the voting age population (all those eighteen and older) but 60.7 percent using the more accurate measure of the voting-eligible population, which excludes noncitizens and felons. In 2008 turnout rose to 56.8 percent for the voting-age population (including noneligible residents) and to 63 percent of the voting-eligible population. Curtis Gans of the Committee for the Study of the American Electorate attributed the 2004 jump to strong emotions about the Bush presidency and unprecedented get-out-the-vote efforts mounted by the parties and their private sector allies.[99] In 2008 Gans traced the national increase to high turnout among Democrats, particularly African American voters, anger against President Bush, fear of the future, and mobilization efforts by the Obama campaign spearheaded by student volunteers.[100]

Many observers believe that the decline in voter participation has been halted. Indeed, the trend ran counter to most theories of why people do not vote. Laws pertaining to registration and voting, said to prevent citizens from going to the polls, had been eased in most states. Federal laws made it far easier for a person to register and to vote for president in 1996, the low point in the trend, than in 1960. A person's lack of education is often put forward as a reason for not voting, but the level of education of U.S. citizens rose as participation declined. Lack of political information is yet another frequently cited explanation, but more Americans than ever are aware of the candidates and their views on public issues, thanks to media coverage and the debates. Finally, close political races are supposed to stimulate people to get out and vote because they think their ballot will make a difference in the outcome. But Gans and others believe that the recent increases could well be temporary.

Why did voting decline after 1960, surge in 1992, decline again in 1996, recover in 2000, and jump in 2004 and 2008? Abramson, Aldrich, and Rohde link the long-term decline to the erosion in political party identification and to lower political efficacy—the belief that citizens can influence what government does.[101] But these authors note that neither party identification nor political efficacy changed significantly in 1992 and 1996 to explain the numbers. Evidence suggests that Perot's presence contributed to the 1992 turnout increase; 14 percent of Perot voters (which translates into nearly 3 million voters, a substantial portion of the larger turnout) indicated in exit polls that without Perot on the ballot, they would not have voted. Neither major party had pushed hard to register new voters in 1992, although there were some nonpartisan turnout efforts, including MTV's "Rock the Vote" feature aimed at young voters, the group with the lowest turnout rates. By 1996, when turnout again declined, the "Motor Voter" bill, which requires states to provide voter registration opportunities through driver's license agencies, among other public offices, had increased registration, and Democrats made a concerted effort to register newly naturalized citizens. In 2004 a high percentage of voters expected the election to be close, and both parties tried hard to get their voters to the polls. These factors may help account for the jump in turnout, but voting in the United States remains low among the disadvantaged and when compared to other industrialized nations. Therefore, we cannot be certain what caused the changes between 1992 and 1996 or 2000 and 2008. It is important to note, however, that even the 2008 turnout was still below that for 1960 and that neither of the long-term causes of the voting decline noted above has been reversed.

Validation

Translating the popular vote into the official outcome is the final stage of the selection process, in which the Electoral College produces the true winner. Until

2000 it had been more than a century since the constitutionally prescribed process failed to do so or produced a winner who was not also the "people's choice," although we had been dangerously close to such an Electoral College *misfire* on a number of occasions.

Despite the separation of the presidential and the vice-presidential balloting in 1804, there remain three possible ways for a misfire to occur. First, the Electoral College does not ensure that the candidate who receives the most popular votes wins the presidency: John Quincy Adams in 1824, Rutherford B. Hayes in 1876, and Benjamin Harrison in 1888 became president even though they finished second in total popular vote to their respective political opponents. The same thing happened in 2000, when Gore won a national plurality of 543,895 votes but lost in the Electoral College.[102] Second, candidates may fail to win an Electoral College majority, thereby throwing selection into the House of Representatives. This situation occurred in 1800, 1824, and 1876.

The 1968 election illustrates a third danger of the Electoral College system: an elector need not cast his or her ballot for the candidate who wins the plurality of votes in the elector's state. This problem of the **faithless elector** occurred eight times in the twentieth century, and in 2004 a Minnesota elector apparently mismarked his ballot and cast votes for John Edwards both as president and vice president. It is not particularly dangerous when isolated electors make an error or refuse to follow the result of their states' popular votes, but widespread desertion would be another matter.[103]

The Electoral College as it operates today violates some major tenets of political equality that are central to our contemporary understanding of democracy. Each person's vote does not count equally: one's influence on the outcome depends on the situation in one's state. For the many Americans who support a losing candidate, it is as though they had not voted at all because under the general-ticket system all the electoral votes of a state go to the candidate with a plurality of its popular votes. Perot received 19,741,048 votes, 18.9 percent of the total cast nationally in 1992, but he won no electoral votes because he did not finish first in any state or in any of the House districts in Maine and Nebraska. Citizens who live in populous, politically competitive states have a premium placed on their votes because they are in a position to affect how large blocs of electoral votes are cast. Similarly, permitting the House, voting by states, to select the president is not consistent with the "one person, one vote" principle that has become a central tenet of American democracy.[104]

Proposals to reform the Electoral College system attempt to remove the possibility of system failures and uphold a more modern understanding of democracy.

They range from the rather modest suggestion of prohibiting faithless electors—votes would be cast automatically—to scrapping the present system and moving to a direct popular election. Intermediate suggestions would nationalize the congressional district plan used in Maine and Nebraska, divide electoral votes proportionally between (or among) the contenders, or provide the popular vote winner with a hundred bonus votes, enough to ensure his or her victory in the Electoral College. No proposal is foolproof, and most must develop guards against new problems.

Is the Electoral College a constitutional anachronism that should no longer be preserved? In the aftermath of the 2000 election, attention once again focused on this eighteenth-century process, with many people stressing its inadequacies and others praising its genius. On December 7, 2000, Rep. Eliot Engel, D-N.Y., proposed two constitutional amendments to change the Electoral College by requiring that electors be allocated either proportionally to the popular vote in each state or to the vote winner in each congressional district. These suggestions were just the latest in a long line of proposals; in fact, "there have been more proposals for Constitutional amendments on changing the Electoral College than on any other subject," more than seven hundred throughout U.S. history.[105] The passage of a constitutional amendment is problematic because national legislators will calculate how the new system will affect their states' influence on the outcome (or their own chances to pursue the office) and vote accordingly. A new reform proposal seeks to sidestep the difficulty of passing a constitutional amendment. The National Popular Vote reform proposal asks states to adopt legislation that awards all of the state's electoral votes to the winner of the *national* popular vote, even if that person did not finish first in the state's balloting. Maryland adopted such legislation in 2007, although the change will not go into effect until enough other states have adopted similar legislation to determine the winner.[106] Hawaii, Illinois, and New Jersey have enacted the same legislation, and five other states have passed the bill in both houses. Although the process is slow, this reform seems to be gaining adherents.

Defenders of the current system note that the most serious misfires occurred during periods of intense political divisiveness (for example, 1824 and 1876), when alternative selection systems would have been just as severely tested. Several of the close calls in the twentieth century, such as those in 1948 and 1968, occurred when political parties were suffering serious internal divisions. An examination of the historical conditions surrounding the misfires shows that only 1888 and 2000 offer clear examples of a popular-vote winner who lost the general election.[107] If popular vote rules had been in place in 2000, the chaos would have been even more widespread because the results would have been challenged in many states with close outcomes, not just in Florida. A national recount would have been far more complex than state-by-state challenges.

Defenders of the present system argue that it has been remarkably successful in producing peaceful resolutions even in tumultuous years. Its virtues include the requirement that candidates not only receive significant popular support but also have support sufficiently distributed geographically to enable the winner to govern. George W. Bush, for example, won thirty states in 2000, including eleven that had voted for Clinton in 1996. Even more significant, because of Bush's strength in the South and the West, "Had the 2000 presidential election been conducted using the new numbers [from the 2000 census] rather than the numbers based on the 1990 census Texas Governor George W. Bush would have defeated Vice President Al Gore by a more comfortable 278–260 margin," a result closer to the 2004 outcome.[108] Ethnic minority groups, it is argued, receive special leverage under the present system because they are concentrated in states with large electoral vote totals and receive attention because their support might make the difference between winning all the electoral votes or none. Finally, some express concern that a system of direct election would encourage the development of minor parties based on regional or ideological interests that might organize in hopes of denying any candidate a majority or winning plurality and thereby force a runoff. Two-party stability, it is suggested, would be threatened.[109]

Analysts differ over the wisdom of retaining the present electoral system, and even the brush with electoral crisis in 2000 did not produce a uniform response. Maintaining government legitimacy is a shared concern. Historically, successful candidates unable to secure a popular vote majority gained legitimacy through an Electoral College majority. This happened twice to Bill Clinton and once to George W. Bush, although Clinton at least won the popular vote plurality. Defenders of the Electoral College believe legitimacy is achieved through continuity with the past, but reformers believe it is achieved through enhancing popular control and avoiding controversy like that surrounding Bush's 2000 victory.

Transitions to Governing

The presidential selection process has been altered many times throughout American history. Some of the informal changes resulting from new practices pursued by the political parties and candidates have been just as important as those resulting from constitutional amendments and statutes. The current system—largely a product of modifications introduced after 1968—stresses the preferences of voters expressed through presidential primaries over those of party professionals, enhances the role of the mass media, and centers on the candidates' ability to raise campaign funds. Front-loading the delegate selection schedule has transformed the dynamics of the early stages of the contest and substantially lengthened the overall process. Despite all this, the winner is still chosen by balloting in the Electoral College, not the national popular vote.

For the individual and election team that prevail in this long, grueling process, victory requires a sudden change in focus. The successful candidate realizes that winning is the means to an end, not an end in itself. Making that transition is sometimes difficult. It involves putting together a team of political executives to staff the new administration as well as establishing a list of program and policy priorities. Much of this is accomplished during the transition, the period between election and inauguration. Many other tasks are tackled during the administration's first six months. Governing, however, offers a new set of problems. Frequently, the techniques that proved successful during the election are simply transferred to those challenges, but such methods are seldom sufficient to ensure success. In the modern presidency, governing involves some of the same activities as getting elected, but the two are far from identical. We review the Obama transition experience in the book's final chapter.

The burning question for everyone is how effective will the president be in leading the nation. Presidents vary along a wide range of dimensions—abilities, interests, personality—even as the office exhibits certain commonalities over time. In chapter 4, we turn to the problem of understanding how a president's personal characteristics influence performance in office, and subsequent chapters focus on presidents' political success. First, however, we examine their relationship with the public between elections, a relationship that has increased in importance in modern times.

SUGGESTED READINGS

Abramson, Paul R., John H. Aldrich, and David W. Rohde. *Change and Continuity in the 1980 Elections.* Washington, D.C.: CQ Press, 1982.

———. *Change and Continuity in the 1984 Elections.* Washington, D.C.: CQ Press, 1986.

———. *Change and Continuity in the 1988 Elections.* Washington, D.C.: CQ Press, 1990.

———. *Change and Continuity in the 1992 Elections.* Washington, D.C.: CQ Press, 1994.

———. *Change and Continuity in the 1992 Elections, rev. ed.* Washington, D.C.: CQ Press, 1995.

———. *Change and Continuity in the 1996 Elections.* Washington, D.C.: CQ Press, 1998.

———. *Change and Continuity in the 1996 and 1998 Elections.* Washington, D.C.: CQ Press, 1999.

———. *Change and Continuity in the 2000 and 2002 Elections.* Washington, D.C.: CQ Press, 2003.

———. *Change and Continuity in the 2004 and 2006 Elections.* Washington, D.C.: CQ Press, 2007.

Alexander, Herbert E., and Anthony Corrado. *Financing the 1992 Election.* Boulder: Westview, 1995.

Bartels, Larry M. *Presidential Primaries and the Dynamics of Public Choice.* Princeton: Princeton University Press, 1988.

Ceaser, James W., and Andrew E. Busch. *Red Over Blue: The 2004 Elections and American Politics.* Lanham, Md.: Rowman and Littlefield, 2005.

Ceaser, James W., Andrew E. Busch, and John J. Pitney Jr. *Epic Journey: The 2008 Elections and American Politics.* Lanham, Md.: Rowman and Littlefield, 2009.

Campbell, Angus, Philip Converse, Warren Miller, and Donald Stokes. *The American Voter,* abr. ed. New York: Wiley, 1964.

Mayer, William G., ed. *In Pursuit of the White House: How We Choose Our Presidential Nominees.* Chatham, N.J.: Chatham House, 1996.

———. *In Pursuit of the White House, 2000: How We Choose Our Presidential Nominees.* Chatham, N.J.: Chatham House, 1999.

———. *The Making of the Presidential Candidates, 2008.* Lanham, Md.: Rowman and Littlefield, 2007.

Nelson, Michael, ed. *The Elections of 1996.* Washington, D.C.: CQ Press, 1997.

———. *The Elections of 2000.* Washington, D.C.: CQ Press, 2001.

———. *The Elections of 2004.* Washington, D.C.: CQ Press, 2005.

———. *The Elections of 2008.* Washington, D.C.: CQ Press, 2009.

Pomper, Gerald M., ed. *The Election of 1996: Reports and Interpretations.* Chatham, N.J.: Chatham House, 1997.

———. *The Election of 2000: Reports and Interpretations.* Chatham, N.J.: Chatham House, 2001.

Wayne, Stephen J. *The Road to the White House 2008.* New York: Wadsworth Publishing, 2007.

RESOURCES ON THE WEB

On the arcane workings of the Electoral College: www.archives.gov/federal-register/electoral-college/about.html.

For up-to-date schedules of the Republican and Democratic Parties' primaries and caucuses: www.thegreenpapers.com.

For thorough analysis of voter turnout: United States Elections Project, http://elections.gmu.edu/voter_turnout.htm.

National Popular Vote reform effort: www.nationalpopularvote.com/index.php.

For a rich collection of presidential election maps, see www.uselectionatlas.org/.

NOTES

1. Besides George Washington, James Monroe is the only candidate to approach this distinction; he won all but one Electoral College vote in 1820. Michael Nelson, ed., *Guide to the Presidency,* 4th ed. (Washington, D.C.: CQ Press, 2007), 2:1819.

2. William Chambers, *Political Parties in a New Nation: The American Experience, 1776–1809* (New York: Oxford University Press, 1963), chap. 2.

3. Jefferson's Republican Party actually served as the basis for the Democratic Party. The Democratic-Republican Party was officially designated the Democratic Party in 1840. Paul David, Ralph Goldman, and Richard Bain, *The Politics of National Party Conventions* (New York: Vintage, 1964), chap. 3.

4. Joseph Charles, *The Origins of the American Party System* (New York: Harper Torch, 1956), 83–94.

5. Other constitutional amendments dealing with presidential selection have expanded participation (Amendments 15, 19, 24, 26), set the term of office (20, 22), and sought to cope with death or disability (20, 25).

6. David, Goldman, and Bain, *National Party Conventions*, 50. The National Republican Party was soon to give way to the Whigs, with many Whig supporters joining the Republican Party when it was formed in the 1850s (57–59).

7. Ibid., 61.

8. First-ballot convention decisions have been surprisingly prevalent. Through 2008 the two major parties selected their candidates on the first ballot at fifty-nine of eighty-five conventions. Many of the multiballot conventions were held from 1840 to 1888, when sixteen of the twenty-two went past the first ballot. What distinguishes the post-1952 era is that *none* of the twenty-six conventions went past one ballot.

9. Richard C. Bain and Judith H. Parris, *Convention Decisions and Voting Records*, 2nd ed. (Washington, D.C.: Brookings, 1973), 1–6.

10. In 2008, forty-one states scheduled primaries for both parties, although in two states the parties voted on different days. An excellent source on the process and calendar is www.thegreenpapers .com/P08/events.phtml.

11. "Because 1956 was the first time that the Republicans were both the incumbent party and the one that met second, it is when the tradition of the Democrats having the later nomination was fully replaced with one of giving that privilege to the incumbents." Bruce E. Altschuler, "Scheduling the Party Conventions," *Presidential Studies Quarterly* 36 (December 2006): 662.

12. Naturalized citizens, such as California governor Arnold Schwarzenegger, who was born in Austria, do not meet this requirement. There is some question whether persons born abroad of American citizens—for example, George Romney, former governor of Michigan and 1968 presidential contender, who was born of American parents in France—are also legally barred from the presidency.

13. Bureau of the Census, "Population by Sex, Age and U.S. Citizenship Status, 2004" *National Population Estimates, Current Population Survey, March 2004*, Table 1.1, www.census.gov/population/ socdemo/foreign/ppl-176/tab01-1.xls.

14. John Aldrich, "Methods and Actors: The Relationship of Processes to Candidates," in *Presidential Selection*, ed. Alexander Heard and Michael Nelson (Durham: Duke University Press, 1987).

15. Before Richard Nixon's selection in 1960, the last incumbent vice president to be nominated was Martin Van Buren in 1836.

16. Joseph A. Pika, "Bush, Quayle, and the New Vice Presidency," in *The Presidency and the Political System*, 3rd ed., ed. Michael Nelson (Washington, D.C.: CQ Press, 1990). Also see Joseph A. Pika, "The Vice Presidency: New Opportunities, Old Constraints," in *The Presidency and the Political System*, 6th ed., ed. Michael Nelson (Washington, D.C.: CQ Press, 2000); Joseph A. Pika, "Dick Cheney, Joe Biden, and the New Vice Presidency," *The Presidency and the Political System*, 8th ed. Michael Nelson (Washington, D.C.: CQ Press, 2009).

17. Ronald D. Elving, "The Senators' Lane to the Presidency," *Congressional Quarterly Weekly Report*, May 20, 1989, 1218.

18. For a statement of informal expectations from 1959, see Sidney Hyman, "Nine Tests for the Presidential Hopeful," *New York Times*, January 4, 1959, Sec. 5, 1–11.

19. Michael Nelson, "Who Vies for President?" in Heard and Nelson, *Presidential Selection*, 144.

20. With an eligible incumbent in the White House, in 2004 Republicans held twenty-six primaries (down from forty-two in 2000), and canceled five. The Democrats held thirty-six primaries.

21. See Nonprofit Voter Engagement Network, *America Goes to the Polls: A Report on Voter Turnout in the 2008 Presidential Primary*, www.nonprofitvote.org/Download-document/America-Goes-to-the-Polls-2008.html.

22. Austin Ranney, "Changing the Rules of the Nominating Game," in *Choosing the President*, ed. James David Barber (Englewood Cliffs, N.J.: Prentice Hall, 1974), 71.

23. Barbara Norrander, "The End Game in Post-Reform Presidential Nominations," *The Journal of Politics* 62 (November 2000): 999–1013.

24. See the useful table "Chronological Cumulative Allocation of Delegates," www.thegreenpapers .com/P08/ccad.phtml.

25. Arthur Hadley, *The Invisible Primary* (Englewood Cliffs, N.J.: Prentice Hall, 1976). For a valuable update, see Emmett H. Buell Jr., "The Invisible Primary," in *In Pursuit of the White House*, ed. William G. Mayer (Chatham, N.J.: Chatham House, 1996).

26. One study argues that party endorsements have become even more important than candidates' position in the polls in determining the nominee. Marty Cohen, David Karol, Hans Noel, and John Zaller, *The Party Decides: Presidential Nominations Before and After Reform* (Chicago: University of Chicago Press, 2008). Also see the same authors' chapter, "The Invisible Primary in Presidential Nominations, 1980–2004," in William G. Mayer, ed., *The Making of the Presidential Candidates, 2008* (Lanham, Md.: Rowman and Littlefield, 2007), chap. 1.

27. Congressional Research Service, "The Presidential Campaign Election Fund and Tax Checkoff: Background and Current Issues," March 2000, updated and included as Table 4-1 in The Campaign Finance Institute's final report of the Task Force on Financing Presidential Nominations, *Participation, Competition, Engagement, September 2003*, http://www.cfinst.org/president/pdf/CFI_Chapter4.pdf; David D. Kirkpatrick, "Death Knell May Be Near for Public Election Funds," *New York Times*, January 23, 2007, www.nytimes.com/2007/01/23/us/politics/23donate.html?ex=1183348800&en=c2cec 39b639a56dc& ei=5070.

28. In prior election cycles, John Connally, Steve Forbes, Maurice Taylor, Orrin Hatch, and George W. Bush—all Republicans—refused prenomination public funding. On 2008, see Kirkpatrick, "Death Knell."

29. In 2008, individuals were limited to contributions of $2,300 to a presidential candidate for each election, up from the previous $1,000 limit (the nomination and general election are considered separate contests), $5,000 to a political action committee (a group that contributes to more than one candidate), $28,500 to the national committee of a political party, and a total contribution of no more than $108,200 over two years. Presidential candidates are free to spend an unlimited amount of their own and their immediate family's money on their campaigns, but if they accept public financing, their contributions to their own campaigns are limited to $50,000 per election. See the Federal Election Commission brochure on "Contributions" for the limits set for 2009–2010, http://www.fec.gov/pages/brochures/contrib .shtml#Chart.

30. The lower totals, the lowest since creation of the system in 1976, reflected the absence of Bush and Kerry in 2004 and Clinton and Obama in 2008. All could have easily qualified for the funding. See press release from the Federal Election Commission, February 3, 2005, and July 16, 2008. www.fec.gov/press/.

31. The difference in convention costs is made up by contributions from individuals and organizations to the convention organizing committees in each city. See http://www.opensecrets.org/pres08/ convcmtes.php?cycle=2008.

32. Anthony Corrado, "Financing the 1996 Elections," in *The Election of 1996*, ed. Gerald M. Pomper (Chatham, N.J.: Chatham House, 1997).

33. Corrado, "Financing the 2000 Elections," 98.

34. Fund-raising totals cited are from the Center for Responsive Politics, whose totals are higher than those from the FEC. See www.opensecrets.org/presidential/index_2004.asp. FEC totals can be found in a press release of February 3, 2005, www.fec.gov/press/press2005/20050203pressum/20050203pressum .html.

35. Not all individual contributions are small, and it is legal for political action committees to help finance nomination campaigns, but their contributions are not matched by federal funds as in the case of individuals.

36. It is not clear, however, whether the additional financial resources produce victory or whether contributors simply choose to give their money to the leading candidate.

37. Richard Berke, "In G.O.P. Presidential Field, a Race to Raise Money Is On," *New York Times*, February 2, 1995, A1.

38. Thomas B. Edsall and Dan Balz, "Kerry Shaded by Edwards in Fundraising Reports Fuel Reassessment," *Washington Post*, April 3, 2003, A3.

39. Adam Nagourney, "G.O.P. Deserts McCain, and a 40-Year Habit," *New York Times*, July 16, 2007, www.nytimes.com/2007/07/16/us/politics/16web-nagourney.html?_r=1&oref=slogin.

40. See www.cfinst.org/events/event.aspx?EventID=18.

41. President Bush's fund-raising efforts for 2004 drew various kinds of criticism. See, for example, Editorial, "The $2000 Hot Dog," *Washington Post*, June 22, 2003.

42. From the text of July 18, 2002, press release announcing creation of the Task Force on Financing Presidential Nominations, www.cfinst.org/pr/prRelease.aspx?ReleaseID=23. For additional data on the nominating system, see Corrado and Green, "The Current Presidential Finance System."

43. The exceptions were George McGovern, who defeated front-runner Edmund Muskie in 1972; Jimmy Carter, who surpassed Hubert Humphrey in 1976; Michael Dukakis, who bested the early leader Gary Hart in 1988; and Bill Clinton, who came from far behind to win in 1992.

44. In 1984 the minimum was 20 percent, a rule that favored the front-runner, Walter Mondale. Complaints from defeated candidates Jesse Jackson and Gary Hart resulted in lowering the qualifying level to 15 percent for the 1988 contest, and that rule was continued in 1992, 1996, 2000, 2004, and 2008. Most Republican contests have been conducted under "winner take all" rules, although some states use proportional rules for both parties.

45. Alan Greenblatt and Rhodes Cook, "Nominating Process Rules Change," *Congressional Quarterly Weekly Report*, August 17, 1996, 2299. For the 2000 election, see Andrew E. Busch, "New Features of the 2000 Presidential Nominating Process: Republican Reforms, Front-Loading's Second Wind, and Early Voting," in *In Pursuit of the White House 2000*, ed. William G. Mayer (New York: Chatham House, 2001).

46. Marjorie Randon Hershey, "The Campaign and the Media," in *The Election of 2000*, ed. Gerald M. Pomper (Chatham, N.J.: Chatham House, 2001), 47.

47. C. Anthony Broh, *A Horse of a Different Color: Television's Treatment of Jesse Jackson's 1984 Presidential Campaign* (Washington, D.C.: Joint Center for Political Studies, 1987), 4.

48. For discussion of the primary contests in 2000 and election results, see William G. Mayer, "The Presidential Nominations," in Pomper, *The Election of 2000*.

49. Broh, *A Horse of a Different Color*, 44.

50. Exceptions to this pattern can be found when two candidates end the preconvention period fairly even, which McGovern and Humphrey did in 1972, Ford and Reagan did in 1976, and Mondale and Hart did in 1984; in each case, however, the preconvention leader took the nomination.

51. Judith Parris, *The Convention Problem: Issues in Reform of Presidential Nominating Procedures* (Washington, D.C.: Brookings, 1972), 110; Terri Susan Fine, "Presidential Nominating Conventions in a Democracy," *Perspectives on Political Science* (Winter 2003): 32–40.

52. Edwin Diamond, Gregg Geller, and Chris Whitley, "Air Wars: Conventions Go Cable," *National Journal*, August 31, 1996, 1859. In 2004 the major networks carried only three hours of prime-time convention coverage, less than one hour a night and a far cry from the once continuous coverage typical of the 1950s and 1960s.

53. "No elector has ever been prosecuted for failing to vote as pledged." From U.S. Electoral College FAQ, www.archives.gov/federal-register/electoral-college/faq.html#popular. For a list of the state laws, see U.S. National Archives and Records Administration, www.archives.gov/federal-register/electoral-college/laws.html.

54. FEC press release, "Public Funds in Presidential Campaigns," February 3, 2005, www.fec.gov/press/press2005/20050203pressum/20050203pressum.html. Nominees receiving full funding may accept other direct contributions only to meet legal and accounting fees, so George W. Bush's enormous fund-raising advantage during the prenomination phase in 1999–2000 could not be repeated for the general election phase.

55. See Fred Wertheimer, president of Democracy 21, "Opening Remarks," conference on the Bipartisan Campaign Reform Act, June 23, 2003; found on the organization Web site under "BCRA and Other Campaign Finance Laws," www.democracy21.org/.

56. Linda Greenhouse and David D. Kirkpatrick, "Justices Loosen Ad Restrictions in Campaign Finance Law," *New York Times*, June 26, 2007, www.nytimes.com/2007/06/26/washington/26scotus.html.

57. Alexander and Bauer, *Financing the 1988 Election*, Table 2-1. Herbert Alexander and Anthony Corrado, *Financing the 1992 Election* (Boulder: Westview, 1995), chap. 5, Table 5-1; Federal Election Commission, *The Presidential Public Funding Program* (Washington, D.C., 1993), 31.

58. Corrado, "Financing the 2000 Elections," 107.

59. Ibid., 109. In 2000 independent expenditures by political groups favored Gore by a margin of seven to one, with Planned Parenthood leading the way.

60. Wertheimer, "Opening Remarks."

61. FEC press release, "Public Funds" (2004). Also see the records reported by the Center for Responsive Politics at http://www.opensecrets.org/pres08/indexp.php.

62. Although presidential candidates are free to refuse public funds, no major party nominee had done so in the general election through 2004, perhaps because the maximum contribution limitations made raising money from individuals and groups more difficult. Candidates may also have thought the public favors the use of public, rather than private, funds. This changed dramatically in 2008 when Obama reversed his previous public position and refused public funding.

63. Center for Responsive Politics http://www.opensecrets.org/pres08/totals.php?cycle=2008.

64. Center for Responsive Politics, "With Help from RNC, McCain Closed Money Gap In Final Stretch," *Capital Eye*, December 5, 2008, http://www.opensecrets.org/news/2008/12/with-help-from-rnc-mccain-clos.html.

65. The Twenty-third Amendment, ratified in 1961, gave the District of Columbia the right to participate in presidential elections. Previously, District residents were excluded. Their inclusion accounts for there being three more electoral votes (538) than the total number of senators and representatives (535).

66. For election results and a brief account of the events surrounding the Florida outcome, see Gerald M. Pomper, "The Presidential Election," in Pomper, *The Election of 2000*, 125–135. For an in-depth journalistic account of the Florida situation, see *Deadlock: The Inside Story of America's Closest Election*, comp. Political Staff of the *Washington Post* (New York: Public Affairs, 2001).

67. Gore received 266 votes. One elector from the District of Columbia, Barbara Lett-Simmons, who should have cast her ballot for Gore and Lieberman, instead cast a blank ballot as a means of protesting the lack of D.C. statehood and a vote in Congress. Therefore the two-party total is not 538. A copy of the ballot can be viewed at the Electoral College Web site of the National Archives, www.archives.gov/federal_register/electoral_college/2000_certificates/vote_dc.html.

68. New York and Pennsylvania each lost two House seats. Connecticut, Illinois, Indiana, Michigan, Mississippi, Ohio, Oklahoma, and Wisconsin each lost one. Arizona, Florida, Georgia, and Texas each gained two seats, and California, Colorado, Nevada, and North Carolina each gained one. Because of

widespread criticism following the 1990 census, the Census Bureau agreed to conduct a postcensus survey to determine the extent to which some population groups had been undercounted. The results of that study should have led to adjustments in congressional representation, but the secretary of commerce recommended following the initial census findings. A similar debate followed the 2000 census. Utah filed suit to have its residents serving as missionaries abroad included in the count, which would give it the additional seat awarded to North Carolina. In *Utah v. Evans* (2002) the Supreme Court decided in favor of North Carolina.

69. In 1992 Clinton amassed 370 electoral votes by winning thirty-two states, each state that had voted for Dukakis in 1988 and all but one of the twelve where the previous Democratic nominee had won at least 45 percent of the vote. Clinton totaled 379 electoral votes in 1996, winning twenty-nine of the same states and adding two longtime Republican strongholds—Arizona and Florida.

70. Gore lost New Hampshire by 7,300 votes; Nader garnered 22,198 there. Nader also received 97,488 votes in Florida, thousands more than Gore needed for victory. Bush lost New Mexico by 366 votes; Buchanan received 1,392 there. In Wisconsin, Bush lost by 5,708, while Buchanan secured 11,471. See official 2000 election results at www.fec.gov/pubrec/2000presgeresults.htm.

71. Angus Campbell et al., *The American Voter*, abr. ed. (New York: Wiley, 1964).

72. For similar figures for the 2000 election see Paul R. Abramson, John H. Aldrich, and David W. Rohde, *Change and Continuity in the 2000 and 2002 Elections* (Washington, D.C.: CQ Press, 2003), 171. The Harris Poll, using a different question and methodology, set identification in early 2004 at 33 percent Democrat, 28 percent Republican, and 24 percent independent. The Harris Poll® #15, "Democrats Still Hold a Small Lead in Party Identification," February 7, 2004, www.harrisinteractive.com/harris_poll/index.asp?PID=444.

73. Pew Center for Research on the People & the Press, "Democrats Hold Party ID Edge Across Political Battleground," October 30, 2008, http://pewresearch.org/pubs/1015/democratic-party-identifica tion-swing-states.

74. Gerald M. Pomper, "The Presidential Election," in *The Election of 1988: Reports and Interpretations,* ed. Gerald M. Pomper (Chatham, N.J.: Chatham House, 1989), 136.

75. Offsetting gains in nonwhite voting, white fundamentalist Christians have gained significance in national politics. This group has become solidly Republican and in 1988 was nearly as large a proportion of the voting population as blacks (9 percent versus 10 percent). See poll results reported in Gerald M. Pomper, "The Presidential Election," in Pomper, *The Election of 1996*, 134.

76. "Election Results 2008," *New York Times,* November 5, 2008, http://elections.nytimes.com/2008/results/president/exit-polls.html.

77. James W. Ceaser and Daniel DiSalvo, "The Magnitude of the 2008 Democratic Victory: By the Numbers," *The Forum* 6 (Issue 4, 2008), http://www.bepress.com/forum/vol6/iss4/art8.

78. Marjorie Randon Hershey, "The Campaign and the Media," in Pomper, *The Election of 1988*, 78.

79. Ibid., 80–83; Paul J. Quirk, "The Election," in Pomper, *The Election of 1988*, 76.

80. Nelson, "The Election: Turbulence and Tranquility," in Nelson, *The Election of 1996*, 58; Marion R. Just, "Candidate Strategies and the Media Campaign," in Pomper, *The Election of 1988*, 91–96.

81. Voter Research and Surveys exit polls as reported in Paul J. Quirk and Jon K. Dallager, "The Election: A 'New Democrat' and a New Kind of Presidential Campaign," in *The Elections of 1992,* ed. Michael Nelson (Washington, D.C.: CQ Press, 1993), 81.

82. Exit poll conducted by Voter News Service and reported in Michael Nelson, "The Election: Turbulence and Tranquility in Contemporary American Politics," in *The Elections of 1996,* ed. Michael Nelson (Washington, D.C.: CQ Press, 1997), 57.

83. Pomper, "The Presidential Election," in Pomper, *The Election of 2000*, 146.

84. ABC News Survey, conducted October 9–November 4, 2004, archived on *National Journal*, www.nationaljournal.com/members/polltrack/2004/races/whitehouse/04wh2004misc.htm#12.

85. Pew Research Center for the People & the Press, "Inside Obama's Sweeping Victory," November 5, 2008, http://pewresearch.org/pubs/1023/exit-poll-analysis-2008.

86. Campbell et al., *The American Voter*, chap. 7.

87. For 1960s data, see Gerald M. Pomper, *Voters' Choice: Varieties of American Electoral Behavior* (New York: Dodd, Mead, 1975), chap. 8. For 1970s data, see Norman Nie, Sidney Verba, and John Petrocik, *The Changing American Voter* (Cambridge: Harvard University Press, 1979), chap. 7.

88. Pomper, "The Presidential Election," in Pomper, *The Election of 2000*, 146.

89. Abramson, Aldrich, and Rohde, *Change and Continuity in the 2000 and 2002 Elections*, chaps. 6 and 7.

90. Paul R. Abramson, John H. Aldrich, and David W. Rohde, *Change and Continuity in the 2004 Elections* (Washington, D.C.: CQ Press, 2006), 149.

91. Katherine Q. Seelye, "Moral Values Cited as a Defining Issue of the Election," *New York Times*, November 4, 2004, www.nytimes.com/2004/11/04/politics/campaign/04poll.html?ei=5070&en=19005b.

92. Abramson, Aldrich, and Rohde, *Change and Continuity in the 2004 Elections*, 142, 158–159.

93. Pew Research Center for the People & the Press, "Inside Obama's Sweeping Victory," November 5, 2008, http://pewresearch.org/pubs/1023/exit-poll-analysis-2008.

94. Martin Wattenberg, "Personal Popularity in U.S. Presidential Elections," *Presidential Studies Quarterly* 34 (March 2004): 146.

95. Pomper, "The Presidential Election," in Pomper, *The Election of 2000*, 142.

96. Abramson, Aldrich, and Rohde, *Change and Continuity in the 2004 Elections*, 176.

97. See the transcript of this debate and others at www.debates.org/pages/trans88c.html.

98. The 1992 turnout represented an increase of about 13 million voters over the 1988 total. Twenty-three candidates shared the votes, although only four—Bush, Clinton, Perot, and the Libertarian Party candidate, Andre Marrou—were on ballots in all fifty states. FEC press release, January 14, 1993.

99. Center for the Study of the American Electorate press release, November 4, 2004, www.fairvote.org/reports/CSAE2004electionreport.pdf. For a later report with more complete data and based on the eligible voting population, see Michael P. McDonald, "Up, Up and Away! Voter Participation in the 2004 Presidential Election," *The Forum* 2 (Issue 4, December 2004), www.bepress.com/cgi/viewcontent.cgi?article=1058&context=forum. Also see the Web site of United States Elections Project, http://elections.gmu.edu/Voter_Turnout_2004.htm.

100. Curtis Gans, "African-Americans, Anger, Fear and Youth Propel Turnout to Highest Level Since 1960," Center for the Study of the American Electorate, December 17, 2008, http://www1.american.edu/ia/cdem/csae/pdfs/2008pdfoffinaledited.pdf. Also see Michael P. McDonald, "The Return of the Voter: Voter Turnout in the 2008 Presidential Election," *The Forum* 6 (Issue 4, December 2008), http://www.bepress.com/forum/vol6/iss4/art4.

101. Abramson, Aldrich, and Rohde, *Change and Continuity in the 2004 Elections*, chap. 4.

102. Official results can be found at www.fec.gov/pubrec/2000presgeresults.htm.

103. In 1960, 1968, 1972, 1976, and 1988, single electors in Oklahoma, North Carolina, Virginia, Washington, and West Virginia, respectively, failed to cast their ballots for the candidate receiving the popular vote plurality in their states. For complete results of Electoral College voting, see Nelson, *Guide to the Presidency*, 2: 1820–1844; see 1819 for a list of faithless electors and the FEC Web site for the D.C. results in 2000.

104. Numerous efforts emerged in the wake of the 2000 election to shed light on the unfairness of the current system. To explore the over- and underrepresentation of citizens depending on state of residence, see www.thegreenpapers.com/Census00/ FedRep.phtml?sort=Elec#Elec.

105. See www.archives.gov/federal_register/electoral_college/faq.html#tie.

106. John R. Koza et al., *Every Vote Equal: A State-Based Plan for Electing the President by National Popular Vote* (Los Altos, Calif.: National Popular Vote Press, 2006). The campaign's progress can be tracked at www.nationalpopularvote.com/index.php.

107. William C. Kimberling, "Electing the President: The Genius of the Electoral College," *FEC Journal* (Fall 1988): 16.

108. Sean Scully, *Washington Times*, December 29, 2000, A12. Gore carried all but two of the states that lost House seats, and Bush won all of the states that stood to gain seats except California.

109. Ibid., 19–20.

CHAPTER 3

Public Politics

Woodrow Wilson throws out the first ball on opening day of the baseball season in 1916. Wilson helped to usher in the modern public presidency.

For more than a century, students of the presidency have argued that the chief executive's continuing relationship with the American public is a major factor in governing the nation. Writing in 1900, Henry Jones Ford concluded that only presidents can "define issues in such a way that public opinion can pass upon them decisively."[1] Woodrow Wilson, anticipating his own approach to the office, echoed that sentiment: "His [the president's] is the only national voice in affairs. Let him once win the admiration and confidence of the country and no other single force can withstand him; no combination of forces will easily overpower him."[2]

As discussed in chapter 1, this preeminent position was strengthened during the second half of the twentieth century. In 1960 Richard Neustadt explained how the presidents' "public prestige," their "standing with the public outside Washington," influences the decisions of other government officials and nongovernmental elites, including members of Congress and the bureaucracy, state governors, military commanders, party politicians, journalists, and foreign diplomats.[3] By the mid-1980s Samuel Kernell was arguing that **"going public"**—issuing campaign-like appeals for citizen support—rather than the traditional strategy of bargaining with other elites—had become the key to presidential success in the modern era.[4] Broadcast television was once seen as the most powerful tool for going public, but Kernell and Matthew A. Baum suggested in 1999 that the rise of cable television made traditional network appeals more difficult. Hundreds of channels of alternate programming meant that presidents were losing the captive audiences they used to command when all three major networks preempted their regular schedules to carry presidential appearances.[5] In addition, the Internet has become an effective way to target presidential communication to specific constituencies. No matter the means or the difficulty involved, presidents cannot afford to stop courting voters after the returns are in on election day; modern chief executives must woo the American public between elections just as they do during election seasons.

Despite a president's best efforts, maintaining public support is often difficult. Approval ratings can change quickly and can be influenced by the state of the economy and crises abroad—events that are sometimes unrelated to specific presidential action. In the week after the terrorist attacks on the World Trade Center and the Pentagon, George W. Bush's Gallup approval rating shot up 35 points, reaching a high of 90 percent in September 2001. The subsequent war in Iraq, however, took its toll. Even as he ran for reelection in 2004, his approval rating hovered around 50 percent, and he won with just 50.7 percent of the popular vote. His approval rating rose to 57 percent shortly after his inauguration, but fell steadily thereafter—plummeting to a low of 25 percent the month before Barack Obama's November 2008 election as president. By the time Bush left office in January 2009 his approval rating had rebounded slightly to 34 percent.[6] Bush's father, George H. W. Bush, suffered a similar fate. He enjoyed an 89 percent approval rating during the Persian Gulf War, only to have it dwindle to 32 percent—largely because of a faltering economy. After defeating the incumbent in 1992, Bill Clinton failed to generate high levels of public support during his first three years as chief executive but left office in 2001 with the highest approval rating of any departing president since the advent of public opinion polls.[7] Even after he was impeached, Clinton maintained high job approval ratings—a factor that some observers attributed to the strong economy, which may have aided his acquittal in the Senate.[8] Obama entered office with a 68 percent Gallup approval rating, compared with George W. Bush's initial rating of 57 percent. A Gallup poll conducted May 1–3, 2009, just after the end of Obama's first hundred days in office showed only a one point drop from his initial approval rating: 67 percent; a Gallup poll conducted May 7–9, 2001, showed Bush down four points to 53 percent.

This chapter begins with an analysis of enduring public attitudes toward the presidency and then considers the ways chief executives try to hold the support of the American people. These include the use of public appeals, targeted communications to interest groups and party activists, and efforts to use the media to the president's advantage. We conclude the chapter by arguing that these tactics have helped to create a "permanent campaign" that presidents wage between elections.

Public Attitudes toward the Presidency

Citizens relate to the presidency on many levels. At the conscious level, people develop attitudes toward three major components of a political system: the political community of which they are a part; the regime, or formal and informal "rules of the game" followed in the constitutional system; and the authorities, the public officials who hold positions in the government structure.[9] If these attitudes are sufficiently strong and positive, the public may follow its leaders even if it does not like a particular incumbent or the policies that leader advocates.

The president, it can be argued, is the focus of public attitudes in each of these three areas. Like the British monarch, the U.S. chief executive is the symbol of the nation, a personification of government capable of inspiring feelings of loyalty and patriotism, particularly in times of crisis when the leader becomes the rallying point for national efforts. Franklin D. Roosevelt's political friends and foes alike turned to him for leadership when the Japanese attacked Pearl Harbor in December 1941. The same support arose when Clinton directed that cruise missiles strike Iraq in 1993 and when Bush launched a full-scale invasion of Iraq in 2003. Calls to support the president quickly drown out critical voices—at least in the short run.

Because presidents are central figures in the constitutional system, they can benefit from upholding the accepted rules of the game or suffer from violating them. Many Americans felt that Richard Nixon violated his constitutional obligations as well as basic democratic values by placing himself above the law during the Watergate scandal; evidence indicated that he participated in a cover-up designed to hide the truth about an illegal break-in directed by White House aides. The Monica Lewinsky scandal, however, showed that many Americans seemed to make a distinction between the types of abuses of power that Nixon engaged in and Clinton's efforts to cover up a sexual affair with Lewinsky. Most viewed Clinton's affair as a private matter that had nothing to do with his job as president.[10]

Finally, presidents are major actors in the policy-making process. The positions they adopt elicit support or opposition, and their overall performance in office becomes the object of citizens' evaluations. Again, Clinton showed that Americans could make a distinction between job performance and personal approval. As he was leaving office in January 2001, a Gallup poll showed a 65 percent job approval rating but only a 41 percent personal approval rating. An April 2000 Gallup poll was even more striking: 59 percent job approval, but only 29 percent personal approval. President Obama's early personal approval ratings were even higher than his job approval ratings. He entered office with a 78 percent personal approval rating, according to Gallup, and a 68 percent job approval rating.

Fred Greenstein has suggested that presidents meet a variety of psychological needs of the citizenry. As a cognitive aid, the president can make government and politics comprehensible. By focusing on the president's activities, citizens simplify a distant and complex world. The president also provides an outlet for feelings experienced by supporters and opponents, giving citizens the opportunity to develop and express emotions about politics. On the subconscious level, some citizens may seek vicarious participation, a desire to identify with a powerful political figure much as people do with fictional figures and entertainment personalities. Presidents symbolize national unity as well as stability and predictability, providing citizens with psychologically satisfying feelings that may meet fundamental needs for membership and reassurance. Finally, presidents serve as lightning rods within the political system, figures to blame for bad times and to credit for good times.[11] Because presidents play a central role in the nightly dramas communicated on television news—not to mention the Internet and around-the-clock cable news outlets such as CNN, Fox News, and MSNBC—their importance as objects of psychological feelings may be greater today than ever before.

Beyond basic beliefs and psychological needs, the public also has views about the day-to-day operation of the political system—in particular, the major issues of the day and the policies the government should follow in dealing with them. These views, generally assumed to be less stable and enduring than beliefs about the political culture, are often described as matters of "public opinion." A citizen's attitudes on policy issues and presidential performance depend on his or her identity with a particular group, such as a political party, and his or her social, economic, and geographic background. As the nation's leading political figure, the president is expected to develop and help put into effect policies, perhaps controversial policies, that are binding on the entire populace. People respond favorably or unfavorably to each chief executive's particular personality and political style and to the events that occur while a president is in office. People also assess presidents by the way they relate to particular groups—political parties as well as social (religious, ethnic, racial), economic (business, labor), and geographic divisions of the population.

Clearly, many diverse factors affect public opinion of the president. At times people see the chief executive as the embodiment of the nation; on other occasions people link the president with a particular issue or policy they favor or oppose. After examining the symbolic importance accorded the presidency, we turn to political socialization and how people develop their attitudes toward the presidency. We then look more closely at public opinion polls.

Symbolic Dimensions of the Presidency

Ceremony and pomp surround the presidency. A presidential inauguration resembles the coronation of a king, complete with the taking of an oath in the presence of notables and "the hailing by the multitudes."[12] Public appearances are accompanied by a display of the special presidential seal and the playing of "Hail to the Chief" as the president arrives. News conferences are conducted under a set of rules designed to communicate deference and respect as much as elicit hard news.

Particular occasions have been elevated to ritualistic status. The State of the Union message, for example, allows the president to outline an agenda for Congress and the nation. Woodrow Wilson resurrected this ceremony after more than a century of disuse, and today it is an annual occasion for high drama and solemn pronouncements aimed as much at the prime-time television audience as the political elites in attendance. Members of Congress, Supreme Court justices, the cabinet, and the diplomatic corps as well as distinguished visitors gather in the House chamber and chatter expectantly until the sergeant-at-arms solemnly announces the president's arrival, at which point the audience respectfully rises to its feet and applauds. Following a formal introduction from the Speaker of the House, there is another standing ovation. After the speech, a phalanx of congressional leaders accompanies the president as he leaves the hall, and members reach out along the way to shake hands or just to touch the presidential person.

These outward manifestations of respect, made part of recurrent governing rituals, indicate the near reverence accorded the position of president. Respect for the *presidency* as distinct from the *president*, the current officeholder, is deeply ingrained in American political culture. George Washington and his advisers gave the office dignity by enhancing its ceremonial functions and designing a set of "republican rituals," for which no direct precedents existed, based on their exclusive experience with monarchy.[13] But Washington's major contribution to the presidency was to imbue the office with nearly mythical stature. At one time, Washington's likeness was so widely displayed that it became a virtual icon, the picture of a venerated saint displayed by fervent believers in hopes of deriving blessings.[14] The hero worship lavished on Washington during his lifetime and the subsequent cult that developed in commemorating his service to the nation ensured that the presidency will always be associated with the nation's own sense of moral virtue and collective destiny.[15]

In the late nineteenth century, Washington's birthday became a day of national celebration second only to the Fourth of July. In many states, Abraham Lincoln's birthday, too, came to be celebrated as a holiday. Eventually, the two were combined into Presidents' Day. Every February, elementary school teachers regale their classes with stories about these presidents, whose youthful endeavors illustrate the fundamental virtues of truthfulness ("Father, I cannot tell a lie"), honesty (walking miles to return change), and hard work (wilderness surveyor and rail-splitter). In like ways, we celebrate the lives of Washington's successors, and we also expect them to live up to the heroic qualities of their predecessors.

Consistent with this symbolic role, the nation routinely turns to the president to perform a variety of ceremonial chores, many of them minor, such as lighting the national Christmas tree and issuing proclamations on the observance of special days. But Americans also call upon presidents to perform more important symbolic tasks, such as helping citizens deal with their collective grief when disaster strikes. President Bush expressed the feelings of millions when he publicly mourned the thousands of deaths caused by the terrorist attacks on September 11, 2001, memorialized the crew of the lost space shuttle *Columbia* in February 2003, and expressed sympathy after the nation's deadliest mass shooting at Virginia Tech in April 2007. Likewise, President Clinton provided solace and reassurance in the face of sudden, inexplicable death after the bombing of the federal building in Oklahoma City on April 19, 1995.

The presidency, more than any other aspect of political life, links Americans with both the past and the future. In focusing on the current White House occupant, citizens simultaneously derive a sense of fulfillment from past accomplishments and reassurance about the future. Presidents often help to evoke such feelings of continuity through symbolism. When Clinton gave his farewell address on January 18, 2001, he was flanked by busts of Lincoln and FDR. When Bush took the oath of office two days later, he used the same 1767 Bible used in the inauguration ceremonies of George Washington, Warren Harding, Dwight D. Eisenhower, Jimmy Carter, and his father, George H. W. Bush. As Bush took the oath of office, former presidents Carter, Bush, and Clinton sat behind him. Obama evoked the memory of Lincoln throughout the 2008 presidential campaign. He announced his candidacy in front of the Old State Capitol building in Springfield, Illinois, where Lincoln had announced his candidacy in 1858. He retraced part of Lincoln's train trip from

Philadelphia to Washington, D.C., for the inauguration, spoke in front of the Lincoln Memorial on the Saturday before being sworn in on the same Bible Lincoln used at his first inaugural, and chose Lincoln's luncheon menu and replicas of his White House china for the post-inaugural meal in the Capitol rotunda.[16]

Barbara Hinckley has argued that presidents and their speechwriters are highly attuned to the public's expectations of a chief executive. In turn, the White House projects "a symbolic presentation of the presidential office" expressed through the chief executive's public actions and statements.[17] Her study traced the Truman through Reagan administrations and showed that with remarkable consistency, the picture portrayed to the public emphasized several common themes: the president, the American people, and the nation were presented as indistinguishable from each other and as together carrying out most of the work of "government"; Congress, when mentioned, was usually dismissed rather than recognized as an equal branch of government; identifiable population groups were pictured as sharing in the larger purposes that unite the nation; political and electoral activity was far less prominent in presidential discourse than references to religious objects such as God and the Bible; and presidents were presented as being without peers and enjoying a unique relationship with the public.[18]

As Hinckley suggested, there is always the possibility that the public might be able to reshape the presidency and its position in the constitutional order by altering expectations of the office and its occupants. After the Democrats' humiliating defeat in the 1994 midterm elections, for example, it looked as if Congress might be able to assert itself as a prime force through the Republicans' "Contract with America." Although House Speaker Newt Gingrich, R-Ga.—the chief architect of the contract and the leader of the "Republican revolution"—dominated the headlines during his first hundred days as Speaker, he quickly lost his momentum.[19] Then, in the famous budget battle of 1995–1996, President Clinton reasserted himself. Republicans called for sharp budget cuts that would have affected major entitlement programs such as Medicaid, Medicare, and Social Security. Clinton called the cuts irresponsible and rallied the opposition to the Republican plan. Deadlock over the budget led to government shutdowns in November and December 1995 and in January 1996. By a margin of two to one, the public blamed the Republicans for the shutdowns, and Clinton emerged victorious from the budget battle. One poll showed that Gingrich's approval rating had plummeted to 25 percent, while Clinton's had risen to 52 percent. Had Congress won instead, the stage might have been set for a long-term shift in the balance of power between Congress and the president—one that might have undermined the president's symbolic position as the nation's leader.

Such a scenario is unlikely. Even if Congress had won, it is hard to imagine the presidency being displaced from its preeminent position—at least for long. Individual presidents may face periods of weakness and defeat, but the power of the presidency itself endures. As we have seen, enormous pressures for continuity have developed around the presidential office. Expectation of heroic performance and belief in the identity between presidents and the nation are attitudes deeply embedded in the political culture. Collectively, these beliefs about the presidency provide the incumbent with a remarkably durable base of popular support.

It is not surprising, then, that the president is the public official most likely to be correctly identified in surveys. Traditionally, presidents have also enjoyed general respect and admiration. In Gallup polls asking Americans to name the man, living anywhere in the world, whom they most admire, the president of the United States has almost always been the first choice.[20] Despite his declining job approval ratings, respondents chose George W. Bush every year of his presidency until 2008, when the president-elect, Barack Obama, won the distinction by a substantial margin. Likewise, despite the Whitewater scandal and the Lewinsky affair, Clinton remained the most admired man in the world in every Gallup poll from 1993 through 2000 (he tied with Pope John Paul II in 2000, a year when there was relatively little consensus among Americans about what man they most admired). First ladies have historically topped the list of most admired women. Hillary Clinton earned that distinction every year of her husband's presidency, as did Laura Bush in 2001. Senator Clinton, however, topped the list for the remainder of the Bush presidency.[21]

The initial basis for admiration of the president is formed in childhood through a process social scientists call "political socialization." Early work on the development of childhood attitudes toward the president showed that children viewed the president as both powerful and benevolent—a "good" person who cares about people, wants to help them, and wants to "get things done." Moreover, the president personified government for children. Until they were teenagers, most children were not even aware that the president shared the running of government with Congress and the federal judiciary.[22]

Tracking Public Opinion

Since 1938 the Gallup organization periodically has polled a cross section of Americans on whether they approve or disapprove of the way the president is handling the job. The emphasis of the question is on performance in office rather than personal qualities, a sort of continuing referendum on how the president is handling the job.[23] These polls can be accessed online at www.gallup.com. Many other organizations also conduct polls, including some that measure presidential approval ratings. In addition to independent pollsters keeping a finger on the pulse of public opinion, every president since Richard Nixon has retained his own paid polling consultants.[24] Earlier presidents—Franklin Roosevelt, for example— secretly sought polling data from unpaid, unofficial advisers.[25] White House pollsters go far beyond simple tracking of presidential approval. As political scientist Diane Heath has written, presidential pollsters "helped their administrations isolate constituencies by focusing on what linked individuals to the president and the administration's policies."[26] The White House can gather highly specific polling data on everyone from homeowners to born-again Christians. At the height of the energy crisis in the 1970s, President Carter's pollsters even created polling categories based on the type of home heating the respondent used.[27] By focusing on specific demographic groups and identifying issues that resonate with them, presidents are able to engage in highly targeted public appeals.

Presidents also use polling and focus groups to test language that they plan to use in speeches.[28] The Reagan administration used focus groups in 1987 and 1988 to help plan the president's State of the Union address, his speech to Congress about the summit meeting with Soviet leader Mikhail Gorbachev, and his response to the Iran-contra affair. Using such focus groups helped the White House to fashion messages that were both appealing and believable.[29] Bill Clinton made extensive use of polls and focus groups in formulating his agenda. Some observers describe the Clinton White House as driven by polls.[30] Molly Andolina and Clyde Wilcox have noted that Clinton often frustrated opponents by his "ability to cut right or left, depending on prevailing sentiments." They point out that in his second term he adeptly embraced issues that enjoyed popular support so that even in the face of a Senate impeachment trial in February 1999, 69 percent of the respondents of a Pew Research Center survey liked Clinton's policies.[31]

George W. Bush was known for publicly scoffing at those who tailor policy to fit the latest poll results. He praised people "who are willing to stand on principle; people not driven by polls or focus groups; . . . people who stand for what they believe no matter what the critics may say."[32] As political scientist Kathryn Dunn Tenpas noted, Bush pledged throughout his 2000 presidential campaign not to govern by public opinion polls. "Shackled by that promise," she wrote, "President Bush and his staff have shrouded his polling apparatus, minimizing the relevance of polls and denying their impact." Yet Tenpas notes that public records and interviews with major players in the Bush administration called into question the administration's "purportedly 'anti-polling' ethos" and showed "an administration closely in keeping with historical precedent."[33] The Obama White House has used polling and focus more openly to help sell the administration's economic policies and gauge public reaction to issues such as the government bailout of financial institutions.[34]

Job approval ratings of presidents almost always decline as their administration progresses. Paul Brace and Barbara Hinckley have called this depletion of public support a **decay curve**.[35] Since polling began, Clinton is the only president whose average Gallup job approval rating was higher for his last year in office (60 percent) than for his first (48.8 percent) (see Figure 3-1). The decay that most presidents experience in their approval ratings can be attributed to the deflation of unrealistically high expectations of performance. The curve typically bottoms out near the thirtieth month of an initial term. Brace and Hinckley suggest that this decay normally occurs "irrespective of the economy, the president, or outside events." If a president is fortunate enough to be reelected, an uncertain prospect at best, the second-term decline usually begins earlier and follows a steeper path.

Beyond this cycle, however, Brace and Hinckley recognize that events capturing the public's attention may increase or diminish presidential support. In general, events that "dramatize conflict in the nation," even if the president has taken no action to trigger them, are likely to reduce support. Events that "unify the nation around its symbols" are likely to increase support. President Bush's approval ratings soared after September 11 and spiked upward when the United States invaded Iraq in March 2003. Still, the decay curve was evident. Bush's Gallup approval rating dropped consistently from a high of 90 percent in September 2001 to 57 percent in the March 3–5, 2003, poll—a steady decay of about six points every three months.[36] It then jumped to 69 percent in a March 24–25, 2003, Gallup poll taken just after the start of the war in Iraq but fell back to 50 percent within six months, staying in that range through his reelection in 2004. It then dropped steeply to 25 percent by October 2008 before rebounding slightly.[37] Such trends suggest that domestic or international events beyond the control of presidents may conspire to increase or decrease their public support, though some presidents may be responsible for their own good or bad fortune by taking actions that trigger positive or negative public responses.[38]

To the extent that presidents rely on public support for policy success, the decay curve suggests that they are well advised to "hit the ground running" and accomplish as much as they can as early as they can in their administrations.[39] Along with public support, other pieces of political "capital," such as a mandate from a strong electoral margin and congressional support, are also likely to be strongest at the start of a president's term.[40] David Gergen, an adviser to presidents Nixon, Ford, Reagan, and Clinton, recognized this phenomenon early on. As a member of Reagan's transition team in 1980, he wrote a detailed memorandum comparing the first hundred days of every administration since FDR's. Gergen showed that the successful presidents were those who immediately established a clear and simple agenda and used their capital to achieve it.[41] Reagan followed Gergen's advice and framed his entire legislative agenda around just four major issues that the administration carefully promoted and implemented. In contrast, both Jimmy Carter and Bill Clinton—despite a Congress controlled by their own party—largely squandered their first months in office.

Like Reagan, George W. Bush charted a clear-cut legislative agenda for his first hundred days in office. For Bush, those days were especially important. He came to office without a clear electoral mandate (indeed, he lost the popular vote to Al Gore), without strong support in Congress (he had a small Republican majority in the House, but the Senate was evenly divided between Republicans and Democrats), and his initial Gallup job *dis*approval ratings were at 25 percent, the highest of any new president since polling began. His approval ratings were also bifurcated by a distinct partisan wedge, which political scientist Gary Jacobson identified as the largest for any newly elected president in polling history. According to Jacobson's analysis of the twenty-eight Gallup and CBS News/*New York Times* presidential approval polls of Bush taken before September 11, 2001, "Bush's approval ratings averaged 88 percent among self-identified Republicans but only 31 percent among Democrats. This 57-point difference marked Bush as an even more polarizing figure than the former record holder, Bill Clinton (with an average partisan difference in approval of 52 points for the comparable period of his administration)."[42]

In contrast, Obama came to office in 2009 with the highest approval ratings of any new president in thirty years. He also faced the greatest economic crisis since the Great Depression of the 1930s. His first major legislative success was an $878 billion economic recovery bill that he signed into law on February 17. Even though the economy initially dominated the president's agenda, some observers—such as *New York Times* columnist David Brooks—expressed concern that Obama was tackling too many issues. As Brooks wrote on March 19, the president wanted to solve not only the economic crisis but, simultaneously, "the four most complicated problems facing the nation: health care, energy, immigration and education."[43] Only time will tell how successful the president will be in dealing with these issues, or whether he will choose to delay focusing on some of them.

Figure 3-1 shows results of the Gallup poll on presidential performance from Kennedy through Obama. An examination of the figure shows evidence of the decay curve for every president except Clinton. Starting in the mid-1960s, it became common for presidential approval ratings to fall below 50 percent, and even incoming presidents confronted lower initial ratings. Eisenhower and Johnson had approval ratings of 78 percent when Gallup first gathered information about them as president, and Kennedy had an approval rating of 72 percent—even though he received only 49.7 percent of the popular vote in the 1960 election.[44] Obama was the first president since Carter to have an initial job approval rating of more than 60 percent; in comparison, Reagan's was only 51 percent. Until George W. Bush, whose first-year average of 66.4 percent approval was skewed upward by the events of September 11, there had been a similar decline in average first-year ratings from 70.1 percent for Kennedy's first year to 48.8 percent for Clinton's. Some of this decline may be attributable to cynicism borne of Vietnam, Watergate, Iran-contra, and Whitewater, and the ability of television to demystify the presidency. The decline may also reflect a persistent trend toward tighter presidential elections, often coupled with a lack of enthusiasm for either candidate, and "divided government," in which one party controls the White House and another controls Congress. Neither Clinton in 1992 or 1996 nor Bush in 2000 received 50 percent of the popular vote. Even Reagan's "landslide" in 1980—with 90.9 percent of the electoral vote—was based on only 50.7 percent of the popular vote. For whatever reason, Americans seemed warier of new presidents than in times past—less willing to give them the benefit of the doubt and more apt to withhold support until they prove themselves. Obama, at least initially, seemed to be an exception to that rule.

Rallying Public Support

Presidents are not passive objects of public attitudes; instead, presidents and their aides take the initiative in shaping public perceptions. Over time, the White House has developed several specialized staff units devoted to maintaining favorable public relations and for promoting its agenda on Capitol Hill, with interest groups, and with members of the president's own party.[45] In performing these tasks, aides take actions and fashion appeals designed to win the support of different kinds of audiences, including other elites, the public at large, and specific constituencies.

The Rise of the Public Presidency

We now take public appeals by the president for granted, but, as noted in chapter 1, scholars such as Jeffrey Tulis contend that the rise of the "rhetorical"

FIGURE 3-1 Presidential Approval, 1961–2009

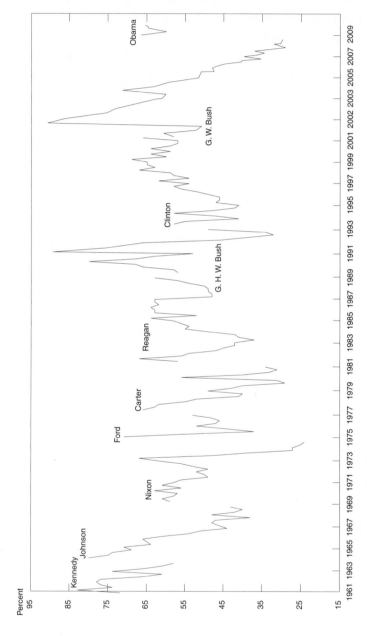

SOURCE: Based on data from the Gallup Poll (www.gallup.com).

NOTE: Question: "Do you approve or disapprove of the way _____ (last name of president) is handling his job as president?" Shown is the percentage who "approved," averaged by quarter. Individual survey results were graphed in previous editions of *Vital Statistics on American Politics*. G. W. Bush data are through April 15, 2007.

presidency is really a twentieth-century phenomenon.[46] Arguably, the now common-place practice of presidents "going public" to build public support for specific legislative initiatives is one of the most significant changes of the modern presidency.[47] As presidents have embraced public appeals, the source of presidential power has expanded from narrowly defined constitutional underpinnings to a broader plebiscitary base.[48] (For an alternate view, see the revisionist account of political scientist Mel Laracey.[49])

Tulis argues that presidents avoided the widespread use of public appeals in the nineteenth century because they adhered to a fundamentally different understanding of our political order from the one commonly held today. Their avoidance of public appeals reflected the founders' distrust of "pure" or "direct" democracy. Although the founders believed that public *consent* was a requirement of republican government, they also believed that the processes of government should be insulated from the whims of public *opinion*. They attempted to instill "deliberation" in government through indirect elections, separation of powers, and an independent executive. In such a system, public appeals by the president were proscribed because they were thought to "manifest demagoguery, impede deliberation, and subvert the routines of republican government."[50] Policy rhetoric by presidents—to the extent that it existed—was primarily written and principally addressed to Congress, as opposed to modern-day policy rhetoric, which is primarily spoken and principally addressed to the people. It was "*public* (available to all) but not thereby *popular* (fashioned for all)."[51]

Presidents avoided "going public," which is specifically designed to whip up public opinion, because it went against the existing interpretation of the constitutional order. That is not to say that other sorts of popular appeals were never made. Government-sponsored partisan newspapers flourished in the early part of our history and were clearly a means of generating public support—often by ridiculing the opposition with highly inflammatory articles.[52] *The Federalist Papers,* published in the New York press and widely distributed in bound volumes, are early examples of public appeals. Indeed, Federalists made a point of befriending influential printers, thereby forming a network for the distribution of information favorable to the Federalist cause.[53] Once in power, Federalists were accused of thwarting the circulation of opposition papers through control of the post office.[54] Arguably, however, the authors of these early examples designed them primarily to build public consent for broadly based structures—partisan newspapers for emerging political parties, and *The Federalist Papers* for a new form of government—rather than as more direct tools for mobilizing public opinion for congressional passage of specific policy initiatives.[55] Securing legislation remained an elite process of bargaining.

Nineteenth-century presidents did not maintain total public silence. They made occasional speeches to the people and even made some tours around the country (called "swings around the circle"). But public speeches were not as important as public appearances on those tours. President Washington, for example, initiated a "grand tour" of two months' duration by visiting the South in 1791, a region where suspicions of central authority had run strong during the constitutional ratification campaign. Washington himself emphasized the importance of "seeing and being seen" on the tour. Although he gave public remarks, Tulis emphasizes that they contained only "general articulations of republican sentiment, not even a clear enunciation of principle."[56]

Indeed, eighteenth- and nineteenth-century presidential speeches had an overall character very different from presidential speeches given today: They were largely ceremonial and usually devoid of policy content. They were also much less frequent. Tulis calculated that from George Washington through William McKinley, presidents averaged thirteen public speeches a year—80 percent or more of them very brief "thank you" remarks. The first eleven presidents averaged three public speeches a year.[57] In comparison, Clinton averaged one public speech almost every other day during his first three years in office.[58] To underscore the very different nature of rhetorical "common law" that existed in the nineteenth century, Tulis points out that Andrew Johnson was the first president to engage in a full-scale popular appeal over the heads of Congress for the passage of legislation and that he had an article of impeachment brought against him for doing so.[59]

Tulis identifies Theodore Roosevelt and Woodrow Wilson as catalysts for the new rhetorical presidency. He cites Roosevelt's public campaign to win passage of the Hepburn Act, which gave the Interstate Commerce Commission authority to regulate railroad shipping rates, as the first example of a president securing legislation with the help of going public.[60] Use of the **"bully pulpit"** dovetailed neatly with Roosevelt's broad "stewardship theory" of presidential power. (See chapter 1.) Like Roosevelt, Wilson believed that presidents had powers beyond those specifically enumerated in the Constitution, and he saw public opinion as an important source of that additional power.[61] He expanded the use of rhetoric and used it in new ways. He was the first elected president to have engaged in a full-scale speaking tour as part of the general election campaign.[62] Once in office, Wilson changed the norms of presidential rhetoric. He was largely responsible for the shift to policy rhetoric primarily spoken and principally addressed to the people. When Wilson delivered his State of the Union report orally—the first president to do so since John Adams—he had clearly fashioned his message for the people even though he presented it to Congress. One of Wilson's most dramatic appeals for public sup-port—his whistle-stop train tour to promote the League of Nations—was cut short in Colorado when he suffered a stroke on September 26, 1919.

Presidential Appeals

Appeals for public support are now a routine part of presidential governance. Pres-idents use that support as a bargaining chip with Congress—a way to persuade (or coerce) it to follow their leads. Barack Obama embraced that strategy as soon as he entered the White House. He quickly took to the road to campaign for his policy agenda. Many of the stops were in the so-called swing states of Arizona, Colorado, Florida, Illinois, and Indiana in just two weeks in February. George W. Bush had done the same thing in the early days of his administration. After using his first address to a joint session of Congress on February 27, 2001, to mobilize national support for his agenda, President Bush took off on speaking tours to promote its centerpiece, a $1.6 trillion tax cut, to specific audiences. In the two days following his address to Con-gress, Bush gave speeches touting his tax cut in Arkansas, Georgia, Iowa, Nebraska, and Pennsylvania. The explicit purpose of these speeches was to urge the American people to put pressure on Congress to pass the president's initiatives.

Speeches such as those given by Obama and Bush on their speaking tours are now commonplace. Unlike major addresses, such as the annual State of the Union and other prime-time television speeches, minor addresses such as those given on the road allow the president to target appeals to specific constituencies and generate local media coverage. As can be seen in Figure 3-2, the number of minor addresses increased dramatically starting in the Reagan years. Kernell has noted that both Clinton and George W. Bush averaged a minor address almost every other day.[63]

Corresponding with the increase in "going public" is the growth in presidential travel, which also began under Reagan (see Figure 3-3). It reflects the presidents' permanent campaign for public support.[64] Even Clinton's inability to run for a third term did not deter him from campaign mode. Bush followed suit. He crisscrossed the country to stump for his tax cut proposals in 2001 and 2003 and barnstormed for fellow Republicans before the 2002 midterm elections, visiting fifteen states in just the last five days before the election.[65] Media observers noted that Bush pre-ferred these public appeals to wooing individual legislators as Lyndon Johnson famously did.[66] Such appeals do not always work. Bush hit the road to win support for Social Security reform in 2005, but the proposal went nowhere, despite the speeches and White House efforts to market the president's call for reform.[67]

FIGURE 3-2   Presidential Addresses, 1933–2003 (Yearly Averages for First Three Years of First Term)

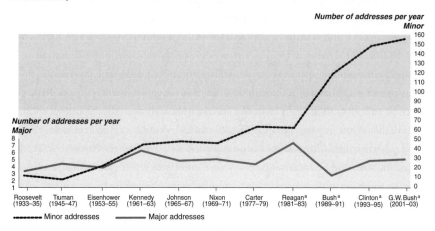

SOURCE: Samuel Kernell and Gary C. Jacobson, *The Logic of American Politics* (Washington, D.C.: CQ Press, 2000), 241.

NOTE: To eliminate public activities inspired by concerns of reelection rather than governing, only the first three years have been tabulated. For this reason, Gerald Ford's record of public activities during his two-and-one-half years of office has been ignored.

a. Includes television addresses only.

Unlike his predecessors, Obama made innovative uses of new technology to further his agenda. He even created a new White House post, director of new media.[68] In particular, the Obama White House has used online social networking to instigate offline community organizing. It took Obama's campaign e-mail list, renamed it "Organizing for America," and used it to ask 13 million supporters to go door-to-door with petitions in support of administration policy, a process that generated still more e-mail addresses. E-mail recipients were also asked to host house parties to inform neighbors of administration policies, such as the economic stimulus package.[69] When Congress voted on important issues like Obama's proposed budget, Organizing for America sent e-mails urging recipients to contact their members of Congress to support the legislation.[70] In his first year in office, Bush had done this the old-fashioned way: through speeches. In Fargo, North Dakota, Bush had urged a cheering, flag-waving crowd to put pressure on their senators: "If you like what you hear today, maybe e-mail some of the good folks from the United States Senate from your state," Bush said. "If you like what you hear, why don't you just give 'em a call and write 'em a letter."[71]

In addition to mobilizing grassroots support through e-mail appeals, Obama also used innovative ways to target other messages to specific constituencies. He delivered his weekly radio address on YouTube; appeared on *The Tonight Show with*

FIGURE 3-3   Days of Political Travel by Presidents, 1933–2003 (Yearly Averages for First Three Years of First Term)

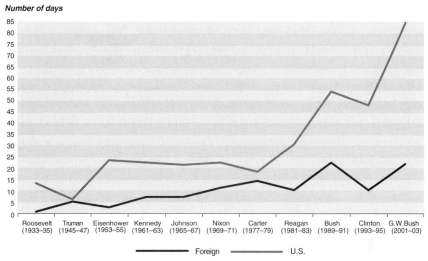

Number of days

| Roosevelt (1933–35) | Truman (1945–47) | Eisenhower (1953–55) | Kennedy (1961–63) | Johnson (1965–67) | Nixon (1969–71) | Carter (1977–79) | Reagan (1981–83) | Bush (1989–91) | Clinton (1993–95) | G.W.Bush (2001–03) |

━━━━━ Foreign   ━━━━━ U.S.

SOURCE: Samuel Kernell and Gary C. Jacobson, *The Logic of American Politics* (Washington, D.C.: CQ Press, 2000), 243.

NOTE: To eliminate public activities inspired by concerns of reelection rather than governing, only the first three years have been tabulated. For this reason, Gerald Ford's record of public activities during his two-and-one-half years of office has been ignored.

Jay Leno, becoming the first sitting president to appear on a late night talk show; and showed up on everything from ESPN, where he filled out his brackets for the NCAA Men's Basketball Championship, to a music awards show on Spanish-language Univision (Spanish-speaking voters are a key to winning swing states in 2012). Obama even held a "virtual" town hall meeting. People submitted questions to the White House Web site, and visitors to the site were asked to vote on which questions they wanted the president to answer. To submit a question or to vote, people had to register at the White House Web site—thereby providing still more names and e-mail addresses to add to the Organizing for America mailing list. Voting on the questions also provided feedback to the White House on which issues were most salient to the public. Hundreds of thousands of people submitted questions for the town hall and some 3.6 million cast votes.[72]

President Obama also traveled to nine foreign nations during his first one hundred days in office. Such travel reflects another change associated with modern presidents: they travel outside the United States more than their predecessors did. Political scientist Richard Rose has dubbed this phenomenon "going international." As Rose puts it, presidents can no longer do their jobs simply by staying in the

Obama's appearance on The Tonight Show with Jay Leno *marked the first time that a sitting U.S. president had appeared on a late night talk show.*

United States. "Whereas Herbert Hoover spent only three days abroad in his term of office and Franklin Roosevelt spent only nine days abroad in his first term, Richard Nixon spent fifty-nine days abroad in his first four years in office, and Jimmy Carter fifty-six days."[73] According to Mark Knoller, a CBS News reporter who gathers statistics on presidential travel, George W. Bush surpassed those numbers in his first two-and-a-half years in office with sixty-five days of foreign travel to thirty-two nations by August 2003.[74] By the time he left office, Bush had visited seventy-five nations, several more than once.[75] Foreign trips highlight the president's role as head of state and can paint a picture of the president as diplomat and peacemaker. Nixon's dramatic trips to China and the Soviet Union in 1972 (an election year) were beamed back live to American television with newly developed satellite technology.[76] Reagan's trips abroad provided many memorable television moments, including his emotional visit to the Normandy beaches of France, which became the backdrop for dramatic reelection ads in 1984.

Aside from foreign travel, "going international" has also come to include efforts by presidents to monitor and build public opinion abroad. Reagan was the first to do this in a systematic way.[77] The Reagan administration made a concerted effort to reach an international audience in 1981–1982 to deflect criticism of the president's decision to deploy nuclear weapons in Europe. This extensive public relations campaign in Western Europe included a speech by Reagan transmitted live by satellite and timed to air in prime time on European television.[78] President Obama held a televised town hall meeting in Strasbourg, France, before attending an April 2009 NATO summit.

George W. Bush arguably took going international to new heights. After the September 11, 2001, terrorist attacks he created the Coalition Information Center (CIC), an around-the-clock White House communications operation to build public support abroad, especially among Muslims in the Middle East, for the war on terrorism. James Wilkinson, who served as its director until 2003, coordinated daily press briefings at CIC offices around the world, including Washington, London, Islamabad, and Kabul, and stressed the need to respond rapidly to breaking news everywhere. "It may be 3 o'clock in the morning in the United States," Wilkinson explained, "but somewhere in the world, a journalist is on deadline."[79] The never-ending news cycle created by globalization required a twenty-four-hour news operation at the White House. In January 2003 the White House expanded the CIC and turned it into the Office of Global Communications directed by Tucker Eskew. In the days leading up to the U.S. invasion of Iraq, the office issued a daily bulletin called "The Global Messenger" to counter Iraqi "propaganda" with "truthful, accurate and effective messages."[80] The White House disbanded the office in 2005 and transferred its functions to the under secretary of state for public diplomacy.

The Bush administration also hired a Washington-based public relations firm called the Lincoln Group to plant pro-American articles in Iraqi newspapers. The stories appeared to be written by Iraqis, but were actually drafted by the Pentagon, and Iraqi newspapers were paid to publish them.[81] The Pentagon's U.S. Special Operations Command also awarded contracts worth $300 million to the Lincoln Group and two other organizations "to develop slogans, advertisements, newspaper articles, radio spots and television programs to build support for U.S. policies overseas."[82] The Lincoln Group, at the direction of the Pentagon, even hired Iraqi religious leaders to participate in the propaganda efforts.[83] A March 2006 Pentagon study concluded that the military policy of paying Iraqi newspapers to print positive stories did not violate military policy and could continue unless the Pentagon chose to change the policy.[84]

Appeals by Surrogates

Presidential **surrogates,** ranging from the vice president and members of the cabinet to party officials and political consultants, also promote the president's agenda through speaking tours, satellite interviews with local media outlets, and nationwide television appearances on the Sunday morning talk shows and cable outlets such as CNN, MSNBC, and Fox News. Nixon was one of the first presidents to aggressively choreograph the use of these surrogates as part of a broader strategy of going public. He sought to build, as his chief of staff, H. R. Haldeman, put it, "a stable of television personalities from within the Administration."[85]

Nixon was also one of the first presidents to use late-night talk shows and other entertainment outlets to promote himself and his agenda. Before becoming president, he appeared on the popular Jack Paar television talk show in 1963 to chat, play the piano, and help rebuild his image after his stinging loss to Pat Brown in the 1962 California gubernatorial race. He made a one-line ("sock it to me") cameo appearance on *Rowan and Martin's Laugh-In* during the 1968 presidential campaign. Once in the White House, Nixon hired a full-time staffer named Al Snyder, a former television executive from New York, to book television appearances for administration officials, but until Obama no sitting president actually appeared on a late night talk show. Snyder placed Vice President Spiro Agnew on the *Tonight Show with Johnny Carson* and Attorney General John Mitchell on the *Dick Cavett Show* and even arranged for the White House communications director, Herb Klein, to co-host the Cavett show. Snyder also booked more traditional appearances on programs such as *Meet the Press* and arranged local media appearances by administration officials along with advising them where and how to get the best media exposure when they traveled around the country.[86] Another Nixon staffer, Virginia Savell, coordinated speaking tours by administration surrogates. In Nixon's first year in office, she arranged for surrogate speakers to crisscross the country promoting everything from Nixon's proposed family assistance plan to postal reform.[87]

Surrogates—whether traveling around the country on speaking tours or appearing on television—follow a carefully scripted "line of the day" that is part of the broader message the administration is trying to convey at that point in time. When George W. Bush focused on education reform during his first week in office, his surrogates followed suit. Education secretary Roderick Paige made the rounds on the morning shows and cable news outlets, as did Vice President Dick Cheney and White House chief of staff Andrew Card. Republican members of Congress joined in, as did other proponents of education reform. In everything from public speeches to background interviews with reporters, administration surrogates stressed education reform. At the same time, the White House arranged for photo opportunities, such as that of the president reading to children at a local school.

The point of such activities is to convey a carefully orchestrated message that is reinforced by different people in a variety of contexts. Such coordination was clearly on display on December 19, 1998, the day the House of Representatives voted to impeach President Clinton. In a morning statement to reporters, White House press secretary Joe Lockhart three times decried "the politics of personal destruction." House minority leader Richard Gephardt repeated the line that morning in a speech on the floor of the House. So, too, did the president in his Rose Garden speech after the impeachment vote.

One advantage of surrogates is that they can be used to target very specific constituencies. Another way of targeting specific constituencies is through links with interest groups, as we discuss in the next section.

Targeted Communications: Presidents and Interest Groups

Presidents have come to recognize the value of targeting appeals to organized interests and mobilizing interest groups to support presidential policy. Liaison with such groups is now an important part of governance. As Mark A. Peterson has written, "Working with (as well as working against) interest groups to piece together support among the public and in Congress played a large role in the [Clinton] administration's political and policy strategies."[88] People who organize to advocate a particular interest are highly attentive to public issues affecting their members. These groups also have ongoing links with Congress and the bureaucracy that provide them with policy-making influence. It is not surprising, therefore, that they are a prime target of presidential communication. For example, presidents give major public addresses on business to conventions of the National Association of Manufacturers or the Chamber of Commerce of the United States and on labor relations to meetings of the American Federation of Labor–Congress of Industrial Organizations (AFL-CIO). Chief executives also dispatch surrogates to meet with these groups and to promote the administration's programs. White House aides serve as a channel for private communications with group representatives and will sometimes arrange meetings with the president.

Interest groups want to hear about current matters of public policy, but they also want to be reassured that the president is sympathetic to the problems group members face. Not surprisingly, chief executives pay particular attention to the groups that helped them get elected. They hope to convert their electoral coalition into one that helps them govern as well. Democratic presidents typically have focused on labor unions and civil rights organizations; Republicans have concentrated on business and professional organizations. Presidents also know that as the leader of the nation, they are supposed to represent *all* the people, not just those who supported their election. Chief executives cannot afford to ignore prominent interest groups, even those politically opposed to them.

Presidents have established channels for routine communication with particular groups through systematic White House liaison. Truman used David Niles, formerly on FDR's staff, as a liaison with blacks and Jews.[89] Eisenhower, who cultivated an image of being above politics, deemphasized, but did not completely ignore, group relations, and the Kennedy and Johnson administrations designated White House staff members to work with Jews, Catholics, and other groups. Gradually, however, the range of group ties became more predictable. Presidents since Nixon have assigned aides to work with eight population groups: business, labor, Jews, consumers, blacks, women, Hispanics, and the elderly.[90] Most of these ties are pursued through the Office of Public Liaison, a White House staff unit first conceived and implemented in the Nixon administration (under the direction of Charles Colson) and officially consolidated and named an independent staff unit under Gerald Ford.[91] George W. Bush also made a concerted effort to cultivate ties with conservative Christians.[92] In keeping with its innovative use of new technology, the Obama administration is using the White House Web site to invite direct citizen communication with the Office of Public Liaison (see http://www.white house.gov/administration/eop/opl/).

The Office of Public Liaison has been a part of each administration since Nixon's. People who serve in the liaison office not only articulate the demands of interest groups inside White House circles but also rally the support of interest groups behind the president's programs. Despite this dual purpose, there is little doubt that the office exists primarily to further the president's wishes rather than those of interest groups.[93]

Targeted Communications: Presidents and Political Parties

Outreach to political parties is also an important part of the modern public presidency. Presidents since Truman have assigned staff to serve as liaisons with their political parties.[94] As early as the Nixon administration, this staff was referred to as the Office of Political Affairs, although it did not become a freestanding entity listed in the *U.S. Government Organization Manual* until the Reagan administration.[95] By 2008 the office had become controversial. John McCain, the 2008 Republican presidential nominee, pledged to abolish the office if elected; Henry A. Waxman, D-Calif., the Democratic chair of the House Oversight and Government Reform Committee, issued a report in October 2008 that recommended its elimination. Nevertheless, President Obama chose to retain the office.[96]

As political scientist Kathryn Dunn Tenpas has noted, the Office of Political Affairs changes a good deal from president to president, but all share at least three core functions. First, the office serves as a formal liaison to national, state, and local party organizations as well as to congressional campaign committees. Such a liaison is a two-way street. On the one hand, it allows the White House to monitor the actions of relevant political actors and receive input from them. On the other hand, it provides an opportunity for the White House to mobilize political support from these actors. Harry S. Dent—head of Nixon's Office of Political Affairs—mobilized state Republican chairs to lobby U.S. senators from their states to vote for Clement Haynsworth, Nixon's Supreme Court nominee, in 1969 and to orchestrate a grassroots letter-writing campaign in behalf of the nomination.[97] The office made similar efforts in behalf of George H. W. Bush's Supreme Court nominees, David Souter and Clarence Thomas, in 1990 and 1991. The office also uses such ties to promote the president's legislative agenda, building *support* for presidential initiatives and mobilizing *opposition* to programs the president does not support. For example, the office may use pressure from party activists to help gain votes for cloture and help guard against veto overrides, and it may also apply grassroots pressure on members of Congress to vote against legislation. Creating a groundswell of grassroots opposition can also make it easier for the president to oppose certain policies. G. H. W. Bush used the Office of Political Affairs very effectively to help stop campaign finance reform.[98] It also appeared that the office may have tried to politicize the hiring and firing of U.S. attorneys under George W. Bush. When Sara M. Taylor, who had served as Bush's political affairs director from 2003 to 2007, was subpoenaed to answer questions about the allegations before the Senate Judiciary Committee after she left her post, President Bush invoked executive privilege, and Taylor refused to answer most questions.[99]

Second, the office serves as liaison with major supporters of the president, including private citizens who have donated money to support the president's political activities. If such a supporter requests a signed photo from the president or a White House tour, the Office of Political Affairs arranges it. Some alleged that the Clinton administration went beyond this simple sort of constituent service and improperly used the office to raise funds and reward donors. A 1998 report by the House Committee on Government Reform and Oversight, chaired by Rep. Dan Burton, R-Ind., pointed to efforts by members of Clinton's Office of Political Affairs to create a computerized White House database to identify potential donors and share the information with the Democratic National Committee. "This is the President's idea and it's a good one," Marsha Scott, a member of the office, wrote in a draft memorandum to White House chief of staff Mack McLarty in 1994. She wrote that the database would be used to "identify and contact key supporters in all fifty states" and would allow the White House to identify, by early 1995, "key financial and political folks in each state who can work with us."[100] Another memo, dated October 25, 1994, noted that the president wanted the database to correlate contributions from individuals and their invitations to, and attendance at, White House events.[101] In other words, the Office of Political Affairs used the list to reward donors with invitations to meet the president, attend White House functions, or spend the night in the Lincoln Bedroom.

Finally, the office engages in what Tenpas calls "electioneering." This function includes planning early reelection strategies for presidents in their first terms. Tim Kraft engaged in such planning in the Carter administration before becoming Carter's campaign manager for the 1980 election, just as Ed Rollins and Lee Atwater worked in the office during the first Reagan administration before moving over to the 1984 Reagan-Bush campaign headquarters.[102] Ken Mehlman served as the director of George W. Bush's political affairs office before managing Bush's 2004 reelection campaign.[103] Often the office looks for ways to expand the president's electoral base in anticipation of a reelection bid. It was especially important for Clinton to expand his electoral base because he won the White House in 1992 with just 43 percent of the popular vote in a three-way race. George W. Bush—winning the White House with roughly 48 percent of the popular vote—was in a similar situation when he first took office in 2001. In addition to engineering reelection strategies, the office uses presidential resources to help elect members of Congress from the same political party as the president. During the 2002 midterm elections, Bush's eleven-person office scheduled campaign appearances by leading Republican celebrities, such as former New York mayor Rudolph Giuliani, to help regional candidates raise money and win votes.[104] Typically, the office arranges presidential appearances in the candidate's home state or congressional district, coordinates photo opportunities for the candidate at the White House, and maintains liaison with House and Senate campaign committees.

Presidents try to influence the outcome of midterm congressional elections, even though the president's party usually loses seats in these contests.[105] The Democrats under Clinton in 1998 and the Republicans under Bush in 2002 bucked that trend. Normally, however, the president is limited in what can be accomplished, especially in elections for the House of Representatives. For one thing, the sheer number of contests (435 every two years) precludes participation in many of them. (Bush's efforts in the 2002 midterm elections have been called "unprecedented," with a record ninety campaign appearances, yet he still made personal campaign appearances for only twenty-three congressional candidates.)[106] For another, good evidence shows that the off-year House elections are primarily local, not national, events. Scholars who have examined off-year congressional elections report the same basic finding: how people vote has more to do with their evaluations of the congressional candidates than with their assessment of the president.[107] The 2006 midterm elections may be an exception to that rule: discontent with President Bush's handling of the war in Iraq, coupled with a series of widely publicized scandals, appears to have motivated many people to vote against Republicans. As a result, the GOP lost control of both houses of Congress. Exit polls indicated that 60 percent of the voters in 2006 cast their vote based on national rather than local issues.[108] The White House countered that the loss of twenty-eight House seats and six Senate seats was close to the average loss suffered by the president's party during the sixth year of the president's term, and identical to the average losses in a wartime midterm.[109]

Another valuable asset for congressional candidates in midterm elections is incumbency. Incumbents benefit from previous campaign experience, close relationships with voters, greater knowledge of issues, and superior financial resources, all of which give them a considerable advantage over their opponents.[110] Redistricting also helped to make House seats safer. The 2002 and 2004 House elections, for example, were the least competitive since World War II.[111] Presidents who attempt to campaign against sitting members of Congress therefore face very difficult odds. Bush in 2002 was aided by the fact that there were few vulnerable House seats to defend and, most significant, that the redistricting after the 2000 census favored Republicans.[112] That, coupled with his record number of campaign appearances and his tireless fund-raising (the president attended seventy-five fund-raisers, taking in a record $144 million), led to a gain of six seats in the House.

Incumbency was somewhat less beneficial for House Republicans in 2006. Corruption charges were a major reason. Many Republicans were linked to the lobbyist Jack Abramoff, who pled guilty to felony charges of fraud, tax evasion, and conspiracy to bribe public officials. Rep. Randy "Duke" Cunningham, R-Calif., resigned and was subsequently convicted for taking some $2.4 million in bribes. Former House majority leader Tom DeLay, R-Texas, was indicted on charges of conspiring to violate election law and money laundering. And it was revealed shortly before the election that Rep. Mark Foley, R-Fla., had sent sexually oriented e-mails and instant messages to teenage male House pages. Twenty incumbent House Republicans, six of whom were caught up in corruption charges, lost their reelection bids, but not a single incumbent Democrat in either the House or Senate lost; it was the first time in American history that a political party maintained all of its seats in both houses. In spite of the Republican losses in 2006, 94.5 percent of all incumbents seeking reelection were successful.[113]

TABLE 3-1   Losses by President's Party in Midterm Elections, 1862–2006

Year	Party holding presidency	President's party: gain/loss of seats in House	President's party: gain/loss of seats in Senate
1862	R	−3	8
1866	R	−2	0
1870	R	−31	−4
1874	R	−96	−8
1878	R	−9	−6
1882	R	−33	3
1886	D	−12	3
1890	R	−85	0
1894	D	−116	−5
1898	R	−21	7
1902	R	9[a]	2
1906	R	−28	3
1910	R	−57	−10
1914	D	−59	5
1918	D	−19	−6
1922	R	−75	−8
1926	R	−10	−6
1930	R	−49	−8
1934	D	9	10
1938	D	−71	−6
1942	D	−55	−9
1946	D	−55	−12
1950	D	−29	−6
1954	R	−18	−1
1958	R	−47	−13
1962	D	−5	3
1966	D	−47	−4
1970	R	−12	2
1974	R	−48	−5
1978	D	−15	−3
1982	R	−26	1
1986	R	−5	−8
1990	R	−10	−1
1994	D	−55	−9
1998	D	4	0
2002	R	8	1
2006	R	−30	−6

SOURCE: Harold W. Stanley and Richard G. Niemi, *Vital Statistics on American Politics, 2007–2008* (Washington, D.C.: CQ Press, 2007).

NOTE: Entry is the difference between the number of seats won by the president's party in that midterm election and the number of seats won by that party in the preceding general election. Because of changes in the overall number of seats in the Senate and House, in the number of seats won by third parties, and in the number of vacancies, a Republican loss is not always matched precisely by a Democratic gain, or vice versa.

a. Although the Republicans gained nine seats in the 1902 elections, they actually lost ground to the Democrats, who gained twenty-five seats after the increase in the overall number of representatives after the 1900 census.

Senatorial midterm elections usually offer a somewhat better opportunity for presidents to influence results. A third of the Senate's one hundred seats are at stake every two years, so the chief executive can concentrate on these contests in a way not possible for House races. Bush made campaign appearances for sixteen Republican Senate candidates in 2002, and the Republican Senatorial Campaign Committee launched an aggressive series of television ads attacking Democratic incumbents for failing to support homeland security.[114] That combination—together with high turnout among Republican voters—led to the Republicans' picking up two Senate seats in 2002 (enough to shift control in the Senate to Republicans), but they lost six seats in 2006. Although sitting senators are in the same position as House members in being able to bring their names to the attention of constituents, incumbency is not as advantageous for a senator as it is for a House member. Senators represent an entire state rather than a small district, and the prestige associated with being a senator means races will be hard fought. Challengers are much more visible to the electorate than are those who run against House incumbents. Popular presidents, therefore, are better able to help candidates who challenge incumbent senators of the opposite party by increasing the challengers' visibility through public association. Midterm election outcomes also depend on the condition of the national economy and the president's standing in public opinion polls at the time of the elections.[115] Voting in these contests tends to be *negative;* that is, those who disapprove of the president's performance in office are more likely to vote in such elections than those who approve.[116] Gary Jacobson contends that the president's role in congressional elections is essentially indirect: the state of the economy and the president's ratings in the public opinion polls influence the caliber of candidates who run in congressional elections. If, for example, these are not favorable, the opposition party will be able to field an unusually large proportion of formidable challengers with well-financed campaigns, and the president's party in Congress may lose a considerable number of seats.[117] Democrats fared miserably in the 1994 midterm elections when Bill Clinton's Gallup approval ratings came near their lowest point—fluctuating between 39 percent on September 6 and 48 percent on October 22. On the other hand, Democrats fared unusually well in the 1998 midterm elections when Clinton's approval ratings remained consistently high, hovering near 66 percent despite the looming threat of impeachment. (See Table 3-1.) Bush's approval rating just before the 2002 elections was (at 63 percent) not quite as high as Clinton's in 1998, but it still tied with Ronald Reagan's 1986 rating "for second highest in any postwar midterm election."[118] In comparison, Bush's approval ratings hovered around 37 percent in the days leading up to the 2006 midterm elections.

The President and the Media

Historically, the most important link between the president and the American public has been the press. In the early years of the Republic, the press was as partisan as it is in many European countries today. The partisan press reached its peak during the presidency of Andrew Jackson, when federal officeholders were expected to subscribe to the administration organ, the *Washington Globe*, which was financed primarily by revenues derived from the printing of official government notices.[119]

The partisan press began to decline during the presidency of Abraham Lincoln. The establishment of the Government Printing Office in 1860 destroyed the printing-contract patronage that had supported former administration organs.[120] The invention of the telegraph led to the formation of wire services, which provided standardized and politically neutral information to avoid antagonizing the diverse readerships of the various subscribing newspapers. Advertising provided newspapers with a secure financial base independent of the support of presidential administrations. By the end of the nineteenth century, "news about the White House was transmitted to the public by independent, nonpartisan news organizations," a factor that continues to affect relationships between the president and the press today.[121]

Not until 1896, though, did the White House become a regular beat for reporters. Not surprisingly, given their role in establishing the public presidency, both Woodrow Wilson and Theodore Roosevelt formalized innovative ties with those reporters in the early part of the twentieth century. Roosevelt began the practice of meeting with them (often during his late afternoon shave). In 1902 he had a pressroom built in the new west wing of the White House and began having an aide, William Loeb, give daily press briefings. Wilson continued the practice of daily press briefings (conducted by Joseph Tumulty) and became the first president to hold regularly scheduled press conferences. He held his first in the East Room of the White House on March 15, 1913—just eleven days after his inauguration—for 125 reporters.[122]

In the twentieth century, several media took their place beside newspapers as important channels between the president and the people. Radio became a dominant force in communications in the 1920s, as did television in the 1950s. By the end of the century, cable and satellite technology had dramatically increased the number of potential sources of news and commentary, and the Internet had revolutionized the way people communicate and gather information. The emergence of broadcast technology, coupled with the array of "new media" (cable, satellite technology, and the Internet) by century's end, allowed presidents to communicate messages directly to the people rather than having their messages relayed (and interpreted) by journalists.

Presidential Media

Today, an enormous variety of media cover the words and actions of the U.S. president. These media differ in the ways they deal with executive branch developments and in their target audiences. They also vary in importance to chief executives and their programs. Over the past fifty years, the way Americans get information has undergone a fundamental change. In 1959, 57 percent of the public claimed to get most of its news from newspapers, and 51 percent from television (more than one response was allowed in the survey); only 19 percent claimed to get their news from television alone. By 1997 only 37 percent cited newspapers as a principal source, and 69 percent cited television; 47 percent claimed to get their news only from television.[123] A Gallup poll conducted March 29–30, 2003, found television to be the main source of information about the war with Iraq for 86 percent of the respondents (3 percent said newspapers were their main source, 6 percent said the radio, and 4 percent said the Internet).[124] This pattern developed with the spread of television ownership: only 9 percent of households had television sets in 1950, a figure that grew to 87 percent by 1960 and 98 percent by 1980.[125] As one would expect, White House attention to television coverage rose over the same period.

In addition, the White House must be attentive to the most influential media figures—a select group of columnists, elite reporters, anchors of the broadcast news, and executives of the media organizations. Indeed, there is substantial evidence that the stated views of news commentators and experts have a greater impact on citizens' policy preferences than the president's own comments.[126]

Syndicated columnists earn White House attention because they reach powerful audiences outside government, including business and labor leaders, lobbyists, and academics, as well as top officials in government—members of Congress, members of the bureaucracy, judges, governors, and mayors. These columnists influence views on the political feasibility of a president's proposed programs. They deal in matters of opinion rather than just factual developments affecting the presidency. "They are guaranteed space, they have no assigned topics, they are freed from the pressure of breaking news stories at deadline, and they have the opportunity to introduce their own perspectives into their stories."[127]

Television anchors such as Katie Couric, Charles Gibson, and Brian Williams are important to the president because of the respect they command and the size of the audiences they reach (about 26 million people each weekday night).[128] They are joined now by the twenty-four-hour cable news networks and their coterie of anchors and commentators. According to Gallup, the percentage of Americans who say they watch cable news networks daily rose from 23 percent in 1995 to 40 percent in 2008, and the percentage who say they watch network news daily fell from 62 percent in 1995 to 34 percent in 2008. Most significant is the dramatic rise in the Internet as a source of news. In 1995 only 3 percent said that they used the internet daily as a source of news. By 2008 that number had risen to 31 percent.[129]

Because far more people watch television than read newspapers, the information the ordinary citizen receives about the presidency depends on what is included in the evening news and covered on cable outlets such as CNN, Fox News, and MSNBC and the Internet. At the same time, television coverage of the presidency has serious limitations: newscasts devote very little time to the most important stories (about seventy-five seconds on average); emphasis is placed on events that are visually exciting; a focus on the president personalizes complex developments; and broadcasts usually lack in-depth reporting and analysis.[130] Sound bites of the president speaking on the evening network newscasts shrank from an average of forty-two seconds in 1968 to less than seven seconds in 1996.[131]

Cable provides additional television outlets for presidents. C-SPAN carries many presidential speeches in their entirety, as well as White House press briefings. Cable news channels also offer a degree of expanded coverage, but the actual news stories are similar in length to those on the evening newscasts. Most significant, cable has given presidential surrogates many more venues to state their cases. When Fox and MSNBC joined the cable news lineup in 1996, they relied heavily on talk shows to fill their airtime. Such shows are cheap to produce and require limited resources. They are also popular with viewers—so much so that CNN followed suit and expanded the number of its talk shows in 2001.

Helping to shape both print and broadcast coverage are the bureau chiefs and other media executives who determine which stories are covered, how they are handled, which reporters will cover the White House, and who should be represented in "pools" that travel with the president to cover significant events. The White House press corps is also an important determinant of what will be reported and how it will be reported. These are the reporters assigned to the White House itself. They attend the daily press briefings, travel with the president, and have as their primary responsibilities the task of reporting what the president is doing. Some members of the press corps are especially influential. Reporters for the *New York Times* and the *Washington Post* are examples because of the readership of their papers; in addition to public officials and important people in the private sector, their readers are the other Washington reporters.[132] The *Times,* in particular, is known to influence network news decisions about which stories to cover.[133] Also significant are the reporters for the wire services—Associated Press (AP) and United Press International (UPI)—because they provide coverage of the president for newspapers across the country. Collectively, the press corps frames most of what we read and see about the president.

Cable, satellite technology, and the Internet also provide unparalleled opportunities for direct communication with the American people. In the 1992 presidential campaign, Bill Clinton very effectively followed a strategy of "narrowcasting"— using media outlets such as MTV, the *Arsenio Hall Show, Phil Donahue,* and Don Imus's radio talk show to transmit direct, targeted messages to particular constituencies, tactics he and his successors brought to the White House. Presidents have learned, however, that these new media have their limits. They cannot be used at the expense of cultivating ties with established White House reporters.

Presidents and reporters alike now face new competition from ordinary citizens. The Internet has democratized the process through the extensive use of online blogs and innovations such as YouTube and Facebook. Meanwhile, cell phone technology allows instant text messaging. The Obama administration has attempted to use these new channels of communication to its advantage.

We turn next to the two White House staff units that deal most directly with the press and communications planning: the Press Office and the Office of Communications.

The White House Press Office

Franklin Roosevelt officially created the **White House Press Office** in 1933. As we have seen, a routinized White House relationship with the press had been in place since Theodore Roosevelt directed William Loeb to provide daily briefings for reporters. Every president after TR assigned a member of his staff to deal with the press, with Herbert Hoover being the first to hire an aide, George Akerson, for whom the press was the *sole* responsibility. Akerson served from 1929 to 1931 and was the equivalent of a modern-day **press secretary,** although that post was not formally created until FDR came to office in 1933.

The Press Office is in the West Wing and maintains day-to-day contact with the reporters assigned to cover the White House. The Press Room (where daily briefings take place) and space for reporters are located downstairs in an area that used to house a swimming pool. Junior staff has space next to the Press Room in what is called the Lower Press Office. Senior staff members, including the press secretary, have their offices upstairs. Altogether the Press Office consists of about twenty people, some of whom specialize in a certain issue area such as foreign affairs. These include several deputy press secretaries as well as the junior staffers who write press releases and do other sorts of research. The most visible (and most senior) member of the Press Office is the press secretary.

The press secretary is the most important person in the executive branch for day-to-day contact with the presidential media. Typically holding two daily briefings, the press secretary provides routine information on executive branch appointments and resignations, on presidential actions and policies, and on the president's schedule—visits, meetings, and travel plans. By the end of an administration there may have been more than two thousand such briefings. In addition, the press secretary holds private meetings with select reporters to provide background information to explain the president's actions on a particular problem or program.

Press secretaries try to balance serving the interests of three constituencies: the president, members of the White House staff, and members of the media.[134] The secretary can perform well only if granted continuous access to, and the confidence of, the president so journalists may assume that the news comes from the chief executive. If presidents try to be their own press secretaries, as may have been true of Lyndon Johnson, even a capable and influential person such as Bill Moyers will not succeed in managing the message.[135] When secretaries are excluded from White House decisions, as appeared to be the case with Clinton's first press secretary, Dee Dee Myers, their credibility suffers.

The modern era's press secretaries varied in effectiveness. Among those considered successful are Stephen Early (FDR), James Hagerty (Eisenhower), Jody Powell (Carter), and Mike McCurry (Clinton). Some, such as Hagerty and Powell, were effective because their presidents kept them informed on virtually everything going on in the White House. But sometimes even well-informed press secretaries do not want to know everything. After leaving office, Mike McCurry admitted that he purposely stayed out of the loop so that he could truthfully respond that he did not know all the answers concerning the Monica Lewinsky affair.[136] On the other hand, Nixon's press secretary, Ron Ziegler, was so out of the loop that he, like Myers, lost credibility with reporters. This was true even before the Watergate affair when, after months of denying any White House involvement, Ziegler was forced to declare those denials "inoperative." Indeed, Nixon purposely diminished the importance of the press secretary when he became president. White House reporters considered Nixon's choice of Ziegler—who was only twenty-nine years old and had no background in journalism—a slap in the face.[137] Another secretary who did not have a particularly good relationship with reporters was Larry Speakes, who became Reagan's press spokesman when James Brady was shot and incapacitated in the assassination attempt on the president. After leaving office, Speakes provoked cries of outrage when he admitted in his memoirs that he had manufactured presidential quotes during Reagan's Iceland summit meeting with Soviet leader Mikhail Gorbachev in November 1985. Fearing that Reagan was being upstaged, Speakes created a public relations solution to the problem, and the fabricated quotes were given prominent attention back home.[138]

The White House Office of Communications

Richard Nixon created the **White House Office of Communications** in 1969.[139] Its functions are quite different from those of the Press Office. As originally conceived, the Office of Communications had four primary goals: (1) long-range communications planning, (2) the coordination of news from all the many departments and agencies of the executive branch, (3) outreach to local media, and (4) oversight of presidential surrogates. The Press Office is largely *reactive;* it responds to the questions and needs of the White House press corps. The Office of Communications, on the other hand, is primarily *proactive;* it is responsible for setting the public agenda and making sure that all the players on the presidential team are adhering to that agenda. This includes setting the "line of the day" and choreographing presidential photo opportunities.

The precise jurisdiction of the Office of Communications has varied somewhat from administration to administration. Outreach to local media has at times been subsumed by a subunit of the Press Office. In fact, the Press Office itself has at times been a subunit of the Office of Communications (and vice versa). For at least part of the administrations of former presidents Reagan, Bush, and Clinton, the Office of Communications became an umbrella term for a variety of offices supervised by the communications director. At various times, this body included the Press Office as well as the Offices of Planning, Speechwriting, Advance, Public Liaison (outreach to interest groups), Media Affairs (outreach to local media), Political Affairs (outreach to members of the president's political party), and Public Affairs (liaison with public information officers throughout the executive branch).

For Nixon, a primary motivation in creating the office was to install a mechanism for bypassing the critical filter of the White House press corps. Outreach to local media, the coordination of surrogate speakers, and the use of venues such as television, radio, and mass mailings to communicate directly with the people were all a part of that effort. For presidents since Reagan, the emphasis has been on long-range communications planning, and tactics of circumvention are often part of that plan. As mentioned above, George W. Bush's administration not only maintained the Office of Communications but also, for a time, a new Office of Global Communications designed to reach a worldwide audience. Vice President Cheney, who had considerable experience with communications planning as White House chief of staff for President Ford, maintained that it is essential for the White House to manage presidential news. "That means that about half the time the White House press corps is going to be pissed off," Cheney admitted, "and that's all right. You're not there to please them. You're there to run an effective presidency. And to do that, you have to be disciplined in what you convey to the country. The most powerful tool you have is the ability to use the symbolic aspects of the presidency to promote your goals and objectives." That means the White House has to control the agenda. "You don't let the press set the agenda," Cheney emphasized. "They like to decide what's important and what isn't important. But if you let them do that, they're going to trash your presidency."[140] Responsibility for controlling the communications agenda rests with the Office of Communications and a variety of other communications advisers—some of whom are not officially members of the White House staff.

Such sharing of communications responsibilities is not unusual. In his first term, President Reagan benefited greatly not only from the skill and experience of communications director David Gergen, who had also served in the Nixon and Ford administrations, but also from the talents of James A. Baker III and Michael Deaver, other members of the White House staff who carefully managed the president's media and public image. This team was especially adept at selecting the "line of the day," often as part of a broader "theme of the week," and creating "photo opportunities" featuring the president to highlight it. As Donald Regan later wrote: "[Deaver] saw—designed—each presidential action as a one-minute or two-minute spot on the evening network news, or picture on page one of the *Washington Post* or the *New York Times,* and conceived every presidential appearance in terms of camera angles. . . . Every moment of every appearance was scheduled, every word was scripted, every place where Reagan was expected to stand was chalked with toe marks."[141] Reagan, the former Hollywood actor, followed the script masterfully. The administration of George W. Bush also proved to be adept at staging photo opportunities, including his May 2003 "tail-hook" landing in an S-3B Viking Navy jet on the USS *Abraham Lincoln.* President Bush told reporters that he had flown the jet himself en route to the ship. Initially, the White House said that the president had to take the jet because the ship was out of helicopter range. It turned out,

Photo-ops such as Bush's "tail-hook" landing on the USS Abraham Lincoln *in May 2003 are designed to convey specific images to the public. These images of the president in his "top gun" gear are intended to reinforce the message of a strong, courageous leader in control.*

however, that the ship was in easy helicopter range—only thirty miles off the coast of California, with cameras carefully positioned so as not to see the coastline.[142] Nevertheless, photographs of Bush in his "top gun" gear conveyed the image of a strong, courageous leader in control. In the long term, however, the photo op, which included a huge "Mission Accomplished" sign, backfired when the war in Iraq dragged on for years. Some attempts at image making do not work—just ask 1988 Democratic presidential nominee Michael Dukakis, who looked ridiculous when his aides arranged a photo op of him driving a tank.

Presidential Press Conferences

Presidents cultivate their own ties with reporters—often through off-the-record sessions when traveling on *Air Force One* and during other informal gatherings, but the presidential press conference is the best-known avenue for interaction between presidents and reporters. FDR perfected the art of the press conference. He held a total of 998 while president—an average of almost 7 a month. His gatherings were informal—usually held in his office—but there was strict control over how reporters could use material from the press conferences, as there had been since President Wilson first began the practice of regular press conferences in 1913. Despite the control, FDR's system—as Samuel Kernell has pointed out—was one of "hard news, openly conveyed."[143]

The emergence of broadcast media and their desire to cover press conferences eroded the intimacy of these interactions between presidents and reporters. It also reduced the White House's dependence upon reporters to communicate the president's views to the public. Radio and television became ways to reach the masses directly. Indeed, press conferences came to be used more to meet the people than to meet the press when President Kennedy began the practice of televising them live in 1961. (Eisenhower had allowed filming, but the White House controlled which clips could be broadcast.) As President Nixon's chief of staff bluntly put it in a 1970 White House memo: "The President wants you to realize and emphasize to all appropriate members of your staff that a press conference is a TV operation and that the TV impression is really all that matters."[144] Nixon also began the practice of prime-time televised news conferences. Kennedy's were almost always held at either 11: 00 A.M. or 4: 00 P.M. Lyndon Johnson never held one after 4: 50 P.M. Nixon changed that. He preferred 9: 00 P.M. Back in the age when the networks preempted regularly scheduled programs to cover such conferences, that time guaranteed a large audience. It was also just late enough that it was difficult for the morning newspapers to dissect the president's performance. By the next evening's network news programs it was already "old" news. George H. W. Bush and Bill Clinton both held most of their press conferences during midday rather than prime-time evening hours. Although their sessions were less widely viewed—CNN was the principal source of coverage—these two presidents held press conferences quite frequently and therefore earned points with reporters for their accessibility. George W. Bush held only seventeen formal press conferences during his first term, the lowest number for any president in the television age. His father held eighty-four during the same period of time.[145] By the time Bush left office he had given a total of fifty solo press conferences.[146] Presidents supplement press conferences with more informal exchanges with reporters. These informal exchanges give presidents greater control because they can stop the questioning at any point. In addition, President Bush held many joint press conferences with foreign leaders, both in the United States and abroad, but these events also give more control to the president than solo press conferences. Questions are more apt to focus on the subjects being discussed by the leaders, and half the questions are addressed to the other participant.

Without the strict ground rules that gave earlier presidents control over what information reporters could use from press conferences, recent presidents facing live television coverage of their press conferences have sought other ways to minimize risks. Members of the president's staff draw up a list of questions reporters are likely to ask, together with suggested answers and supporting information. Some presidents hold full-scale mock news conferences for practice. Reagan, for example, liked two-hour practices, dividing the time between foreign policy and domestic policy. Staff would point out errors and critique the president's performance. On the day of the news conference, photos of the reporters expected to attend were fixed to their likely places on a seating chart, and difficult questions were reviewed.[147] The emphasis, in short, shifted to performance.

President Nixon liked to emphasize the appearance of risk he was taking in such performances. He likened himself to "the man in the arena" facing hostile adversaries when he confronted the press. To symbolize his lack of fear of these adversaries, he sometimes held press conferences with no podium to shield him from reporters. But, overall, presidents control the interchange at these conferences. At times, the White House limits questions to domestic policy or foreign policy, and presidents can always refuse to answer certain questions on the grounds that the subject matter is too sensitive for public discussion, a frequent response to foreign and military questions.

The success of a press conference depends on the skills of the president. President Eisenhower came across badly in them. He appeared to have trouble expressing himself clearly and grammatically and displayed meager knowledge about many vital issues of the day. Revisionist accounts have suggested that he may have used this as a tactic to avoid sensitive issues.[148] President Johnson also came across poorly in formal televised press conferences. On the other hand, FDR and Kennedy were masters of the press conference. Roosevelt had a keen sense of what was newsworthy and even suggested reporters' lead stories to them. He also prepared members of the press for actions he took on controversial problems by educating them initially with confidential background information; consequently, reporters tended to support his decisions because they understood his reasoning. Kennedy, who had served a brief stint as a newspaperman and enjoyed the company of reporters, used his press conferences to great advantage; his ability to field difficult questions impressed not only the members of the press but also the public. Clinton did not have the close relationship with reporters that Roosevelt and Kennedy enjoyed, but he also performed well in press conferences, as has Obama. Most people who have studied or been involved in modern-day press conferences have concluded that they serve primarily the president rather than the media. As George Reedy, Johnson's press secretary, pointed out, a president rarely receives an unexpected question on an important issue in a conference, and should that happen, the president could respond with a witty or a noncommittal remark.[149] Michael Grossman and Martha Kumar summarize the president's advantage as follows: "The President decides when to hold a conference, how much notice reporters will be given, who will ask the questions, and what the answers will be."[150]

In managing their relationships with the media, presidents must take into account their particular strengths and weaknesses. Nicknamed the Great Communicator, Reagan benefited enormously from his previous professional experience in radio, films, and television. To take advantage of those skills, the president frequently addressed the nation on prime-time television and used a series of Saturday radio broadcasts to explain and justify his administration's policies. The administration also avoided or restricted the use of other media formats that President Reagan did not handle as well as prepared speeches, specifically those that required him to give spontaneous answers to questions. He did not participate in call-in shows and seldom invited reporters to the White House for informal, on-the-record question and answer sessions. Reagan seldom would answer impromptu questions from reporters at photo sessions, and he held fewer press conferences in eight years than President Carter did in four. Nationally televised speeches were Reagan's best vehicle for communicating his views to the American people.

Relations between the President and the Media: Conflict or Collusion?

It is common for presidents to view the press unfavorably. George Washington, whom journalists treated rather well, was inclined not to run for a second term because of what he considered a critical press.[151] Since then, virtually all presidents have expressed outrage, indignation, resentment, or consternation over their treatment in the media. In turn, members of the press have criticized the way presidents have handled media relations. Typically, chief executives are accused of "managing" the news and, as their terms in office progress, of isolating themselves from the media and the public. Some, such as Johnson and Nixon, were also charged with deliberately lying to the media and the public, as was Clinton, when questioned about his relationship with Monica Lewinsky. George W. Bush was accused of misleading the public when he included an unsubstantiated charge in his 2003 State of the Union address that "Saddam Hussein recently sought significant quantities of uranium from Africa." The charge raised the specter of Iraq as a nuclear threat and was part of Bush's effort to convince Congress and the American people that war with Iraq was justified. Bush's own secretary of state had already dismissed that particular claim as not credible, and CIA director George J. Tenet later admitted that those words "should never have been included in the text written for the president."[152]

There is little question that a built-in conflict exists between the president and the media. Chief executives want to suppress information they feel will endanger the nation's security or put their administrations in a bad light. George W. Bush was livid when newspapers published details of his secret wiretap program designed to combat terrorism. On the other hand, members of the media are eager for news, however sensitive it may be. And, as a president's approval ratings fall—as Bush's did in his second term—press coverage becomes harsher. A president's lame-duck status also leads to more dismissive coverage.[153] Another source of tension between presidents and the press is the latter's penchant for what might be called "attack journalism": stories focused on scandal.[154]

Despite the potential for conflict, there is a basis for cooperation between presidents and the press that ultimately produces a collusive relationship.[155] Quite simply, the two are mutually dependent: neither presidents nor the press can perform their jobs without the assistance of the other, and cooperation is, therefore, beneficial to both. The president must be able to communicate with the public through the media, and the media must have the administration's cooperation if they are to cover the most important official in the national government and give the public an accurate assessment of presidential activities. Moreover, the White House offers a range of media services designed to seduce reporters into favorable coverage. The product is an *exchange relationship,* a set of negotiated terms for the interaction between the media and the president that favors the White House and disadvantages the public.[156] As David Broder has argued, "We have been drawn into a circle of working relationships and even friendships with the people we are supposed to cover. The distinction between press and government has tended to become erased."[157]

Grossman and Kumar have argued that the general relationship between the president and the media goes through certain predictable phases.[158] During the initial period of "alliance," both parties agree that the focus should be on the new administration's appointees and its proposed goals and policies—the presidency is "open"; reporters are likely "to have their phone calls answered, to be granted interviews, and to get information that has not been specifically restricted."[159] During the second phase, "competition," the president wants to concentrate on portraying members of his administration as part of a happy team, committed to common goals and policies, while the media focus on conflicts among personalities in the administration and controversies over policies.[160] Presidents restrict access to themselves and others in the administration and may even go on the attack against especially critical reporters or organizations. The final phase of presidential-media relationships is "detachment." Surrogates manage the news, and presidents appear only in favorable settings scheduled to coincide with major events. The media, in turn, engage in more investigative reporting and seek information from sources other than the White House.

The Clinton administration's relationship with the press did not seem to follow the typical phases identified by Grossman and Kumar. The period of "alliance" was unusually brief, and relations became obviously strained within a matter of months. Clinton also got off to a rocky start with the White House press corps by pointedly circumventing them and restricting their access. The period of "competition" set in early, and Clinton exacerbated it by offering outspoken criticism of the press on several occasions, including a bitter public exchange with Brit Hume of ABC News on June 12, 1993, and a first-year-ending interview with *Rolling Stone* magazine in which he blamed the media for giving a false impression of his administration.[161] One study found that television news coverage provided more negative than positive comments for all but one of Clinton's first sixteen months in office. In fact, nearly three-quarters of all network reporters' assessments of Clinton during that period were judged negative.[162]

Many people in the executive branch help presidents deal with the media, but the media also have their share of resources. A large number of reporters cover the White House, many of whom have expertise in substantive areas such as law, science, welfare, and defense policy.[163] Nevertheless, members of the media may not use their skills to full advantage. Journalists covering the presidency generally lack confidence in dealing with the substance of policies and consequently focus their coverage on four areas in which they feel most comfortable: administration scandals, internal dissension, a public gaffe or tactical blunder, and the ebb and flow of electoral contests and public opinion polls.[164] The result is unintended collusion between the presidency and the media that keeps the public less, rather than more, informed about American government. This line of criticism, focused on journalistic norms and practices, goes beyond those who believe that particular presidents received less vigorous scrutiny than they deserved. For example, some observers have suggested that poor journalism led to Reagan's vaunted "Teflon coating," a term commonly used during his presidency to suggest that negative stories did not seem to stick to Reagan.[165]

The ever-increasing speed with which news is reported—and the emergence of a never-ending news cycle—has arguably made the media less careful in what they convey about the president and other political figures. In their haste to keep up with the opposition, news organizations often pick up and report breaking news stories without independent corroboration. As Bill Kovach and Tom Rosenstiel have written: "Information is moving so fast, news outlets are caught between trying to gather new information and playing catch-up with what others have delivered ahead of them. The result for any news organization is a set of flexible standards that are often bent beyond recognition as the organization relies on another's reportage."[166] The Internet, in particular, has altered the way news is reported. The traditional old media had served as a gatekeeper of what news was reported. With the Internet, however, virtually anyone can post a story.

Conclusion: The Permanent Campaign

The rise of the public presidency corresponds with the development of the **permanent campaign**. Sidney Blumenthal popularized that phrase in a 1982 book of the same name, but the phrase had been used before—notably in a transition memo from adviser Pat Caddell to President-elect Jimmy Carter in 1976.[167] Blumenthal noted that the traditional distinction between *campaigning* and *governing* had broken down and that the resulting permanent campaign had remade government "into an instrument designed to sustain an elected official's popularity."[168] More recently, Hugh Heclo described the permanent campaign this way:

[P]ermanent campaign is shorthand for an emergent pattern of political management that the body politic did not plan, debate, or formally adopt. It is a work of inadvertence, something developed higgledy-piggledy since the middle of the twentieth-century. The permanent campaign comprises a complex mixture of politically sophisticated people, communication techniques, and organizations—profit and nonprofit alike. What ties the pieces together is the continuous and voracious quest for public approval.[169]

The Clinton presidency is a quintessential example of the permanent campaign in action.[170] Charles O. Jones noted that Clinton remained in full campaign mode even in his final year in office. "Here was a prime example of the campaigning style of governing, practiced by a virtuoso," Jones wrote.[171] George W. Bush and Barack Obama both followed suit.

The White House staff units discussed in this chapter are important tools for waging that campaign. The problem with such tactics is that campaigning—by its very nature—is *adversarial*, while governing is—or at least should be—largely *collaborative*. As Heclo puts it, "Campaigning is self-centered, and governing is group-centered."[172] When the permanent campaign becomes the predominant governing style, however, collaboration becomes difficult. Bush's embrace of the unitary executive, discussed in chapter 1, also served to undercut collaboration.

Samuel Kernell has noted that the elite bargaining community that used to collaborate to produce policy is neither as isolated from public pressure nor as tightly bound together by established norms of behavior as it used to be.[173] He contends that presidents once promoted their programs primarily by negotiating with other political elites in Congress and the executive branch, but today they more often choose to "go public" by circumventing those elites and appealing directly to the American people for support.[174] Presidents make these appeals through the means we have discussed in this chapter: public speeches, public appearances, and political travel, coupled with targeted outreach using White House staff units such as the Office of Communications and the Office of Public Liaison. The new media are now an important component of such appeals.

SUGGESTED READINGS

Brace, Paul, and Barbara Hinckley. *Follow the Leader: Opinion Polls and Modern Presidents.* New York: Basic Books, 1992.

Cohen, Jeffrey E. *The Presidency in the Era of 24-Hour News.* Princeton: Princeton University Press, 2008.

Cornwell, Elmer E. *Presidential Leadership of Public Opinion.* Bloomington: Indiana University Press, 1965.

Edwards, George C., III. *The Public Presidency: The Pursuit of Popular Support.* New York: St. Martin's Press, 1983.

Eisinger, Robert M. *The Evolution of Presidential Polling.* New York: Cambridge University Press, 2003.

Grossman, Michael Baruch, and Martha Joynt Kumar. *Portraying the President: The White House and the News Media.* Baltimore: Johns Hopkins University Press, 1981.

Hinckley, Barbara. *The Symbolic Presidency: How Presidents Portray Themselves.* New York: Routledge, 1990.

Kernell, Samuel. *Going Public: New Strategies of Presidential Leadership,* 4th ed. Washington, D.C.: CQ Press, 2006.

Kumar, Martha Joynt. *Managing the President's Message: The White House Communications Operation.* Baltimore: Johns Hopkins University Press, 2007.

Maltese, John Anthony. *Spin Control: The White House Office of Communications and the Management of Presidential News,* 2nd rev. ed., Chapel Hill: University of North Carolina Press, 1994.

Ornstein, Norman J., and Thomas E. Mann, eds. *The Permanent Campaign and Its Future.* Washington, D.C.: American Enterprise Institute, 2000.

Patterson, Bradley H., Jr. *The White House Staff: Inside the West Wing and Beyond.* Washington, D.C.: Brookings Institution Press, 2000.

Shapiro, Robert Y., Martha Joynt Kumar, and Lawrence R. Jacobs, eds. *Presidential Power: Forging the Presidency for the Twenty-first Century.* New York: Columbia University Press, 2000.

Tulis, Jeffrey K. *The Rhetorical Presidency.* Princeton: Princeton University Press, 1987.

Notes

1. Henry Jones Ford, *The Rise and Growth of American Politics: A Sketch of Constitutional Development* (New York: Macmillan, 1900), 283.

2. Woodrow Wilson, *Constitutional Government in the United States* (1908; reprint, New York: Columbia University Press, 1961), 68.

3. Richard E. Neustadt, *Presidential Power: The Politics of Leadership* (New York: Wiley, 1960), 86–107.

4. Samuel Kernell, *Going Public: New Strategies of Presidential Leadership,* 4th ed. (Washington, D.C.: CQ Press, 2006).

5. Matthew A. Baum and Samuel Kernell, "Has Cable Ended the Golden Age of Presidential Television?" *American Political Science Review* 93 (March 1999): 99–114.

6. For a complete summary of Bush's approval ratings by Gallup and other organizations, see www.pollingreport.com.

7. The numbers in this paragraph are based on Gallup polls. The latest Gallup polls can be found on the Web at www.gallup.com. Summaries of polls from a variety of polling organizations can be found at www.pollingreport.com. President Clinton's final Gallup job approval rating, based on nationwide surveys taken on January 5–7, 2001—before Clinton pardoned fugitive financier Marc Rich—was 65 percent. Other polls showed similar results: CNN/*Time* (64 percent), CBS (68 percent), and NBC/*Wall Street Journal* (66 percent). Ronald Reagan came closest with his final Gallup job approval rating of 63 percent. For an account of Clinton's early low poll ratings, see George C. Edwards III, "Frustration and Folly: Bill Clinton and the Public Presidency," in *The Clinton Presidency: First Appraisals,* ed. Colin Campbell and Bert A. Rockman (Chatham, N.J.: Chatham House, 1996).

8. Molly W. Andolina and Clyde Wilcox, "Public Opinion: The Paradoxes of Clinton's Popularity," in *The Clinton Scandal and the Future of American Government,* ed. Mark J. Rozell and Clyde Wilcox (Washington, D.C.: Georgetown University Press, 2000), 171–194.

9. David Easton, *A Systems Analysis of Political Life* (New York: Wiley, 1965), chaps. 10–13.

10. Andolina and Wilcox, "Public Opinion," 189. For example, a CBS/*New York Times* poll conducted September 22–23, 1998, showed that 65 percent of those surveyed felt the affair was a private matter (83 percent of Democrats thought it was a private matter, as opposed to 67 percent of independents, and 40 percent of Republicans). See also Robert J. Spitzer, "The Presidency: The Clinton Crisis and Its Consequences," in Rozell and Wilcox, *The Clinton Scandal and the Future of American Government,* 3–4.

11. Fred I. Greenstein, "What the President Means to Americans: Presidential 'Choice' between Elections," in *Choosing the President,* ed. James David Barber (Englewood Cliffs, N.J.: Prentice Hall, 1974), 144–146.

12. Joseph E. Kallenbach, *The American Chief Executive: The Presidency and the Governorship* (New York: Harper and Row, 1966), 275.

13. Barry Schwartz, *George Washington: The Making of an American Symbol* (Ithaca: Cornell University Press, 1987), 58–63.

14. Schwartz's discussion of the various public portrayals of Washington and their iconography is especially valuable.

15. Schwartz, *George Washington,* especially part 2.

16. ABC News, "Obama Will Eat Like Lincoln on Inauguration Day," January 10, 2009, available online at http://blogs.abcnews.com/politicalpunch/2009/01/obama-will-eat.html.

17. Barbara Hinckley, *The Symbolic Presidency: How Presidents Portray Themselves* (New York: Routledge, 1990), 130.

18. Ibid., 131–133.

19. Colin Campbell, "Demotion? Has Clinton Turned the Bully Pulpit into a Lectern?" in *The Clinton Legacy*, ed. Colin Campbell and Bert A. Rockman (New York: Chatham House, 2000), 56.

20. Findings of the Survey Research Center at the University of Michigan in the mid-1960s indicated that of all the occupations in the United States, including "famous doctor," "president of a large corporation like General Motors," "bishop or other church official," "Supreme Court justice," and "senator," more than half the adults named the president as the most respected.

21. Results by year for both most admired man and most admired woman can be found at www.pollingreport.com.

22. Fred I. Greenstein, *Children and Politics* (New Haven: Yale University Press, 1965); Robert Hess and Judith Torney, *The Development of Political Attitudes in Children* (Chicago: Aldine, 1967); David Easton and Jack Dennis, *Children in the Political System: Origins of Political Legitimacy* (New York: McGraw-Hill, 1969).

23. Paul Brace and Barbara Hinckley, *Follow the Leader: Opinion Polls and Modern Presidents* (New York: Basic Books, 1992), 19.

24. Diane J. Heath, "Presidential Polling and the Potential for Leadership," in *Presidential Power: Forging the Presidency for the Twenty-first Century*, ed. Robert Y. Shapiro, Martha Joynt Kumar, and Lawrence R. Jacobs (New York: Columbia University Press, 2000), 382.

25. Robert M. Eisinger, *The Evolution of Presidential Polling* (New York: Cambridge University Press, 2003), 3.

26. Heath, "Presidential Polling," 384.

27. Ibid., 387.

28. Ibid., 392.

29. John Anthony Maltese, *Spin Control: The White House Office of Communications and the Management of Presidential News*, 2nd rev. ed. (Chapel Hill: University of North Carolina Press, 1994), 213–214.

30. Carl M. Cannon, "Hooked on Polls," *National Journal*, October 17, 1998, 2438 ff.

31. Andolina and Wilcox, "Public Opinion," 183.

32. "Remarks by President George W. Bush at the National Republican Congressional Committee Dinner," March 15, 2007.

33. Kathryn Dunn Tenpas, "Words vs. Deeds: President George W. Bush and Polling," *The Brookings Review* 21 (Summer 2003): 32–35; www.brook.edu/press/review/summer2003/tenpas.htm.

34. Jeff Zeleny, "Obama's Political Protector, Ever Close at Hand," *New York Times*, March 9, 2009, A1.

35. Paul Brace and Barbara Hinckley, "Public Opinion Polls: The New Referendum," in *Understanding the Presidency*, ed. James P. Pfiffner and Roger H. Davidson (New York: Longman, 1997), 125. See also Brace and Hinckley, *Follow the Leader*. An earlier study that made a similar finding about the decay of presidential support was John Mueller, *War, Presidents, and Public Opinion* (New York: Wiley, 1973).

36. Jeffrey M. Jones, "Bush Approval Ratings One Year after the Peak," *Gallup Tuesday Briefing*, October 1, 2002, www.gallup.com; supplemented by approval ratings posted at www.gallup.com.

37. See www.pollingreport.com.

38. Brace and Hinckley, *Follow the Leader*, 23–24, 32, 24.

39. James P. Pfiffner, *The Strategic Presidency: Hitting the Ground Running*, 2nd rev. ed. (Lawrence: University Press of Kansas, 1996).

40. Paul C. Light, *The President's Agenda: Domestic Policy Choice from Kennedy to Clinton*, 3rd ed. (Baltimore: Johns Hopkins University Press, 1999).

41. Maltese, *Spin Control*, 180.

42. Gary C. Jacobson, "The Bush Presidency and the American Electorate," in *The Presidency of George W. Bush: An Early Assessment*, ed. Fred I. Greenstein (Baltimore: Johns Hopkins University Press, 2003), 199.

43. David Brooks, "Perverse Cosmic Myopia," *New York Times*, March 20, 2009, A27.

44. Johnson's first approval ratings came just after President Kennedy was assassinated in 1963. On taking office in January 1965, after being elected in his own right, Johnson's approval rating was 71 percent.

45. Bradley H. Patterson Jr., *The White House Staff: Inside the West Wing and Beyond* (Washington, D.C.: Brookings Institution Press, 2000). See also Charles E. Walcott and Karen M. Hult, *Governing the White House: From Hoover through LBJ* (Lawrence: University Press of Kansas, 1995), chaps. 3 and 10.

46. Jeffrey K. Tulis, *The Rhetorical Presidency* (Princeton: Princeton University Press, 1987).

47. Kernell, *Going Public*, chap. 2.

48. Jeffrey K. Tulis, "The Two Constitutional Presidencies," in *The Presidency and the Political System*, 6th ed., ed. Michael Nelson (Washington, D.C.: CQ Press, 2000), 115–116.

49. Mel Laracey, *Presidents and the People: The Partisan Story of Going Public* (College Station: Texas A&M University Press, 2002).

50. Tulis, *The Rhetorical Presidency*, 95.

51. Ibid., 46; see, generally, chaps. 1 and 2.

52. See, for example, Richard L. Rubin, *Press, Party, and Presidency* (New York: Norton, 1981); Culver H. Smith, *The Press, Politics, and Patronage* (Athens: University of Georgia Press, 1977).

53. Robert A. Rutland, *The Newsmongers* (New York: Dial Press, 1973), 58.

54. Frank Luther Mott, *American Journalism* (New York: Macmillan, 1941), 119–120.

55. Laracey, however, contends that every president from 1800 to 1860 "supported a newspaper that was regarded as at least the semiofficial voice of his administration" and that those newspapers are "the forgotten way of going public" for many nineteenth-century presidents—especially those from Andrew Jackson through Abraham Lincoln (1829–1865). Nevertheless, Laracey admits that from Ulysses S. Grant through the second administration of Grover Cleveland (1869–1897), presidents did not engage in the tactic of going public. See Laracey, *Presidents and the People*, 8, 146.

56. Tulis, *The Rhetorical Presidency*, 69.

57. Based on Table 3-1 in Tulis, *The Rhetorical Presidency*, 64.

58. Samuel Kernell and Gary C. Jacobson, *The Logic of American Politics*, 4th ed. (Washington, D.C.: CQ Press, 2008), 347.

59. Tulis, *The Rhetorical Presidency*, 91–93.

60. Ibid., 106.

61. James W. Caesar, *Presidential Selection: Theory and Development* (Princeton: Princeton University Press, 1979), 181–184.

62. Tulis, *The Rhetorical Presidency*, 182.

63. Kernell, *Going Public*, 4th ed., 12–23.

64. For a discussion of the permanent campaign and its impact on presidential governance, see Norman J. Ornstein and Thomas E. Mann, eds., *The Permanent Campaign and Its Future* (Washington, D.C.: American Enterprise Institute, 2000).

65. John C. Fortier and Norman J. Ornstein, "President Bush: Legislative Strategist," in *The George W. Bush Presidency*, 166.

66. Elizabeth Wilner, "This President Hits the Road, Not the Phones," *Washington Post*, May 29, 2005, B1.

67. Ibid.

68. Eric Benderoff, "Macon Phillips: The man behind WhiteHouse.gov," *Chicago Tribune*, February 24, 2009, available online at http://www.chicagotribune.com/business/chi-tue-macon-phillips-new-mediafeb24,0,6751735.story. One minute after Obama was sworn in as president, Macon Phillips, the director of new media, began a blog on the newly designed White House Web site. See: http://www.whitehouse.gov/blog/change_has_come_to_whitehouse-gov/.

69. "Obama e-mails push stimulus; Democratic strategists fire up post-election grassroots effort," *Grand Rapids Press*, January 31, 2009, A2.

70. Jon Ward, "Obama ramps up high-tech pitch for budget," *Washington Times*, March 26, 2009, A6.

71. "Bush Tax Cuts Clear First Hurdle," *World News Tonight*, ABC, March 8, 2001.

72. James Oliphant and Frank James, "Obama Hosts 'Virtual' Town Hall," *Baltimore Sun*, March 27, 2009, 19A.

73. Richard Rose, *The Postmodern President*, 2nd ed. (Chatham, N.J.: Chatham House, 1991), 38.

74. E-mail from Mark Knoller to John Anthony Maltese, September 13, 2003.

75. E-mail from Mark Knoller to the John Anthony Maltese, October 11, 2008.

76. For an account of the public relations aspects of Nixon's trip, see Margaret Macmillan, *Nixon and Mao: The Week that Changed the World* (New York: Random House, 2007), especially chap. 17.

77. Maltese, *Spin Control*, 195.

78. Mark Hertsgaard, *On Bended Knee: The Press and the Reagan Presidency* (New York: Farrar Straus, 1988), 273.

79. Quoted in Johanna Neuman, "Response to Terror: Public Diplomacy Is Shaped in President's Ornate War Room," *Los Angeles Times*, December 22, 2001, A3. See also John Anthony Maltese, "The Presidency and the News Media," in *Media Power, Media Politics*, ed. Mark J. Rozell (Lanham, Md.: Rowman and Littlefield, 2003), 4–5.

80. Elaine Monaghan, "U.S. Set to Bombard Globe with Words," *The Times* (London), March 20, 2003, 4.

81. Jeff Gerth and Scott Shane, "U.S. Said to Pay to Plant Articles in Iraq Papers," *New York Times*, December 1, 2005, A1.

82. Matt Kelley, "3 groups have contracts for pro-U.S. propaganda; Deals for work in Iraq and elsewhere worth up to $300M," *USA Today*, December 14, 2005, 5A.

83. David S. Cloud and Jeff Gerth, "Iraqi clerics found on Pentagon payroll; $144,000 paid for propaganda work," *International Herald Tribune*, January 2, 2006, 1.

84. Thom Shanker, "No Breach Is Seen in Planting U.S. Propaganda in Iraq Media," *New York Times*, March 22, 2006, 12. For a more complete account, see Daniel Schulman, "Mind Games," *Columbia Journalism Review*, May/June 2006.

85. Memo, H. R. Haldeman to Herb Klein, March 20, 1969, in "Memos/Herb Klein (March 1969)," Box 49, H. R. Haldeman Files, Nixon Presidential Materials Project. For a thorough discussion of the use of presidential surrogates from Nixon through Clinton, see Maltese, *Spin Control*.

86. Maltese, *Spin Control*, 34, 222.

87. Ibid., 35.

88. Mark A. Peterson, "Clinton and Organized Interests: Splitting Friends, Unifying Enemies," in Campbell and Rockman, *The Clinton Legacy*, 147.

89. Joseph A. Pika, "Interest Groups and the White House under Roosevelt and Truman," *Political Science Quarterly* (Winter 1987-1988): 647–668.

90. Joseph A. Pika, "Interest Groups and the Executive: Presidential Intervention," in *Interest Group Politics*, ed. Allan J. Cigler and Burdett A. Loomis (Washington, D.C.: CQ Press, 1983), 318. Also see Mark A. Peterson, "The Presidency and Organized Interests: White House Patterns of Interest Group Liaison," *American Political Science Review* (September 1992): 612–625; Joseph A. Pika, "Opening Doors for Kindred Souls: The White House Office of Public Liaison," in *Interest Group Politics*, 3rd ed., ed. Allan J. Cigler and Burdett A. Loomis (Washington, D.C.: CQ Press, 1991); Martha Joynt Kumar and Michael Baruch Grossman, "Political Communications from the White House: The Interest Group Connection," *Presidential Studies Quarterly* (Winter 1986): 92–101; Walcott and Hult, *Governing the White House*, chap. 6; and Bradley H. Patterson Jr., *The Ring of Power: The White House Staff and Its Expanding Role in Government* (New York: Basic Books, 1988), chap. 14.

91. For a discussion of Colson and his tactics as Nixon's liaison with interest groups, see Maltese, *Spin Control*, 38, 82–84.

92. James Harding, "Preaching to the Converted," *Washington Post*, January 4, 2003, A1; Jim Vande-Hei, "Pipeline to the President for GOP Conservatives; Give and Take Flows Through Public Liaison Aide," *Washington Post*, December 24, 2004, A15.

93. Kumar and Grossman, "Political Communications," 98.

94. Patterson, *The Ring of Power*, 230.

95. Kathryn Dunn Tenpas, "Institutionalized Politics: The White House Office of Political Affairs," *Presidential Studies Quarterly* (Spring 1996): 511.

96. Carol E. Lee, "White House Political Office Will Remain," *Politico*, November 21, 2008, available online at http://www.politico.com/news/stories/1108/15880.html.

97. John Anthony Maltese, *The Selling of Supreme Court Nominees* (Baltimore: Johns Hopkins University Press, 1995), 77.

98. Tenpas, "Institutionalized Politics," 514.

99. Jon Ward, "Bush limits access to ex-aides; Asserts executive privilege again in probe of U.S. attorney firings," *Washington Times*, July 10, 2007, A1.

100. House Committee on Government Reform and Oversight, *Investigation of the Conversion of the $1.7 Million Centralized White House Computer System, Known as the White House Database, and Related Matters*, 105th Cong., 2nd sess., 1998, H. Rept. 105 828, 43–44, http://www.mega.nu:8080/ampp/whodb.pdf.

101. Ibid., 44.

102. Tenpas, "Institutionalized Politics," 512.

103. Elisabeth Bumiller, "Preparing to Raise the Curtain on 2004," *New York Times*, June 23, 2003, A17.

104. Cynthia Kopkowski, "Politicians Hitch Bandwagon to Stars," *Atlanta Journal-Constitution*, July 20, 2002, 1A.

105. Losses by the president's party in midterm elections have been remarkably predictable. In the thirty-five midterm elections from 1862 through 1998, the president's party lost seats in the House of Representatives in thirty-two (1902, 1934, and 1998 are the exceptions) and in the Senate in twenty-one of the elections. Harold W. Stanley and Richard G. Niemi, *Vital Statistics on American Politics, 1999–2000*, 5th ed. (Washington, D.C.: CQ Press, 2000), Table 1-16, 48.

106. Fortier and Ornstein, "Congress and the Bush Presidency," 39.

107. Thomas Mann presents his findings on the 1974 elections in *Unsafe at Any Margin: Interpreting Congressional Elections* (Washington, D.C.: American Enterprise Institute, 1978), 92; Lyn Ragsdale presents her findings on the 1978 elections in "The Fiction of Congressional Elections as Presidential Events," *American Politics Quarterly* (October 1980): 375–398.

108. "Exit polls: Bush, Iraq key to outcome," CNN, November 8, 2006, www.cnn.com/2006/POLITICS/11/08/election.why/index.html.

109. Peter Baker, "Rove Remains Steadfast in the Face of Criticism," *Washington Post*, November 12, 2006, A1.

110. David Leuthold, *Electioneering in a Democracy: Campaigns for Congress* (New York: Wiley, 1968).

111. Alan I. Abramowitz, Brad Alexander, and Matthew Gunning, "Incumbency, Redistricting, and the Decline of Competition in U.S. House Elections," *Journal of Politics* 68 (February 2006): 75.

112. Jacobson, "The Bush Presidency and the American Electorate," 11–12. Indeed, Jacobson argues that redistricting is largely responsible for the Republican gains in 2002. Also see Gary C. Jacobson, "Terror, Terrain, and Turnout: Explaining the 2002 Midterm Elections," *Political Science Quarterly* 118 (Spring 2003): 1.

113. Eric M. Uslaner, "The 2006 Midterm Elections in the United States and the Consequences for Policy-Making in the 110th Congress," working paper, Department of Government and Politics, University of Maryland.

114. Fortier and Ornstein, "Congress and the Bush Presidency," 39–40.

115. Edward Tufte, "Determinants of the Outcomes of Midterm Congressional Elections," *American Political Science Review* (September 1975): 812–826.

116. Samuel Kernell, "Presidential Popularity and Negative Voting: An Alternative Explanation of the Midterm Decline of the Presidential Party," *American Political Science Review* (March 1977): 44–66.

117. Gary Jacobson, *The Politics of Congressional Elections* (Boston: Little, Brown, 1983),138 ff. Jacobson argues that the 2002 midterm election results were "entirely consistent" with such a model. He further adds: "Contrary to a great deal of postelection commentary, the results of the 2002 midterm congressional elections were neither surprising nor historically anomalous" (Jacobson, "Terror, Terrain, and Turnout," 1).

118. Jacobson, "Terror, Terrain, and Turnout," 3.

119. James Pollard, *The Presidents and the Press* (New York: Macmillan, 1947), chap. 1.

120. William Rivers, *The Opinion-Makers* (Boston: Beacon Press, 1967), 7.

121. Michael Baruch Grossman and Martha Joynt Kumar, *Portraying the President: The White House and the News Media* (Baltimore: Johns Hopkins University Press, 1981), 19.

122. Elmer E. Cornwell, *Presidential Leadership of Public Opinion* (Bloomington: Indiana University Press, 1965), 17; Stephen Hess, "Press Relations," in *Encyclopedia of the American Presidency,* ed. Leonard W. Levy and Louis Fisher (New York: Simon and Schuster, 1994), 1230.

123. *TV Dimensions 2000* (New York: Media Dynamics, 2000), 245.

124. "Poll Topics & Trends: Media Use and Evaluation," www.gallup.com.

125. Harold W. Stanley and Richard G. Niemi, *Vital Statistics on American Politics,* 5th ed. (Washington, D.C.: CQ Press, 1995), Table 2-1, 47.

126. Benjamin I. Page, Robert Y. Shapiro, and Glenn R. Dempsey, "What Moves Public Opinion?" *American Political Science Review* (March 1987): 23–43; and Donald L. Jordan, "Newspaper Effects on Policy Preferences," *Public Opinion Quarterly* (Summer 1993): 191–204. Page, Shapiro, and Dempsey examined the impact of television reports, whereas Jordan concentrated on the effects of newspapers.

127. Grossman and Kumar, *Portraying the President,* 209–210.

128. Stanley and Niemi, *Vital Statistics on American Politics,* 5th ed., Table 2-2, 48–49.

129. Lymari Morales, "Cable, Internet Sources Gaining in Popularity," *Gallup,* December 15, 2008, available online at http://www.gallup.com/poll/113314/Cable-Internet-News-Sources-Growing-Popularity.aspx.

130. There are some notable exceptions to this rule. The *NewsHour with Jim Lehrer,* broadcast nightly by PBS, takes an hour to examine two or three topics in depth; ABC's *Nightline* looks at one topic for half an hour. PBS's *Washington Week in Review* invites major political reporters to analyze the significant news developments of the previous week; and CNN provides continuing coverage as well as expanded focus on Washington, as on *Inside Politics.*

131. Baum and Kernell, "Has Cable Ended the Golden Age?" 99.

132. Stephen Hess, *The Washington Reporters* (Washington, D.C.: Brookings, 1981), chap. 2; Leon Segal, *Reporters and Officials* (Lexington, Mass.: D. C. Heath, 1973), chap. 1.

133. Hess, *The Washington Reporters,* 31.

134. Grossman and Kumar, *Portraying the President,* chap. 5.

135. M. L. Stein, *When Presidents Meet the Press* (New York: Messner, 1969), 166.

136. John F. Kennedy Jr., "Mike McCurry's About-Face," *George,* March 1999, 78.

137. Maltese, *Spin Control,* 24, 29.

138. Larry Speakes, *Speaking Out: Inside the Reagan White House* (New York: Scribner's, 1988), 136, 153.

139. For a full account of the office and its precursors, see Maltese, *Spin Control.*

140. Interview with John Anthony Maltese, March 10, 1989, Washington, D.C., quoted in Maltese, *Spin Control,* 2.

141. Donald T. Regan, *For the Record* (New York: Harcourt Brace Jovanovich, 1988), 248.

142. William Douglas, "Bush's 'Great Image,'" *Newsday,* May 2, 2003, A06; Dana Milbank, "Explanation for Bush's Carrier Landing Altered," *Washington Post,* May 7, 2003, A20; Elisabeth Bumiller, "Keepers of Bush Image Lift Stagecraft to New Heights," *New York Times,* May 16, 2003, 1.

143. Kernell, *Going Public,* 63.

144. Quoted in Maltese, *Spin Control,* 44.

145. Project for Excellence in Journalism, "All the President's Pressers," October 16, 2006; www.journalism.org/node/2409.

146 Christina Bellantoni, "Obama Sets Record in News Conferences," *The Washington Times,* November 27, 2008, A8. In addition to the forty-nine solo press conferences referenced in this article, President Bush gave a final solo press conference on January 12, 2009.

147. Patterson, *The Ring of Power,* 174.

148. Fred I. Greenstein, *The Hidden-Hand Presidency: Eisenhower as Leader* (New York: Basic Books, 1982), 66–70.

149. George Reedy, *The Twilight of the Presidency* (New York: New American Library, 1970), 164.

150. Grossman and Kumar, *Portraying the President,* 244.

151. Pollard, *The Presidents and the Press,* 14.

152. David E. Sanger and James Risen, "C.I.A. Chief Takes Blame in Assertion on Iraqi Uranium," *New York Times,* July 12, 2003, A1; Christopher Marquis, "How Powerful Can 16 Words Be?" *New York Times,* July 20, 2003, sec. 4, 5.

153. Howard Kurtz, "The Press, Turning Up Its Nose at Lame Duck," *Washington Post,* February 5, 2007, C1.

154. Larry J. Sabato, *Feeding Frenzy: Attack Journalism and American Politics* (Baltimore: Lanahan, 2000).

155. Grossman and Kumar, *Portraying the President,* chap. 1.

156. Michael Grossman and Francis Rourke, "The Media and the Presidency: An Exchange Analysis," *Political Science Quarterly* (Fall 1976): 455–470. Also see Timothy E. Cook and Lyn Ragsdale, "The President and the Press: Negotiating Newsworthiness at the White House," in Nelson, *The Presidency and the Political System,* 6th ed.

157. Quoted by Patterson in *The Ring of Power,* 170.

158. Grossman and Kumar, *Portraying the President,* chap. 11.

159. Ibid., 178.

160. This tendency first became apparent during the second year of the Reagan administration when reporters began to ask him more embarrassing questions, such as why he did not set an example by making more generous donations to private charities. They also appeared not to take seriously the president's statement that members of his administration were one big happy family.

161. Martha Joynt Kumar, "President Clinton Meets the Media: Communications Shaped by Predictable Patterns," in *The Clinton Presidency: Campaigning, Governing, and the Psychology of Leadership,* ed. Stanley A. Renshon (Boulder: Westview, 1995), 167–171.

162. Study conducted by Robert Lichter of the Center for Media and Public Affairs as reported in Howard Kurtz, "The Bad News about Clinton," *Washington Post,* September 1, 1994, D1.

163. Stephen Hess showed that in 1978, 73 percent were college graduates and 33 percent had graduate degrees (*The Washington Reporters,* 83); Leo Rosten reported that in 1936, 51 percent were college

graduates and 6 percent had an advanced academic degree; see *The Washington Correspondents* (New York: Harcourt, Brace, 1937), 159–160.

164. James Fallows, "The Presidency and the Press," in *The Presidency and the Political System,* 3rd ed., ed. Michael Nelson (Washington, D.C.: CQ Press, 1990).

165. Hertsgaard, *On Bended Knee.*

166. Bill Kovach and Tom Rosenstiel, *Warp Speed: America in the Age of Mixed Media* (New York: Century Foundation Press, 1999), 51.

167. Sidney Blumenthal, *The Permanent Campaign* (New York: Simon and Schuster, 1982); see also Ornstein and Mann, *The Permanent Campaign and Its Future,* vii.

168. Blumenthal, *The Permanent Campaign,* 7.

169. Hugh Heclo, "Campaigning and Governing: A Conspectus," in Ornstein and Mann, *The Permanent Campaign and Its Future,* 15.

170. George C. Edwards III, "Campaigning Is Not Governing: Bill Clinton's Rhetorical Presidency," in Campbell and Rockman, *The Clinton Legacy,* 33.

171. Jones, "Preparing to Govern in 2001," 185.

172. Heclo, "Campaigning and Governing," 11.

173. Kernell, *Going Public,* 23.

174. Ibid., 2.

CHAPTER 4

Presidential Character and Performance

In a dramatic moment intended to halt media reports and rumors, on January 26, 1998, President Clinton denies having had a sexual relationship with "that woman," Monica Lewinsky. He was later forced to publicly apologize for lying about the relationship and to defend himself against impeachment charges.

President George W. Bush left office at noon on January 20, 2009. As they always do at the end of a term, the media and learned academics devoted considerable time to reviewing the president's performance and assessing his legacy. The public shares in this fascination with presidents. We dwell on their accomplishments, deconstruct their decisions, and speculate on their place in history, making it all seem very personal, a reflection of the president's strengths, weaknesses, emotional needs, and attitudes. The reality is more complex than that, but the design of American government enhances the importance of a president's individual qualities.

Observers make a connection between the personal qualities of presidents and their performance in office, but the link is not always clear. When William Jefferson Clinton left office at the completion of a controversial eight-year roller-coaster ride on the national scene, he left behind many lingering questions centered on his personal character and judgment. Retrospective evaluations of his legacy recognized the mixed nature of his performance as president, a record of "striking strengths [and] glaring failures."[1] Foremost among the latter was his sexual relationship with former White House intern Monica Lewinsky, which became the focus of a special prosecutor's investigation.[2] The investigation resulted in the Republican-controlled House passing articles of impeachment against Clinton on charges of perjury and obstruction of justice. But the Senate acquitted him, and he completed his term in office. (See chapter 5.) Could we have predicted Clinton's performance in office? Did we know enough about his personal background and previous experience in elected office to have anticipated his record of dramatically alternating highs and lows?

As George W. Bush's time in the White House drew to a close, different questions arose from those that surrounded Clinton. In what ways did Bush's background, experience, and outlook affect his performance as a wartime president? As Fred Greenstein has suggested, Al Gore, had he won the 2000 election, would probably have reacted to the 9/11 terrorist attacks much the same way as Bush, but it is less clear that a President Gore would have launched a preemptive invasion of Iraq.[3] And Iraq proved costly to Bush. As we saw in chapter 3, during Bush's two terms, the public's approval of his performance declined from all-time highs to dramatic lows. Even after Republicans suffered defeat in the 2006 midterm elections, Bush continued on a path in Iraq that was widely rejected. Did his persistence reflect a personality-based inability to admit mistakes—a pattern comparable to that found for Presidents Wilson, Hoover, and Johnson—or did it arise from a different view of the consequences for America's international interests?

The presidency invites such speculation because its occupants wield enormous power in a one-person office rather than as part of a collective institution. Moreover, during the last third of the twentieth century, enormous attention was devoted to the psychological makeup of chief executives. Many analysts attributed the conduct of the Vietnam War (1965–1973) and the Watergate scandal, in which White House aides covered up illegal activities committed to help the president get reelected, to the unique emotional needs of Presidents Lyndon Johnson and Richard Nixon.[4] As the nation approached the 2008 election, people were speculating on what Rudolph Giuliani, Barak Obama, or Mitt Romney would be like as president. How would Hillary Clinton's eight years as first lady amidst enormous controversy shape her performance? Could John McCain overcome his penchant for angry outbursts to exercise balanced judgment from the Oval Office?

In this chapter we look more closely at what kinds of people have served as president and how their personal qualities may have shaped their conduct. We are especially concerned with presidents' backgrounds, skills, psychological traits, and management styles and how these factors influence their performances in office. We therefore examine the abilities and attitudes that presidents develop before entering office, ways in which their personalities affect how they do the job, and their habitual modes of working. We also look at how presidents interact with their staffs, those assistants whose positions were created to extend presidents' personal capabilities. To conclude, we take a closer look at the factors that shaped Bill Clinton and George W. Bush's performance in office, and we offer a preliminary assessment of Barack Obama.

Determinants and Evaluations of Performance

For generations, historians and political scientists have argued about how important a leader's characteristics are for understanding and explaining events. Does one, for example, place great significance on the intelligence, stature, and wisdom of Abraham Lincoln in explaining the Union's ultimate victory? Or was victory the product of forces beyond Lincoln's control, such as the changing nature of modern warfare in an industrial age, which favored the North? Did the United States and the Soviet Union avert nuclear war during the Cuban missile crisis of 1962 because of the decision style adopted by John F. Kennedy? Or was the outcome the result of organizational routines for crisis management and other random occurrences perhaps not intended by either side during the confrontation? The larger questions are, therefore, just how much importance should one ascribe to the president's personal characteristics, and are these elements powerful predictors of performance in office?

Specialists have not reached agreement on the importance of these factors, although there is widespread belief that it does indeed matter—and probably a great deal—who is president. As Fred Greenstein argues, "If some higher power had set out to design a democracy in which the individual on top mattered, the result might well resemble the American political system."[5] Every four years the nation devotes enormous effort and resources to selecting a leader, and this confidence in the difference an individual can make is revealed when citizens insist they "voted for the person, not the party." Public attention focuses on the presidency, with the mass media personalizing the solution to public problems and portraying presidents as the embodiment of the larger political process. Moreover, presidents and their media advisers encourage personalization when they highlight traits the public regards as desirable.

Not everyone agrees that presidents' individual characteristics are critical to understanding their accomplishments. The alternative is to stress the environment within which presidents operate as the truly significant determinant of outcomes. The most influential interpretation in this tradition is the work of Stephen Skowronek, whose analysis rests on comparison of presidents in decidedly different time frames. Thus Thomas Jefferson, Andrew Jackson, Abraham Lincoln, Franklin Roosevelt, and Ronald Reagan shared common "leadership tasks" associated with the decline and reconstruction of the links among societal interests and the political parties essential to a political order. Similarly, James Monroe, James K. Polk, Theodore Roosevelt, and Lyndon Johnson had more in common with each other— the position they inherited in relation to the dominant political order—than with their immediate predecessors and successors. Although the title of Skowronek's principal work—*The Politics Presidents Make*—emphasizes the role of leadership, the unfolding evolution of larger forces in American social and political life defines the tasks presidents confront and severely limits the possibilities they enjoy at the beginning of their terms.[6]

Nevertheless, there is broad consensus among students of the presidency that each chief executive brings to the job a combination of attitudes, skills, strengths, and shortcomings that will influence the performance in office and may at times have an enduring effect on the nation's history. Disagreement still exists on the relative significance of these causal factors and exactly how they are related to job performance and policy outcomes. A number of analysts have suggested ways to conceptualize these issues; a modified, considerably simplified diagram based on two of the most prominent treatments is presented in Figure 4-1.

All presidents bring to the job enduring personality traits as well as attitudes and beliefs toward a wide range of political structures, institutions, and relationships. These personal characteristics and attitudes take shape within a distinctive social context—family situation, place in the community, educational experience,

FIGURE 4-1   Relationship of Background to Performance

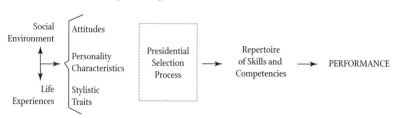

SOURCES: Bert A. Rockman, *The Leadership Question* (New York: Praeger, 1984), 189; Fred I. Greenstein, *Personality and Politics* (New York: Norton, 1975), 27.

and so on. In addition, their adult professional experiences prior to entering office, particularly as they relate to role demands of the presidency, produce a personal style that may be more or less congruent with the demands of serving as chief executive. The presidential selection process filters out personal styles, skills, and competencies that are not role appropriate. Ultimately, presidents may be more or less likely to produce successful outcomes as these individual traits interact with the situations the presidents confront. In concentrating on the importance of leaders' individual characteristics, one recognizes that presidents are in the position to have potentially decisive impacts on political events. Even if the environment—forces beyond the control of the individual leader—has a determinative effect on events, "environments are always mediated by the individuals on whom they act."[7]

Just as analysts disagree over the determinants of presidential behavior, so too do they disagree over how to evaluate a president's performance, although the general public and professional presidency watchers engage in evaluations all the time. Polls provide current, short-term assessments of public approval (discussed in chapter 3), and journalists constantly assess the administration's record in dealing with Congress or in addressing particular policy areas. Certain evaluation points have become institutionalized: for example, the end of an administration's first hundred days in office (a carryover from FDR's first term) always produces a spate of articles. Other evaluation points are at midterm and on departure from office.[8] In other words, the public, journalists, and academics are constantly engaged in *contemporary evaluation* of presidential performance.

Scholars and others use a variety of criteria to evaluate presidential performance. Bruce Buchanan has drawn broad distinctions between subjective and objective criteria. Judgments based on subjective grounds emphasize the "appearance and demeanor" of leadership, including success in projecting the image of integrity and charisma; the "moral desirability of a president's means or ends"; and the pragmatic test of self-interest—the extent to which the president contributed to a citizen's well-being. Objective criteria, on which professionals are more likely to make their evaluations, focus on presidential skill in making things happen, especially short-term successes, or on the lasting results produced for the nation.[9] A number of works on the record of achievements by the Reagan administration adopted the long view in assessing its legacy. As Bert Rockman put it, politicians can "leave greater or lesser footprints. Assessing the depth and durability of those marks is hazardous while the administration under evaluation is still in power. The real answers will come later—much later." [10]

Bill Clinton's conduct reawakened concern with **presidential character,** a term with many contradictory meanings. James Pfiffner seeks to help the public address this murky area: how should Americans assess the personal failures of presidents when they lie about trivial or important matters, violate marriage vows, or intentionally seek to deceive the public?[11] Pfiffner reviews numerous instances of presidential untruths in terms of the teller's intent and the seriousness of the lie, a recognition that evaluation of this conduct depends heavily on context. Although the public widely regards telling the truth as a moral obligation, Pfiffner accepts the possibility of a "justified lie."[12] Therefore, lies to protect the national security, concerning trivial matters (for example, describing one's personal history or illustrating a point), or to prevent embarrassment and preserve political viability are less serious than those used to cover up important facts or deceive the public on policy matters. Pfiffner's discussion of Clinton's marital infidelity is placed in the context of other presidents known to have committed similar acts or suspected of doing so: Franklin Roosevelt, Dwight Eisenhower, John Kennedy, and Lyndon Johnson.[13]

Efforts to evaluate presidential performance and conduct are not new. Since 1948 scholars, primarily historians, have been asked on several occasions to "rate" American presidents. In essence they were to assess the "depth and durability" of presidential footprints and provide a *historical evaluation.* Table 4-1 shows the results of six of these efforts. Each poll was structured a bit differently and surveyed a different panel of "experts."[14] Yet one finds considerable consensus among participants on the top ten and the bottom ten, with the exception of Nixon, whose reputation has undergone a marked resurgence since his death in 1994. Because of the similar results across polls, Robert Murray and Tim Blessing concluded that historians "had in mind more than vague and uncritical generalities when they evaluated presidential performances."[15] Assessments of the more recent presidents are particularly susceptible to change with the passage of time. Note how Eisenhower moved from twentieth place in 1962 to ninth in the Lindgren-Calabresi poll in 2000 and eighth in the 2009 C-SPAN poll. Harry S. Truman's standing among professionals was already strong by 1962 and has remained so. Reagan's evaluation by historians has improved from below average to the borderline between average and above average.[16] As he left office, Clinton finished in the middle of the pack at number twenty-four, a couple positions behind George H. W. Bush, but moved to fifteenth in the 2009 C-SPAN rankings. George W. Bush placed seventh from the bottom, in thirty-sixth place, in the same rankings.[17]

In addition to analyzing 846 completed surveys, Murray and Blessing conducted sixty in-depth interviews with historians to determine their evaluative criteria. The most important personal trait contributing to presidential achievement, in

TABLE 4-1 Ratings of U.S. Presidents

Schlesinger poll (1948)	Schlesinger poll (1962)	Maranell-Dodder poll (1982)	Murray-Blessing poll[a] (1982)	Lindgren-Calabresi poll (2000)	C-SPAN poll (2009)
Great 1. Lincoln	*Great* 1. Lincoln	*Accomplishments of administration* 1. Lincoln	*Great* 1. Lincoln	*Great* 1. Washington	1. Lincoln
2. Washington	2. Washington	2. F. Roosevelt	2. F. Roosevelt	2. Lincoln	2. Washington
3. F. Roosevelt	3. F. Roosevelt	3. Washington	3. Washington	3. F. Roosevelt	3. F. Roosevelt
4. Wilson	4. Wilson	4. Jefferson	4. Jefferson	*Near great* 4. Jefferson	4. T. Roosevelt
5. Jefferson	5. Jefferson	5. T. Roosevelt	*Near great* 5. T. Roosevelt	5. T. Roosevelt	5. Truman
6. Jackson	*Near great* 6. Jackson	6. Truman	6. Wilson	6. Jackson	6. Kennedy
Near great 7. T. Roosevelt	7. T. Roosevelt	7. Wilson	7. Jackson	7. Truman	7. Jefferson
8. Cleveland	8. Polk Truman (tie)	8. Jackson	8. Truman	8. Reagan	8. Eisenhower
9. J. Adams	9. J. Adams	9. L. Johnson	*Above average* 9. J. Adams	9. Eisenhower	9. Wilson
10. Polk	10. Cleveland	10. Polk	10. L. Johnson	10. Polk	10. Reagan
Average 11. J.Q. Adams	*Average* 11. Madison	11. J. Adams	11. Eisenhower	11. Wilson	11. L. Johnson
12. Monroe	12. J.Q. Adams	12. Kennedy	12. Polk	*Above average* 12. Cleveland	12. Polk
13. Hayes	13. Hayes	13. Monroe	13. Kennedy	13. J. Adams	13. Jackson
14. Madison	14. McKinley	14. Cleveland	14. Madison	14. McKinley	14. Monroe
15. Van Buren	15. Taft	15. Madison	15. Monroe	15. Madison	15. Clinton
16. Taft	16. Van Buren	16. Taft	16. J.Q. Adams	16. Monroe	16. McKinley
17. Arthur	17. Monroe	17. McKinley	17. Cleveland	17. L. Johnson	17. J. Adams
18. McKinley	18. Hoover	18. J.Q. Adams	*Average* 18. McKinley	18. Kennedy	18. G.H.W. Bush
19. A. Johnson	19. B. Harrison	19. Hoover	19. Taft	*Average* 20. J.Q. Adams	19. J.Q. Adams
20. Hoover	20. Arthur Eisenhower (tie)	20. Eisenhower	20. Van Buren	21. G.H.W. Bush	20. Madison
21. B. Harrison	21. A. Johnson	21. A. Johnson			21. Cleveland
		22. Van Buren			22. Ford
		23. Arthur			23. Grant

(Continued)

TABLE 4-1 (Continued)

Schlesinger poll (1948)	Schlesinger poll (1962)	Maranell-Dodder poll (1982)	Murray-Blessing poll[a] (1982)	Lindgren-Calabresi poll (2000)	C-SPAN poll (2009)
Below average	Below average	24. Hayes	21. Hoover	22. Hayes	24. Taft
22. Tyler	22. Taylor	25. Tyler	22. Hayes	23. Van Buren	25. Carter
23. Coolidge	23. Tyler	26. B. Harrison	23. Arthur	24. Clinton	26. Coolidge
24. Fillmore	24. Fillmore	27. Taylor	24. Ford	25. Coolidge	27. Nixon
25. Taylor	25. Coolidge	28. Buchanan	25. Carter	26. Arthur	28. Garfield
26. Buchanan	26. Pierce	29. Fillmore	26. B. Harrison	Below average	29. Taylor
27. Pierce	27. Buchanan	30. Coolidge	Below average	27. Harrison	30. B. Harrison
Failure	Failure	31. Pierce	27. Taylor	28. Ford	31. Van Buren
28. Grant	28. Grant	32. Grant	28. Reagan	29. Hoover	32. Arthur
29. Harding	29. Harding	33. Harding	29. Tyler	30. Carter	33. Hayes
			30. Fillmore	31. Taylor	34. Hoover
			31. Coolidge	32. Grant	35. Tyler
			32. Pierce	33. Nixon	36. G.W. Bush
			Failure	34. Tyler	37. Fillmore
			33. A. Johnson	35. Fillmore	38. Harding
			34. Buchanan	Failure	39. W.H. Harrison
			35. Nixon	36. A. Johnson	40. Pierce
			36. Grant	37. Pierce	41. A. Johnson
			37. Harding	38. Harding	42. Buchanan
				39. Buchanan	

SOURCES: Harold W. Stanley and Richard G. Niemi, *Vital Statistics on American Politics, 1999–2000* (Washington, D.C.: CQ Press, 2000), Table 6-2, 244–245; and James Lindgren and Steven Calabresi, "Rating the Presidents of the United States, 1789–2000: A Survey of Scholars in Political Science, History and Law," *Constitutional Commentary* 18 (Winter 2001): 583–605 (Sponsored by Federalist Society and *Wall Street Journal*); C-SPAN 2009 Historians Leadership Survey, http://www.c-span.org/PresidentialSurvey/presidential-leadership-survey.aspx.

NOTE: These ratings result from surveys of scholars and range in number from 49 to 846.

a. The rating of President Reagan was obtained in a separate poll conducted in 1989.

the view of the participating historians, was decisiveness; intelligence, particularly the capacity for growth, and integrity were close behind.[18] Greatness, many seemed to feel, is achieved by those leaders able to exercise moral, inspirational leadership, who have "a capacity for creative innovation and an imagination that was fired by a clear vision of the future."[19] James MacGregor Burns's discussion of leadership emphasizes similar abilities as the source of "transformational" leadership, by which presidents appeal to the higher goals and motives of followers to achieve true change.[20] Greenstein suggests that a president's job performance is shaped by six qualities: proficiency as a *public communicator; organizational capacity* to rally colleagues and structure activities; *political skill* insofar as it is linked to a *vision* of public policy; *cognitive style* in processing advice and information; and *emotional intelligence,* by which he means the ability to manage one's own emotions for constructive purposes.[21]

As Greenstein makes clear, it is now necessary to factor an additional consideration into assessing performance: modern presidents no longer govern alone. Since the 1930s they have been assisted by a large number of aides appointed to serve in the **Executive Office of the President.** Aides have the capacity to amplify a president's personal capabilities; mobilizing such efforts is a new dimension of the job just as public communications have taken on a much greater significance than they had prior to the twentieth century.

To examine the importance of individual characteristics, we turn first to a discussion of the backgrounds from which presidents have been drawn. As depicted in Figure 4-1, a president's life and occupational experiences are distant from the actual service in office and should therefore have only limited power to explain performance. Nevertheless, the patterns uncovered tell us something about leadership in America.

What Manner of Person?

Each president brings to the office a cumulation of life experiences derived from a position in American society and previous professional experience. The selection process, rather than producing a random sampling of Americans, favors some backgrounds over others. After reviewing the historical pattern for social background and education, scholars have found, not surprisingly, that presidents have disproportionately been drawn from traditionally dominant groups in American society. It is less clear, however, just what this has meant for performance in office.

Social Background

Although there is no single indicator of social status on which all Americans would agree, occupation is probably the most important criterion for social ranking in the United States.[22] Moreover, the occupation of an individual's father provides a reasonably accurate picture of his or her class origins. By analyzing such origins, one can determine the extent to which presidents have achieved their positions of power as a result of their own abilities or the advantages of family background.[23] The presidency has long been cited as an example of how ability can enable individuals to overcome disadvantages and rise to power. But the reality of presidents' personal histories, argues Edward Pessen, contradicts "the log cabin myth" and demonstrates that "the political race here as elsewhere has usually been won by those who had the advantage of starting from a favorable position."[24] Pessen characterized the family background of each president through Reagan in terms of six basic groupings: upper-upper and lower-upper, upper-middle and lower-middle, upper-lower and lower-lower.[25] In making his evaluations, Pessen compared the presidents' family backgrounds with the economic and social conditions that existed at the time rather than using a permanent yardstick.

Five distinguished American families have produced ten presidents, more than one-fifth of the total. Included were John Adams and his son John Quincy Adams; James Madison and Zachary Taylor, who had grandparents in common; William Henry Harrison and his grandson Benjamin Harrison; cousins Theodore and Franklin Roosevelt; and George H. W. Bush and his son, George W. Bush. All five families meet Pessen's criteria for upper-class status. It is also not uncommon for presidents to come from politically prominent families, also more often than not upper-class. John Tyler was the son of a Virginia governor; William Howard Taft's father served as secretary of war, attorney general, and ambassador to Austria and Russia; and John Kennedy's father was the chairman of the Securities and Exchange Commission and ambassador to Great Britain. Franklin Pierce's father was governor of New Hampshire (though Pessen locates the family between the lower-upper and upper-middle classes). George H. W. Bush's father accumulated a fortune working on Wall Street before being elected to the Senate from Connecticut. (See Table 4-2 for presidents' social class distribution.)

Other chief executives from upper-class origins but whose fathers did not hold high political office include George Washington, Thomas Jefferson, James Monroe, James K. Polk, and Woodrow Wilson. Pessen ranks Chester Arthur as upper-middle class. A number of presidents, including Pierce, Rutherford B. Hayes, Grover Cleveland, Warren G. Harding, Calvin Coolidge, and Truman, fall into a special bridge

TABLE 4-2   Pessen's Analysis of Presidential Social Class

Social Class	President
Upper-Upper	G. Washington, T. Jefferson, J. Madison, J.Q. Adams, W.H. Harrison, J. Tyler, Z. Taylor, B. Harrison, T. Roosevelt, W.H. Taft, F.D. Roosevelt, George H.W. Bush*, George W. Bush*
Middle-Upper	J. Polk, J. Kennedy
Lower-Upper	J. Adams, J. Monroe, W. Wilson
Lower-Upper/	F. Pierce, R. Hayes, G. Cleveland, W. Harding,
Upper-Middle	C. Coolidge, H. Truman
Upper-Middle	A. Jackson, M. Van Buren, J. Buchanan, U.S. Grant, C. Arthur, W. McKinley, H. Hoover, L. Johnson, G. Ford, J. Carter
Middle	A. Lincoln, D. Eisenhower, R. Reagan, W. Clinton*, B. Obama*
Lower-Middle	M. Fillmore, J. Garfield, R. Nixon
Upper-Lower	A. Johnson
Lower-Lower	None

SOURCE: Edward Pessen, *The Log Cabin Myth: The Social Backgrounds of the Presidents* (New Haven: Yale University Press, 1984), 68.

*Presidents rated by author, not by Pessen. Table updated by the authors.

category between upper-class and middle-class origins. Altogether, Pessen considers sixteen presidents to be drawn from upper-class roots (the Bushes would make eighteen) and six more as bordering on this exclusive group—a total of twenty-four, more than half of all those who have served in the White House.

Ten presidents are in Pessen's upper-middle category, leaving only seven who can be regarded as drawn from middle- or lower-class roots; Bill Clinton and Barack Obama would make nine. The presidents most socially disadvantaged include Andrew Johnson, whose father held a variety of jobs, including janitor and porter at an inn; Millard Fillmore, probably the only president truly born in a log cabin as the son of a dirt farmer; and James Garfield, whose father pulled the family into prosperity through manual labor as a canal worker in the Midwest. Despite the stories about Lincoln's modest background, his father owned more property and livestock at the time of Abraham's birth than did the majority of his neighbors, and his prominence continued to grow.

Three twentieth-century presidents—Eisenhower, Nixon, and Reagan—were the sons of poor men who tried numerous jobs without much success. Eisenhower's father was a mechanic in a creamery for a time after an investment failed; Nixon's father was a streetcar conductor in Columbus, Ohio, before trying his luck as a painter, carpenter, glass worker, and sheep rancher; and Reagan's father worked on and off as an itinerant shoe salesman. Clinton's father, a traveling salesman, died before his son was born, and Clinton's mother became a nurse anesthetist. His grandfather, with whom he lived until age four, was first the town iceman and later a neighborhood grocer, and his stepfather was a car salesman. Obama's father was a graduate student who abandoned his family and returned home to Kenya. During his teenage years, Obama lived with his grandparents, a sales manager and bank employee. The fathers of Lyndon Johnson, Gerald Ford, and Jimmy Carter met mixed success in business: Johnson's father traded in commodities and livestock; Ford's stepfather (the president was born Leslie King and adopted as Gerald R. Ford Jr.) operated a paint and lumber business; and Carter's father founded a successful peanut warehouse.

Although presidents have come from diverse backgrounds, those with upper-class origins have been the most prevalent, and most others were drawn from prosperous and socially respected backgrounds. Even so, the trend over time has been toward more modest origins. The first six chief executives came from socially, and in many cases politically, prominent families. Not wholly by coincidence, they served during the period when presidential candidates were nominated by congressional caucus. After both political parties adopted the national nominating convention in the early 1830s, candidates from less-privileged backgrounds also began to make it to the White House. Fillmore, Lincoln, Andrew Johnson, and Garfield—four presidents with humble origins—are concentrated in the period 1850–1880. Since then, presidents have come from both upper-class (the two Roosevelts, Taft, Wilson, Kennedy, and the Bushes) and modest family circumstances (Truman, Eisenhower, Nixon, Reagan, Clinton, and Obama).

Education

Education is often closely correlated with social class. Most U.S. presidents have been well educated. Only nine of the forty-three individuals (Cleveland served two, nonconsecutive terms) had no formal instruction at a college or university. Moreover, the trend has been toward chief executives with greater college training. Of the eighteen who occupied the presidency in the twentieth century, only Truman did not attend an institution of higher learning.[26] The schools presidents attended are among the most highly regarded in the nation. Harvard University leads the list with seven chief executives as alumni—the two Adamses, the two Roosevelts, Kennedy, and George W. Bush (an MBA; Obama has a Harvard law degree). Alma maters of other presidents include major private universities such as Princeton (Madison and Wilson), Yale (Taft and the two Bushes; Ford and Clinton also have Yale law degrees), Stanford (Herbert Hoover), Georgetown (Clinton), Columbia

(Obama), and a number of prestigious smaller private colleges, such as Allegheny (William McKinley), Amherst (Coolidge), Bowdoin (Pierce), Dickinson (James Buchanan), Hampden-Sidney (W. H. Harrison), Kenyon (Hayes), Union (Arthur), and Williams (Garfield). Well-known public universities also figure among presidents' alma maters: Miami University of Ohio (Benjamin Harrison), the University of Michigan (Ford), the University of North Carolina (Polk), William and Mary (Jefferson, Monroe, and Tyler), and the two service academies, Annapolis (Carter) and West Point (Ulysses S. Grant and Eisenhower). Twentieth-century presidents hailing from families with more modest social standing attended less-prestigious institutions: Johnson attended Southwest Texas State Teachers College (now Texas State University–San Marcos); Nixon graduated from Whittier College in California before attending Duke University Law School; Reagan majored in economics and sociology at Eureka College in Illinois.

That so many presidents attended prestigious institutions of higher learning probably has less to do with innate abilities or career aspirations than with family status or a desire to improve their economic and social positions. An example is James Garfield, the son of a canal construction worker, who died when Garfield was two. Garfield managed, after a long struggle for education, to graduate from Williams College and become the principal of a church school before being admitted to the bar and eventually going into politics. More presidents attended private than public schools because private schools were established earlier, particularly in the northeastern states, such as New York and Massachusetts, which have produced ten presidents, and the midwestern states, such as Ohio, which has produced six. Although most citizens today would probably agree that a college education is essential if presidents are to understand the complex problems confronting the nation, no direct correlation exists between quality of institution or years of training and performance.

Career Experience

Although the family occupational backgrounds of the presidents are fairly broad, their own careers prior to and outside politics have been much less diverse. Twenty-six of the forty-three chief executives practiced law at some time. Other occupations include the military (W. H. Harrison, Taylor, Grant, and Eisenhower), education (Wilson and L. Johnson), journalism (Harding and Kennedy), engineering (Hoover), and entertainment (Reagan). Washington and Madison were gentleman farmers. Carter combined farming with his family peanut business after giving up his career as a navy engineer to return to Georgia when his father died. George

W. Bush was an oilman and managing general partner of a baseball team. Two presidents who pursued less-prestigious careers before entering public life were Truman, who, in addition to trying his hand at farming, was a haberdasher and a railroad timekeeper, and Andrew Johnson, who was a tailor. It is not surprising that so many presidents were lawyers, because that profession is closely linked with political careers. Law is a prestigious occupation, rewards skill in interpersonal negotiation and conciliation as well as verbal and argumentative facility, and enables its practitioners to return to private life more readily than is true of medicine or engineering, for example.[27] Since World War II, however, fewer chief executives have come from the law; of the thirteen presidents, only four—Nixon, Ford, Clinton, and Obama—were lawyers. As increasing numbers of people from nonlegal backgrounds—business and teaching, in particular—become senators and governors (the positions from which today's presidents often are recruited), still more presidents without legal training may occupy the White House.

Only three presidents, career military officers, had not held public office before becoming president. Taylor, Grant, and Eisenhower were thrust into the vortex of presidential politics because of heroic exploits in the Mexican War, the Civil War, and World War II, respectively. As professional military men they had not even been involved in partisan activities. Taylor, elected as the Whig candidate in 1848, had never voted before in a presidential election and had no party affiliation.[28] Grant, the Republican Party candidate elected in 1868, had voted for James Buchanan, the Democratic standard-bearer in 1856, and had political views that have been described as "obscure."[29] Even more perplexing for party leaders was Eisenhower, the Republican Party candidate in 1952 and 1956, whom a number of liberal Democratic leaders had tried to draft for their party's nomination in 1948.[30]

For most U.S. chief executives, the road to the presidency involved a long apprenticeship in public office with careers usually begun at lower levels of the political system when they were in their twenties or thirties. Andrew Johnson and Coolidge began their public careers as city aldermen or councilmen. Others were first elected to county offices: John Adams was a highway surveyor; Truman a member of the county court, an administrative, not a judicial, position. Some presidents, including Jackson, Buchanan, Cleveland, McKinley, and Taft, entered public service as prosecuting or district attorneys; others, such as Hayes and Benjamin Harrison, served as city solicitors or attorneys. Clinton began his career in 1976 as Arkansas's attorney general. Several chief executives—Jefferson, Lincoln, the two Roosevelts, and Obama among them—began their public careers as state legislators.

The typical career pattern for these presidents was to move up the political ladder by winning offices representing progressively larger constituencies. Approximately two-thirds of the presidents served in either the House of Representatives or the Senate or both. Exceptions include Wilson, who spent most of his adult life as a professor of government and then as president of Princeton University; in 1910, at age fifty-four, he was elected governor of New Jersey, just two years before winning the presidency. Reagan was primarily a radio, movie, and television performer until his fifties, when he became active in national politics in Barry Goldwater's 1964 presidential campaign. In 1966 he was elected to the first of two terms as governor of California; in 1980 he was elected president. George W. Bush became governor of Texas in 1994 at age forty-seven and was reelected in 1998. Neither Taft nor Hoover held any elective office before being chosen president. Taft served as a judge at the county, state, and federal levels, and later became governor general of the Philippines and secretary of war. Hoover chaired the Commission for Relief in Belgium after World War I; oversaw prices, production, and distribution of food during World War I as U.S. food administrator; and served as secretary of commerce under Harding and Coolidge.

Most presidents come to the White House from another high public office (see chapter 2). Typical positions include the vice presidency, state governorships, Senate seats, and appointive executive office. From one era to the next, these offices have varied in the extent to which their occupants have been favored or disfavored in their pursuit of the presidency.

How is experience related to performance? Most observers assume experience can make a president more or less familiar with the problems confronting the nation as well as with the institutions and people who must collectively address these problems. Moreover, an earlier career in elective office may enable individuals to develop the skills necessary for exercising leadership—bargaining skills, facility in public speaking, and the ability to persuade or inspire others. Candidates, therefore, usually argue that their particular blend of experience—whether in state, national, or nonpublic sectors—has made them best qualified for the position.

Background-Performance Links

How have scholars linked these biographical characteristics to presidential performance? Have they discovered systematic patterns that would enable the public to predict which candidates will enjoy greatest success in office? Unfortunately, there are no simple answers.

Our review shows that most presidents achieved political success with a substantial boost from their family circumstances, advantages that included political and social standing as well as educational and professional opportunities unavailable to most of their fellow citizens. "The common characteristic [of presidents] . . . for all their dissimilarities in other respects, has been the essential conservatism of their social, economic, and political beliefs. . . . [A]ll of them were champions of the prevailing order," according to Pessen.[31] Because the selection process is not neutral toward social class, it seems likely that most presidential aspirants will sustain the status quo.

Two sociologists, E. Digby Baltzell and Howard G. Schneiderman, have more specifically sought to link class origin with performance in office. They correlate Pessen's analysis of class origins with a ranking of presidential performance based on the Murray-Blessing survey of American historians described earlier.[32] Their conclusion challenges some of the myths surrounding the presidency. "There has been . . . not only a high correlation between high social origins and getting to the presidency, as Pessen clearly has shown, [but] once elected to office, men of privileged origins have performed far better than those of lower social status."[33] Of the eight presidents ranked by historians as great or near great, five were from upper-class families (Washington, Jefferson, T. Roosevelt, Wilson, and FDR), two from the upper-middle class (Jackson and Truman), and only one from the middle and lower classes (Lincoln, who is generally ranked number one). In contrast, no presidents drawn from the upper class are found among those regarded by historians as failures (A. Johnson, Buchanan, Grant, Harding, and Nixon). Overall, Baltzell and Schneiderman find that eleven of the fifteen upper-class presidents included in their study (73 percent) were judged to have performed above average in office, while only six of the twenty-one presidents drawn from below the upper class (29 percent) were comparably rated.[34] Although it does not provide a clear explanation for how background is translated into success, the Baltzell-Schneiderman analysis suggests that an upper-class background does make a difference: "Our best aristocratic traditions have stressed *doing* a better job rather than the prevalent, middle-class ideology which has always stressed *getting* a better job."[35]

Richard Neustadt was a forceful advocate of electing an experienced politician to the presidency. As he has argued since 1960, when the first edition of his influential book *Presidential Power and the Modern Presidents* appeared, "The Presidency is no place for amateurs."[36] Neustadt's observation seemed to capture the difficulties Eisenhower experienced in office, although evaluations of Ike's performance have risen over time. As articulated in some of Neustadt's later editions, experience enhances presidents' self-confidence, which in turn makes it easier for them to make the choices about power that are critical to success. Yet "the quality of experience" may count "more than the quantity," an admission Neustadt made after two highly experienced presidents, Lyndon Johnson and Richard Nixon, seemed to flounder if not fail in office. Neustadt ultimately concluded that "the variety of experience is such that none of it can be applied predictively with confidence."[37] Bert Rockman reaches a similar conclusion after looking at the length and types of government experience in relation to performance. In comparing the government experience of the top ten and bottom ten presidents as ranked by an expert panel, the bottom ten actually had modestly *greater* government experience than the top ten (16.9 mean years versus 15.1) and more than twice as many years of congressional experience (7.6 mean years versus 3.7).[38] Experience, it appears, offers no guarantee of success.

We are left with fundamental uncertainties about how life experience may have a bearing on performance. In addition to social class and career experience, there has also been considerable interest in the psychological traits presidents bring to the office, the subject of the next section.

Psychological Characteristics of U.S. Presidents

In October 1972, just before voters were to choose between Richard Nixon and George McGovern, political scientist James David Barber drew attention to the inherent shortcomings of evaluating a candidate's life experience when deciding how to vote. Barber made a prediction. The person who would win had grown up as part of a Republican family in a small town. He had excelled in school, studied piano, had a younger brother rowdier than himself, and had been elected president of his college class. Following military service during World War II, he had attended graduate school and followed an uncertain career path until gaining election to Congress in a contest marked by anticommunist appeals. After two terms in the House and service in the Senate, he was considered a member of his party's liberal wing and respected for hard work and independent thinking. The description fit both Nixon and McGovern. Despite the similarities in life experiences, few doubted that the two would make very different presidents.[39]

The similarity between the major party candidates in 1972 was uncanny even in light of the broadly similar backgrounds from which presidents are drawn. Yet no two people, regardless of how similar their life circumstances, will bring identical personalities to the office. They bring a set of distinctive psychological characteristics, features that may loom large under the intense pressures focused on the presidency. Psychological traits are more proximate to presidential behavior than life experiences, but that does not make them easier to study or evaluate. Fred Greenstein points out that psychologists view personality as a complex phenomenon, involving diverse factors such as how people adapt to the world by screening reality (cognition), how they express feelings (affect), and how they relate to others (identification).[40] These structures are likely to be deeply rooted, making it even more necessary to infer their existence rather than to observe them directly. Analysts, in short, introduce personality as a construct to account for the regularities in a person's behavior. For these reasons, examinations of psychological characteristics are more uncertain and subjective than examinations of professional experience and social backgrounds.

Despite these problems, political scientists and historians have used psychological concepts to help explain why political figures behave as they do, a field of study known as **psychobiography.** Several presidents, including Wilson, L. Johnson, Nixon, Carter, and Clinton, have been the subjects of such biographies.[41] These studies tend to concentrate on childhood experiences, particularly relationships with parents, and how such experiences shaped the presidents' self-perceptions, degree of self-confidence, and psychological needs.

Even with the upsurge in interest, analysts remain divided on how to conduct these studies and the theoretical framework within which they should be conducted. Two broad approaches can be adopted: single-subject case studies and multi-subject case studies. The former seek to develop a comprehensive analysis of the full array of behaviors manifested by one person, with particular attention paid to explaining the origins of recurrent patterns. The latter also rely on close examination of biographical materials but seek to draw conclusions from similarities found among several actors' behavior.[42] An example of a single-subject case study is Alexander George and Juliette George's comprehensive work on Woodrow Wilson, which attempts to explain his strikingly complex and contradictory behavior. Barber's study, *The Presidential Character,* has identified similarities between Wilson's conduct and that of three other presidents—Hoover, L. Johnson, and Nixon—so they may be treated as examples of a similar personality type.

Practitioners of these two styles of inquiry disagree on how analysis should proceed.[43] There are multiple, competing theories of personality and a lack of established rules on how such research should be conducted. Particularly bothersome to many is the extent to which researchers may inject subjective evaluations into the collection and interpretation of case study materials. Although the research remains controversial, it would be unrealistic to overlook the importance of personality in trying to understand the presidency, because this office imposes fewer constraints on the occupant's behavior than does any other in American government.[44] In other words, presidents have great opportunities to be themselves in performing their day-to-day responsibilities.[45] Their emotional fitness for the job is therefore enormously important.

Barber's Approach to Studying Personality

In 1972 Barber made another forecast, more famous than his election prediction, one that brought considerable attention to him and the study of presidential personality. He predicted Nixon would be susceptible to the same "danger" Wilson, Hoover, and Johnson had been, namely, "adhering rigidly to a line of policy long after it had proved itself a failure."[46] Given the right set of circumstances, Nixon was likely to pursue a self-defeating plan of action even in the face of mounting evidence of its likely failure. The causes were rooted in his personality—his emotional needs—no less than they had been for the other three men. Nixon's conduct during Watergate, the extended investigations conducted by Congress during 1973 and 1974 into questionable campaign practices of the 1972 election, seemed to validate the prediction and the method on which it was based.

Was Barber's prediction lucky, or had he uncovered the secret of how to predict presidential performance based on systematic personality analysis? If so, the next step would be to make such insights available to voters before an election to produce more informed decisions.

Barber's work attempts to identify broad character patterns that will predict general patterns of presidential conduct in office. Central to his analysis are three personal characteristics—*character, world view,* and *style*—and two environmental conditions—*power situation* and *climate of expectations*. Together these elements determine the likelihood of presidential success. Character, the most important of Barber's analytic constructs, develops during childhood and is expressed in two analytic dimensions: energy and affect. Presidents may be active or passive in terms of the effort invested in their jobs; they also may be positive or negative about their positions. Both dimensions influence performance.

The resulting four-cell typology is presented in Figure 4-2, with the principal personality trait Barber identified for each type. **Active-positives** exhibit personal growth and adaptability; they enjoy their work and find it a challenge to use power productively as a means to pursue goals beneficial to others. Their success rests on a fundamental sense of self-confidence expressed in goal-oriented behavior. Yet they are flexible in their pursuit of goals and willing to change or abandon them rather than suffer a costly political defeat. In short, they are pragmatic

FIGURE 4-2   Barber's Typology of Character

		Affect	
		Positive	Negative
Activity Level	Active	**Adaptive:** self-confident; power used as means to achieve beneficial results	**Compulsive:** power as a means to self-realization; "driven"; problem managing aggression
	Passive	**Compliant:** seek to be loved; easily manipulated; low self-esteem	**Withdrawn:** respond to sense of duty; avoid power; low self-esteem

SOURCE: James David Barber, *The Presidential Character: Predicting Performance in the White House*, 4th ed. (Englewood Cliffs, N.J.: Prentice Hall, 1992).

politicians. Barber's active-positives include FDR, Truman, Kennedy, Ford, Carter, George H. W. Bush, and Clinton.[47]

Active-negative presidents also invest a great deal of energy in being president, but unlike their active-positive counterparts, they do not appear to derive enjoyment from serving in the office. Rather than exercising political power for the benefit of the citizenry, active-negative chief executives seem to seek power for its own sake, exhibiting compulsiveness as if they are driven to pursue a political career instead of doing it for pleasure. This behavior arises from a poor self-image and lack of self-confidence, traits caused by painful childhood experiences; they seek power and domination over others as compensation for their own lack of self-esteem. In this pursuit, active-negatives may come to believe that the policies they favor are morally right, vital to the nation's interest, and impossible to compromise. They may pursue a course of action even if it obviously is not working, exhibiting a pattern of "rigidification" that can ultimately cause their own political failure. Thus they constitute a great danger to the nation. Barber classifies four twentieth-century presidents as active-negatives: Wilson, Hoover, Johnson, and Nixon.

Passive-positive presidents are not in politics to seek power either for the betterment of the American people or to compensate for their own sense of inadequacy. Rather, they choose politics because they are, in Barber's terms, "political lovers." They genuinely enjoy people and want to help them by doing small favors; in return, they feel wanted and loved. Barber suggests that passive-positive presidents have low self-esteem combined with a superficial optimism about life; they tend to let others set goals for them and find it difficult to make decisions. The danger they pose is one of drift, leaving the affairs of state undirected. Barber identifies three passive-positive chief executives: Taft, Harding, and Reagan.

Passive-negative presidents combine two characteristics one would *not* expect to find in the person who attains the nation's highest office: an unwillingness to invest much energy in that office and a lack of pleasure in serving. Such persons pursue public service because they believe it is something they *ought* to do. They have a fundamental sense of uselessness and compensate for it by dutifully agreeing to work on behalf of their fellow citizens. Exemplifying passive-negative chief executives are Coolidge and Eisenhower.

Barber examines two other personal factors that influence presidential behavior but play a smaller role in his analysis than character. **World view** consists of a president's "politically relevant beliefs, particularly his conceptions of social causality, human nature, and the central moral conflicts of the time."[48] Rather than dealing with specific policy issues, these attitudes are general in nature and therefore more likely to have wide applicability. Barber sees them as developed primarily during adolescence.

Style is the president's "habitual way of performing three political roles: rhetoric, personal relations, and homework."[49] Style focuses on how presidents typically work with words, people, and substantive problems. These patterns are developed largely during early adulthood, particularly in conjunction with the president's "first independent political success," which usually occurs in college or in a first elective or appointive office. **Character** colors both world view and style but does not determine them in any direct way.

Barber analyzed the life histories of presidents from Taft through George H. W. Bush. These analyses are summarized in Figure 4-3. Some of his classifications have been highly controversial, but after 1972 journalists sought out his views of each candidate during presidential elections, and he offered inauguration-eve predictions of how the new president would perform.

Barber also made a tentative analysis of Clinton as an active-positive.[50] Another analyst, Stanley A. Renshon, offered a "preliminary assessment" of Clinton based on events of the presidential campaign and Clinton's first year in office, and those arguments have been expanded subsequently.[51] Renshon concluded that Clinton could be a hybrid type within Barber's framework, a borderline active-negative with a "strong need to be validated." Clinton, argued Renshon, had developed an idealized view of himself—his skills, his accomplishments, and his motives. "Most people wish to think well of themselves but Bill Clinton appears to have come to believe the *best* of himself and to have discounted evidence from his own behavior that all is not as he believes it to be." Unlike active-negatives who use power to overcome low estimates of themselves," Renshon suggests "it is also possible that political leaders

FIGURE 4-3   Barber's Characterization of Modern Presidents

		Affect	
		Positive	Negative
Activity Level	Active	Franklin Roosevelt Harry Truman John F. Kennedy Gerald R. Ford Jimmy Carter George H.W. Bush William J. Clinton George W. Bush*	Woodrow Wilson Herbert Hoover Lyndon Johnson Richard Nixon
	Passive	William H. Taft Warren Harding Ronald Reagan George W. Bush*	Calvin Coolidge Dwight Eisenhower

SOURCE: James David Barber, *The Presidential Character: Predicting Performance in the White House,* 4th ed. (Englewood Cliffs, N.J.: Prentice Hall, 1992). For Barber's views on Clinton, see the *News & Observer* (Raleigh, N.C.), January 17, 1993.
*Possible characterization (not evaluated by Barber).

might well use power to validate high estimates of themselves," something Barber had not anticipated and Clinton might embody.[52] Fred Greenstein, writing toward the end of Clinton's presidency, agreed: "The ever-smiling, hyperactive Clinton has all of the outward signs of an active-positive character. Yet his actions, particularly his astonishing recklessness in the Monica Lewinsky affair, reveal him to be as emotionally deficient as any classically active-negative president."[53]

Reactions to Barber

Because Barber's work was widely popularized in the press, it is important to assess its analytic quality. Academics have been especially critical, suggesting it suffers from the fundamental problem common to all studies in the field—reductionism, paying "insufficient attention to the full range of possible psychological and non-psychological determinants of behavior."[54] Insufficient attention is given to the impact of the environment on presidents, including the nature of the problems they confront, the political support they enjoy, and the constraints within which they operate.

Barber's classification of presidents also has been questioned. The behavior patterns associated with his character types fit some presidents grouped into the same cell better than others. For example, evidence on Eisenhower published after Barber completed his analysis suggests Ike was a more active president than was generally recognized when he was in office.[55] Hoover's reluctance to use extensive federal aid to restore the economy might better be understood as arising from his world view rather than unresolved emotional needs.[56] Another study, using markedly different methods, finds Reagan's personality to be most similar to those of Franklin Roosevelt and Kennedy, although Barber considered Reagan a passive-positive and the other two active-positives.[57] Barber acknowledged that no president fits any type perfectly, that each is a mixture of all four types.[58] Nevertheless, he argued that a dominant pattern can be identified.

Was Barber guilty of positing an ideal personality type that may also conceal a partisan bias? When Barber's study first appeared, all the active-positives were liberal Democrats. Republicans Ford and G. H. W. Bush were subsequently added. What the approach may favor, however, is the heroic model of presidential leadership, which assigns principal responsibility for solving national problems to the White House. Barber recognized that not all active-positives will be successful in office and may pose risks for the political system; their "hunger for and attention to results" may lead them to challenge structures and norms the public believes are better preserved than overturned.[59] FDR's effort in 1937 to alter the structure of the Supreme Court by increasing its membership to as many as fifteen posed a challenge to the tradition of checks and balances and illustrates this possible danger.[60]

Can types other than active-positives achieve substantial success? Jeffrey Tulis argues that in Barber's terms Lincoln should be considered an active-negative, but few would argue that his stewardship of the nation during the Civil War was unsuccessful.[61]

In sum, Barber's work does not represent a panacea to a nation searching for effective leaders. Like most social science, Barber's work is best thought of in terms of probabilities, not certainties. He aspired to present voters with the kind of information on candidate backgrounds and records that would improve the likelihood of informed electoral choices, but the kind of research necessary for personality analysis is difficult to undertake at any time and perhaps most difficult in the heat of an electoral contest. Journalists may be able to improve their coverage of candidates' records and identify behavior patterns of concern, but the chance of conducting a complete study of candidates' personalities in the midst of a campaign is negligible. Nor is it clear who in our society should be given such inordinate influence as to declare some personalities "fit" and others "unfit" for office. Therefore, the practical value of Barber's work remains an open question.[62]

Despite these criticisms of Barber, continuing to study the personalities of presidents and their emotional fitness for the position is of critical importance. Perhaps the most compelling justification comes from those who have experienced the power of presidential personalities firsthand. Clark Clifford, a longtime Washington power broker who served in the Truman and Johnson administrations, voiced the prevailing wisdom among government veterans: "The executive branch of our government is like a chameleon. To a startling degree it reflects the character and personality of the president."[63]

Management Styles of Modern Presidents

Presidents do not govern alone. Those serving before Franklin Roosevelt drew heavily on the assistance of cabinet secretaries and the bureaucracies they headed. Since Roosevelt, another source of advice and assistance—political and policy specialists—has emerged to supplement the traditional sources. To what extent do presidents use these various sources of assistance? How do they structure their advisory systems and make decisions? Should we, in fact, think of the presidency as an individual-dominated office where personality reigns supreme or as a collective that might actually control and constrain the impact of a president's ambitions and goals?[64] This section provides a brief discussion of the development of presidential staffing and the management styles presidents use with these assistants.

Just as important as attitudes drawn from life experiences, and skills developed in previous careers, is a president's aptitude for management. Aides have the potential to magnify presidents' skills, compensate for their shortcomings, and reduce the impact of dangerous personality traits.

The Development of Presidential Staffing

The presidential staff has grown substantially since Congress authorized its modern structure in 1939. Today the Executive Office of the President houses a wide range of expert staff units, including the well-known Office of Management and Budget, Council of Economic Advisers, and National Security Council (all discussed more fully in later chapters), as well as the lesser-known Office of U.S. Trade Representative, Office of Science and Technology Policy, and others. Perhaps best known, and certainly most notorious in Washington circles, is the White House Office, a unit that has traditionally emphasized the president's personal and political concerns.

Like his predecessors, FDR had a limited number of aides, many in clerical positions who were borrowed from other parts of the federal bureaucracy. Looking for a justification to expand these resources, in 1936 he appointed a blue-ribbon group of public administration professors, headed by Louis Brownlow, to study the modern president's management needs. The resulting structure, based on recommendations from that group but reorganized many times since, has always been viewed as a response to the Brownlow Commission's defining sentence: "The President needs help." As Roosevelt and others recognized, the president required additional "eyes and ears" as well as brains to help discharge the ever-growing list of responsibilities placed at the White House door. Presidential staffing is an attempt to help presidents avoid "overload," the possibility that job demands will exceed the capacity of any individual, whose time and ability are finite. The staff can *amplify* the capabilities one person brings to the presidency, but it also can *buffer* the direct impact of a president's personality on performance. Presidents have been given great latitude in their use of staff resources, a flexibility that ensures responsiveness to new problems and perceived needs.

Staff size, although a recurrent political issue, is difficult to monitor with precision. Best estimates place the size of today's Executive Office at approximately seventeen hundred employees.[65] Moreover, the percentage of positions at higher levels of policy-making responsibility appears to have increased substantially over the years.[66] Staff growth has been accompanied by a shift in influence, with one analyst going so far as to suggest that the new structure constitutes a "presidential branch" of government distinct from the larger executive branch.[67] Clearly, presidents can draw on a wide range of assistance outside and within the presidency.

Presidential Management Styles

Style is no doubt an overused term in describing characteristic patterns of presidential behavior, but a number of analysts have focused on how presidents structure and use their advisory systems in making decisions. We term these behavior patterns a president's **management style.** Alexander George identified three personality factors that determine management style: the executive's habitual ways of dealing with information (acquiring, storing, retrieving, evaluating, and using it); the president's sense of competence in dealing personally with problems, which in turn determines the tasks delegated to others; and the president's orientation toward conflict, particularly the tolerance for competition and dissent among advisers.[68]

Because it reflects personality characteristics and distinctive traits, each president's management style is by definition unique. Until the 1970s presidents chose to operate within one of three broad advisory structures, with multiple variations reflecting their management styles.[69] Presidents since Reagan (and arguably since Nixon) have adopted a "standard model" of staff structure centered on established routines for reporting information, coordinating policy decisions, and staffing implementation.[70] The **formalistic** pattern emphasizes clear division of labor among staff assistants, well-defined procedures, and a carefully controlled flow of information to the president, usually through a chief of staff, who tries to deflect problems not worthy of presidential attention. Truman, Eisenhower, and Nixon constructed and operated such systems, although differences in operation reflected the unique combination of needs and contributions each brought to the presidency. Ford and Carter initially tried to work without a chief of staff, but internal disorder eventually forced them to reverse that course. Every president since has appointed a chief of staff, and the hierarchical model became the standard for modern presidents. The **competitive** pattern, typified by FDR, encouraged conflict among advisers and thrived on diversity of opinion, with the president reserving ultimate judgment to himself. Conflict is endemic to decision making within the American government, but Roosevelt encouraged even more of it. Under a **collegial** system, emphasis is on group problem solving, teamwork, and shared responsibility for outcomes, with the president participating in the process and choosing among identified options. Kennedy, particularly during the Cuban missile crisis, typified this style, and elements can be found in later administrations.

Richard Johnson's three models are a starting point for describing how the staff systems work. Presidents might follow more than one pattern or construct hybrid combinations. Ford followed a collegial pattern in domestic policy but was more formalistic in foreign policy.[71] Carter's system was described as a mixture of collegial and formalistic.[72] Reagan constructed a variant of the formalistic and collegial models during his first term when he relied heavily on three senior aides (the "troika"), a system that drew considerable praise from many observers, particularly when its successor in the second term became less collegial and notably less successful.[73] Clinton's style, discussed later in the chapter, evolved from a highly undisciplined, sometimes collegial style to a somewhat more disciplined collegial pattern. George W. Bush adopted a formal style with himself at the "hub of a quadrangle" of senior aides who had ready access to him; others list six aides with direct access.[74] Bush employed systematic delegation from the outset, but abandoned it on occasion.[75] Many observers speculated on how President Obama would manage the White House, especially because he named an assertive chief of staff, Rahm Emanuel, who needed to coordinate a large number of other prominent advisers who oversee major problem areas including environmental, health, and technology policy.[76] It is important to note that the size of government, as well as the number and complexity of issues that confront modern presidencies, have forced "every modern president to rely at least to some extent on formalistic procedures."[77]

In general, formalistic structures place more modest demands on presidential time and knowledge. Delegating a larger range of tasks conserves time and may increase the probability that experts will deal with the problem. Because much of the work is processed in written form, the formal system is less appropriate for presidents who prefer to rely on group interaction, discussion, and even argument as part of the decision-making process. Competitive and collegial structures place heavier demands on the president, who not only must rely largely on his own substantive knowledge in making choices among competing alternatives but also must be able to monitor a policy-making process inherently political in nature. Advisers and the areas they represent push hard for the president to adopt their solutions, and the maneuvers used to gain an advantage are believed to be the keys to success. Unfortunately, winning such battles may come at the expense of good decisions.

Democratic presidents, using FDR as a model, tend to adopt a more interactive advisory system, sometimes described as a "spokes-in-a-wheel" system, with the president at the center of several principal aides in and out of the White House. Such a system encourages dispute and argumentation. Republican presidents, following Eisenhower's lead, have operated within a more structured system, in which the chief executive relies on a single chief of staff or a limited number of advisers and on systematic review processes. This approach is thought less susceptible to political maneuvering. Over time, partisan staffing differences have diminished as consensus developed on what the White House needs. But it is important to remember that informal structures also shape how the White House operates,[78] and staffs may be more or less faithful to the formal models they create. Ultimately, if the advisory system reflects the kind of personality variables identified by Alexander George, the system will be modified to meet the incumbent's particular needs.

Multiple Advocacy: Learning a Decision Process

The best-known effort to prescribe a specific decision process for presidents to follow is George's system of **multiple advocacy**.[79] In essence, he suggested that presidents should be able to learn a set of techniques to follow in managing advisers and making decisions. Although recognizing that a given president may find this style "uncongenial to his cognitive style and work habits," George believed the advantages would make it worthwhile for a president to consider. For example, Nixon found it painful to be the object of direct, face-to-face argument among his advisers, but he might have modified the system advocated by George to derive its benefits.[80]

George defined multiple advocacy as a *mixed* system—benefiting from both centralized and decentralized features—that tries to ensure that the president benefits from a wide review of policy options and hears a variety of viewpoints before making a final decision. It tries to build on the inevitable conflict among individual advisers and bureaucratic agencies by channeling that conflict in productive ways. The overall process must be structured so every relevant viewpoint receives a fair hearing. One of the major tasks, then, in operating such a system is monitoring the breadth of options being considered and the opportunities that advocates of such views have to be heard. To operate in this system, the president requires a full-time assistant, a "custodian-manager" who acts as an "honest broker" among the advisers pushing their positions on the president and ensures that several crucial tasks be performed, namely to "collect and analyze information, formulate policy problems, identify and appraise alternative options," and coordinate efforts across government departments.[81]

George hoped that systematic review of options, one of the claimed benefits of a formalistic system, could be achieved under multiple advocacy, with the added benefit of the open debate and discussion encouraged by competitive and collegial systems.[82] The president should act as a magistrate—"one who listens to the arguments made, evaluates them, poses issues and asks questions, and finally judges which action to take either from among those articulated by advocates or as formulated independently by himself after hearing them."[83] Consistent with this role, presidents need to suppress the urge to announce their own preferences early in the process and ensure that they remain faithful to the premise on which the system rests, the guarantee of giving an equal hearing to all views.

Such a process can be time-consuming, and George recognized that presidents would have to decide when it should be used. There may be times when they already know the policy they wish to pursue, and because constitutional responsibility in the American executive is unitary rather than collective, presidents can always exercise individual discretion. Paul Kowert raises another issue: "while some leaders thrive on diversity of opinion, others are immobilized by it," so "leaders must guard not only against too little advice, but also against too much."[84] If overwhelmed by information, a leader might withdraw from contentious issues and allow policy to drift into "deadlock," a plausible interpretation of Reagan's inaction in the face of growing budget deficits (see chapter 9) and the exchanges of arms for hostages that lay at the heart of the Iran-contra incident (see chapter 10).[85]

Even George did not believe that use of a multiple advocacy system and the magistrate presidential style that accompanies it can ensure good decisions. Rather, he urged its adoption as a way to improve the quality of information made available to presidents and to prevent the bad decisions that result from faulty procedures.[86]

Understanding Presidents: Bill Clinton and George W. Bush

Explaining presidential behavior and linking its determinants to performance is like putting together the pieces of a puzzle, but a puzzle whose final shape is uncertain. One way to illustrate how background, experience, personality, and management style shape behavior and performance is to take an in-depth look at individual cases. It is too soon to provide a final evaluation of George W. Bush's effectiveness in office, and even judgments about Clinton are still difficult to make, but we can trace major features of their lives and explore ways in which they potentially affected performance. Clinton and Bush offer strikingly contrasting personal portraits. Clinton's ambition to be president can be traced to his teenage years; he systematically prepared to launch his political career at an early age. Bush was the classic "late-bloomer" and speaks openly of a life-changing event at forty. He did not enter politics until age forty-seven. Clinton was elected to office as a "new Democrat" seeking to move his party toward more moderate positions, but he encountered scathing criticism during his first year for being a vintage liberal. Bush ran as a "compassionate conservative" and a "different kind of Republican" but was highly attentive to his conservative base. Although a product of the 1960s, an era known for its revolt against established power structures and social norms, Clinton, the first "baby boomer" president, has been consistently criticized for compromising with power centers, first in Arkansas and later in Washington. Bush, heir to one of the great political family traditions in American life, was always the iconoclast who challenged traditional authority but resisted the lure of 1960s-style rebellion. A booster of family values and a devout Baptist, Clinton confronted repeated charges of marital infidelity, culminating in the Lewinsky scandal. Bush is a born-again Christian who acknowledges an earlier problem with alcohol and making unspecified mistakes during his "irresponsible youth." Filled with nostalgic pride for his small-town roots, Clinton burned with ambition to succeed on larger stages. Bush claims small-town Texas as his adopted home despite the ready access he has always had to larger stages. The following are snapshots of their lives.

Clinton's Early Life and Prepresidential Career

Bill Clinton entered life in the wake of tragedy. Shortly before the birth of William Jefferson Blythe III (Clinton's original name) in 1946, his father drowned in a roadside ditch following a car accident while driving from Chicago to Hope, Arkansas. The newly widowed Virginia Blythe, a wartime bride, completed her training as a nurse anesthetist in New Orleans, leaving her son with her parents for his first two years. Although his grandmother doted on Bill, her hot temper offset his grandfather's universal friendliness, traits later displayed by the adult Bill Clinton.

When Bill was four, his mother married Roger Clinton, a car dealer (also known to deal in bootleg liquor) whose first wife had divorced him because of abuse. The new family settled in Hot Springs, Arkansas, a resort town where gambling and prostitution were openly pursued. For the next twelve years, the future president lived in two very different worlds: a public world centered on school and church, in which he earned plaudits as a model citizen, and a private, turbulent world in which his stepfather had become an abusive alcoholic. After repeated episodes of abuse, Virginia divorced her second husband (Bill provided testimony in the trial) only to remarry him three months later. During the interlude, Bill Blythe changed his last name to Clinton so that it would be the same as Roger Clinton's, his younger half-brother.

Inevitably, this unhappy family life heavily influenced Bill Clinton's personality. He assumed the part of "family hero," one of the roles commonly found among children of alcoholics. Characteristically, this child assumes responsibility for protecting the family and serves as its redeemer to the outside world by winning awards and praise.[87] Clinton did both, once intervening to stop his stepfather from abusing his mother, and bringing glory to the family through his high school successes. As a Boys' Nation delegate, in a memorable moment captured on film, the sixteen-year-old shook the hand of President John F. Kennedy. Children of alcoholics also have an "exaggerated need to be agreeable"[88] and can be predisposed to develop addictive behavior of their own, in Clinton's case, a sexual addiction.[89]

Clinton attended Georgetown University's School of Foreign Service and became a campus leader, reflecting "his political skills, his ability to think on his feet, to build coalitions and networks."[90] Even as a young man Clinton cultivated potentially helpful contacts through an internship on Capitol Hill, work in political campaigns, and selection as a Rhodes Scholar at the height of the Vietnam War. Like many other male college students of the era, Clinton developed a strategy to avoid military service by entering the Reserve Officers Training Corps (ROTC) at the University of Arkansas, where he promised to enroll in the law school in the fall of 1969. His draft board canceled his induction, but instead of entering law school, Clinton returned to England and was saved by the new lottery system for selecting inductees—Clinton's high number was never called. Later, political opponents charged that he had dodged the draft.

When he returned to the United States in 1970, Clinton entered the prestigious Yale University Law School. He gained valuable campaign experience in a Connecticut Senate race and in Texas as state coordinator for presidential candidate George McGovern in 1972. These campaigns widened his network of contacts to a new generation of political activists, heavily motivated by antiwar sentiments and the desire to reform the American political and economic systems. The other lasting effect from his time at Yale was a romance with Hillary Rodham, a no less brilliant and far more focused law school classmate.

After serving for less than a year on the faculty of the University of Arkansas Law School, Clinton challenged the incumbent U.S. representative and ran an aggressive, imaginative campaign, but lost by 4,000 votes. Hillary Rodham left the House Judiciary Committee's Watergate investigation team, moved to Arkansas during Clinton's campaign, and they married soon after. In 1976 he easily won election as Arkansas's attorney general and served as Jimmy Carter's state campaign chairman at the same time. This began Clinton's meteoric rise. He won the governorship in 1978 with 63 percent of the vote, becoming the youngest U.S. governor in four decades.[91] Clinton's first two-year term as governor, much like his first two years as president—were marked by an overly ambitious, highly idealistic agenda of initiatives. His young staff ruffled feathers in the Arkansas establishment and was unable to discipline Clinton's "loose, free-ranging management style," which included off-the-cuff comments to the press, an inability to adhere to a schedule, and excessive accessibility to any and all visitors.[92] Successes were scarce, and the governor's ratings slipped.

Clinton lost badly in the next election. The experience was reportedly devastating, triggering months of soul-searching about what had gone wrong, as he unenthusiastically entered private law practice. He regained the governorship in 1982 and secured reelection in 1984, 1986, and 1990, after the term was lengthened to four years.

Clinton's return to power was eerily similar to later chapters in his political career: he turned to political consultant Dick Morris. Then, as later, when he would advise Clinton in 1995 after the devastating Republican victories in the 1994 midterm elections, Morris urged Clinton to moderate his positions, to become more pragmatic and less idealistic. Another feature of that comeback is familiar. To regain public support, Clinton apologized to Arkansans for mistakes he had made as a young governor, essentially admitting that he had become "too big for his britches." A similar drama of apology and personal penance was played out in 1998–1999 as the Lewinsky scandal produced his initial nonapologetic televised address to the nation in August, followed by gradually increasing statements of regret.

Clinton began his pursuit of the presidency by chairing the National Governors Association and addressing the Democratic National Conventions in 1980, 1984, and 1988. He had almost sought the 1988 presidential nomination himself, agonizing for weeks over whether to run. He disappointed a gathering of friends who had come to Little Rock anticipating an announcement after a female aide confronted him with a long list of women whose past relationships with him would be probed by the press.[93] But that setback was only temporary. Clinton announced his candidacy in fall 1991, thereby reversing a campaign promise to Arkansans that he would finish out his full term as governor.

Evaluating Clinton's Performance

The most troubling questions about the Clinton presidency concern the Lewinsky affair:

Why would someone who had achieved his lifelong dream needlessly jeopardize it? Why would an inherently cautious politician with an obvious need for public affirmation follow such a careless private path? . . . Why would someone with a deep distrust of his political enemies give them so much ammunition with which to attack? Why would someone with a near photographic memory, who could immediately recall a telephone number that he had not dialed in thirty years, seem so incapable of remembering and learning from history and his own mistakes?[94]

Speculation on these and related questions gripped the nation for fourteen months as the drama of the president and the intern unfolded. Clinton was chastised for "a severe lack of self-discipline" and "defective impulse control,"[95] as well as "a self-delusion of invincibility" that fed his recklessness and could be traced to recurring traits in his character.[96] The Clinton experience reaffirms the importance of not electing presidents who are "emotionally handicapped," as Fred Greenstein describes Johnson, Nixon, Carter, and Clinton. As he points out, "in the real world, human imperfection is inevitable, but some imperfections are more disabling than others."[97] Although Clinton went to great lengths to show the nation he was effectively discharging his duties throughout the ordeal of his investigation and impeachment, many believe that the nation's life and business were disrupted and that Clinton's legacy would have been greater had he not had to devote endless hours to his legal defense.

We can draw some confident conclusions about Clinton's service as president. Clinton was the first president born after World War II, the first "to live in a relentless real-time media culture that magnified his every mistake," and the first elected president to be impeached.[98] He was a man of contradictions: "considerate and calculating, easygoing and ambitious, mediator and predator"; "sincere and deceptive at the same time"; "indecisive, too eager to please, and prone to deception" but also "indefatigable, intelligent, empathetic, and self-deprecating."[99] He projected "relentless optimism" and "great resilience" in the face of repeated setbacks inflicted on him by the media, his political opponents, and himself.[100] His political skills were prodigious, acknowledged even by some of his harshest critics, who recognized a "talent for language that is rare in politicians" and an "extraordinary gift for intimacy" revealed in his capacity to relate to people, to listen to their concerns, and to empathize with their problems.[101] Newt Gingrich, a longtime adversary, described Clinton as "'the best tactical politician, certainly of my lifetime.'"[102] There was, as well, near universal praise for his native intelligence and natural abilities as well as his energy.[103] Bert Rockman declared that Clinton is that "rare combination of a complex policy thinker and a sophisticated thinker about politics."[104] Perhaps it is precisely because of Clinton's prodigious talents that disappointment was widespread about his performance when he left office. But, as we noted earlier, his ratings have improved since then.

Did Clinton offer the public, the press, and politicians a consistent policy vision? His harshest critics questioned whether he had any lasting principles that directed his activity.[105] Others suggested that policy reversals and waffling arose "partly because he cannot make up his own mind and partly because he wants to please the last group to have spoken to him"[106] or because his especially sophisticated mind enabled him to view policy matters from multiple angles.[107] Ideological consistency was never a hallmark of Clinton's political career, and he frequently abandoned positions and allies when necessary. Clinton believed in an activist government and, more than any other policy area, supported intervention in civil rights. Yet even that lifelong commitment was sorely tested in 1995 when he ordered a review of government-sponsored affirmative action programs (ultimately ordering few changes) and supported welfare reform before the 1996 election. His initiative to improve race relations, launched in 1997 and intended as a centerpiece of his second term, floundered on the national fascination with impeachment.[108]

Impatient activism and resilience were hallmarks of Clinton's service. Like Jimmy Carter, Clinton was accused of failing to set priorities among his many first-year initiatives, resulting in a serious overload of the congressional and public agendas. This overload is reminiscent of the problems encountered during his first year as governor. He has admitted to feeling "an urgent sense to do everything he could in life as quickly as possible" because of his father's death at age twenty-eight.[109]

More than anything else, Clinton had the capacity to bounce back from adversity, evident in the 1992 New Hampshire primary, when Clinton labeled himself the "Comeback Kid," following three major prepresidential crises[110] and twice during his presidency, after Democrats lost a congressional majority in November 1994 and during the extended inquiry that led to his impeachment in 1998. Crises triggered periods of introspection and self-correction, a capacity that helped him as president. Even when he was wrong, he had the laudable ability "to admit his own failings" and make pragmatic adjustments.[111] No less than other presidents, Clinton learned how to be president on the job; he also learned much about himself.

George W. Bush's Life

If Bill Clinton's lifetime challenge was to overcome the absence of a father, the challenge for George W. Bush was to escape his father's shadow.[112] Born in Connecticut, where his father was completing college at Yale after returning from World War II, George W., as the family always called him, adopted Texas as his home. Midland was the site of his childhood and his career in the oil industry, though he also spent time in Houston. Bush is the eldest of four sons and one daughter. His closest sibling, Robin, died of leukemia at age four, an especially traumatic time for Bush (then seven) and his parents. In fact, this event has been portrayed as a critical moment in his life. Barbara Bush, his mother, slipped into an extended period of depression after her daughter's death and George W. took it on himself to keep her company and cheer her up, an effort leading to his habitual clowning and role as the family's "ebullient cutup." As a result of the close bond between Bush and his mother, family members suggest he possesses more of her "blunt outspokenness," "irreverence and readiness with a joke," and spontaneity than he does his father's "guarded, dignified" personality.[113] Although he may have idealized his father and sought his approval, he frequently jousted verbally and collided with his mother.[114]

There were two realities in Bush's childhood. On the one hand, he "grew up as the first son in a large, generationally extended family with wealth on all sides," enjoying the benefits of privilege, such as a New England summer home, and family ties hardly imaginable to most Americans.[115] On the other hand, descriptions of Bush's childhood in Midland sound like vintage Americana. Little League, picnics, and adventures with brothers and friends with Bush in the lead characterize the president's memories of those years. Bush attended public schools through seventh grade, spending one of those years in Houston, where he later attended an exclusive private school for two years. At that point his life took on a shadowlike quality, retracing the footsteps of his illustrious father. Bush entered his father's and grand-father's prep school alma mater, Phillips Exeter Academy in Andover, Massachusetts, to complete his high school years before moving on to Yale. He was an indifferent student at Andover, falling far short of his father's achievements as senior class president and captain of the baseball team. George W. worked his way onto the baseball and basketball teams but was much more of a social leader, expressing opinions on everything (hence his nickname "Lip").[116] Although mediocre grades meant he was concerned about getting into Yale, where his grandfather, father, and uncles were educated, Bush entered as a legacy in 1964. Again, academics were not his major concern—he became president of his fraternity, known on campus as the "party fraternity," and like his father he was selected for membership in Skull and Bones, Yale's most elite secret society. Classmates recall Bush as fun loving, lacking pretense, and outspokenly supporting the Vietnam War in the face of over-whelming campus opposition, but not a scholar.

Like Clinton who also graduated from college in 1968, Bush confronted the draft and found an avenue that kept him out of direct fire. This decision became one of the more controversial features of his early life, with charges leveled that he received favorable treatment as the son of a member of Congress. Two weeks before his col-lege graduation, the point at which his draft deferment would run out, Bush applied to the Texas Air National Guard and was immediately sworn in despite a waiting list. Some allege that strings were pulled; Bush argues that he wanted to follow in his father's footsteps and be a fighter pilot.[117] (The elder Bush was the youngest commis-sioned officer in the Navy during WWII and returned home a hero after earning the Distinguished Flying Cross.) What followed were two years of training and a four-year commitment to part-time service. His unit was not sent overseas, and Bush com-pleted his military obligation while working in a variety of jobs back home, none with much gusto, while he partied in Texas with considerable gusto.

In 1975 Bush graduated from Harvard Business School, where he is remem-bered for his iconoclastic behavior—pinching snuff, dressing shabbily, disdaining those aspiring to a career on Wall Street. After graduation he held several entry-level jobs in the Midland oil business. Bush and his family refer to these as his "nomadic" years, when he seemed to lack direction or purpose.

At age thirty-one Bush showed the first indication of personal political ambi-tion. Over the years, he had worked in an impressive list of political campaigns, including three of his father's and two other Republican senatorial campaigns.[118] When an unexpected retirement opened the House seat in West Texas, Bush, once again following in his father's footsteps, declared his candidacy and won the Republican nomination in a June 1978 runoff against a Reagan-backed conservative.[119] In the midst of the campaign, he married Laura Welch, a librarian who had known Bush in elementary school but had not seen him again until a blind date put them together. His Republican adversary set the groundwork for the Democratic opponent, who charged Bush with being a privileged product of the eastern establishment and out of step with bedrock values of West Texas. Bush won 47 percent of the vote but lost the election. Reportedly, he concluded that his own political career would have to be delayed until his father was out of politics, a long wait because at that point George H. W. Bush was preparing to seek the Republican presidential nomination.

Perhaps in preparation for the day he could turn to a career in public service, the central feature of the family ethos of "making one's mark in the world," Bush looked to business as a way to create financial security and free himself to run for political office.[120] Like his father, he entered the oil business in Midland, establishing a small independent oil drilling company. Bush no doubt benefited from his name and family contacts in winning the support of investors for such a high-risk venture—it did not hurt to be the son of the U.S. vice president. The business was not successful, limping along from year to year without any major finds and suffering from depressed oil prices. This was all part of a "nagging pattern that marked his life until past the age of forty: once again, he had followed his father's path but failed to achieve his father's success."[121] At a critical time when losses were mounting and his corporation was millions in debt, the corporate assets were bought out, the debts assumed, and Bush was given stock and options of Harken Oil and Gas, a large Dallas firm whose board Bush joined. Again, the suggestion has been made that this success was the result of Bush's name and special contacts. Even more controversial was the sale of his entire stock holdings in the company in 1990, eight days before the announcement of major losses reduced the stock price by 25 percent. The Securities and Exchange Commission conducted an investigation into whether Bush had engaged in insider trading, profiting from the privileged information available to a board member. No impropriety was found, although Bush's opponent in the 1994 Texas governor's race alleged otherwise.[122]

Bush's sudden turn in fortunes coincided with the turning point in his life: he gave up alcohol the morning after a boisterous fortieth birthday party in 1986. And, on the heels of a 1985 conversation with Rev. Billy Graham, he became more religious.[123] As the *Washington Post*'s close study of the president's life concludes, Bush was abusing alcohol though he was not an alcoholic—more a fraternity binge drinker than someone with an addiction. But alcohol had begun to cause problems for him, including a 1976 charge of driving under the influence in Maine.[124] Bush sought to seize control of his life. "By doing so he would finally begin to close the gap between what was expected of him and what he had achieved."[125] Developing self-discipline was probably not an overnight occurrence but involved foreswearing alcohol, establishing a vigorous exercise routine, and learning to harness his energy productively.[126] Ultimately, "focus, will power, perseverance and resilience" were the traits that enabled Bush to complete a personal transformation that Stanley Renshon attributes to his own strengths, not others.[127]

His major independent success followed the 1988 presidential election, when George W. joined his father's presidential campaign headquarters, working closely with political consultant Lee Atwater and serving as principal liaison with evangelical Christian leaders and groups.[128] Bush put together an investment group that purchased the Texas Rangers baseball team and began the process of fashioning an identity distinctive from his father's. He served as the managing partner, the public face of the team. He handled public relations, built and maintained consensus among members of the management team he assembled, and used baseball as the way to become "a man of the people."[129] He oversaw the financing and planning for a new ballpark that ushered in an era of team success and greatly enhanced the value of the franchise. When the partnership sold its interest in 1998, Bush's original investment of $606,302 was worth more than $15 million.[130] By then, however, he had already reaped other benefits, riding his newfound identity to the Texas governorship.

Bush's Prepresidential Political Career

Although he unsuccessfully ran for Congress in 1978 and worked in numerous campaigns, Bush had never held elected or appointed public office until he became governor of Texas in 1995. He had considered running for the position in 1990 but ultimately agreed with advice from his mother and principal strategists that the time was not right, particularly with his commitment to the Rangers.[131] With his father's defeat in 1992, however, Bush was able to run for office with less fear of the criticisms he had encountered in the congressional campaign. Moreover, his success with the Rangers had established a separate persona for him as a Texas businessman.

His race against incumbent Ann Richards, who had memorably parodied his father at the 1988 Democratic nominating convention, was remarkably similar to that against Al Gore six years later. Like Gore, Richards seemed intent on provoking Bush into an undisciplined verbal mistake. Bush never took the bait and remained tightly "on message" throughout the campaign, focused on the issues he chose to emphasize and sticking with broad themes rather than policy details. Richards had difficulty defending her record, and none of the rumors about Bush's wrongdoing in his youth or his questionable business dealings ever produced a major embarrassment. Bush won, 53 percent to 46 percent.

In 1998 Bush became the first Texas governor to be reelected to a four-year term (most previous governors had served for two years) when he defeated a weak opponent, 69 percent to 31 percent. The election was particularly noteworthy for the strong support Bush received from Hispanic voters and women, taken as an indication that he would run a strong national campaign if nominated for president. In fact, there had been open discussion about Bush's national ambitions during the campaign.[132] His presidential aspirations, however, were relatively new. "Unlike almost any other serious presidential candidates in modern memory, no one who knew him [earlier in life] envisioned George W. Bush in the White House."[133] By one measure, Bush brings to the presidency "the scantiest record in public office of any modern President." But that record does not recognize his "two decades apprenticing as a kind of *de facto* political consultant."[134] Nor does it take into account the opportunity to be a participant-observer in his father's three-decade political career. To focus on Bush's elected experience misses the full extent of his substantial "political" experience.

Bush as President

George W. Bush brought a diverse set of skills and experiences to the White House. On a personal level, he is gregarious, unpretentious, persistent, and highly adaptable. By all accounts, his interpersonal skills are outstanding. There is universal acknowledgment of how well he relates to a wide range of people, using humor and warmth as a way to make them comfortable, win their support, and mold coworkers into a team. This trait was a central feature of his success in business and politics. As did Clinton, Bush has moved through life creating networks of contacts that later played a major role in his financial and political success. He seems to elicit considerable personal loyalty. For example, his chief political adviser, Karl Rove, first joined him in the unsuccessful 1978 congressional race, and Bush's closest financial advisers were longtime friends and associates, such as Donald Evans, his first commerce secretary.[135] His humor prevents him from personalizing battles or taking himself too seriously, yet he was a determined competitor in politics no less than in sports.

By acknowledging some skeletons in his closet, particularly his partying as a youth, and by changing his behavior, Bush showed a capacity for self-reflection and personal growth, even though the changes were long-delayed. In terms of Barber's typology, Bush appears best described as an active-positive. He exudes strong self-esteem, invests reasonably high levels of energy in discharging his duties, and seemed to enjoy the position of president. He appeared self-confident, and why not? After all, "how many Americans who at the age of forty were running a failing business and drinking too much turned their lives around so completely that within a dozen years they became not just a two-time governor of the nation's second-most populous state but also a serious contender for [and winner of] the White House?"[136]

Bush's pedigree connotes privilege—Andover, Yale, Harvard—yet his manner was decidedly populist. This could arise from discomfort with his own roots or the trappings of elitism, either conservative or liberal in origin.[137] He did not appear to agonize over decisions—if anything, he had a tendency to be impulsive, a potential weakness in the past, partially managed by his wife.[138] Some evidence suggests that he tended to be impatient with policy details,[139] and critics questioned his intellectual ability. A fuller reading of his past would recognize that when engaged, he has considerable mental ability, which he demonstrated in his youth by mastering mountains of baseball statistics, in young adulthood by learning the intricacies of flying jet fighters, and later in overseeing the minutiae of his father's 1988 presidential campaign.[140] It would be fairer to say that he did not always apply that ability to its fullest. In that respect, Bush may resemble Reagan, an instinctive politician more comfortable with themes than specifics, somewhat incurious, and always ready to delegate. Like Reagan, Bush relied on gut instinct to make some decisions, particularly in evaluating people. Also like Reagan, Bush brought a CEO style to the presidency but with important differences. Bush's style was honed during his period as managing partner of the Rangers and reflects a stronger commitment to aggressive pursuit of clearly set goals. Bush's higher energy levels also made him less susceptible than Reagan to the danger of failing to monitor subordinates closely enough. Much like Reagan, Bush kept the presidency in perspective; he enjoyed the job but also enjoyed his time away from it, an ability probably underrated by journalists and academics.

If you closed your eyes and listened to speeches of George W. Bush and his father, you would immediately note the similarities—the broken syntax, the occasionally labored delivery, the mangled vocabulary. Both men, however, demonstrated that they could rise to the occasion when it was important to perform well with a set speech, and George W. gained far more experience in working with the media and the public in the baseball business than his father did in his many government posts. Did George W. Bush possess the communication skills necessary for modern presidents to be successful? For much of his first year, Bush avoided the media, holding no prime-time press conferences until after 9/11 and relying on his White House staff to ensure that the administration's message structured media coverage. He relied on informal exchanges with the press and did not address the nation from the Oval Office until the night of September 11, 2001. Once Bush found his voice, his direct, genuine delivery of speeches resonated effectively with most Americans, and he "became a compelling public presence" in delivering a series of forceful addresses following the terrorist attacks.[141] Did the content of his speeches provide more "vision" than was found in his father's? The knock on the elder Bush was the "vision thing," as he once dismissed it. Even after eight years, George W.'s world view was still a bit of a mystery, a montage of traditional conservative themes, laden with evangelical Christian overtones, and rejection of the liberal excesses found in the baby boom generation.[142] "Compassionate conservatism," Bush's own term for his philosophy during the 2000 presidential campaign, somehow got lost along the way despite the many policy proposals and concrete actions.

In two areas, the economy and foreign policy, Bush's first-term record was far bolder than expected given the narrowness of his election victory and the absence of a mandate. With two large swipes of the tax-cutting knife, Bush reversed Clinton's legacy of reduced federal deficits and revealed himself to be a firm believer in supply-side economic theory. A slow economic recovery after the brief recession in 2001 led him to replace virtually his entire team of economic advisers; it fell to the new team to sell the second round of tax cuts as a jobs-and-growth plan, which was heavily attacked during the president's 2004 reelection bid. In foreign affairs Bush was "leading a revolution" by reorienting the conduct and the substance of American foreign policy. Even before 9/11, the administration made clear its willingness to act through unilateral, rather than multilateral, strategies. After 9/11, by word and by deed the administration asserted U.S. primacy in the world through a redefinition of national strategy and its aggressive use of force, particularly in Iraq where all major world powers except Britain opposed military action.[143] In contrast to economic policy, Bush stuck with his foreign policy team throughout the first four years, even though their voices were often discordant, with those of Defense Secretary Donald Rumsfeld and Secretary of State Colin Powell the loudest. Powell left early in the second term, and Rumsfeld stayed until after the midterm election losses of November 2006.

Given the lack of administration consensus, it fell to the president to confidently steer a course intended to redefine America's place in the world. Neither domestic nor foreign publics accepted this new vision (see chapter 10).

John Burke provides an especially thorough review of accounts provided by journalists and academics of the Bush administration's decision-making style, particularly in regard to Afghanistan and Iraq. Burke concludes that although the design of the policy-making system had the potential to combine benefits from both the hierarchical and collegial styles of management, Bush's performance and that of his advisers fell far short of this ideal. In particular, the president failed to exercise control over Secretary Rumsfeld and Vice President Cheney, thereby tolerating their repeated evasions of the policy-making system centered on the National Security Council. Condoleezza Rice, national security adviser during the first administration, was an effective policy coordinator until Iraq became the dominant foreign policy issue, and then she lost control. Senior officials and those lower in the bureaucracy who questioned administration policy were seen not as the source of important views that needed to be considered, but as disloyal. And Bush's own performance was questioned: he was viewed as fully engaged on practical questions of how to get things done but not whether they should be undertaken; as having a distinct preference for short conversations rather than longer, more searching arguments; and as overly reliant on a narrow circle of advisers rather than reaching out for additional perspectives.[144] In short, the first MBA to serve in the White House may not have fully lived up to his training. A second evaluation by Andrew Rudalevige agrees with many of Burke's points, adding that decisions were often based on ideology rather than fact, the reflection of a president confident in his own beliefs and stressing decisiveness.[145]

Another area of performance also drew criticism. Based on the first term, it was unclear whether Bush fully appreciated how presidents must teach the public and fashion a broad consensus behind national goals, a special challenge given Bush's proposals for significant policy departures.[146] Three second-term issues occasioned similar questions. In 2005 Bush devoted enormous effort to building public understanding of the Social Security crisis as a way to win acceptance of his preferred reform, individual retirement accounts. Although the president pursued a legislative strategy that allowed him to assemble a bipartisan coalition, he seemed to misread the depth of Democrats' opposition to his reform's centerpiece, and neither side was willing to negotiate.[147] During the debate on immigration reform in 2007, Bush was unwilling to compromise with Republican conservatives who abandoned their own president's reform proposals. And on Iraq, Bush pursued the surge strategy in the winter of 2006–2007 instead of adopting the carefully constructed plan for a bipartisan strategy fashioned by former secretary of state James Baker and former representative Lee Hamilton as part of the Iraq Study Group. At the time, these decisions seemed to repeat errors of political judgment or represented stubborn refusals to compromise even when defeat seemed likely. As conditions improved in Iraq, however, Bush's confidence in the surge seemed justified.

Without experience of his own at the federal level, Bush chose notably experienced hands to help him, including his vice president. Cheney handled many challenging tasks: overseeing the transition, guiding the administration's legislative agenda through Congress, fashioning an energy strategy, and helping to revise the nation's defense doctrine. But Cheney's performance was highly controversial, raising questions about Bush's reliance on this source of help. The competence and outlook of a president's team is especially important for a CEO-style executive; with the exception of Cheney's role, Bush's performance suggests he seldom, if ever, delegated the final say on administration policies. "Unlike Reagan, who often could not decide between his oft-feuding friends, or Clinton, who always saw every side to an argument, Bush quickly earned a reputation among his advisers for decisiveness,"[148] overruling public positions of Rumsfeld, Powell, and others during the early months of the administration (see chapter 6).

Bush's personal resilience and his capacity to rally the nation were sorely tested by 9/11, and the public clearly decided that he passed the test of leadership as evidenced in the record outpouring of support. The terrorist attacks were a classic example of how "a leader's intentions and real world constraints" interact "in turning point events."[149] Renshon argues that Bush was transformed by the event. His "personal anguish" provided "strong emotional fuel to an already high level of resolve . . . on bringing those responsible, and their allies, to justice."[150] Bush and his administration suddenly had a sense of mission. The 9/11 attacks were a transformational experience in Bush's life similar to his midlife awakening. As Renshon summarizes, "After several false starts, occupational cul-de-sacs, and personal lapses, Mr. Bush seemed finally to have arrived at his life's destination. He had won the highest political office in the land, and now had an urgent mission to accomplish."[151] Commentators and historians will help define his success.

What to Expect from Obama

Barack Obama's path to the presidency was unlike that of any other chief executive, traditional or modern. This point is inevitably true for the son of a black man and a

President Obama's father came to the United States from Kenya to attend college at the University of Hawaii, where he met and married Stanley Ann Dunham, Obama's mother. The president has visited his Kenyan relatives several times, including this trip in 2006.

white woman, making him the first black president in American history. The president's early years also included far greater exposure to multicultural influences than most Americans experience, including four years of immersion in a non-Western culture followed by eight more in ethnically diverse Hawaii. A month's visit to Kenya just before he entered law school sought to resolve a lifelong confusion about his heritage, but it was not until he became firmly entrenched in Chicago that his identity as a black man became clearer. As David Maraniss (also the biographer of Bill Clinton) argues, "Hawaii and Chicago are the two main threads weaving through the cloth of Barack Obama's life. Each involves more than geography." [152] Hawaii shaped the boy; Chicago was the proving ground for his political skills. Much like Clinton's experience, Barack Obama's father—or more precisely his absence—stands at the center of the president's childhood; as a result, the president has been shaped by a series of strong women—his mother, his grandmother, and now his wife, Michelle. Restlessness characterizes his own life as well as those of his closest relatives—father, mother, grandparents—who were remarkably mobile.

On the day he was sworn into office, Obama registered many firsts, summarized again by Maraniss:

The first president to enter the White House with a literate and introspective memoir behind him, Obama is his own book of firsts. He is the first president with a foreign father. He is the first president to grow up in Hawaii, the 50th state. He is the first president whose parents earned doctoral degrees. He is the first president who once could speak the Indonesian language. He is the first president who was president of the Harvard Law Review. He is the first president who was a hapa, as they are called in Hawaii, with parents of different races. He is the first president who has a sister from Asia and a sister from Africa and a wife from the black working-class South Side of Chicago. And he is the first African American president, yet one with no slaves but a few slaveholders in his ancestry.[153]

Americans have become familiar with parts of this odyssey but are still learning much about their forty-fourth president.

The president's father, also named Barack Hussein Obama, arrived in the United States from Kenya as a student at the University of Hawaii in 1959, the first African student admitted to the school. A self-confident intellectual with an impressively deep speaking voice and political ambitions in Kenya, he impregnated and then married Stanley Ann Dunham, an unconventional first-year student originally from Kansas, whom he met in a Russian language class. The new family soon added a son, known during childhood as Barry. When Barry was two, his father left the family behind to pursue a graduate degree at Harvard University, much as he had left behind a child and pregnant wife when he moved from Kenya. Divorce followed within a year, and Barry saw his father only once more, a month-long visit to Hawaii when he was ten. The need to understand his heritage led Obama on a pilgrimage to Kenya when he learned more about his now-deceased father's frustrations and a life that fell short of the idealized image of greatness that Barack had carried throughout childhood.

After Ann Dunham remarried, this time to an Indonesian graduate student, the family left the United States, and Barry attended school from ages six to ten in Jakarta, Indonesia, a period little described in his speeches or writings.[154] It was during this time that his mother would wake Obama early in the morning to instruct him in a variety of subjects as a way to compensate for limitations in his Indonesian education. Barry returned to Hawaii in 1971 to live with his maternal grandparents and attend the Punahou School, a private college prep school where he was one of very few black students. His grandparents had moved frequently during their marriage, living in California, Texas, Oklahoma, and Washington State. His grandfather, a salesman, initially managed a furniture store and later sold insurance. His grandmother met with greater success, rising through the administrative ranks to become a vice president in a local bank. When Ann Dunham Soetoro returned from Indonesia with Barry's half-sister, Maya Soetoro, the family was reunited while his mother completed her education. She later returned to Indonesia to conduct research and begin her work with local artisans. Barack chose to remain behind, but mother and son worked at maintaining contact.[155] Soetoro later worked for the U.S. Agency for International Development and the Ford Foundation as a specialist in providing financial support for local artisans in Pakistan, India, and New York City, completing her Ph.D. in anthropology along the way.

Barry stayed behind to complete high school and play basketball, his true love, giving no indication of his future in politics. Unlike Clinton, there were no leadership roles or efforts to build networks that would later help him secure power. Nor was he a distinguished student—he got B's—enough to keep eligible to play basketball. He has acknowledged in his memoir, *Dreams from My Father*, that there was lots of partying, which included the use of illegal drugs. Obama attended Occidental College for two years and completed his undergraduate degree at Columbia University. By the time he arrived in New York City, he had shifted from using Barry to Barack.[156] He also developed greater self-discipline in his studies and his physical conditioning.[157] Arguably, his first independent political success came at Occidental when he delivered a speech during a rally supporting divestment from South Africa, a moment he reports in his autobiography. After a few brief post-graduation jobs, he became a community organizer in Harlem before moving to Chicago to do much of the same for three years. There, he learned first-hand about the power of black ministers, came to better understand his place in black America, and developed skills at grass-roots coalition building as he carried the message of self-help to groups that had been ignored by the political power structure.[158] But he came to realize that his impact was limited, something he sought to change. His big leap was to Harvard Law School where he was elected to serve as president of the *Harvard Law Review*, the first black student to serve in that capacity. One key to his success was the ability to speak with members of several competing camps among students, ranging from conservative ideologues to black radicals. As Laurence Tribe, the nationally known faculty member explained of Obama, who worked for him as a research assistant, "He just seems to have the surest way of calmly reaching across what are impenetrable barriers to many people."[159] Following graduation, he moved to Chicago to practice civil rights law and teach at the University of Chicago's law school.

He met his future wife, also a Harvard Law graduate, during a summer internship with an influential Chicago law firm. His persistence paid off when she overcame her initial reluctance and agreed to date him. Michelle Robinson was firmly rooted in Chicago's working-class black community, and she provided a foundation and steadiness that had been missing throughout most of Barack's life. They married in 1990 and settled in a mixed-race, mixed-income neighborhood not far from the University of Chicago.[160]

Chicago became the foundation for Obama's political career when at age thirty-five he won a seat in the Illinois Senate after navigating difficult political waters in 1996. He served in the Illinois legislature for eight years, widened his network of contacts, and established a respectable record of accomplishments while displaying considerable political ambition. In 2000 he lost a primary campaign in an effort to unseat a black Democratic incumbent in the U.S. House of Representatives; in 2001 he considered running for attorney general but withdrew from the campaign; in 2002 he began planning his campaign to wrest the U.S. Senate seat from the Republicans and secured the nomination against six opponents; he won the Illinois Senate seat in a race against Alan Keyes after the campaign of a wealthier Republican opponent collapsed when it was revealed he had frequented sex clubs. Obama waltzed to victory in 2004, a success that was capped by his first appearance on the national stage, his keynote address to the Democratic National Convention that electrified delegates in Boston and party loyalists around the country. Two years after entering the Senate, he declared himself a candidate for president, the final leg of a long journey, both geographically and personally.

Obama's prepresidential political experience was modest. Two of his four years in the Senate were spent on the presidential campaign trail and although he had star power in Washington, D.C., his role in Congress was modest, befitting a freshman. On the campaign trail, however, his short service in the Senate was portrayed as an asset—he had not yet succumbed to the allures of the nation's capital but had been there long enough to understand the many ways it needed to be changed. Moreover, Obama's personal gifts—confidence and intelligence, commanding and inspiring rhetoric, an unflappable manner, and a straightforward approach to solving problems—quickly laid to rest doubts about inexperience. His personal story— the focus of his speech to Democrats in 2004—reveals admirable persistence, enormous self-assurance, and a generous dollop of good luck, something one can neither inherit nor consciously develop as a skill. He proved remarkably successful in luring high-powered politicians from governors' mansions and the U.S. Senate into his cabinet, a sign that he inspires those with whom he works.

Obama is still untested as a manager. Senators seldom move directly from Capitol Hill to the White House (Obama is only the third in U.S. history), and managing a Senate staff pales in comparison to managing the Executive Office of the President, let alone the entire executive branch. Some observers expressed concern about the large number of prominent advisers that he assembled and whether the resulting clash of egos might prove difficult to tame. The early months of most administrations are the most difficult, beset with the pains of getting acclimated to new challenges, new team members, and new pressures. Presidency watchers will be observing closely to see how decisions are made and which aides and appointees emerge as the most powerful figures in the Obama administration. Will Obama be a delegator or someone who tries to do too much? Will he find time to think and work through issues, or will he be so heavily involved in selling his reform proposals that he loses the chance to improve them?

Although personally comfortable with international issues and well-liked overseas, Obama also is untested in high-pressure international negotiations. Perhaps his experience as a community organizer and in Chicago's bare-knuckle politics will prove readily transferable. Obama might also prove to be a fast learner or come to rely on able aides around him. The domestic challenges he confronts are enormous, but so are those on the international front, including one war winding down (Iraq), another heating up (Afghanistan), nuclear threats rising in Iran and North Korea, and pressures to redesign the international financial system. No president has entered office with a more challenging agenda, and international challenges are not even his worst problems. Indeed, the nation's hopes seem to rest heavily on this one man.

Conclusion: Seeking Presidential Success

Paul Quirk has posed a deceptively simple question: What does a president need to know? Quirk identifies a list of presidential competencies that could serve as the basis for making decisions about how best to allocate the president's time, energy, and talent as well as that of the White House staff and the innermost group of presidential advisers.[161] In Quirk's view, presidents require a minimal level of *substantive familiarity* so they can make intelligent choices among policy options. Moreover, presidents need a degree of *process sensibility* that reflects familiarity with how government decisions are made and carried out, as well as with how such systems might best be designed. Finally, presidents need the capacity for *policy promotion,* the means to achieve their goals through bargains with other Washington elites and through appeals for broad public support. Every president brings a different mix of personal competencies to the job and needs to compensate for personal weaknesses or to complement strengths with the help of others. In Quirk's view, it is critical that each president have a well-designed strategy for how to succeed, what Quirk terms *strategic competence.* This strategy involves decisions on how to allocate time, energy, and talent in relation to mastering substantive issues, delegating tasks, and establishing the prerequisites for successful delegation—for example, selecting personnel.[162]

How are these competencies developed? Implicitly, Quirk seems to suggest that experience in government at the federal level is a critical qualification for presidents. Without it, they have difficulty developing adequate levels of process sensibility and substantive familiarity. But Quirk's advice is directed more to presidents than to voters. Above all else, Quirk urges presidents to approach the office self-consciously, with an eye to developing a management strategy—know yourself and take the steps necessary for effectiveness. Only in this way can a president hope to achieve a measure of success. It is not clear how readily presidents will accept such advice. Are they likely to recognize their own shortcomings? One might expect that any newly elected president, imbued with ambition and flush with success, will proceed to the task of governing filled with self-confidence. Moreover, one might expect those presidents whose personalities drive them to pursue achievement will be least likely to undertake self-analysis.

In many respects, this chapter has explored a question similar to the one posed by Quirk: *What personal qualities make a successful president?* As we have seen, there are no simple answers. Competencies may be part of the solution, but so are temperament and attitudes. As this chapter demonstrates, we can only speculate on how the qualities necessary for success are derived from family background, career experience, personality, and beliefs. This is true in no small measure because success is the product of these personal qualities interacting with the constraints and opportunities of situations. Despite this fundamental uncertainty, there remains a pervasive confidence that the president's personal qualities have the utmost effect on performance in office, and, therefore, the American people are likely to continue their search for men and women with heroic qualities.

Suggested Readings

Barber, James David. *The Presidential Character,* 4th ed. Englewood Cliffs, N.J.: Prentice Hall, 1992.

George, Alexander L., and Juliette George. *Woodrow Wilson and Colonel House: A Personality Study.* New York: John Day, 1956.

————. *Presidential Personality and Performance.* Boulder: Westview, 1998.

Greenstein, Fred I. *Personality and Politics: Problems of Evidence, Inference, and Conceptualization.* New York: Norton, 1975.

————. *The Presidential Difference: Leadership Style from FDR to Clinton.* New York: Free Press, 2000.

Hargrove, Erwin. *Jimmy Carter as President: Leadership and the Politics of the Public Good.* Baton Rouge: Louisiana State University Press, 1988.

Kearns, Doris. *Lyndon Johnson and the American Dream.* New York: Harper and Row, 1976.

Maraniss, David. *First in His Class: The Biography of Bill Clinton.* New York: Simon and Schuster, 1995.

Mazlish, Bruce. *In Search of Nixon: A Psychohistorical Inquiry.* Baltimore: Pelican, 1973.

Pfiffner, James P. *The Character Factor: How We Judge America's Presidents.* College Station: Texas A&M University Press, 2004.

Renshon, Stanley A. *High Hopes: The Clinton Presidency and the Politics of Ambition.* New York: New York University Press, 1996.

————. *In His Father's Shadow: The Transformations of George W. Bush.* New York: Palgrave MacMillan, 2004.

Rockman, Bert A. *The Leadership Question: The Presidency and the American System.* New York: Praeger, 1984.

Schultz, William Todd. *Handbook of Psychobiography.* Oxford; New York: Oxford University Press, 2005.

Resources on the Web

C-SPAN, American Presidents: Life Portraits, www.americanpresidents.org/.

Miller Center of Public Affairs, American President: An Online Reference Resource, http://millercenter.org/academic/americanpresident.

White House site on American presidents, http://www.whitehouse.gov/about/presidents/.

Notes

1. Todd S. Purdum, "Striking Strengths, Glaring Failures," *New York Times,* December 24, 2000, A1.

2. When word of the alleged affair swept the nation in January 1998, Clinton publicly denied having a sexual relationship with "that woman," a position he also maintained in a legal deposition in a civil suit for sexual harassment that Paula Jones, a former Arkansas state employee, filed against him. But after a sustained grand jury investigation into whether his testimony constituted perjury, Clinton grudgingly admitted in a nationally televised speech on August 17, 1998, the relationship had been "wrong" and "not appropriate." This brief, 10 P.M. address concluded a day in which the president had answered questions for four hours before Kenneth Starr, the independent counsel appointed to look into allegations of wrongdoing. For a detailed analysis of the speech in light of Clinton's life, see David Maraniss, *The Clinton Enigma* (New York: Simon and Schuster, 1998). Jones's lawyers had been informed of the existence of secret tape recordings of telephone conversations between Lewinsky and Linda Tripp that described the affair. The lawyers were then able to probe the relationship and elicit the president's denial. Lewinsky had been working in the White House during the fall of 1995. One evening, a flirtatious relationship with the president turned into a sexual encounter in the Oval Office suite, followed by nine others over the next eighteen months. Excruciating details of these encounters were provided in Starr's report to the U.S. House of Representatives in September 1998. This report formed the basis for Clinton's subsequent impeachment.

3. Fred I. Greenstein, review of Stanley A. Renshon, *In His Father's Shadow: The Transformations of George W. Bush,* in *Presidential Studies Quarterly* 35 (September 2005): 623.

4. The most influential of these interpretations was offered by James David Barber, *The Presidential Character: Predicting Performance in the White House*, 4th ed. (Englewood Cliffs, N.J.: Prentice Hall, 1992).

5. Fred I. Greenstein, *The Presidential Difference: Leadership Style from FDR to Clinton* (New York: Free Press, 2000), 3.

6. Stephen Skowronek, *The Politics Presidents Make: Leadership from John Adams to George Bush* (Cambridge: Harvard University Press, 1993). For another work that deals with the importance of a president's environment, defined in a different way, see Bert A. Rockman, *The Leadership Question: The Presidency and the American System* (New York: Praeger, 1984).

7. Fred I. Greenstein, "Can Personality and Politics Be Studied Systematically?" *Political Psychology* 13, no. 1 (1992): 109. For a general discussion of studying personality and politics with special attention to the presidency, see Fred I. Greenstein, *Personality and Politics: Problems of Evidence, Inference, and Conceptualization*, 2nd ed. (New York: Norton, 1975); and Rockman, *The Leadership Question*.

8. See, for example, Colin Campbell and Bert A. Rockman, eds., *The Clinton Legacy* (Chatham, N.J.: Chatham House, 2000).

9. Bruce Buchanan, *The Citizen's Presidency* (Washington, D.C.: CQ Press, 1987), 102–104. Buchanan proposes a set of "competent process standards" that are more susceptible to empirical verification (108–134).

10. Bert A. Rockman, "Conclusions: An Imprint but Not a Revolution," in *The Reagan Revolution?* ed. B. B. Kymlicka and Jean V. Matthews (Chicago: Dorsey, 1988), 205. Other works in this vein, important because of the significance attributed to the Reagan experience, include the following: Larry Berman, ed., *Looking Back on the Reagan Presidency* (Baltimore: Johns Hopkins University Press, 1990); Sidney Blumenthal and Thomas Byrne Edsall, eds., *The Reagan Legacy* (New York: Pantheon Books, 1988); Charles O. Jones, ed., *The Reagan Legacy: Promise and Performance* (Chatham, N.J.: Chatham House, 1988); and John L. Palmer, ed., *Perspectives on the Reagan Years* (Washington, D.C.: Urban Institute, 1986).

11. James P. Pfiffner, *The Character Factor: How We Judge America's Presidents* (College Station: Texas A&M University Press, 2004).

12. Ibid., 19. See the table on page 21.

13. Ibid., 82–90. Pfiffner concludes that Clinton was reckless and irresponsible in his behavior and that he extended the effect of his lies by telling them to cabinet members and White House staff aides he knew would repeat the untruths. But the lies "did not constitute the same level of institutional threat to the polity that Watergate and Iran-Contra did." Ibid., 139.

14. Arthur Schlesinger's initial effort polled 55 scholars, and his second included 75, with historians constituting the greater part of each group. Gary Maranell and Richard Dodder's poll included results from 571 historians. The Murray-Blessing poll was based on 846 responses to a nineteen-page, 180-question survey sent to 1,997 Ph.D.-holding American historians with assistant professor rank (an additional 107 responses were returned late). The Lindgren-Calabresi survey included 78 presidential scholars from history, political science, and law with an explicit attempt to balance the sample based on ideology. The most recent poll by C-SPAN asked sixty-five historians and presidential specialists to evaluate all presidents on ten dimensions with a cumulative score and one for each dimension. For information on poll samples, see Henry J. Abraham, *Justices and Presidents* (New York: Oxford University Press, 1985), appendix B. For discussion of these efforts as well as their own, see Robert K. Murray and Tim H. Blessing, *Greatness in the White House: Rating the Presidents, Washington through Ronald Reagan*, 2nd updated ed. (University Park: Pennsylvania State University Press, 1994), chaps. 1 and 2. The ranking of Ronald Reagan was completed in 1988–1990 and is reported in this updated edition.

15. Murray and Blessing, *Greatness in the White House*, 24.

16. Tim H. Blessing and Anne A. Skleder, "Top Down: A General Overview of Present Research on Ronald Reagan's Doctrinal Presidency," in *Reassessing the Reagan Presidency*, ed. Richard S. Conley

(Lanham, Md.: University Press of America, 2003), 30. The authors report the results of an unpublished poll about Reagan similar to the poll conducted in 1990.

17. C-SPAN 2009 Historians Leadership Survey, http://www.c-span.org/PresidentialSurvey/presidential-leadership-survey.aspx.

18. Murray and Blessing, *Greatness in the White House*, 41–43, and appendix 8, 139. The personal traits conducive to success also were examined in terms of how they changed for different times. For the modern era, 1945 to the present, respondents ranked intelligence first and integrity second, with other qualities in declining order: sensitivity to popular demands, charisma, previous political experience, pleasing physical appearance, intense patriotism, and an aristocratic bearing.

19. Ibid., 63.

20. James MacGregor Burns, *Leadership* (New York: Harper and Row, 1977).

21. Greenstein, *The Presidential Difference*, 5–6.

22. Donald Matthews, *The Social Background of Political Decision Makers* (New York: Random House, 1954), 23.

23. Edward Pessen, *The Log Cabin Myth: The Social Backgrounds of the Presidents* (New Haven: Yale University Press, 1984), 56–57.

24. Ibid., 171.

25. Ibid., 56–63. Pessen views a family's class as a combination of wealth and possessions, income and occupational prestige, lifestyle, status, influence, and power. He recognizes, moreover, that analysts' characterizations are subjective.

26. Truman attended night classes at the Kansas City Law School, but it was a proprietary institution not then affiliated with a university. It is now part of the Law School of the University of Missouri–Kansas City.

27. Max Weber, "Politics as a Vocation," in *Max Weber: Essays in Sociology*, ed. H. H. Gerth and C. W. Mills (New York: Oxford University Press, 1946), 85.

28. Hugh Montgomery-Massingberd, ed., *Burke's Presidential Families of the U.S.A.* (London: Burke's Peerage, 1975), 250.

29. Ibid., 320.

30. Robert Donovan, *Conflict and Crisis: The Presidency of Harry S Truman, 1945–48* (New York: Praeger, 1977), chap. 40. It should also be noted that military officers have demonstrated leadership skills and may be called on to develop substantial political skill while building careers or in dealing with foreign leaders. Eisenhower, for example, did both.

31. Pessen, *The Log Cabin Myth*, 171.

32. E. Digby Baltzell and Howard G. Schneiderman, "Social Class in the Oval Office," *Society* 26 (September/October 1988): 42–49. The ranking of presidential performance used in this study was conducted by Robert K. Murray and Tim H. Blessing and was first published in the *Journal of American History* 70 (December 1983): 535–555.

33. Baltzell and Schneiderman, "Social Class in the Oval Office," 47.

34. W. H. Harrison and Garfield were not rated because of the brief time they served in office.

35. Baltzell and Schneiderman, "Social Class in the Oval Office," 49.

36. Richard E. Neustadt, *Presidential Power and the Modern Presidents* (New York: Free Press, 1991), 151.

37. Ibid., 205.

38. Rockman, *The Leadership Question*, 212. Rockman uses a performance ranking compiled by the *Chicago Tribune* in 1982.

39. We are indebted to Leonard P. Stark for this account and continuing stimulation on the subject of presidential personality. See his senior honors thesis, "Personality and Presidential Selection: Evaluating Character and Experience in the 1988 Election" (University of Delaware, 1991), 47–48. Barber's article was "The Question of Presidential Character," *Saturday Review*, September 23, 1972, 62–66.

40. Greenstein, *Personality and Politics,* 3.

41. Alexander L. George and Juliette George, *Woodrow Wilson and Colonel House: A Personality Study* (New York: John Day, 1956); Doris Kearns Goodwin, *Lyndon Johnson and the American Dream* (New York: Harper and Row, 1976); Bruce Mazlish, *In Search of Nixon: A Psychohistorical Inquiry* (Baltimore: Pelican, 1973); Betty Glad, *Jimmy Carter: In Search of the Great White House* (New York: Norton, 1980); and Stanley A. Renshon, *High Hopes: The Clinton Presidency and the Politics of Ambition* (New York: NYU Press, 1996). For an excellent biography of Clinton that provides psychological insights but is not informed by psychological theory, see David Maraniss, *First in His Class: A Biography of Bill Clinton* (New York: Simon and Schuster, 1995).

42. For an extended discussion, see Greenstein's treatment of these issues in *Personality and Politics,* chaps. 3 and 4, as well as the introduction.

43. See, for example, Alexander L. George's discussion of Barber's book *The Presidential Character* in George, "Assessing Presidential Character," *World Politics* 26 (January 1974): 234–282. This essay is reprinted with several related essays in Alexander L. George and Juliette George, *Presidential Personality and Performance* (Boulder: Westview, 1998), 145–197.

44. For recent efforts to rebut critics, see Betty Glad, "Political Leadership: Some Methodological Considerations," in *Political Leadership for the New Century: Personality and Behavior Among American Leaders,* ed. Linda O. Valenty and Ofer Feldman (Westport, Conn.: Praeger, 2002), 9–23; Paul A. Kowert, "Where 'Does' the Buck Stop? Assessing the Impact of Presidential Personality," *Political Psychology* 17 (September 1996): 421–452.

45. Although the call of conservatives during the Reagan years was "let Reagan be Reagan," Clinton's aides had begun the practice during his gubernatorial years of "protect[ing] Clinton from Clinton." See Maraniss, *The Clinton Enigma,* 60.

46. Barber, *The Presidential Character,* 34.

47. James David Barber, "Predicting Hope with Clinton at Helm," *News & Observer* (Raleigh, N.C.), January 17, 1993. Barber did not offer a preliminary evaluation of George H. W. Bush.

48. Barber, *The Presidential Character,* 5.

49. Ibid.

50. Barber, "Predicting Hope."

51. Stanley A. Renshon, "A Preliminary Assessment of the Clinton Presidency: Character, Leadership, and Performance," *Political Psychology* 15, no. 2 (1994): 375–394. Also see a slightly revised version of the paper in *The Clinton Presidency: Campaigning, Governing, and the Psychology of Leadership,* ed. Stanley A. Renshon (Boulder: Westview, 1995), 57–87. Also see Renshon, *High Hopes.*

52. Renshon, "Preliminary Assessment," 381, 380, 382.

53. Greenstein, *The Presidential Difference,* 255.

54. Greenstein, *Personality and Politics,* 19.

55. Fred I. Greenstein, *The Hidden-Hand Presidency* (New York: Basic Books, 1982). Barber, however, responded that the new evidence confirms his original analysis even more fully. See Barber, *The Presidential Character,* 522–525.

56. See George, "Assessing Presidential Character"; and Michael Nelson, "The Psychological Presidency," in *The Presidency and the Political System,* 4th ed., ed. Michael Nelson (Washington, D.C.: CQ Press, 1995).

57. Dean Keith Simonton, *Why Presidents Succeed: A Political Psychology of Leadership* (New Haven: Yale University Press, 1987), 151–152.

58. Barber, *The Presidential Character,* 487.

59. Ibid., 298.

60. Ibid., 296–299.

61. Jeffrey Tulis, "On Presidential Character," in *The Presidency in the Constitutional Order*, ed. Jeffrey Tulis and Joseph M. Bessette (Baton Rouge: Louisiana State University Press, 1981), 283–313.

62. For another effort at guiding electoral choice, see Stanley A. Renshon, *The Psychological Assessment of Presidential Candidates* (New York: New York University Press, 1996).

63. Clark Clifford, "The Presidency as I Have Seen It," in *The Living Presidency*, ed. Emmet John Hughes (New York: Coward, McCann, and Geoghegan, 1973), 315, cited by Greenstein in *The Presidential Difference*, 189.

64. This dichotomy is captured by Peri E. Arnold, "The Presidency as Individual and Collective," *The Review of Politics* 49 (Summer 1987): 432–434, a review of Colin Campbell, *Managing the Presidency: Carter, Reagan and the Search for Executive Harmony.*

65. U.S. Office of Personnel Management, "Federal Civilian Employment and Payroll by Branch, Selected Agency, and Area, January 2007," Table 9, www.opm.gov/feddata/html/2007/january/table9.asp.

66. Joseph A. Pika, "Management Style and the Organizational Matrix: Studying White House Operations," *Administration and Society* 20, no. 1 (May 1988): 11.

67. John Hart, *The Presidential Branch: From Washington to Clinton* (Chatham, N.J.: Chatham House, 1995).

68. Alexander L. George, *Presidential Decisionmaking in Foreign Policy* (Boulder: Westview, 1980), 139–168.

69. See Richard Tanner Johnson, *Managing the White House* (New York: Harper and Row, 1974). Also see Johnson, "Presidential Style," in *Perspectives on the Presidency*, ed. Aaron Wildavsky (Boston: Little, Brown, 1975).

70. Charles E. Walcott and Karen M. Hult, "White House Structure and Decision Making: Elaborating the Standard Model," *Presidential Studies Quarterly* 35 (June 2005): 303–318.

71. Roger Porter, "A Healing Presidency," in *Leadership in the Modern Presidency*, ed. Fred I. Greenstein (Cambridge: Harvard University Press, 1988), 218.

72. George, *Presidential Decisionmaking*, 159.

73. Colin Campbell, *Managing the Presidency: Carter, Reagan, and the Search for Executive Harmony* (Pittsburgh: University of Pittsburgh Press, 1986), 93–111; James Pfiffner, *The Strategic Presidency: Hitting the Ground Running* (Chicago: Dorsey, 1988), 30–37; and Buchanan, *The Citizen's Presidency*, 124–133.

74. Stanley A. Renshon, *In His Father's Shadow: The Transformations of George W. Bush* (New York: Palgrave MacMillan, 2004), 126–127 and 256, n 96. Others have suggested that Bush recreated a "troika" with aides Andrew Card, Karen Hughes, and Karl Rove, or that there were six aides with direct access to him: those three plus Vice President Cheney, Condoleezza Rice, and Alberto Gonzales. See Andrew Rudalevige, "'The Decider': Issue Management and the Bush White House," in *The George W. Bush Legacy*, ed. Colin Campbell, Bert A. Rockman, and Andrew Rudalevige (Washington, D.C.: CQ Press, 2007), 135–163.

75. See especially the dramatic case of Bush's decision, at Cheney's urging, to deny foreign terrorism suspects access to U.S. courts, as described in Barton Gellman and Jo Becker, "'A Different Understanding with the President,'" *Washington Post*, June 24, 2007, A1.

76. Karl Rove, "The Obama White House Might Be a Crowded Mess," *Wall Street Journal*, January 29, 2009, http://online.wsj.com/article/SB123318823268126605.html.

77. Alexander L. George and Eric Stern, "Presidential Management Styles and Models," in George and George, *Presidential Personality and Performance*, 263.

78. Walcott and Hult, "White House Structure and Decision Making," 313.

79. Alexander L. George, "The Case for Multiple Advocacy in Making Foreign Policy," *American Political Science Review* 66 (September 1972): 751–785. Also see George, *Presidential Decisionmaking*, chap. 11.

80. George, *Presidential Decisionmaking*, 203, 203–204.

81. Alexander L. George and Eric K. Stern, "Harnessing Conflict in Foreign Policy Making: From Devil's Advocate to Multiple Advocacy," *Presidential Studies Quarterly* 32 (September 2002): 490.

82. Discussions of the standard model (hierarchical) frequently link its purported benefits to systematic review of options by diverse advisers, a vital element of multiple advocacy. Walcott and Hult, "White House Structure and Decision Making," 314–316.

83. Ibid., 201.

84. Paul A. Kowert, *Groupthink or Deadlock: When Do Leaders Learn from Their Advisers?* (Albany: State University of New York Press, 2002), 4, 23.

85. Ibid., chap. 6.

86. George, *Presidential Decisionmaking,* 204.

87. Maraniss, *First in His Class,* 38.

88. Greenstein, "Two Leadership Styles," 358.

89. Jerome D. Levin, *The Clinton Syndrome: The President and the Self-Destructive Nature of Sexual Addiction* (Rocklin, Calif.: Prima, 1998), 5.

90. Maraniss, *First in His Class,* 88.

91. Ibid., 357.

92. Ibid., 362.

93. Maraniss, *The Clinton Enigma,* 14.

94. Ibid., 42–43.

95. Greenstein, *The Presidential Difference,* 174, 199.

96. Maraniss, *The Clinton Enigma,* 43.

97. Greenstein, *The Presidential Difference,* 200.

98. Purdum, "Striking Strengths," A1.

99. Maraniss, *First in His Class,* 124, 199, 355.

100. Purdum, "Striking Strengths," A13.

101. Michael J. Kelly, "A Man Who Wants to Be Liked, and Is: William Jefferson Blythe Clinton," *New York Times,* November 4, 1992, A1; Michael J. Kelly, "The President's Past," *New York Times Magazine,* July 31, 1994, 25.

102. Quoted in Purdum, "Striking Strengths," A1.

103. Jann S. Wenner and William Greider, "The Rolling Stone Interview: Bill Clinton," *Rolling Stone,* December 9, 1993, 40.

104. Bert A. Rockman, "Leadership Style and the Clinton Presidency," in *The Clinton Presidency: First Appraisals,* ed. Colin Campbell and Bert A. Rockman (Chatham, N.J.: Chatham House, 1996), 9; and Maraniss, *First in His Class,* 347.

105. Kelly, "President's Past," 45.

106. Graham K. Wilson, "The Clinton Administration and Interest Groups," in Campbell and Rockman, *The Clinton Presidency: First Appraisals,* 220.

107. Rockman, "Leadership Style," 355.

108. Jason DeParle and Steven A. Holmes, "A War on Poverty Subtly Linked to Race," *New York Times,* December 26, 2000, A1.

109. Maraniss, *First in His Class,* 293, 349.

110. The three were the suicide of fellow Rhodes scholar Frank Aller, which came on the heels of Clinton's own personal torment over the Vietnam draft; his crushing defeat when he sought reelection after his first term as governor; and the arrest of his half-brother, Roger Clinton, for cocaine dealing. The latter episode produced an extensive round of counseling and the family's first open discussion of how it had been affected by his stepfather's alcoholism. During this period Clinton reportedly recognized how his own dislike of personal conflict and his desire to please were linked with his family experience. Ibid., 422.

111. Greenstein, "Two Leadership Styles," 357.

112. Two multipart series on the life and preparation of George W. Bush, originally published in the *Washington Post* in 1999 and 2000, provide much of the background for this sketch. Both can be found on the paper's Web site, http://www.washingtonpost.com/wp-srv/onpolitics/shoulderbox/bushseries 1999.htm. Separate installments are cited where appropriate. There are also several book-length analyses of Bush, including Renshon, *In His Father's Shadow*.

113. Lois Romano and George Lardner Jr., "Part 2: Tragedy Created Bush Mother-Son Bond," *Washington Post*, July 26, 1999, A1.

114. Renshon, "In His Father's Shadow," in *Handbook of Psychobiography* ed. William Todd Schultz (Oxford; New York: Oxford University Press, 2005), 327–330.

115. Hugh Heclo, "The Bush Political Ethos" (paper prepared for the conference on "The George W. Bush Presidency: An Early Assessment," Woodrow Wilson School, Princeton University, April 25–26, 2003), 2.

116. Romano and Lardner, "Part 3: A So-So Student but a Campus Mover," *Washington Post*, July 27, 1999, A1.

117. Romano and Lardner, "Part 4: At Height of Vietnam, Bush Picks Guard," *Washington Post*, July 28, 1999, A1.

118. Renshon, "In His Father's Shadow," 325–326.

119. Romano and Lardner, "Part 5: Young Bush, A Political Natural, Revs Up," *Washington Post*, July 29, 1999, A1.

120. Heclo, "The Bush Political Ethos," 5.

121. Romano and Lardner, "Part 6: Bush Name Helps Fuel Oil Dealings," *Washington Post*, July 30, 1999, A1.

122. Ibid.

123. The reawakening of Bush's spirituality can also be traced to his participation in a weekly men's Bible study group organized in Midland. See Hanna Rosin, "Applying Personal Faith to Public Policy," *Washington Post*, July 24, 2000, A1.

124. This incident was revealed late in the 2000 campaign by a Fox-affiliate news reporter in Maine, temporarily throwing the Bush campaign off-balance. In 1976 Bush admitted to drinking too many beers at a local bar in Kennebunkport and being pulled over for driving erratically. He was fined $150 and had his driving privileges suspended in Maine for thirty days. They were not restored until 1978 because he was unable to attend a required rehabilitation program. Bush explained that he had not revealed the incident earlier because he sought to protect his daughters from learning of their father's dangerous behavior. See Dan Balz, "Bush Acknowledges 1976 DUI Arrest," *Washington Post*, November 3, 2000, A1; and Steven A. Kurkjian and David Armstrong, "Bush Downplayed Drinking: '78 Comments Got License Back," *Boston Globe*, November 4, 2000, A11.

125. Romano and Lardner, "Part 1: Bush's Life-Changing Year," *Washington Post*, July 25, 1999, A1. Bush has resolutely refused to answer reporters' questions on whether he engaged in illegal drug use. He has unequivocally declared his faithfulness to his wife but has not assumed a similar position on drug usage. Needless to say, this stance spurs media curiosity. For an extensive examination of this question and how it became an issue in the 2000 election, see Felicity Barringer, "When an Old Drug Question Becomes New News," *New York Times*, August 22, 1999.

126. Heclo, "The Bush Political Ethos," 18.

127. Renshon, "In His Father's Shadow," 341.

128. Rosin, "Applying Personal Faith," A1.

129. Dana Milbank, "Dispelling Doubts with the Rangers," *Washington Post*, July 25, 2000, A1.

130. Romano and Lardner, "Part 7: Bush's Move Up to the Majors," *Washington Post*, July 31, 1999, A1.

131. Ibid.

132. Exit polls showed Bush winning 46 percent of the Hispanic vote, an all-time high for a statewide Republican candidate. See R. G. Ratcliffe, "Election 98: Bush Leads Statewide GOP Blitz," *Houston Chronicle*, November 4, 1998, A1.

133. Romano and Lardner, "Part 1: Bush's Life-Changing Year," A1.

134. Heclo, "The Bush Political Ethos," 6–7.

135. Lois Romano, "A Fierce Loyalty Marks Bush's Inner Circle," *Washington Post*, July 26, 2000, A1. On Evans, see Elisabeth Bumiller, "Texas Pals Are Still Sharing Adventures," *New York Times*, May 26, 2003, www.nytimes.com/2003/05/26/ national/26LETT.html.

136. Ivo H. Daalder and James M. Lindsay, "The Bush Revolution: The Remaking of America's Foreign Policy" (paper presented at the conference on "The George W. Bush Presidency: An Early Assessment" Woodrow Wilson School, Princeton University, April 25–26, 2003), 7.

137. Hanna Rosin, "Bush's Resentment of 'Elites' Informs Bid," *Washington Post*, July 23, 2000, A1.

138. See the story of Bush's deciding to run for governor in Romano and Lardner, "Part 7: Bush's Move Up to the Majors," A1.

139. See the experience of Joseph Allbaugh, Bush's campaign manager in 1994, as reported in ibid.

140. Heclo, "The Bush Political Ethos," 19.

141. Fred I. Greenstein, "The Leadership Style of George W. Bush" (paper presented at the conference on "The George W. Bush Presidency: An Early Assessment," Woodrow Wilson School, Princeton University, April 25–26, 2003), 12, 16.

142. For a thoughtful discussion of the generational and Christian influences on Bush's thinking, see the two articles by Hanna Rosin published in the *Washington Post* (cited in notes 123 and 137).

143. Daalder and Lindsay, "The Bush Revolution," 1.

144. John P. Burke, "From Success to Failure? Iraq and the Organization of George W. Bush's Decision Making," in *The Polarized Presidency*, ed. George C. Edwards III and Desmond S. King (Oxford; New York: Oxford University Press, 2007), 173–212.

145. Rudalevige, " 'The Decider,' " 151–156.

146. In their thoughtful evaluations of the Bush administration, both Greenstein and Heclo identify Bush's ability to fashion public and international support for the administration's policy visions as the principal unanswered question for this presidency. Greenstein, "The Leadership Style of George W. Bush," 25; Heclo, "The Bush Political Ethos," 25–26.

147. Jason D. Mycoff and Joseph A. Pika, *Confrontation and Compromise: Presidential and Congressional Leadership, 2001–2006* (Lanham, Md.: Rowman and Littlefield, 2007), chap. 7.

148. Ibid., 21.

149. Glad, "Political Leadership."

150. Renshon, *In His Father's Shadow*, 142.

151. Ibid., 145.

152. David Maraniss, "Though Obama Had to Leave to Find Himself, It Was Hawaii that Made His Rise Possible," *Washington Post*, August 24, 2008, 22. On Obama's childhood, also see Jennifer Steinhauer, "Charisma and a Search for Self in Obama's Hawaii Childhood," *New York Times*, March 17, 2007, http://www.nytimes.com/2007/03/17/us/politics/17hawaii.html?_r=1.

153. David Maraniss, "Restless Searcher on an Improbable Path," *Washington Post*, January 20, 2009, A4.

154. For a fascinating look at which parts of Obama's life have been explored by himself and the media, see Slate.com's interactive timeline constructed by Christopher Beam and Chris Wilson at http://www.slate.com/id/2196908.

155. Janny Scott, "A Free-Spirited Wanderer Who Set Obama's Path," *New York Times*, March 14, 2008, http://www.nytimes.com/2008/03/14/us/politics/14obama.html?pagewanted=1.

156. Richard Wolffe, Jessica Ramirez, and Jeffrey Bartholet, "When Barry Became Barack," *Newsweek,* March 31, 2008, http://www.newsweek.com/id/128633/page/1.

157. Janny Scott, "Obama's Account of New York Years Often Differs From What Others Say," *New York Times,* October 30, 2007, http://wwww.nytimes.com/2007/10/30/us/politics/30obama.html.

158. Serge Kovaleski, "Obama's Organizing Years, Guiding Others and Finding Himself," *New York Times,* July 7, 2008, http://www.nytimies.com/2008/07/07/us/politics/07community.html.

159. As quoted in Amanda Ripley, "Obama's Ascent," *Time,* November 3, 2004, http://www.time.com/time/magazine/article/0,9171,750742-2,00.html.

160. Kenneth T. Walsh, "Obama's Years in Chicago Politics Shaped His Presidential Candidacy," *U.S. News and World Report,* April 11, 2008, http://www.usnews.com/articles/news/campaign-2008/04/11/obamas-years-in-chicago-politics-shaped-his-presidential-candidacy.html?PageNr=1.

161. Paul Quirk, "Presidential Competence," in *The Presidency and the Political System,* 7th ed., ed. Michael Nelson (Washington, D.C.: CQ Press, 2003), 158–189; and Paul Quirk, "What Must a President Know?" *Transactional Society* 23 (January/February 1983).

162. Quirk, "Presidential Competence."

CHAPTER 5

Legislative Politics

During his first address to a joint session of Congress, President Obama sought to boost the confidence of the American people by promising that "though we are living through difficult and uncertain times ... we will rebuild, we will recover, and the United States of America will emerge stronger than before."

Presidents can not govern alone, but the necessary partnership with Congress is often uneasy, and relations between the president and Congress frequently provide the nation with high political drama. These two branches must cooperate to pass laws, adopt budgets, enter into international treaties, declare wars, and appoint officials to the executive branch. In most cases, the institutions must find a compromise position but sometimes engage in painful confrontations. Before reviewing the full context of legislative-executive relations, we briefly review four particularly contentious cases drawn from the Clinton and Bush years.

Four Confrontations in Interbranch Relations

When Bill Clinton and the Republican-controlled Congress could not reach agreement on a new budget, the federal government shut down twice during the winter of 1995–1996. Even more dramatic was the winter of 1998–1999, when Clinton became only the second president in American history to be impeached by the House and survive a Senate trial. George W. Bush signed a massive tax-cut bill into law on June 7, 2001, fulfilling a campaign pledge, but in the process lost a Republican majority in the Senate. Finally, when Republicans lost control of Congress during the midterm elections of 2006, Bush confronted an effort led by Democrats to force changes in U.S. policy toward Iraq.

The Budget Battle, 1995–1996

Both the president and Congress must approve national budgets. When they disagree over spending priorities, conflict can easily escalate. On November 17, 1995, the Republican-controlled 104th Congress enacted a bill designed to balance the budget by 2002 through spending cuts in several major programs—Medicare, Medicaid, and other welfare programs—as well as education, job training, and environmental protection. The bill also would have cut taxes by $245 billion during the same period. Democrats objected, but were outvoted in both the House and the Senate.[1] President Clinton, who supported the goal of a balanced budget, vetoed the bill, and subsequent negotiations with Republican leaders of Congress failed to produce an agreement on how to achieve that goal. To put greater pressure on the president, congressional Republicans refused to authorize the government to borrow funds needed to pay its obligations, raising the threat that the U.S. government would fail to honor its debts.

At the heart of this confrontation was a philosophical disagreement over the role of the federal government. Clinton and the Republicans both wanted a balanced budget, but they offered different time frames (Clinton ten years, Congress seven years) and did not agree on the size of tax and spending cuts. And the president rejected Republican demands to reduce the federal commitment to major social programs.

Before the two sides reached a political truce, the government shut down twice: 800,000 federal employees stayed home November 14–20, 1995, and 280,000 from December 16 to January 5, 1996. Permanent appropriations did not become final until April 1996.[2] In their struggle with Clinton, Republicans believed he would accept their terms rather than allow the government to shut down or default on its obligations. To everyone's surprise, Clinton proved resolute. Secretary of the Treasury Robert Rubin was able to use certain trust funds under his control to prevent default. Clinton's response laid the groundwork for his reelection in 1996 as the public placed more of the blame for the shutdowns on Congress than on the president.

The Impeachment Battle, 1998–1999

The Constitution empowers Congress to remove a president from office, a step never taken in American history. But it has been attempted twice, most recently with Bill Clinton. On December 19, 1998, the House approved two articles of impeachment against him. By a 228-206 vote, the House accused the president of lying under oath while giving testimony to a grand jury in August 1999 and, by a 221-212 vote, accused him of obstructing justice by hiding his improper relationship with a White House intern. These votes came at the end of a lengthy investigation by independent counsel Kenneth Starr. He had expanded his investigation of Clinton's involvement in Whitewater, a failed land development project in Arkansas, to include other subjects of alleged wrongdoing.[3] Starr questioned Clinton's testimony in connection with a civil suit brought against him by Paula Jones, a former Arkansas state employee who had accused Governor Clinton of making unwanted sexual advances in 1991. To document a pattern of sexual harassment with other state or federal employees, Jones's lawyers posed questions to the president about his relationship with former White House intern Monica Lewinsky. When Clinton denied the existence of that relationship in a court deposition and subsequently misrepresented it to the public and a grand jury, the ground was set for a constitutional confrontation.

Starr subpoenaed Clinton and deposed him by closed-circuit television on August 17, 1998, the first instance of such testimony by a sitting president. In September the independent counsel filed a report with Congress (and released it, replete with salacious details, to the public) that formed the basis for the House Judiciary Committee's recommendation, in a straight party vote, that the House conduct an impeachment inquiry. Throughout this saga, the meaning of "high crimes and misdemeanors," the constitutional grounds for removing a president, remained a central question. Advocates of removal believed that Clinton had undermined the "rule of law" enforced by the courts; defenders of the president believed that personal misconduct did not constitute a threat to the Republic.[4] "Clinton turned the struggle into a question of whether a president who was performing well should be removed for actions unconnected to his official duties."[5]

The Senate began the impeachment trial on January 7, 1999. Thirteen Republican members of the House served as managers and had three days to present their case; the president's legal team responded over three days. Although the House managers were distressed that Republicans in the Senate seemed less committed to removal than they were, Majority Leader Trent Lott realized how difficult it would be to generate the two-thirds majority needed for removal when the Democrats held forty-five seats. Test votes showed that only one Democrat might cross party lines, not the dozen needed for conviction. When the House managers wanted a long list of witnesses to publicly testify to the president's immoral behavior, the Senate instead approved a short list of witnesses who were deposed in private, and their videotaped testimony was available only to Senate members.[6] In the end, neither article of impeachment received even a majority vote on February 12, when the Senate concluded its consideration. The president survived, but impeachment will always help define his place in history.

Bush's 2001 Tax Cut Victory and Senate Setback

George W. Bush entered office with something no Republican president had enjoyed since 1955—a Republican majority in the House and the Senate. Despite repeated success in winning presidential elections and controlling the White House for two extended periods (1969–1977 and 1981–1993), the Republicans had not controlled both elected branches of government since the two years following Dwight D. Eisenhower's first electoral victory in 1952. But Bush's working majorities were small: nine votes in the House and only one in the evenly divided Senate, a vote to be cast by the vice president in the event of a tie.[7] Bush's hotly contested electoral victory was expected to produce a difficult working relationship with Democrats in Congress, and Bush initially promoted bipartisanship and projected a nonconfrontational tone, the so-called "charm offensive."[8] Ultimately, however, the president proposed a relatively aggressive agenda that would rise or fall based largely on Republican votes. In short, he sought to "hit the ground running" with a focused legislative agenda that could be accomplished while his influence remained high.[9]

House Republicans were especially unified during the early months, adopting Bush's budget proposals and most of his $1.6 trillion tax-cut proposal with only modest changes. Senate Republicans proved less cooperative when two moderates refused to support the proposed budget because of the large tax cut, and Arizona senator John McCain, Bush's opponent for the Republican nomination in 2000, continued to assert his independence.[10] But, with the support of several moderate Democrats, Bush achieved his primary legislative priority and campaign promise—tax relief. The cuts were close to the original proposal ($1.35 trillion), as were many of the details. Bush stressed the historic nature of the moment when he noted at the signing ceremony, "Tax relief does not happen often in Washington. . . . In fact, since World War II, it has happened only twice: President Kennedy's tax cut in the 60's and President Reagan's tax cuts in the 1980's."[11]

Many Republicans worried about the long-term consequences of this victory. Sen. James M. Jeffords, R-Vt., announced on May 24, just two days before the House and Senate approved the tax-cut bill, that he would become an independent and vote with the Democrats for organizational purposes. His decision meant that Republicans would lose control of the Senate and give the Democrats an opportunity to define the agenda, block nominations, conduct investigations, and derail administration-sponsored legislation. Jeffords objected to bullying tactics used by the White House and Republican leaders to pressure him to adhere to the party line in critical votes. He was also reportedly disappointed that the president had not committed more money for special education, a program of particular concern to him as chair of the Health, Education, Labor, and Pensions Committee.[12] Jeffords's public statement emphasized the growing distance between the Republican Party's national agenda and his own brand of Republicanism, which stressed the principles of "moderation, tolerance, and fiscal responsibility."[13] Bush, many argued, had placed such emphasis on maintaining support from the party's conservative wing that moderates felt their views on abortion, the environment, energy, judicial appointments, and missile defense were already being ignored and would not be respected in the future. Although the Republicans gained a Senate seat in 2002 and thereby regained a majority, the earlier victory had proved costly.

Democrats Oppose Bush's Iraq War

In 2006 the Democrats took back control in the House and Senate. Fresh from their election victories, members of the new majorities were determined to change policy in Iraq by shifting the combat role from U.S. forces to the Iraqis and bring U.S. forces home. Shortly after the 110th Congress was sworn in, President Bush announced on January 10, 2007, in a prime-time speech to the nation, a new strategy of his own—"the surge." The plan would commit 28,500 additional U.S. combat troops who would employ different tactics in an effort to reduce sectarian violence and build confidence in the new Iraqi government. Democrats were unconvinced that the strategy would work and instead described it as an "escalation," a term drawn from the Vietnam era. Some critics feared that the new policy would widen the war and lead to conflict with Syria and Iran. Strong voices in the antiwar movement urged the Democrats to force the president to cancel the surge and withdraw all American forces from Iraq. Pledging to remain true to the public's verdict in the previous election, Democrats faced a range of possibilities:

Should Congress deny Bush the funds he would need to increase the U.S. forces in Iraq? Should it give him the money, but with a slew of conditions and strings attached? Should it limit the number of troops? Cut off the funding for the war completely? Or simply issue a politically devastating vote of no confidence, with lawmakers from both parties joining in, and hope that's enough to get Bush to back down?[14]

At the heart of this confrontation was the president's constitutional authority to exercise his powers as commander in chief versus Congress's constitutional authority to shape policy.

Democrats were also divided and failed to shape a common policy. On February 16, House Democrats, joined by a limited number of Republicans, voted 246-182 in favor of a nonbinding resolution that opposed the troop increase. Senate Republicans used procedural tactics to block a similar effort. Liberal Democrats urged their colleagues to cut off funding for the war, impose mandatory deadlines for withdrawal, or require another congressional vote to reauthorize the use of force rather than rely on the favorable October 2002 vote. Moderate colleagues were less willing to force the president's hand and were fearful of endangering the forces already in place. Even Republicans critical of the president's policies were unwilling to adopt language that allowed Congress to "micromanage" the war and reduce the president's control.

The political conflict at home continued on with funding bills serving as the main battlefield. Bush needed additional money to continue the war and Democrats kept adding provisions that were unacceptable to the president, resulting in a May 1 veto, only his second to that point. Neither the House nor the Senate could muster the two-thirds vote required for an override. After extensive negotiations with the White House, Congress met the president's demand to remove timelines for withdrawing troops from Iraq and established instead eighteen benchmarks for the Iraqi government to meet. The bill required the president to provide Congress with July and September reports on Iraqi performance in meeting these benchmarks.

Democrats continued their efforts to force a change in policy, this time using the Defense Department's authorization and appropriations bills for fiscal year 2008 as the vehicle for pressuring the White House.[15]

What do these four cases demonstrate? The solutions to major national problems require that Congress act in concert with the president, but Congress is seldom a fully cooperative partner in shaping solutions, which sets the stage for the kind of dramatic confrontations detailed above. This chapter traces the development of the chief executive's legislative role in the twentieth century and analyzes the constitutional relationship between the president and Congress. A discussion of the president's formal legislative powers and a description of presidential strategies to influence legislation follow. The chapter then analyzes what factors contribute to the success and failure of presidents in gaining their legislative goals.

Development of the President's Legislative Role

The Constitution, in Article 1, section 8, grants Congress seventeen powers that cover a wide range of subjects—for example, levying and collecting taxes, borrowing money, and regulating foreign and interstate commerce—as well as the power to choose the means to execute the enumerated powers. Clearly, the framers expected Congress, not the president, to have primary responsibility for formulating national policy and the president's legislative role to be secondary. Until the twentieth century, most presidents limited their involvement in the congressional process. Even Thomas Jefferson and Abraham Lincoln, the two most inclined to lead Congress, encountered strong opposition, and their activism did not alter the pattern of congressional supremacy.[16]

Theodore Roosevelt and Woodrow Wilson greatly expanded the presidency's legislative role early in the twentieth century as the national government responded to rapid industrialization and urbanization. Roosevelt worked closely with congressional leaders and sent several messages to Congress that defined a legislative program. He saw it as the duty of the president to "take a very active interest in getting the right kind of legislation."[17] Wilson, who as a political science professor had argued that strong presidential leadership of Congress was needed if the nation were to cope with its growing problems, took the lead in defining his program's goals, helped formulate bills, reinstated the practice abandoned by Jefferson of personally delivering the State of the Union message to Congress, used cabinet members to build congressional support for bills, and personally lobbied for some of his most important measures, such as the Federal Reserve Act and the Clayton Antitrust Act.[18] (See chapter 1.)

Franklin D. Roosevelt undertook the next major expansion of the president's legislative role. Taking office in 1933, with the economy mired in the Great Depression, FDR called Congress into a special session; during a hundred-day period the president proposed, and Congress passed, legislation to meet the economic crisis. Together they overhauled the banking system, authorized a program of industrial self-government under the National Recovery Administration, buttressed farm income with the Agricultural Adjustment Act, regulated financial markets under the Truth in Securities Act, and created the Tennessee Valley Authority, a program of comprehensive development of one of the nation's most depressed areas. This period of unprecedented activity established the practice of assessing a new president's first one hundred days.

During the remainder of his first term, FDR continued to develop measures to promote soil conservation and restrict excess agricultural production; guarantee labor the right to organize and bargain collectively; and establish a system of social insurance to protect people against the loss of work due to economic slowdowns, physical disability, or old age. FDR established the expectation that the president would be actively involved at all stages of the legislative process by submitting a legislative program to Congress, working for its passage, and coordinating its implementation. Today's presidents behave much like FDR: they send Congress messages that analyze problems and outline proposed solutions, assign aides to monitor the bills and lobby for passage, and ensure adherence to a common legislative program for the executive branch enforced through a central clearance process monitored by the Office of Management and Budget (OMB).[19] They threaten to veto legislation that fails to meet presidential demands or that they regard as unwise or contrary to their purposes. Harry S. Truman and Dwight Eisenhower institutionalized the president's legislative role by creating structures and processes to assist in carrying it out on a systematic basis with help from the Bureau of the Budget (which later became the OMB) and the White House staff.[20]

By the mid-1960s it appeared to some observers that the presidency dominated the legislative process. In 1965 Samuel P. Huntington wrote, "[T]he congressional role in legislation has largely been reduced to delay and amendment." Tasks such as taking the initiative in formulating legislation, assigning legislative priorities, generating support for legislation, and determining final content had "shifted to the executive branch," which, in Huntington's view, had gained "at the expense of Congress."[21] Others argued that Congress remained vitally important to the process by constantly modifying and altering policy through appropriations, amendments, and renewals of statutory authorizations.[22]

But Congress and the president are not engaged in a zero-sum game in which the power of one decreases as the power of the other increases. Since 1933 Congress has increased its power by vastly expanding the subjects on which it legislates. During this same time, presidents also assumed greater responsibility as innovators of policy. In three brief periods of intense legislative activity—1933–1937, 1964–1965, and 1981—activist presidents (FDR, Lyndon Johnson, and Reagan) led responsive Congresses in the adoption of major changes in domestic policy. In foreign policy, Congress responded to presidential leadership in establishing the role of the United States in world affairs during and immediately after World War II.

At times Congress has reacted to what was viewed as excessive presidential power. During the 1970s, for example, Congress expanded its control over the executive branch through increased use of the **legislative veto** (see chapter 6), sought to curb presidential use of military force abroad with the War Powers Resolution (see chapter 10), and strengthened its ability to determine federal spending by redesigning the congressional budget process (see chapter 9).

All presidents since FDR, with the possible exception of Eisenhower, have aspired to lead Congress as a way to lead the nation. Some have succeeded temporarily; others have been totally unsuccessful. For example, in 1981 Reagan took command of bipartisan conservative congressional majorities, which passed his taxing and spending proposals and sharply altered the course of domestic social and economic policy the nation had followed since the 1930s.[23] But his period of dominance was short-lived; congressional critics of his policies regrouped in 1982, support among the Republicans sagged, and legislative concerns shifted as budget deficits soared to unprecedented levels. Reagan discovered, as had Roosevelt in 1937 and Johnson in 1966, that congressional approval of a president's program is not automatic. Congressional support must be cultivated and maintained and can rapidly disappear when conditions change. Reagan's immediate successor, George H. W. Bush, offered modest, rather than sweeping, initiatives, but he, too, could not develop sustained congressional support from a Democrat-controlled Congress. In contrast, congressional Democrats enacted much of Clinton's initial legislative agenda with only limited Republican help.[24] When Republicans won control of Congress in 1994, Clinton's agenda and strategies changed drastically, leading to prolonged battles.

Despite his much-publicized calls to reduce partisan conflict, George W. Bush initially advanced a markedly conservative legislative agenda, reflecting Republican control of Congress. When Senator Jeffords left the party, the administration was forced to reexamine its agenda and its tactics for winning congressional support. The terrorist attacks of September 11, 2001, strengthened the president's hand, and Bush scored major successes on education reform, tax cuts, prescription drug coverage for Medicare, and foreign policy leadership. With the restoration of one-party government after the 2002 elections, he moved forward with his original agenda but with little success. Bush's top priority after being reelected in 2004 was to reform Social Security, an initiative that never came to a vote on Capitol Hill. After the Democrats' election victories during the mid-term elections of 2006, Iraq moved to center stage and became the focus of congressional challenges to the president's authority as commander in chief.[25] House Republicans abandoned the president in fall 2008 when the administration proposed a $700 billion rescue package (termed a "bailout" by its critics) for the banking system. Although the House later reversed course and Congress reluctantly approved a hastily designed plan, Bush was clearly a lame-duck president entering his final months in office unable to address the nation's most serious economic crisis since the Great Depression.

President Obama also found Congress skeptical about his economic plans. He secured passage of a massive economic stimulus bill in February 2009 without a single Republican vote in the House but with three critical Republican votes in the Senate. The Republican moderates—Arlen Specter of Pennsylvania, who a few months later switched parties, Olympia Snowe of Maine, and Susan Collins of Maine— secured important concessions from the Democrats and helped the majority party fend off a threatened Republican filibuster. Similar partisan showdown votes looked inevitable as the debate about the fiscal year 2010 budget moved forward amidst concern that the large projected deficit, well in excess of a trillion dollars, would wreak economic havoc. Central to this debate were questions about the administration's proposals for significant increases in federal spending for education, energy independence, and health care, major new legislative initiatives included in the president's proposed budget. Even though Obama was exerting leadership in the midst of an economic crisis, Congress refused to be a passive partner.

The Presidential-Congressional Relationship

Institutional competition between Congress and the presidency arises from the Constitution's separation of powers, but the Constitution also mandates a sharing of powers: joint action is required to authorize programs, appropriate money to pay for them, and levy taxes to provide the funds. Neither branch can achieve its goals or operate the government without the other. Since 1970, however, presidential-congressional relations have been highly competitive because of heightened distrust between the branches and intensified party differences between presidents and members of Congress. Charles O. Jones describes the relationship as one in which "these separated institutions often *compete* for shared powers."[26]

Competition by Design: The Separation of Powers

James Madison's *Federalist* No. 51 makes it clear that the framers had intended presidential-congressional conflict:

To what expedient . . . shall we finally resort, for maintaining in practice the necessary partition of power among the several departments, as laid down in the constitution? The only answer that can be given is . . . by so contriving the interior structure of the government as its several constituent parts may, by their mutual relations, be the means of keeping each other in their proper places. . . .

In order to lay a due foundation for that separate and distinct exercise of the different powers of the government, which to a certain extent is admitted on all hands to be essential to the preservation of liberty, it is evident that each department should have a will of its own. . . .

But the great security against a gradual concentration of the several powers in the same department consists in giving to those who administer each department the necessary constitutional means and personal motives to resist the encroachments of the others. . . . Ambition must be made to counteract ambition. The interests of the man must be connected with the constitutional rights of the place.[27]

The pattern of presidential-congressional relations has not been static. Some analysts point to a cyclical pattern of power aggrandizement by Congress or the presidency and a resurgence by the other that has operated from the Republic's beginning.[28] In the nineteenth century the institutional surges and declines oscillated evenly within well-defined boundaries, but U.S. economic, social, and technological transformations and emergence from international isolation during the twentieth century created conditions that more frequently called for executive, rather than legislative, leadership. The president can act more quickly, more decisively, and more consistently than Congress, which has difficulty ascertaining its institutional will and coherently pursuing its goals. Therefore, it can be argued that in the twentieth century, presidential surges have resulted in permanent expansions of executive power and presidential aggrandizements, such as Johnson's use of the war powers to involve the United States in the Vietnam War (see chapter 10) and Nixon's sweeping claims of executive privilege and his frequent impoundments of appropriated funds (see chapter 6).

During the 1970s Congress reasserted its constitutional authority in several areas and launched internal reforms, which continued throughout the 1980s and 1990s, that enhanced its legislative power.[29] Yet the nation found it needed presidential leadership to deal with difficult problems such as severe inflation, persistent budget deficits, economic interdependence, and international terrorism. Divided government prevailed throughout most of this period, giving congressional leaders the opportunity to challenge the policies of presidents from the other party. For example, Republicans followed their victory in the 1994 midterm elections with a new collective assertiveness that threatened to undermine Clinton's leadership. Under Newt Gingrich, the aggressive, ideologically conservative Speaker, House Republicans took action within the first hundred days of the new Congress on the ten priorities outlined in the *Contract with America,* an election manifesto most Republican candidates for the House had endorsed. Even this novel strategy to regain the legislative initiative did not restore congressional ascendancy, as Senate Republicans pursued more moderate priorities and Clinton developed effective defensive tactics.[30]

The conflict between Congress and the presidency is not driven by partisan divisions alone. Even with a Congress controlled by his own party, George W. Bush self-consciously sought to recover some of the ground his predecessors lost to assertive Congresses in the years following Watergate. "The result has been the broadest expansion of White House power in decades: Bush has resisted sending documents or witnesses to Capitol Hill, imposed restrictions on access to the papers of former presidents and rapidly filled the confirmation pipeline with conservative candidates for judgeships."[31] Vice President Cheney refused to submit information to the Government Accounting Office (renamed the Government Accountability Office) when it sought documents on the energy task force he chaired in 2001.[32] The administration refused to allow Tom Ridge, director of Homeland Security, to testify before Congress to answer questions about the administration's antiterrorism strategy. Despite claiming a commitment to cooperation, the administration dragged its feet and then was highly restrictive in its sharing of information with the investigation by the National Commission on Terrorist Attacks Upon the United States, usually called the 9-11 Commission. And the administration invoked **executive privilege**—denying information to Congress to preserve the quality of advice the president receives—when it refused a House committee's request for documents related to a terminated Justice Department investigation.[33] Critics have been so concerned about decisions to delay declassifying documents from past administrations and making it easier to classify current information that they have concluded, "[T]his White House is obsessed with secrecy."[34] One legal expert wrote, "Bush wanted to not only revitalize executive privilege but also expand the scope of that power substantially."[35]

Conflicts Based on Constituency and Electoral Differences

In addition to institutional competition born of the separation of powers, conflict stems from the difference in the constituencies of the members of Congress and the president. The 535 congressional members represent constituencies that vary in geographic area, population, economic structure, and social composition. Every member depends for reelection on distinctive, constituency-based political forces, making all members necessarily narrow-minded on at least some policy choices. Their perspective on the national interest is shaped by their constituency's interests.

Congressional parties have the potential to overcome constituency-based fragmentation, but creating party unity is a struggle. Party leaders cannot command their members' votes, although the centralizing reforms of the 1980s and 1990s that were most evident in the House have given the Speaker limited power to speak on the chamber's behalf. The Senate majority leader remains heavily dependent on a stubbornly independent membership and the minority party's insistence on being fully consulted. The national interest emerges in Congress through bargaining among members and blocs of members responsive to particular interests.

In contrast, presidents claim the entire nation as their constituency and can say they speak on behalf of the national interest or act for various inarticulate and unorganized interests not adequately represented in Congress. Presidents can resist the demands of well-organized particular interests by posing as champions of the national interest, even though there may be times when they, too, respond to such pressures.

From 1946 to 1972 presidents took advantage of intraparty divisions to forge temporary majority coalitions to pass specific measures with bipartisan support. Congressional policymaking was deliberate, incremental, or piecemeal, and largely reactive to presidential leadership. Congress could not maintain consistency in its actions in different policy areas or cohesiveness within those areas. Speed, efficiency, consistency, and cohesiveness usually were lacking, except in a crisis.

After Nixon, however, presidents had less success in playing the national interest card, and party cohesion in Congress rose dramatically with a majority of one party confronting a majority of the other.[36] In part, this change was a reflection of the realignment of the South into a heavily Republican region so that the *conservative coalition,* the traditional alliance of Republicans with conservative southern Democrats, declined. It also reflected the growing capacity of party leaders to define a policy agenda with a distinctive ideological cast.

Changes in electoral politics also have widened the gap between presidents and Congress. Members of Congress are political entrepreneurs who routinely seek reelection through constituency-based electoral coalitions largely independent of party labels. Incumbents have been remarkably successful: Since 1954 "an average of 93 percent of the House incumbents and 84 percent of the Senate incumbents who sought reelection were successful."[37] Members are nominated in direct primaries, their campaigns are financed heavily from nonparty sources, and they sustain electoral support through activities unrelated to party, such as providing service to constituents. Unlike parliamentary executives whose electoral success is directly linked to their party colleagues, presidents gain election on their own and seem to have less and less impact on the success of their copartisans in Congress. Presidential coattails—congressional seats won by candidates of the president's party because of strong public support—have nearly disappeared, and there are fewer seats in which the presidential victor's margin of victory exceeds that of the congressional candidates.[38] Clinton and Bush both entered office with *negative coattails;* their parties lost seats in Congress in the 1992 and 2000 elections. Republicans made modest gains in 2004: three seats in the House, and four in the Senate. By contrast, when Obama took office, Democrats had added twenty-one seats in the House and seven in the Senate, with one more—the seat in Minnesota—unresolved well into 2009 as the 225-vote margin of victory was challenged in the courts. At most, the presidential vote has exerted only a small influence on the congressional vote in recent elections, certainly less than partisanship or incumbency.[39] This separation of presidential and congressional electoral coalitions means presidents can exert little leverage on members of their own parties by appealing to their shared electoral fates, and the potential to influence members of the opposition party has declined as well.

Divided Party Control of Government

Recent presidents have confronted a major strategic dilemma. Under the best of conditions, when a president's party controls both houses of Congress, party loyalty is a weak link. Even this connection is not available to a president faced with a Congress controlled by the opposition party. Since 1933 Democratic presidents have had to deal with an opposition Congress in 1947–1948 and 1995–2001, and Republican presidents have confronted full opposition control in all years except 1953–1954, 1981–1986, 2001–2002, and 2003–2006 (see Table 5-1).

Analysts differ sharply in their assessments of the consequences of divided partisan control. The critics of divided government argue that it renders unworkable the Constitution's already cumbersome and inefficient separation-of-powers structure.[40] Critics blame the large federal budget deficits of the late 1980s and 1990s on divided government, in which each branch has a stake in the failure of the other.[41] These critics also charge that divided government undermines electoral accountability because it is impossible for voters to hold either party responsible for policies adopted and results achieved since the last election.

TABLE 5-1   Partisan Control of the Presidency and Congress, 1933–2010

Dates	Presidency	Congress
1933–1946	Democratic	Democratic
1947–1948	Democratic	Republican
1949–1952	Democratic	Democratic
1953–1954	Republican	Republican
1955–1960	Republican	Democratic
1961–1968	Democratic	Democratic
1969–1976	Republican	Democratic
1977–1980	Democratic	Democratic
1981–1986	Republican	Republican (Senate) Democractic (House)
1987–1992	Republican	Democratic
1993–1994	Democratic	Democratic
1995–2000	Democratic	Republican
2001 (through 6/6)	Republican	Republican
2001 (after 6/6)[a]	Republican	Democractic (Senate) Republican (House)
2003–2006	Republican	Republican
2007–2008	Republican	Democratic
2009–2010	Democratic	Democratic

a. One Republican senator officially changed his affiliation to independent and voted with the Democrats.

Other researchers draw different conclusions. After a systematic empirical analysis of significant legislation and congressional investigations since World War II, David Mayhew concluded that it does not make "much difference whether party control of the American government happens to be unified or divided."[42] Morris Fiorina, acknowledging that divided government results in more "conflictual" presidential-congressional relations, suggests that its consequences are not "necessarily bad."[43] Divided government may limit the potential for social gain through public policy, but it also limits potential loss through government mistakes, and divided government is the American electorate's way of establishing the type of coalition governments common in multiparty systems.[44] Divided government is more of a problem when the parties' policy preferences are polarized and there is little prospect for bipartisan cooperation, but action is possible even under these circumstances, if the party controlling Congress wields a supermajority that can override presidential vetoes.[45] It is clear that divided government has dominated presidential-congressional relations for most of the last quarter of the twentieth century and reemerged in the twenty-first century. For his first two years in office at least, Obama enjoyed solid Democratic majorities in Congress. And the academic debate continues.[46]

Despite efforts to overcome internal fragmentation and fashion more coherent policy, Congress finds it difficult to compete with the relative decisiveness, cohesion, and consistency of the presidency as a national policy-making institution. Congress's oft-mentioned weaknesses—loosely structured congressional parties, party leaders with limited power, the absence of party discipline in congressional voting, the competition among strong committees and subcommittees, and the ambitions of individual members to enhance their reelection chances and to advance to higher office—may have been altered, but the fundamental problems remain. The short-lived experiment with Congress-centered party government under Gingrich in 1995 is a case in point: many party members, worried about reelection, defied party leadership and moved to the center in 1996.

Even an internally fragmented Congress can be assertive, but its thrust is to negate or restrain, not direct, presidential action. At present, Congress values the function of "representation" over that of "lawmaking,"[47] which means it is responsive primarily to constituency interests and well-organized interest groups. It also means Congress is more comfortable with distributive policies and programs, which provide widespread benefits, than with redistributive policies, which change society's allocation of wealth and power. Ironically, presidents have assumed responsibility for exercising the lawmaking function that translates electoral mandates into policies with broad societal impact but often encounter the kind of resistance Bush did on Social Security.

Patterns of Presidential-Congressional Policymaking

To make national policy, the president and Congress must resolve conflicts. Some analysts have identified patterns in this relationship, which vary according to issues, presidential leadership styles, and political context. Presidents tend to prevail in foreign and military policy—for example, Bush's success on Iraq—and on those issues to which they attach high priority, such as Johnson's Great Society program.[48] Congress usually dominates on domestic policy, as it did in the 1970s, when it passed major legislation on the environment, consumer protection, and occupational safety; it also dominates on public works. Stalemate, in which differences prevent policy from moving forward, characterized much of the energy legislation proposed by presidents in the 1970s, as well as proposals for reducing the federal budget deficit in the 1980s and 1990s and reforming Social Security in the 1990s and 2000s.

Occasionally, a proposal may be stalemated for years and then move rapidly to passage as conditions change or a new president takes office. Proposals for national health insurance had languished in Congress since first advanced by President Truman in 1946. The political climate turned favorable for liberal social legislation in 1964 and 1965, after President Kennedy was assassinated. Responding to Johnson's forceful leadership, Congress enacted legislation authorizing national health insurance for the elderly (Medicare). But progress at one point does not ensure later gains. An effort to establish national health care under the leadership of Bill and Hillary Clinton collapsed in 1993–1994, leading to a series of more limited proposals over the next decade to provide prescription drug coverage for senior citizens and revise Medicare under Bush.

Presidential ambition and leadership style can be important causes of conflict. An activist president committed to an extensive legislative program, such as FDR or Lyndon Johnson, normally tries to dominate Congress, whereas a less activist president, such as Eisenhower, Ford, and George H. W. Bush, may be more inclined to cooperate with Congress or accept considerable congressional initiative in program development. The competitive setting affects how forceful a president will be. Presidents in the last two decades of the twentieth century confronted a significantly different strategic environment, one that curtailed their ambitions. Instead of seeking major legislative accomplishments of their own, they selectively facilitated pursuing items on the legislative agenda of the majority party, most often the opposition. Reagan, Bush, and Clinton were also forced to use veto threats more frequently than their predecessors to trigger negotiations.[49] Clinton, a moderate with an ambitious reform agenda, initially attempted to dominate Congress through the Democratic majority and its more liberal leaders, angering a small, but influential group of moderate and conservative Democrats.[50] After Republicans gained congressional majorities in 1995, Clinton positioned himself as the moderate force between liberal Democrats and conservative Republicans (the so-called "triangulation" strategy), which enabled him to make alliances with any legislative group. For example, Clinton and congressional Republicans fashioned a major reform of national welfare policies in 1996 that angered many Democrats. Yet the latter rallied to his defense during the impeachment controversy.

George W. Bush entered office with a more ambitious legislative agenda than expected, given his narrow electoral victory. On some matters, most notably education reform, he sought common ground with Democrats, but on most issues (developing a national energy strategy and environmental policies, reforming Social Security, cutting taxes, reviewing national defense) he relied on support from conservative Republicans and a few conservative to moderate Democrats.[51] Bush consistently depended on the cohesive House Republicans to deliver a conservative version of his legislation that would prevail in negotiations with the more moderate Senate. Although many thought his legislative strategy would have to adjust to changing circumstances, it never seemed to happen. The partisan strategy dominated; bipartisanship was the exception.[52] Iraq proved to be a major weight on Bush's second term; continued American battlefield deaths and the apparent lack of progress lowered the president's public approval ratings and generated early discussions about his **lame-duck** status. Neither Social Security reform nor tax code simplification, the two major legislative goals of the second term, gained support in Congress, and the Democratic majorities elected in November 2006 quickly asserted their own priorities.

Presidents have two sets of tools, used simultaneously, to accomplish legislative goals: (1) formal powers vested in the presidency by the Constitution and by statute, and (2) informal resources inherent in the office. In the next two sections, each is examined separately.

The President's Formal Legislative Powers

Article II, section 3, of the Constitution authorizes the president to call Congress into special session; it also requires that he "from time to time give to the Congress information of the state of the Union, and recommend to their consideration such measures as he shall judge necessary and expedient." Article I, section 7, makes presidents direct participants in the legislative process by providing that the president approve or disapprove (through the veto) "every bill" and "every order, resolution, or vote to which the concurrence of the Senate and House may be necessary." These formal legislative powers are augmented by statutory delegations of authority to the president and to administrative agencies.

Messages to Congress and Agenda Setting

Although contemporary presidents have not gained much leverage by calling special congressional sessions, they have derived substantial power from their constitutional duty to report on the state of the nation and to recommend legislation. Since passage of the Budget and Accounting Act of 1921 and the Employment Act of 1946, Congress has required that presidents annually submit messages explaining and justifying their budgets and reporting on the economy's condition. The State of the Union address and these fiscal messages enable presidents to set the congressional agenda by assessing the nation's problems and laying before Congress a comprehensive legislative program reflecting the president's goals and priorities. The messages are also efforts to enlist public opinion behind those priorities. Now delivered during a prime-time, televised speech to both houses of Congress and members of the cabinet, the Supreme Court, and the Joint Chiefs of Staff as well as ambassadors from around the world, the modern State of the Union address is a far cry from the tedious reading of a lengthy speech by a congressional clerk that occurred as late as Teddy Roosevelt's administration.

Individual members of Congress still introduce a multitude of bills independently of the president, but the chief executive is in a position to substantially influence, if not dominate, the congressional agenda. In a comprehensive review of how presidents helped set the congressional agenda from 1953 to 1996, George C. Edwards and Andrew Barrett concluded that the president generates about one-third of "the total number of significant bills on the congressional agenda," ranging from a high of 68.6 percent under Kennedy in 1961–1963 to a low of 0 percent under Clinton in 1995–1996, and "presidential initiatives are more likely than congressional initiatives to become law," with the success rate nearly twice as high under unified, rather than divided, government.[53] Additional research has demonstrated that presidents fashion their agendas to fit the constraints of party support in Congress and the budget, and they respond to public concerns within the context of election cycles.[54]

Only infrequently does Congress seek to seize the full agenda-setting power. During the G. H. W. Bush administration, the Democratic majority advanced proposals in areas the president did not address, such as civil rights and immigration. Even more dramatically, Speaker Gingrich did much the same for Republicans following their 1994 victory, when Clinton's 1995 State of the Union address provided few specific legislative proposals and adopted a defensive posture toward the conservative agenda.[55] But these efforts to replace presidential leadership with an agenda generated by Congress proved difficult to sustain. Clinton reemerged to steer legislative action in 1996 by taking advantage of the unpopularity of Republican tactics that closed the government and by co-opting much of the Republicans' agenda as his own.[56] Thus both recent efforts to wrest the agenda-making power from the president were short-lived.

The Veto Power

The Constitution establishes a major legislative role for presidents by requiring their approval of measures passed by Congress (Article 1, section 7, paragraph 2).

Within ten days (Sundays excepted) after a bill or joint resolution is presented to the White House, the president must either (1) sign it into law; (2) disapprove or veto it and return it to the house of Congress in which it originated along with a message explaining this action; or (3) take no action on it, in which case it becomes law without the president's signature at the end of ten days. If Congress adjourns within that ten-day period and the president does not sign a measure awaiting action, then it does not become law and the president has exercised a **pocket veto.** The president's action is final because adjournment prevents a measure from being returned to Congress for reconsideration and a possible override.

The veto is the president's ultimate legislative weapon; it carries the weight of two-thirds of the members of each house because that is what is required to overturn a veto. In his classic treatise *Congressional Government,* Woodrow Wilson noted the importance of the veto even when Congress dominated the national government: "For in the exercise of his power of veto, which is, of course, beyond all comparison, his most formidable prerogative, the President acts not as the executive but as a third branch of the legislature."[57] Andrew Jackson adopted a broad interpretation of the veto power, one giving him the right to reject legislation on the basis of its wisdom, merit, or equity as well as on constitutional grounds.[58] Presidents since 1933 have espoused this "tribunative" view of the veto and have used it often.

The data in Table 5-2 demonstrate a more extensive use of the veto by Roosevelt, Truman, and Eisenhower than by their successors. The data also show that from 1961 through 1995 Democratic presidents vetoed fewer bills than did the Republicans, not unexpected because Democrats controlled Congress throughout much of that time—the Senate from 1961 through 1980 and 1987 through 1994, and the House from 1961 through 1994. President Clinton exercised no vetoes during the 103rd Congress, controlled by his own party, "the first time since the 32nd Congress (1851–1852) and the administration of Millard Fillmore that an entire Congress served without prompting a presidential rejection."[59] George W. Bush accomplished the same feat when he served for five and a half years before casting his first veto in September 2006; he vetoed the embryonic stem cell research bill. His second veto was exercised on Iraq appropriations, as described at the beginning of this chapter, and others occurred as Democrats' priorities clashed with the president's.

The veto power affects policy negatively and positively. It is negative by nature; once used, it signifies an impasse between the president and Congress, and prior policy is unchanged. Sometimes presidents find the veto the best means of emphatically communicating their intentions to Congress even when it goes against the

TABLE 5-2   Presidential Vetoes of Bills, 1933–2009

President	Regular vetoes	Pocket vetoes	Total	Number of vetoes overridden	Percentage of vetoes overridden
FDR (1933–1945)	372	263	635	9	1.4
Truman (1945–1953)	180	70	250	12	4.8
Eisenhower (1953–1961)	73	108	181	2	1.1
Kennedy (1961–1963)	12	9	21	0	0.0
Johnson (1963–1969)	16	14	30	0	0.0
Nixon (1969–1974)	26	17	43	7	16.3
Ford (1974–1977)	48	18	66	12	18.2
Carter (1977–1981)	13	18	31	2	6.5
Reagan (1981–1989)	39	39	78	9	11.5
G. H. W. Bush (1989–1993)[a]	29	15	44	1	2.3
Clinton (1993–2001)	37	1	38	2	5.3
G. W. Bush (2001–2009)	11	1	12	4	33.0

SOURCE: Office of the Clerk, U.S. House of Representatives http://clerk.house.gov/art_history/house_history/vetoes .html.

a. G. H. W. Bush attempted to pocket veto two bills during intrasession recess periods. Congress considered the two bills enacted into law because of the president's failure to return the legislation. The bills are not counted as pocket vetoes in this table.

wishes of a large legislative majority. Many of Ford's and Reagan's vetoes, for example, were intended to signal their view that the liberal Democratic Congress was engaging in "allegedly wasteful spending."[60] The positive aspect of the veto lies in its use as a bargaining tool to "shape, alter, or deter legislation."[61] By threatening to exercise the veto, presidents can define the limits of their willingness to compromise. They can state in advance what they will and will not accept, hoping to coax concessions from Congress and thereby reduce the likelihood of a showdown over a bill or to "stimulate serious bargaining."[62] Threats can be issued either publicly or privately; and presidents may have a greater or lesser "propensity to veto."[63] More generally, veto threats have become a major means for presidents to force opposition majorities to make policy concessions in the "high-intensity partisan environment" that has characterized Washington since the Reagan administration.[64]

Republican congressional leaders worked hard to avoid presenting George W. Bush with objectionable legislation that he might veto.[65] But another explanation for the strikingly small number of vetoes Bush issued is the expanded use of **presidential signing statements,** "pronouncements issued by the president at the time a congressional enactment is signed that . . . identify provisions of the legislation with which the president has concerns," stating the president's alternative constitutional interpretation, and often directing the administration on how it should implement (or not implement) the law.[66] The Constitution stipulates that vetoes must be accompanied by a statement of the president's objections, but there is no comparable requirement that he make a statement when he signs a bill into law. This practice began under James Monroe in the early nineteenth century, but became more prominent after Reagan began using statements to articulate disagreements with Congress that could become part of the legislative history of a law.

Bush's use of signing statements became controversial when some legal scholars alleged that the practice was tantamount to a **line item veto,** the power that some governors can exercise to strike down portions of a law with which they disagree rather than veto the entire bill.[67] In *Clinton v. City of New York* (1998) the Supreme Court struck down the federal statute that provided presidents with a line item veto. George W. Bush issued 161 signing statements challenging more than 1,100 provisions of law, a major assertion of presidential prerogative.[68] (Barack Obama issued three signing statements in slightly over two months in office, none of them controversial.) Others have argued, however, that Bush's statements were largely rhetorical, intended for public relations purposes, and were designed to change understandings of presidential power rather than negate particular legal provisions.[69] At the request of Congress, the Government Accountability Office conducted a close study of nineteen signing statements issued by Bush in 2006 and determined that nearly a third involved instances of the administration not carrying out provisions according to law. "In all those instances, presidential signing statements had asserted that congressional demands were encroaching on Bush's prerogatives to control executive branch employees as he sees fit and to receive effective services from his employees."[70]

The President's Informal Legislative Influence

In 1960 Richard Neustadt startled students of the presidency when, in his now celebrated treatise *Presidential Power,* he asserted that the formal powers of the president amounted to little more than a clerkship. The Constitution, Neustadt argued, placed the president in a position of mostly providing services to other participants in national politics. "Presidential power," Neustadt declared, "is the power to persuade."[71] As the preceding examination of the president's formal legislative powers suggests, this is often the case in presidential relations with Congress. It is not enough for presidents to present a legislative program to Congress; they also must persuade congressional majorities to enact each statutory component of it. To do so, they employ mostly informal methods of influence. These tools can be used to exert indirect and direct pressure. Presidents may engage in bargaining, arm-twisting, and confrontation as general modes of working with Congress.

Indirect Influence

Presidents attempt to influence Congress indirectly through appeals to the public and by enlisting interest group support. A careful appeal, usually launched with a major public address, can generate pressure that causes Congress to act. Presidents are more likely to use popular appeals successfully in a crisis that appears to require congressional action. Success is less likely when public opinion is divided and substantial opposition to the president's position exists. In any case, presidents use such appeals selectively. Congress may object to the president's "going over its head" to the people too frequently because in doing so the president attacks, directly or by implication, the members' wisdom and motives.

George W. Bush used his first televised address to a joint session of Congress on February 27, 2001, to launch an aggressive, campaign-style strategy to win support for his major legislative proposals. The administration had already displayed impressive organization by focusing in successive weeks on education, religious faith-based charities, and tax cuts, critical elements of the Bush program. Moreover, it developed talking points for Republican members of Congress so the party message would be in harmony.[72] Bush followed up by visiting states where he had run well in 2000 and where influential Democratic votes were located—Arkansas, Florida, Georgia, Iowa, Louisiana, Nebraska, North Dakota, Pennsylvania, and South Dakota. The president clearly wanted supporters attending the rallies to contact their Washington representatives. As Bush's spokesman explained, "Every day, in every way, whether it's at the White House or it's in travel, the president looks at how to get his plan across to the voters so voters can get their message to the Senators and congressmen."[73] The result of this carefully choreographed effort was the major tax-cut victory. But when Bush tried to repeat this formula for success in 2005 with a much larger campaign to reform Social Security, the effort failed. After launching the campaign in his State of the Union address, Bush visited twenty-nine states in an effort to convince the public that Social Security faced a crisis and that his proposal for individual retirement accounts was the best solution.[74] Polls showed that the public believed a problem existed, but not that the president's solution was best.[75] In fact, at the end of the sixty-day period, approval for how he was handling the issue had dropped from 41 percent to 29 percent.[76] Instead of agreeing to negotiate on details, the Democrats refused to discuss the issue, and by the end of 2005 it was gone from the White House agenda.[77]

Direct Influence

In their direct efforts to persuade Congress, presidents use two informal tools. They may grant or withhold services and amenities at their disposal as rewards for support or sanctions for lack of it, and they may become personally involved in the legislative process. Presidents vary greatly in their skills at exploiting these resources.

Favors. Bestowing or denying favors to members of Congress gives presidents a measure of leverage. Such favors may be given to an individual member or to important people in his or her constituency, or the favor may be of benefit to the constituency itself.[78] Favors given as rewards to congressional members include appointments with the president and other high-ranking officials; letters or telephone calls from the president expressing thanks for support; campaign assistance in the form of cash from the party's national committee, a presidential visit to the constituency, or a presidential endorsement; the opportunity to announce the award of federal grants to recipients in the constituency; invitations to be present at bill-signing ceremonies, to attend White House social functions, and to accompany the president on trips; and White House memorabilia such as pens and photographs. Favors for influential congressional constituents include appointments, appearances by administration officials at organization meetings, invitations to social functions, mailings on important occasions such as anniversaries, memorabilia, and VIP treatment such as White House mess privileges. To some extent, all members of Congress share in such benefits, but the president's supporters have readier access to them and feel more comfortable asking for them than do others.

The most important constituency-related rewards are jobs and projects. Congressional recommendations by members of the president's party greatly influence the selection of U.S. district court judges, U.S. attorneys, U.S. marshals, customs collectors for ports of entry, and a variety of lesser positions. Projects often regarded as rewards include military installations; research and administrative facilities; public works such as buildings, dams, and navigational improvements to rivers and harbors; government contracts with local firms; grants to local governments and educational institutions; and the deposit of federal funds in banks. Presidents cannot direct projects exclusively to their supporters, but they can exercise discretion whenever possible. As some federal activities are reduced in size, eliminated, or turned over to state governments, their potential for use as bargaining chips declines.

Involvement in the Legislative Process. Presidents can help themselves by becoming personally involved in the legislative process, but doing so requires knowledge and skill that are products of their political background, experience, and leadership style. To turn participation in the process to an advantage, a president should have knowledge of Congress and the Washington community, a sense of timing, a willingness to consult with congressional leaders and to give them notice in advance of major actions, sensitivity to the institutional prerogatives of Congress and to the personal and political needs of its members, and a balance between firmness and flexibility in resolving differences with Congress.

No president has ever possessed all of these skills. By most accounts, however, Lyndon Johnson exhibited more than any other modern president and made the most effective use of his involvement in the legislative process. He believed that constant, intense attention by presidents and their administrations was necessary to move their legislative programs through Congress.[79] His success in persuading Congress to enact the unfinished agenda of President Kennedy's New Frontier program and his own Great Society bills makes his approach to Congress a good example for study. It should be noted, however, that Johnson's legislative triumphs were aided in no small measure by contextual factors. In the aftermath of the Kennedy assassination, public support for the New Frontier measures was high, and Johnson's landslide victory in the 1964 election also brought him large, liberal Democratic majorities in the House and the Senate.

Johnson grounded his legislative strategy in intimate knowledge of Congress as an institution and of its most influential members.[80] He knew whom to approach on specific issues and how to do so. Johnson also placed considerable emphasis on proper timing, waiting to send bills to Congress until the moment seemed right for the maximum support and least opposition. He sent bills singly, rather than in a package, so opposition would not develop automatically around several measures at once. In addition, he took care to consult with important senators and representatives in formulating legislation. Before sending a bill to Congress, the president and his top aides would hold a briefing for congressional leaders to explain its features. Cabinet secretaries were made responsible for the success of legislation in their areas, and the White House coordinated their efforts. Finally, when crucial votes were approaching on Capitol Hill, Johnson made intense personal appeals to the members whose votes served as cues for others and to members who were identified as uncommitted or wavering. Johnson sought to build congressional coalitions in support of his proposals. Through an analysis of head counts, used by Johnson's congressional liaison office to track House members' positions on bills over time, Terry Sullivan found that the Johnson administration built coalitions not just by mobilizing friends, but even by "converting hard core opponents."[81]

When the Vietnam War changed the political context, Johnson's approach to congressional relations proved less effective. The president lost much of his touch with Congress as he became increasingly involved in foreign policy matters and as the momentum of the Great Society gave way to the unpopularity of the war. The loss of forty-eight Democratic seats in the House in the 1966 midterm elections also adversely affected Johnson's ability to push bills through Congress. Despite changes in the political environment, today's presidents might still benefit from emulating Johnson's approach: gain detailed knowledge of Congress, respect its constitutional prerogatives, remain sensitive to its members' personal and constituency needs, and create the organizational and political capacity to build coalitions.

Although President Clinton lacked Washington experience, he had a close and cooperative relationship with the Democratic leadership during the 103rd Congress (1993–1994).[82] His legislative achievements were substantial. In both 1993 and 1994 he won on 86.4 percent of the floor votes in Congress on which he took a position.[83] The list of major legislation enacted was impressive: his economic program, which included a major deficit reduction; family and medical leave legislation; reauthorization and revision of the Elementary and Secondary Education Act; expansion of Head Start; motor-voter legislation; national service legislation; the Brady gun control bill; a comprehensive anticrime bill; the North American Free Trade Agreement (NAFTA); and legislation extending and expanding the General Agreement on Tariffs and Trade (GATT). Much of this list consists of Democratic initiatives that had been blocked during twelve consecutive years of Republican presidents.[84] Clinton failed, however, to secure passage of bills to reform health care and welfare, largely his own, rather than broadly shared, initiatives. Even though he was productive legislatively and attempted to address the problems of declining middle-class incomes and economic dislocation stemming from changes in the U.S. economy and the globalization of markets, he received no political benefit from the voters in 1994.[85] Congenial relations with Congress were a distant memory by the time of the impeachment hearings, and Clinton's high first-year success rate on floor votes had hit a record low of 36.2 percent in 1995.[86] Clinton's experience demonstrates that presidential congeniality cannot compensate for philosophical differences, partisan divisions, and an assertive opposition.

Surrounded by politicians and students, President George W. Bush signed the No Child Left Behind Act, which expanded federal influence over local schools. Flanking Bush are Democrats George Miller and Ted Kennedy (on the left) and Republican John Boehner who worked across party lines to secure congressional approval.

Bush and Congress. George W. Bush, a Washington outsider without legislative experience, campaigned on a clear, limited agenda led by his promise to cut taxes and reform education, the issues most emphasized during his first year in office. Despite its controversial size and specific provisions, Bush secured passage of a $1.3 trillion, multiyear tax cut in May 2001, having relied on unified Republican support in the House and a few moderate Democrats in the narrowly divided (50–50) Senate. Education reform also seemed destined for early success based on a bipartisan coalition until Senator Jeffords left the Republican Party. With the Senate now controlled by the Democrats, action on education reform was delayed until the fall, and major provisions were modified to accommodate the new majority. By that time, the atmospherics in Congress had changed yet again. The terrorist attacks of September 11, 2001, ushered in a nearly unprecedented era of "hyper-bipartisanship," characterized by warm relations and regular meetings among all four party leaders and the president as well as near-unanimous votes on using force in Afghanistan, providing law enforcement officials with additional powers to combat terrorism (the Patriot Act), rebuilding New York City, and enhancing airport security.[87]

That degree of cooperation did not last long. Early in 2002 Bush and the Democrats locked horns over trade promotion authority, the new name for fast-track trade authority that allows presidents to negotiate trade agreements that will be moved through Congress quickly and without amendments. Bush ultimately won the battle in a dramatic 215-214 vote in the House.[88] The bigger battle, however, was over creation of a Department of Homeland Security, originally a Democratic proposal advanced in 2000 but embraced by the Bush administration in summer 2002 (see chapter 6). This issue stood at the center of congressional politics during the lead-up to the midterm elections, with Senate Democrats insisting on a set of worker and union protections rejected by House Republicans and the president. When no final action could be taken, Bush made this the signature issue for the fall campaign when he launched an unprecedented effort in behalf of Republican candidates, contributing to victories that doubled the Republican advantage in the House to twelve votes and regained a Republican majority in the Senate. In the election aftermath, a lame-duck session of Congress approved the Bush version of a Department of Homeland Security.

Moving toward reelection in 2004, Bush's public approval rose, and the Republican Congress remained supportive, if sometimes restive.[89] Even the situation in Iraq looked brighter when the first democratic elections were held in January 2005. But then things seemed to fall apart for the administration. Buoyed by a successful reelection in which he secured a narrow but clear victory, Bush set forth to shape his legacy by modernizing Social Security. By the end of the summer, however, when public doubts about the president's formula remained strong, Republican members of Congress made it clear that they were unwilling to risk their political futures for the legacy of someone who would never again face the voters. Then Hurricane Katrina struck New Orleans and the Gulf Coast, shifting public attention, triggering an enormous but unknown financial commitment for the federal government, and highlighting the administrative failures of FEMA, the Federal Emergency Management Agency.

But the disarray did not stop there. Conservative Republicans forced the administration to withdraw the nomination of White House counsel Harriet Miers for a vacancy on the Supreme Court, and Lewis Libby, the vice president's chief of staff who also held a position on the National Security Council, was indicted on perjury charges stemming from the investigation into the leak of a CIA operative's name to the press.[90] The news from Iraq once again was gloomy, and the president's public approval ratings resumed their decline. The press revealed the operation of a warrantless eavesdropping program conducted by the National Security Agency, which was listening in to Americans' phone conversations. The Republican-controlled Congress flexed its muscles: the Patriot Act was reauthorized for only a brief period in order to continue debate with the administration over potential abuse of Americans' civil liberties (it was eventually renewed). Senator McCain led a crusade to establish an antitorture policy toward enemy captives as a way to protect American military personnel who might also be captured, but the administration asserted the right to determine when the limits would be observed. In addition, the growing demand that the administration get its act together by firing ineffective staff eventually led to the resignation of Andrew Card, the White House chief of staff. Congress accomplished little for the rest of the year, and in 2007 the arrival of Democratic majorities created an even more assertive Congress.

Modes of Presidential-Congressional Relations

In their relations with Congress, presidents follow certain modes or patterns of behavior: bargaining, arm-twisting, and confrontation. Bargaining is the predominant mode, and occasionally the president bargains directly with members whose support is deemed essential to a bill's passage. In May 1981, for example, the Reagan administration agreed to revive a costly program to support the price of sugar in exchange for the votes of four Democratic representatives from Louisiana (where sugar is a major crop) on a comprehensive budget reduction bill.[91]

Presidents usually try to avoid such explicit bargains because they have limited resources for trading, and the desire among members for these resources is keen. Moreover, Congress is so large and its power so decentralized that presidents cannot bargain extensively over most bills. In some instances, the president may be unable or unwilling to bargain. Fortunately, rather than a quid pro quo exchange of favors for votes, much presidential-congressional bargaining is implicit, generalized trading in which tacit exchanges of support and favors occur.

If bargaining does not result in the approval of their proposals, presidents may resort to stronger methods, such as arm-twisting, which involves intense, even extraordinary, pressure and threats. In one sense, it is an intensified extension of bargaining, but it entails something more—a direct threat of punishment if the member's opposition continues. Among modern presidents, Johnson was perhaps the most frequent practitioner of arm-twisting. When gentler efforts failed, or when a once-supportive member opposed him on an important issue, Johnson resorted to tactics such as deliberate embarrassment, threats, and reprisals. In contrast, Eisenhower was most reluctant to pressure Congress. Arm-twisting is understandably an unpopular tactic and, if used often, creates resentment and hostility.

Still, judicious demonstration that sustained opposition or desertion by normal supporters will exact costs strengthens a president's bargaining position.

Presidents unable to gain support through bargaining and arm-twisting may adopt a confrontational strategy. Confrontation might consist of appeals to the public, direct challenges to congressional authority, assertion of presidential prerogative, or similar tactics. Nixon confronted Congress often and more sharply than any other modern president. Disdaining the role of legislative coalition builder, he saw himself as deserving congressional support by virtue of his election mandate and his constitutional position as chief executive. The most visible confrontation occurred between 1971 and 1973, when he challenged congressional spending decisions at variance with his budget proposals by impounding more than $30 billion that Congress had appropriated. Nixon also claimed Congress could not question thousands of executive branch officials or have access to routine documentary information.

A strategy of confrontation is unlikely to result in sustained congressional responsiveness to presidential initiatives. Congress has constitutional prerogatives and constituency bases of support that enable it to resist presidential domination. The imperatives for cooperation between the two branches are so great that most presidents try to avoid such confrontations, entering them only when the presidency's constitutional integrity is at issue.

To oversee this system of bargaining, negotiation, and occasional confrontation, Eisenhower established the White House Office of Legislative Affairs, staffed by knowledgeable specialists who lobbied legislators in behalf of the administration's program. Every administration since has maintained such a unit. Although some administrations have made subtle changes in assignments and techniques, the activities have become largely institutionalized, reflecting a clear set of expectations about how staffers will conduct the job. With such a staff in place, there is continuity in legislative-executive relations and a reduction in the variation resulting from presidents' individual abilities and skills.[92]

Explaining Presidents' Legislative Success

If all presidents approach Congress with the same formal powers and informal tools of influence and use well-established staff arrangements to oversee day-to-day relations, what accounts for their legislative successes or failures? Studies have identified at least six factors that affect presidents' ability to achieve their legislative goals: partisan and ideological support in Congress, popular support, style in dealing with Congress, the contexts in which they must operate, cyclical trends in presidential-congressional relations, and the content of their domestic program. It is not possible to assess the relative importance of each factor thoroughly, but all have come into play since 1933, when FDR inaugurated the modern legislative presidency. The first five factors will be examined here; the sixth, in chapter 8.

Congressional Support

Support in Congress depends heavily on the size and cohesiveness of a president's party strength there. George Edwards has shown that from 1961 through 1986, three Democratic and three Republican presidents consistently received strong support on roll call votes from their parties' congressional members.[93] John Kessel notes that since the Reagan administration, presidents' partisans have provided higher levels of support. From 1953 through 1980 presidents received support 66 percent of the time from fellow partisans in the House and Senate, but that level rose to 75 percent from 1981 through 1996.[94] Edwards and Jon Bond and Richard Fleisher have found, however, that support may vary by issue. Historically, Republican presidents have received stronger support overall on foreign policy legislation than on domestic policy issues, primarily because of increased backing from liberal Democrats on foreign issues.[95]

It is interesting to note that partisan support for presidents in Congress apparently owes little to the storied effect of presidential coattails. The ability of presidents to transfer their electoral appeal to congressional candidates of their parties declined steadily from 1948 to 1988.[96] Even in 1984, when Reagan won a landslide victory over the Democratic candidate, Walter Mondale, the measurable coattail effect was weak, but stronger than in 1980 and 1988.[97] Edwards attributes the decline to increased split-ticket voting, the reduced competitiveness of House seats, and the electoral success of incumbents since 1952.

Despite the shorter coattails in presidential election years, some presidents have sought to improve their chances of success by campaigning for candidates from their own party during midterm elections. Such efforts are usually unsuccessful, but in 2002 George W. Bush demonstrated that it can be done (see chapter 3). Bush sought to transfer his own relatively high public approval to Republican candidates by personalizing the election. By doing so, he could claim partial credit for bucking the historical trend in which members of the president's party lose seats in the midterm election, a trend violated over the past century only in 1934 and 1998.[98] The same was not true in 2006. Bush's approval rating had plunged, and Republican candidates were more anxious to distance themselves from the president than to receive an endorsement. Despite their efforts, they lost seats and control of Congress.

Because presidents cannot rely on full support from their own party members, they must build coalitions by obtaining support from some opposition members.[99] Coalition building is especially important when the opposition controls one or both houses—the situation for most presidents since 1969. Several factors other than party membership influence congressional voting decisions, including constituency pressures, state and regional loyalty, ideological orientations, and interest group influence.[100] On many occasions, presidents have received crucial support from the opposition. Eisenhower successfully sought Democratic votes on foreign policy matters; Republicans contributed sizable pluralities to the enactment of civil rights legislation in the 1960s; conservative Democrats, mainly from the South, often supported the domestic policy proposals of Nixon and Ford; conservative Democrats in the House were essential to Reagan's 1981 legislative victories; Clinton depended on Republican support for the passage of NAFTA and GATT; and George W. Bush received critical, though limited, support from Democrats on his tax-reduction and education-reform proposals. Obama's economic stimulus package passed the Senate only after concessions were made to three Republican members. Despite continuing instances when presidents assemble bipartisan coalitions to achieve legislative goals, there is evidence that over the past two decades the opportunity to build bipartisan coalitions has sharply declined. Internal congressional reforms and heightened unity among partisans in Congress have made the task of winning in Congress much more difficult.[101]

In summary, congressional support for the president is built primarily on fellow partisans, but party affiliation by itself is seldom a sufficient basis for the enactment of the president's program. When constituency, regional, and ideological pressures reduce the number of partisan backers, the president must try to attract support from opposition members by appealing to these same pressures. A president's legislative success is, therefore, "mainly a function of the partisan and ideological makeup of Congress."[102]

Popular Support

The prestige, or popular support, of presidents also affects congressional responses to their policies. It has been widely observed that a popular president enjoys substantial leeway in dealing with Congress, and a president whose popularity is low or falling is likely to encounter considerable resistance. Bond and Fleisher argue, however, that popular support is only marginally related to presidential success on congressional floor votes.[103] Similarly, Edwards finds that public approval is a background resource that provides presidents with leverage, but not control, over Congress.[104]

Although popularity is clearly, if marginally, related to congressional support for the president's legislative program and can be used as a tool of influence, it cannot be easily manipulated. There are factors, such as the erosion of popular support over time and the economy's condition, over which the president has no control.[105] Presidents can take advantage of their popularity when it is high to influence congressional opinion, as Johnson did in 1964 and 1965 and Reagan did in 1981 and, to a lesser extent, in 1985 and 1986 (his popularity then plummeted because of the Iran-contra affair). George W. Bush sought to draw upon his strong approval ratings in this way in 2003 but had to retreat on the size and content of his tax-cut proposals and lost on the issue of oil drilling in Alaska's Arctic National Wildlife Refuge.

Presidential Style and Legislative Skills

The president's style in dealing with Congress has long been considered an important determinant of legislative success. Style encompasses the degree to which presidents are accessible to members; their interactions with, and sensitivity to, the members; and the extent of their involvement in the legislative process.[106]

Modern presidents have varied greatly in their accessibility. Johnson and Ford were usually available to members and leaders, whereas Nixon was remote and inaccessible most of the time. Kennedy and Reagan frequently sought contact through telephone calls. George H. W. Bush maintained a wide range of congressional friends and acquaintances but was criticized for not consulting enough with influential party and committee leaders. During his first two years, Clinton was so accessible and made such efforts to cultivate personal relationships that his effectiveness may have been impaired.[107] That accessibility lessened when he was working with an assertive Republican majority and with Democrats who distanced themselves from a president they regarded as a political liability. George W. Bush met with a broad cross-section of representatives and senators during his first months in office—more than ninety members in his first week, including many Democrats.[108] In those early days Bush tried to set a nonconfrontational tone in the nation's capital, and his relations with Democratic leaders improved markedly for several months after 9/11. Obama began his presidency by consulting broadly with Democrats and Republicans in fashioning his economic proposals, going so far as to meet with the House Republican membership on Capitol Hill just one week after his swearing in. Although accessibility on demand is not feasible because of the pressures on a president's time, it enhances congressional support if members know they can reach the president on matters of great importance to them. Accessibility to congressional leaders of both parties is particularly important if the president is to work effectively with Congress.

It is not clear how much interpersonal relations influence congressional support, but they are a distinctive part of a chief executive's style and affect the disposition of leaders and members toward the president. If nothing else, popularity with members of Congress can improve relations even when there are sharp differences over issues. If the president has strained personal relations, sustained congressional support will be difficult to achieve even when the president's party has a majority and many members share his goals.

Similarly, presidential involvement in the legislative process varies. Kennedy, Johnson, Ford, and Reagan maintained close interest in the course of legislation, and Johnson actively directed its progress on occasion. In contrast, Eisenhower, Nixon, and Carter were more detached. George H. W. Bush displayed a varied pattern of interest in the progress of legislation, ranging from detachment to active engagement, as during the 1991 budget negotiations. Clinton developed a reputation for making concessions so early in negotiations that he drew criticism for making it "too easy" for his opponents.[109] George W. Bush delegated most of these decisions to the experts in his administration, relying more heavily on his vice president's advice and assistance than did most of his predecessors. Unlike most vice presidents, Dick Cheney had an office on both the Senate and House sides of the Capitol building. Known briefly as the "fifty-first senator" because of his critical role in casting the tie-breaking vote before Republicans lost the Senate majority in 2001, Cheney attended weekly Republican policy meetings in the House and the Senate and regularly made himself available to listen to congressional concerns. Conventional wisdom holds that presidents' legislative skills are major determinants of congressional support for their programs, but empirical analyses provide little support for that argument. According to Edwards and others, presidential legislative skills are effective at the margins of congressional coalition building, not at the core.[110] Presenting a somewhat different argument, Mark Peterson states that presidents have some, but not unlimited, control over the timing, priorities, and size of their programs. By clearly establishing their priorities and adjusting their "ambitions to fit the opportunities of the day," he concludes, presidents can be perceived as successful leaders of Congress.[111] Some observers believed that Obama overestimated his ability to win congressional support for his ambitious first-year proposals.

Contextual Factors

Most students of presidential-congressional relations agree that contextual factors over which the president has virtually no control—such as the structure of political institutions and processes, public opinion, the alignment of political and social forces, economic and social conditions, and long-term trends in the political system—are more important than individual legislative skills as determinants of congressional decisions. For example, the cultural context of American politics is a source of frustration for presidents attempting to influence Congress. Edwards posits that phenomena such as extremely high and often contradictory public expectations of presidential performance, individualism, and skepticism of authority are powerful constraints on presidential leadership.[112] Bond and Fleisher argue that Congress-centered variables, such as the partisan and ideological predispositions of members and leaders, determined by the outcome of the last election, are of greater importance than presidency-centered variables in explaining presidential influence in Congress.[113]

Taking a middle position, Peterson provides the most comprehensive and extensive analysis of contextual factors affecting presidential success in Congress. He identifies four contexts that shape congressional action on presidential programs: (1) the "pure context," which includes the "institutional properties" of Congress, political parties, and interest groups and over which the president has little influence and no control; (2) the "malleable context," which consists of "dynamic" political conditions resulting from electoral cycles and economic conditions and over which the president has "greater but unpredictable influence" and no control; (3) the "policy context"—a context the president can influence and to some extent control by making "strategic choices" in developing an agenda—which includes the consequence of various proposals for the political system, the relative importance of proposals for presidential policy goals, and the controversiality of proposals; and (4) the "individual context," which includes personal attributes, such as style and skills, and the choices the president makes concerning the organization of the presidency for the exercise of influence that distinguish the president and the administration.[114]

However one defines and classifies the contexts that affect the president's influence or success in Congress, it is important to recognize that they function to provide both constraints upon and opportunities for the exercise of presidential leadership. To a considerable extent, the president can do little to alter most of these contexts. What a president can do is take maximum advantage of the opportunities they present. In doing so, the chief executive can act as a facilitator who encourages change but not as a director who determines it.

Cyclical Trends

Long-term cyclical fluctuations in presidential and congressional power also appear to affect the fate of specific presidential programs. In 1933 FDR initiated a period of presidential ascendancy that lasted until Nixon and the Watergate scandal. During that time Congress made extensive delegations of power to the president and to executive branch agencies; presidents assumed responsibility for legislative leadership; Congress acquiesced in presidential domination of foreign and military policy; and the public looked to the presidency more than to Congress to solve the nation's problems.[115] The president and Congress clashed often during that period, but the dominant trend was one of presidential aggrandizement. When conflict occurred, Congress usually took defensive stands against presidential assertiveness.[116]

Angered over the conduct of the war in Southeast Asia and President Nixon's claims of budget impoundment powers and executive privilege, in 1973 Congress moved to reassert its constitutional prerogatives. Seizing the opportunity afforded by Nixon's preoccupation with Watergate and the plunge in public support, Congress enacted the War Powers Resolution of 1973, the Budget and Impoundment Control Act of 1974, and the National Emergencies Act of 1976, major elements in a resurgence designed to restrain presidential power.[117] In 1974 the House Judiciary Committee approved three impeachment charges against Nixon, who resigned on August 9 before the House could act on them. His two immediate successors, Gerald Ford and Jimmy Carter, had to deal with a Congress intent on curbing presidential power and retaining the constitutional parity with the president it had at least partially regained. This period of congressional resurgence was marked by increased skepticism of claims for presidential prerogatives, careful scrutiny of presidential proposals, demands for more extensive White House consultation with congressional leaders, and more exacting senatorial confirmation hearings on presidential appointments.

With Reagan, Congress was more willing to accept presidential policy leadership and less assertive in insisting on its institutional prerogatives. The presidential-congressional relationship did not, however, return to the one that prevailed under the "imperial presidency."[118] (See chapter 1.) Reagan's relationship with Congress bent, but did not break, in 1987, following Democratic successes in the 1986 congressional elections and public disenchantment with his detached leadership, which the Iran-contra affair revealed as resting on too much delegation of presidential authority.

Presidents George H. W. Bush and Clinton had stormy relationships with Congress over the budget. In fall 1990 Bush became embroiled in a battle with members from both parties over the deficit in the 1991 budget. In October, a coalition of very liberal Democratic and very conservative Republican House members rejected a bipartisan plan negotiated by the administration and congressional leaders. Amid bitter exchanges within both parties, a compromise was reached. But even as that battle ended, a new one began, as most congressional Democrats and some Republicans sharply questioned Bush's handling of the Persian Gulf crisis and pressed him for a congressional vote of approval before initiating military action against Iraq. Although the administration insisted it had authority to initiate such action, Congress passed a resolution authorizing the use of U.S. forces to implement UN resolutions calling on Iraq to leave Kuwait or face economic sanctions and, if necessary, military action. Clinton's struggle was far more bitter and protracted. His battle with Congress over the 1996 budget escalated to new extremes with the two government shutdowns. The remainder of 1996 proved to be a temporary, election-year truce that provided new grist for postelection congressional investigations of Clinton-Gore fund-raising abuses. Conflict between the president and Congress escalated to new heights in 1998–1999 with the impeachment inquiry.

Early in his presidency George W. Bush's principal problem was with his own party's moderates. After announcing his intention to pursue an inclusive approach to working with Congress, one that would rest on cooperation with Democrats, Bush increasingly relied on a strong conservative base in the House to achieve his goals, and Republican moderates felt excluded. Many members of Congress came to believe that Bush was seeking to assert executive prerogatives at the expense of congressional powers. The administration's repeated refusals to share information even with the Republican-controlled Congress, to allow White House staff to testify before Congress, and to accept congressional limits in the conduct of the war on terror became a concern to Capitol Hill Democrats and Republicans alike. In fact, three Republican senators—John McCain of Arizona, Lindsey Graham of South Carolina, and John Warner of Virginia—challenged the administration over its use of torture in dealing with prisoners held at the U.S. naval base in Guantánamo Bay. During a hearing of the Personnel Subcommittee of the Senate Armed Services Committee conducted in 2005, a Defense Department lawyer was unable to respond to questions about Congress's power to legislate regarding combatants during time of war. As Jack Rakove points out, "It defies belief, not to say political common sense, to send a senior lawyer to a serious congressional hearing, to confess that the only part of the Constitution with which he is familiar is Article II," the one that deals with presidential power.[119] But the error was symbolic: the executive was unconcerned with Congress's authority and intent on asserting its own. For many observers of Washington politics, Bush represented a new incarnation of the imperial presidency that had been so closely associated with Presidents Johnson and Nixon.[120]

Conclusion

The experiences of recent presidents in their relations with Congress provide a few lessons. These presidents found success far from automatic. Success requires consultation before and during legislative consideration and a willingness to negotiate and bargain with Congress. Legislative proposals must be coordinated between the White House and the executive departments and agencies. More important, cooperation between the president and congressional leaders and between the institutional presidency and Congress is essential. The constitutional separation of powers does not allow the two branches to operate independently; rather, it requires that they exercise their shared powers jointly.[121]

The constitutional separation of powers requires cooperation but ensures conflict. The framers sought to prevent tyranny by establishing a balance between executive and legislative power. But this relationship is continually in flux. First one branch has expanded its authority; then the other branch has reasserted its prerogatives, recaptured lost powers, and acquired new ones. The cycle of institutional aggrandizement, decline, and resurgence reflects certain strengths and weaknesses in the presidency and Congress and the respective abilities of the branches to respond to social forces, economic conditions, and political change.

The need for presidential-congressional cooperation is clear, but there are few ways of obtaining it other than through consultation involving persuasion and bargaining. Presidents cannot command congressional approval of their proposals any more than Congress can direct presidents in the exercise of their constitutional powers. The threat of government stalemate is always present, and more often than not policy is an unsatisfactory compromise of presidential and various congressional viewpoints.

The relationship between the president and Congress will always be characterized by a degree of stability provided by the Constitution as well as by adaptations to social, economic, and political change.

SUGGESTED READINGS

Bond, Jon R., and Richard Fleisher. *The President in the Legislative Arena.* Chicago: University of Chicago Press, 1990.

———, eds. *Polarized Politics: Congress and the President in a Partisan Era.* Washington, D.C.: CQ Press, 2000.

Conley, Richard S. *The Presidency, Congress, and Divided Government.* College Station: Texas A&M University, 2003.

Edwards, George C., III. *At the Margins: Presidential Leadership of Congress.* New Haven: Yale University Press, 1989.

———. *On Deaf Ears: The Limits of the Bully Pulpit.* New Haven: Yale University Press, 2006.

Fiorina, Morris. *Divided Government.* 2nd ed. Boston: Allyn and Bacon, 1996.

Fisher, Louis. *Constitutional Conflicts between Congress and the President.* Rev. 5th ed. Lawrence: University Press of Kansas, 2007.

Jacobson, Gary C. *A Divider, Not a Uniter: George W. Bush and the American People.* New York: Longman, 2006.

Jones, Charles O. *Separate but Equal Branches: Congress and the Presidency.* 2nd ed. Chatham, N.J.: Chatham House, 2000.

———. *The Presidency in a Separated System.* 2nd ed. Washington, D.C.: Brookings Institution Press, 2005.

Mayhew, David R. *Divided We Govern: Party Control, Lawmaking, and Investigations, 1946–2002.* 2nd ed. New Haven: Yale University Press, 2005.

Mycoff, Jason, D., and Joseph A. Pika. *Confrontation and Compromise: Presidential and Congressional Leadership, 2001–2006.* Lanham, Md.: Rowman and Littlefield, 2007.

Peterson, Mark A. *Legislating Together: The White House and Capitol Hill from Eisenhower to Reagan.* Cambridge: Harvard University Press, 1990.

Rudalevige, Andrew. *The New Imperial Presidency: Renewing Presidential Power after Watergate.* Ann Arbor: University of Michigan Press, 2006.

Shull, Steven A., ed. *The Two Presidencies: A Quarter-Century Assessment.* Chicago: Nelson-Hall, 1991.

Spitzer, Robert J. *The Presidential Veto: Touchstone of the American Presidency.* Albany: State University of New York Press, 1988.

———. *President and Congress: Executive Harmony at the Crossroads of American Government.* New York: McGraw-Hill, 1993.

Sundquist, James L. *The Decline and Resurgence of Congress.* Washington, D.C.: Brookings, 1981.

Thurber, James A., ed. *Rivals for Power: Presidential-Congressional Relations.* 3rd ed. Lanham, Md.: Rowman and Littlefield, 2006.

Wayne, Stephen J. *The Legislative Presidency.* New York: Harper and Row, 1978.

Notes

1. Alissa J. Rubin, "Congress Readies Budget Bill for President's Veto Pen," *Congressional Quarterly Weekly Report,* November 18, 1995, 3512.

2. Alfred Hill, "The Shutdowns and the Constitution," *Political Science Quarterly* (Summer 2000): 274. Also see Peri E. Arnold, "Bill Clinton and the Institutionalized Presidency," in *The Postmodern Presidency,* ed. Steven E. Schier (Pittsburgh: University of Pittsburgh Press, 2000), 28–31.

3. Starr also investigated the firing of White House employees in the travel office ("Travelgate"), the potential abuse of FBI files by the Clinton White House ("Filegate"), and the suicide of White House counsel Vincent J. Foster.

4. "Mr. Ruff for the Defense," editorial, *New York Times,* January 20, 1999, A30.

5. Arnold, "Bill Clinton and the Institutionalized Presidency," 31.

6. Evan Thomas, "Acquittal: The Inside Story," *Newsweek,* February 22, 1999, 24–31; Kirk Victor and Carl M. Cannon, "Promise and Peril," *National Journal,* January 23, 1999, 170–175.

7. The results of the 2000 congressional elections: House Republicans 221, House Democrats 212, Independents 2, one voting with each party caucus; Senate Republicans 50, Senate Democrats 50. The Senate tie produced a Democrat-controlled Senate for three weeks while Vice President Gore voted with the Democrats, followed by Republican control after inauguration day, when Vice President Cheney voted with the Republicans.

8. Susan Crabtree, "Bush's Charm Offensive Suffers Slight Setback," *Roll Call,* February 5, 2001; Mark Lacey, "Bush to Attend Democratic Caucuses," *New York Times,* January 27, 2001, A11; David E. Sanger and Alison Mitchell, "Bush, the Conciliator, Meets with Democrats," *New York Times,* February 3, 2001, A10.

9. James P. Pfiffner, *The Strategic Presidency,* rev. 2nd ed. (Lawrence: University Press of Kansas, 1996), ix. For a full discussion of the "cycle of decreasing influence" that underlies the need to "move it or lose it" at an administration's outset, see Paul C. Light, *The President's Agenda: Domestic Policy Choice from Kennedy to Reagan,* rev. ed. (Baltimore: Johns Hopkins University Press, 1991), 36–37.

10. Richard E. Cohen and David Baumann, "The GOP's Drive to Deliver," *National Journal,* May 12, 2001, 1402–1403. Ultimately, five Democrats supported the Bush budget plan, which included a large tax cut. The partisan conflict was intense, however, with Vice President Cheney casting two tie-breaking votes to keep the budget on track.

11. David E. Sanger, "President's Signature Turns Broad Tax Cut, and a Campaign Promise, into Law," *New York Times,* June 8, 2001, A18.

12. Frank Bruni and David E. Sanger, "Bush Defends His Stance Despite Stinging Defection," *New York Times,* May 25, 2001, A18; Katharine Q. Seelye and Adam Clymer, "Senate Republicans Step Out and Democrats Jump In," *New York Times,* May 25, 2001, A1.

13. Transcript of James M. Jeffords's announcement, *New York Times,* May 25, 2001, A18.

14. David Nather, "Waging War on the Surge," *CQ Weekly Online,* January 15, 2007, 170–177, http://library.cqpress.com/cqweekly/weeklyreport110-000002428775.

15. Liriel Higa, "A Withdrawal-Free Supplemental," *CQ Weekly Online,* May 28, 2007, 1598–1600, http://library.cqpress.com/cqweekly/weeklyreport110-000002520622; Richard Cohen, "Congressional Chronicle-The Fog of War," *National Journal,* June 2, 2007; Brian Friel, "Congress-Temperatures Rising on Iraq," *National Journal,* June 9, 2007.

16. Stephen J. Wayne, *The Legislative Presidency* (New York: Harper and Row, 1978), 8–12.

17. Theodore Roosevelt, *Autobiography* (New York: Macmillan, 1913), 292.

18. Woodrow Wilson, *Constitutional Government in the United States* (1908; reprint, New York: Columbia University Press, 1961).

19. Richard E. Neustadt, "The Presidency and Legislation: The Growth of Central Clearance," *American Political Science Review* (September 1954): 641–670.

20. Richard E. Neustadt, "The Presidency and Legislation: Planning the President's Program," *American Political Science Review* (December 1955): 980–1018; Wayne, *The Legislative Presidency;* Larry Berman, *The Office of Management and Budget and the Presidency* (Princeton: Princeton University Press, 1979); Light, *The President's Agenda.*

21. Samuel P. Huntington, "Congressional Responses to the Twentieth Century," in *The Congress and America's Future,* ed. David B. Truman (Englewood Cliffs, N.J.: Prentice Hall, 1965), 23.

22. Ronald C. Moe and Steven C. Teel, "Congress as Policy-Maker: A Necessary Reappraisal," *Political Science Quarterly* (Fall 1970): 443–470; John R. Johannes, *Policy Innovation in Congress* (Morristown, N.J.: General Learning Press, 1972); Gary Orfield, *Congressional Power: Congress and Social Change* (New York: Harcourt Brace Jovanovich, 1975).

23. In the Senate the Republicans had a 53–47 majority. In the House the 192 Republicans, who voted together on the major elements of Reagan's economic legislation in a remarkable display of cohesion,

were joined by a sizable bloc of conservative southern Democrats called the "Boll Weevils." In both chambers, Republicans and conservative Democrats maintained voting cohesion that enabled the majorities to enact the Reagan program.

24. For example, Clinton's budget proposals in 1993 passed by a single vote in both the House and the Senate without any support from Republicans. Barbara Sinclair, "Trying to Govern Positively in a Negative Era," in *The Clinton Presidency: First Appraisals*, ed. Colin Campbell and Bert A. Rockman (Chatham, N.J.: Chatham House, 1996), 121. Also see Barbara Sinclair, "The President as Legislative Leader," in *The Clinton Legacy*, ed. Colin Campbell and Bert A. Rockman (Chatham, N.J.: Chatham House, 2000), 72–83.

25. On Bush's relations with Congress, see Jason D. Mycoff and Joseph A. Pika, *Confrontation and Compromise: Presidential and Congressional Leadership, 2001–2006* (Lanham, Md.: Rowman and Littlefield, 2007).

26. Charles O. Jones, *The Presidency in a Separated System* (Washington, D.C.: Brookings, 1994), 16.

27. Alexander Hamilton, John Jay, and James Madison, *The Federalist Papers* (New York: Modern Library, 1938), 335–337.

28. Lawrence C. Dodd, "Congress and the Quest for Power," in *Congress Reconsidered*, ed. Lawrence C. Dodd and Bruce I. Oppenheimer (New York: Praeger, 1977), 298–302.

29. James L. Sundquist, *The Decline and Resurgence of Congress* (Washington, D.C.: Brookings, 1981); Richard S. Conley, *The Presidency, Congress, and Divided Government: A Postwar Assessment* (College Station: Texas A&M University Press, 2003), 20, 24–26.

30. David S. Cloud, "Republicans Pushing the Envelope with Confrontational Approach," *Congressional Quarterly Weekly Report*, August 5, 1995, 2331–2334.

31. Mike Allen, "Counsel to Assertive Presidency," *Washington Post*, May 19, 2003, A17.

32. In December 2002 a federal district court decision denied that the GAO had standing to force release of the disputed documents, but a district judge ruled in favor of releasing information sought by the Sierra Club and Judicial Watch, a public interest group. When the Bush administration refused to comply, the Supreme Court reviewed the case and returned it to the federal appeals court. That court ruled on May 10, 2005, that the federal open meetings law did not apply to the activities of nongovernment participants in policy-making discussions unless they were voting members of an advisory committee or in position to veto committee recommendations. In short, the administration's position was upheld. News Release, Judicial Watch, May 10, 2005, www.judicialwatch.org/5309.shtml. See the appeals court decision at http://caselaw.lp.findlaw.com/data2/circs/dc/025354b.pdf.

33. Joel D. Aberbach, "The State of the Contemporary American Presidency: Or, Is Bush II Actually Ronald Reagan's Heir?" in *The George W. Bush Presidency: First Appraisals*, ed. Colin Campbell and Bert A. Rockman (Chatham, N.J.: Chatham House, 2003), chap. 11.

34. "Secrecy: The Bush Byword," editorial, *New York Times*, March 28, 2003, http://www.nytimes.com/2003/03/28/opinion/secrecy-the-bush-byword.html?scp=4&sq=March+28%2C+2003+editorial&st=nyt.

35. Mark J. Rozell, *Executive Privilege: Presidential Power, Secrecy, and Accountability*, rev. 2nd ed. (Lawrence: University Press of Kansas, 2002), 147.

36. Conley, *The Presidency, Congress, and Divided Government*, 22.

37. Paul R. Abramson, John H. Aldrich, and David W. Rohde, *Change and Continuity in the 2004 and 2006 Elections* (Washington, D.C.: CQ Press, 2007), 213. For 2006, a year when both the House and Senate changed hands, the success rates were still high: 94.1 percent of House incumbents and 78.6 percent of the Senate incumbents were reelected. Ibid., 266.

38. Conley, *The Presidency, Congress, and Divided Government*, 14–19.

39. Abramson, Aldrich, and Rohde, *Change and Continuity*, 263.

40. Among the classic criticisms of divided government, see James L. Sundquist, "Needed: A Political Theory for the New Era of Coalition Government in the United States," *Political Science Quarterly* (Winter 1988-1989): 613–635; Lloyd N. Cutler, "To Form a Government," *Foreign Affairs* 59 (Fall 1980): 126–143; Cutler, "Now Is the Time for All Good Men," *William and Mary Law Review* 30 (Fall 1989): 387–402; and Michael L. Mezey, *Congress, the President, and Public Policy* (Boulder: Westview, 1989).

41. Gary W. Cox and Samuel Kernell, "Conclusion," in *The Politics of Divided Government*, ed. Gary W. Cox and Samuel Kernell (Boulder: Westview, 1991), 242–243. Also see Mathew D. McCubbins, "Government on Lay-Away: Federal Spending and Deficits under Divided Party Control," in Cox and Kernell, *The Politics of Divided Government*, 113–153.

42. David R. Mayhew, *Divided We Govern: Party Control, Lawmaking, and Investigations, 1946–1990* (New Haven: Yale University Press, 1991), 198. The 2005 edition covers 1946–2002.

43. Morris Fiorina, *Divided Government*, 2nd ed. (Boston: Allyn and Bacon, 1996), 107, 108.

44. Ibid., 110; chap 7.

45. David R. Jones, "Party Polarization and Legislative Gridlock," *Political Research Quarterly* 54 (March 2001): 125–141.

46. For a good review of the findings, see John J. Coleman, "Unified Government, Divided Government, and Party Responsiveness," *American Political Science Review* 93 (December 1999): 821–835.

47. Roger H. Davidson, Walter J. Oleszek, and Francis E. Lee, *Congress and Its Members*, 11th ed. (Washington, D.C.: CQ Press, 2007), chap. 1.

48. The main components of the Great Society were the Economic Opportunity Act of 1964, which launched a "war on poverty"; the Civil Rights Act of 1964; the Voting Rights Act of 1965; the Elementary and Secondary Education Act of 1965; and the Medicare Act of 1965.

49. Conley, *The Presidency, Congress, and Divided Government*, 44–45.

50. This discussion follows Sinclair, "Trying to Govern Positively," 91–119.

51. Juliet Eilperin, "Bush to Woo Democratic Rank-and-File," *Washington Post*, January 22, 2001, A1; Barbara Sinclair, "Bipartisan Governing: Possible, Yes; Likely, No," *PS: Political Science and Politics* 34 (March 2001): 81–83.

52. Barbara Sinclair, "Living (and Dying?) by the Sword: George W. Bush as Legislative Leader," in *The George W. Bush Legacy*, ed. Colin Campbell, Bert A. Rockman, and Andrew Rudalevige (Washington, D.C.: CQ Press, 2008), 164–187.

53. George C. Edwards III and Andrew Barrett, "Presidential Agenda Setting in Congress," in *Polarized Politics: Congress and the President in a Partisan Era*, ed. Jon R. Bond and Richard Fleisher (Washington, D.C.: CQ Press, 2000), 120, 122, 127.

54. Matthew Eshbaugh-Soha, "The Politics of Presidential Agendas," *Political Research Quarterly* 58 (June 2005): 257–268; Jeff Yates and Andrew Whitford, "Institutional Foundations of the President's Issue Agenda," *Political Research Quarterly* 58 (December 2005): 577–585.

55. David S. Cloud, "Lack of New Proposals Reflects New Dynamic on the Hill," *Congressional Quarterly Weekly Report*, January 28, 1995, 259–260; Donna Cassata, "Swift Progress of 'Contract' Inspires Awe and Concern," *Congressional Quarterly Weekly Report*, April 1, 1995, 909–912.

56. Carroll J. Doherty, "Clinton's Big Comeback Shown in Vote Score," *Congressional Quarterly Weekly Report*, December 21, 1996, 3427–3428.

57. Woodrow Wilson, *Congressional Government* (1885; reprint, New York: Meridian, 1956), 53.

58. Joseph E. Kallenbach, *The American Chief Executive* (New York: Harper and Row, 1966), 354.

59. Mark A. Peterson, "The President and Congress," in *The Presidency and the Political System*, 6th ed., ed. Michael Nelson (Washington, D.C.: CQ Press, 2000), 476.

60. Richard S. Conley and Amie Kreppel, "Toward a New Typology of Vetoes and Overrides," *Political Research Quarterly* 54 (December 2001): 845.

61. Robert J. Spitzer, *The Presidential Veto: Touchstone of the American Presidency* (Albany: State University of New York Press, 1988), 100–103.

62. Janet Hook, "Avalanche of Veto Threats Divides Bush, Congress," *Congressional Quarterly Weekly Report*, September 22, 1990, 2991. Hook cites an OMB spokeswoman as stating that the Bush administration had issued 120 veto threats since January 1989.

63. Rebecca E. Deen and Laura W. Arnold, "Veto Threats as a Policy Tool: When to Threaten?" *Presidential Studies Quarterly* 32 (March 2002): 36–37; John B. Gilmour, "Institutional and Individual Influences on the President's Veto," *Journal of Politics* 64 (February 2002): 198–218.

64. Barbara Sinclair, "Hostile Partners: The President, Congress, and Lawmaking in the Partisan 1990s," in Bond and Fleisher, *Polarized Politics*, 144. For a rational choice analysis of these interactions, see Charles M. Cameron, *Veto Bargaining: Presidents and the Politics of Negative Power* (New York: Cambridge University Press, 2000).

65. Sinclair, "Living (and Dying?) by the Sword," 180.

66. Phillip J. Cooper, "George W. Bush, Edgar Allan Poe, and the Use and Abuse of Presidential Signing Statements," *Presidential Studies Quarterly* 35 (September 2005): 516–517.

67. Ibid. Popular concern about the practice grew after an article was published in the *Boston Globe*. Charlie Savage, "Bush Challenges Hundreds of Laws; President Cites Powers of his Office," *Boston Globe*, April 30, 2006, www.boston.com/news/nation/articles/2006/04/30/bush_challenges_hundreds_of_laws.

68. T. J. Halstead, "Presidential Signing Statements: Constitutional and Institutional Implications," Congressional Research Service, September 20, 2006, updated April 13, 2007, www.coherentbabble .com/signingstatements/CRS/CRS-RL33667-4-07.pdf. Halstead's count is somewhat different from that of Christopher Kelley who has catalogued the statements and the challenged provisions at www.coherentbabble .com/signingstatements/FAQs.htm#1.%20%20What%20are%20presidential%20signing%20statements.

69. Curtis A. Bradley and Eric A. Posner, "Presidential Signing Statements and Executive Power," *Constitutional Commentary* 23 (Winter 2006): 307–358.

70. The GAO identified 160 provisions that had been challenged in signing statements. Of these, they focused on nineteen. Jonathan Weisman, "'Signing Statements' Study Finds Administration Has Ignored Laws," *Washington Post*, June 19, 2007, A4.

71. Richard E. Neustadt, *Presidential Power: The Politics of Leadership* (New York: Wiley, 1960), 10.

72. Dave Boyer, "White House, GOP on Hill in Harmony," *Washington Times*, February 14, 2001, A1. On the speech, see Dan Balz, "President Begins His Toughest Sell," *Washington Post*, February 28, 2001, A1.

73. Ari Fleischer as quoted by Scott Shepard, Cox News Service, March 4, 2001. Also see Mike Allen, "It's Campaign 2001: President Hits the Trail to Pitch Tax, Education Plans," *Washington Post*, March 2, 2001, A6.

74. The campaign was well documented on the White House Web site, including a map and videos of the president's appearances at http://georgewbush-whitehouse.archives.gov/infocus/social-security/map.html. President Bush made three appearances in Florida, two in Kentucky, and two in Pennsylvania.

75. Adriel Bettelheim, "Bush's Rough Choice on Social Security: Backtrack or Take Flak," *CQ Weekly*, March 7, 2005, 550.

76. Matthew Esbaugh-Soha and Jeffrey S. Peake, "The Contemporary Presidency: 'Going Local' to Reform Social Security," *Presidential Studies Quarterly* 36 (December 2006): 689–705.

77. Mycoff and Pika, *Confrontation and Compromise.* chap. 7.

78. Joseph A. Pika, "White House Office of Congressional Relations: A Longitudinal Analysis" (paper presented at the annual meeting of the Midwest Political Science Association, Chicago, April 20–22, 1978). See also the discussion in Kenneth E. Collier, *Between the Branches: The White House Office of Legislative Affairs* (Pittsburgh: University of Pittsburgh Press, 1997), 16–22, chap. 4.

79. Lyndon B. Johnson, *Vantage Point* (New York: Holt, Rinehart and Winston, 1971), 448; Doris Kearns Goodwin, *Lyndon Johnson and the American Dream* (New York: Harper and Row, 1976), 226.

80. George C. Edwards III, *Presidential Influence in Congress* (San Francisco: Freeman, 1980), 117–120. For the origins of Johnson's knowledge of the Senate, see Robert A. Caro, *The Years of Lyndon Johnson: Master of the Senate* (New York: Knopf, 2002).

81. Terry Sullivan, "Headcounts, Expectations, and Presidential Coalitions in Congress," *American Journal of Political Science* (August 1988): 567. Elsewhere, Sullivan demonstrates that head counts are a valuable presidential tool for signaling congressional supporters and for obtaining information from them. "Explaining Why Presidents Count: Signaling and Information," *Journal of Politics* (August 1990): 939–962.

82. Sinclair, "Trying to Govern Positively," 96–100.

83. Steve Langdon, "Clinton's High Victory Rate Conceals Disappointments," *Congressional Quarterly Weekly Report*, December 31, 1994, 3619.

84. Conley, *The Presidency, Congress and Divided Government*, chap. 7.

85. Sinclair, "Trying to Govern Positively," 121.

86. Jon Healey, "Clinton Success Rate Declined to a Record Low in 1995," *Congressional Quarterly Weekly Report*, January 27, 1996, 193.

87. John C. Fortier and Norman J. Ornstein, "Congress and the Bush Presidency" (paper presented at the conference on "The Bush Presidency: An Early Assessment," Woodrow Wilson School, Princeton University, April 25–26, 2003), 24, 26.

88. Ibid., 34.

89. For example, House Republican conservatives refused to acquiesce to the Bush administration's compromise on intelligence reform. See Mycoff and Pika, *Confrontation and Compromise*, chap. 3.

90. Andrew Rudalevige, "The Contemporary Presidency: The Decline and Resurgence and Decline (and Resurgence?) of Congress: Charting a New Imperial Presidency," *Presidential Studies Quarterly* 36 (September 2006): 518–519.

91. Laurence L. Barrett, *Gambling with History* (Garden City, N.Y.: Doubleday, 1983), 334.

92. The most thorough study of this staff unit is by Kenneth Collier, *Between the Branches: The White House Office of Legislative Affairs* (Pittsburgh: University of Pittsburgh Press, 1997). Also see the discussion in John H. Kessel, *Presidents, the Presidency, and the Political Environment* (Washington, D.C.: CQ Press, 2001), 30–52.

93. George C. Edwards III, *At the Margins: Presidential Leadership of Congress* (New Haven: Yale University Press, 1989), chap. 3.

94. Kessel, *Presidents, the Presidency, and the Political Environment*, 26.

95. Edwards, *At the Margins*, 68–69; Jon R. Bond and Richard Fleisher, *The President in the Legislative Arena* (Chicago: University of Chicago Press, 1990), 171–175.

96. Gary C. Jacobson, *The Electoral Origins of Divided Government* (Boulder: Westview, 1990), 80–81.

97. Gary C. Jacobson, *The Politics of Congressional Elections*, 3rd ed. (New York: HarperCollins, 1992), 161–162.

98. Fortier and Ornstein, "Congress and the Bush Presidency," 39–40. On midterm losses, see Abramson, Aldrich, and Rohde, *Change and Continuity*, 228.

99. Sullivan, "Headcounts, Expectations, and Presidential Coalitions in Congress," 573–582.

100. John W. Kingdon, *Congressmen's Voting Decisions* (New York: Harper and Row, 1981); Aage R. Clausen, *How Congressmen Decide* (New York: St. Martin's Press, 1973).

101. Conley, *The Presidency, Congress, and Divided Government*, 3–83.

102. Bond and Fleisher, *The President in the Legislative Arena*, 221.

103. Ibid., 182.

104. Edwards, *At the Margins*, 124–125.

105. John E. Mueller, *War, Presidents, and Public Opinion* (New York: Wiley, 1973).

106. Wayne, *The Legislative Presidency*, 166.

107. Elizabeth Drew, *On the Edge* (New York: Simon and Schuster, 1994), 54, 266.

108. Mark Lacey, "Bush to Attend Democratic Caucuses," *New York Times*, January 27, 2001, A11.

109. Drew, *On the Edge*, 266. For a more positive review of Clinton's personal effectiveness, see Pfiffner, *The Strategic Presidency*, 180.

110. Edwards, *At the Margins*, 211. Also see Bond and Fleisher, *The President in the Legislative Arena*, 219; Bert A. Rockman, *The Leadership Question: The Presidency and the American Political System* (New York: Praeger, 1984), 214.

111. Mark A. Peterson, *Legislating Together: The White House and Capitol Hill from Eisenhower to Reagan* (Cambridge: Harvard University Press, 1990), 267.

112. Edwards, *At the Margins*, 8–15.

113. Bond and Fleisher, *The President in the Legislative Arena*, 220–234.

114. Peterson, *Legislating Together*, 92–94, chaps. 4 and 5.

115. Arthur M. Schlesinger Jr., *The Imperial Presidency* (Boston: Houghton Mifflin, 1973).

116. For an alternative view stressing legislative rather than executive dominance, see Keith E. Whittington and Daniel P. Carpenter, "Executive Power in American Institutional Development," *Perspectives on Politics* 1 (September 2003): 495–513.

117. Sundquist, *The Decline and Resurgence of Congress*.

118. In the second edition of *The Imperial Presidency* (Boston: Houghton Mifflin, 1989), Schlesinger maintains that Reagan moved two-thirds of the way toward restoring the imperial presidency. He met two of Schlesinger's "tests"—extensive presidential war making and heavy reliance on secrecy—but Reagan did not direct his powers against administration critics (451, 457).

119. Jack N. Rakove, "Taking Prerogative Out of the Presidency: An Originalist Perspective," *Presidential Studies Quarterly* 37 (March 2007): 85.

120. Rudalevige, "The Contemporary Presidency."

121. This is the central theme of Peterson's *Legislating Together*, in which he advocates a "tandem institutions" perspective on presidential-congressional relations.

CHAPTER 6

Executive Politics

Presidents rely not only on members of their cabinet for policy advice but on aides in the White House and staff units in the Executive Office of the President. Here President Obama discusses the economy in the Oval Office with (left to right) Vice President Joe Biden, Director of OMB Peter Orszag, White House Chief of Staff Rahm Emanuel, and National Economic Director Lawrence Summers.

Americans commonly think of the president as the "chief executive" of the federal government, held responsible for its many activities and responsibilities. If government fails to meet popular expectations, the president takes the blame. In the wake of 9/11, the president and his administration took responsibility for preventing another terrorist attack and for minimizing the consequences if one should occur. To accomplish this goal, President Bush proposed on June 6, 2002, and signed into law on November 25, legislation creating the Department of Homeland Security. As he declared, "We're taking historic action to defend the United States and protect our citizens from the dangers of a new era."[1] The mammoth new department, described by some as a "superagency," consolidated twenty-two agencies and units from other departments into a single entity with 170,000 or more workers, making it the federal government's third biggest department. This move was the largest single government reorganization since the creation of the Department of Defense in 1947.

FIGURE 6-1   Organizational Chart of the Department of Homeland Security, 2003

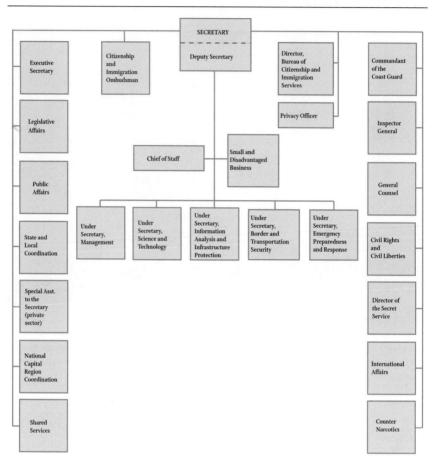

SOURCE: www.dhs.gov

The department's primary mission is to (1) prevent terrorist attacks within the United States; (2) reduce the country's vulnerability to terrorism; and (3) minimize the damage and assist in the recovery from terrorist attacks that do occur within the nation's borders. To accomplish these goals, the department was organized into five directorates: Border and Transportation Security, Emergency Preparedness and Response, Information Analysis, Infrastructure Protection and Management, and Science and Technology. Complaints about the department's unwieldiness and poor performance during the Hurricane Katrina disaster resulted in the directorates disappearing but made the organization chart even more complex.[2] Several units, including the Coast Guard and Secret Service, were not originally in a directorate and still answer directly to the secretary (see Figure 6-1). Even with the changes introduced in 2003 and subsequently, it was recognized that success would require extensive coordination with other federal agencies as well as with state and local officials, all of whom participate in securing the homeland.

Creation of a huge federal bureaucracy was not the president's original solution. On October 8, 2001, he chose Pennsylvania governor Tom Ridge to serve as director of the Office of Homeland Security, a one-hundred-person White House staff unit, and to oversee the Homeland Security Council, an interdepartmental coordinating committee designed to function much like the long-established National Security Council. Ridge, however, encountered resistance from his government colleagues when he proposed reorganizing their efforts, struggled to create new systems such as the color-coded alert system, and was drawn into protracted battles with Congress over its right to exercise oversight of his activities.[3] Congressional Democrats were especially critical of Bush's less than bold approach. By early May 2002, a bipartisan, bicameral proposal to create a new department had emerged, and later in the month Sen. Joseph Lieberman, D-Conn., secured approval from the Government Affairs Committee, which he chaired. Bush's sudden endorsement of the proposal surprised most observers, but by doing so, he regained the initiative on this high visibility issue. Although the turf battles proved long and bitter, Bush ultimately got most of what he sought, with numerous bureaucratic units moving into the new structure, some projected to prosper and others to suffer from the move. Among the agencies that moved were the Coast Guard (from Transportation), the Secret Service (from Treasury),[4] the Customs Service (from Treasury),[5] the Border Patrol (from Justice), the newly created Transportation Security Administration (from Transportation),[6] FEMA (the Federal Emergency Management Agency, an independent agency),[7] the Office of Domestic Preparedness (from Justice), the National Domestic Preparedness Office (from the FBI), the Computer Security Division (from Commerce), and the National Communications System (from Defense).

Deciding which units should be housed in the new structure was probably the easy part, even if it seemed hard at the time; assembling a management team on short notice and pulling all the pieces into a coherent whole presented a greater challenge. As public administration experts pointed out, it took nearly four decades for the military forces to work effectively in a single department; the Department of

Transportation (created in 1967) continues to founder from the fragmentation caused by multiple congressional committees favoring different modes of transportation; the Department of Energy, created in 1977 as a response to the oil crisis, also suffers from a fragmented congressional committee structure and deeply embedded organizational cultures difficult to mold into one.[8] Secretary Ridge's challenge was enormous. According to the White House, "88 congressional committees and subcommittees have jurisdiction over issues related to homeland security, and . . . that gives the Homeland Security Department a lot of congressional bosses to work with—and answer to—in its drive to make America safer."[9] This legislative cross-section included all senators and 95 percent of the House members in the 107th Congress. In addition, the newly assembled pieces of the department brought with them established relationships with organized interests that hoped to protect the access and services they enjoyed under the old arrangements, and a few newly organized interests as well.[10] To help the secretary create a coherent department, the administration battled throughout the fall with the Democrat-controlled Senate and public workers' unions to "give the new agency's executives a free hand to reshuffle personnel and change the way employees are hired, paid, promoted and disciplined."[11] Ridge, then, confronted a nearly unprecedented task with nearly unprecedented powers.

It was no surprise that the reorganization did not solve all problems. Secretary Ridge left government service and was replaced by Michael Chertoff, a former federal appeals court judge, whose leadership of the department was stressful. The first crisis was Hurricane Katrina in September 2005 when problems within FEMA became all too apparent. FEMA's director resigned, and the agency's mistakes both before and after the hurricane underwent microscopic review. To his credit, Chertoff had proposed a wide range of reorganization proposals even before the hurricane.[12] When implemented, they looked to one observer like an "extreme makeover" of the department.[13] They included trimming one layer of bureaucracy between the secretary and units responsible for airport, seaport, bridge, and subway security; streamlining FEMA's responsibilities and establishing clearer capacity to coordinate federal, state, and local actions; creating a new office to integrate intelligence and analysis from the department's ten intelligence units. Later controversies over enforcing immigration laws, allowing a company based in Dubai to manage U.S. seaports, and changing the formula for allocating grants to state and local governments embroiled Chertoff in further battles. He was, however, able to retain FEMA in his department. All the while, Congress continued to battle over who should exercise oversight over the department's programs.[14]

After President Bush and his administration were severely criticized for a delayed and ineffective response to Hurricane Katrina in August 2005, the president made certain that he met with victims of subsequent natural disasters. Here he tours a home destroyed by the California fires of October 2007.

Like Bush with his struggles to provide homeland security, most modern presidents have encountered difficulties in their efforts to direct the executive branch, whether it be working with existing entities or creating new ones. John F. Kennedy lamented the inertia of the State Department, and Ronald Reagan made his campaign attack on an overgrown federal bureaucracy one of his presidency's enduring themes. Presidents proposing to harness the potential of government to deliver much-needed services must overcome the cynical belief that bureaucracy is the problem, not the solution. Bill Clinton's proposal to solve the nation's health care problems fell victim to the charge that it would create a bloated federal bureaucracy. Richard Rose, who has studied the president as a manager, has remarked that the "president's title of chief executive is a misnomer; he can more accurately be described as a nonexecutive chief."[15] The essence of Rose's argument is that, even within the executive branch, presidential powers of command are limited and that a president's success as an administrator depends greatly on the ability to win the trust of others. Presidents therefore confront an enormous challenge. The public expects them to produce results but is unsure of government's role, not wanting it to become too intrusive. Given this gap between expectations and powers, it should not be surprising that presidents gravitate toward instruments of unilateral power that provide them with greater leverage over the government. But, as noted in chapter 1, George W. Bush's exercise of these unilateral powers created controversy.

This chapter examines the president's responsibilities as chief executive and the factors that affect administrative performance. It opens with a discussion of the president's executive role, its constitutional, legal, and administrative foundations. It then explores the president's relationships with the executive branch and the cabinet. After establishing that the president's powers of command over the units of the executive branch are limited, the chapter analyzes the formal powers and managerial tools that modern presidents have available for discharging administrative duties.

The President as Executive

The president's executive role is grounded in ambiguous language in Article II of the Constitution, which says "the executive Power" is vested in the president, who is directed to "take Care that the Laws be faithfully executed." The president may also "require the Opinion, in writing, of the principal Officer in each of the executive Departments" and "grant Reprieves and Pardons." Modern presidents have tended to interpret these provisions broadly and have derived substantial additional powers from them. In addition to these constitutionally based powers, presidents have received extensive delegations of statutory authority from Congress.

Yet presidents confront a paradox. Although they enjoy considerable formal legal powers and head a vast, complex military and civilian bureaucracy, their ability to direct that bureaucracy toward the achievement of the administration's policy objectives and program goals is frequently limited. To understand that paradox, we must examine the constitutional relationship of the presidency to the legislative and judicial branches as well as the nature of the federal bureaucracy and the president's relationship to it.

In administration as in so many other areas, presidents require the cooperation of Congress because only Congress can authorize government programs, establish agencies to implement the programs, and appropriate funds to finance them.[16] Presidents, however, find that congressional cooperation may be difficult to obtain because, regardless of party loyalties, presidents and members of Congress have different constituency and institutional perspectives. There are also occasions when the exercise of presidential power must be acceptable to the judiciary. In short, presidential power is not self-executing, and it is subject to restraint.

Although the federal bureaucracy—which today consists of fifteen cabinet departments and scores of special agencies, with a total workforce of more than 4 million civilian and military employees—is called the executive branch, it is really the creation of the legislative branch. When Congress establishes federal departments and agencies, its members are responding not only to presidential needs and requests, but also to demands and pressures from various constituency forces, interest groups, and the general public. As a result, the structure of the federal bureaucracy tends to reflect the political fragmentation and committee jurisdictions of Congress, which often leads, as with Homeland Security, to multiple committees overseeing the activities of the same department. Presidents do not look down upon subordinate administrative units from a position at the apex of a pyramid of authority; instead, they confront a complex and confusing array of departments and agencies with varying degrees of independence.

In addition, presidents deal with career civil servants who staff bureaucratic units and constitute a permanent federal government. These civil servants respond to demands from interest groups and to direction from congressional committees as well as to presidential leadership. Most modern presidents have entered office believing—or they soon become convinced—that they cannot take the support and loyalty of the bureaucracy for granted, but must constantly strive to earn both.[17]

The president's task as the nation's chief executive, therefore, is much more than issuing commands or finding ways to bring a large complex bureaucracy under operational control. The president must secure congressional cooperation while suppressing the executive branch's natural tendencies toward conflict with the legislative branch and must give direction to the bureaucracy so that it will help accomplish the administration's goals. As the functions of the federal government expanded from the New Deal onward, the task of defining objectives and coordinating their achievement has become more difficult for presidents.

The President and the Executive Branch

Presidents need help in discharging their ill-defined executive power, but the Constitution provided them with few sources of assistance. Presidents quickly discover that the reality of their relations with the federal bureaucracy bears little resemblance to the idealized vision that many hold of presidents issuing orders and bureaucrats carrying them out. Presidential appointees to posts in the government, collectively known as **political executives,** are expected to assist the president. Department secretaries and agency administrators appointed by the president are charged with directing the work of the career employees, coordinating the operations of their component bureaus, and developing and maintaining links with other federal departments and agencies as well as with state and local governments. The vice president, exercising his constitutional responsibility to preside over the Senate, was originally more an officer of Congress than a source of help to the president, but, as discussed below, that position changed dramatically in the second half of the twentieth century. Today, the president's greatest assistance in managing the federal bureaucracy comes from the staff housed in the White House Office and FDR's creation, the **Executive Office of the President** (EOP). Roosevelt convinced Congress to create the EOP to help him define objectives, convert them into operating programs, allocate resources to the agencies administering the programs, and coordinate the implementation of programs within the federal government and among federal, state, and local governments.

Tension among the president, presidential agents, and the bureaucracy has been present in every modern administration. It exists, at least in part, because of what Hugh Heclo has identified as the distinction between "political leadership in the bureaucracy" and "bureaucratic power."[18] The direction and effectiveness of the political leadership presidents provide depend on their personalities, leadership style, and values as well as on external events and conditions. In contrast, bureaucratic power is relatively permanent, not dependent on personalities and transitory factors. That power belongs to the career civil servants who make up the permanent government.

At least five general factors contribute to bureaucratic power and shape presidential-bureaucratic relations: the size, complexity, and dispersion of the executive branch; bureaucratic inertia and momentum; executive branch personnel; the legal position of the executive branch; and the susceptibility of executive branch units to external political influence. Major consequences of the interaction of these factors are presidential frustration and a pattern of policymaking often sharply at odds with the norm of democratic accountability; it is a system that obscures those responsible for a policy and a decision.

Size, Complexity, and Dispersion of the Executive Branch

The scope of federal government activities has exploded since 1933, tremendously increasing the number of agencies and the range of programs they administer. Federal spending for 2008 was $2.98 trillion, and federal employees numbered more than 2.67 million civilians and about 1.4 million active duty military personnel. Federal employees oversee domestic programs that reach into every community in the nation and touch the lives of individuals from birth to death. Many of those programs are delivered by nonfederal employees: one estimate sets the total number of jobs associated with federal government programs at almost 15 million when the contract employees, grant recipients, and state and local employees working on government funding are included.[19] Strategies designed to ensure national security extend U.S. military and foreign policy activities around the world. Providing leadership and direction to such a far-flung bureaucracy is difficult. It would be so even if the president could command prompt and unquestioning obedience.

The multiplicity of agencies and programs creates an additional obstacle to effective leadership. Overlapping jurisdictions lead in some cases to duplication of efforts and in others to contradictory efforts; one even finds competition among government agencies. Presidents must be coordinators. When they define goals for a policy area, they most often deal not with single administrative units but with many. Even after twenty-two administrative units were consolidated into the Department of Homeland Security, the military services, the FBI, and the CIA remain outside units whose cooperation and coordination are critical to success. A rigorous review of intelligence failures that preceded the 9/11 attacks identified competition within the intelligence community as a major problem, but the changes were modest—a new position to coordinate the intelligence community's efforts and yet an additional intelligence agency, making a total of sixteen.[20]

The tremendous size of the federal bureaucracy means its activities are widely dispersed. Presidents, their aides, and their principal political appointees are at the center of government. The people who operate programs, deliver services to individuals, and regulate the conduct of businesses and other organizations are at the periphery. These people, most of them civil servants, are there when a new president and staff take office and will be there after the political executives depart.

Bureaucratic Inertia and Momentum

Bureaucratic inertia means it is hard to get a new government activity started, and once it is under way, it is even more difficult to stop it or even significantly redirect it. In short, "bureaucracies at rest tend to stay at rest and bureaucracies in motion tend to stay in motion."[21] Much of this inflexibility arises because of organizational routines—prescribed operating procedures that have worked successfully in the past—or interest group efforts to preserve established programs.

The momentum of ongoing programs especially frustrates presidents. Government commitments are reflected in public laws, the amount of money allocated for those activities in annual appropriations, and the number of civil service and military employees who carry out the activities. In 2006 mandatory expenditures constituted about 62 percent of the government's budget. The principal mandatory items included interest on the national debt; entitlement programs such as Social Security, Medicare, and Medicaid; federal retirement and veterans' benefits; and unemployment compensation. Even the remaining, discretionary portion of the budget is highly resistant to cuts because of support from groups benefiting from those expenditures. Presidents can influence the shape of the federal budget, but major changes usually require years to be implemented. From one year to the next, presidents tend to be limited to incremental changes.

Given their fixed terms of office and the usual scope of their objectives, presidents find the incremental adjustments possible through annual budgeting inadequate. For members of the permanent government, the time perspective is much different; they can afford to be patient. In the budget process, they fight to maintain their "base," which is their current appropriation, and to add as large an increment to it as possible.[22] Over time, small annual increases are transformed into large permanent gains. Bureaucratic momentum therefore works to the advantage of the permanent government and acts as a constraint on presidents who attempt to counter it. President Reagan and his successors tried to overcome the effects of incremental budgeting by means of a top-down process that restricted total government spending and forced agencies and their supporters to accept cuts or limited growth.[23]

The large number of career federal employees pressures the president to maintain ongoing programs. Major reductions in personnel or redirection of their activities are economically and politically costly. People will oppose actions that threaten to deprive them of their jobs or that require them to move, undergo additional training, or reduce their sense of security and importance. Most presidents can make only modest adjustments in the size and mission of the federal workforce. Clinton was somewhat more successful in this regard than other modern presidents, eventually eliminating more than 300,000 jobs at the end of seven years as part of the "reinvent government" effort led by Vice President Al Gore.[24]

Bureaucratic Personnel

Presidents must depend on both political appointees and career officials to operate the federal bureaucracy. Until 1883, when the Pendleton Act created the federal civil service, no distinction existed between the two groups. Presidents could theoretically appoint all members of the federal bureaucracy, a spoils system of tangible rewards for party members who had supported the election winner. With the creation and steady expansion of the civil service system, which opened government jobs to all citizens based on their qualifications, presidential control of government personnel declined, and the characteristics and roles of appointed and career officials became more distinctive, often hindering presidential direction of programs. In 2002 George W. Bush argued that protecting the American homeland was so critical that it required jettisoning some of the worker protections that had become part of the civil service system. The proposal became a major issue in the midterm elections that fall and was later included in the legislation that created the Department of Homeland Security. Democrats have sought to remove the special provisions and restore the traditional civil service protections.[25]

The political executives—those appointed by the president and charged with directing the careerists—are a weak substitute for the old patronage-based system and constitute what Hugh Heclo has called a "government of strangers."[26] Aside from cabinet officers, a few important subcabinet appointees, and the heads of major independent agencies, these political executives are largely unknown to the president and one another. Only loosely do they constitute a presidential team able to provide direction to the bureaucracy. "Although party is still the glue that seems to hold administrations together, this glue's consistency is much thinner than ever before and its holding power is greatly reduced."[27]

Cabinet selection involves the president directly in an attempt to build support for the administration by including representatives of various constituencies in the party and the country.[28] Presidents sometimes appoint personal friends to especially important cabinet departments because of the close counseling relationship involved.[29] But selection of other political executives is affected by multiple and often conflicting pressures: loyalty to the president, party membership, technical competence, the wishes of the cabinet member under whom the appointee will serve, and the demands of congressional members, interest groups, and state and local party leaders. Moreover, anyone subject to Senate confirmation must be acceptable to the relevant committee members and have a sparkling clean financial and personal background.

When done with care and planning, recruiting people to serve in an administration has the potential to be an instrument of control over policy, a tool of administrative management, and an important component of presidential relations with Congress, interest groups, and political parties. Consequently, the process is highly political. Presidents since Eisenhower have used personnel staffs located in the White House to run the appointment process, a group now more formally identified as the Office of Presidential Personnel.[30] The personnel process is always chaotic at the start of a new administration because of the many positions to be filled, pressures for jobs from campaign workers and party members, and uncertainty about how to proceed. The number of inquiries from job seekers can be crushing, reaching as many as fifteen hundred a day.[31] Eventually the search becomes more systematic,[32] and the office typically will coordinate the filling of about five thousand positions during a presidential term.[33] Over time, centralization of appointment decisions in the Office of Presidential Personnel has increased presidential control and bureaucratic responsiveness, but the consequences have been costly. As Thomas Weko points out, centralization permits job seekers, interest groups, members of Congress, and campaign contributors to press their claims directly on the White House staff, transferring into the White House conflicts once waged outside it, provoking conflict between the appointments staff and the administrative units, and diminishing the importance of program considerations.[34]

The process also depends on an active president who provides sustained support for the selection of appointees. President Reagan excelled in this regard. The Reagan White House exercised tight control over recruitment, filling sensitive positions with loyal individuals committed to the president's ideology. Cabinet members could not conduct independent searches for subcabinet officials. Prospective appointees were screened for policy views, political and personal backgrounds, and, if considered necessary, expertise. The Reagan administration took a long time to get its political executives in place (the next three administrations took even longer), but the result was tighter control over the executive branch and greater cohesion within it than other modern presidents have achieved.[35]

Bill Clinton's experience illustrates the difficulty presidents encounter. The Clinton personnel operation had almost three hundred employees during the transition and more than one hundred in the Presidential Personnel Office in March 1993. The operation's objective was to create a competent staff that also responded to the claims and demands of campaign workers and contributors and represented the diverse blocs, movements, and constituencies that had brought electoral victory. The operation's political success was reflected in the diversity of the appointees, recruited to reflect EGG—"ethnicity, gender and geography."[36] The preoccupation with diversity, ethical concerns, and a series of botched nominations, however, resulted in a slowed appointment pace that brought criticism from Congress, Democratic constituency groups, and the media.[37]

Because the outcome of the 2000 election long remained in question, George W. Bush's search for personnel got off to a late start. Even so, the administration was only a week behind Clinton's record in selecting the cabinet and was actually faster in naming the White House staff.[38] But there were other sources of delay. At the hundred-day mark, Bush was well behind Reagan and Clinton in getting appointees in place. With 488 top appointments to make, Bush had announced 177 candidates, but only 60 names had been submitted to the Senate, and of those, only 29 had been confirmed. "Indeed, as of December 31, 2002, and despite nearly heroic efforts at both ends of Pennsylvania Avenue, the Bush administration had become the slowest in modern history to fill its top jobs."[39] Candidates were delayed by the need to fill out extensive questionnaires, complete financial disclosure forms, and undergo background investigations.

With each new administration the confirmation process has grown longer. Some problems are self-inflicted. Several of President Barack Obama's nominees withdrew from consideration because of revelations about their past conduct. Tom Daschle, nominated for secretary of the Health and Human Services Department and slated to play the leading role in health care reform, withdrew after reports that he had failed to pay taxes on a limousine service provided by a client. Obama needed three tries to get a commerce secretary before Gary Locke was confirmed. Bill Richardson, the first nominee, withdrew because of a grand jury investigation into state contracts awarded to prominent campaign contributors in New Mexico. Judd Gregg, a Republican senator from New Hampshire, was a surprise nominee, but he then announced that his disagreements with the administration's economic strategy were too numerous and too deep for him to move forward. Nancy Killefer, slotted to be the Office of Management and Budget (OMB) chief performance officer, withdrew after revelations about her personal finances. One nominee who made it through despite financial problems was Treasury Secretary Timothy Geithner, who had failed to pay taxes on some of his previous income, a political problem because Geithner would oversee the Internal Revenue Service in his new job.

After these embarrassments, the administration applied still greater care in reviewing potential nominees' personal finances. Several candidates for subcabinet positions (second- or third-level jobs in the departments) withdrew rather than undergo intense and prolonged scrutiny or suffer further delay. Candidates were required to fill out a sixty-three-item questionnaire that asked, among other things, whether they had ever written an embarrassing e-mail, demanded copies of all resumés submitted for any jobs over the previous ten years, and copies of every speech candidates had ever delivered. The materials were then inspected (*vetted* is the Washington term) by the White House, the FBI, the IRS, and the Office of Government Ethics. For positions subject to Senate confirmation, each congressional committee uses its own questionnaire.

The political executives who successfully navigate this gauntlet are often amateurs in the precarious world of Washington politics, lacking the political knowledge and substantive skills needed to provide effective leadership. They quickly discover their dependence on top-level career executives and lower-ranking civil servants for information and advice. That support is obtained only by paying a price, however, in the form of loyalty to the agency and support for its programs within the administration, before Congress, and with the public. Members of the president's team suddenly find themselves striking a balance between the often conflicting claims of the White House and the agencies they lead. In general, it takes twelve to eighteen months for political executives to master their jobs. Their average tenure, however, is only two years. The high turnover rates make it difficult to develop teamwork within departments and agencies. Cabinet secretaries are continually adapting to new assistants, and people on the same administrative level barely get to know one another. One result is that expectations and roles are in flux, and coordination and control problematic.

Political executives, who look upward to the president for support and direction and downward to the permanent government for support and services, are imperfect instruments for presidential control of the bureaucracy. They can best serve the president by winning the trust of the careerists, but to do so means maintaining a considerable degree of independence from the White House.

Conflicts between the White House and the career executives arise for understandable reasons. The relatively secure tenure of upper-level civil servants (as opposed to the expendability and shorter tenure of political executives) allows them to take a more gradual approach to resolving problems and to pursue their objectives obliquely and by indirection, generating less opposition. In contrast, political executives, urged on by the White House, tend to pursue their goals quite directly and to see virtue in conflict. In addition, civil servants must remain politically neutral to remain civil servants; they are therefore cautious about becoming identified with a political party or appointee. Presidential appointees, many of whom are unfamiliar with bureaucratic ways, often mistake such caution for opposition or disloyalty. This viewpoint is reinforced by the high value career executives place on maintaining their relationships with clientele group representatives, congressional members and staff, and individuals outside the Washington community who are involved in, or knowledgeable about, their agencies' programs.

To correct perceived deficiencies in the career service and to increase presidential control over the higher civil service (those in GS-16 and higher positions), the Carter administration engineered the passage of the Civil Service Reform Act (CSRA) of 1978. The CSRA established the Senior Executive Service (SES), a professional managerial corps of career civil servants whose members are eligible for financial bonuses. It also increased the ability of political executives to transfer career officials within and between agencies and to raise the number of noncareerists in the SES and lower positions.[40] Another provision of the CSRA replaced the three-person bipartisan Civil Service Commission with the single-headed Office of Personnel Management (OPM), which gave the president more control over the career service. Reagan's first director of the OPM, Donald J. Devine, aggressively implemented a partisan vision of leadership.[41] Neither of Reagan's immediate successors, George H. W. Bush and Bill Clinton, used politicization of the career service as extensively as Reagan did to direct the executive branch.

These Carter-era reforms have come under administration and congressional scrutiny. As Paul Light testified before the House Government Reform Committee, "The federal government has had twenty-five years of experience under the 1978 reforms with decisively mixed results," and some analysts believed that only comprehensive reforms could fix the problems.[42] George W. Bush's administration originally challenged civil service practices in security-related departments (Homeland Security and Defense) and then proposed a "management agenda" that stressed evaluating agency performance in achieving five governmentwide initiatives and broadcasting the results publicly on a Web-based scorecard.[43] The most controversial feature of the agenda was requiring that outside companies be invited to compete for contracts to provide "commercial activities" performed by government workers, a process similar to "contracting out" or "outsourcing." Red flags went up on Capitol Hill and in government agencies when it seemed the Bush administration was aiming to open nearly 900,000 government positions to competitive bidding. The target number was reduced by half, and the targets varied from agency to agency. Although the final effort was significantly smaller than originally feared, many observers remained concerned about the motives behind the Bush effort.[44]

Legal Arrangements

The ambiguous legal position of the executive branch is the fourth factor that affects a president's control over the bureaucracy. Although the Constitution charges presidents with responsibility for executing the laws, their legal position as chief executive is somewhat unclear because Congress has—with presidential approval—delegated authority to, and imposed duties directly on, other administrative officials. In some cases, such as independent regulatory commissions and the Federal Reserve Board, presidents have no formal power to direct agency actions or set agency policy. Their influence is based on budgetary and appointment powers and persuasive abilities. For cabinet members, heads of independent agencies, and other political executives with operating authority to whom Congress has directly delegated power, the situation is ambiguous. As chief executive, the president, by virtue of the Constitution's "take care" clause, can command the decisions of subordinates. In doing so, however, the president risks confrontation with Congress and with the clientele groups and individuals affected by the administrative units involved. In addition, the Supreme Court long ago ruled that the president must not interfere with the performance of a "purely ministerial" duty that does not involve the exercise of discretion or judgment.[45] Nor may the president prevent the execution of the law by subordinates.

Congress has provided administrative officials with broad delegations of discretionary authority because legislation can seldom be drafted in sufficient detail to cover all contingencies. Legislators also have made vague and general grants of power because it is politically advantageous to shift difficult and potentially unpopular decisions to the bureaucracy. The Supreme Court has approved such delegations with the proviso that they be accompanied by clear statutory guidelines.[46] The Court's insistence on specific statutory standards has, however, seldom been followed by Congress or by the lower courts.[47] The standards the Court uses have tended to be vague and unspecific, such as "just and reasonable rates," "excess profits," and "the public interest, convenience, and necessity." In spite of judicial review of the fairness of administrative procedures and judicial reference to the legislative history of statutes as found in congressional committee hearings, reports, and floor debates, administrative officials retain substantial discretionary authority that complicates the president's task of controlling the bureaucracy.

Susceptibility to External Influence

Although presidents try to impose control on the federal bureaucracy, the effort frequently falls short. The reach of appointees chosen on the basis of party and personal loyalty is limited. As a result, the federal bureaucracy is susceptible to other outside forces and depends upon them for political support. For some agencies, outside support is essential when a president fundamentally challenges their programs or ranks them low on the administration's priority list, which may threaten their funding. In addition, executive branch units confronted with external criticism and political pressure may find little support within an administration concerned with negative publicity and political fallout. If presidential support is lacking, the agency must look elsewhere for help in maintaining its authority, funding, and personnel. It turns to the public, especially to the individuals and groups affected by its programs, and it turns to Congress, particularly the committees or subcommittees with jurisdiction over its legislative authorizations and appropriations.

The regulations that agencies promulgate and enforce, or the benefits and services they deliver, provide the basis for the development of enduring ties between them and their clientele groups. An agency without a well-organized clientele is in a precarious position. Clientele groups can publicize an agency's accomplishments and defend it against attack. In exchange, the agency administers its programs with a manifest concern for the clientele's interests. The agency consults with clientele group officials and with individual notables attentive to its activities. Such outsiders often participate in agency decision making through informal personal contacts and advisory councils and panels. Agencies seldom draft guidelines and regulations or award grants without extensive external participation and consultation. There is also a two-way flow of personnel between agencies and clientele organizations. These mutually beneficial relations are characteristic of most domestic policy areas in the federal government.

For example, the National Education Association (NEA) and several other education interest groups provide support and protection to the Department of Education in exchange for access and information. The NEA led the congressional effort to elevate the former U.S. Office of Education to departmental status in 1979 and the battle to prevent the abolition of the fledgling department during the Reagan administration. Department of Education political executives have found employment with the NEA and other education interest groups; on occasion, those lobbies have helped to recruit or have provided agency staffers.

Agencies also find it easy and convenient to develop strong ties to the congressional committees or subcommittees that oversee them. Congressional requests for consideration on appointments and grants, suggestions concerning program administration, and inquiries in behalf of constituents are quickly acknowledged. Congressional influence with the agencies strengthens the committee members in their constituencies.[48] Bureaucrats use their connections with committee members to effect changes in their statutory authority and gain favorable treatment during budget negotiations. Agencies may use their committee ties to obtain more funds than the president has recommended or to modify their activities in a way not fully in accord with presidential preferences.

Agencies are not, however, totally resistant to presidential directives; agencies and the president need each other to accomplish their goals. If the true test of presidential power is the power to persuade, one of the best measures of an agency's strength is the degree to which a president must "bargain with it in order to secure its cooperation."[49]

The President and the Cabinet

Most modern presidents have come to office announcing their intention to make more extensive use of the cabinet as a collective decision-making body than the previous incumbent did, pledges generally applauded by the media and academics. Yet, with the exception of Dwight Eisenhower, presidents have not used their cabinets as vehicles of collective leadership. As MaryAnne Borrelli summarizes, "Cabinet government is a promise made by candidates, an ideal endorsed by presidents-elect, and a practice abandoned by presidents."[50]

This gap between expectation and experience suggests the public and most political leaders lack understanding of the cabinet. In point of fact, the Constitution places executive authority, ultimately, in the president alone. The notion of **collective leadership** or **collegial leadership**—typically found among cabinet members in parliamentary systems, who share leadership responsibility as a group—is incompatible with constitutional reality and inconsistent with American practice. The president is not first among equals; rather, he (or she) is the person in charge. Cabinet members are presidential appointees, serving at the president's pleasure. The president is not obliged to consult them as a group or to act according to their preferences. Colin Powell, Bush's first secretary of state, was reputed to have lost many battles over policy to administration hard-liners. He explained, "In the end, the president decides and we execute."[51] The cabinet has no formal constitutional or legal standing. It exists by custom, and presidents may use it as little or as much as they see fit. Clinton met with his entire cabinet only twice from the beginning of 1998 to May 1999.[52] According to White House chief of staff Andrew Card, the Bush cabinet met about once every two to three months during the first term.[53] The Bush system, however, was designed to implement White House directives, not to facilitate consultation, which became clear when the White House staff unit responsible for coordinating cabinet input was "effectively eliminated" in the second term.[54]

Yet the cabinet does have political significance. Members are the principal spokespersons for administration policy. They are also the top political executives expected to provide direction for those federal commitments deemed so important as to warrant cabinet-level status. Management tasks may be growing more important to cabinet members as their service in the job has become longer. Whereas the average tenure of cabinet members in the Nixon administration was 1.73 years, the service of Clinton's cabinet members was 3.36 years by the middle of 1999, the culmination of a six-administration trend of lengthening service.[55] Finally, cabinet composition has great symbolic value as a means of representing major social, economic, and political constituencies in the administration's highest councils.[56] Newly elected presidents try to select cabinet members whose presence will unify those constituencies behind the new administration.

Political experience, group identification, and technical expertise are important criteria for selecting cabinet members. Appointees to head certain departments, such as agriculture, generally must be acceptable to clientele groups. In choosing the secretaries of defense and the Treasury, presidents may give special weight to the candidates' expertise and experience. Generalist administrators, however, often are named to head the Departments of Commerce, Health and Human Services, Housing and Urban Development, and Transportation. A study covering eight administrations found that on average, two-thirds of presidents' initial cabinet appointees since FDR have been "Washington outsiders" less familiar with their departments' program responsibilities and that presidents tend to appoint more experienced managers ("insiders") as replacements for their first picks. Similarly, one finds the emphasis on group relations and "liaison" backgrounds early in administrations with the percentage of "generalists" increasing as the term progresses.[57] Among Bush's original fifteen cabinet secretaries, nearly a third were insiders. Seven came from "liaison" backgrounds; eight could be viewed as "generalists"; five had held significant roles in the presidential campaign; nine had previous executive branch experience; four were current or previous members of Congress; and seven had experience in state or local government.[58]

Most modern presidents develop close ties with the appointees Thomas Cronin refers to as the inner cabinet—the heads of the Departments of State, Defense, Treasury, Justice, and now Homeland Security. The activities and responsibilities of these departments are of the highest priority—foreign relations, civil rights, national security, the condition of the economy, and the administration of justice. Moreover, they cut across the concerns of the public and all members of Congress. These are the matters that dominate the president's time and attention.[59] The heads of the other departments usually constitute the outer cabinet.[60] Their departments have more sharply focused activities, and their leaders find themselves acting as advocates for clientele and congressional interests within the administration.[61] Frequently, those pressures conflict with the president's broader priorities. It is helpful to view President Obama's cabinet appointments in light of the inner/outer distinction.

Obama depended heavily on government insiders to staff his initial cabinet, people with previous elective or appointed experience. (See Table 6-1.) All five secretaries heading inner cabinet departments had extensive experience in government

TABLE 6-1   Backgrounds of Barack Obama's Initial Cabinet, 2009

Appointee	Former public position
Inner Cabinet	
Secretary of Defense	
Robert M. Gates	Secretary of Defense in Bush administration
Attorney General	
Eric H. Holder	Deputy attorney general
Secretary of State	
Hillary Rodham Clinton	Senator from New York
Secretary of the Treasury	
Timothy Geithner	President, Federal Reserve Bank of New York
Secretary of Homeland Security	
Janet Napolitano	Governor of Arizona
Outer Cabinet	
Secretary of Agriculture	
Tom Vilsack	Governor of Iowa
Secretary of Commerce	
Gary Locke	Governor of Washington
Secretary of Education	
Arne Duncan	Chief executive, Chicago Public Schools
Secretary of Energy	
Steven Chu	Director, Lawrence Livermore National Lab, Nobel laureate
Secretary of Health and Human Services	
Kathleen Sibelius	Governor of Kansas
Secretary of Housing and Urban Development	
Shaun L. S. Donovan	Housing commissioner, New York City
Secretary of the Interior	
Ken Salazar	Senator from Colorado
Secretary of Labor	
Hilda L. Solis	U.S. representative, California
Secretary of Transportation	
Ray LaHood	U.S. representative, Illinois
Secretary of Veterans Affairs	
Eric K. Shinseki	U.S. Army general, retired
Nondepartment Cabinet-level Positions	
Vice President	
Joseph R. Biden	Senator from Delaware
Ambassador to the United Nations	
Susan E. Rice	Assistant secretary of state
EPA Administrator	
Lisa P. Jackson	Chief, New Jersey Department of Environmental Protection
OMB Director	
Peter Orszag	Director, Congressional Budget Office
U.S. Trade Representative	
Ron Kirk	Mayor of Dallas
White House Chief of Staff	
Rahm Emanuel	U.S. representative, Illinois

SOURCE: Compiled by authors from public sources.

service, and two were elected officials. One, Secretary of Defense Robert Gates, was a holdover from the Bush administration and one of two Republicans included in the new cabinet; the other is Ray LaHood, and a third had been invited to join. The remainder of the cabinet included three governors, two House members, and one senator. Appointees without previous elected experience were notable for their technical expertise—a Nobel laureate in physics, chief executive of one of the nation's largest public school systems, a retired general, and an expert in urban housing—and three of these had also worked for government in the past. Some commentators complained it would be difficult for this group to deliver "change," Obama's signature campaign promise. But others were reassured that Obama had not chosen novices to lead the administration.

Presidents often try to use the cabinet as a decision-making body early in their administrations, but most eventually abandon the effort and rely on the White House staff instead.[62] They find that most cabinet members are concerned primarily with issues affecting their departments and that competition for the president's attention often occurs between cabinet members. Cabinet meetings are unsatisfactory devices for focused, analytical discussion of major issues. At best they can serve as forums for informal discussion of issues and problems and for the exchange of information. Presidents and their aides in the EOP are the only source of cohesion and policy coordination. Individual cabinet members feel loyal to the president *and* to the permanent governments within their departments. These conflicting loyalties inhibit the development of an informal sense of unity and purpose, without which the cabinet cannot realize its potential as a formal advisory body and policy-making mechanism.[63]

In most administrations one or two cabinet members tend to stand out and to develop close ties with the president. During Reagan's second term, Attorney General Edwin Meese III and Secretary of the Treasury James A. Baker III enjoyed considerable leeway in pursuing their own agendas without aggressive interference from the White House staff, provided they did not conflict with the president's ideological precepts.[64] Treasury Secretaries Lloyd Bentsen and Robert Rubin enjoyed independent stature in the Clinton administration because of their political and business experience, respectively.[65]

At the start of George W. Bush's administration, observers noted the influence of Vice President Dick Cheney, whose broad responsibilities and access apparently gave him more clout than any of the cabinet members, especially after Bush publicly contradicted positions taken by Secretary of State Colin L. Powell and EPA administrator Christine Todd Whitman (one of the first members of the original group to leave) during his first hundred days. After 9/11 Bush became a wartime president, a development that narrowed his circle of cabinet interactions.[66] The "war cabinet"— Cheney, Card, Powell, national security adviser Condoleezza Rice, Secretary of Defense Donald Rumsfeld, Secretary of the Treasury Paul O'Neill, and CIA director George Tenet—met daily with the president. This team of inner cabinet members, several of their senior aides, and certain White House assistants helped the president manage the immediate aftermath of the disaster and prepare the nation for a war on terrorism.[67]

Presidents generally look beyond the cabinet for policy advice. Since its creation in 1947, the National Security Council (NSC) and its staff have been used extensively by presidents for foreign and military policy matters (see chapter 10). In economic policy areas, presidents work closely with the chair of the Council of Economic Advisers, the OMB director, the secretary of the Treasury, and the chair of the Federal Reserve Board (see chapter 9). In domestic policy areas, which involve primarily the outer cabinet departments, domestic policy staffs and OMB have provided assistance to the president in policy formulation (see chapter 8), and cabinet committees, interagency committees, and policy councils have been employed to coordinate policymaking and implementation.

Cabinet committees, usually appointed on an ad hoc basis to handle specific problems, can focus quickly on them. Interagency committees, which operate mostly at the agency and subcabinet levels, may achieve a measure of coordination, but their work is often hampered by competition between agencies and by a lack of status and visibility.

Policy councils help presidents highlight particular problems. Nixon introduced a domestic council designed to perform many of the same services as the NSC, and Ford created the Economic Policy Board. Both units have appeared under various names in successor administrations. Reagan established seven cabinet councils in addition to the NSC to help move issues upward to the cabinet and then the president; that group was later reduced to two, the Economic Policy Council and the Domestic Policy Council. George H. W. Bush continued to utilize the Economic Policy Council and the Domestic Policy Council, but with apparently limited effectiveness due to squabbling and rivalries among his advisers.[68] Clinton began his presidency with three policy staff units in the White House: the National Economic Council, the Domestic Policy Council, and the Office of Environmental Policy, headed by a presidential assistant or deputy assistant.[69] In addition, he had three high-level advisers on policy: Ira Magaziner, George Stephanopoulos, and first lady Hillary Rodham Clinton. The fragmentation of advice that this structure produced reflected Clinton's desire to be at the center of an informal, collegial policy-making process, which he ran like a continuous seminar. With respect to selling and implementing his policy choices, however, Clinton preferred a more formal structure.[70]

Obama, like his predecessor, retained the Domestic Policy Council and the National Economic Policy Council (NEC) as White House coordinating units at the beginning of his administration and staffed each with trusted campaign advisers. Consistent with all other presidents since Truman, he also utilized the National Security Council structure to help coordinate national security policy. Obama's principal innovation was the appointment of "policy czars," White House aides who were given broad responsibility for coordinating major policy initiatives throughout the government. Positions were carved out for energy and climate change, health care reform, technology promotion, urban affairs, national security policy, and economic policy. Helping the middle class and coordinating the rescue of the automobile industry (the "car czar") were mentioned as additional possibilities.[71] In essence, the president was expanding a longtime strategy: to assign a White House aide the responsibility to coordinate government action across departments and agencies. In some areas, the aide would enjoy staff support and prestige associated with a long-standing council, such as the NSC, but in other areas the effort would be new. Much depended on the personalities of the assistants and how cooperative the cabinet secretaries would prove to be. Lawrence H. Summers, former Treasury secretary under Clinton and career mentor to Secretary Geithner, was the most prominent of these czars and was expected to emerge as the major force fashioning a plan to combat the recession. Summers was officially director of the NEC but could exercise far broader powers than his predecessors in earlier administrations.

The Vice President

George W. Bush's most controversial management innovation was the power delegated to Vice President Cheney, whose unprecedented influence could ultimately have negative consequences for an office that emerged from the shadows during the Carter administration. Historically, vice presidents were given little to do either by the Constitution or the presidents with whom they served. The position's constitutional powers are limited: preside over the Senate, cast a vote only in the event of a tie, and succeed the president in the event of removal by "Death, Resignation, or Inability to discharge the Powers and Duties of the said Office."[72] Tie-breaking votes have been rare: only 244 in history. Cheney cast eight of those votes, six coming during the 2001–2003 period when the Senate's partisan balance was almost even.[73]

Nine vice presidents have succeeded to the presidency, constituting nearly a quarter of the nation's forty-four presidents. The Constitution's guidelines on succession are not very clear. In the event of the predecessor's death, would the new president be the "president" or the "acting president"? John Tyler asserted the former and in 1841 established the precedent that has been followed since. What happens in the event of a vacancy in the vice presidency? That question was answered in 1967 with adoption of the Twenty-fifth Amendment. In addition, over the years Congress has provided three different succession scenarios if neither the president nor vice president is able to serve. For the nation's first ninety-four years, the successor was the Senate's president pro tempore, followed by the Speaker of the House. For the next six decades, it was members of the cabinet in order of their office's creation. The most recent succession act, adopted in 1947, calls for the Speaker of the House, followed by the president pro tempore, followed by the cabinet secretaries in the order of their office's creation, which means the Secretary of Homeland Security comes last, although that was not true for the first four years of that position's history when it was placed eighth.

What do vice presidents do? For many years, they were largely forgotten by presidents and public alike, dispatched around the world to attend ceremonial events and funeral services, and given the job of launching highly partisan attacks (beneath the dignity of the president) during political campaigns. Jimmy Carter and Walter Mondale are credited with modernizing the job to be an integral part of the president's support staff.[74] Mondale met regularly with the president, attended senior staff meetings, had a staff of his own, was given important assignments, and was treated with respect rather than derision. His successors—George H. W. Bush, Dan Quayle, and Al Gore—sought to build on that foundation, although Gore seemed to be Cheney's most influential predecessor.

At the outset of the administration, Cheney was by far the most experienced person on the team. He had served seven years in the Nixon-Ford White House, including one as Nixon's chief of staff. He then had ten years in the House of Representatives and rose through the ranks to become minority whip. Cheney next served as secretary of defense for nearly four years, heading the department during the Persian Gulf War. After George H. W. Bush's loss in 1992, Cheney became a multimillionaire as the chairman and CEO of Halliburton Company, an international oil services firm, his position when George W. Bush asked him to oversee the committee to select the Republican vice-presidential candidate. Cheney was Bush's surprise choice.

All of this experience meant that Cheney was far more familiar with the ways of Washington than was his boss, and there is ample evidence that he used this knowledge to its fullest advantage to influence critical policy decisions of the Bush administration. After an extensive review of Cheney's record, the *Washington Post* concluded that he had "shaped his times as no vice president has done before."[75] Among his better-known areas of involvement were Supreme Court nominations, tax proposals, federal regulations, energy policy, and the conduct of the war on terror. Most important, Cheney enjoyed his boss's confidence, advising him in private and standing by his side in public. Much of Cheney's influence was behind the scenes: "The president is 'the decider,' as Bush puts it, but the vice president often serves up his menu of choices."[76] Cheney's fingerprints (seldom obvious) are alleged to have been on many of the most controversial actions of the Bush administration: establishing an eavesdropping program on international phone conversations of Americans outside of judicial control; using military commissions to process foreign terrorism suspects outside the international protocols set by the Geneva Conventions; authorizing use of interrogation techniques on terrorism suspects that fall outside the Geneva Conventions (in other words, using torture to extract information); pushing consistently for higher tax cuts for the wealthiest segment of the public; leaking to the media the identity of Valerie Plame, a CIA operative and the wife of diplomat Joseph Wilson, an outspoken critic of the Bush administration's Iraq policy. The leak ultimately led to the conviction of I. Lewis "Scooter" Libby, Cheney's chief of staff, for perjury and obstruction of justice.

Before he assumed office, Vice President Joseph Biden openly criticized Cheney's abuse of executive power and questionable policy positions on using torture as a means to protect the homeland from further terrorist attacks. Biden is likely to return to the Mondale model of the vice presidency—serve as an influential general adviser, assume responsibilities as assigned by the president, and operate within more conventional definitions of the job.[77] At the outset of the Obama administration, he was asked to head the task force charged with improving the condition of the middle class, oversee implementation of the economic stiumulus package, and deliver important foreign policy messages to audiences overseas.[78] In short, Biden was heavily involved in the major decisions of the Obama presidency and asked to take the lead on selected issues.

Presidential Control of the Bureaucracy

Although presidents face substantial obstacles in seeking to control policymaking and implementation, they do have resources for this effort. They have substantial powers granted by the Constitution, delegated by Congress, and derived from the nature of their office. The most important are the powers to appoint and remove subordinates, to issue executive orders, and to prepare the annual federal budget and regulate expenditures.

Appointment and Removal

The Constitution gives the president broad powers of appointment (Article II, section 2, paragraph 2), but it makes high-ranking officials subject to senatorial confirmation, and it authorizes Congress to vest the appointment of lower officials in the president, in department heads, or in the courts. Congress determines whether the Senate must confirm an appointment. The Senate can also narrow the president's discretion in making appointments by establishing detailed qualifications for various offices. Congress cannot, however, give itself the power to appoint executive officials.[79] Neither can it force the president to make an appointment to a vacant position.[80] The president's appointive powers also are constrained by political considerations and practices such as senatorial courtesy, whereby senators effectively have veto power over certain administrative and judicial appointments from their home states.

The Senate generally has given presidents considerable leeway in the appointment of top-level executives. But confirmation is not automatic, and the Senate has used rejections to express disapproval of specific individuals or practices.[81] Since Watergate (1972–1974), the Senate has tended to be more careful and procedurally consistent in examining nominees' backgrounds, qualifications, and relevant policy views. Enhanced vigilance has made the confirmation process "more tedious, time-consuming, and intrusive for the nominees," a situation exacerbated by interparty conflict.[82] For example, the Senate finally confirmed Richard C. Holbrooke as U.S. permanent representative to the United Nations in August 1999 after a fourteen-month odyssey that included two federal ethics investigations, four hearings conducted by the Senate Foreign Relations Committee, and "holds"—objections to a nominee that delay action—placed by several Republican senators in an effort to wrest concessions from the administration on unrelated matters. The Bush administration never succeeded in securing Senate approval for John R. Bolton's appointment to the same position despite two sets of hearings held by the Senate Foreign Relations Committee (2005 and 2006) and multiple efforts to end a Democratic filibuster on the floor of the Senate. The prospect of such a tortuous and contentious process sometimes causes candidates to withdraw from consideration or decline invitations to serve.[83]

At the beginning of his term, George W. Bush had about 1,200 full-time positions subject to Senate confirmation to fill.[84] He confronted unusual hurdles in doing so. Not only were the nominations delayed by the 2000 election controversy, but also the new Senate was initially bogged down in a 50-50 stalemate, then experienced a change in the majority party from Republican to Democratic in June 2001, and finally experienced confusion after September 11. All of this slowed the Bush administration in selecting top appointees. During Bush's first year in office, it took an average of 181 days for nominees to be confirmed, up from Clinton's 174 days and Reagan's 142. Much of the blame for tardy action could be laid at the feet of Congress, but after two years some positions still had not been filled, delays that could reflect efforts to select candidates whose policy views were compatible with the president's.[85]

The Obama administration's record may turn out to be worse. By mid-May 2009, 85 nominated candidates awaited confirmation and 111 had been approved for the 486 top positions subject to Senate confirmation.[86] Such delays could have devastating consequences on effectiveness. For example, the Department of the Treasury, where Secretary Geithner faced unprecedented challenges to fix the financial crisis, had twenty-three such positions to fill. Ten weeks into the administration, only one person other than himself had been confirmed and through the administration's first one hundred days the total stood at only four. Without a senior leadership team, the department was likely to flounder.

The Constitution also empowers the president to make appointments when the Senate is in recess. This power ensured government continuity when transportation was difficult and Congress met only part of the year. Such **recess appointments** must be confirmed by the end of the Senate's next session, but the appointee serves in the interim. Senators often object to recess appointments to high-level positions because they feel inhibited from thoroughly examining people who have already begun their duties. Presidents make surprisingly frequent use of recess appointments: Reagan made 240 recess appointments, George H. W. Bush made 77, Bill Clinton 140, and George W. Bush 110 in his first term.[87] This strategy enables presidents to get the person they want without making policy compromises, but the tactic may come at a cost. President Clinton made extensive use of appointments to acting positions after Republicans gained control of the Senate in 1995 and he encountered problems getting nominees approved, but in some instances Republican senators retaliated by refusing to approve other nominees. George W. Bush adopted the strategy with John Bolton. When Republicans were unable to defeat the Democrats' filibuster of Bolton's nomination as UN ambassador, a congressional battle that lasted from April through June 2005, the president named Bolton the "permanent representative" to the UN, a post he held from

August 1, 2005, to December 4, 2006. Renewed efforts to get Bolton confirmed were destined for failure after the Democrats took back the Senate in the 2006 midterm elections.

Complementing the appointment power, and fundamental to presidential control of the executive branch, is the removal power. Without the ability to remove subordinate officials on performance or policy grounds, presidents cannot be held fully responsible for their actions or for a department's or agency's failure to achieve presidential objectives. The Constitution is silent, however, concerning the removal of executive officials other than through impeachment, a cumbersome process limited to conviction for "Treason, Bribery, or other high Crimes and Misdemeanors."

Presidents have clashed with Congress over the removal power. The post–Civil War conflict between President Andrew Johnson and Congress over Reconstruction policy involved the removal power. In 1867 Congress brought impeachment proceedings against Johnson for violating the Tenure of Office Act, which it had passed over his veto. That statute authorized all persons appointed with the advice and consent of the Senate to continue to hold office until the president appointed, and the Senate confirmed, a successor. Johnson tried to remove Secretary of War Edwin Stanton without permission. Although Johnson survived the impeachment trial by one vote, the issue of the removal power remained unresolved. (Congress repealed the Tenure of Office Act in 1887.)

The Supreme Court dealt directly with the removal power in a decision involving a challenge to Woodrow Wilson's summary removal of a postmaster.[88] The Court invalidated an 1876 law that required the Senate's consent for a postmaster's removal. It held that the Constitution gave the president the removal power and Congress could not place restrictions on its exercise. Nine years later, however, the Court upheld the provisions of the Federal Trade Commission Act that limited the grounds for removal of its members.[89] The Court ruled that the president's unqualified power of removal is limited to "purely executive offices" and that Congress may prescribe conditions for the removal of officials performing "quasi-legislative" and "quasi-judicial" functions. The Court has not, however, fully clarified the meaning of these terms. A dramatic instance of the removal power occurred in August 1981, when Reagan fired 11,400 striking members of the Professional Air Traffic Controllers Organization. A U.S. court of appeals upheld the action, interpreting it as a discharge of the president's obligation to enforce a statute prohibiting strikes by federal employees.[90] In 2007 Senate Democrats, reluctantly joined by several Republicans, sought to force President Bush to remove Alberto Gonzales when controversy about

Hundreds of alleged terrorists were detained at the American naval base in Guantánamo Bay, Cuba, setting off a worldwide storm of criticism directed at U.S. violation of human rights.

the firing of eight U.S. attorneys, allegedly on "political grounds," embroiled the attorney general in sustained controversy. After several ineffective appearances before the Senate Judiciary Committee, Gonzales submitted his resignation in August 2007. The president accepted, expressing appreciation for his longtime aide's hard work and bitterness at what he saw as mistreatment of Gonzales.

Executive Orders and Direct Action

Recent presidents have used executive orders and presidential memoranda to take dramatic action during their initial hours and days in office. Moments after delivering his first inaugural address, Reagan used a presidential memorandum to freeze federal hiring to support his contention that big government was the problem, not the solution. Clinton issued an executive order on ethics while still on Capitol Hill after delivering his first inaugural and then used high visibility presidential memoranda over the next several days to reverse the previous administration's prohibition on abortion counseling. George W. Bush issued three memoranda on his first inauguration day, followed by several more in the next week to emphasize high-level policy priorities, including the redefinition of relationships between faith-based programs and the government.[91] These examples illustrate a long-standing presidential practice: to accomplish goals by using a variety of unilateral instruments or direct administration, including executive orders, directives, memoranda, proclamations, policy instructions, and interpretations of congressional intent.

Under a strict interpretation of separation of powers, presidents have no direct legislative authority. From the beginning, however, they have issued orders and directives on the basis of Article II. Most modern presidents have followed Theodore Roosevelt's "stewardship" theory of executive power (see chapter 1), which holds that Article II confers on them inherent power to take whatever actions they deem necessary in the national interest unless prohibited by the Constitution or by law. Executive orders have been a primary means of exercising this broad presidential prerogative power. "They are presidential edicts, legal instruments that create or modify laws, procedures, and policy by fiat," and have helped push "the boundaries of presidential power by taking advantage of gaps in constitutional and statutory language that allow them to fill power vacuums and gain control of emerging capabilities."[92]

Reliance on such strategies is especially common in crucial policy areas such as civil rights, economic stabilization, and national security,[93] or when conflict with Congress means action cannot be accomplished through legislation. In civil rights, Franklin Roosevelt established a Fair Employment Practices Commission in 1943 to prevent discriminatory hiring by government agencies and military suppliers. In 1948 Harry Truman ended segregation in the armed forces by executive order. In March 1961 John Kennedy issued a sweeping order creating the Equal Employment Opportunity Commission and giving it broad enforcement powers. Lyndon Johnson went further, requiring by executive order preferential hiring of minorities by government contractors.

An economic crisis often triggers unilateral action. FDR established broad precedents for the use of executive orders to achieve economic stability, and a number of his successors have followed suit. During World War II, he issued executive orders to establish the Office of Price Administration (OPA) and the Office of Economic Stabilization and to give them extensive powers over prices, wages, and profits. The OPA also rationed scarce consumer goods such as meat, butter, shoes, tires, and gasoline. As a basis for his actions, Roosevelt cited his responsibility to respond to the "unlimited emergency" created by the war. The Emergency Price Control Act of 1942 provided retroactive statutory endorsement for the establishment of the emergency

TABLE 6-2 Executive Orders, 1969–May 15, 2009

President/years in office	Total executive orders issued by administration	Executive orders per year
Richard Nixon (1969–1974)	346	62.9
Gerald R. Ford (1974–1977)	169	67.6
Jimmy Carter (1977–1981)	320	80.0
Ronald Reagan (1981–1989)	381	47.6
George H. W. Bush (1989–1993)	166	41.5
William J. Clinton (1993–2001)	364	45.5
George W. Bush (2001–2009)	290	36.3
Barack H. Obama (2009–May 15, 2009)	19	19.0

SOURCE: See www.archives.gov/federal-register/executive-orders/disposition.html.

agencies and the measures they implemented. In 1970, in the face of persistent inflation, Congress passed the Economic Stabilization Act, which authorized the president to issue orders that would control wages and prices, but with few criteria to
guide these actions. On August 15, 1971, Nixon issued an executive order imposing a
ninety-day freeze on nonagricultural wages and prices and establishing the Cost of
Living Council to administer the controls. An October 15 order extended the controls and established additional machinery to aid in administering them.[94]

Presidents also have used executive orders and national security directives to
guide foreign policy. In 1942, for example, FDR issued an executive order requiring
the internment of all persons of Japanese ancestry living in the Pacific coastal
states, seventy thousand of them U.S. citizens. The Supreme Court upheld this
massive deprivation of civil liberties on the basis of the commander in chief
clause.[95] George W. Bush responded to the 9/11 attacks with a series of executive
orders enabling him to wield wartime powers.

Among the seven most recently completed administrations, Jimmy Carter made
the heaviest use of executive orders; presidents since 1981 have used them less (see
Table 6-2). In the three months following 9/11, President Bush issued more executive orders than he had in the previous eight months, and several of them proved
especially controversial.[96]

There is some disagreement over whether presidents confronted by a Congress
controlled by the opposition party will make heavier use of executive orders. For
example, year-to-year totals show that Clinton's use of executive orders actually
declined rather than increased when he confronted a hostile Republican Congress
after 1995, although he may still have used executive orders as a way to make
progress on major policy initiatives.[97] In his exhaustive study of executive orders,

Kenneth Mayer traces the pattern of their use from 1936 through 1995 and concludes that the issuance of orders "rises and falls in response to significant events."[98] The onset of war, for example, triggers new administrative arrangements and regulations governing economic controls and wartime mobilization, just as peace requires their removal. The focus of executive orders has also changed over time. Orders dealing with executive branch administration, foreign affairs, and domestic policy increased during the 1936–1999 period.[99] Finally, Democrats make more use of executive orders than Republicans; more orders are issued at the end of a term and when the president's public support is low than under the opposite conditions; and more orders are issued when the president's party is in the congressional majority, a counterintuitive finding.[100] Mayer estimates that about one of every seven executive orders is significant—that is, it attracts media, congressional, or scholarly notice; triggers litigation; or represents a meaningful policy departure.[101]

Phillip J. Cooper argues that the focus should be on the content, rather than the quantity, of such actions and the reasons presidents use them. In particular, recent administrations use "presidential memoranda" alongside, and interchangeably with, executive orders; and Clinton is credited with issuing 536 presidential memoranda, many more than his predecessors.[102] Unlike executive orders, memoranda do not have to be published in the *Federal Register,* in which rules and orders appear, nor is there a procedure for developing them, thereby making them simpler to issue. Ultimately, the question will be whether Congress and others will accept such assertions of presidential prerogative. In fact, unilateral presidential action can be reversed. During the Korean War, the Supreme Court invalidated Truman's seizure of the steel industry on the grounds that he had not used the machinery established in the Taft-Hartley Act of 1947 to avert a strike.[103] More recently, we have the example of successor presidents reversing an action of their predecessors, as Clinton and George W. Bush did.[104] Obama followed suit in 2009, issuing executive orders during his first two days in office. The orders reversed Bush administration practices on government secrecy, outlawed the use of torture in questioning suspected terrorists, and set a date for closing the controversial detention facility in Guantánamo Bay, where such suspects had been held. He later issued another executive order that reversed the Bush policy that had severely limited stem cell research.[105]

From 1932 until 1983 Congress exerted a measure of control over executive lawmaking with the legislative veto. Provisions added to certain statutes gave Congress the power to review and reject executive orders or administrative regulations authorized by the legislation. The legislative veto took various forms. It allowed disapproval of regulations by concurrent resolution or by simple resolution of either house or by action of a committee of either house. In its most common form, the legislative veto required that the proposed action lie before Congress for a specified period—usually sixty or ninety days—during which either chamber could disapprove it. The president's reorganization authority, which Congress first authorized in 1939, carried such a procedure. Other major statutes that had a form of legislative veto include the War Powers Resolution of 1973, the Budget and Impoundment Control Act of 1974, the Federal Elections Campaign Act of 1974, and the National Emergencies Act of 1976. More than 250 statutes provided for some type of legislative veto before the Supreme Court declared it unconstitutional in 1983.

In *Immigration and Naturalization Service v. Chadha* the Court held that the one-house legislative veto provision of the Immigration and Nationality Act was an unconstitutional breach of the separation of powers.[106] The Court reasoned that the veto involved "the exercise of legislative power" without "bicameral passage followed by presentment to the President." In other words, such actions were not subject to presidential concurrence or veto. Initial reaction to the decision was that it was not a definitive ruling and that somehow Congress would find a way statutorily to control executive branch lawmaking.[107] Although the Court threw out past practices, Congress has required agencies to obtain approval from the appropriations committees before taking specified actions and used informal agreements with agencies to achieve the same goal.[108]

Congress has also employed the joint resolution of approval before an executive action can be taken.[109] For example, the Reorganization Act Amendments of 1984 provide that a presidentially prepared reorganization plan submitted to Congress cannot take effect unless approved by a joint resolution within ninety days. This provision places the burden on the president rather than on Congress, and the president has only a specific number of days in which to act. In effect, the joint resolution of approval works like a one-house legislative veto: if either house refuses to approve an action, it cannot be taken. The major disadvantage of the device for Congress is that it requires much time, and extensive use of it would threaten the congressional agenda with legislative gridlock.

Presidents and Money

Presidents have substantial financial powers, delegated by Congress, that they use in their efforts to control the bureaucracy. The most important is the power to formulate the budget, which controls the amount of spending by federal departments and agencies. The budget establishes the president's spending priorities, sets the timing of program initiatives, and distributes rewards to, and imposes sanctions on, executive branch units.[110] By controlling the total amount of the budget, the president can try to influence the economy's performance (see chapter 9).

Presidential use of the executive budget developed in the twentieth century. The enormous increase in expenditures during World War I, and the task of managing the sizable national debt that resulted, convinced Congress of the need for an executive budget. The Budget and Accounting Act of 1921 made the president responsible for compiling department and agency estimates and for submitting them annually to Congress in the form of a budget. The statute established the Bureau of the Budget (BOB), in the Treasury Department, to assist the president in assembling and revising the estimates. The statute barred departments and agencies from submitting their funding requests directly to Congress as they had done previously.

The initial emphasis in the development of the federal budget process was on control of expenditures and prevention of administrative abuses.[111] During the 1930s the emphasis shifted from control to management. The budget was seen as a means of evaluating and improving administrative performance. The transfer of the BOB in 1939 from the Treasury Department to the new Executive Office of the President symbolized the management orientation. The BOB was to become the president's management arm. A decade later, the government adopted a performance budget organized by functions and activities rather than by line items representing objects of expenditure.

The most recent development in budgeting is its orientation toward planning. This emphasis attempts to link annual budgeting, geared to the appropriations process in Congress, to long-range planning of government objectives. The limited success of the planning orientation is reflected in the rapid arrival and departure of budgeting systems, such as the program planning budgeting system and zero-base budgeting.[112] The budgeting process, as it had developed by the early 1970s, embodied all three orientations—control, management, and planning—but it was least effective as a planning device.

Because the annual budget process is inherently incremental and subject to restrictions and conditions imposed by Congress, the executive budget has only limited utility as an aid to presidential decision making. The budget cycle forces the president and Congress to act according to a timetable that stretches from twenty-two months before the start of the fiscal year (October 1) through the ensuing year. Congress and the bureaucracy are concerned primarily with how large an increase or decrease will be made in a department's or an agency's budget. From 1982 to 1997, huge federal deficits accompanied by strong public resistance to tax increases caused presidential and congressional budget decisions to be focused primarily on reducing spending. The emergence of a budget surplus in 1998 ushered in a debate between Republicans and Democrats over the need for tax cuts. Republicans won the struggle in 2001, when George W. Bush engineered a massive tax cut to be spread over eleven years, and then accelerated in the additional cuts of 2003. But when the threat of deficits emerged in mid-2001, questions again arose about the government's capacity to plan effectively, and several Democrats seeking the presidency in 2004 proposed that the tax cuts be rolled back. Faced with a severe economic recession, Obama proposed dramatically increased federal spending, delayed taking action on his campaign promise to increase taxes on the wealthiest Americans, but also discussed the need to return to a more responsible budget plan in the future.

Congress makes its own budget decisions. It limits total spending through resolutions proposed by the budget committees in each house. Although the congressional budget total is usually fairly close to the president's, the priorities in the two budgets often differ sharply. Deficit politics constrained Bill Clinton when he attempted to use his first budget as a vehicle for policy change.[113] Although Congress narrowly (with no Republican support) accepted most of his five-year plan (1994–1998) to reduce the deficit by almost $500 billion, it embarrassed Clinton by rejecting a $16 billion package to stimulate the economy.[114] In 1995 the first Republican-controlled Congress in forty years ignored the administration's budget, which did not contain proposals for eventually eliminating the deficit, and adopted a budget resolution that projected a balanced budget in fiscal year 2002. Nearly two years of budget battles were finally resolved in a 1997 agreement on how to balance the budget.[115] George W. Bush, in contrast, found a cooperative Congress controlled by his own party during the first half of 2001 and secured passage of his tax cut.

In addition to budgeting, presidents have certain discretionary spending powers that increase their leverage over the bureaucracy. They have substantial nonstatutory authority, based on understandings with congressional appropriations committees, to transfer funds within an appropriation and from one program to another. The committees expect to be kept informed of such "reprogramming" actions.[116] Fund transfer authority is essential to sound financial management, but it can be abused to circumvent congressional decisions. In 1970 Nixon transferred funds to support an extensive unauthorized covert military operation in Cambodia. Nevertheless, Congress has given presidents and certain agencies the authority to spend substantial amounts of money on a confidential basis, the largest and most controversial being for intelligence activities.

Presidents have exercised a measure of expenditure control through the practice of impounding or returning appropriated funds to the Treasury Department. Beginning with George Washington, presidents routinely impounded funds to achieve savings when actual expenditures fell short of appropriations.[117] They withheld funds when authorized or directed to do so by Congress to establish contingency reserves or impose a ceiling on total expenditures. Presidents from FDR through Lyndon Johnson also impounded some of the funds Congress had added, over their objections, for various programs. Although such actions often drew congressional criticism, they did not lead to confrontation because they occurred infrequently and were generally focused on expenditures for specific programs or projects. Congress recognized that circumspect use of impoundments helped its members resist pressure for increased spending.[118]

Impoundment became a major constitutional issue during the Nixon administration. Sweeping impoundments in domestic program areas, especially agriculture, housing, and water pollution control, led to charges that the president arbitrarily and illegally had substituted his spending priorities for those of Congress. Nixon's impoundments involved larger amounts, violated explicit congressional instructions to spend the funds, and were designed to terminate entire programs rather than individual projects. In short, Nixon used impoundment as the primary weapon in a battle with Congress over domestic spending priorities. He did not bargain or negotiate but imposed his priorities by fiat. Congress struck back with the Budget and Impoundment Control Act of 1974, which established procedures for congressional review by requiring the president to report all impoundments to Congress. Proposals to rescind appropriated funds, that is, to return them to the Treasury, must be approved by both houses within forty-five days. The original power of either house to disapprove proposals to defer spending to the next fiscal year disappeared when the Supreme Court invalidated the legislative veto.

In 1996 Clinton was the beneficiary of the Republican Party's promise in its 1994 election manifesto, the Contract with America, to establish a line-item veto for the president's use in fighting the budget deficit, a power many governors enjoy. Clinton was the first, and probably the last, president to have this power. The Line-Item Veto Act authorized the president to cancel specific spending items or tax breaks rather than veto an entire appropriation bill if the budget was in deficit. Presidential decisions would stand unless overturned by a two-thirds vote in both houses of Congress. The Court invalidated this statute in 1998,[119] but not before

Clinton invoked the authority eighty-two times. In 2006 and 2007 some congressional Republicans supported George W. Bush's request for expedited rescission powers comparable to a line-item veto but requiring affirmative majority votes in both houses of Congress, a design he hoped the Court would not strike down.[120]

Presidential Management of the Bureaucracy

In addition to their formal powers, modern presidents have relied on managerial tools in their efforts to coordinate and direct executive branch operations. Three major tools—staffing, reorganization, and planning—have been employed with mixed results. This is not to argue that the public sector is inhospitable to modern management techniques, but to suggest that political forces significantly affect their use.[121]

Staffing

As discussed in chapters 1 and 4, the institutionalized presidency has grown steadily as presidents have used staff to direct the executive branch and fulfill its many functions. From the vantage point of the Oval Office it may sometimes seem that there are "people, people everywhere but none to do his will."[122] Although recent administrations have used presidential staffs and the cabinet in different ways, the long-term trend has been toward increasing reliance on a strong, sizable, centralized White House staff to protect the political interests of presidents, to act as their principal policy advisers, and to direct (as opposed to monitor and coordinate) the implementation of presidential priorities by the bureaucracy. Centralizing power in the White House may appear to have been a *linear* process, but Andrew Rudalevige effectively argues that centralization is *contingent* on the president's needs, the shifting environment, and estimates of the full range of available strategies for accomplishing presidential goals.[123]

Critics of this development argue that centralization has undercut the cabinet's advisory potential, narrowed the president's perspective on policy choices, and inhibited effective and responsive bureaucratic performance. Stephen Hess cautions that reliance on a centralized White House staff has been "self-defeating."[124] Experiences under Nixon and Reagan support this view. Yet Ford and Carter both tried a decentralized model of White House staffing and abandoned it in favor of hierarchical alternatives.

George H. W. Bush adopted the hierarchical model of organization. Former New Hampshire governor John Sununu served as White House chief of staff, functioning as the guardian of the president's political interests, serving as his link to conservatives, and often appearing to set the administration's course on domestic social policy issues. In these roles, Sununu was the target of considerable congressional and media criticism that ultimately made him a liability.[125]

The Clinton White House reflected the leadership of a highly intelligent, energetic, enthusiastic, and enormously self-confident president who lacked self-discipline, assumed many personal responsibilities, had difficulty focusing his goals and managing his efforts, and was reluctant to delegate. Clinton entered office with no plan for organizing the White House and proceeded to staff it largely with consultants from his campaign and friends and political associates from Arkansas.[126] The staff lacked the Washington experience and political stature that might have prevented damaging early missteps such as the botched nominations of Zoë Baird and Kimba Wood to be attorney general, the conflict with Congress over ending discrimination against gays in the military, and the defeat of the administration's economic stimulus bill.

Clinton's first chief of staff, Thomas F. McLarty III, was replaced in June 1994 by Leon Panetta, the OMB director, who brought much-needed order. Panetta and his successors, Erskine Bowles and John Podesta, established control over the flow of communications and personal access to the president.[127] A greater degree of centralization and formal organization proved a necessity to counteract Clinton's lack of discipline. Clinton also demonstrated the ability to recognize his failings and take corrective action. White House staff at the start of Clinton's second term were more pragmatic and less ideological and had more Washington experience than their first-term counterparts.[128]

George W. Bush followed a modified version of the "spokes-in-a-wheel" White House structure so successful during Reagan's first term. In this model, a limited number of aides have access to a president who freely delegates responsibilities. Like Reagan, Bush had three principal aides. Andrew Card was Bush's first chief of staff, a position that has become so prevalent across both Republican and Democratic administrations as to warrant being described as "institutionalized." He was joined by Karl Rove, the political strategist, and Karen Hughes, the press and public relations adviser. Card, who began his government service in the Reagan administration, had served as deputy chief of staff and secretary of transportation in the G. H. W. Bush administration. Rove and Hughes were longtime aides to George W. Bush in Texas.[129] Hughes left after two years, and Card resigned in April 2006 under pressure when a mishandled Supreme Court nomination, the bungled response to Hurricane Katrina, and severely declining polls triggered calls for a staff shakeup. Despite his early departure, Card had served longer than any chief of staff in nearly a half-century, testifying to the pressure-cooker nature of the job.[130] Until his resignation in August 2007, Rove remained an influential White House figure, broadly responsible for political affairs. Investigators probed Rove's role in the outing of Valerie Plame, the firing of U.S. attorneys, the establishment of a shadow e-mail system that staff could use for political purposes, and pressure on government employees to help Republican allies.[131]

Two other advisers played a special role in the Bush administration. Vice President Cheney was given some of the most challenging assignments in the administration, including relations with Congress, developing a national energy strategy, and being a full participant (some would say the major architect) of the administration's policies to counter terrorism and the proliferation of weapons of mass destruction. Condoleezza Rice, first as national security adviser and then secretary of state, was a public spokesperson called upon to explain and justify policies. As the administration responded to 9/11, Rice spent considerable time brokering discussions between two of the most forceful members of the Bush cabinet, Secretary of State Powell and Secretary of Defense Rumsfeld. Finally, Alberto Gonzales, during his time as White House counsel, also had ready access to President Bush.

In striking contrast to Clinton, Bush, the first president with an MBA, emerged as a "disciplined delegator," who drew upon the services of his able aides from the outset.[132] Critics, however, raised the same question they had asked about Reagan and Eisenhower: when presidents delegate, who's really in charge? For critics, it seemed that Vice President Cheney was exercising more responsibility than his constitutional superior, an issue fueled by several health crises Cheney experienced during the administration's first months,[133] the president's absence from Washington on 9/11, and the vice president's prominence in policy-making circles.

Since the Reagan administration, the presidency has become increasingly centralized and politicized. Terry Moe defends these developments as an inescapable consequence of the expectations that impinge upon the presidency.[134] A similar conclusion emerged from a 1986 symposium featuring eight former White House chiefs of staff (or their functional equivalents), who served presidents from Eisenhower through Carter. In their views, "the demands for activism and the requirements of self-reliance encourage presidents to look favorably upon the kinds of services provided by a rationalized White House run by a strong chief."[135] At its outset, the Obama administration appeared to be squarely in this pattern, sending every indication that a hard-charging chief of staff, aided by a number of policy czars, would seek to run the government from the White House. Although it is possible to argue that the twin crises of foreign wars and domestic recession created the need for such a centralization of decision making, Moe's research suggests that the Obama administration was simply falling into line with recent practice.

Reorganization

It is almost an article of faith among political leaders and public administration theorists that executive reorganization can increase presidential power over the bureaucracy. Johnson, Nixon, and Carter believed the performance of the executive branch could be improved and the bureaucracy brought to heel through such changes. Johnson's efforts were, however, inconsequential, and Nixon's were interrupted by his resignation. By most accounts, the results of Carter's reorganization project—by far the most extensive—were modest.[136]

Organizational structure and administrative arrangements are significant because they reflect values and priorities and affect access to decision makers. The location and status of an administrative unit—as a department, an independent agency, or a component of a department—symbolize the importance of its goals and the interests it serves. Administrative arrangements also can contribute to or frustrate the achievement of accountability to Congress and the public. Reorganizing, however, does not necessarily result in increased operational efficiency, greater program effectiveness, or enhanced public accountability. There is no ideal form for a government agency or a consistent set of prescriptions for organizing the executive branch. One set of standard prescriptions tends to centralize authority; another tends to disperse it. The most profound consequences of organizational change are not in the "engineered realm of efficiency, simplicity, size, and cost of government"; rather, they lie in the areas of "political influence, policy emphasis, and communication of governmental intentions."[137] For example, the placement of the Occupational Safety and Health Administration in the Department of Labor rather than in the Department of Health, Education, and Welfare led to an initial focus of regulations on mechanical, rather than biological, hazards in the workplace. Experience has shown that although the rationale for reorganization is couched in the rhetoric of economy and efficiency, the crucial factors in decisions to reorganize are power, policy, and symbolic significance.

In 1939 Congress authorized presidents to propose executive reorganization plans that take effect after sixty days unless disapproved by both houses. When extending that authority in 1949, Congress allowed either house to disapprove such plans. Congress continued to renew the reorganization authority with little change until 1973, when it was allowed to lapse in the conflict with Nixon over his efforts to centralize control of the executive branch. In 1977 Carter requested and received renewal of the authority with provision for veto by either house. The Supreme Court decision striking down the legislative veto necessitated changes in the review process that made Congress a full partner in reorganizations, but the authority lapsed in 1984 and was not renewed.[138] George W. Bush wanted to use reorganization as a strategy and requested restoration of the president's permanent reorganization authority. But in the absence of congressional action, Bush had to follow the normal legislative process, as happened in creating the Department of Homeland Security. (The same process was used earlier to create the Departments of Energy, Education, and Veterans Affairs.)[139]

Carter's reorganization achievements exceeded those of his immediate predecessors and of his successors but fell far short of the thorough restructuring of the executive branch and reduction in the number of agencies he had promised. Congress passed legislation that established the Departments of Energy and of Education and allowed five reorganization plans to take effect. Carter and his staff were unprepared for the jurisdictional conflicts that accompanied congressional consideration of reorganization proposals.[140] The president also lacked a well-conceived, comprehensive, politically defensible strategy. The Carter experience indicates that reorganization has its uses, but they are more in the realm of policy and politics than management improvement.

The Clinton administration ignored reorganization in favor of extensive personnel reductions called for in Vice President Gore's *National Performance Review Report*, along with the report's recommendations to cut red tape, enhance customer satisfaction, empower employees, and eliminate unneeded functions. That report broke sharply with the administrative management paradigm that had dominated presidential efforts to manage the bureaucracy since the Brownlow Committee report of 1937. That philosophy, which the reports of the Hoover Commission (1949) and the Ash Council (1971) also embodied, "emphasized the need for democratic accountability of departmental and agency officers to the President and his central management agencies and through these institutions to the Congress."[141] In its stead, the Gore report embraced the entrepreneurial management paradigm popularized by David Osborne and Ted Gaebler in *Reinventing Government*.[142] These writers call for a "cultural and behavioral shift in the management of government" from a bureaucratic to an entrepreneurial government. In their view, public agencies are entrepreneurial organizations competing in a market environment in which success is determined by customer satisfaction. Clinton's reinvention effort evolved over time and in two later phases shifted attention to reducing government's cost and then to attacking complex problems, such as finding ways to create and maintain "safe communities," a highly complex issue for government to tackle.[143] Clinton's departure from administrative orthodoxy sparked extensive discussion among academics,[144] but in the short run, few conclusions can be drawn about his novel strategy.

George W. Bush made the Clinton strategy his own by adding a few distinctive features. He sought to reduce government employment by ultimately making at least half of the federal jobs subject to competitive bidding from the private sector, and he hoped to realize this goal by establishing numerical targets for outsourcing jobs—5 percent of commercial-like jobs in 2002 increasing to 15 percent by the end of fiscal 2003.[145] Small reorganizations were introduced in agencies throughout the government and justified as improving performance. The administration called for a new "pay for performance" system that would not provide annual pay increases for civil service employees. They introduced this system for members of the Senior Executive Service and proposed extending it more generally.[146]

Planning

Aaron Wildavsky defined planning as "current action to secure future consequences."[147] Foresight in anticipating problems and developing solutions is the essence of effective planning. Long-range planning is a hallmark of successful corporate management, but the federal government cannot make that claim. Presidents have engaged in long-range planning with only limited success. As noted, attempts to combine annual budgeting with comprehensive planning through the program planning budgeting system and zero-base budgeting have not succeeded. Both approaches entailed comprehensive attempts to relate spending decisions to long-term consequences. Each required extensive amounts of information and analyses that were never integrated with budget decisions, and bureau and agency officials did not find it worthwhile to take either process seriously. Their fatal defect was neglect of the hard political choices involved in the budget process.

Nixon had introduced a similar technique that focused on goals, called management by objectives, to strengthen his oversight of the executive branch. He directed twenty-one departments and agencies to prepare rank-order lists of their principal objectives. After OMB reviewed the lists, the president approved objectives for each reporting unit. These presidential objectives then became the standard for monitoring the units' performances. Management by objectives focused first on immediate objectives, then on intermediate objectives that could be achieved in a fiscal year, and finally on long-term goals.[148] Other than to continue multiyear budgeting introduced by Carter, Reagan demonstrated little interest in planning. He appeared to believe that domestic policy planning was socialistic and incompatible with a free market economy. G. H. W. Bush, although neglecting domestic policy planning, was committed to, and actively involved in, foreign and defense policy planning. Generally, planning in these areas has been more successful than in domestic policy, and future presidents will always need to engage in national security planning. Clinton's proposals for reforming health care and the welfare system included planning that linked them to the five-year deficit reduction that was integral to the 1994 budget. But he exhibited little planning after the Republicans assumed control of Congress in 1995. Moving toward a balanced budget then became the overriding concern. In the administration's final years, creating a legacy was more important than planning.

With a heavy emphasis on pursuing legislative victories during its early months, the George W. Bush administration did not show much attention to planning, with the notable exception of developing a coherent energy policy. Just two weeks into the new administration, Bush named Cheney to head a task force that released its recommendations on May 17, 2001, after meeting largely in secret. The administration's proposals primarily focused on ways to increase the supply of energy rather than conserve its use—encouraging oil and natural gas exploration, building electric transmission infrastructure, encouraging the use of coal, and supporting nuclear power generation.[149] But the complex plan met enormous resistance in the face of electric outages in California, rising gas prices, and concerns about environmental protections. Questions arose about whether an "energy industry that put its financial backing solidly behind Bush's election has received a plan that offers support for every major form of energy production and distribution."[150] The symbolic core of the proposals was to open the Arctic National Wildlife Refuge to oil exploration. The Senate repeatedly rejected it in dramatic showdown votes over three separate Congresses.

One could also argue that Bush's effort to reform Social Security, launched amidst much fanfare in 2005, was an effort in long-range planning. Unique among government programs, Social Security is required by law to plan on a seventy-five-year timeline, but that requirement reduces confidence in the policymakers' ability to project so far ahead. Ultimately, the Bush plan failed to gain congressional approval.

Conclusion

Can the president lead the executive branch? Many of the studies discussed here raise doubts.[151] Although presidents have substantial formal powers and managerial resources, they wrestle with the problem of controlling their own branch of government. Their capacity to direct its many departments and agencies in the implementation of presidential policies is limited by bureaucratic complexity and fragmentation, conflict between the presidency and the bureaucracy, external pressure and influence on the bureaucracy, and the extreme difficulty of establishing an effective management system within the government.

Important milestones in this effort can be found throughout the twentieth century. Roosevelt created the Executive Office of the President in 1939, providing his successors with a critical group of presidential loyalists and policy experts independent of bureaucratic pressures. Johnson's enthusiastic endorsement of the program planning budgeting system in 1966 started a series of experiments in using the budget as a planning instrument. Nixon's centralization of decisions in the White House is a strategy others have emulated. Carter established the potential as well as the limits of using reorganization as a management tool, and his sponsorship of the Civil Service Reform Act of 1978 created a new cadre of presidential allies in the civil service.

Reagan came closest to assembling these instruments of control into a coherent administrative strategy, a consensus that prevails a quarter-century after he assumed office.[152] Reagan's centralized control of appointments fashioned a relatively unified "team" by making ideological compatibility with his goals the principal criterion for selection. Reagan also used cabinet councils as a means to link the White House staff with the cabinet officials in directing policy efforts. Most important, he used the budget to enforce his spending priorities on departments and agencies. In the face of strong pressures to reduce spending, he reversed the traditional pattern of budget preparation from the bottom up, in which agencies attempt to protect their bases, and instituted top-down budgeting, with presidential and OMB decisions being determinative.[153] Finally, Reagan attempted to accomplish policy change administratively by establishing procedures for OMB review of regulations, diminishing the intensity of regulatory enforcement, and reinterpreting agency functions and relations with clientele in accordance with the administration's ideology.[154]

Each president faces anew the challenges of asserting control. Although Reagan's successes did not extend to his successors, they provided guidance for future efforts. George W. Bush and his White House aides were attentive students and launched a comprehensive effort to establish presidential control, but its results were mixed. Similar struggles await Barack Obama.

Suggested Readings

Arnold, Peri E. *Making the Managerial Presidency: Comprehensive Reorganization Planning, 1905–1980*. Princeton: Princeton University Press, 1986.

Borrelli, MaryAnne. *The President's Cabinet: Gender, Power, and Representation*. Boulder: Lynne Rienner, 2002.

Campbell, Colin. *Managing the Presidency: Carter, Reagan, and the Search for Executive Harmony*. Pittsburgh: University of Pittsburgh Press, 1986.

Cohen, Jeffrey E. *The Politics of the U.S. Cabinet: Representation in the Executive Branch, 1789–1984*. Pittsburgh: University of Pittsburgh Press, 1988.

Cooper, Phillip J. *By Order of the President: The Use and Abuse of Executive Direct Action*. Lawrence: University Press of Kansas, 2002.

Cronin, Thomas E. *The State of the Presidency*. 2nd ed. Boston: Little, Brown, 1980.

Fisher, Louis. *Constitutional Conflicts between Congress and the President*. 3rd ed., rev. Lawrence: University Press of Kansas, 1991.

Hart, John. *The Presidential Branch: From Washington to Clinton*. 2nd ed. Chatham, N.J.: Chatham House, 1995.

Hess, Stephen. *Organizing the Presidency*. 3rd ed. Washington, D.C.: Brookings, 2002.

Light, Paul C. *Thickening Government: Federal Hierarchy and the Diffusion of Accountability*. Washington, D.C.: Brookings, 1995.

Mayer, Kenneth R. *With the Stroke of a Pen: Executive Orders and Presidential Power*. Princeton: Princeton University Press, 2001.

Nathan, Richard P. *The Administrative Presidency*. New York: Wiley, 1983.

Pfiffner, James P. *The Strategic Presidency*. 2nd ed. Lawrence: University Press of Kansas, 1996.

———. *The Managerial Presidency*. 2nd ed. College Station: Texas A&M University Press, 1999.

Warshaw, Shirley Anne. *Powersharing: White House–Cabinet Relations in the Modern Presidency*. Albany: State University of New York Press, 1996.

Weko, Thomas J. *The Politicizing Presidency: The White House Personnel Office, 1948–1994*. Lawrence: University Press of Kansas, 1995.

Resources on the Web

Archive of CRS Reports: http://digital.library.unt.edu/govdocs/crs/.
Office of Personnel Management: http://www.opm.gov/.
Executive Orders: http://www.archives.gov/federal-register/executive-orders/.

Notes

1. John Mintz, "Homeland Agency Launched; Bush Signs Bill to Combine Federal Security Functions," *Washington Post*, November 26, 2002, A1.

2. The most recent DHS organization chart can be found at http://www.dhs.gov/xlibrary/photos/orgchart-web.png.

3. Brookings Press Briefing, July 15, 2002, "Brookings Report Urges Congress to Revise President Bush's Homeland Security Proposal," www.brookings.edu/~/media/Files/events/2002/0715homeland%20security/20020715homeland.pdf. Also see David Gunter et al., *Protecting the American Homeland* (Washington, D.C.: Brookings Institution Press, 2002).

4. Spencer S. Hsu, "A Public Coup for the Secret Service: Agency May Gain Clout after a Move to Planned Homeland Security Department," *Washington Post*, August 14, 2002, A27.

5. Edward Walsh, "Changing Customs: Can Free Trade Flourish with Focus on Terrorism?" *Washington Post*, July 26, 2002, A31.

6. Sara Kehaulani Goo, "Fledgling TSA Offers Lessons: Lawmakers Urged Not to Ask Too Much of New Department," *Washington Post*, July 22, 2002, A13.

7. Walter Pincus, "FEMA's Influence May Be Cut under New Department," *Washington Post*, July 24, 2002, A17.

8. Sydney J. Freedberg Jr., Corine Hegland, and Margaret Kriz, "Repeating the Past?" *National Journal*, June 14, 2002, http://nationaljournal.com/members/news/2002/06/0614nj2.htm.

9. Richard E. Cohen, Siobhan Gorman, and Sydney J. Freedberg Jr., "The Ultimate Turf War," *National Journal*, January 3, 2003, http://nationaljournal.com/members/news/2003/01/0103nj1.htm.

10. Siobhan Gorman, Sydney J. Freedberg Jr., and Peter H. Stone, "New Department, New Special Interests," *National Journal*, December 6, 2002, www.nationaljournal.com/members/news/2002/12/1206nj7.htm.

11. Christopher Lee and Stephen Barr, "New Agency, New Rules—and a Cost: Bush Gets Management Freedom, and a Measure of Mistrust among Workers," *Washington Post*, November 14, 2002, A31.

12. Greta Wodele, "Homeland Overhaul May Spur Budget Troubles," *National Journal*, July 18, 2005, http://nationaljournal.com/members/news/2005/07/0718tdissue.htm.

13. Paul C. Light, "Homeland Security's Extreme Makeover," *Christian Science Monitor*, October 12, 2005, 9.

14. Martin Kady II, "Three Years On, Homeland Security Turf Wars Persist," *CQ Weekly Online*, June 26, 2006, 1776–1777, http://library.cqpress.com/cqweekly/weeklyreport109-000002312160.

15. Richard Rose, "Government against Subgovernments: A European Perspective on Washington," in *Presidents and Prime Ministers*, ed. Richard Rose and Ezra N. Suleiman (Washington, D.C.: American Enterprise Institute, 1980), 339.

16. For a view that regards presidents as much more than passive participants in agency design, see David E. Lewis, *Presidents and the Politics of Agency Design* (Stanford: Stanford University Press, 2003).

17. James P. Pfiffner challenges this viewpoint and maintains that presidents tend to overestimate the opposition they will get from the bureaucracy. See Pfiffner, "Political Appointees and Career Executives: The Democracy-Bureaucracy Nexus in the Third Century," *Public Administration Review* (January-February 1987): 57–65.

18. Hugh Heclo, *A Government of Strangers* (Washington, D.C.: Brookings, 1977), 7.

19. Paul C. Light, "The New True Size of Government," Research Brief Number 2, Organizational Performance Initiative, Wagner Graduate School of Public Service, New York University, August 2006, http://wagner.nyu.edu/performance/files/True_Size.pdf.

20. Jason D. Mycoff and Joseph A. Pika, *Confrontation and Compromise: Presidential and Congressional Leadership, 2001–2006* (Lanham, Md.: Rowman and Littlefield, 2007), chap. 3.

21. Francis E. Rourke, *Bureaucracy, Politics, and Public Policy*, 3rd ed. (Boston: Little, Brown, 1984), 32.

22. Aaron Wildavsky, *The New Politics of the Budgetary Process*, 2nd ed. (New York: HarperCollins, 1992), 87–88.

23. David A. Stockman, *The Triumph of Politics: Why the Reagan Revolution Failed* (New York: Harper and Row, 1986).

24. Paul C. Light, *Thickening Government: Federal Hierarchy and the Diffusion of Accountability* (Washington, D.C.: Brookings, 1995), 32–33.

25. Patrick Yoest, "Homeland Authorization Bill Defies Veto Threat," *CQ Weekly Online*, May 14, 2007, 1442, http://library.cqpress.com/cqweekly/weeklyreport110-000002510510.

26. Heclo, *A Government of Strangers*.

27. G. Calvin MacKenzie, "Partisan Presidential Leadership: The President's Appointees," in *The Parties Respond: Changes in American Parties and Campaigns*, 4th ed., ed. L. Sandy Maisel (Boulder: Westview, 2002), 267.

28. Jeffrey E. Cohen, *The Politics of the U.S. Cabinet: Representation in the Executive Branch, 1789–1984* (Pittsburgh: University of Pittsburgh Press, 1988), chaps. 3, 4.

29. Thomas E. Cronin, *The State of the Presidency*, 2nd ed. (Boston: Little, Brown, 1980), 282.

30. Bradley H. Patterson and James P. Pfiffner, "The White House Office of Presidential Personnel," *Presidential Studies Quarterly* 31 (September 2001): 415–439.

31. James P. Pfiffner, *The Strategic Presidency*, 2nd ed. (Lawrence: University Press of Kansas, 1996), 57.

32. G. Calvin Mackenzie, *The Politics of Presidential Appointments* (New York: Free Press, 1981).

33. Patterson and Pfiffner, "The White House Office," 420.

34. Thomas J. Weko, *The Politicizing Presidency: The White House Personnel Office, 1948–1994* (Lawrence: University Press of Kansas, 1995), 149–151, 157.

35. Richard P. Nathan, *The Administrative Presidency* (New York: Wiley, 1983), 74–76.

36. Joel D. Aberbach, "A Reinvented Government, or the Same Old Government?" in *The Clinton Legacy*, ed. Colin Campbell and Bert A. Rockman (New York: Chatham House, 2000), 120.

37. Weko, *The Politicizing Presidency*, 100–103.

38. John P. Burke, "The Bush Transition in Historical Context," *PS: Political Science & Politics* 35 (March 2002).

39. Testimony of Paul C. Light before the Government Reform Committee, U.S. House of Representatives, May 3, 2003, 8, http://www.brookings.edu/testimony/2003/0505governance_light.aspx.

40. Mark W. Huddleston and William W. Boyer, *The Higher Civil Service in the United States: Quest for Reform* (Pittsburgh: University of Pittsburgh Press, 1996); Edie N. Goldenberg, "The Permanent Government in an Era of Retrenchment and Redirection," in *The Reagan Presidency and the Governing of America*, ed. Lester M. Salamon and Michael S. Lund (Washington, D.C.: Urban Institute Press, 1984), 381–404.

41. Chester A. Newland, "A Midterm Appraisal—The Reagan Presidency, Limited Government, and Political Administration," *Public Administration Review* (January-February 1983): 15–16.

42. Light, Testimony, 1.

43. John Maggs, "Compete or Else," *National Journal*, July 11, 2003, http://nationaljournal.com/members/news/2003/07/0711nj1.htm. For the scorecard designed under Bush, see http://www.whitehouse.gov/omb/budintegration/scorecards/agency_scorecards.html.

44. Office of Management and Budget, "Competitive Sourcing: Conducting Public-Private Competition in a Reasoned and Responsible Manner," July 2003, http://www.whitehouse.gov/omb/procurement/comp_sourc_addendum.pdf. For commentary, see Jia Lynn Yang, "An Evolving Civil Service," *National Journal*, July 11, 2003, http://nationaljournal.com/members/news/2003/07/0711nj4.htm.

45. *Kendall v. United States*, 37 U.S. (12 Pet.) 524 (1838).

46. *Panama Refining Co. v. Ryan*, 293 U.S. 338 (1934); *Schechter Poultry Co. v. United States*, 295 U.S. 495 (1935).

47. Louis Fisher, *Constitutional Conflicts between Congress and the President*, 3rd ed. (Lawrence: University Press of Kansas, 1991), 98; Theodore J. Lowi, *The End of Liberalism*, 2nd ed. (New York: Norton, 1979), chap. 5.

48. Morris P. Fiorina, *Congress: Keystone of the Washington Establishment*, 2nd ed. (New Haven: Yale University Press, 1989).

49. Rourke, *Bureaucracy, Politics, and Public Policy*, 74.

50. MaryAnne Borrelli, *The President's Cabinet: Gender, Power, and Representation* (Boulder: Lynne Rienner, 2002), 15.

51. "Grading the Cabinet," *National Journal*, January 24, 2003, http://nationaljournal.com/members/news/2003/01/0124nj1.htm.

52. Carl M. Cannon, "The Old-Timers," *National Journal*, May 22, 1999, 1387.

53. "The Cabinet's Keeper," *National Journal*, January 24, 2003, http://nationaljournal.com/members/news/2003/01/0124nj2.htm.

54. Andrew Rudalevige, " 'The Decider': Issue Management and the Bush White House," in *The George W. Bush Legacy* ed. Colin Campbell, Bert A. Rockman, and Andrew Rudalevige (Washington, D.C.: CQ Press, 2007), 147.

55. Cannon, "The Old-Timers," 1388. The average tenure of cabinet members for the past six administrations based on data from Shirley Ann Warshaw reported in *National Journal* was Nixon 1.73 years, Ford 2.04, Carter 2.47, Reagan 3.27, G. H. W. Bush 2.52, and Clinton 3.36.

56. Cohen, *The Politics of the U.S. Cabinet*, 173–176.

57. Borrelli, *The President's Cabinet*, 46–52. This pattern held true for seven of the eight administrations included in the study, with G. H. W. Bush being the exception. Because Bush had been elected as a sitting vice president after eight years of Republican control, Borrelli suggests that Bush drew on his extensive network of experienced acquaintances and that the pool of outsiders was depleted. Borrelli's research covered administrations from FDR through Bush II, except for Truman, Kennedy, and Johnson. Also see Nelson W. Polsby, "Presidential Cabinet-Making Lessons for the Political System," *Political Science Quarterly* (Spring 1978): 15–25.

58. Borrelli, *The President's Cabinet*, 72–74.

59. Cronin, *The State of the Presidency*, 270–272.

60. Ibid., 282–285.

61. In *The Politics of the U.S. Cabinet*, Cohen finds a distinction between the older and the newer outer departments based on "the importance of interests in creating the department and on the complexity of its interest group environment" (144). The older departments—agriculture, commerce, labor, and interior—were created in response to demands from single interests that continue to provide them with some protection from presidential control. The newer departments tend to operate in "more complex interest group environments" that may result in "intradepartmental conflict among advocates of the competing interests" (138, 139).

62. Pfiffner, *The Strategic Presidency*, 41–42, 65–66; Stephen Hess, *Organizing the Presidency*, 2nd ed. (Washington, D.C.: Brookings, 1988), 200; Shirley Anne Warshaw, *Powersharing: White House-Cabinet Relations in the Modern Presidency* (Albany: State University of New York Press, 1996), 228–233.

63. Richard F. Fenno Jr., *The President's Cabinet* (New York: Vintage Books, 1959), 132.

64. Ronald Brownstein and Dick Kirschten, "Cabinet Power," *National Journal*, June 28, 1986, 1582–9.

65. James A. Barnes, "Like His Home-State Razorbacks . . . Clinton's Cabinet Plays to Win," *National Journal*, April 9, 1994, 852–853. Also see Warshaw, *Powersharing*, 198–227.

66. For discussions of pre-9/11 management practices, see Lizette Alvarez and Eric Schmitt, "Cheney Ever More Powerful as Crucial Link to Congress," *New York Times*, May 13, 2001, A1. On the general operation of the administration, see John F. Harris and Dan Balz, "Conflicting Image of Bush Emerges," *Washington Post*, April 28, 2001, A1. Also see Alexis Simendinger, "Stepping into Power," *National Journal*, January 27, 2001, 246–248.

67. Karen M. Hult, "The Bush White House in Comparative Perspective" (paper delivered at the conference on "The George W. Bush Presidency: An Early Assessment," Woodrow Wilson School, Princeton University, April 25–26, 2003), 20. For a detailed account of Bush's decision making in the aftermath of 9/11, see Bob Woodward, *Bush at War* (New York: Simon and Shuster, 2002).

68. Andrew Rosenthal, "Sununu's Out and Skinner Is In, but White House Troubles Persist," *New York Times*, February 11, 1992, A1, A13. Also see Burt Solomon, "Bush's Renovated Inner Circle Has a Bit of a Reaganesque Look," *National Journal*, February 8, 1992, 346–347.

69. John Hart, *The Presidential Branch: From Washington to Clinton*, 2nd ed. (Chatham, N.J.: Chatham House, 1995), 91.

70. Margaret C. Hermann, "Advice and Advisers in the Clinton Presidency: The Impact of Leadership," in *The Clinton Presidency: Campaigning, Governing, and the Psychology of Leadership*, ed. Stanley A. Renshon (Boulder: Westview, 1995), 157, 159.

71. Will Englund, "Czar Wars: Who's on Obama's Front Line," *National Journal Special Report*, http://nationaljournalspecialreport.com/NatJournal_CzarWars.pdf.

72. U.S. Constitution, Article II, section 1.

73. Senate Historical Office, "Occasions When Vice Presidents Have Voted to Break Ties in the Senate," March 13, 2008. www.senate.gov/artandhistory/history/resources/pdf/VPTies.pdf.

74. Paul C. Light, *Vice-Presidential Power: Advice and Influence in the White House* (Baltimore: Johns Hopkins University Press, 1983).

75. Barton Gellman and Jo Becker, "A Different Understanding with the President," *Washington Post*, June 24, 2007, A1.

76. Jo Becker and Barton Gellman, "A Strong Push From Backstage," *Washington Post*, June 26, 2007, A1.

77. Joseph A. Pika, "Dick Cheney, Joe Biden, and the New Vice Presidency," in *The Presidency and the Political System*, 9th ed., ed. Michael Nelson (Washington, D.C.: CQ Press, 2009).

78. Will Englund, "What Kind of Vice President Will Biden Be?" *National Journal*, March 7, 2009, http://www.nationaljournal.com/njmagazine/nj_20090307_9943.php.

79. *Buckley v. Valeo*, 421 U.S. 1 (1976).

80. In 1973 President Nixon named Howard J. Phillips acting director of the Office of Economic Opportunity (OEO), an agency Nixon planned to dismantle. Phillips began to phase out its programs and withhold funds from it. Sen. Harrison A. Williams, D-N.J., took legal action to force Nixon either to submit Phillips's name to the Senate for confirmation or to stop dismantling the OEO. A U.S. court of appeals ruled that Phillips was illegally holding office and enjoined him from further actions. See James P. Pfiffner, *The President, the Budget, and Congress: Impoundment and the 1974 Budget Act* (Boulder: Westview, 1974), 116–117. The effort was thwarted, but the decision did not settle the issue.

81. Three notable examples are the Senate's rejection of former senator John Tower, R-Texas, to be secretary of defense in 1989; its long delay in acting on the nomination of Dr. Henry Foster Jr. to be surgeon general of the United States; and its narrow support in 2001 for former senator John Ashcroft, R-Mo., to become attorney general. Tower had antagonized several of his former colleagues during his service in the chamber and was objectionable to many Democratic senators because of his hawkish views. Foster, a distinguished obstetrician and gynecologist, became a political football in the debate over abortion. The White House Personnel Office, in an inexplicable blunder, neglected to ask Foster if he had ever performed abortions until after Clinton announced the nomination on February 2, 1995. When Foster gave three different answers and explained them as due to a faulty memory, abortion opponents made the nomination a cause célèebre, and Sens. Robert Dole and Phil Gramm, both Republican presidential hopefuls, tried to outdo each other in their opposition to the nomination by threatening to keep it from coming to a vote in the Senate. The abortion issue then became entwined with Foster's credibility. Following confirmation hearings at which Foster performed very credibly, the Senate Labor and Human Resources Committee on May 24, 1995, approved the nomination by a 10–8 vote. A successful Republican filibuster prevented the nomination from coming to an up or down vote of the full Senate. Ashcroft was a vehemently outspoken opponent of abortion who Democrats suspected would not enforce the laws. After a surprisingly bitter debate, unusual in that senators seldom criticize one of their own, the full membership confirmed Ashcroft by a vote of 58 to 42.

82. Christopher J. Deering, "Damned if You Do and Damned if You Don't: The Senate's Role in the Appointment Process," in *The In-and-Outers*, ed. G. Calvin McKenzie (Baltimore: Johns Hopkins University Press, 1987), 119. Also see G. Calvin McKenzie, ed., *Innocent until Nominated* (Washington, D.C.: Brookings, 2001).

83. Anthony Lake withdrew from consideration as nominee to head the CIA in March 1997 after concluding that he would be subjected to endless delays and partisan criticism. Juliana Gruenwald, "Tenet Appears Likely to Win Confirmation as CIA Chief," *Congressional Quarterly Weekly Report*, March 22, 1997, 712–714. On the Holbrooke nomination, see Philip Shenon, "Holbrooke Nomination Passes One Hurdle but Faces Another," *New York Times*, July 1, 1999, A6; Philip Shenon, "Let's Slow Down on Holbrooke's Case, Lott Says," *New York Times*, July 23, 1999, A9; Eric Schmitt, "When Nomination Turns to Wrangling to Impasse," *New York Times*, July 28, 1999, A16; Miles A. Pomper, "Holbrooke Confirmed as U.N. Envoy," *CQ Weekly*, August 7, 1999, 1961–1962.

84. Senate Committee on Governmental Affairs, *Policy and Supporting Positions* (Washington, D.C.: GPO, 2000), also known as the "plum book." For a fuller discussion, see Bradley H. Patterson and James P. Pfiffner, "The White House Office of Presidential Personnel," *Presidential Studies Quarterly* 31 (September 2001): 420. Patterson and Pfiffner identify 1,125 full-time positions subject to confirmation, including 185 ambassadors, 94 U.S. attorneys, 94 U.S. marshals, 15 in international organizations, and 4 in the legislative branch.

85. On the hurdles confronted by candidates, see Paul C. Light, "The Last Word Make It Easier to Say 'Yes,'" *Government Executive*, December 15, 2002, http://www.govexec.com/features/1202/1202lastword.htm. On the attention devoted to nominees' records, see James A. Barnes, "White House: Bush's Insiders," *National Journal*, June 25, 2001.

86. The *Washington Post* maintained a running tally of positions at "Head Count," http://projects.washingtonpost.com/2009/federal-appointments.

87. Pamela C. Corley, "Avoiding Advice and Consent: Recess Appointments and Presidential Power," *Presidential Studies Quarterly* 36 (December 2006): 671.

88. *Myers v. United States*, 272 U.S. 52 (1926).

89. *Humphrey's Executor v. United States*, 295 U.S. 602 (1935).

90. Fisher, *Constitutional Conflicts*, 79.

91. Phillip J. Cooper, *By Order of the President: The Use and Abuse of Executive Direct Action* (Lawrence: University Press of Kansas, 2002), 15, 81–83. By April 4, 2001, Bush had revoked six of Clinton's executive orders. Hult, "The Bush White House in Comparative Perspective," 27 n. 77.

92. Kenneth R. Mayer, *With the Stroke of a Pen: Executive Orders and Presidential Power* (Princeton: Princeton University Press, 2001), 4.

93. For excellent discussions of presidential use of executive orders in the areas of information secrecy and intelligence organization as well as in civil rights, see ibid., chaps. 5, 6.

94. *Amalgamated Meat Cutters v. Connally*, 337 F. Supp. 737 (1971).

95. *Hirabayashi v. United States*, 320 U.S. 581 (1943); *Korematsu v. United States*, 323 U.S. 214 (1944).

96. Hult, "The Bush White House in Comparative Perspective," 27.

97. For an interpretation that Clinton relied more heavily on such instruments after the Republicans controlled Congress, see Aberbach, "A Reinvented Government," 128; and Alexis Simendinger, "The Paper Wars," *National Journal*, July 25, 1998, 1732–1739. Some reports confuse distinctions among the different forms of unilateral presidential action rather than adhering to the definition of executive orders maintained by the National Archives and Records Administration.

98. Mayer, *With the Stroke of a Pen*, 70.

99. Ibid., Table 3.3, 82.

100. Ibid., 102.

101. Kenneth R. Mayer and Kevin Price, "Unilateral Presidential Powers: Significant Executive Orders, 1949–99," *Presidential Studies Quarterly* 32 (June 2002): 375.

102. Cooper, *By Order of the President*, 13, 90–91.

103. *Youngstown Sheet and Tube Co. v. Sawyer*, 343 U.S. 579 (1952).

104. Lawrence R. Jacobs and Robert Y. Shapiro, "Public Opinion in Clinton's First Year: Leadership and Responsiveness," in Renshon, *The Clinton Presidency*, 201.

105. A comprehensive list of executive orders from January 1937 can be accessed at http://www .archives.gov/federal-register/executive-orders/.

106. *Immigration and Naturalization Service v. Chadha*, 462 U.S. 919 (1983).

107. Joseph Cooper, "Postscript on the Congressional Veto," *Political Science Quarterly* (Fall 1983): 427–430; Barbara Hinkson Craig, *The Legislative Veto: Congressional Control of Regulation* (Boulder: Westview, 1983), 139–150; Fisher, *Constitutional Conflicts*, 152.

108. Fisher, *Constitutional Conflicts*, 150–152.

109. Louis Fisher, "Judicial Misjudgments about the Lawmaking Process: The Legislative Veto Case," *Public Administration Review* (November-December 1985): 709–710.

110. Richard M. Pious, *The American Presidency* (New York: Basic Books, 1979), 256–257.

111. Allen Schick, "The Road to PPB: The States of Budget Reform," *Public Administration Review* (December 1966): 243–258.

112. Wildavsky, *The New Politics of the Budgetary Process*, 436–440.

113. Allen Schick, *The Federal Budget: Politics, Policy, Process* (Washington, D.C.: Brookings, 1995), 2–4.

114. Bob Woodward, *The Agenda: Inside the Clinton White House* (New York: Simon and Schuster, 1994).

115. Daniel J. Palazzolo, *Done Deal? The Politics of the 1997 Budget Agreement* (Chatham, N.J.: Chatham House, 1999).

116. Louis Fisher, *Presidential Spending Power* (Princeton: Princeton University Press, 1979), chap. 4.

117. Ibid., 148.

118. Vivian Vale, "The Obligation to Spend: Presidential Impoundment of Congressional Appropriations," *Political Studies* (1977): 508–532.

119. *Clinton v. City of New York*, 524 U.S. 417 (1998). The case can be found at http://supct .law.cornell.edu/supct/html/historics/USSC_CR_0524_0417_ZS.html.

120. Steven T. Dennis, "A Promise for a Line-Item Vote," *CQ Weekly Online*, January 22, 2007, 252–252, http://library.cqpress.com/cqweekly/weeklyreport110-000002433724.

121. Peri Arnold concludes his authoritative study of "the managerial presidency" by observing that "no modern president has fully managed the executive branch." He further argues that the "managerial conception of the presidency is untenable" because it "places impossible obligations on presidents" and creates unrealistic "public expectations of presidential performance." Peri E. Arnold, *Making the Managerial Presidency: Comprehensive Reorganization Planning, 1905–1980* (Princeton: Princeton University Press, 1986), 361–362.

122. Andrew Rudalevige, *Managing the President's Program: Presidential Leadership and Legislative Policy Formulation* (Princeton: Princeton University Press, 2002), 7.

123. Ibid.

124. Hess, *Organizing the Presidency*, 230–231.

125. Jack W. Germond and Jules Witcover, "Bush Left with Little Room for Error," *National Journal*, December 22, 1990, 3104.

126. Fred I. Greenstein, "Political and Political Leadership: The Case of Bill Clinton," in Renshon, *The Clinton Presidency*, 141, 142.

127. Burt Solomon, "Clinton's New Taskmaster Takes Charge," *National Journal,* August 6, 1994, 1872.

128. Todd S. Purdum, "The Ungreening of the White House Staff," *New York Times,* December 22, 1996, E10.

129. Karen Hughes returned to Texas in July 2002. For a discussion of the Bush staff system, see Hult, "The Bush White House in Comparative Perspective."

130. Mark Leibovich, "Pressure Cooker: Andrew Card Has the Recipe for Chief of Staff Down Pat," *Washington Post,* January 5, 2005, C1.

131. Tom Hamburger, "Inquiry of Rove brings unit out of obscurity," *Seattle Times,* April 24, 2007, http://seattletimes.nwsource.com/html/politics/2003678550_investigate24.html.

132. Alexis Simendinger, "Stepping into Power," *National Journal,* January 27, 2001, 247.

133. Stuart Rothenberg, "There's No Question about Who's in Charge at Bush's White House,"*Roll Call,* March 26, 2001, www.rollcall.com.

134. Terry M. Moe, "The Politicized Presidency," in *The New Direction in American Politics,* ed. John E. Chubb and Paul E. Peterson (Washington, D.C.: Brookings, 1985), 235–271.

135. Samuel Kernell, "The Creed and Reality of Modern White House Management," in *Chief of Staff: Twenty-Five Years of Managing the Presidency,* ed. Samuel Kernell and Samuel L. Popkin (Berkeley: University of California Press, 1986), 228.

136. John R. Dempsey, "Carter Reorganization: A Midterm Appraisal," *Public Administration Review* (January–February 1979): 74–78; Arnold, *Making the Managerial Presidency,* chap. 10.

137. Herbert Kaufman, "Reflections on Administrative Reorganization," in *Setting National Priorities: The 1978 Budget,* ed. Joseph A. Pechman (Washington, D.C.: Brookings, 1977), 403.

138. Harold C. Relyea, "93026: Executive Branch Reorganization," *CRS Issue Brief,* updated December 6, 1996, www.fas.org/spp/civil/crs/93-026.htm

139. Harold C. Relyea, "Executive Branch Reorganization and Management Initiatives," *CRS Issue Brief for Congress,* updated September 23, 2003, http://digital.library.unt.edu/govdocs/crs/permalink/meta-crs-4579:1.

140. Dempsey, "Carter Reorganization," 75.

141. Ronald C. Moe, "The 'Reinventing Government' Exercise: Misinterpreting the Problem, Misjudging the Consequences," *Public Administration Review* (March–April 1994): 112.

142. David Osborne and Ted Gaebler, *Reinventing Government: How the Entrepreneurial Spirit Is Transforming the Public Sector from Schoolhouse to State House, City Hall to Pentagon* (Reading, Mass.: Addison-Wesley, 1992), 111.

143. Donald F. Kettl, *Reinventing Government: A Fifth Year Report Card,* Center for Public Management Report 98-1 (Washington, D.C.: Brookings, September 1998).

144. In "The 'Reinventing Government' Exercise," Ronald Moe argues that Clinton's effort substitutes results for processes and amounts to abandonment of public law as the basis of political accountability (112). Political scientist James Q. Wilson doubts whether in the era of big government "political accountability can any longer be equated with presidential power." James Q. Wilson, "Reinventing Public Administration," *P.S.: Political Science and Politics* (December 1994): 671. Well-known management consultant Peter Drucker called for a new theory that "asks what the proper functions of government might be and could be . . . [and] what results government should be held accountable for." Peter Drucker, "Really Reinventing Government," *Atlantic Monthly,* February 1995, 61.

145. Joel D. Aberbach, "The State of the Contemporary American Presidency: Or, Is Bush II Actually Ronald Reagan's Heir?" in *The George W. Bush Presidency: First Appraisals,* ed. Colin Campbell and Bert A. Rockman (Chatham, N.J.: Chatham House, 2003), chap. 11.

146. Paul Singer, "By the Horns," *National Journal,* March 25, 2005, http://nationaljournal.com/members/news/2005/03/0325nj1.htm.

147. Aaron Wildavsky, *Speaking Truth to Power* (Boston: Little, Brown, 1979), 120.

148. Richard Rose, *Managing Presidential Objectives* (New York: Free Press, 1976), chap. 6.

149. Peter Behr, "Energy Plan to Fuel Long Fight; at Issue Is Environmental Cost of Plentiful, Cheaper Power," *Washington Post,* May 15, 2001, A9.

150. Peter Behr, "Bush Places His Bet on Energy Industry," *Washington Post,* May 18, 2001, E1.

151. See, for example, Arnold, *Making the Managerial Presidency;* Colin Campbell, *Managing the Presidency: Carter, Reagan, and the Search for Executive Harmony* (Pittsburgh: University of Pittsburgh Press, 1986); and Rose, *Managing Presidential Objectives.* Also see Walter Williams, *Mismanaging America: The Rise of the Anti-Analytic Presidency* (Lawrence: University Press of Kansas, 1990).

152. Nathan, *The Administrative Presidency.*

153. Allen Schick, "The Budget as an Instrument of Presidential Policy," in Salamon and Lund, *The Reagan Presidency and the Governing of America,* 113.

154. Lester M. Salamon and Alan J. Abramson, "Governance: The Politics of Retrenchment," in *The Reagan Record,* ed. John L. Palmer and Isabell V. Sawhill (Cambridge, Mass.: Ballinger, 1984), 97; Joseph A. Pika and Norman C. Thomas, "The President as Institution Builder: The Reagan Case," *Governance* (October 1990): 444–447.

CHAPTER 7

Judicial Politics

The members of the U.S. Supreme Court look on as Justice John Paul Stevens swears in Chief Justice John G. Roberts Jr. on October 3, 2005. Clerk of the Court William Suter holds the Bible.

On February 5, 2009, news broke that seventy-five-year-old U.S. Supreme Court justice Ruth Bader Ginsburg had undergone surgery for pancreatic cancer. Doctors discovered the cancer early, and it had not spread, but the news led to speculation that Ginsburg might decide to retire, perhaps as early as the end of the current Supreme Court term. Even if she did not retire, it remained likely that Barack Obama would have the opportunity to appoint at least one justice to the Supreme Court. Justice John Paul Stevens turned eighty-nine on April 20, 2009, making him just one year and ten months shy of the oldest Supreme Court justice ever to serve—Oliver Wendell Holmes Jr., who retired at the age of ninety years and ten months in January 1932. Justices Anthony Kennedy and Antonin Scalia will both be seventy-seven years old by the end of Obama's first term. In addition, some Court observers believed that David Souter, a relative youngster of sixty-nine when Obama was sworn in, was eager to return to New Hampshire—and they were right.

On May 1, 2009, Souter announced that he would retire at the end of the term. Although he was appointed by a Republican president, George H. W. Bush, Souter was giving a Democrat the opportunity to name his replacement. President Obama made it clear that he was looking for a nominee who was not only dedicated to the rule of law and mindful of the limits of the judicial role, but also had empathy for how the law affects real people in their daily lives. Souter, Ginsburg, and Stevens, along with Justice Stephen Breyer, constituted the liberal bloc on the Supreme Court, so Obama's choice to replace Souter (or any of the other three members of that group) will likely make little difference in terms of voting patterns on the Court. But an Obama replacement for either of the two remaining Reagan appointees—Scalia (a stalwart of the conservative bloc of four justices) or Kennedy (a centrist swing vote)—could make a big difference and provoke a huge confirmation battle.

This chapter examines the relationship between the president and the federal courts. The first section analyzes the most important influence the president exerts over these courts: the power to nominate their members. The chapter then explores other means by which the chief executive affects the business of the courts; and finally, it examines the reverse situation: how the federal courts, and the Supreme Court in particular, influence the actions of the president.

Presidential Appointment of Federal Judges

Perhaps the greatest impact the president can have on the courts is the selection of federal judges who share the administration's policy goals. These judges include not only the nine justices of the U.S. Supreme Court, but also more than eight hundred judges who sit on lower federal courts. The Constitution established (and requires) one Supreme Court. It authorized (but did not require) Congress to create lower federal courts. Congress created lower courts almost immediately through the Judiciary Act of 1789, and that system has grown and evolved since then. All federal judges are nominated by the president, confirmed by the Senate, and serve "during good Behaviour." In other words, they have life tenure subject to impeachment or resignation. Once they are on the bench, federal judges can influence judicial policymaking for years, usually many more than the president who appoints them. This is no small matter because judges may rule on controversial issues such as gay marriage, the right to die, abortion, affirmative action, school prayer, and the rights of criminal defendants.

One might think that impartial judges who objectively apply the law according to set standards of interpretation should all arrive at the same "correct" outcome in cases that come before them. In practice, judges hold very different views about how to interpret legal texts. Moreover, judges are human beings who are influenced, at least in part, by their backgrounds, personal beliefs, and judicial philosophies. As a result, different judges can—and do—reach different conclusions when confronted with the same case. Presidents therefore work hard to nominate judges with a judicial philosophy similar to theirs. Interest groups—well aware of the impact judges can have on policy—also take keen interest in these nominees. So, too, does the Senate, which has the power to confirm or reject nominees.

Selection of Lower Federal Court Judges

There are two basic types of lower federal courts: trial courts, which are called U.S. district courts, and appellate courts, called U.S. courts of appeals.[1] These courts are distinct from state courts. The United States has an overlapping system of state and federal courts, and each state structures its own court system. As a result, the country has fifty-one court systems—one at the federal level and one for each of the fifty states. State courts usually hear cases involving state law, and federal courts hear cases involving federal law. Sometimes a single action can provoke cases in both state and federal court. Timothy McVeigh violated federal law when he blew up the Federal Building in Oklahoma City and was therefore tried in federal court. But he could also have been tried in state court for violating state law against murder. Moreover, a case involving state law that begins in state court can be appealed to federal court if it involves a *federal question.* A federal question exists if a state law is alleged to violate federal law, a U.S. treaty, or the U.S. Constitution. It can also exist if police or prosecutors are alleged to have violated the constitutional rights of a criminal defendant. A person convicted in state court because of evidence gathered from an unreasonable search and seizure or a coerced confession could appeal to federal court. If there is no federal question, however, the highest state court remains the court of last resort. The manner of selecting state court judges varies from state to state and is completely unrelated to federal judicial selection.

Federal criminal and civil cases originate in U.S. district courts, which try the cases. Each of these courts has jurisdiction over a geographic area called a district. Each district falls within the boundary of a single state, and, by tradition, judges who come from that state are appointed to a district's courts.[2] Every state has at least one district. Those with heavier caseloads have more than one, and Congress occasionally adds new districts to accommodate increased caseloads. Because district courts are the point of entry to the federal judicial system, they hear more cases than any other kind of federal court. Currently more than six hundred judges staff ninety-four district courts.

The courts of appeals are intermediate appellate courts between the district courts and the Supreme Court. Each has jurisdiction over a geographic area called a circuit, made up of several districts. There are twelve regional circuits: one for the District of Columbia and eleven numbered circuits covering the rest of the country. Unlike districts, the numbered circuits have jurisdiction over several states: the First Circuit, for example, covers Maine, Massachusetts, New Hampshire, and Rhode Island. The circuit courts hear appeals from the trial courts and decide whether the trial court made a legal error in trying the case. In other words, courts of appeals answer questions of *law* rather than questions of *fact.* Unlike in proceedings in the district courts, there are no witnesses, no testimony, and no jury. Judges on the courts of appeals base their rulings on written legal arguments called briefs and on oral arguments presented by lawyers representing each side of the case. A panel of three judges usually hears appeals. A majority vote of the panel is necessary to overturn a lower court ruling, and the court of appeals issues a written opinion explaining its ruling.

Only about one-sixth of the litigants from the district courts appeal, so the caseload for the courts of appeals is significantly less than the caseload for the district courts. Even though they hear fewer cases than the district courts, the courts of appeals are very influential because of their power to set precedents that are binding on the lower courts in their circuits. Because the U.S. Supreme Court accepts such a minuscule number of cases from the courts of appeals for review, the courts of appeals are effectively the court of last resort in more than 99 percent of the cases that come before them.[3] Therefore, appointments to these courts are especially significant.

In theory, the appointment process for lower federal courts is the same as for the Supreme Court: the president nominates, and the Senate either confirms or rejects. In practice, presidents have traditionally had less control over the selection of lower federal court judges than over the selection of Supreme Court justices. This is especially true at the district court level because of a practice called **senatorial courtesy.** This informal rule has existed since the early days of George Washington's administration. It means that the Senate (out of courtesy) will generally refuse to confirm people to federal positions who do not have the support of the senators from the state where the vacancy exists.

Senatorial courtesy was institutionalized in the 1940s through the development of the so-called **blue slip** procedure.[4] Both senators, regardless of party affiliation, from the state where the vacancy occurs receive a letter from the chairman of the Senate Judiciary Committee asking for advice about the nominee. Enclosed is a form, printed on blue paper, for the senator to comment on the nominee. Although senators may put their support or opposition in writing and return the form, it is understood that failure to return the blue slip amounts to a veto that will prevent committee hearings on the nominee—a de facto invocation of senatorial courtesy that usually blocks the nomination.[5]

The Senate has not always agreed on whether home-state senators *not* of the president's party should be able to block a nomination. During certain periods, the committee counted only blue slip vetoes from senators of the president's party.[6] At other times, either home-state senator, regardless of party, could scuttle a nomination. Shifting standards sometimes reflect partisan politics. During the last six years of the Clinton administration, when a Democrat controlled the White House and Republicans controlled the Senate, Judiciary Committee chairman Orrin Hatch of Utah routinely allowed blue slips from home-state Republicans to prevent hearings on many Democratic nominees. In other words, he allowed home-state senators who were not of the same political party as President Clinton to block his nominees. Once George W. Bush became president in 2001, however, Hatch abruptly shifted gears and sought to weaken the power of the blue slip. With a Republican in the White House, Hatch wanted to discount the veto power of home-state Democrats, saying that support of a home-state Republican should overcome opposition of a home-state Democrat. The *New York Times* called Hatch's turnabout both ironic and audacious: opposition Republicans had for six years "routinely obstructed" Clinton's judicial nominations and were now trying to remove the possibility that opposition Democrats could do the same to Bush.[7]

As a result of senatorial courtesy and the blue slip, presidents traditionally turn to home-state senators for advice about whom to nominate. Home-state senators of the president's party have the most influence, but some presidents have also sought advice from home-state senators of the opposition party. (Even when they do so, presidents very rarely appoint judges of the opposing party.) In the early days of the Republic—when communication was slow and difficult and the president was more isolated and removed from the various states than today—seeking advice made sense. It assumed that home-state senators were better able to select qualified individuals than the president because they knew more about the existing pool of candidates. Over time, however, senators came to treat district court appointments as a form of patronage. Robert F. Kennedy, who served as attorney general in his brother's administration, went so far as to call it "senatorial appointment with the advice and consent of the Senate."[8]

G. Alan Tarr has pointed out that senatorial courtesy has influenced the type of individuals appointed to district courts. Because these appointments have long served as a form of political patronage for home-state senators of the president's political party, it is not surprising that roughly 95 percent of all district court judges appointed during the past hundred years have come from the same political party as the appointing president. Tarr also notes that "district court judges have usually 'earned' their positions by active party service in their state prior to appointment."[9]

In an attempt to ensure the quality of these judges, the American Bar Association (ABA) created its Standing Committee on Federal Judiciary in 1946 to review the qualifications of all federal judicial nominees.[10] Republicans on the Senate Judiciary Committee embraced the ABA's role—partly to block some of President Harry Truman's Democratic nominees. When Republican president Dwight D. Eisenhower entered office in 1953, he established a formal link between the White House and the ABA. The ABA would review the qualifications of all potential nominees before the president nominated anyone.

By the 1980s, however, Republicans had come to view the ABA with suspicion. Once a conservative organization, the ABA had become more liberal over time. Republicans were especially angry that in 1987 four of the fifteen members of the ABA's standing committee had rated Ronald Reagan's failed Supreme Court nominee Robert Bork "not qualified." In March 2001 President Bush severed the White House link with the ABA—something his father had threatened to do in 1991. In a letter to ABA president Martha W. Barnett, White House counsel Alberto R. Gonzales, who became Bush's second-term attorney general, wrote: "We will continue to welcome suggestions from all sources, including the ABA. The issue at hand, however, is quite different: whether the ABA alone—out of the literally dozens of groups and many individuals who have a strong interest in the composition of the federal courts—should receive advance notice of the identities of potential nominees in order to render prenomination opinions on their fitness for judicial service."[11]

When Democrats regained control of the Senate from June 2001 through the 2002 midterm elections, and again after the 2006 midterm elections, they reinstated a role for the ABA by promising not to hold hearings on Bush's judicial nominees until the Senate Judiciary Committee received their ABA ratings. Shortly after taking office, President Obama overturned Bush's decision to sever the relationship between the White House and the ABA. Democrats argue that the ABA ratings validate a nominee's professional qualifications and maintain that Bush's attempt to bypass the ABA was part of an effort to appoint more ideologically extreme judges to the bench. Democrats also point out that many of the White House lawyers assigned to judicial selection in the Bush administration were affiliated with the conservative Federalist Society, an organization formed in 1982 in response to the perception that liberal ideology dominated law schools and the legal profession.[12] Critics of the Federalist Society have called it "a clearinghouse for the selection of conservative law clerks, government political appointees, judges, and other key policymaking spots in the Bush administration."[13] But critics of the ABA claim it is also an ideological clearinghouse; the only difference being that it favors liberal appointees. A recent scholarly study reinforces that perception by showing that liberal nominees were more likely to receive the highest ABA rating of "well qualified" than conservative nominees.[14]

Since the Carter administration, presidents have exerted greater control over the selection of lower federal court judges than they used to, especially at the level of the courts of appeals. Some view this control as an attempt by presidents to appoint more ideological judges. Ironically, President Carter was attempting to institute merit selection of federal judges. He created the Circuit Court Nominating Commission by executive order in 1977. The commission diminished the role of senators in the selection of courts of appeals judges by taking control of the screening process for nominees. Under the new system, the commission would submit a short list of qualified nominees to the president, who would then nominate someone from that list.[15] Carter also urged senators to create, voluntarily, nominating commissions to advise him on the selection of district court judges from their states. By 1979 senators from thirty-one states had created such commissions.[16] The changes were made to help ensure that the awarding of judgeships would be based on qualifications and not used as political patronage.

Despite Carter's emphasis on merit in judicial selection, his appointments were partisan: over 90 percent of his district court appointments and just over 82 percent of his appeals court appointments were Democrats.[17] Carter also practiced affirmative action when selecting judges. He made a deliberate effort to place women, African Americans, and Hispanics on the federal judiciary—appointing more of each than had been placed on the bench by all previous presidents combined.[18]

Ronald Reagan transformed the selection process when he took office in 1981. He abolished Carter's commission system and seized control of the selection process as part of an effort to identify nominees that reflected his administration's ideology. He created the President's Committee on Federal Judicial Selection, staffed by representatives of the White House and the Justice Department, to conduct the screening—which included extensive interviews of all leading candidates. Sheldon Goldman called it "the most systematic judicial philosophical screening of candidates ever seen in the nation's history."[19] Reagan's attorney general, Edwin Meese III, bluntly said the appointments were meant to "institutionalize the

Reagan revolution so it can't be set aside no matter what happens in future presidential elections."[20] By the time he left office, Reagan had set a new record for the number of lower federal judges appointed: 290 district court judges and 78 appeals court judges.[21] George H. W. Bush appointed almost 200 additional federal judges during his four years as president.

Presidents Carter, Reagan, and Bush all benefited from legislation that significantly expanded the number of federal judges. President Clinton did not. During Clinton's eight years in office, Congress created only 9 additional seats—as compared with 85 under Bush, 85 under Reagan, and 152 under Carter.[22] Clinton also faced a Senate controlled by opposition Republicans during his last six years in office. In 1997 Republican senators orchestrated an unprecedented slowdown of the confirmation process to protest what they called Clinton's "activist" (liberal) nominees. Such charges may have reflected partisan hyperbole more than fact. Studies suggest that Clinton's nominees were actually quite moderate, even the nominees confirmed before Republicans took control of the Senate.[23] Clinton's appointees also had the highest ABA ratings of the past four presidents.[24]

As a result of the Republican slowdown, 10 percent of seats on the federal judiciary were vacant by the end of 1997. Twenty-six seats had remained empty for more than eighteen months, and one-third of the seats in the Ninth Circuit were empty. In March 1997 House majority whip Tom DeLay suggested that congressional Republicans should begin efforts to impeach liberal federal judges.[25] Such tactics provoked outcries. Even Chief Justice William Rehnquist, a conservative appointed by Reagan, criticized the Senate for its slowdown in his annual State of the Judiciary report. "The Senate is surely under no obligation to confirm any particular nominee," Rehnquist wrote, "but after the necessary time for inquiry, it should vote him up or vote him down."[26]

In part because of Rehnquist's criticism, Senate Republicans backed away from their slowdown, and the backlog of vacancies eased in 1998. But the delaying tactics returned in 1999 and continued through the rest of the Clinton presidency. By then, Republicans hoped to postpone confirmations until a Republican president was elected. They were especially concerned with appeals court appointments. In 2000 the Senate confirmed only thirty-nine of eighty-one judicial nominees Clinton put forward, and two other nominees withdrew. Nominations of forty-two judicial candidates remained unconfirmed when Clinton left office in January 2001—thirty-eight of them had never received a Judiciary Committee hearing.[27]

Despite the slowdowns and the lack of new judicial seats to fill, Clinton appointed 366 judges to the district courts, courts of appeals, and Supreme Court during his eight years in office. By the end of Clinton's second term, the number of his appointees serving on the courts narrowly surpassed the number of Reagan-Bush appointees still serving, 42.7 percent to 40.7 percent.[28] Even more than Carter had done, Clinton diversified the bench through these appointments. He appointed 108 women and 61 African Americans: more of each than Ford, Carter, Reagan, and Bush combined had appointed in nineteen years.[29] (See Table 7-1.) But Republicans had the opportunity to make significant inroads when George W. Bush took office in 2001. By the end of his second month in office, Bush had ninety-four judicial vacancies to fill, including twenty-eight on appellate courts.[30] Bush assigned Alberto Gonzales an active role in judicial selection, and in the first two months of the Bush presidency, Gonzales interviewed some fifty potential nominees.[31] The Bush administration was eager to fill the vacancies quickly while Republicans (with the tie-breaking vote of Vice President Cheney) still held marginal control of the Senate. They especially feared that Strom Thurmond, the ninety-eight-year-old Republican senator from South Carolina, might die or resign because of ill health before the 2002 elections. If that happened, the Democratic governor of South Carolina would name a replacement. But none of Bush's judicial nominees was confirmed before Senator Jeffords defected from the Republican Party and threw control of the Senate to the Democrats in June 2001.

By October 2001 Bush had submitted sixty judicial nominations, but the Senate had confirmed only eight. Now Republicans accused Democrats of slowing down the confirmation process, charged that judicial vacancies would hamper the war on terrorism, and mounted a Senate filibuster against a foreign-aid spending bill as retaliation for the confirmation slowdown. Democrats denied that they had deliberately slowed down the confirmation process as Republicans had done under Clinton, pointing out that they had controlled the Senate for only four months and that the legislative agenda had been interrupted during that time by the terrorist attacks of September 11 and the anthrax scare on Capitol Hill.[32] The charges and countercharges further polarized the two sides. Democrats charged Bush with nominating ideologically extreme judges and blocked his nominations of Charles Pickering and Priscilla Owen to the Fifth Circuit Court of Appeals. President Bush, emboldened by his skyrocketing public approval after September 11, charged Democrats with obstructionism and turned the "vacancy crisis" on the federal bench into a campaign issue during the 2002 midterm elections.[33]

Republicans regained control of the Senate in the midterm elections, and it appeared that Bush's nominees would be approved. Bush quickly renominated Pickering and Owen. Senate Democrats showed a willingness to vote for moderate

TABLE 7-1 Race, Ethnicity, and Gender of Appointments to the U.S. District Courts and Courts of Appeals, by Administration (Nixon to G. W. Bush)

President	Total appointments	Male	Female	White	African American	Hispanic	Asian	Native American
G. W. Bush (2001–2009)	320	251 (78.4%)	69 (21.6%)	263 (82.2%)	24 (7.5%)	29 (9.1%)	4 (1.3%)	0
Clinton (1993–2001)	366	259 (70.8%)	107 (29.2%)	274 (74.9%)	61 (16.7%)	25 (6.8%)	5 (1.4%)	1 (0.3%)
G. H. W. Bush (1989–1993)	185	148 (80.0%)	37 (20.0%)	165 (89.2%)	12 (6.5%)	8 (4.3%)	0	0
Reagan (1981–1989)	368	340 (92.4%)	28 (7.6%)	344 (93.5%)	7 (1.9%)	15 (4.1%)	2 (0.5%)	0
Carter (1977–1981)	258	218 (84.5%)	40 (15.5%)	202 (78.3%)	37 (14.3%)	16 (6.2%)	2 (0.8%)	1 (0.4%)
Ford (1974–1977)	64	63 (98.4%)	1 (1.6%)	58 (90.6%)	3 (4.7%)	1 (1.6%)	2 (3.1%)	0
Nixon (1969–1974)	224	223 (99.6%)	1 (0.4%)	215 (96%)	6 (2.6%)	2 (0.9%)	1 (0.4%)	0

SOURCE: Drawn from tables 2 and 4 in Sheldon Goldman et al., "Picking Judges in a Time of Turmoil: W. Bush's Judiciary During the 109th Congress," *Judicature* 90 (May–June 2007), 272 and 282; and from table 6.1 (for Ford and Nixon) from Sheldon Goldman, *Picking Federal Judges: Lower Court Selection from Roosevelt through Reagan* (New Haven: Yale University Press, 1997), 227–229. Figures for George W. Bush courtesy of Sheldon Goldman.

nominees—all nine Democrats on the Senate Judiciary Committee voted in favor of Edward Prado, a Bush nominee to the Fifth Circuit Court of Appeals—but they continued their vow to block "ideological extremists." To do so, they resurrected a tool used by Republicans in 1968 to block Lyndon Johnson's nomination of Abe Fortas to be chief justice of the United States: the filibuster. Under Senate Rule 22, it takes a vote of three-fifths of the entire Senate, sixty votes, to end a filibuster. Because Republicans could not muster the necessary sixty votes, Democrats succeeded in blocking ten nominations—prompting a Republican threat to change Senate rules regarding filibusters, a strategy dubbed the "nuclear option," so Democrats could no longer use them against judicial nominees. The standoff was resolved when seven moderate senators from each party, the so-called "Gang of 14," brokered a compromise that allowed judicial filibusters only in "extraordinary circumstances" and put off any formal changes in the filibuster rule until after the 2006 midterm elections. The compromise allowed the Senate to vote on several nominees whom Democrats had blocked by filibuster. In return, the seven Republicans who worked out the compromise agreed not to object if Democrats filibustered two other Bush nominees. When the Senate reverted to Democratic control in 2007, Republicans again complained that confirmations were proceeding too slowly.[34] Others retorted that President Bush had been slow to nominate while trying to find nominees who could be confirmed.[35] By the time he left office, Bush had appointed 261 judges to the district courts, 59 judges to the courts of appeals, and 2 justices to the Supreme Court for a total of 322 lifetime judicial appointments.

President Obama's first judicial nominee, David Hamilton, enjoyed the support of the Republican home-state senator, Richard Lugar of Indiana, and Obama insiders said that the president chose Hamilton, whom they described as a moderate, to fill a seat on the U.S. Court of Appeals for the Seventh Circuit because he wanted to "put the history of confirmation wars behind us."[36] Some Republicans were not convinced. Most GOP senators on the Judiciary Committee boycotted the hearing on Hamilton's nomination because they said it was moving too quickly and they did not have adequate time to prepare for the hearing.[37] A group of conservative Republicans, including former attorney general Edwin Meese, came out against Hamilton, describing him as "soft on crime, radically pro-abortion, and hostile towards religion."[38]

Earlier, all forty-one Republican senators had signed a letter to President Obama urging that he consult with them about whom to nominate and that he renominate some of the individuals put forward earlier by President Bush who were not confirmed by the Senate. They also threatened to act to "preserve the rights of our colleagues" if home-state Republicans lost their power under senatorial courtesy to block nominees.[39] Some interpreted this as a threat to filibuster. Sen. Patrick Leahy, D-Vt., chairman of the Senate Judiciary Committee, subsequently announced that the practice of senatorial courtesy would not be changed, although he did stop use of the "anonymous hold"—a practice whereby a senator could anonymously block a nomination.[40] The change meant that senators who block a nomination must do so publicly. Only time will tell how the judicial confirmation process will play out under President Obama, but early signs suggest that confirmation wars are brewing.

Selection of Supreme Court Justices

The president clearly dominates the process of selecting members of the Supreme Court. Despite the constitutional admonition that the Senate offer "advice and consent" on presidents' nominees, the extent to which presidents seek advice from senators on whom to nominate is minimal. A rare exception came in 1874, when President Ulysses S. Grant formally sought the advice of Senate leaders before nominating Morrison Waite to be chief justice. Bill Clinton is said to have consulted influential Senate Republicans about Ruth Bader Ginsburg in 1993 and Stephen Breyer in 1994 before nominating them.[41] Both were easily confirmed.

Although presidents have only recently come to appreciate and take full advantage of their ability to influence judicial policymaking through *lower* federal court appointments, they have long recognized the importance of Supreme Court appointments. Through its power of judicial review, the Court has the authority—when a legitimate case or controversy is brought before it—to review actions of the other branches of government and the states and to strike down those that violate the Constitution.

First used by the Supreme Court to strike down legislation in *Marbury v. Madison* (1803), the power of judicial review is a critical part of the U.S. system of checks and balances.[42] Judicial review is a way to police the actions of other government actors and ensure that they act in accordance with the Constitution. It prevents temporary legislative majorities from invading the rights of minorities and keeps strong-willed presidents from thwarting the Constitution. It is, in other words, a protection against "tyranny of the majority" and other abuses of power by government officials.

But judicial review also entails a certain amount of risk. After all, it is up to a simple majority of the Court to determine what the Constitution means and whether a government action violates it. The task may seem easy, but it is not.

Many provisions of the Constitution are notoriously vague and ambiguous. As a result, they are susceptible to different interpretations. As we saw in chapter 1, the ambiguity of Article II has led to considerable disagreement over the scope of presidential power. Such ambiguity extends to many other provisions of the Constitution. For example, what does "equal protection" mean? "Unreasonable searches and seizures"? "Cruel and unusual punishment"? The First Amendment says that Congress shall make no law abridging freedom of speech. But what is "speech"? Does it include libel? Campaign contributions? False advertising? Obscenity? Advocacy to overthrow the government? Flag burning? Nude dancing? All of these questions have come before the Court, and reasonable and well-meaning people have disagreed about how to answer them.

The real danger of judicial review lies in the possibility that a majority of the Court might take advantage of the Constitution's ambiguities to impose its own will. Under the guise of upholding the Constitution, five unelected judges could choose to impose policies they support and nullify those they do not. Judges from both ends of the political spectrum are susceptible to that temptation. Some observers say that is what happened when a conservative majority on the Court struck down government attempts to regulate business in the early twentieth century, or when a liberal majority in the 1960s and 1970s used an unenumerated "right of privacy" to strike down state laws that banned abortion and the use of contraceptives.[43]

Even when the Court is doing its best to apply the Constitution fairly and accurately, answers to many constitutional questions remain a matter of judgment. It is precisely for that reason that Supreme Court appointments matter so much. The Court's decisions are of vital interest to the president because they affect presidential programs, the operation of the entire political system, and the functioning of U.S. society in general. Presidents seek to affect those decisions through their appointments to the Court, and they tend to approach these nominations with great care.

Nominee Qualifications. Generally speaking, presidents and their aides look at three broad categories of qualifications when screening nominees: professional, representational, and doctrinal.[44] The Constitution offers no guidance, as it contains no specific qualifications for being a Supreme Court justice. This deficiency stands in stark contrast to the very specific constitutional qualifications for the president, senators, and representatives. Because federal law has not mandated specific qualifications either, it "is legally possible, though scarcely conceivable, that a non-citizen, a minor or a non-lawyer could be appointed to the Court."[45]

Despite the lack of legally mandated qualifications, presidents recognize the importance of a nominee's professional experience. Although President Bush severed the official relationship between the White House and the American Bar Association in 2001, the ABA ratings of nominees continued to be a way for senators and the public to gauge the professional merits of a nominee. The ABA bases its ratings largely on the nominee's professional qualifications. So, too, do others who assess whether an individual is fit to serve on the Supreme Court. Every justice who has served on the Court has been a lawyer, and high professional standards have been a basic criterion when selecting and confirming nominees.[46]

Representational qualifications include the partisan affiliation of potential nominees, their geographic region, and factors such as race, gender, and ethnicity. With rare exceptions, presidents appoint justices from their own political party. Early in the nation's history, geographic balance was also a major consideration for presidents when deciding upon a nominee because Supreme Court justices had the onerous responsibility of "riding circuit"—traveling around the country to preside over appeals in lower federal courts of the particular circuit to which they were assigned. Prior to the Civil War, presidents tried to have at least one justice from each of the circuits. When Congress abolished the requirement of circuit riding in 1891, the main reason for geographic balance disappeared. Still, presidents make some effort to represent different parts of the country on the Court. Occasionally, a president tries to use a Court appointment to curry favor with a particular region of the country. Herbert Hoover and Richard Nixon tried to appoint southerners to the Court as a way to build electoral support in the South.[47]

Religion, race, gender, and ethnicity have joined geography as representational concerns. Although the Court has historically had a distinctly white, male, and, until recently, Protestant bias, a "Catholic seat" has existed by tradition since 1836, as has a "Jewish seat" since 1916 (except for 1969 to 1993). When Obama took office in 2009, five Catholics, two Jews, and two Protestants were sitting on the Court. The appointments of John G. Roberts Jr. and Samuel A. Alito Jr. secured a Catholic majority for the first time in the Court's history. Since 1967 an African American has been a member, and since 1981 at least one woman. Both Bush I and Bush II as well as Clinton gave serious consideration to appointing the first Hispanic to the Court. Such an appointment would help to build support for the president's party among the growing Hispanic population in pivotal electoral states such as California, Florida, and Texas.

Doctrinal qualifications refer to the perception that a nominee shares the president's political philosophy and approach to public policy issues, a critical issue given the Court's power to interpret the Constitution and exercise judicial review. Some presidents, such as Ronald Reagan and George W. Bush, made doctrinal considerations a central part of their screening process. Although Reagan's appointment of Sandra Day O'Connor was driven largely by representational concerns, he was careful to select a woman who fit his doctrinal qualifications. His elevation of Rehnquist to chief justice, his appointments of Antonin Scalia and Anthony Kennedy, and his unsuccessful nominations of Robert Bork and Douglas Ginsburg were motivated largely by doctrinal considerations. Bush's appointments of Roberts and Alito were also motivated by doctrinal considerations and resulted in a new 5-4 majority that shifted the balance on the Court.

In contrast, Clinton was somewhat less concerned with doctrinal representation. Although applauded for their representational impact, Ruth Bader Ginsburg and Stephen Breyer actually drew some criticism from liberal Democrats who were distressed that the first Democratic president since Lyndon Johnson with the opportunity to fill vacancies on the Court (Carter made no appointments) picked candidates with moderate, mainstream—rather than activist, liberal—constitutional views. Both justices were Democrats who were more liberal than Reagan's nominees, but in the interest of avoiding a confirmation battle in the Senate, Clinton selected experienced, moderate federal appeals court judges rather than ideologues to fill the Court vacancies. Ginsburg and Breyer had strong support from both liberals and conservatives on the Senate Judiciary Committee, and the two won easy confirmation.

Initial Screening and Selection. As David Yalof points out, different presidents go about screening and selecting potential Supreme Court nominees in different ways. Even within a single administration, Yalof identifies a number of factors that influence the president's selection process. These include (1) the timing of the vacancy, (2) the composition of the Senate, (3) the public approval of the president, (4) attributes of the outgoing justice, and (5) the realistic pool of candidates available to the president.[48] If the vacancy occurs early in their terms, presidents are usually in a stronger position politically than if the vacancy occurs closer to the end of their terms. If the vacancy occurs shortly before their reelection campaigns or toward the end of their second terms, presidents may be more limited in the type of nominee they can send to the Senate and may feel compelled to nominate a more moderate, consensus candidate. The same is true if the opposition party controls the Senate or if a president's approval ratings are low. Choice of a successor may also be more limited if the outgoing justice represents a particular religious or demographic group or if the president feels that a particular region of the country needs representation on the Court. And, obviously, presidents are limited by the available pool of candidates and may find it difficult to find a nominee who fits the precise mix of professional, doctrinal, and representational concerns they would like.

Since 1853 the Justice Department has had formal responsibility for identifying and recommending potential nominees. Historically, the attorney general, the head of the Justice Department, played the primary role in this process. As Yalof notes, however, the growth and bureaucratization of both the White House and the Justice Department have led to the emergence of specialized staff units assigned to vet potential nominees.[49] The Office of White House Counsel, created as part of the president's personal staff during the Truman administration, now participates in vetting nominees, as do the chief of staff and other White House officials. The FBI is responsible for conducting background checks.

In some administrations, overlapping responsibilities between the White House and the Justice Department have led to internal power struggles over what type of judges to nominate. When Justice Lewis Powell resigned from the Court in 1987, Attorney General Meese and other Justice Department officials pushed for a staunchly conservative nominee: Robert Bork. White House counsel Arthur B. Culvahouse and chief of staff Howard Baker wanted a moderate consensus nominee. The Justice Department won, but the Senate went on to defeat the Bork nomination in a highly contentious confirmation battle.[50]

Many people have a desire to influence the nomination decision, including other lawyers. The legal community includes professional organizations such as the ABA, whose ratings can affect how the public and the Senate perceive the nominees. Other legal groups, as well as individual lawyers, also participate in the selection process. They may suggest nominees to the president or announce their evaluations of the person the president nominated. Coalitions of lawyers sometimes sign letters of support for, or of opposition to, specific nominees. Even Supreme Court justices themselves occasionally participate in the process by recommending a potential nominee to the president or even lobbying publicly for a candidate. Chief Justice William Howard Taft (1921–1930) was particularly active in that regard, and Chief Justice Warren Burger suggested the nomination of Harry Blackmun in 1970 and O'Connor in 1981.[51] Interest groups also lobby for and against the initial selection of nominees, although these groups are usually more active during the confirmation process. As early as the 1880s, interest groups recognized how directly the Supreme Court could affect them, and they began to take an active interest in the Senate confirmation of nominees.[52] They also began to lobby presidents before nominations were announced.[53] Today, they sometimes announce their views on nominations even before vacancies on the Supreme Court occur.

Senate Confirmation. Once nominated by the president, a candidate to the Supreme Court must be confirmed by the Senate. Confirmation needs only a simple majority vote. If one excludes consecutive nominations of the same individual by the same president for the same seat on the Court and President Reagan's 1987 nomination of Douglas Ginsburg, which was announced but never formally submitted to the Senate, 150 nominations were submitted to the Senate prior to David Souter's May 1, 2009, announcement that he planned to retire. Of these 150 nominations, 7 of the nominees declined, 1 died before taking office, and 1 expected vacancy failed to materialize. In addition, Bush's nomination of Roberts to fill O'Connor's seat was withdrawn before Senate action and submitted to fill the chief justice's seat. Of the 140 remaining nominations, 114 were confirmed by the Senate. The other 26 may be classified as "failed" nominations because Senate opposition blocked them: the Senate rejected 12 by roll-call vote, voted to postpone or table another 5, and passively rejected 5 others by taking no action. Presidents withdrew the remaining 4 in the face of certain Senate defeat. The number of "failed" nominations rises to 27 if Douglas Ginsburg is included.

The most recent of these failed nominations was Harriet Miers, nominated to replace O'Connor in 2005. Miers quickly came under fire: some critics said she was not sufficiently qualified, and prominent representatives of Bush's constituency complained that she was not conservative enough.[54] She withdrew before any Senate hearings took place. All told, the failure rate of Supreme Court nominees is higher than any other appointive post requiring Senate confirmation.[55] Six nominations (including Douglas Ginsburg) have failed just since 1968, a clear reflection of the concern for the profound effect Supreme Court appointments can have on public policy.

Confirmation is also a test of presidential strength. "Weak" presidents—those who are unelected, those who face a Senate controlled by the opposition, and those in their final year in office—are statistically less likely to secure confirmation of their Supreme Court nominees. An unusually long period of divided government (with the White House controlled by one party and the Senate by another) has added to the contentiousness of confirmation battles. From 1969 through 2009, different parties controlled the Senate and the White House for twenty-five out of forty years. Also contributing to intense confirmation battles are the ongoing public policy debates over controversial issues such as race, abortion, and same-sex marriage—something that journalist E. J. Dionne has called a "cultural civil war."[56]

TABLE 7-2   Failed Supreme Court Nominees

Nominee and year of nomination	President and party	Composition of Senate	Action
John Rutledge, 1795[a]	Washington (F)	19 F, 13 DR	Rejected 14-10
Alexander Wolcott, 1811	Madison (DR)	28 DR, 6 F	Rejected 24-9
John J. Crittenden, 1828	J. Q. Adams (NR)	28 J, 20 NR	Postponed 23-17
Roger B. Taney, 1835	Jackson (D)	20 D, 20 W	Postponed 24-21
John C. Spencer, 1844	Tyler (W)	28 W, 25 D	Rejected 26-21
Reuben H. Walworth, 1844[b]	Tyler (W)	28 W, 25 D	Postponed 27-20
Edward King, 1844[c]	Tyler (W)	28 W, 25 D	Postponed 29-18
John M. Read, 1845	Tyler (W)	28 W, 25 D	No action
George W. Woodward, 1845	Polk (D)	31 D, 25 W	Rejected 20-19
Edward A. Bradford, 1852	Fillmore (W)	35 D, 24 W	No action
George E. Badger, 1853	Fillmore (W)	35 D, 24 W	Postponed 26-25
William C. Micou, 1853	Fillmore (W)	35 D, 24 W	No action
Jeremiah S. Black, 1861	Buchanan (D)	36 D, 26 R	Rejected 26-25
Henry Stanbery, 1866	A. Johnson (R)	42 U, 10 D	No action
Ebenezer R. Hoar, 1869	Grant (R)	56 R, 11 D	Rejected 33-24
George H. Williams, 1873	Grant (R)	49 R, 19 D	Withdrawn
Caleb Cushing, 1874	Grant (R)	49 R, 19 D	Withdrawn
Stanley Matthews, 1881	Hayes (R)	42 D, 33 R	No action
William Hornblower, 1893	Cleveland (D)	44 D, 38 R	Rejected 30-24
Wheeler H. Peckham, 1894	Cleveland (D)	44 D, 38 R	Rejected 41-32
John J. Parker, 1930	Hoover (R)	56 R, 39 D	Rejected 41-39
Abe Fortas, 1968[d]	Johnson (D)	64 D, 36 R	Withdrawn
Clement Haynsworth, 1969	Nixon (R)	58 D, 42 R	Rejected 55-45
G. Harrold Carswell, 1970	Nixon (R)	58 D, 42 R	Rejected 51-45
Robert H. Bork, 1987	Reagan (R)	55 D, 45 R	Rejected 58-42
Douglas Ginsburg, 1987[e]	Reagan (R)	55 D, 45 R	Withdrawn
Harriet Miers, 2005	G. W. Bush (R)	55 R, 44 D, 1 I	Withdrawn

SOURCE: John Anthony Maltese, *The Selling of Supreme Court Nominees* (Baltimore: Johns Hopkins University Press, 1995), 3. Updated by author.

NOTES: F = Federalist, DR = Democratic-Republican, NR = National-Republican, D = Democrat, W = Whig, R = Republican, J = Jacksonian, U = Unionist, and I = independent. Tyler, Fillmore, and Andrew Johnson were not elected.

a. Rutledge was an associate justice. The Senate rejected his nomination to be chief justice.

b. Reuben Walworth's nomination was later withdrawn.

c. Tyler renominated Edward King, who then withdrew. Some list him as having failed twice.

d. Fortas was an associate justice.

e. Ginsburg withdrew before his nomination was officially submitted to the Senate.

Interest groups fan the flames through their efforts for and against nominees. In the twentieth century interest groups led the opposition to almost all the nominees rejected by the Senate or forced to withdraw. John J. Parker, a southern court of appeals judge nominated by Herbert Hoover in 1930, fell victim to the combined opposition of the American Federation of Labor and the National Association for the Advancement of Colored People (NAACP), who viewed him as antilabor and racist. Labor and the NAACP again joined forces to defeat two Nixon nominees: Clement Haynsworth, a federal court of appeals judge from South Carolina, in 1969 and G. Harrold Carswell, a federal court of appeals judge from Florida, in 1970.[57] Johnson's nomination of Abe Fortas to be chief justice in 1968 was bitterly attacked by conservative groups because of his liberal decisions in obscenity cases and suits concerning the rights of the accused in criminal proceedings.[58] A major effort by civil rights, women's, and other liberal groups contributed to Judge Bork's defeat in 1987.[59] In contrast, Miers withdrew her name before many interest groups had taken a stand. Much of the opposition to her came from the conservative base of the Republican Party.

Other problems may arise. Some people considered Fortas's acceptance of a legal fee from a family foundation and his advising President Johnson on political matters to be unethical activities for a justice of the Supreme Court.[60] Haynsworth was criticized for ruling on cases in which he had a personal financial interest. Much of the opposition to Carswell from members of the bar, particularly law professors, stemmed from his perceived lack of professional qualifications. Sen. Roman Hruska, R-Neb., Carswell's leading supporter in the Senate, made the situation worse when he tried to make the nominee's mediocrity a virtue by saying on national television that mediocre people needed representation on the Supreme Court. Suddenly, Carswell was a national joke. This, coupled with some shockingly racist statements Carswell had made when running for public office ("I believe the segregation of the races is proper and the only practical and correct way of life in our states," and "I yield to no man . . . in the firm, vigorous belief in the principles of white supremacy, and I shall always be so governed") doomed Carswell's nomination.[61]

Active involvement by interest groups in every Supreme Court confirmation process dates back only to the 1960s or so. Although organized interests attempted to block Senate confirmation of a nominee as early as 1881, their success in blocking three confirmations in three years marked a turning point. Since then, interest groups have taken an active stand on virtually every Supreme Court nominee, although their involvement accelerated dramatically with Bork in 1987. Starting with that nomination, interest groups moved beyond testifying at confirmation hearings and mobilizing their members to lobby their senators to launching a full-fledged public relations offensive, including television, radio, and print ads; mass mailings; and phone banks to sway public opinion. They also attempted to influence reporters and editorial writers through the use of press briefings and fact sheets they aggressively distributed.

Interest group action corresponded with the increased visibility of Senate Judiciary Committee hearings and floor votes on nominees. Prior to the twentieth century, the confirmation process was shrouded in secrecy. The committee held hearings behind closed doors and rarely even kept records of its proceedings. As the *New York Times* wrote in 1881, the "Judiciary Committee of the Senate is the most mysterious committee in that body, and succeeds better than any other in maintaining secrecy as to its proceedings."[62]

At that time, the committee usually deliberated without hearing from any witnesses. Interest groups seldom participated in this phase of the process (none testified until 1930), and no nominee appeared before the committee until Harlan Fiske Stone in 1925. Nominees actually thought it improper to answer any questions and maintained almost complete public silence. When a reporter from the New York *Sun* asked Louis Brandeis about his nomination in 1916, Brandeis quickly replied: "I have nothing to say about anything, and that goes for all time and to all newspapers, including both the *Sun* and the moon."[63] Presidents, too, maintained almost complete public silence about their nominees. When the full Senate finally voted on a nominee, it almost always did so in closed session and often with no roll call vote. The secrecy effectively minimized the influence of interest groups and any others concerned about the outcome of a nomination. So, too, did the fact that senators then were not popularly elected but chosen by state legislators. The lack of public participation removed the potential threat of retaliation against senators that the electorate now enjoys and on which interest groups can capitalize.

The situation changed in the twentieth century. Ratification of the Seventeenth Amendment to the Constitution in 1913 provided for the direct election of senators, and Senate rules changes in 1929 opened floor debate on nominations. Public opinion now mattered in a very direct way to senators—they were dependent upon it for reelection. The Senate began to use public Judiciary Committee hearings as a way of both testing and influencing public opinion. Since 1981 Judiciary Committee hearings have been broadcast live on television for the entire world to see. The emergence of the modern "public presidency" (see chapter 3) also led to greater involvement by presidents in promoting their nominees. As specialized staff units developed in the White House, they, too, came to be used as a way to secure support for nominees and thereby increase the likelihood of Senate confirmation. Today, the Office of Communications, the Office of Public Liaison, the Office of Political Affairs, and other staff units are all used in this manner.[64]

At the end of the day, after opponents find fault with a nominee's qualifications or record and supporters claim the opposite, it all comes down to ideology. How will the nominee vote if confirmed? The president tries to predict how the nominee will perform, but judicial appointees may fail to vote the way the president had hoped. Reagan and George H. W. Bush appointed six justices to the Supreme Court with the avowed hope of overturning *Roe v. Wade* (1973), the controversial abortion rights decision.[65] Three of those appointees went on to uphold *Roe.*[66] Dwight D. Eisenhower lamented his appointment of Earl Warren as chief justice because of Warren's liberal voting record on the bench, and Harry Truman—never one to mince words—was furious when Tom Clark, who had been Truman's attorney general, did not vote on the Court as the president had hoped. "I don't know what got into me," Truman later fumed. "He was no damn good as Attorney General, and on the Supreme Court . . . it doesn't seem possible, but he's been even worse. He hasn't made one right decision that I can think of. . . . It's just that he's such a dumb son of a bitch."[67] Despite White House chief of staff John Sununu's prediction to G. H. W. Bush that David Souter would be a "home run" for conservatives, Souter turned out to be one of the most liberal members of the Court. The in-depth screening of judicial nominees tends to minimize such "mistakes"—so far, both Roberts and Alito are voting in line with what one would expect from George W. Bush appointees—but no one can completely predict the behavior of individuals once they sit on the Court.

Other Presidential Influences on the Federal Courts

The appointment of federal judges is the primary method by which presidents affect the courts, but presidents have other ways to influence judicial activities. The first is through the solicitor general, whom Robert Scigliano calls "the lawyer for the executive branch."[68] The second is through legislation that affects the operation of the Supreme Court—a means Congress, too, has tried to use to its advantage and the president's disadvantage. The third is through the enforcement—or nonenforcement—of court decisions.

Role of the Solicitor General in the Appellate Courts

The **solicitor general,** appointed by the president with the advice and consent of the Senate, is a major player in setting the agenda of the federal appellate courts. First, the solicitor general determines which of the cases the government loses in the federal district courts will be taken to the courts of appeals. Second, of the cases the government loses in the lower courts, the solicitor general decides which to

President Obama introduces Sonia Sotomayor on May 26, 2009, as his nominee to replace David Souter on the U.S. Supreme Court.

recommend that the Supreme Court hear. Unlike the courts of appeals, which must take cases properly appealed to them, the Supreme Court chooses the cases it hears.[69] The Court is more likely to take cases proposed by the solicitor general than by other parties.

Once the Court accepts a case involving the federal government, the solicitor general decides the position the government should take and argues the case before the Court. Thus "the Solicitor General not only determines whether the executive branch goes to the Supreme Court but what it will say there."[70] And what it says there usually advances the policy goals of the incumbent president.[71] Moreover, the solicitor general's influence is not restricted to cases in which the federal government itself is a party. He or she also decides whether the government will file an amicus curiae (friend of the court) brief supporting or opposing positions by other parties who have cases pending before the Court.

Amicus filings by the solicitor general increased dramatically in the twentieth century. Steven Puro, who analyzed the briefs filed from 1920 through 1973, found that 71 percent occurred in the last twenty years of that period.[72] He concluded that whether by its own initiative or as a result of an invitation from the Court, the federal government participated as amicus in almost every major domestic question before the Court since World War II. Particularly prominent is the government entrance into the controversial issues of civil liberties, civil rights, and the jurisdiction and procedures of the courts.

When the federal government becomes involved in a case before the Supreme Court, it is usually successful. Scigliano's analysis of Court opinions chosen at ten-year intervals beginning in 1800 shows that the United States has consistently won 62 percent or more of its litigation there. Its record as amicus is even more impressive. Puro found that in the political cases he examined, when the federal government participated, it supported the winning side almost 74 percent of the time. An analysis of race discrimination employment cases from 1970 to 1981 showed that the government won 70 percent of the cases in which it was a direct party and 81.6 percent of those in which it filed amicus briefs.[73]

Much has been written about why solicitors general are so successful in their appearances before the Supreme Court. Kevin T. McGuire argues that it really boils down to one thing: litigation experience.[74] They are the prototypical "repeat player." Solicitors general or members of their staff argue far more cases than any other party, including any law firm in the country. They therefore develop a great deal of expertise in dealing with the Court. This expertise translates into high quality briefs and an intimate understanding of the workings of the Court. Solicitors general may also build up credit with the Court because they help the justices manage their caseload by holding down the number of government appeals. Christopher Zorn also notes that amicus filings by the solicitor general "are highest when both the administration and the Court share similar policy preferences, and drop off substantially when those preferences diverge." Zorn concludes that, like other litigants, "The solicitor general appears to explicitly take into account the probability that his position will be received favorably by the Court when formulating his litigation strategies."[75]

The Reagan administration used the solicitor general's office particularly aggressively to promote its conservative policy agenda.[76] In tandem with Reagan's appointments to the Supreme Court and lower federal courts, Solicitor General Rex Lee led this "other campaign" to persuade the Supreme Court to change previous rulings on matters such as abortion, prayer in the public schools, busing, affirmative action, the rights of the accused in criminal cases, and federal-state relations.[77] Lincoln Caplan argued that this activity marked a shift away from the solicitor general's traditional posture of restraint to a posture of aggressively pushing the Court to take cases that advanced the administration's social policy agenda. The result, according to Caplan, was a temporary loss of the justices' trust in the solicitor general's presentation of facts and interpretation of the law.[78] Succeeding presidents did not use the solicitor general's office this way. Richard L. Pacelle Jr. has noted the many constraints solicitors general now face:

In trying to assist the Court as tenth justice or fifth Clerk, while fulfilling the president's agenda as "attorney general as policy maker" or pursuing the Justice Department's more neutral obligations as the "attorney general as law enforcement officer," the solicitor general has to balance a number of roles. In attempting to fulfill these roles, the solicitor general has several potentially competing constituencies to satisfy. When these factors move in the same direction, there are opportunities for the solicitor general, but that was rare in the last half-century, as divided government has been the rule.[79]

Legislation Affecting the Supreme Court

The president also can affect the actions of the Supreme Court through legislation. Presidential authority to propose bills to Congress and to work for their adoption, as well as the power to oppose measures favored by members of Congress and, if necessary, to veto them, means the president can influence legislation affecting the Court. At the same time, Congress can pass legislation concerning the Court that threatens the president's power.

In 1937 Franklin Roosevelt became actively involved in trying to get Congress to exercise its power to expand the size of the Supreme Court. The Constitution grants Congress the power to establish the number of justices, and Congress has changed it several times. Historically, however, Congress has done so without prompting from the president. Sometimes it has altered the size of the Court in an effort to thwart a particular president. In the latter days of the John Adams administration, the lame-duck Congress—still controlled by the Federalists—passed the Judiciary Act of 1801. That act reduced the number of justices from six to five in an attempt to prevent the incoming president, Democratic-Republican Thomas Jefferson, from appointing a replacement for ailing justice William Cushing. (Because justices have life tenure, the size of the Court would not actually decrease until a justice left the bench.) The Democratic-Republicans quickly repealed the 1801 law and restored the number of justices to six when they took control of Congress later that year. In 1807 the Democratic-Republican Congress increased the number of justices to seven to accommodate population growth in Kentucky, Tennessee, and Ohio. The Federalists' attempt to thwart President Jefferson failed, and he went on to name three justices. Ironically, Justice Cushing recovered and lived until 1810; his successor was named by James Madison, not Jefferson.

Congressional manipulation of the size of the Court so as to affect presidential appointments also occurred in the 1860s. The 1863 Judiciary Act expanding the Court from nine to ten members enabled Abraham Lincoln to appoint Stephen J. Field, who subsequently supported the president on war issues. Shortly thereafter, the Radical Republicans, who controlled Congress, passed legislation reducing the number of justices to prevent Lincoln's successor, Andrew Johnson, from naming justices they feared would rule against the Reconstruction program. Soon after Ulysses S. Grant was inaugurated in March 1869, the size of the Court was again expanded; this expansion, plus a retirement, enabled Grant to appoint Justices William Strong and Joseph P. Bradley. Both voted to reconsider a previous Supreme Court decision, *Hepburn v. Griswold*, that had declared unconstitutional the substitution of paper money for gold as legal tender for the payment of contracts. The new decision validated the use of "greenbacks" as legal tender.[80] The three successive changes in the size of the Court within a six-year period brought the results Congress desired.

Roosevelt's "Court packing" proposal was different from these earlier examples because of his aggressive efforts to promote congressional action. Frustrated by the invalidation of much of the early New Deal legislation—between January 1935 and June 1936 the Court had struck down eight separate statutes—Roosevelt proposed legislation in early 1937 that would permit him to appoint one justice, up to six in number, for each sitting member of the Court who failed to retire voluntarily at age seventy. Buoyed by his landslide electoral victory in 1936, and confident that the Democrat-controlled Congress would follow his lead, Roosevelt announced the proposal at a press conference without consulting with members of Congress. Samuel Kernell points to it as an early, failed attempt at "going public."[81] Although FDR contended that the additions were necessary to handle the Court's caseload, it was patently clear that his real purpose was to liberalize the Court. The proposal stimulated outrage from members of the bar, the press, and many of Roosevelt's political supporters in Congress who were angered that they had not been consulted about it. At this point, Justice Owen J. Roberts, a centrist who had been aligned with four conservative colleagues in striking down New Deal legislation, began to vote with the other four justices to uphold the legislation and give FDR the new majority he had been seeking. The unpopularity of Roosevelt's proposal, Justice Roberts's mitigating action (which observers dubbed "the switch in time that saved nine"), and the sudden death of Majority Leader Joseph Robinson of Arkansas, who was leading the president's effort in the Senate, resulted in Congress's failure to adopt the Court-packing plan. Kernell calls it "FDR's most stunning legislative failure in his twelve years in office."[82] Yet Roosevelt won the legal battle anyway. Once Roberts switched his vote, conservative members—now in the minority—began to leave the Court. By the time he died, Roosevelt had managed to appoint all but one of the nine justices and secure a majority willing to uphold his policies.

In addition to its power to change the size of the Court, Congress can also pass legislation altering its appellate jurisdiction.[83] President Bush proposed and the Republican-controlled Congress passed the Military Commissions Act of 2006, which stripped federal courts of jurisdiction to hear habeas corpus petitions from detainees at Guantánamo Bay. When he signed the act into law on October 17, 2006, Bush called it "one of the most important pieces of legislation in the war on terror."[84] A three-judge panel for a U.S. court of appeals voted 2-1 to uphold the law, but in 2008 the U.S. Supreme Court reversed by a 5-4 vote in *Boumediene v. Bush.*[85] The 2008 Republican Party platform endorsed jurisdiction-stripping in other areas. Noting that "a Republican Congress enacted the Defense of Marriage Act, affirming the right of states not to recognize same-sex 'marriages' licensed in other states," the platform urged Congress to "use its Article III, section 2 power [to withdraw appellate jurisdiction] to prevent activist federal judges from imposing upon the rest of the nation the judicial activism in Massachusetts and California."[86] Courts in both states had ruled that laws banning same-sex marriage violated each state's constitution. Iowa followed suit in April 2009, and four days later the Vermont legislature overrode the governor's veto of a law allowing same-sex marriage.[87] In 2004 the Republican-controlled House of Representatives had passed H.R. 3313, a bill to withdraw jurisdiction from the federal courts over the Defense of Marriage Act, but the bill then stalled in the Senate. This was not the only time that members of Congress have attempted to strip the Supreme Court of its power to hear certain types of hot-button cases. In the 1980s Sen. Jesse Helms, R-N.C., proposed legislation to remove the Court's appellate jurisdiction to hear cases involving school prayer. (Helms was angered that the Court had declared state-sponsored prayer in public schools a violation of the establishment clause requirement of a separation between church and state.) Helms's effort failed, as have the vast majority of jurisdiction-stripping proposals.

Presidents occasionally urge Congress to propose constitutional amendments to overturn Court rulings or lobby for the passage of legislation that might undermine existing rulings. Republican presidents Reagan and G. H. W. Bush sought to overturn *Roe v. Wade* by pressuring Congress to propose a constitutional amendment outlawing abortion. Although unsuccessful in this effort, both presidents signed legislation that limited use of federal funds for abortions and made access to abortions more difficult. Bush also supported a constitutional amendment to overrule a controversial Supreme Court decision, *Texas v. Johnson* (1989), that permitted flag burning as a form of protected symbolic speech.[88] George W. Bush called for a constitutional amendment to define marriage as the legal union of one man and one woman.

Enforcement of Court Decisions

The federal courts have the authority to hand down decisions on cases within their jurisdiction, but they have no independent power to enforce their decisions. Lacking both the power of the purse and of the sword, the Supreme Court depends upon the executive branch to enforce its rulings. President Eisenhower called out federal troops in 1957 to enforce court-ordered school desegregation in Little Rock, Arkansas. The order was an outgrowth of the Court's landmark *Brown v. Board of Education* (1954) ruling that overturned the "separate but equal" doctrine of *Plessy v. Ferguson* (1896).[89]

Sometimes less forceful action by the president helps to bring about compliance with Supreme Court rulings. President Kennedy, in a June 1962 press conference, publicly supported the Court's controversial ruling in *Engel v. Vitale*, which banned state-sponsored prayer in public schools, and set an example for others to follow.[90] Presidents also set an example by complying with court orders aimed at them. Immediately after the Court held in 1952 that President Truman's seizure of the steel mills was unconstitutional, the president ordered the mills restored to private operation.[91] Likewise, President Nixon complied with the Court's 1974 ruling in *United States v. Nixon* that he turn over to a federal district court tapes of his conversations with executive aides.[92] That action produced evidence of the president's involvement in the Watergate affair, which led to the House Judiciary Committee's approving three articles of impeachment against him and ultimately to Nixon's resignation.

Some presidents have defied—or threatened to defy—the Court. The fear that President Jefferson's secretary of state, James Madison, would (with the president's blessing) defy a court order to deliver commissions that would seat some Federalist judges (but weaken the Court) probably influenced John Marshall's opinion in *Marbury v. Madison*. Marshall gave the Jefferson administration what it wanted—it did not force delivery of the commissions—but did so by creating the power of judicial review. More blatantly, President Lincoln once ignored a federal court ruling that declared his suspension of habeas corpus unconstitutional.[93] But Lincoln's response was an exception to the rule, for chief executives typically have enforced judicial decisions, even when they would have preferred not to do so. When the justices struck down the Gun Free School Zones Act in *United States v. Lopez* (1995), President Clinton strongly criticized the decision and ordered Attorney General Janet Reno to come up with other ways to keep guns out of schools, but he did not defy the ruling.[94]

That approach changed under George W. Bush. As discussed in chapter 1, Bush embraced a theory of presidential power known as the unitary executive. A core element of that approach is the idea of "coordinate construction"—that presidents have the power to interpret the Constitution just as courts do. Rather than veto the legislation or wait for courts to rule on their constitutionality, Bush quietly used "signing statements" to indicate that he would not enforce those provisions of laws he found problematic. By the time he left office, Bush had challenged more than 1,100 specific provisions of bills he signed.[95] For example, he used signing statements to signal that he would not enforce the provision of the Patriot Act that required the president to report to Congress when the executive branch secretly searches homes or seizes private papers. Another signing statement said that he reserved the right to ignore the McCain amendment forbidding U.S. officials to use torture.[96] Sometimes the signing statements were so general that it was not clear what provisions the president might choose not to enforce. But when Congress passed a law requiring the attorney general to submit to Congress a detailed list of provisions of bills that were not being enforced by the administration, Bush used a signing statement to reiterate presidential authority to withhold information from Congress—including such a list—whenever he deemed it necessary.[97] The use of signing statements, the embrace of coordinate construction, and his strong criticism of "activist" judges, suggested Bush's willingness to substitute his judgment of how the Constitution should be interpreted for that of the federal courts.

Moreover, Bush's expansive view of presidential war power held that presidents have broad authority to act unilaterally to promote the nation's interests. Taken to its extreme, this meant that presidents, in some instances, could take actions contrary to the Constitution. If that were the case, it followed that presidents could claim the authority to disobey the courts in such instances (as Lincoln did with regard to habeas corpus). Bush strongly asserted the view that his subordinates in the executive branch should not report directly to Congress. As noted by the ABA's Task Force on Presidential Signing Statements, he did so repeatedly "even though there is Supreme Court precedent to the effect that Congress may authorize a subordinate official to act directly or to report directly to Congress."[98] When Congress passed a law requiring that government scientists report their findings directly to

Congress so that they could not be censored by the administration, Bush used a signing statement to prevent enforcement of the law.

Judicial Oversight of Presidential Action

Through its power of judicial review, the Supreme Court has the ability to invalidate presidential actions and those of other parts of the executive branch. This is a significant check on presidential power, but has been infrequently used. The founders originally left open the question of who had the final power to interpret the Constitution. If, as Jefferson contended, each branch has the authority to interpret the Constitution as far as its own duties are concerned, then the president would be the judge of the constitutionality of executive actions. As a result of *Marbury v. Madison,* however, the Supreme Court has the power to make the final judgment on such matters. Although *Marbury* was decided in 1803, the Court did not declare a presidential action unconstitutional until after the Civil War.

Only a handful of presidents have been the objects of major Court decisions invalidating their actions. Even when invalidating a specific presidential action, the Court has often endorsed a broad reading of presidential power. For example, the Court, as previously noted, invalidated President Truman's seizure of steel mills during the Korean War.[99] Truman argued that government seizure to keep open the steel mills, which were involved in a labor dispute that threatened to shut them down, was essential to the war effort. But in seizing the mills, Truman ignored the provisions of the Taft-Hartley Act, which had passed over his veto. The law permitted the president to obtain an injunction postponing for eighty days a strike that threatened the national safety and welfare. Instead, he issued an executive order seizing the mills, based on his authority under the Constitution and U.S. law and as commander in chief. The steel companies protested the seizure as unconstitutional, and the case went to the Supreme Court.

By a 6-3 vote, the Court invalidated the president's move. Although six justices voted against the specific action in question, six justices (three in the majority plus the three dissenters) explicitly recognized that presidents have a range of "inherent" power to take actions not explicitly authorized by the Constitution. The dissenters said that power was broad enough to cover Truman's seizure of the mills. The other three who recognized some degree of inherent power stressed that such power is not absolute and that it was not broad enough to cover a situation such as this in which the president went against the will of Congress. Even though the case invalidated an action taken by a specific president, it set a precedent that actually *expanded* presidential power through the Court's recognition of inherent power.

Similarly, a unanimous Court in *United States v. Nixon* ruled against President Nixon's refusal to surrender subpoenaed White House tapes to Watergate special prosecutor Leon Jaworski.[100] In refusing to surrender the tapes, Nixon claimed the existence of an "executive privilege" relating to private conversations between chief executives and their advisers. Although the Court rejected Nixon's specific claim of privilege, it recognized for the first time that the principle of executive privilege did have constitutional underpinnings. As with *Youngstown*, the Court ruled against a specific exercise of presidential power while at the same time expanding the general scope of presidential power.[101]

The Court has been especially deferential to presidential power in the realm of foreign affairs. In *United States v. Curtiss-Wright Export Corp.* (1936), the Court suggested that presidents might have a wider degree of discretion in foreign affairs than they do in domestic affairs.[102] Justice George Sutherland went so far as to call the president "the sole organ of the federal government in the field of international relations."[103] Similarly, the Court has recognized that presidents have broad power to respond to military emergencies and wage war even without a congressional declaration of war. In *The Prize Cases* (1863) the Court recognized President Lincoln's power to impose a military blockade on Southern ports—an act of war—even though Congress had not yet spoken.[104] During World War II, the Court upheld broad executive power to impose the forced relocation of Japanese Americans and others of Japanese ancestry to federal detention centers.[105] In 1981 the Court upheld the power of the president to seize Iranian assets and use them as a bargaining chip to help free American hostages held in the 1970s.[106] But the Court limited efforts by the Bush administration to curtail the civil liberties of detainees at Guantánamo Bay. In *Hamdan v. Rumsfeld* (2006) the Court ruled 5-3 (Chief Justice Roberts did not participate) that the president did not have inherent power to require that the detainees be tried by military commission rather than in federal court.[107] Although the decision was a setback for his administration, President Bush introduced and the Republican-controlled Congress promptly passed legislation that authorized the use of such tribunals and curtailed the habeas corpus rights of detainees—an action that the Supreme Court then struck down in *Boumediene v. Bush*.[108]

In addition to establishing general parameters of presidential power, Supreme Court decisions can have significant repercussions on the fate of particular presidents. Two such decisions had a particular bearing on Bill Clinton. Had it not been for a 1988 ruling upholding (over the lone dissent of Antonin Scalia) the constitutionality of the independent counsel law, and a unanimous 1997 ruling that

allowed a sexual harassment lawsuit against the president by Paula Jones to proceed while he was still in office, Clinton might have been spared the independent
counsel investigation by Kenneth Starr and the impeachment trial brought about
as a result of the Monica Lewinsky scandal.[109]

Conclusion

The relationship between the presidency and the judiciary can be described as a
balancing act. The judiciary has the power to hand down rulings that have a direct
effect on presidents and their policies, but presidents can influence the federal
courts through the power to nominate judges to serve on them. Both have long-
term consequences. Supreme Court rulings are not easy to overturn. Those based
on the Constitution can be overruled only by the Court itself or through the passage
of a constitutional amendment. The president's power to appoint can also be far-
reaching. Federal judges, unlike members of Congress and the political appointees
of the executive branch, serve for life. That fact all but guarantees that judicial nominees will continue to be closely scrutinized and, in all likelihood, hotly contested.

Suggested Readings

Abraham, Henry. *Justices, Presidents, and Senators: A History of U.S. Supreme Court
Appointments from Washington to Clinton.* 4th ed. Lanham, Md.: Rowman and Little-
field, 1999.
Baum, Lawrence. *The Supreme Court.* 9th ed. Washington, D.C.: CQ Press, 2006.
Caldeira, Gregory, and John Wright. "Lobbying for Justice." *American Journal of Political Sci-
ence* 42 (April 1998).
Caplan, Lincoln. *The Tenth Justice: The Solicitor General and the Rule of Law.* New York: Random
House, 1987.
Comiskey, Michael. *Seeking Justices: The Judging of Supreme Court Nominees.* Lawrence: Univer-
sity Press of Kansas, 2004.
Epstein, Lee, and Thomas G. Walker. *Constitutional Law for a Changing America: Institutional
Powers and Constraints.* 6th ed. Washington, D.C.: CQ Press, 2007.
Gerhardt, Michael J. *The Federal Appointments Process: A Constitutional and Historical Analysis.*
Durham: Duke University Press, 2000.
Goldman, Sheldon. *Picking Federal Judges: Lower Court Selection from Roosevelt through Reagan.*
New Haven: Yale University Press, 1997.
Goldman, Sheldon, Elliot Slotnick, Gerard Gryski, and Gary Zuk. "Clinton's Judges: Summing
Up the Legacy." *Judicature* 84 (March-April 2001).
Goldman, Sheldon, Elliot Slotnick, Gerard Gryski, Gary Zuk, and Sara Schiavoni. "W. Bush's
Judiciary: The First Term Record." *Judicature* 88 (May-June 2005).

Johnson, Timothy R., and Jason M. Roberts. "Presidential Capital and the Supreme Court Confirmation Process." *Journal of Politics* 66 (August 2004).

Maltese, John Anthony. *The Selling of Supreme Court Nominees.* Baltimore: Johns Hopkins University Press, 1995.

O'Brien, David M. *Judicial Roulette.* New York: Priority Press, 1988.

Pacelle, Richard L., Jr., *Between Law and Politics: The Solicitor General and the Structuring of Race, Gender, and Reproductive Rights Litigation.* College Station: Texas A&M University Press, 2003.

Salokar, Rebecca Mae. *The Solicitor General: The Politics of Law.* Philadelphia: Temple University Press, 1992.

Wittes, Benjamin. *Confirmation Wars: Preserving Independent Courts in Angry Times.* Lanham, Md.: Rowman and Littlefield, 2006.

Yalof, David Alistair. *Pursuit of Justices: Presidential Politics and the Selection of Supreme Court Nominees.* Chicago: University of Chicago Press, 1999.

Notes

1. In addition to the district courts and the courts of appeals, there are several specialized courts, including the U.S. Court of International Trade and the U.S. Court of Federal Claims.

2. The District of Columbia and U.S. territories, such as Guam, also have district courts.

3. G. Alan Tarr, *Judicial Process and Policymaking,* 2nd ed. (New York: West/Wadsworth, 1999), 40.

4. David M. O'Brien, *Judicial Roulette* (New York: Priority Press, 1988), 70.

5. Howard Ball, *Courts and Politics: The Federal Judicial System,* 2nd ed. (Englewood Cliffs, N.J.: Prentice Hall, 1987), 199.

6. Ibid., 199–200.

7. "Doing Business in the Senate," editorial, *New York Times,* June 19, 2001, A22.

8. O'Brien, *Judicial Roulette,* 33.

9. Tarr, *Judicial Process,* 75.

10. Sheldon Goldman, *Picking Federal Judges: Lower Court Selection from Roosevelt through Reagan* (New Haven: Yale University Press, 1997), 86; see also Joel B. Grossman, *Lawyers and Judges: The ABA and the Politics of Judicial Selection* (New York: Wiley, 1965), chap. 3.

11. Quoted in Neil A. Lewis, "White House Ends Bar Association's Role in Screening Federal Judges," *New York Times,* March 23, 2001, A13. For a scholarly assessment of the ABA's ratings, see Susan Brodie Haire, "Rating the Ratings of the American Bar Association Standing Committee on Federal Judiciary," *Justice System Journal* 22, no. 1 (2001): 1–17.

12. Thomas B. Edsall, "Federalist Society Becomes a Force in Washington; Conservative Group's Members Take Key Roles in Bush White House and Help Shape Policy and Judicial Appointments," *Washington Post,* April 18, 2001, A4.

13. Thomas B. Edsall, "Liberals Form Counter to Federalist Society," *Washington Post,* August 1, 2001, A5.

14. Richard L. Vining Jr., Amy Steigerwalt, and Susan Navarro Smelcer, "Bias and the Bar: Evaluating the ABA Ratings of Federal Judicial Nominees," (paper presented at the annual meeting of the Midwest Political Science Association, Chicago, April 2009).

15. Larry C. Berkson and Susan B. Carbon, *The United States Circuit Judge Nominating Commission: Its Members, Procedures, and Candidates* (Chicago: American Judicature Society, 1980).

16. Alan Neff, *The United States District Judge Nominating Commissions: Their Members, Procedures, and Candidates* (Chicago: American Judicature Society, 1981).

17. Harry P. Stumpf, *American Judicial Politics*, 2nd ed. (Upper Saddle River, N.J.: Prentice Hall, 1998), Tables 6-2 and 6-3, 180–183.

18. Goldman, *Picking Federal Judges*, 282; Stumpf, *American Judicial Politics*, 183.

19. Sheldon Goldman, "Reagan's Judicial Legacy: Completing the Puzzle and Summing Up," *Judicature* 72 (April-May 1989): 319–320.

20. Quoted in O'Brien, *Judicial Roulette*, 61–62.

21. Goldman, *Picking Federal Judges*, Tables 9.1 and 9.2. The total number of federal judicial appointments with life tenure rises to 372 if Reagan's four Supreme Court appointments are included. It rises slightly higher if one includes his appointments of non–Article III judges who staff specialized courts and do not have life tenure.

22. Alliance for Justice Judicial Selection Project, "2000 Annual Report," 3, www.afj.org/jsp.

23. Ronald Stidham, Robert A. Carp, and Donald Songer, "The Voting Behavior of President Clinton's Judicial Appointees," *Judicature* 80 (July-August 1996): 16–20. See also Alliance for Justice Judicial Selection Project, "2000 Annual Report," 4–5; Sheldon Goldman and Elliot Slotnick, "Picking Judges under Fire," *Judicature* 82 (May-June 1999): 265–284; Nancy Scherer, "Are Clinton's Judges 'Old' Democrats or 'New' Democrats?" *Judicature* 84 (November-December 2000): 151–154.

24. Goldman and Slotnick, "Picking Judges under Fire," 282.

25. Michael Kelly, "Judge Dread," *New Republic*, March 31, 1997, 6.

26. John H. Cushman Jr., "Senate Imperils Judicial System, Rehnquist Says," *New York Times*, January 1, 1998, A1.

27. Alliance for Justice Judicial Selection Project, "2000 Annual Report," 5.

28. Ibid., 2.

29. Ibid., 1. See also Sheldon Goldman et al., "Clinton's Judges: Summing Up the Legacy," *Judicature* 84 (March-April 2001): 228–254.

30. "ABA a Key Player on Federal Bench," editorial, *Chicago Sun-Times*, March 27, 2001, 31.

31. Bennett Roth, "Change in Judicial Appointments Signaled by Bush; Clinton Nominees Are Pulled," *Houston Chronicle*, March 21, 2001, A1.

32. Helen Dewar, "Foreign Aid Bill Held Up by GOP; Senators Demand Action on Nominees," *Washington Post*, October 13, 2001, A3.

33. See John Anthony Maltese, "Confirmation Gridlock: The Federal Judicial Appointments Process under Bill Clinton and George W. Bush," *The Journal of Appellate Practice and Process* 5 (Spring 2003): 1–28.

34. Carl Tobias, "Republicans Threaten to Shut Down the Senate, Charging that Democratic Consideration of Judicial Nominees Is Too Slow: Are These Charges Accurate?" *FindLaw*, June 20, 2007, http://writ.news.findlaw.com/commentary/20070620_tobias.html.

35. Robert Barnes and Michael Abramowitz, "Conservatives Worry About Court Vacancies," *Washington Post*, June 10, 2007, A4.

36. Neil A. Lewis, "Moderate Is Said to Be Pick for Court," *New York Times*, March 17, 2009, A14.

37. Associated Press, "GOP Senators Boycott Hearing on Obama Judicial Nominee," April 1, 2009, available at http://www.foxnews.com/politics/2009/04/01/gop-senators-boycott-hearing-obama-judicial-nominee/.

38. Jim Meyers, "Conservatives Warn About Obama Judicial Nominee," *Newsmax.com*, March 20, 2009, http://www.newsmax.com/insidecover/judge_hamilton_warning/2009/03/20/194328.html.

39. Letter from all forty-one Republican senators to President Obama, March 2, 2009, http://republican.senate.gov/public/index.cfm?FuseAction=blogs.view&blog_id=3c522434-76e5-448e-9ead-1ec214b881ac.

40. "Leahy Gives Blue Clue," *Alliance for Justice: Justice Watch,* March 12, 2009, http://afjjustice watch.blogspot.com/2009/03/leahy-gives-blue-clue.html.

41. Joan Biskupic, "The Next President Could Tip High Court," *USA Today,* March 30, 2004, 1A.

42. *Marbury v. Madison,* 5 U.S. 137 (1803).

43. *Lochner v. New York,* 198 U.S. 45 (1905); *Roe v. Wade,* 410 U.S. 113 (1973); *Griswold v. Connecticut,* 381 U.S. 479 (1965). See Robert H. Bork, *The Tempting of America* (New York: Free Press, 1990), for a criticism of both lines of cases.

44. Robert Scigliano, *The Supreme Court and the Presidency* (New York: Free Press, 1971), chap. 4.

45. Joel B. Grossman and Stephen L. Wasby, "The Senate and Supreme Court Nominations: Some Reflections," *Duke Law Journal* (August 1972): 559 n. 8.

46. All Supreme Court justices have been lawyers, but not all have had law school degrees. Law schools as we know them did not exist in the early part of the nineteenth century, and a majority of the lawyers learned the profession through apprenticeship into the early part of the twentieth century. See David M. O'Brien, *Storm Center: The Supreme Court in American Politics,* 5th ed. (New York: Norton, 2000), 34.

47. See John Anthony Maltese, *The Selling of Supreme Court Nominees* (Baltimore: Johns Hopkins University Press, 1995), chaps. 4, 5.

48. David Alistair Yalof, *Pursuit of Justices: Presidential Politics and the Selection of Supreme Court Nominees* (Chicago: University of Chicago Press, 1999), 4–5.

49. Ibid., 7, 12–13.

50. Ethan Bronner, *Battle for Justice: How the Bork Nomination Shook America* (New York: Norton, 1989), 29–36; Mark Gitenstein, *Matters of Principle: An Insider's Account of America's Rejection of Robert Bork's Nomination to the Supreme Court* (New York: Simon and Schuster, 1992), 28–37.

51. Lawrence Baum, *The Supreme Court,* 9th ed. (Washington, D.C.: CQ Press, 2006), 31.

52. Scott H. Ainsworth and John Anthony Maltese, "National Grange Influence on the Supreme Court Confirmation of Stanley Matthews," *Social Science History* 20 (Spring 1996): 41–62.

53. For early examples of lobbying, see Maltese, *The Selling of Supreme Court Nominees,* 47–49, 53.

54. William Kristol, "Disappointed, Depressed and Demoralized: A Reaction to the Harriet Miers Nomination," *The Weekly Standard,* October 3, 2005, www.weeklystandard.com/Content/Public/Articles/000/000/006/166quhvd.asp.

55. P. S. Ruckman Jr., "The Supreme Court, Critical Nominations, and the Senate Confirmation Process," *Journal of Politics* 55 (August 1993): 794. If the two nominations withdrawn on a technicality are included, the failure rate rises to 19.5 percent.

56. E. J. Dionne, "A Town Hall Meeting: A Process Run Amok—Can It Be Fixed?" *ABC News Nightline,* ABC, October 16, 1991.

57. For case studies of these three nominations, see Maltese, *The Selling of Supreme Court Nominees,* chaps. 1, 4, 5.

58. It should be noted that liberal groups protested Associate Justice William Rehnquist's nomination for chief justice in 1986 because of his alleged insensitivity to the rights of minorities and women. He was ultimately confirmed, but the thirty-three votes against him were the most ever cast against a confirmed justice up to that point.

59. See Patrick B. McGuigan and Dawn M. Weyrich, *Ninth Justice: The Fight for Bork* (Washington, D.C.: Free Congress Foundation, 1990); and Michael Pertschuk and Wendy Schaetzel, *The People Rising: The Campaign Against the Bork Nomination* (New York: Thunder's Mouth Press, 1989).

60. Robert Shogan, *A Question of Judgment: The Fortas Case and the Struggle for the Supreme Court* (New York: Bobbs-Merrill, 1972).

61. Maltese, *The Selling of Supreme Court Nominees,* 14, 16.

62. "The Electoral Count," *New York Times*, January 30, 1881.

63. Quoted in Alpheus Thomas Mason, *Brandeis: A Free Man's Life* (New York: Viking, 1946), 467.

64. See Maltese, *The Selling of Supreme Court Nominees*, for accounts of these developments.

65. *Roe v. Wade*, 410 U.S. 113 (1973).

66. O'Connor, Kennedy, and Souter. *Planned Parenthood of Southeastern Pennsylvania v. Casey*, 505 U.S. 833 (1992).

67. Quoted in David M. O'Brien, *Storm Center: The Supreme Court in American Politics*, 5th ed. (New York: Norton, 1993), 84.

68. Scigliano, *The Supreme Court and the Presidency*, chap. 6. See also Lincoln Caplan, *The Tenth Justice: The Solicitor General and the Rule of Law* (New York: Random House, 1987); Rebecca Mae Salokar, *The Solicitor General: The Politics of Law* (Philadelphia: Temple University Press, 1992).

69. The Supreme Court's discretion has changed over time and since 1988 is almost absolute. Cases now come to the Court almost exclusively by way of a writ of certiorari. To grant "cert" (agree to hear a case), four of the nine justices must vote to accept review. See Craig R. Ducat, *Constitutional Interpretation*, 7th ed. (Belmont, Calif.: West, 2000), 31.

70. Scigliano, *The Supreme Court and the Presidency*, 172.

71. Christopher Zorn, "Information, Advocacy, and the Role of the Solicitor General as Amicus Curiae" (working paper, Emory University, 1999), 1.

72. Steven Puro, "The United States as Amicus Curiae," in *Courts, Law, and Judicial Processes*, ed. S. Sidney Ulmer (New York: Free Press, 1981), 220–230.

73. Scigliano, *The Supreme Court and the Presidency*, chap. 6; Puro, "The United States as Amicus Curiae"; Karen O'Connor, "The Amicus Curiae Role of the U.S. Solicitor General in Supreme Court Litigation," *Judicature* 66 (December-January 1983): 261.

74. Kevin T. McGuire, "Explaining Executive Success in the U.S. Supreme Court," *Political Research Quarterly* 51 (June 1998): 522.

75. This situation is to be contrasted with the paucity of experience attorneys general have before the Court: traditionally, they argue only one case before their terms are over. For an interesting account of Robert Kennedy's first appearance before the Court two years after he became attorney general, see Victor Navasky, *Kennedy Justice* (New York: Athenaeum, 1980), chap. 6.

76. Caplan, *The Tenth Justice*.

77. Elder Witt, *A Different Justice* (Washington, D.C.: Congressional Quarterly, 1986), chaps. 6, 7.

78. Caplan, *The Tenth Justice*, 79–80, 255–256.

79. Richard L. Pacelle Jr., *Between Law and Politics: The Solicitor General and the Structuring of Race, Gender, and Reproductive Rights Litigation* (College Station: Texas A&M University Press, 2003), 265.

80. *Hepburn v. Griswold (First Legal Tender Case)*, 75 U.S. (8 Wall.) 506 (1870); *Knox v. Lee, Parker v. Davis (Second Legal Tender Case)*, 79 U.S. (12 Wall.) 457 (1871).

81. Samuel Kernell, *Going Public*, 4th ed. (Washington, D.C.: CQ Press, 2007), 134.

82. Ibid.

83. For a useful review of this power, see Gerald Gunther, "Congressional Power to Curtail Federal Court Jurisdiction: An Opinionated Guide to the Ongoing Debate," *Stanford Law Review* 36 (1984): 895. The most famous Supreme Court case involving this issue is *Ex parte McCardle*, 74 U.S. 506 (1869).

84. "President Signs Military Commissions Act of 2006," text of remarks at signing ceremony, October 17, 2006,www.whitehouse.gov/news/releases/2006/10/20061017-1.html.

85. *Boumediene v. Bush*, 553 U.S. — (2008). See Michael C. Dorf, "A Federal Appeals Court Upholds the Jurisdiction-Stripping Provisions of the Military Commissions Act of 2006, but Overlooks the Possibility of an Evolving Conception of Habeas Corpus," *FindLaw*, February 28, 2007, http://writ.news.findlaw.com/dorf/20070228.html.

86. "2008 Republican Platform," 53, http://platform.gop.com/2008Platform.pdf.

87. Keith B. Richburg, "Vermont Legislature Legalizes Same-Sex Marriage," *Washington Post*, April 7, 2009, http://www.washingtonpost.com/wp-dyn/content/article/2009/04/07/AR2009040701663.html.

88. *Texas v. Johnson*, 491 U.S. 397 (1989).

89. *Brown v. Board of Education*, 347 U.S. 483 (1954); *Plessy v. Ferguson*, 163 U.S. 537 (1896).

90. Stumpf, *American Judicial Politics*, 429; *Engel v. Vitale*, 370 U.S. 421 (1962).

91. *Youngstown Sheet and Tube Co. v. Sawyer*, 343 U.S. 579 (1952).

92. *United States v. Nixon*, 418 U.S. 683 (1974).

93. *Ex parte Merryman*, 17 Fed.Cas. 144 (1861).

94. Stumpf, *American Judicial Politics*, 429; *United States v. Lopez*, 514 U.S. 549 (1995).

95. For a list of signing statements by Presidents Bush and Obama, see http://www.coherentbabble.com/listGWBall.htm. In 2006 the American Bar Association Task Force on Presidential Signing Statements issued a report on President Bush's use of the practice. See, "Report," August 2006, www.abanet.org/media/docs/signstatereport.pdf.

96. "Report," 16.

97. Ibid., 17.

98. Ibid., 16.

99. *Youngstown Sheet and Tube Co. v. Sawyer.* See Maeva Marcus, *Truman and the Steel Seizure Case: The Limits of Presidential Power* (Durham: Duke University Press, 1994).

100. *United States v. Nixon.*

101. For accounts of executive privilege, see Raoul Berger, *Executive Privilege: A Constitutional Myth* (Cambridge: Harvard University Press, 1974); Mark J. Rozell, *Executive Privilege: The Dilemma of Secrecy and Democratic Accountability* (Baltimore: Johns Hopkins University Press, 1994).

102. *United States v. Curtiss-Wright Export Corp.*, 299 U.S. 304 (1936).

103. See Lee Epstein and Thomas G. Walker, *Constitutional Law for a Changing America: Institutional Powers and Constraints*, 6th ed. (Washington, D.C.: CQ Press, 2007), 263–267.

104. *The Prize Cases*, 67 U.S. 635 (1863).

105. *Korematsu v. United States*, 323 U.S. 214 (1944). See Peter Irons, *Justice at War: The Story of the Japanese-American Internment Cases* (New York: Oxford University Press, 1983).

106. *Dames & Moore v. Regan*, 453 U.S. 654 (1981).

107. *Hamdan v. Rumsfeld*, 126 S.Ct. 2749 (2006).

108. 2600; *Boumediene v. Bush.*

109. *Morrison v. Olson*, 487 U.S. 654 (1988); *Clinton v. Jones*, 520 U.S. 681 (1997). For a discussion of the Lewinsky scandal, see Mark J. Rozell and Clyde Wilcox, eds., *The Clinton Scandal and the Future of American Government* (Washington, D.C.: Georgetown University Press, 2000).

CHAPTER 8

The Politics of Domestic Policy

President Obama aggressively campaigned for congressional approval of his economic stimulus plan by traveling across the nation to highlight the problems of home foreclosures, unemployment, and inadequate health care. This town hall meeting occurred in Fort Myers, Florida, on February 10, 2009.

One big surprise in the 2008 election was the return to prominence of domestic issues, led by the economy. Heading into the election year, most observers expected the Iraq War to again take center stage, as it had in 2006. Indeed, Iraq was an important part of the Democrats' nomination contest, with Barack Obama gaining an advantage over his opponents for their votes supporting the war. But foreign policy, terrorism, and homeland security took a backseat to domestic issues as the economy quickly declined in September and October 2008. This was a return to pre–September 11 politics.

Bill Clinton in 1992 was the first president since FDR to win election with a campaign focused almost exclusively on domestic problems. One of Clinton's sharpest criticisms of his predecessor, President George H. W. Bush, was that he had neglected serious social and economic conditions in the United States while concentrating on foreign policy. Al Gore and George W. Bush also focused on domestic issues in the election of 2000. September 11 redirected the nation's attention, but as conditions in the Iraq war seemed to be improving, domestic needs again came to the forefront.

Whether they want to or not, presidents confront a vast array of domestic problems, issues, and demands for government action. As soon as they take office, they must consider numerous complex and costly programs competing for limited funds. Many of these programs enjoy the support of powerful interest groups and congressional leaders. Whatever the administration does (or fails to do) in response to public demands is likely to cost the president political support.

Presidents face a congested public policy agenda, the result of interrelatedness, overlapping, and layering of issues.[1] Political scientists have used many ways to bring order to this bewildering array of policy issues, but the most widely used classification scheme, or typology, is Theodore Lowi's division of policies into three categories: distributive, regulatory, and redistributive.[2] He based his categories on the identity of those affected by the policies—from individuals to society as a whole—and the likelihood that the government will have to exercise coercion to implement the policy.

Distributive policies have the most diffused impact. They affect specific groups of people and provide individualized benefits. They have low visibility, produce little conflict, and are not likely to require the application of coercion. Examples of distributive policies include agricultural price supports, public works projects, and research and development programs. **Regulatory policies** affect large segments of society and involve the application of coercion. Although regulatory issues tend to be highly technical, they often are quite visible and controversial. Examples include pollution control, antitrust violations, and occupational safety and health requirements. **Redistributive policies** have the broadest impact on society. They involve the transfer of resources (wealth and income) from certain groups to others. They require coercion, are highly visible, and usually are accompanied by social or class conflict. Examples of redistributive policies include Social Security and tax reform.

Lowi argued that the type of policy determines the focus and behavior of political actors. The politics of distributive policy involves limited presidential and extensive congressional participation and decision making that relies heavily on logrolling—the mutual exchange of support for legislation. Regulatory policy politics creates moderate presidential and substantial congressional interest and involvement, with frequent conflict between the president and Congress. Redistributive policy politics often is fraught with ideological disputes and presidential-congressional conflict. Presidents tend to be most involved with redistributive policy issues, and they are involved whether the government is seeking to expand or to limit the scope of its activities.

Steven Shull has used Lowi's policy typology to examine presidential and congressional roles in domestic policy formation. He found "some differences in presidential and congressional behavior . . . along lines anticipated by the 'theory'" and that "modest empirical distinctions" existed among the three policy categories.[3] The principal problem with Lowi's typology is the difficulty in making it operational for purposes of measurement. The problem arises because an issue may change its designation over time, starting out, for example, as a redistributive issue and becoming distributive. That is what happened to Title I of the Elementary and Secondary Education Act of 1965 (ESEA), a program of federal assistance to local school districts for economically disadvantaged children. As a new program, it sparked controversy because of its redistributive effects, but over time it became a routine distribution of federal funds that was part of the established structure of school finance. When ESEA was reauthorized in 2002 as the No Child Left Behind Act, it became more regulatory in nature as it compelled school districts across the nation to adhere to a new set of federal requirements. In other words, Lowi's categories are not fixed in time. Shull concluded that Lowi's typology is not as useful as substantive classification based on policy content.

John Kessel has used policy content to classify domestic policy into areas involving social benefits, civil liberties, natural resources, and agriculture.[4] Each area entails a specific type of politics and its own temporal pattern, both of which have implications for presidential participation. The politics of social benefits, such as housing and the Social Security retirement program, involves the allocation of resources. In this way, it is similar to Lowi's distributive and redistributive categories. Presidents use the distribution of social benefits to build public support. As a result, they tend to pay most attention to social benefits as they approach reelection; afterward, the winners are much less concerned with these benefits. Civil rights involve a pattern of politics that is regulatory and highly sensitive because of differing conceptions of fairness. Presidents are most likely to act on civil rights issues immediately after election because these issues are highly controversial and because campaign promises must be fulfilled. The politics of natural resources, which includes environmental protection, is primarily regulatory, and agriculture mostly involves allocation. The temporal patterns in natural resource and agricultural policy politics are a function of long-range developments and presidential participation is limited.

Whether one approaches domestic policy using Lowi's analytical typology or Kessel's substantive classifications, it is clear that as a practical matter presidents can become fully involved with only a small number of problems and issues. The Lowi and Kessel approaches suggest that in domestic policy, presidents tend to focus on matters such as maintaining the financial integrity of the Social Security system, reforming welfare, and dealing with major civil rights proposals. They do not take up all major redistributive, social benefit, and civil rights issues, and may consciously avoid those issues that could involve enormous financial or political costs. They are unlikely to become bogged down with established distributive policies or with the technicalities of economic and social regulation. Jimmy Carter harmed himself politically when he tangled with Congress over eighteen water projects he regarded as unnecessary. Other presidents have been content to leave the distribution of "pork barrel" projects to Congress. Although George W. Bush initially vowed to cut such pork in half (from $16 billion in fiscal 2001 to $8 billion under his proposed budget), he backed off in the summer of 2001 to avoid a fight with Congress. In Bush's transportation spending bill alone, the House had added some nine hundred local pork barrel projects. Later in his term, Bush resumed his battle with a Democratic Congress over **earmarks,** spending directed to home-district or home-state projects by members of Congress that frequently have not been approved by formal votes in the normal legislative process.

Earmarks were a prominent issue during the 2008 election. John McCain vowed to end the practice and elicited a similar commitment from Barack Obama, who promised to roll them back to 1994 levels, that is, before the Republicans regained control of Congress. Once elected, however, Obama accepted the large number of earmarks—nearly nine thousand by some counts—included in the final version of the fiscal year 2009 appropriations bill. Obama said that this was business carried over from the previous year and that henceforth he would reject them. His explanation opened him up to criticisms of having a double standard.[5] Legislators love earmarks because they "bring home the bacon" to constituents, but budget reformers like McCain argue that they constitute wasteful spending that the nation can ill afford.

The range and complexity of domestic problems and issues produce a policy congestion that makes coordination the essential presidential function in this area. Coordination has been complicated, however, by the interrelatedness of domestic, economic, and national security policy. If, on the one hand, presidents attempt to coordinate specific policies through simplification—say, by proposals to balance the budget or reorganize the bureaucracy—they encounter the opposition of powerful forces mobilized around those policy issues. Ronald Reagan's 1982 proposals to move toward a balanced budget by reducing Social Security cost-of-living allowances provide an excellent example. Opposition from the "gray lobby" (senior citizens) and most members of Congress quickly stymied the idea. If, on the other hand, presidents fail to maintain the initiative in coordinating complex policies effectively, they not only risk losing popular and congressional support but also have to deal with interest group opposition. This scenario played out early in Clinton's first term when he lost control of his health care proposal. Lack of coordination in selling the proposal to Congress and the public allowed opponents to pick the plan apart. As cracks appeared, opponents took control of the agenda, thereby dooming the president's proposal.

Health care reform is one of President Obama's top priorities. Learning from Clinton's experience, he began the effort by convening a White House summit on health care that assembled members of Congress and representatives from all the major interests that would be affected by reform in an attempt to establish a common commitment to moving forward. Sen. Edward Kennedy, D-Mass., under treatment for a malignant brain tumor, provided an emotional boost to the effort. The administration linked controlling health care costs to restoring the nation's economy. As always, however, negotiating the details of change will be the key to success, and Obama appointed a health care czar to serve as the point person for this effort. As head of the White House Office on Health Reform, Nancy-Ann DeParle would coordinate efforts with Secretary of Health and Human Services Kathleen Sebelius.

But reform, even with the president's full support, is not easy to achieve, as demonstrated by several cases from the second term of George W. Bush. In 2005 Bush tackled the long-term problem of keeping Social Security solvent, that is, ensuring that enough money will be available to meet commitments to retirees over the next seventy-five years. His central recommendation—that younger workers be allowed to create personal retirement accounts—generated intense opposition from the largest lobbying group in the United States, the AARP, and unified resistance by congressional Democrats.[6] Bush's proposed reform of immigration policy illustrates the interrelatedness of issues. Immigration affects Hispanics, an important and growing domestic constituency; has a direct bearing on labor needs in important industries; and is a critical issue to many nations around the world, as they attempt to prevent terrorist attacks. Congress, confronted with competing pressures, refused in 2007 to follow the president's lead and fashion bipartisan, comprehensive reform. Obama's effort on health care will be yet another test of a president's capacity to reform major domestic policies.

The Domestic Policy Process

The domestic policy process consists of actions that culminate in the development and presentation of legislative proposals to Congress, the issuance of executive orders and regulations, and the preparation and submission of annual budgets. There is a cyclical regularity to much of the policy process because annual events such as the delivery of the State of the Union, budget, and economic messages define the broad outlines of the president's program.[7] (Although these events occur at approximately the same time each year, the full cycles last longer than a year. The budget for the fiscal year beginning on October 1, 2009, for example, had its origins in the budget review process conducted in spring 2007.) Formal events for proposing policy, such as the president's annual submission of the budget, are supplemented by the emergence of policy proposals at other times during the year. Such proposals may emerge due to unexpected events or because of forces outside the White House.

Policy Streams

The process of setting the president's domestic policy agenda can be understood as the convergence in the White House of three tributary streams: the first identifies *problems and issues* requiring attention; the second produces *proposed solutions* to the problems; and the third carries the *political factors* that establish the context for policymaking. According to John Kingdon, these three streams operate largely, but not absolutely, independently of one another. Problems and solutions develop separately and may or may not be joined, and political factors may change regardless of whether policymakers have recognized a problem or whether a potential solution exists.[8]

The First Stream: Problems and Issues. Problems and issues move onto the president's domestic policy agenda either because their seriousness and high visibility make it impossible to avoid them or because of presidential initiative. Examples of unavoidable problems that force the president to react include matters such as energy shortages, a failing economy, high rates of inflation and unemployment, the emergence of major threats to public health, problems resulting from increased drug abuse, and parental dissatisfaction with the quality of education. Other times, presidents act more proactively by adding items they believe are instrumental to the achievement of their goals.

Once enough influential people, inside and outside the government, think something should be done about a certain problem or issue, it is likely that the president will react by adding the item to the administration's domestic agenda.[9] This pressure may occur as a consequence of changes in economic and social indicators, such as rates of inflation, unemployment, energy costs, infant mortality, and students' scores on various standardized tests. Decision makers in the presidency, the bureaucracy, Congress, the private sector, and state and local governments routinely monitor changes in a large array of indicators. Whether these changes add up to a problem appropriately addressed by the federal government is a matter of interpretation. That interpretation takes place in the context of the symbolic significance of the matter, the personal experiences of the president and the other decision makers with it, and the relationship of the subject to other problems and issues.

The president and other decision makers may be moved to recognize a condition as a compelling problem because of a "focusing event," such as a disaster or a crisis. The near meltdown of a reactor at the Three Mile Island power plant in western Pennsylvania in March 1979 thrust nuclear safety to the forefront of the domestic agenda; prior to this event, safety proponents had struggled for years with little success to call attention to the issue. The massive power outage that left eight states in the dark in August 2003 drew attention to the vulnerability of the nation's aging electrical grid and brought debate over a proposed energy bill to the forefront. The terrorist attacks of September 11, 2001, forced the issue of domestic security onto the agenda and led to quick passage of the USA PATRIOT Act. The devastation wrought by Hurricane Katrina in August 2005 triggered a debate on governments' preparedness for responding to natural disasters; the consensus was that "disaster response policy [became] a significant political disaster for Bush."[10] And the severe economic recession that emerged during 2008 (see chapter 9) allowed the Obama administration to link several major policy initiatives to long-term needs of the economy, specifically, establishing cost-effective universal health care, committing to energy independence through green technologies, and strengthening the nation's education system to enhance competitiveness in a global economy.

On occasion, presidents have no choice but to deal with a problem, even though they may prefer not to do so. The 1992 riots in Los Angeles forced a reluctant George H. W. Bush to propose legislation to aid the damaged city, and events in Somalia, Haiti, and Bosnia forced Bill Clinton to devote more attention than he wished to foreign policy. Similarly, the collision of a U.S. Navy surveillance aircraft with a Chinese F-8 interceptor over the South China Sea in April 2001 and the subsequent detention of the U.S. flight crew by the Chinese government forced George W. Bush to focus attention on the diplomatic standoff. Hurricane Katrina pushed all other domestic problems, including Social Security reform, off the national agenda.

Some problems and issues remain on the agenda through successive presidential administrations. Feasible solutions may not have been found, solutions may have been tried unsuccessfully, or the problem may have been "solved" only to reemerge in a different form. Health care exemplifies such an issue. Harry S. Truman proposed a comprehensive national health insurance program in 1945 as an additional Social Security benefit.[11] The American Medical Association and major business groups successfully attacked the proposal as "socialized medicine." Both John F. Kennedy and Lyndon B. Johnson advanced proposals for national health insurance, and in 1965 Congress responded partially with Medicare, a health insurance plan for Social Security retirees age sixty-five and older. Since then, pressures have continued for a plan that would provide universal coverage. In the 1970s Richard Nixon and Jimmy Carter supported universal coverage, as opinion polls showed that a majority of the population favored some kind of national health insurance program. During the recession in the early 1990s, health care reform became a salient issue as millions of workers either lost or feared losing health insurance along with their jobs. Bill Clinton made the need for health care reform one of the central issues in his 1992 presidential campaign, and it became one of the principal goals of the domestic policy agenda in his first two years, although his 1,342-page plan failed to pass Congress. At the urging of George W. Bush, prescription drug coverage was added to Medicare in 2003, but health care reform remained a priority in the 2004 and 2008 elections. Rising costs have a direct impact on workers and employers, especially during difficult economic times, and an estimated 45 million Americans lack any form of health insurance.[12]

Sometimes presidents have broader discretion to determine which problems and issues to emphasize. In such cases, three goals affect the selection of problems and issues to address: reelection (for a first-term president), historical achievement (legacy), and a desire to shape public policy.[13] Presidents vary in the emphasis they place on these goals. Nixon's willingness to propose innovative policies for welfare reform and revenue sharing, even at the expense of alienating some of his conservative supporters, reflected his concern with historical achievement.[14] As he approached his reelection campaign, Carter shifted from making agenda decisions on the basis of his beliefs to making them on the basis of politics. Second-term presidents, including George W. Bush, are usually seen as focused on their historical legacy.

The Second Stream: Solutions. Once a problem or an issue has been recognized, the availability of a solution becomes an important determinant of whether it rises to a high position on the president's agenda.[15] Solutions take several forms, ranging from *direct actions,* such as legislative proposals or executive orders, to *symbolic actions,* such as appointment of a study commission or a task force, to *no action.* Problems can have several solutions, and a single solution can be applied to more than one problem. Some solutions come attached to a problem; others are consciously selected from among competing alternatives. Most solutions come from ideas generated outside the presidency because of the time constraints facing executive advisers and the small size of the institution of the presidency in relation to the policy-making environment as a whole. Aside from the presidency, the principal sources of policy ideas are Congress, the bureaucracy, interest groups, universities, think tanks (research institutes), and state and local governments. Within the presidency, the incumbent's campaign promises are a source of policy proposals and a benchmark for evaluating externally generated ideas.[16] Obama's pledge to raise taxes only on those with incomes above $250,000 is an example. The president's domestic policy staff and other units in the Executive Office of the President might develop new ideas once the president is in office, but these aides often become bogged down in day-to-day problems.

Many of the ideas that emerge as proposed solutions to problems on the president's agenda have been circulating among members of **issue networks.** Issue networks are groups of individuals and organizations trying to shape certain policies. Such networks might consist of members of Congress and their legislative aides, bureaucrats, interest groups, the media, scholars and other experts in research organizations, and representatives of state and local government. Together they promote specific ideas and proposals, such as campaign finance reform, energy policy, and a patients' bill of rights. Issue networks are motivated by their participants' desire to advance personal and organizational interests and to influence public policy in accordance with the groups' values. Network participants study, analyze, and discuss problems and solutions among themselves, and they attempt to inform and influence the major decision makers in government, the most important of whom is the president.

The process by which policy ideas develop, advance, and either succeed or fail is often lengthy and generally diffuse. John Kingdon describes it as a "policy primeval soup" in which ideas are continually bumping into one another and surviving, dying, combining, or emerging into new forms.[17] The ideas that do manage to become incorporated into a president's specific policy proposal are evaluated according to three criteria: economic, political, and technical feasibility.

The *economic feasibility,* or cost, of a potential solution is especially important, as demands for federal expenditures far outweigh the government's capacity to supply the necessary funds. Few proposals for major new spending programs survive in an era of resource constraints. Proposals that restrain or reduce spending are more attractive to a president struggling to control the budget deficit. A proposal's *political feasibility* is determined initially by its compatibility with the values and interests of other important decision makers, particularly those in Congress. Ultimately, a proposal must gain the acquiescence, if not the acceptance, of the public and the relevant interest groups. A proposal's *technical feasibility*—the question of its workability—does not receive as much attention as its economic and political costs. Some ideas—such as proposals for welfare reform that maintain reasonably high payments, reduce inequities between recipients in different states and between recipients and the working poor, and do not increase the cost to the government—are economically and politically attractive but unworkable in practice. Presidents Nixon and Carter made this discovery, much to their dismay, after the failure of their major efforts to achieve welfare reform.[18] Financial costs may rule out a proposal that is politically and technically feasible, such as rapid cleanup of toxic waste sites. Political costs may prevent acceptance of a workable proposal that is compatible with a tight budget, such as freezing Social Security cost-of-living increases. Eventually, a short list of presidential proposals emerges from a multitude of potential solutions.

The Third Stream: Political Factors. The last of Kingdon's three policy-making streams is the one carrying political factors.[19] Such factors affect the setting and implementation of the president's agenda, and they include the balance of political forces, events within the government, and the national mood.

The *national mood* is a somewhat amorphous term, difficult to define. It is not identical to public opinion, nor can it be ascertained through survey research. National mood is perhaps best described as the perception among decision makers that a consensus exists, or is building, among various attentive publics and political activists for specific government policies. Politicians sense this mood in suggestions, requests, and other communications from interest groups, state and local government officials, corporate executives, and politically active citizens; in news media coverage of events; and in editorial commentary. The national mood also reflects the influence of social movements such as civil rights, environmentalism, and family values. Without a favorable national mood, major new policies are unlikely to be adopted. In short, the national mood is a reflection of the politically relevant climate or temper of the times. Counting on a national mood that supports "change," his campaign mantra, President Obama began to push several major reforms through the system and took bold steps to remedy the economic emergency.

Considerably more concrete than the national mood is the extent of consensus and conflict that determines the *balance of political forces.* The prospects for adoption of a proposed policy change depend on the balance of organized interests and other forces, but assessing the balance on any issue is largely a matter of informed guess-work. The complex pattern of pluralistic political forces and the fragmentation of government authority combine to provide a strong advantage to the *opponents* of policy change. Often, heavy political costs are associated with just raising an issue for consideration, let alone obtaining adoption of a proposal. This problem arises when the administration attempts to change existing government programs, most of which have powerful clientele groups ready to defend them. Clientele interests, in triangular alliances with agencies that administer the programs and congressional subcommittees with jurisdiction, engage in bargaining and logrolling to maintain and enhance the programs. To overcome government's natural inertia, a strong constituency for political change must be mobilized; without it, a proposal will encounter great difficulty. The Carter administration's efforts to enact a national energy policy were unsuccessful despite widespread shortages of fuels until compromises made the proposal acceptable to the oil industry and consumer interests. Clinton's proposal for health care reform failed because strong opposition from a variety of special interests tipped the balance of political forces against the proposed change. George W. Bush succeeded in convincing the public that Social Security was running out of money, but groups representing seniors worked strenuously against his preferred solution.

Events within government are the third major political factor shaping the president's policy agenda. The principal event is a presidential election, which can produce fundamental changes in the agenda. The 1980 election brought Ronald Reagan to the presidency and gave the Republicans control of the Senate after a quarter-century in the minority and was certainly such an event. An ideologically defined, conservative agenda replaced the liberal agenda in effect since the New Deal. Similarly, the 1994 election, in which the Republicans captured control of both houses of Congress for the first time in forty years, profoundly reshaped President Clinton's domestic agenda. Much of the revised agenda consisted of defensive reactions to Republican proposals to curtail affirmative action and reverse regulatory policies affecting the environment, occupational health and safety, and business and financial practices. Moreover, Clinton dropped health care reform from his list and reshaped his welfare reform proposals to compete with Republican plans. The 2006 midterm elections returned Democrats to the majority in the House and Senate, setting up the potential for agenda clashes between the White House and Congress. Divided government has also made implementing policy more difficult. From 1969 through 2009, the same political party controlled the White House and both houses of Congress for only ten out of forty years.[20]

Two researchers looking at presidential action on crime issues over a fifty-year period concluded that the president's electoral cycle is the single strongest determinant of when such a discretionary policy issue becomes part of the president's agenda.[21] Matthew Eshbaugh-Soha argues that the political composition of Congress and the condition of the federal budget determine both the number and significance of policies the president might propose; budget and political constraints lead presidents to emphasize unimportant or short-term policies.[22] Obama determined that higher government spending was needed to combat the recession and counted on the broad public support registered in the election to enable him to pass an ambitious reform agenda.

Jurisdictional matters are another intragovernmental factor that may affect agenda setting. Disputes over bureaucratic and committee turf often delay or prevent action, although jurisdictional competition occasionally accelerates consideration of a popular issue. In addition, a proposal may be structured so it will be handled by a committee or an agency favorably disposed to it.

In sum, the most significant domestic policy actions are likely to occur when the national mood and election outcomes combine to overcome the normal inertia produced by the balance of political forces and the fragmentation of government authority among numerous bureaucratic and congressional fiefdoms. Once items begin to rise on the agenda, however, organized political forces attempt to shape policy proposals to their advantage or to defeat the proposals outright. Despite the tools at their disposal, presidents largely remain "prisoners of circumstance" in domestic policy. For George W. Bush those circumstances were largely shaped by the events of 9/11 in New York City and Washington, D.C., as well as the hurricane winds of August 2005 in New Orleans.[23] For Barack Obama the economic problems, bad as they are, may favor significant policy initiatives.

Resources and Opportunities

Successful policy leadership results from advancing appropriate solutions to specific problems under favorable political circumstances. Relatively few policy proposals can receive presidential attention and consideration. Some are not compatible with an administration's overall objectives and ideology, but many otherwise acceptable proposals never become part of the president's agenda because limited resources cannot be devoted to them. Quite simply, presidents must establish priorities.[24] Presidents establish priorities through what political scientist Paul Light calls a "filtering process," which maintains an orderly flow of problems and solutions to the president and merges them to produce policy proposals. The objectives of the process are to control the flow so that important problems, issues, and

Presidents sometimes use executive orders to establish policies in areas that would otherwise bog down in prolonged congressional debate. In this instance, President Obama signed Executive Order 13505 on March 9, 2009, which reversed the Bush administration's severe restrictions on using federal funds to support stem-cell research through the National Institutes of Health.

alternatives receive attention without overloading the president and to ensure that policy proposals are formulated with due regard to relevant political factors. As they are melded into presidential decisions, problems and solutions pass through two filters: resources and opportunities.

Resources: Political Capital. One of the president's most important resources is **political capital,** the reservoir of popular and congressional support with which presidents begin their terms. As they make controversial decisions, presidents "spend" some of their capital, a resource they can seldom replenish. Presidents must decide which proposals merit the expenditure of political capital and in what amounts. Reagan, for example, was willing to spend his capital heavily on reducing activities of the federal government, cutting taxes, and reforming the income tax code, but not on antiabortion or school prayer amendments to the Constitution. Material resources determine which proposals for new programs can be advanced and the emphasis to be placed on existing programs.

Clinton began his presidency lacking sufficient political capital to enact his ambitious agenda.[25] Although he won a clear Electoral College victory and had a

6 percent vote margin over incumbent president George H. W. Bush, he received only 43 percent of the popular vote because of Ross Perot's third-party candidacy. Immediately after the election, the Republican Senate leader, Bob Dole, pointedly claimed to speak for the 57 percent of the electorate who had opposed Clinton. Furthermore, although Clinton's victory temporarily ended twelve years of divided government, the potential for ending presidential-congressional stalemate over domestic policy was diminished by the Republicans' gain of ten House seats. Moreover, the centrist New Democrat stance Clinton adopted to win election was not shared by a majority of congressional Democrats, who were considerably more liberal. Finally, the damage to Clinton's image done in the campaign by allegations of sexual misconduct and avoidance of military service in Vietnam reduced the public's trust and support. These factors limited the capital Clinton had to spend on advocating potentially controversial domestic policies.

George W. Bush also entered office with limited political capital. In the 2000 presidential election, he lost the popular vote to Al Gore and took power only after a protracted dispute over which candidate had won Florida's electoral votes. In addition, he faced the highest disapproval rating of any incoming president since polling began—25 percent according to the Gallup Poll.[26] In May 2001 he lost the marginal control of the Senate that Republicans had enjoyed since January after Sen. James Jeffords, R-Vt., defected and became an independent. The return to divided government, which lasted until the 2002 midterm elections, made the passage of Bush's initiatives more difficult. But Bush proceeded confidently, as if he had a mandate for his conservative agenda. "I know the value of political capital," Bush said just before his inauguration, "how to earn it and how to spend it."[27] He swiftly advanced a few proposals that enjoyed broad support, such as tax cuts and education reform. After 9/11 Bush sought—with mixed success—to parlay his high public approval ratings into support for his domestic policy initiatives.

Two days after he was reelected, Bush again spoke of his prospects during a press conference. "I earned capital in the campaign, political capital, and now I intend to spend it. . . . [Y]ou've heard the agenda: Social Security and tax reform, moving this economy forward, education, fighting and winning the war on terror."[28] But Bush's approval ratings began a downward slide caused by Iraq, a White House scandal, a botched Supreme Court nomination, and faulty relief efforts after Hurricane Katrina.[29] As a result, neither of his top two domestic priorities was realized, and the chance to regain capital in the 2006 midterm election disappeared.

Obama entered office with a solid electoral victory based on the promise of change as well as public hopes that he was the right candidate to repair the economy. His campaign excited millions of first-time and young voters, and he seemed to embody a new beginning on many fronts—in race relations, bipartisan discussions of common problems, and international negotiations. Expectations were especially high as he entered the White House with a Democrat-controlled Congress, potentially setting him up for a backlash if results are disappointing. Riding on the crest of electoral victory and widespread popularity, he advanced an ambitious agenda that ran the risk of overreaching. Carter and Clinton had swamped Congress with too many proposals during their first two years in office, but neither of them had enjoyed as much public support as Obama, who was counting on his ability to link his policy initiatives together as necessary to strengthen the economy in both the short and long term.

Opportunities. In addition to resources, Light argues, presidents need **opportunities** to formulate the agenda. These opportunities are often described metaphorically as windows: they open for a while and then close. They may be scheduled or unscheduled. Scheduled opportunities to shape the agenda occur in conjunction with the annual cycle of presidential messages to Congress (State of the Union, budget, and economic report), the congressional calendar, and action-forcing deadlines, such as renewals of program authorizations. An administration's greatest opportunity to set the agenda occurs during January and February, when Congress begins a new session and presidents deliver their messages, and in August and September, when Congress returns from recess and earlier proposals can be replaced or modified.[30] Unscheduled opportunities come about as the result of focusing events or changes in political conditions. Both scheduled and unscheduled windows of opportunity eventually close, some sooner than others. An opportunity is more likely to be seized and an issue given a high place on the president's agenda when problems, solutions, and political factors come together.[31] Without a viable solution and in the absence of favorable political conditions, a problem has a limited chance of moving up on the agenda. For example, popular support for biomedical research is substantial, but the slow pace of development of treatments and cures for diseases such as cancer limits presidential attention to the issue.

Opportunities also fluctuate as a presidential term progresses. In a president's first year in office, Congress and the public have high expectations of policy change based on campaign promises and the election mandate. Opportunities tend to be at their peak during a new administration's so-called honeymoon period. In the second and fourth years of a president's term, concern begins to focus on the forthcoming election campaigns, and policy opportunities decline. The third year frequently is regarded as crucial, for the administration is by then experienced, mature, removed from immediate electoral pressures, and anxious to make its mark.[32] Opportunities are most likely to be exploited effectively then and in the first year of a president's second term—assuming there is one. Because a second term is also a final term, the president becomes a **lame duck,** which tends to restrict further policy opportunities. The effects of lame-duck status on presidential initiatives are especially notable following the midterm congressional election in a president's second term. In anticipation of losing control of Congress in the November 2006 elections, Bush asked department secretaries for lists of "initiatives that could be accomplished without congressional approval."[33] Instead, he would employ regulations and other unilateral action powers. Other presidents, including Clinton, used such a strategy.

The patterns in the progression of opportunities conflict as presidents move through their terms. On the one hand, as they acquire experience and expertise, presidents become more effective and therefore increase their policy opportunities. On the other hand, as their congressional and popular support declines through the term, they lose opportunities. Light describes these as cycles of increasing effectiveness and declining influence.[34] It is ironic that as presidents become more skilled at finding opportunities, they become less able to use them.

The Domestic Policy Environment

The most outstanding characteristic of the domestic policy environment is its complexity. Myriad actors—individuals, groups, and other government institutions and agencies—all pursue a seemingly incalculable range of objectives and protect countless interests. Although presidential power is limited, the president is better situated than anyone else to give direction and bring a degree of coordination to the federal government's domestic policies.

The fragmentation of political power and influence that is the hallmark of the U.S. political system is the product of a heterogeneous and pluralistic society and of constitutional arrangements designed to produce deliberate, rather than expeditious, government decision making. Nowhere is the fragmentation of power more apparent and more profound than in the domestic policy environment.

Interest Groups

Outside the government, thousands of interest groups constantly seek to influence policy. They range from organizations concerned with all of the government's activities, such as Americans for Democratic Action, to those focused on a single issue, such as the National Rifle Association (NRA). Interest groups are concerned not only with virtually every government program that distributes benefits to individuals and organizations and regulates their conduct but also with possibilities for new programs. Simply stated, the objectives of interest groups are to secure the adoption of policies beneficial to their members and to prevent the adoption of policies they view as harmful to them. Interest groups operate in all sectors of domestic policy. They include organizations that represent business; labor; the professions; consumers; state and local governments and their subdivisions; public officials; social groupings based on age, sex, race, religion, and shared attitudes and experiences; and groups presenting themselves as protectors of the unorganized public interest. In sum, interest groups represent every aspect of society and help convey our myriad concerns to policymakers.[35] Within the national government, interest groups attempt to exert influence directly on Congress, the bureaucracy, the courts, and the presidency. As we saw in chapter 3, presidents have responded to the growing influence of interest groups by assigning individual White House aides as liaisons to groups in policy areas such as civil rights, education, and health. Interest groups have also attempted to exert influence indirectly, principally by endorsing and making campaign contributions to presidential and congressional candidates and by urging their members to bring pressure to bear on the White House and on their representatives in Congress.

It is difficult to measure the effectiveness of interest group influence on public policy because of multiple points of access to government decision makers; numerous groups usually seek to influence a particular policy or set of related policies; and other powerful forces are also at work. Nevertheless, many believe that the growth in interest group activity since 1965 has contributed substantially to the rise in federal spending on domestic programs and the expansion of federal regulation into noneconomic areas, such as consumer protection, product safety, and occupational safety and health.[36] The demands of interest groups, often asserted as a matter of "right" and defended on grounds of fairness or improvement of quality of life, have strained the federal government's fiscal capacity and created societal conflicts.

Economist Mancur Olson has argued that societies with large numbers of powerful "distributional coalitions" (his term for interest groups) have experienced insupportably high public spending and little or no economic growth as a consequence of those groups' political influence. The groups press for public benefits for their members even though the result may be disadvantageous to the community as a whole. According to Olson, unless an interest group encompasses most of the population, there is "no constraint on the social cost such an organization will find it expedient to impose on the society in the cause of obtaining a larger share of the social output for itself."[37] To a substantial extent, domestic policy politics can become the pursuit of narrow group interests, even at the expense of the general public interest, which is usually unorganized, unarticulated, and difficult to identify or define. The president is better situated, in terms of political resources, than anyone else to define, enhance, and defend the public interest. That is the president's principal challenge in the domestic policy area. Harry Truman, echoing an argument heard since Teddy Roosevelt's presidency, was fond of saying his job was to act as a lobbyist for the American people, most of whom are unrepresented by lobbyists.

Separation of Powers and Federalism

The pattern of interest group activity traditionally has been described as **policy subgovernments,** mutually beneficial triangular relationships among interest groups, administrative agencies, and congressional subcommittees. Subgovernments, and the more open and amorphous issue networks that cut across and intersect with them, contribute to the fragmentation of power and influence in the domestic policy environment. That fragmentation is enhanced by constitutional arrangements dividing power among the government branches and between the national and state governments and by the internal structures of Congress and the federal bureaucracy. The constitutional design, which established a system of "separated institutions sharing powers," was created to prevent the abuse of power.[38]

The framers invented federalism as a means of resolving the seemingly intractable conflict between advocates of a consolidated system of government and the proponents of state sovereignty. Their ingenious compromise, which artfully avoided establishing a precise boundary between national and state powers, has been adapted to the needs of the times by successive generations of political leaders. The current system of federalism still leaves primary responsibility for most basic government services in the hands of the states and their local subdivisions. These services include public education, public health, public safety, and the construction and maintenance of streets, roads, and highways. The federal government has programs that help finance state and local activities in these and other areas, and it exerts a substantial degree of influence on them by virtue of its grant and regulatory programs. For example, even though the federal government provides only 8 percent of the funding spent nationally on kindergarten through twelfth grade public education, the Bush administration and Congress imposed a common system of accountability on all states through the No Child Left Behind program and gained compliance by threatening to withdraw federal funding from states that failed to meet federal regulations.[39] Still, most of the federal government's domestic policy activity does not entail direct federal administration.

Presidential leadership in domestic policy requires the president to work with Congress, federal administrators, and state and local officials. In these relationships, the president has limited power to command and must rely primarily on personal skills as a political leader—principally persuasion and bargaining—to achieve goals.

The structure of authority in Congress has varied over time, with a prevailing tendency toward fragmentation. The reforms of the early 1970s, while strengthening somewhat the majority party leadership in the House, provided individual members with extensive opportunities to influence policy.[40] Consequently, in the following decades Congress often found it difficult to give direction to public policy, and presidents encountered problems in their relations with Congress. Unlike their predecessors in the late 1950s and 1960s, presidents from the mid-1970s to the early 1990s could not easily negotiate agreements with top party leaders and with one or two influential chairs in each house and be confident those agreements would prevail in floor voting. Rather, the presidents had to deal separately, in each chamber, with several committee chairs, subcommittee chairs, and party leaders. Agreements reached at one stage in the legislative process often came undone later.

The congressional environment changed dramatically following the Republican takeover in 1994. In the House, the new majority leadership under Speaker Newt Gingrich, R-Ga., imposed tight discipline on Republican members and committee chairs, all eager to implement a conservative policy revolution.[41] Party government, not seen since the first decade of the twentieth century, seemed to have returned, even though the new Senate predictably was less disciplined than the House. But Clinton repeatedly foiled plans for the conservative revolution, and even the election of George W. Bush in 2000 and the results of the 2002 midterm elections did not ensure a uniform Republican agenda. House Republicans, whipped by the heavy hand of Majority Leader Tom DeLay, remained generally supportive of the administration's goals, but the votes were sometimes costly.[42] Moreover, moderate Republicans in the Senate frequently clashed with the more ideologically unified House majority. The Democratic majority that took control of Congress in 2007 clashed repeatedly with President Bush, a prolonged conflict that kept the party relatively unified in both the House and Senate. With the return of a Democratic president advancing an ambitious agenda, however, pressure may mount to move in directions other than those preferred by the White House, as happened with Presidents Carter and Clinton.

Congressional fragmentation has had mixed effects on the president's involvement in domestic policy. Congress has been unable to counterbalance the presidency by providing alternative policy leadership, but at the same time presidents have found it difficult to lead Congress. Congressional influence has been extensive, if only in a negative sense, because of its inertia and its ability to resist presidential direction.

Fragmentation of a different sort characterizes the federal bureaucracy. As noted in chapter 6, an independent power exists in the bureaucracy that is based in career civil servants, who constitute a permanent government. The members of the permanent government have professional and agency loyalties and close ties to the interest groups that constitute their clientele and to the congressional subcommittees with jurisdiction over their appropriations and the legislation that authorizes their programs. Subgovernments and issue networks comprise members of the permanent government and complicate presidential control of policy development and implementation in or by the bureaucracy. In addition, the fragmentation resulting from the size and complexity of the federal bureaucracy creates enormous problems of management and policy coordination for the president.

The Domestic Policy Apparatus

The need for presidential coordination in domestic policy has been recognized for some time. By developing a domestic policy staff apparatus in the Executive Office of the President (EOP), it was hoped that presidents could provide the necessary level of coordination. The domestic policy staff evolved slowly, in conjunction with the development of the president's legislative role (see chapter 5). This evolutionary process relied initially on the Bureau of the Budget (BOB); eventually it saw the establishment of a separate staff to formulate and implement domestic policy.

BOB: Central Clearance and Legislative Program Planning

From the early nineteenth century until the creation of the Bureau of the Budget in 1921, the president's role in domestic policy formulation was ad hoc and unorganized.[43] In its first year of operation, the BOB established the requirement that all agency legislative proposals for the expenditure of federal funds had to be submitted to it before being sent to Congress. Any proposal the bureau determined not in accord with the president's financial program would not be sent forward to Congress. Moreover, agencies were to inform Congress if any pending legislation had been found not in accord. This procedure, known as **central clearance,** was expanded during Franklin Roosevelt's administration to cover the substantive content of proposed legislation. Early on, central clearance was used to ensure that legislative proposals of various departments and agencies were compatible with the president's overall program goals.[44] Over time, it acquired additional functions, among them supervising and coordinating executive branch legislative initiatives, providing a clear indication to congressional committees of the president's position on proposed legislation, and making various administrative units aware of one another's goals and activities.

Beginning in 1947 the BOB's domestic policy role expanded to include participation in the development of the president's annual legislative program.[45] The bureau's Legislative Reference Division worked directly with Truman's White House staff in reviewing agency recommendations and integrating them into a comprehensive legislative program. The additional responsibilities to formulate policy involved BOB personnel in the pursuit of the president's political goals. Dwight D. Eisenhower delegated even more power to the BOB. When he first took office in 1953, Ike was unprepared to send a legislative program to Congress. He was also less interested in domestic policy than Truman had been. He therefore relied heavily on the BOB to formulate a domestic program. The centralized clearance and planning processes lodged in the bureau were compatible with Eisenhower's penchant for systematic staff operations, so he continued to employ it as a clearinghouse for policy throughout his presidency. By 1960 annual submissions to the BOB of legislative proposals by departments and agencies were commonplace. The result was a highly routinized process nearly impervious to new ideas. This system suited Eisenhower and his limited interest in domestic policy initiatives. It did not suit Kennedy or Johnson, both of whom placed a high priority on domestic policy. To overcome the rigidities and bureaucratic domination of the BOB-based program planning process, JFK and LBJ sought ideas and suggestions from nongovernment sources.[46]

Task Forces and Study Commissions

The mechanism used by Kennedy and Johnson for gathering policy advice was the task force, a group consisting of experts from inside and outside the government. Before his inauguration, Kennedy appointed several such groups to advise him on the major issues and problems the new administration would be facing. The reports of these task forces, and of a number of others appointed after he took office, provided the basis for much of Kennedy's New Frontier program.[47] Although Kennedy remained eager for new ideas and suggestions, he did not rely exclusively on outside sources of advice after the initial round of task forces. Instead, he turned primarily to his cabinet for suggestions.

In spring 1964 President Johnson appointed task forces with the specific mission of developing a distinctive program for his administration. They were made up of outsiders and operated in secret. Johnson was so pleased with their reports, which furnished much of the form and substance of his Great Society program, that he made task forces a regular part of his program development process. The White House staff coordinated task force operations, and the BOB integrated the proposals into the annual legislative program. Johnson favored the task force process because it largely avoided the ordeal of bargaining with departments and agencies and because it was not adulterated by bureaucratic, congressional, and interest group pressures.[48]

The presidents who followed Johnson made little use of task forces. Instead, they relied on more formal advisory bodies, such as commissions and White House conferences, to study issues and problems and to gather outside recommendations. Presidential commissions are broadly representative bodies often appointed to defuse highly sensitive issues. In September 1981, for example, President Reagan appointed the National Commission on Social Security Reform to develop a solution to a Social Security funding crisis. Although the commission did not solve the problem, it provided "cover" under which the principals, Reagan and House Speaker Thomas P. O'Neill, D-Mass., could work out a compromise.[49] As one of his first official actions, President Clinton appointed the Task Force on National Health Care Reform to develop the administration's proposed legislation within a hundred days.[50] Headed by the first lady, Hillary Rodham Clinton, and the senior adviser for policy development, Ira Magaziner, the task force consisted of five hundred experts from inside and outside government, who divided themselves into thirty-four groups and operated secretly. The unprecedented size, the cumbersome secret process, and Hillary Clinton's role made the task force a target for criticism well before it had finished its work. The delay in developing the proposal postponed congressional consideration of it until 1994, when it got caught up in election year politics. The proposal's "complexity, high cost, and obtrusive bureaucracy made it an easy target for Republicans" and contributed to the failure of Congress to enact it.[51]

Shortly after assuming office, President Bush asked Vice President Cheney to chair the National Energy Policy Development Group, a task force charged with developing a new national energy policy. Learning from the Clinton example, the group was kept small and simple—a six-person staff that wrote a 170-page report, far shorter than Clinton's 1,350-page product.[52] Like the Clinton effort, however, the task force became controversial: its recommendations were considered highly favorable to the energy industry, and the White House refused to release information on the commission's membership and its meetings with industry leaders and groups. Court decisions blocked the release of that information to environmental groups and Congress. Shortly after taking office, President Obama formed a task force on helping the middle class and announced new initiatives for cities, women and girls, and science and technology policy. All of these areas were likely to draw heavily for advice on sources outside the government.

Because their membership seeks broad representation and tries to obtain consensus, presidential commissions often issue reports that blur critical issues. Commissions may also make findings and suggestions that embarrass the president, as did the 1970 Scranton Commission report, which blamed campus unrest on President Nixon.

White House conferences bring together groups of experts and distinguished citizens for public forums held under presidential auspices. Their principal function is to build support among experts, political leaders, and relevant interests for presidential leadership to deal with the problems at issue. Neither White House conferences nor presidential commissions have served as the basis for major legislative proposals, but they have given legitimacy to certain presidential undertakings. As the Clinton and Bush cases suggest, task forces, because they are more closed and focused on presidential priorities, are likely to produce controversy about their content and process.

Domestic Policy Staffs

Since Johnson, presidents have used domestic policy staffs in the Executive Office of the President and a politicized Office of Management and Budget (OMB)—the renamed BOB—to develop legislative programs. Nixon established the Domestic Council in 1970 as part of a reorganization of the presidency. The Domestic Council comprised the president, the vice president, the attorney general, and the secretaries of agriculture, commerce, housing and urban development, interior, labor, transportation, Treasury, and health, education and welfare, as well as the director and deputy director of OMB. The council was to be a top-level forum for discussion, debate, and determination of policy analogous to the National Security Council (NSC). (See chapter 10.) Like the NSC, the Domestic Council had a staff of professionals and support personnel. Headed by John Ehrlichman, the presidential assistant for domestic policy, the staff dominated Nixon's domestic policy-making process during the last two years of his first term (1971–1972).[53]

The council conducted its activity through work groups headed by one of six assistant directors. These groups prepared working papers for the president, evaluated departmental proposals for legislation, and participated in drafting presidential messages to Congress and preparing supportive materials for specific legislative proposals. In addition to assisting the president in formulating policy proposals, the Domestic Council advocated, monitored, and evaluated policy.[54] This arrangement, in effect, made Ehrlichman the president's general agent for domestic policy. Under him, the council centralized control over domestic policy in the White House. The president's interests, as defined and expressed by Ehrlichman, took precedence over the interests of departments and agencies, as conveyed by cabinet members and agency heads.

The council's domination of domestic policy did not survive Ehrlichman's departure from the White House in April 1973.[55] The influence of the staff was clearly a function of Ehrlichman's status with the president. Under Ehrlichman's successor, Kenneth Cole, the Domestic Council became more of a service unit, and OMB resumed many of the functions of planning legislative programs.

In addition to the development of a presidential staff for domestic policy, Nixon effected a major transformation in OMB by using it for political purposes. The OMB director became indistinguishable from other high-level presidential assistants, and a layer of political appointees, called "program assistant directors," was placed above OMB's career staff. Nixon's politicization of OMB reduced its ability to serve the institutional needs of the presidency as an impartial professional staff agency and sparked considerable debate.[56]

President Ford used the OMB to facilitate the unusual transfer of power from Nixon to himself after Nixon's resignation, and Ford then relied on it to help plan and coordinate programs in a more traditional and less partisan manner than Nixon had. Initially, Ford intended to give the Domestic Council a major planning role by making Vice President Nelson Rockefeller its chair, but Rockefeller never became Ford's general agent for domestic policy. The long delay in congressional confirmation of Rockefeller's appointment and his conflict with White House chief of staff Donald Rumsfeld appear to have prevented such a development.[57] Ford preferred advice from a wide range of sources and seldom used the Domestic Council for policy planning.[58] President Carter abolished the council shortly after taking office, but he retained a domestic policy staff headed by one of his top aides, Stuart Eizenstat. In some respects, Eizenstat and his staff acquired a policy-making role resembling that of Ehrlichman and the Domestic Council in the Nixon administration. But Eizenstat and his staff members did not dominate the domestic policy process, and they functioned more in the roles of "effective administrator and of contributing advisor."[59]

Ronald Reagan, who came to office with a set, ideologically defined policy agenda and a strong commitment to cabinet government, created a new policy apparatus. The principal units were OMB, the Office of Policy Development (OPD), and seven cabinet councils. OMB's domestic policy involvement was especially crucial during Reagan's first year in office (1981), when the prime objective of drastically reducing the role of the federal government was linked to a budget reduction strategy implemented through use of the congressional budget process (see chapter 9). OMB director David Stockman was the principal architect of the first substantial rollback of the government's domestic programs since the New Deal.

The OPD, the Reagan administration's equivalent of Carter's domestic policy staff, worked through cabinet councils that had jurisdiction over economic affairs, commerce and trade, human resources, natural resources and environment, food and agriculture, legal policy, and management and administration.[60] The councils' members included appropriate cabinet and subcabinet officers and OMB personnel and the White House staff. Each council had a secretariat composed of department and agency representatives and used working groups to provide expertise and analyze issues. The cabinet council system did not, however, become the directing force for domestic policy. Other factors, particularly the president's long-range objectives and budget pressures, determined the agenda from the administration's beginning. Reagan's domestic policy apparatus worked out "details secondary to the president's fixed view of government,"[61] and its influence declined in his second term. Donald Regan, the newly appointed White House chief of staff, moved quickly to bring the three major policy areas—economics, national security, and domestic policy—under his control. Because the two remaining cabinet councils were chaired by Edwin Meese and James Baker, former White House advisers to the president, they enjoyed substantial autonomy to pursue their own policy projects. Overall, the administration's orientation shifted from changing policies to defending them. Having accomplished most of his initial domestic agenda, principally curtailment of the growth of federal agencies and a reduction in spending on them, Reagan concentrated his energies on national security and economic policy objectives.

The same situation continued under George H. W. Bush.[62] The assistant to the president for economic and domestic affairs, Roger Porter, a former Harvard professor, directed the Office of Policy Development. The OPD and the White House Office of Cabinet Affairs provided staff support for the Domestic Policy Council and the Economic Policy Council. Major issues usually bypassed the cabinet council system and were resolved by White House chief of staff John Sununu or the budget director, Richard Darman. Sununu's self-defined role was to protect the conservative integrity of the administration against those who urged the president to pursue more politically pragmatic options, and Darman functioned as a nonideological guardian of the budget and advocate of economic growth. Both intervened frequently on low-level issues. Some cabinet members, such as Secretary of Housing and Urban Development Jack Kemp and Secretary of Transportation Samuel Skinner, however, took the lead in developing major domestic legislative proposals and pushing them in Congress.[63]

The domestic policy process during the first two years of the Clinton administration was frequently frenetic and uncoordinated.[64] The Domestic Policy Council did not meet regularly. Development of health care reform, the principal initiative, was the responsibility of the large task force headed by Hillary Clinton and Magaziner. Cabinet members, such as Health and Human Services secretary Donna Shalala, did not play major roles in developing initiatives.

Although formally lodged in a policy council chaired by a high-level presidential assistant, the policy process was operationally centered in the president himself. Clinton, with his deep interest in domestic policy, presided over numerous wide-ranging and intensive meetings with his advisers that shifted back and forth between various policy alternatives. No single individual, such as the chief of staff, or group comparable to Reagan's Legislative Strategy Group was responsible for resolving disputes, imparting coherence and practicality to the many proposals, and moving them to Congress in a timely manner. Clinton resisted delegating such authority, and despite his intellectual brilliance and energy, he was unable to "ring-master" the domestic policy process effectively on his own.[65]

The situation changed dramatically after the Republicans won majorities in both congressional houses in the 1994 midterm elections. (Republicans had controlled the Senate as recently as 1986, but they had not led the House since 1954.) The new Republican majority largely controlled policymaking through most of 1995, and for a time the "Republican revolution" seemed to live up to its name.[66] Then came the notorious budget battle of 1995–1996, when Republicans pushed for sharp cuts in entitlement programs. President Clinton reasserted himself, exercised his first veto in response to the proposed cuts, and rallied opposition to the Republican plan. House Speaker Newt Gingrich refused to compromise, and the stalemate led to government shutdowns, which the public blamed on the Republicans. In the end, Clinton won the political battle.

Paul J. Quirk and William Cunion noted that the government shutdowns led to a new phase of Clinton's domestic presidency. It began in January 1996 and ran through the eruption of the Monica Lewinsky scandal in January 1998. It was marked by an unusual degree of cooperation between Clinton and the Republican majority in Congress, leading to a "notable amount of significant legislation," including a major overhaul of the welfare system.[67] With the help of political strategist Dick Morris, Clinton followed a centrist strategy of "triangulation" and finally seemed to master the art of domestic policymaking. But cooperation and policy output came to halt in 1998 and 1999 with the Lewinsky scandal and Clinton's impeachment.

In contrast to Clinton's frenetic style, George W. Bush's domestic policy process was highly structured. Bush, unlike any of his predecessors, came to office with a master's degree in business administration (from Harvard Business School). He surrounded himself with high-level advisers with experience not only in government but also as chief executive officers of major businesses. The strength of this business model was its efficiency; Bush insisted on a highly disciplined staff. He was comfortable working with a strong team of advisers, and he proved willing to delegate decision making. Yet he was also willing to assert control.[68]

Domestic policy seemed to be secondary in the Bush administration. Bush's Domestic Policy Council attracted far less attention than the National Security Council, its foreign policy counterpart, where policies on terrorism and Iraq were hammered out. Indeed, the Domestic Council's profile was so low that for a period it was unclear who the director of the council was.[69] John Bridgeland and Jay Lefkowitz were variously described in the media as the director, whereas other accounts identified Margaret L. Spellings (secretary of education in Bush's second term) as the director and the others as her deputies.[70] There is little doubt that Spellings, as director of the Office of Policy Development, supervised the others.[71]

In the view of one insider, it made little difference who headed the council. Domestic policy was dominated by the dictates of domestic politics, and that was the preserve of Karl Rove, the president's principal political adviser and head of the White House Office of Strategic Initiatives.[72] Ron Suskind, quoting extensively from off-the-record interviews and a long exchange with the original director of the Office of Faith-Based and Community Initiatives, John DiIulio—which DiIulio later disavowed—described the Bush White House as evidencing little serious discussion of domestic policy matters. (In the second term, Rove was formally given responsibility for coordinating policy.) Karl Zinsmeister became the Domestic Council's director in June 2006 after his predecessor, Claude A. Allen, was charged with "stealing more than $5,000 in a phony refund scheme" from retail stores.[73] Zinsmeister was best known for his outspoken defense of the administration's Iraq policy, further testimony to the short shrift the administration gave to domestic policy.

Like its predecessors, the Obama administration will establish procedures to coordinate policy making. Melody Barnes, the campaign's domestic policy adviser, was named to head the Domestic Policy Council. She had staff experience in both the House and Senate and had worked at the Center for American Progress, a think tank for progressive Democrats, before joining the campaign. Her expertise centered on civil rights and voting rights, women's health, and religious liberties.[74] But with many high profile advisers located in the White House, some observers wondered who would referee the many expected battles over policy priorities.

Conclusion

Presidents approach the task of making domestic policy with varying amounts of resources and differing policy opportunities. Their domestic policy leadership depends to a large extent on their effectiveness in using the available resources to exploit existing opportunities and create new ones. They are most apt to succeed when the three components of the policy stream—problems, solutions, and politics—converge. A president's ability to bring these three tributary streams together is one indication of effective policy leadership.

Successful policy leadership requires presidents to spend their resources carefully and exploit opportunities skillfully. To do so they must pay particular attention to four strategic factors: goals, priorities, timing, and costs and benefits.

Modest, flexible *goals* usually are easier to achieve than those that are extensive and ideologically derived. So, too, are goals that enjoy substantial support among the public and policy-making elites. In establishing their goals, presidents take such considerations into account along with their own values and beliefs. A primarily pragmatic set of objectives tends to be easier to accomplish than one ideologically derived. Such aims are less likely, however, to have an impact on society than more visionary and comprehensive objectives. In some circumstances, ideological goals may be highly appropriate. For example, Ronald Reagan initially struck a responsive note in Congress and the public with his unabashedly conservative domestic program. Presidents are free to be as pragmatic or as ideological as they wish in establishing their goals. However they decide, the mix they choose affects their policy leadership.

Closely related to goals, *priorities* also affect policy leadership. Presidents who clearly define their priorities generally have been more successful than those who have not done so because the policy process can handle only a few major issues at a time, even though many contend for attention. If a president does not indicate preferences, other participants will pursue their own objectives, possibly to the detriment of the president's. Nor is it realistic for presidents to expect that all of their goals will receive consideration to the exclusion of those of other participants. In this respect a comparison between Carter and Reagan is instructive. Carter developed a lengthy domestic agenda and insisted that all of his goals were vitally important to the nation and deserving of enactment. Congress responded by taking its time in dealing with Carter's program and by pursuing many of its own objectives. Some of Carter's wishes, such as welfare reform and national health insurance, were never adopted; others, such as a national energy policy, were passed in greatly modified form after extensive delay and bargaining. Many congressional Democrats complained that Carter failed to provide them with direction and guidance for his domestic proposals. In contrast, Reagan made his priorities clear from the beginning and continued to do so. Congress had little doubt about which goals Reagan considered vital—and on which he would spend political capital—and which were less important to him. Cutting domestic spending, strengthening national defense, and reducing and reforming taxes took precedence over balancing the federal budget, ending legalized abortion, and restoring school prayer.

Timing, the third strategic consideration in successful policy leadership, is crucial to effective exploitation of opportunities. If opportunities are missed, they may be lost indefinitely. Good timing also involves taking advantage of the regular policy and electoral cycles. Proposals submitted at appropriate times in those cycles have greater likelihood of adoption. Proposals also can be withheld until conditions are ripe for their submission. A proposal with limited support can be moved to the top of the agenda and pushed successfully as the result of a focusing event such as a disaster or a crisis. Presidents able to time the presentation of proposals to coincide with favorable events and conditions are more likely to be effective policy leaders than those lacking such a sense of timing. Two presidents with effective timing of domestic proposals were Franklin Roosevelt, during the first hundred days of the New Deal when the Great Depression provided the rationale for a comprehensive set of economic recovery and reform laws, and Lyndon Johnson, who in early 1964 used the shock of the Kennedy assassination to secure passage of the Civil Rights Act. In contrast, Bill Clinton's poor timing of his health care reform and welfare reform proposals contributed to their failure.

Finally, successful policy leadership requires presidents to be attentive to the *costs and benefits* of raising problems for consideration and posing solutions. As presidents decide which problems and issues to emphasize, they focus on political benefits. They select agenda items according to the prospective electoral, historical, and programmatic benefits of the times.[75] When presidents select solutions for problems they are addressing, their emphasis is on costs.[76] Political costs, assessed in terms of congressional, electoral, bureaucratic, and interest group support, enter presidential calculations at each stage of the process, and presidents and other actors have tended to view political costs in terms of avoiding blame and claiming credit for the outcomes, a pattern already visible in the 1980s and even more prominent in the decades that followed.[77]

Economic costs sharply limit the policy alternatives. Budget pressures force presidents to make hard choices, such as whether to support new programs and which existing programs to emphasize, maintain, or reduce. Technical costs and questions of workability also enter the selection of policy alternatives.

No prescription or formula can guarantee that a president will provide successful domestic policy leadership, in part because some problems, such as the high unemployment rate among African American men, are very difficult to solve, or solutions do not exist. Another reason for the absence of a workable formula is that conditions constantly change. Some problems may be solved only to reemerge in a new form; others may decline in importance. Solutions viable today may not be a few years hence, or solutions may have unanticipated consequences that become problems in their own right. Political conditions, such as the popular mood or control of Congress, are in flux, so strategies may have to be modified frequently. Because many of the requirements of successful policy leadership are not fixed, what worked well for one president may be only partially useful to those who come later.

Even presidents who take office committed to concentrating their energies on domestic policy encounter extensive frustrations. They may enjoy some initial successes, as did Reagan; but the difficulties of accomplishing additional objectives eventually increase, and the sharing of power with Congress, the bureaucracy, and organized interests becomes ever more burdensome. The natural tendency is for presidents to turn their attention to national security or economic policy. In these areas, the challenges are more immediately threatening to the general welfare; the constraints on a president's ability to act, although very real, are not as frustrating; and successful policy leadership appears less elusive. Presidential difficulties in achieving domestic policy progress have mounted so rapidly that Paul Light, a long-time student of presidential policy making, wondered aloud at the end of the Clinton years "whether the presidency as an institution is properly configured for making domestic policy."[78] Taking a long-term look, he found that as the organizational capacity to make policy grew, the actual product—the number of proposals and their scope—declined.

SUGGESTED READINGS

Ainsworth, Scott H. *Analyzing Interest Groups: Group Influence on People and Policies.* New York: W. W. Norton, 2002.

Baumgartner, Frank R., and Byron D. Jones. *Agendas and Instability in American Politics.* Chicago: University of Chicago Press, 1993.

Kessel, John H. *Presidents, the Presidency, and the Political Environment.* Washington, D.C.: CQ Press, 2001.

Kingdon, John W. *Agendas, Alternatives, and Public Policies.* 2nd ed. New York: Longman, 2003.

Lammers, William W., and Michael A. Genovese. *The Presidency and Domestic Policy: Comparing Leadership Styles, FDR to Clinton.* Washington, D.C.: CQ Press, 2000.

Light, Paul C. *The President's Agenda: Domestic Policy Choice from Kennedy to Clinton.* 3rd ed. Baltimore: Johns Hopkins University Press, 1999.

Rudalevige, Andrew. *Managing the President's Program: Presidential Leadership and Legislative Policy Formulation.* Princeton: Princeton University Press, 2002.

Shull, Steven A. *American Civil Rights Policy from Truman to Clinton: The Role of Presidential Leadership.* Armonk, N.Y.: M. E. Sharpe, 1999.

Warshaw, Shirley Anne. *The Domestic Presidency: Policy Making in the White House.* Boston: Allyn and Bacon, 1996.

NOTES

1. The concept of "issue congestion" was developed by Hugh Heclo, "One Executive Branch or Many?" in *Both Ends of the Avenue,* ed. Anthony King (Washington, D.C.: American Enterprise Institute, 1983), 26–58.

2. Theodore J. Lowi, "American Business, Public Policy, Case Studies, and Political Theory," *World Politics* (July 1964): 677–715.

3. Steven A. Shull, *Domestic Policy Formation: Presidential-Congressional Partnership?* (Westport, Conn.: Greenwood Press, 1983), 155; Steven A. Shull, "Change in Presidential Policy Initiatives," *Western Political Quarterly* (September 1983): 497.

4. John H. Kessel, *Presidential Parties* (Homewood, Ill.: Dorsey, 1984), 112–115.

5. J. Newton-Small and Michael Scherer, "Does Obama Have a Double-Standard on Earmarks?" *Time* magazine, February 26, 2009, http://www.time.com/time/politics/article/0,8599,1881855,00.html.

6. Jason D. Mycoff and Joseph A. Pika, *Confrontation and Compromise: Presidential and Congressional Leadership, 2001–2006* (Lanham, Md.: Rowman and Littlefield, 2007), chap. 7.

7. Kessel, *Presidential Parties,* 68–69.

8. The policy-stream metaphor borrows from Paul Light, "The Presidential Policy Stream," in *The Presidency and the Political System,* ed. Michael Nelson (Washington, D.C.: CQ Press, 1984), 423–448; and John W. Kingdon, *Agendas, Alternatives, and Public Policies,* 2nd ed. (New York: HarperCollins, 1995), 85–86.

9. This discussion follows Kingdon, *Agendas,* chap. 5.

10. Christopher H. Foreman Jr., "The Braking of the President: Shifting Context and the Bush Domestic Agenda," in *The George W. Bush Legacy*, ed. Colin Campbell, Bert A. Rockman, and Andrew Rudalevige (Washington, D.C.: CQ Press, 2007), 267.

11. The discussion of the development of the health care issue follows B. Guy Peters, *American Public Policy: Promise and Performance*, 3rd ed. (Chatham, N.J.: Chatham House, 1993), 230–235.

12. Robin Toner, "2008 Candidates Vow to Overhaul U.S. Health Care," *New York Times*, July 6, 2007, www.nytimes.com/2007/07/06/us/politics/06health.html?ex=1186113600&en=2fafcafdf4fa57ca&ei=5070.

13. Paul Light, *The President's Agenda: Domestic Policy Choice from Kennedy to Reagan*, 3rd ed. (Baltimore: Johns Hopkins University Press, 1991), chap. 3; and Light, "The Presidential Policy Stream," 427–428.

14. Ironically, Nixon's preoccupation with the judgment of history helped cut short his presidency. He consistently explained the installation of the secret taping system in the Oval Office as motivated by his desire to have a complete and accurate record for use by historians. That taped record provided the "smoking gun" that led the House Judiciary Committee to vote impeachment charges, which prompted his resignation in August 1974.

15. Kingdon, *Agendas*, 142–143.

16. Jeff Fishel, *Presidents and Promises: From Campaign Pledge to Presidential Performance* (Washington, D.C.: CQ Press, 1984).

17. Kingdon, *Agendas*, 131.

18. Vincent J. Burke and Vee Burke, *Nixon's Good Deed: Welfare Reform* (New York: Columbia University Press, 1974); Laurence E. Lynn Jr. and David D. Whitman, *The President as Policymaker: Jimmy Carter and Welfare Reform* (Philadelphia: Temple University Press, 1981).

19. This discussion is based on Kingdon, *Agendas*, chap. 7.

20. Democrats maintained united government from 1977 through 1980 and again from 1993 through 1994. Republicans maintained united government from the 2002 midterm elections through the 2006 elections.

21. Jeff Yates and Andrew Whitford, "Institutional Foundations of the President's Issue Agenda," *Political Research Quarterly* 58 (December 2005): 577–585.

22. Matthew Eshbaugh-Soha, "The Politics of Presidential Agendas," *Political Research Quarterly* 58 (June 2005): 257–268.

23. Foreman, "The Braking of the President," 282.

24. This discussion follows Light, "The Presidential Policy Stream," 440–446.

25. Paul J. Quirk and Joseph Hinchcliffe, "Domestic Policy: The Trials of a Centrist Democrat," in *The Clinton Presidency: First Appraisals*, ed. Colin Campbell and Bert A. Rockman (Chatham, N.J.: Chatham House, 1996), 264–267.

26. David W. Moore, "Initial Job Approval for Bush at 57 percent, but Highest Disapproval of any President since Polling Began," Gallup Poll release, February 6, 2001, www.gallup.com.

27. Quoted in Ron Fournier, "Bush's Test: To Unite the Great Divide," *Pittsburgh Post-Gazette*, January 21, 2001, A9.

28. Transcript, Bush press conference, November 4, 2004, http://www.nytimes.com/2004/11/04/politics/04BUSHTRANS.html.

29. Gary C. Jacobson, *A Divider, Not a Uniter: George W. Bush and the American People* (New York: Longman, 2006).

30. Light, "The Presidential Policy Stream," 444–445.

31. Kingdon, *Agendas*, 194–195.

32. Kessel, *Presidential Parties*, 60.

33. Rebecca Adams, "Lame Duck or Leap Frog?" *CQ Weekly*, February 12, 2007, 450.

34. Light, *The President's Agenda*, 36–38.

35. For an excellent account of interest groups, see Scott H. Ainsworth, *Analyzing Interest Groups: Group Influence on People and Policies* (New York: W. W. Norton, 2002).

36. Harold Wolman and Fred Teitelbaum, "Interest Groups and the Reagan Presidency," in *The Reagan Presidency and the Governing of America,* ed. Lester M. Salamon and Michael S. Lund (Washington, D.C.: Urban Institute Press, 1985), 299–301.

37. Mancur Olson, *The Rise and Decline of Nations* (New Haven: Yale University Press, 1982), 44.

38. Richard E. Neustadt, *Presidential Power and the Modern Presidents: The Politics of Leadership from Roosevelt to Reagan* (New York: Free Press, 1990), 29.

39. Mycoff and Pika, *Confrontation and Compromise,* chap. 2.

40. Leroy Rieselbach, *Congressional Reform: The Changing Modern Congress* (Washington, D.C.: CQ Press, 1994); Roger H. Davidson, ed., *The Postreform Congress* (New York: St. Martin's Press, 1992).

41. Donna Cassata, "Republicans Bask in Success of Rousing Performance," *Congressional Quarterly Weekly Report,* April 8, 1995, 986, 988, 990; Jennifer Babson, "Armey Stood Guard over Contract," *Congressional Quarterly Weekly Report,* April 8, 1995, 987; and Adam Clymer, "House Party: With Political Discipline It Works Like Parliament," *New York Times,* August 6, 1995, E6.

42. The Republicans angered Democrats by holding open the vote on the Medicare prescription drug bill for nearly three hours rather than the usual fifteen minutes to secure the requisite number of votes.

43. Lester M. Salamon, "The Presidency and Domestic Policy Formulation," in *The Illusion of Presidential Government,* ed. Hugh Heclo and Lester M. Salamon (Boulder: Westview Press, 1981), 179.

44. Richard E. Neustadt, "The Presidency and Legislation: The Growth of Central Clearance," *American Political Science Review* (September 1954): 641–670; Robert S. Gilmour, "Central Clearance: A Revised Perspective," *Public Administration Review* (March–April 1971): 150–158.

45. Richard E. Neustadt, "The Presidency and Legislation: Planning the President's Program," *American Political Science Review* (December 1955): 980–1018; Larry Berman, *The Office of Management and Budget and the Presidency* (Princeton: Princeton University Press, 1979), 42–43; Stephen J. Wayne, *The Legislative Presidency* (New York: Harper and Row, 1978), 103–105.

46. Norman C. Thomas and Harold L. Wolman, "The Presidency and Policy Formation: The Task Force Device," *Public Administration Review* (September-October 1969): 459–471.

47. Text of the reports were published in *New Frontiers of the Kennedy Administration* (Washington, D.C.: Public Affairs Press, 1961).

48. Lyndon B. Johnson, *The Vantage Point* (New York: Holt, Rinehart and Winston, 1971), 326.

49. Paul Light, *Artful Work: The Politics of Social Security Reform* (New York: Random House, 1985), 232.

50. Quirk and Hinchcliffe, "Domestic Policy," 274–275.

51. Ibid., 275.

52. Michael Abramowitz and Steven Mufson, "Papers Detail Industry's Role in Cheney's Energy Report," *Washington Post,* July 18, 2007, A1.

53. Raymond J. Waldman, "The Domestic Council: Innovation in Presidential Government," *Public Administration Review* (May-June 1976): 260–268.

54. Margaret Jane Wyszomirski, "The Roles of a Presidential Office for Domestic Policy: Three Models and Four Cases," in *The Presidency and Policy Making,* ed. George C. Edwards III, Steven A. Shull, and Norman C. Thomas (Pittsburgh: University of Pittsburgh Press, 1985), 134.

55. John Helmer and Louis Maisel, "Analytical Problems in the Study of Presidential Advice: The Domestic Council Staff in Flux," *Presidential Studies Quarterly* (Winter 1978): 52–53.

56. A sharp debate raged over politicization of OMB and the institutionalized presidency generally. Berman, in *The Office of Management and Budget,* argued that politicization damaged, if not destroyed, the

capacity of OMB to serve the institutional needs of the presidency in a professional manner. In contrast, Terry Moe, in a seminal essay, viewed politicization as a logical (indeed necessary) institutional development resulting from the extensive and steady growth of "expectations surrounding presidential performance." See Terry Moe, "The Politicized Presidency," in *The New Direction in American Politics*, ed. John E. Chubb and Paul E. Peterson (Washington, D.C.: Brookings, 1985), 269.

57. Wyszomirski, "The Roles of a Presidential Office," 136–137.

58. Wayne, *The Legislative Presidency*, 123.

59. Wyszomirski, "The Roles of a Presidential Office," 140.

60. For an extended description of the OPD-cabinet council system, see Chester A. Newland, "Executive Office Policy Apparatus: Enforcing the Reagan Agenda," in Salamon and Lund, *The Reagan Presidency*, 153–159. Martin Anderson, who was Reagan's first director of the OPD, provides a participant's perspective on the cabinet councils in *Revolution* (New York: Harcourt Brace Jovanovich, 1988), chap. 19.

61. Newland, "Executive Office Policy Apparatus," 160.

62. This discussion follows Colin Campbell, "The White House and the Presidency under the 'Let's Deal' President," in *The Bush Presidency: First Appraisals*, ed. Colin Campbell and Bert A. Rockman (Chatham, N.J.: Chatham House, 1991), 210–212.

63. Julie Rovner, "On Policy Front, Home Is Not Where Bush's Heart Is," *Congressional Quarterly Weekly Report*, February 2, 1991, 292.

64. This discussion follows Colin Campbell, "Management in a Sandbox," in Campbell and Rockman, *The Clinton Presidency*, 77–80.

65. Ibid., 79.

66. Paul J. Quirk and William Cunion, "Clinton's Domestic Policy: The Lessons of a 'New Democrat,'" in *The Clinton Legacy*, ed. Colin Campbell and Bert A. Rockman (New York: Chatham House, 2000), 208.

67. Ibid., 210–211.

68. Bill Keller, "The Radical Presidency of George W. Bush," *New York Times Magazine*, January 26, 2003, 26.

69. For an account of this confusion, see Timothy Noah, "Who Is the Director of the Domestic Policy Council," *Slate*, posted January 15, 2003, www.slate.com/id/2077046/.

70. Martha Joynt Kumar, "Recruiting and Organizing the White House Staff," *PS: Political Science and Politics* 35 (March 2002): 38.

71. Andrew Rudalevige, "'The Decider': Issue Management and the Bush White House," in Campbell, Rockman, and Rudalevige, *The George W. Bush Legacy*, 144.

72. Ron Suskind, "Why Are These Men Laughing," *Esquire*, January 2003, www.ronsuskind.com/newsite/articles/archives/000032.html; and www.esquire.com/features/ESQ0103-JAN_ROVE_rev_2. DiIulio's original communication is also available at www.esquire.com/features/dilulio.

73. Michael A. Fletcher, "Editor at Conservative Magazine To Be Top Policy Adviser to Bush," *Washington Post*, May 25, 2006, A4. On Allen, see Ian Urbina and David D. Kirkpatrick, "For Ex-Aide to Bush, Quick Fall after Long Climb," *New York Times*, March 14, 2006, A1.

74. See Domestic Policy Council at http://www.whitehouse.gov/administration/eop/dpc/.

75. Light, *The President's Agenda*, 71.

76. Ibid., 134–136.

77. R. Kent Weaver, *Automatic Government: The Politics of Indexation* (Washington, D.C.: Brookings, 1988), chap. 2.

78. Paul C. Light, "Domestic Policy Making," *Presidential Studies Quarterly* 30 (March 2000): 111.

CHAPTER 9

The Politics of Economic Policy

During the Great Depression, Franklin Roosevelt used radio broadcasts from the White House, known as "fireside chats," to persuade the public to support his unprecedented economic policies.

Americans expect presidents to provide peace and prosperity. As George W. Bush left office, neither condition prevailed. The United States was waging costly wars in Iraq and Afghanistan. Even more worrisome was the condition of the economy, which had deteriorated in fall 2008 to such a degree that nearly two-thirds of the public identified it as their principal concern when they chose between Senators John McCain and Barack Obama in the fall election (see chapter 2). So there was little doubt about what President Obama's number one problem was when he took office in January 2009. Some economists feared that the recession had the potential to become a second Great Depression, the prolonged period of massive unemployment that gripped the United States and the world during the 1930s. Conditions worsened during the final months of the Bush administration, which struggled to stem the tide as the nation awaited the inauguration of a new president. There was a sense of suspended animation as the

368

Bush-Obama transition unfolded, eerily similar to the period following the election of 1932 when the nation awaited the arrival of Franklin D. Roosevelt in the White House. What would the president do to address the economic crisis and put the nation back on the path to prosperity?

Answers presume causes. What caused the economic meltdown? A late-summer crisis in the U.S. mortgage market triggered massive losses on stock markets around the globe in fall 2008. Lenders in the United States had been too anxious to make new loans during the mid-decade housing boom, but as workers began to lose their jobs in August 2007 and monthly payments on adjustable rate mortgages began to rise, large numbers of borrowers defaulted not only on their mortgages, but also on car loans and other debts. Several mortgage companies went bankrupt. Housing sales suddenly came to a screeching halt, prices dropped, and the construction industry began laying off workers. The downturn in housing also affected those who manufacture and sell durable goods such as appliances, carpeting, and furniture. Employment levels continued to slide through the next year and, to make matters worse, American consumers were hit with a dramatic rise in oil prices that resulted in increased prices for food and gas.[1] Pressures mounted on banks whose reserves became dangerously low, leading them to halt new loans to businesses and consumers. And the problem became global when securities that rested on the U.S. mortgage market, one form of *derivatives,* declined rapidly in value, causing panic among individuals and institutions that owned the investments.

The Bush administration and the Federal Reserve Board (usually referred to as "the Fed") tried to respond. Their initial actions were piecemeal, aimed at propping up single banks and firms that came under financial pressure. The Wall Street investment bank Bear Stearns was kept out of bankruptcy with a $29 billion package from the Fed, but another firm, Lehman Brothers, was allowed to go bankrupt. Freddie Mac and Fannie Mae, two government-backed companies that are central to the nation's mortgage industry, were tottering. Congress authorized Treasury Secretary Henry Paulson to save the companies with a $200 billion bailout. Nevertheless, the banks were experiencing a growing crisis in liquidity—the ability of consumers and business to borrow money to spend or invest—which had dire consequences for the country. Investment in new plants and enterprises ground to a halt. Consumer purchases of cars and other items declined precipitously. Banks had used up their own reserves and were unable to get new money to lend out. There was fear that depositors would soon start taking their money out of banks and force many of them to fail. The conditions likely to produce an economic depression were lining up like a row of dominoes ready to topple.

Dramatic action was needed. Paulson and Fed chairman Ben Bernanke frantically devised a plan to restore confidence in the banking industry by buying up distressed assets—those based on mortgages that were going into default. The Troubled Asset Relief Program (TARP) would allow the Treasury Department to spend up to $700 billion to stabilize U.S. banks. The cost of the plan, the absence of details (it was originally only three pages long), and the potential consequences for a free-market economy raised red flags on Capitol Hill. Despite predictions of dire consequences, the House of Representatives initially rejected the proposal; even President Bush's own partisans voted overwhelmingly against it. In response the stock market suffered the largest one-day sell-off in the history of the market. The Senate stepped in two days later and approved a modified plan with features that they expected would mollify the House. Two days after that, under pressure from their party leaders and the president, the House reversed course, although a majority of Republicans still voted no. Congress had imposed conditions, insisting on oversight powers and a reduced initial outlay of $350 billion. In fact, Treasury soon reconsidered the original plan and decided not to purchase bad loans; instead, it invested the money in the banks expecting them to start lending to consumers. In essence, the taxpayers became investors in the banks but had little control over how the funds would be used. To the outrage of many, banks did not simply turn around and pump new liquidity into the system. Some continued to conduct business as usual, including staff retreats at expensive resorts and awarding large year-end bonuses to employees.

Among the first moves of the new administration was the attempt to combat the recession. What tools did Obama have? Would he succeed? Economic issues are often at the heart of national politics. They helped account for George H. W. Bush's loss in the 1992 election. The public blamed him for the 1991–1992 recession. Charging that Bush had indeed neglected the economy, Democratic candidate Bill Clinton focused his campaign on economic issues. (A sign stating "It's the Economy, Stupid" hung on the wall of his national campaign headquarters.)[2] That year's independent candidate, Ross Perot, stressed the importance of ending the deficit and reducing the expanding national debt. The electorate responded by choosing Clinton while giving Perot 19 percent of the vote. Not surprisingly, the deficit and other economic issues dominated Clinton's first two years in office, but Clinton got only modest credit for presiding over a period of record economic growth with low inflation that coincided with a near-miraculous transformation in the annual budget from a $290 billion deficit in 1992 to a $69.2 billion surplus in 1998. Clinton enthusiasts hailed this turnaround as a great achievement, but many analysts saw it as the product of luck and the efforts of the long-serving Fed chairman, Alan Greenspan.[3]

Like Obama, George W. Bush had also begun his presidency as the economy was slowing down, but he largely escaped blame for rising unemployment, dramatically lower stock prices, a resurgence in budget deficits to record highs, and declining public confidence in corporate America.[4] The reason was that the events of September 11 caused the nation's economy to reel from damage to its financial infrastructure and dealt an almost fatal blow to the nation's airlines. But it was impossible for the Bush administration to avoid blame for the recession that started in 2007, and as conditions worsened in 2008, economic issues definitely influenced the fall elections. Modern presidents are highly attentive to economic conditions, but that was not always the case. Some presidents who confronted serious economic adversity, such as Martin Van Buren in 1837, Ulysses S. Grant in 1873, Grover Cleveland in 1893, Theodore Roosevelt in 1907, and Warren G. Harding in 1921, did little more than ride out the storm. The electorate, however, reacted by denying reelection to Van Buren and by inflicting sizable losses on the president's party in the midterm congressional elections of 1838, 1874, and 1894. In fact, the existence of a relationship between business cycles and election results was known long before Edward Tufte's precise empirical analysis of the phenomenon.[5] Only since the 1930s, however, have presidents attempted to *control* business cycles through public policy, and the public has come to expect them to do so.

This chapter examines the president's economic policy responsibilities and activities. It begins by distinguishing between actions designed to manage the entire economy (macroeconomic policy) and those meant to control specific aspects of the economy (microeconomic policy). The primary focus of the chapter is on macroeconomic policy. We review presidential efforts to manage the economy from 1933 to 2009 and then describe the politics of macroeconomic policymaking. Next we analyze how the president makes economic policy and how presidents since Dwight D. Eisenhower have handled the problem of coordinating economic policy. The chapter concludes with an assessment of the congressional role in macroeconomic policymaking.

Macroeconomic Policy

Not since the Great Depression of the 1930s have Americans been so keenly aware of the ways that government can intervene to influence the economy, efforts known as **macroeconomic policy.** The government has two principal strategies at its disposal: fiscal policy and monetary policy. Using **fiscal policy,** the government tries to regulate the level of the nation's economic activity by varying taxes and public expenditures. A policy of higher spending and lower taxes—adopted by the Obama administration in 2009—aims to expand the economy; one of less spending and higher taxes—potentially necessary if the economic stimulus is too great—aims to contract it. A **budget deficit,** which occurs when spending exceeds tax revenues, stimulates economic activity, and a **budget surplus** (tax revenues exceed spending) slows the economy. The president and Congress jointly make fiscal policy. They determine expenditures through budgeting and appropriations, and they establish taxes through legislation. **Monetary policy** refers to a government's efforts, through its central bank (in the United States, the Federal Reserve System), to regulate economic activity by controlling the supply of money—currency and credit. An independent agency, the Board of Governors of the Federal Reserve System, makes monetary policy. Although fiscal policy and monetary policy constitute distinct realms of policymaking, administrations seek to coordinate them.

Since the Depression, the goals of macroeconomic policy have remained constant: *to hold down the rate of inflation, to establish and maintain full employment, and to achieve a steady rate of economic growth.* Policymakers, however, have pursued these goals through alternative theories: classical conservative economics, Keynesianism, monetarism, and supply-side economics.

Conservative economic theory lost credibility during the Depression when the administrations of Herbert Hoover and Franklin D. Roosevelt (at the outset) stressed balancing the budget and failed to restore confidence in the economy and produce the desired upturn. FDR quickly discovered that emergency spending and loan programs provided relief and produced a measure of recovery. The ideas of John Maynard Keynes, a British economist Roosevelt met in 1934, offered an explanation for why fiscal stimulus is effective and eventually provided a rationale for deficit spending. Keynes argued that a drop in private demand for goods and services causes an economic decline. A government could stimulate demand by increasing its own expenditures or increasing those of consumers by reducing taxes. The temporary deficits created by fiscal stimulation would be financed by government borrowing and repaid during periods of hyperactivity in the economy. Eventually, the economy's recovery following mobilization during World War II, which was supported by government spending, provided most economists with empirical validation of Keynes's basic theories. Conservative economics, however, retained its hold on many political leaders, such as Eisenhower, who made balanced budgets the goal and regarded fiscal stimulation of lagging demand as an emergency measure.

We saw evidence of these beliefs again in 2009 when the startlingly large projected deficits arising from President Obama's proposed budget alarmed lawmakers committed to the goal of balanced budgets.

While **Keynesianism** was establishing itself as the new orthodoxy, another theory emerged to challenge it. The monetarists, under the leadership of economist Milton Friedman, held that the key to maintaining economic stability lay not in stimulating demand but in limiting the growth rate of the money supply to no more than the growth rate of the economy. Inflation occurs, monetarists claim, when the money supply expands too rapidly. The only remedy for inflation is a painful contraction in the money supply. Monetarists hold that fiscal policy and the size of budget deficits are subordinate to monetary policy and the growth rate of the money supply, which for them constitute the basic means of managing the economy.

Monetarism gained adherents as the limitations of Keynesianism became apparent during the 1970s. Keynesian theory has an inflationary bias—its primary defect as a macroeconomic theory. Decisions on taxing and spending are made by the president and members of Congress—politicians concerned with reelection—and not by professional economists. Consequently, it has proved easier in practice to increase spending and cut taxes, the Keynesian prescription for expansion, than to cut spending and increase taxes, the theory's remedy for inflation. In the 1970s, when inflation became the nation's leading economic problem, political decision makers were unwilling to impose the Keynesian solution. Although the inflationary bias of Keynesianism is a political defect rather than a weakness in the theory itself, this bias nevertheless has made it less attractive than other theories as a guide to policy.

Monetarism, whatever its theoretical merits and limitations, offered a politically palatable way to control inflation through the autonomous **Federal Reserve Board,** which reduces inflation by contracting the money supply. Political officeholders can blame the consequences of monetary contractions—high interest rates and rising unemployment—on the Fed and its amorphous supporters: "Wall Street" investing interests and the banks. But monetarism also became politically unattractive when efforts to control inflation proved especially painful during the late 1970s. By the early 1980s a new theoretical approach, **supply-side economics,** emerged and President Reagan embraced it.

Essentially, supply-side economics is an amalgam of Keynesianism and monetarism.[6] Supply-siders endorse strict monetary restraint as the means of controlling inflation, but they also believe, unlike pure monetarists, that fiscal policy can be used to achieve macroeconomic policy objectives. The supply-siders assert, however, that the Keynesians misdirect government efforts. Instead of stimulating demand through tax cuts for consumers, the supply-siders seek to stimulate supply through tax cuts for businesses and investors that provide incentives to encourage additional investments and enhanced productivity, which in turn increase the supply of goods and services. The additional jobs created ultimately fuel consumer buying, although the focus of the policy is producers, not consumers. Supply-siders are not disturbed by budget deficits resulting from tax-cut incentives. They believe an expanded economy will not be inflationary and eventually will generate enough revenues at lower rates of taxation to balance the budget.

Supply-side economics draws sharp criticism from both liberals and conservatives who doubt the validity of assumptions on which the theory rests. Liberals charge that it is another version of the discredited "trickle down" approach to economic policy, under which tax advantages for the affluent are justified on the grounds that they eventually lead to prosperity for all. Conservatives fear that supply-side tolerance of budget deficits leads to excessive rates of inflation and erodes confidence in the monetary system. Even those critics who would like supply-side policies to work do not believe they can. Experience since 1981 with a massive cut in federal income taxes, phased in over several years and based on supply-side reasoning, supports their pessimism. The economy expanded steadily during the 1980s and 1990s, but a balanced budget was not achieved until 1998, when there was a modest surplus. The Democrats, whose willingness to raise taxes in 1993 helped increase government revenues, claimed credit for this accomplishment. But when signs of an economic slowdown emerged in late 2000, tax cuts became a campaign issue. With a new administration in place, the Republican Congress passed three tax reductions at the urging of President Bush. These cuts provided another opportunity to observe how the federal budget is affected by supply-side policies in the long run. In his memoir, Greenspan harshly criticized this new round of supply-side tax cuts, which were taken with little consideration of how they would increase the deficit.[7] (Committed supply-siders, it should be pointed out, will disagree with this account. In their view, Reagan's tax cuts fueled the economic boom of the 1990s, not the Democrats' commitment to a balanced budget.)

During the 1980s and 1990s federal policymakers were forced to rely more heavily on monetary policy than on fiscal policy to manage the economy. Coping with large and persistent deficits, presidents had little room to increase spending or reduce taxes, actions that would have further expanded the deficit. Moreover, Republicans and Democrats disagreed vehemently over the level and purposes of government spending and the structure of taxes—who pays how much. In this intractable setting, monetary policy instruments became the only viable alternative for macroeconomic management.[8] Although the appearance of budget surpluses seemed to breathe new life into fiscal policy, this revival proved short-lived. The Bush tax cuts adopted in 2001–2003 were so large that the federal government once again began to run a substantial deficit, but administration defenders claimed it stemmed from other sources.

Efforts to Stabilize the Economy, 2008–2009

The severe recession that began in 2007 once again highlighted the unique role played by the federal government in combating nationwide economic problems. Both fiscal and monetary policies sought to counteract the severe contraction in consumption, investment, and jobs experienced by the country. In effect, only the federal government could take action. State and local governments, which are required by law to balance their budgets, are forced to behave like Herbert Hoover did between 1929 and 1932. By contrast, the Fed has the authority to print currency, thereby expanding the money supply, and Congress and the president can adopt expansionary fiscal policies, that is, increase government spending and reduce taxes. Working together, the instruments of both monetary and fiscal policy were put into motion in 2009.

By February 2009 the national unemployment rate stood at 8.1 percent, a figure that translated into 12.5 million unemployed Americans, a level well above what is considered acceptable in the United States. The economy was contracting, not growing, at a rate of 6.2 percent over the final three months of 2008, and both figures were moving in the wrong direction; unemployment was increasing from month to month as more workers received pink slips, and economic activity was declining. The Bush administration and Congress had tried to head off the recession a year earlier with a stimulus package. Tax rebates in the form of U.S. Treasury checks of up to $600 for individuals and $1200 for couples were distributed to eligible tax payers. Businesses could also deduct from their taxes a larger portion of the cost of investments in new equipment. The downside of these actions was that both the annual budget deficit and the national debt (total indebtedness) rose to unprecedented levels, occasioning complaints from those wedded to balanced budgets. Total cost of the package was $168 billion.[9]

The Fed aggressively used monetary policy to combat the worsening economy. It began to cut interest rates in September 2007 on the short-term loans it makes to banks and continued to reduce that rate until it reached zero in December 2008. The Fed backed the bailouts of Bear Stearns and American International Group (AIG), the giant insurance company that has been blamed for many of the riskiest loan transactions that began to echo through the economy. Chairman Bernanke then invented new ways that the Fed could build liquidity back into the system and get money flowing again. By February 2009 the Fed had injected an additional $1.9 trillion in credit throughout the financial system while working first with Paulson and then with Timothy Geithner, Obama's Treasury secretary.[10] Bernanke, a professional economist with a research specialty in the Great Depression, made speeches and appeared frequently before Congress to explain these strategies.

When the economy continued in its tailspin, the Obama administration proposed an even larger stimulus package. The American Recovery and Reinvestment Act of 2009 was approved exactly a year after George W. Bush signed the earlier effort. Rather than lump-sum checks, individuals and couples would have less money withheld from their pay checks up to maximums of $400 and $800 through the end of 2010.[11] Other tax credits were given for child care, college tuition, and home buying. Businesses that invested in clean energy technology could qualify for tax credits, as well. The same bill also increased government spending for targeted projects: public works infrastructure, expanded Medicare and Medicaid payments, increased Pell grants to college students, new energy research, extended benefits for food stamps and the child nutrition program, and financial assistance to state and local governments. The goals of the legislation were twofold: reduce taxes on middle class Americans who, it was hoped, would spend the additional money and create jobs through the targeted spending. This was a classic Keynesian formulation sold by President Obama as a way to improve the country and save jobs at the same time.

The Republicans were not buying. They complained that Democrats had added many of their pet projects onto this almost 1,100-page bill, not as a way to help the economy but as a way to expand government. In the House, not a single Republican voted for any version of the bill. In the Senate, three Republican moderates won concessions from the Democrats, and later conference committee negotiations reduced the overall projected cost of the bill to $789 billion, with $282 billion in tax cuts and $507 billion in additional spending. The three Republican votes made final passage possible, giving the Democrats enough support to fend off a Republican filibuster.[12] The scope of the package, likened by many to Roosevelt's New Deal, was nevertheless challenged by some economists as too small. Again, the package relied on borrowed money and increased the size of the deficit.

Government's Four Strategies to Rescue the Economy

Traditional macroeconomic policy was only part of the effort made by government. The Bush and Obama stimulus packages together totaled $914.9 billion, money essentially spent by *government as a consumer,* one of several roles identified by *CQ Weekly* as a way to describe the many actions taken over twelve months. This was the traditional countercyclical effort prescribed by Keynesian thinking. But the Obama administration also announced two other major initiatives to address the nation's economic problems. An additional financial rescue package would spend the second $350 billion appropriated for TARP and fund a new program titled TALF (Term Asset-Backed Loan Facility) intended to stimulate consumer borrowing. Secretary Geithner also announced an ill-defined public-private partnership to remove bad assets from banks with an unknown cost. The third leg of the administration's economic rescue strategy was designed to help homeowners renegotiate the terms of their mortgages in order to keep them in their homes.

Therefore, in addition to being a direct purchaser and stimulator of services, the government committed even more money to these other roles. At the forefront was *government as an investor* when the Treasury and the Federal Reserve put money into banks (TARP), acquired bad mortgage assets, helped homeowners refinance their mortgages, and provided help to Fannie Mae and Freddie Mac. By February 2009 these commitments were estimated at $1.6 trillion. The Federal Reserve played the role of *government as lender,* pumping nearly $850 billion into banks on a short-term basis, and the Treasury made loans to two U.S. automakers to help them remain in business. Finally, the *government served as guarantor* of loans on bad assets that would otherwise have forced some banks out of business. As *CQ Weekly* sought to make sense out of all these transactions and the overlapping categories, it estimated about $2 trillion had been made in loans and guarantees. The government's efforts to right the economy had already amounted to approximately $4.5 trillion, could double in the long-run if all the guarantees had to be paid, and President Obama kept reminding Americans that this investment might not be enough.[13] The magnitude of the effort testified to the size of the problem.

Microeconomic Policy

Microeconomic policy is a term used to describe government regulation of specific economic activities; it also encompasses antitrust policy, which is designed to prevent business monopolies and stimulate competition. Microeconomic policies focus on specific industries or on economic practices in several industries. They are designed to affect directly the infrastructure of the economy and only indirectly its overall performance. Modern presidents generally have paid less attention to microeconomic than to macroeconomic policy, largely because the impact of the former is more narrowly focused. But in the wake of the financial crisis came a renewed awareness that unregulated economic activities and weak enforcement can have deleterious effects as well as a demand for controls on the practices that brought the American economy to its knees. Much of the public debate from the late 1970s onward focused on the benefits of deregulating major sectors of the economy and the costs of environmental regulations. The Obama administration came to power in the midst of a broad rethinking of those policies—an understanding of why some economic practices must be regulated and a strong commitment to protecting the environment. Microeconomic policy is likely to be an important area of future activity.

Before the Great Depression, presidents were involved exclusively with microeconomic policy and did not regard overall management of the economy as a primary policy responsibility. To preserve competition in the market, Theodore Roosevelt and William Howard Taft vigorously enforced the Sherman Anti-Trust Act of 1890—Roosevelt with great fanfare and Taft with quiet effectiveness. Woodrow Wilson persuaded Congress to establish an independent regulatory agency, the Federal Trade Commission, with extensive authority to regulate anti-competitive and unfair business practices. Roosevelt, Taft, and Wilson believed the federal government should serve as an umpire and act to correct imperfections in the operations of the free market economy.

During the New Deal, Franklin Roosevelt endorsed legislation that established or strengthened independent regulatory agencies: the Securities and Exchange Commission, the Federal Power Commission, the Federal Communications Commission, the Civil Aeronautics Board, and the National Labor Relations Board. These agencies received broad grants of authority to regulate the interstate aspects of specific industries such as trade in stocks and bonds, electric power and natural gas, broadcasting and wire communications, and air transportation, as well as economy-wide activities such as labor-management relations. FDR experimented with government intervention, hoping to improve the operation of certain economic sectors or the overall health of the economy.

FDR's successors varied in their use of microeconomic policies. Presidents Harry S. Truman, Dwight D. Eisenhower, John F. Kennedy, and Lyndon B. Johnson accepted the legitimacy of government regulation of economic activity that had been established by 1940, including antitrust policy. They differed mainly in the intensity with which they enforced regulations and in their willingness to use certain microeconomic policy tools.

Beginning in the late 1960s and continuing into the 1970s, Congress expanded federal regulation of economic activity as a way to achieve non-economic goals, such as a cleaner physical environment, safer automobiles and other consumer products, and a higher degree of safety and health in the workplace. Presidents Richard Nixon and Gerald Ford initially approved the new regulatory activities, but they raised questions when the economic costs of regulation became apparent. A deregulatory movement gained support, endorsed by Ford, Jimmy Carter, and Ronald Reagan. Ford and Carter used the Council of Economic Advisers (CEA) to analyze the impact of regulations on inflation and later to review new rules and regulations with significant economic costs. These actions did not reduce the volume of new regulations or the economic impact of regulation on industry.[14] Carter also supported legislation that deregulated the airline and trucking industries.

Reagan's 1980 campaign pointed to federal regulation as a primary cause of the decline of productivity in the economy. Vice President George H. W. Bush headed the Task Force on Regulatory Relief, which analyzed the economic effects of existing and proposed regulations. The task force also prepared the way for the establishment of a new entity in the Office of Management and Budget (OMB). The mission of the Office of Information and Regulatory Affairs (OIRA) is to review proposed agency regulations. In addition, Reagan mandated by executive order that all major regulations be subjected to cost-benefit analysis, a way to kill or slow regulations. The administration enforced regulations less intensely and pursued cooperative, rather than confrontational, means to achieve compliance.[15] When he became president, G. H. W. Bush maintained Reagan's regulatory review process and involved his own vice president, Dan Quayle, in an antiregulation effort, naming him chair of the Council on Competitiveness, which had broad authority to intervene in drafting federal regulations. Unlike Reagan, Bush did not oppose social regulation—especially occupational safety and environmental protection—and he gave stronger support to economic regulatory policy. Bush appointed moderates to regulatory positions, in sharp contrast to Reagan's practice of naming conservative appointees, who were philosophically opposed to regulation.[16]

The Clinton administration abolished the Council on Competitiveness, left most responsibility for regulatory review in OMB, enhanced public access to decision making, and shifted substantive emphasis. Whereas Reagan and Bush had required that the benefits of regulations outweigh costs, Clinton "required only that benefits justify costs."[17] Regulatory policy initially was not a major concern of the Clinton administration, but it grew in importance as part of the Reinventing Government Initiative headed by Vice President Al Gore. Regulation became a political issue when Republicans, following their takeover of Congress in 1995, introduced legislation designed to provide businesses and individuals with relief from environmental regulation.[18] Clinton threatened to veto Republican bills seeking to return to the Reagan-era justification of proposed rules and make it easier for parties subject to regulations to raise challenges before they were issued.[19] As the Clinton years came to a close, a fateful policy emerged: Congress approved the activities that would ultimately trigger the economic problems nine years later by allowing the sale of financial derivates—securities marketed on the basis of pooled assets such as mortgages—by unregulated entities, including AIG, which had received nearly $170 billion in federal assistance by early 2009 to prevent its collapse.

During the early months of his administration, George W. Bush triggered fears among environmentalists, organized labor, and consumer advocacy groups that he would overturn regulations deemed harmful by business. The administration declared a sixty-day delay while it reviewed new rules approved by the departing president during his final days in office. These included rules to lower the level of arsenic in drinking water, ban road construction and limit logging on 60 million acres of federal forests, require higher efficiency for air conditioners, reduce diesel exhaust in the air, and reduce repetitive-motion injuries in the workplace.[20] Some rules were reversed, grabbing the headlines and allowing critics to suggest Bush would favor business interests, but at first the administration's actions were mixed. OMB's regulatory review applied stringent cost-benefit criteria to proposed regulations, but OMB was forced to act with greater moderation and in a less probusiness manner than it had first assumed.[21] But there can be little doubt about the administration's agenda of reduced regulation. OMB annually solicited suggestions about federal regulations that should be revised or rescinded, receiving seventy-one suggestions in 2001 and nearly four times as many in 2002.[22] In subsequent years, the administration established "a higher threshold for reaching scientific certainty in regulatory decisions, and create[d] new opportunities for outside experts to challenge the government's conclusions about the dangers that a rule is designed to mitigate."[23] OIRA also got involved with rulemaking at an earlier stage in the process.

Since FDR, microeconomic policies have been secondary to macroeconomic policy in all administrations. Following the economic collapse of 2008–2009, however, many saw the need to reestablish vigorous regulation of financial markets and ensure effective enforcement. The Federal Deposit Insurance Corporation (FDIC), which regulates the operations of commercial banks, had no powers to regulate investment banks or nonbanking financial entities such as insurance companies and hedge funds. When those businesses engaged in especially risky transactions, there was no one to blow the whistle and few powers to intervene. The Obama administration, in conjunction with Bernanke, proposed reforms in March 2009 that would create a single regulator responsible to oversee large companies with the potential to damage the economic system, reduce gaps between regulatory authorities, and improve international coordination.[24] The proposal triggered immediate criticism on Capitol Hill. For some, to consolidate so much power in one regulator, even the Fed, was dangerous. In line with that view, Sen. Christopher Dodd, D-Conn., chair of the Senate Banking Committee, felt that a council of financial regulatory agencies should be created to share responsibilities. Few were convinced that the administration's proposals should be quickly put into place, an indication that the financial regulatory debate was likely to linger for quite some time. Microeconomic policies cannot replace fiscal and monetary policies as the primary means by which presidents guide the nation's economy, but there is a new appreciation of their importance.

Presidents and the Economy: 1933–2009

The president's role as manager of the economy dates from FDR's New Deal, with its commitment to use the federal government's power to bring about recovery from the Great Depression. Keynesian economics and its prescription of increased government spending to compensate for inadequate private spending for investment and consumption provided a theoretical justification for government intervention. Ultimately, it was not the New Deal reforms or recovery programs that ended the Depression but the huge increase in government spending during World War II. All of the nation's unused productive capacity—capital facilities and human resources—were mobilized to achieve victory, and government borrowing financed much of that mobilization.

After the war Congress passed the **Employment Act of 1946,** committing the government to the maintenance of "maximum employment, production, and purchasing power." This act translated into law the widespread expectation, developed during the Roosevelt administration, that the government would guarantee to the fullest extent possible a prosperous economy. It also made the president primarily responsible for providing economic policy leadership, although it failed to furnish the office with many new tools for the task. The Employment Act created the CEA and an accompanying staff to provide professional analysis and advice, and it required the president to report annually to Congress on the condition of the economy and to offer proposals for maintaining or improving its health. Ultimate power over the president's economic proposals, however, remained with Congress.

From the end of World War II until the late 1960s, presidents and Congress fought over economic policy. Truman struggled unsuccessfully with Congress over its desire to reduce wartime taxes, but he was somewhat more effective in controlling the inflation that resulted from spending for the Korean War. Eisenhower's conservative policies tended to prevail over the plans of a Democratic Congress to increase domestic spending. The Eisenhower administration was marked by recessions in 1954 and 1958, with a period of economic expansion between them. The Kennedy-Johnson administration fully embraced Keynesian theory, and a 1964 income tax cut had the desired effect of expanding the economy and increasing revenues. It was thought that economic forecasting and management of the economy had developed to the point where it was possible to fine-tune unemployment and the inflation rate.[25]

In 1966, however, economic conditions began to change. Vietnam War expenditures rose rapidly, the deficit increased, and President Johnson shifted his focus from economic expansion to economic restraint. Congress resisted Johnson's requests for higher excise taxes, and for political reasons he did not ask for income tax increases, fearing that Congress would raise embarrassing questions about the war and its cost on the eve of midterm elections. By the time Johnson had requested additional income taxes and Congress had approved a temporary 10 percent income surtax, the economy had begun a prolonged inflationary period that drastically changed conditions that had been relatively stable since 1946. (The first twenty-five years of the post–World War II period were characterized by an inflation rate of approximately 3 percent a year, unemployment that varied between 4 percent and 8 percent, and sustained growth in the gross domestic product.)

Presidents since Johnson have had to contend with a changing and frequently intractable economy. Inflation rates crept upward into double digits in the late 1970s and early 1980s before declining; unemployment remained high by postwar standards into the mid-1990s; and the federal budget ran a deficit every year between 1970 and 1997 (see Table 9-1). Underlying these developments were systemic factors beyond the control of the government: the increased dependence of the economy on foreign sources of raw materials, especially oil; the growing interdependence of the U.S. economy with those of other industrial democracies; the declining productivity of the U.S. economy in relation to foreign competition; the growth and maturation of domestic social welfare programs based on statutory entitlements; and a commitment to improve the quality of the physical environment even at substantial cost to economic growth and productivity.

TABLE 9-1 Inflation, Unemployment, and Federal Budget Deficits/Surpluses, 1970–2008

	Inflation[a]	Unemployment[b]	Deficit/surplus[c]
1970	5.7%	4.9%	$–2.84
1971	4.4	5.9	–23.03
1972	3.2	5.6	–23.37
1973	6.2	4.9	–14.91
1974	11.0	5.6	–6.14
1975	9.1	8.5	–53.24
1976	5.6	7.7	–73.73
1977	6.5	7.0	–53.66
1978	7.6	6.6	–59.19
1979	11.3	5.8	–40.73
1980	13.5	7.1	–73.84
1981	10.3	7.6	–78.98
1982	6.2	9.7	–127.99
1983	3.2	9.6	–207.82
1984	4.3	7.5	–185.39
1985	3.6	7.2	–212.33
1986	1.9	7.0	–221.25
1987	3.6	6.2	–149.77
1988	4.1	5.5	–155.19
1989	4.8	5.3	–152.48
1990	5.4	5.6	–221.23
1991	4.2	6.8	–269.36
1992	3.0	7.5	–290.40
1993	3.0	6.9	–255.11
1994	2.6	6.1	–203.28
1995	2.8	5.6	–164.01
1996	3.0	5.4	–107.51
1997	2.3	4.9	–21.99
1998	1.6	4.5	+69.19
1999	2.2	4.2	+125.6
2000	3.4	4.0	+236.4
2001	2.8	4.7	+128.2
2002	1.6	5.8	–157.8
2003	2.3	6.0	–377.6
2004	2.7	5.5	–412.7
2005	3.4	5.1	–318.3
2006	3.2	4.6	–248.2
2007	2.9	4.6	–160.7
2008	3.9	5.8	–454.8

SOURCES: For budget deficits: Congressional Budget Office Historical Budget Data, Table 1, www.cbo.gov. For data on inflation and unemployment: Department of Labor, Bureau of Labor Statistics, Household Data, Table 1, and History of CPI-U U.S, www.stats.bls.gov/home.htm.

a. Percentage increase in the consumer price index.
b. Percentage of the civilian noninstitutional population sixteen years of age or over.
c. In billions of dollars.

Richard Nixon responded to the changing economic environment by consistently pursuing the classical conservative course of reducing federal spending to balance the budget. In addition, he took the extraordinary step, for a conservative Republican, of freezing prices and wages in August 1971. Roosevelt and Truman had imposed wage and price controls during World War II and the Korean War, but Nixon was the only president to adopt them when the nation was not fully mobilized for war. He acted under authority Congress delegated to the president in the Economic Stabilization Act of 1970, which had passed over his strong objections. The wage and price freeze experience during 1971–1973 suggests that peacetime wage and price controls are at best a temporary means of curbing inflation and that they can quickly become a political liability unless their impact is moderated— Nixon did not suffer the political consequences in 1972, but congressional Republicans did.

Upon taking office in August 1974, President Ford assumed that the principal economic problem confronting the United States was inflation, and he pushed to cut federal spending. Instead, economic conditions changed, and Ford spent his last year as president combating a recession that contributed to his electoral defeat in 1976. Ford's successor, Jimmy Carter, fared little better. Carter initiated an antirecession program of increased federal spending and tax cuts to stimulate business investment. The economy responded almost too quickly, and he was confronted with surging inflation rates that reached double digits during his last two years in office.

Perhaps Carter's most important decision affecting the economy was to select Paul Volcker as chairman of the Federal Reserve Board in 1979. Volcker's appointment reflected Carter's frustration with Keynesian theory's inability to provide solutions to the problem of stagflation, a combination of a stagnant economy and rising prices. Essentially a monetarist, Volcker moved quickly to curb inflation by restraining the growth of the money supply, the first time monetarism had a prominent role in macroeconomic policymaking.

The rate of inflation did not respond quickly to Volcker's efforts to tighten the money supply, but interest rates on consumer loans rose sharply, undoubtedly contributing to Carter's defeat by Reagan in the 1980 election. One of Reagan's campaign pledges had been to restore vitality to the economy through a revolutionary program of major reductions in taxes and spending. Congress responded positively to Reagan's initiatives in 1981 by enacting the largest income tax cut in U.S. history to that point and by reducing domestic spending in nonentitlement programs. Congress also supported Reagan's proposals for a major defense buildup, projected over five years, from 1981 through 1986.

The results of the Reagan administration's macroeconomic policies were mixed. The Fed can claim credit for curtailing inflation, which fluctuated between annual rates of 1.9 percent and 4.3 percent from 1983 through 1988. The economy also began a sustained period of growth that lasted from 1983 through 1990. Before that growth spurt, however, the United States experienced the most severe recession since World War II, with unemployment rising to 10.75 percent in the fourth quarter of 1982. In spite of the prosperity achieved after 1982, unemployment did not drop below 5 percent until fifteen years later.

On the negative side, the Reagan administration's macroeconomic policies produced massive federal budget deficits. The deficits grew rapidly through a conjunction of forces: the recession of 1982 caused revenues to fall and triggered automatic countercyclical spending (such as unemployment compensation); the tax cuts and increased defense spending authorized in 1981 became effective, reducing revenues and increasing some expenditures. The result was a large structural, or permanent, deficit as the increases in federal revenues promised by supply-side advocates failed to materialize and Congress refused to provide sizable additional cuts in nondefense spending. Finally, interest payments rose quickly to pay for government borrowing needed to close the gap between spending and revenues. From $990 billion in 1980, the debt rose to $3.1 trillion ten years later.[26]

Although the deficits proved embarrassing to President Reagan because they violated traditional conservative values of fiscal restraint, they also brought political advantage to the administration. The unprecedented deficit spending put money in the pockets of American consumers, creating additional demand that in turn stimulated the economy and served as the basis for the sustained recovery from the 1981–1982 recession. That recovery was crucial to Reagan's 1984 reelection victory, for voters concluded that his economic policies had worked quite well. The deficits also provided Reagan with an effective argument for restraining the growth of nondefense spending.

George H. W. Bush's victory in the 1988 presidential election was an endorsement of the status quo. The country was prosperous and not at war. The only economic policy mandate Bush received derived from his pledge that there would be "no new taxes." He kept this promise until October 1990, when he faced the prospect of an enormous deficit that would trigger automatic budget cuts. His administration negotiated a budget deal with Congress that would balance the budget by 1996, a goal overwhelmed by unanticipated expenditures for the Persian Gulf War and the costs of bailing out failed savings and loan institutions insured by the federal government.[27] The deficits for fiscal 1991 ($269.36 billion) and 1992

($290.40 billion) were the highest to that point in U.S. history. The recession that began in late 1990 and continued into 1992 meant Congress could neither cut spending nor raise taxes, thus impeding administration and congressional efforts to curb the deficit.

The 1992 election gave a clear indication of voter dissatisfaction with the condition of the economy, but it produced no general agreement on economic policies. Bill Clinton lacked a clear electoral mandate—he received only 43.3 percent of the vote—and he had failed to provide concrete proposals for deficit reduction out of fear of antagonizing the voters. "While concerned about ending deficits, the voters [were] even more concerned with preventing the spending cuts and tax increases necessary to accomplish that goal."[28] During the campaign, Clinton promised an economic stimulus package and a middle-class tax cut; deficit reduction was a distant concern. This plan began to change on December 3, 1992, during his first meeting with Greenspan, who argued that the key to prosperity was convincing Wall Street that the new administration was committed to reducing the budget deficit.[29]

Less than a month after his inauguration, President Clinton moved quickly to address economic problems. His economic program, unveiled on February 17, 1993, contained three parts: deficit reduction; long-term investments in research, education and training, and physical infrastructure; and short-term spending to stimulate the economy. By a single vote in each chamber, Congress passed legislation (called a reconciliation bill) that reduced the deficit by $496 billion over five years, mainly through tax increases on the wealthy. The investment spending proposals were severely reduced or deferred, however, and a Senate filibuster mounted by Republicans killed the stimulus package. Economic conditions improved quickly under Clinton: unemployment dropped, inflation was moderate, and the economy grew at a healthy annual rate.[30] As a result of the 1993 deficit reduction package and a stronger than anticipated economic performance, the budget deficit fell from nearly $300 billion in 1992 to just over $108 billion by 1996,[31] and it turned the corner with a modest surplus in 1998. This goal was reached in just one year, five years earlier than anticipated in the 1997 budget agreement between Clinton and congressional Republicans.[32]

Evaluated in terms of conventional indicators, Clinton's economic policies succeeded, but not fast enough for the voters. In the 1994 congressional elections, regarded as a referendum on Clinton's overall performance, the Democratic Party suffered a stunning defeat as the Republicans gained control over Congress for the first time in forty years. No Republican legislator had voted for the economic package, and the Democrats were branded as the party of high taxes. During the

1996 election and by the end of Clinton's term, however, his contributions to national prosperity seemed to underlie his reelection and the strong public support he received even in the midst of the impeachment controversy (see chapter 5).

Ultimately, "Clinton's fiscal policy served as a laboratory for a change in economic thought." Rather than relying on government deficits to stimulate economic activity, Clinton sought "balanced budgets—or better yet, surpluses—[which] are believed to hold down interest rates, free capital for the private sector and reassure investors about long-term economic stability."[33] The conventional Keynesian strategy for pursuing an expansionary fiscal policy was turned on its head. Ironically, this challenge to traditional economic thinking may have laid the groundwork for George W. Bush's initial legislative victories on economic policy.

Approval of a massive tax cut at the start of the Bush administration reversed a major feature of the Clinton legacy—budget surpluses large enough to pay off the accumulated national debt and maintain solvency for the big-ticket programs of Social Security and Medicare. Clinton had been almost too successful. When estimates of future surpluses grew to $5.6 trillion over ten years, Democrats' arguments against "giving the people their money back" (Bush's central position) were undermined.[34] This debate occurred before 9/11 and its new pressures to increase spending for defense and homeland security. As the economy lagged in the face of economic dislocation and consumer uncertainty, government revenues fell even further and the deficit mounted. From a surplus of $128 billion in fiscal year 2001, the federal budget returned to deficits in FY02 of $158 billion, $378 billion in FY03, what was then an all-time record $413 billion in FY04, followed by declines to $318 billion, $248 billion, and $161.5 billion in FY05, FY06 and FY07. At mid-year 2007, the CBO projected a surplus in 2012. Instead, deficits grew dramatically, reflecting the slowing economy and tax cuts (lower revenues) as well as stimulus efforts (higher spending). The FY08 deficit of $454.8 billion was immediately dwarfed by the record deficit of a projected $1.8 trillion for FY09. President Obama's proposed budget for 2010 called for a $1.2 trillion deficit and was expected to be just under $1 trillion in 2011.[35]

Even before the mammoth effort to stave off another depression, the erosion in federal finances was significant. Democrats point to Bush's tax cuts as the culprit, arguing that they severely reduced federal revenues. New expenditures for homeland security added to the deficit as did the wars in Iraq and Afghanistan even though they had never been part of the annual budget. Those concerned with the rising national debt point to the sudden reversal after Clinton. "It took the federal government 28 years (1970–98) to produce a surplus, but only 4 years to return to deficit."[36] "A policy of endlessly rising deficits . . . constitutes an explicit decision by today's adults to collectively shift the current cost of government from themselves to their children and grandchildren."[37] The national debt ceiling—the limit to which the Treasury is authorized to borrow—was quietly raised on the day after approval of the 2003 tax cuts to $7.384 trillion to accommodate deficit spending accumulating at the rate of more than $1.5 billion a day. By February 2009 the national debt stood at $11.12 trillion, an increase of more than $5 trillion during the Bush presidency.[38] Aware of widespread concern about the rising national debt, Obama convened a White House summit early in his administration focused on restoring budget discipline, but his own projections looking forward ten years still had the annual deficit at around $500 billion, a long way from balance. Bush had tried and failed to solve the gathering crisis in Social Security and Medicare, programs projected to run enormous deficits as the baby boom generation retires and becomes eligible for full benefits with Medicare in 2011. As one study concludes, "[A] significant opportunity to pre-fund future retirement and health benefits was missed" when the Clinton surplus disappeared.[39]

Bush's legacy in economic and budget policy will remain enormously controversial. His commitment to tax reduction was much like Reagan's; unlike Reagan, Bush had a Congress whose majority was unified in supporting the administration for four years. Even a Republican Congress, however, was unwilling to support the spending cuts and radical program redesigns required to restore a balanced budget. In fact, Republicans proved to be no less profligate in their spending than the Democrats. Bush left behind a legacy for his successor much like that bequeathed to Reagan's—fiscal crisis amid a plethora of unattractive policy choices.

The Politics of Macroeconomic Policymaking

Presidents do not make macroeconomic policy in a vacuum or solely according to economic theories. Their decisions in this crucial area are intensely political and are affected by consideration of other policy goals (including microeconomic policy), electoral politics, interest group politics, and bureaucratic politics among institutional participants in the policy-making process. In a very real sense, the United States has a *political* economy, the nation is an economic *polity*, and the president is the focal point of the relationships involved in both.

Policy Politics

The achievement of macroeconomic policy goals is affected by, and has an effect on, other policy goals. National security policy objectives, for example, often have a profound impact on economic policy. In the 1980s substantial increases in defense spending beginning in fiscal year 1982 reflected the consensus that U.S. military strength had declined compared with that of the Soviet Union. These increases hindered efforts to balance the budget. The end of the cold war between the United States and the Soviet Union in late 1991 precipitated a budget struggle over the disposition of the "peace dividend" that congressional Democrats believed should result from the reduction of tensions. In the October 1990 budget agreement between President Bush and Congress, any reductions in either defense or discretionary domestic spending were to be devoted to reducing the deficit. By late 2008 the United States had spent $864 billion on the war on terror, the war in Afghanistan, and the Iraq War, an important contribution to the growing deficits that Obama projected at $130 billion in FY10.[40]

Since 1990 budget-balancing efforts in domestic programs conflicted with commitments made to Social Security beneficiaries, welfare recipients, retired federal employees, and numerous other groups served by federal programs. In addition, the macroeconomic goals of economic growth, increased productivity, and full employment often appeared to be at odds with regulatory policies designed to improve environmental quality, enhance occupational safety and health, increase the safety of automobiles and other consumer products, and protect consumers against a variety of unfair business practices. Fiscal policy frequently served as the arena for resolving trade-offs among these conflicting goals.

Electoral Politics

Macroeconomic policy has important implications for electoral politics. It has long been recognized that presidential administrations and congressional majorities manipulate fiscal policy to produce short-term improvements in economic conditions to enhance their party's election prospects. They may adjust the timing and location of benefits to achieve this end, making policies that amount to marginal adjustments rather than fundamental restructuring of the economic system.

Presidents do not automatically avoid hard political choices and cave in to election pressures from party and special constituencies.[41] Ronald Reagan remained firm throughout his presidency in his commitment to the 1981 income tax cut based on supply-side theory, even though it meant proposing and defending record peacetime budget deficits (of around $200 billion) that were anathema to his conservative supporters. George H. W. Bush reluctantly agreed to tax increases of $146 billion as part of a five-year, $496 billion deficit reduction package. (Opponents attacked him for breaking his "no new taxes" pledge in the 1992 election campaign, and he expressed regret at having done so.) In response to congressional pressures from Republicans and conservative Democrats and to advice from his economic advisers, Bill Clinton abandoned his campaign promise of a tax cut for the middle class and settled for half of the major investments in human resources and infrastructure that were major elements in his proposed 1993 economic program.[42] During his first two-and-a-half years in office, George W. Bush saw 2.5 million jobs disappear during a sluggish recovery. To counter charges that he had ignored problems at home to address those abroad, the president accepted a tax cut in 2003 that was less than half his original proposal and failed to include several important policy changes (such as eliminating double taxation of dividends), calculating that it was the best he could achieve.[43] Obama remained true to his campaign promises of helping the middle-class weather the economic storm. He included proposals in both his stimulus package and initial budget to cut taxes for those who made less than $200,000 per year, as he proposed to phase out the Bush tax cuts for upper-income earners.

Interest Group Politics

In making economic policy, presidents and Congress are subjected to pressures from interest groups, including business, labor, agriculture, the financial community, state and local governments, and foreign governments. The effect of these interests on policy varies according to the issues and the current economic conditions at home and abroad.

Business and labor interests are the most organized and thoroughly entrenched. Businesses use umbrella organizations, such as the Chamber of Commerce of the United States and the National Association of Manufacturers, to exert influence, as well as industry-based trade associations, such as the Automobile Manufacturers Association and the American Gas Association. Individual companies, especially large corporations, also try to shape policy. Businesses usually concentrate their lobbying on microeconomic policies that specifically affect their operations but may also be concerned about areas of macroeconomic policy: inflation, tax burdens, and interest rates. Organized labor encompasses the giant AFL-CIO (American Federation of Labor-Congress of Industrial Organizations) and a host of independent unions. Labor's position on macroeconomic policy issues usually contrasts sharply with that of business. Labor worries more about unemployment than inflation, supports fiscal stimulation of the economy in periods of recession, and opposes the use of monetary restraints to curb inflation. Like business, labor takes great interest in microeconomic policy directly affecting its interests, including regulation of labor-management relations and regulations to promote occupational safety and health.

Agricultural interest groups, though shrinking in membership, remain quite diverse. The American Farm Bureau Federation and the National Grange support conservative policies, while the National Farmers Union and the National Farmers Organization take more liberal stances. Regardless of their ideologies, farm organizations tend to oppose monetary policies that result in high interest rates because the use of credit is an essential part of farm management.

The financial community consists of two principal components, the securities exchanges—Wall Street—and banks and other financial institutions. (Wall Street and financial institutions buy and sell "paper"—government and private financial obligations—and bonds, the longer-term securities.) Wall Street registers its reactions to monetary and fiscal policies—investor confidence—through the prices of corporate stocks traded on the major stock exchanges. Bond prices move up or down inversely with interest rates and reflect monetary policy shifts; interest paid on short-term government and commercial paper also fluctuates as monetary policy changes. Administrations seek to have their policies favorably received by Wall Street and by major banks and other leading financial institutions. A vote of "no confidence" by the financial community in the government's economic policies makes the administration vulnerable to criticism by political opponents and weakens its popular support. As in the broader business world, members of the financial community tend to support conservative fiscal policies and monetary restraint to control inflation. They fear large deficits, whether due to high spending levels or sizable tax cuts. Similarly, some bankers considered the terms associated with the assistance programs received in 2008–2009 as too intrusive, arguing that government was restricting their decisions and providing an incentive for them to pay back the loans as quickly as possible.

With the advent of the Great Society domestic programs in the mid-1960s, state and local governments became vitally interested in macroeconomic policy. The federal government is a source of funding for a wide range of state and local programs in education, welfare and social services, housing and urban development, transportation, and health care. Consequently, many state and local governments, collectively—through national associations, such as the U.S. Conference of Mayors—and individually—through the efforts of members of Congress—have exerted pressure to maintain the flow of federal funds, even though this goal could be accomplished only at the expense of larger and potentially inflationary budget deficits.

Hoping to reduce state and local dependence on federal funding, Presidents Reagan and George H. W. Bush sought a major reordering of federal fiscal responsibilities. This effort failed to accomplish its most revolutionary goals, but it triggered a rethinking of federal aid and its implications for macroeconomic policy.[44] In the face of mounting budget deficits in 1993 and 1994, Republicans and conservative Democrats opposed Clinton's infrastructure spending, which they viewed as more appropriate for state and local governments to fund. Conservatives also demanded that financial responsibility for major redistributive programs be shifted to the states. In 1995 the Republican majority in Congress proposed ending entitlement status for welfare (Aid to Families with Dependent Children) and Medicaid by converting federally funded programs—accompanied by extensive federal rules and regulations—to programs giving block grants to states. States would be freed from most federal controls, but funding would be fixed and would not increase as demands for services expanded. Initially, Clinton opposed these changes by vetoing two Republican versions, but in 1996 he compromised with the Republicans. Much to the dismay of many Democrats, welfare (but not Medicaid) lost its entitlement status and became a block grant program.[45] George W. Bush proposed changes in Medicaid that would largely accomplish the Republicans' 1995 goal, but Obama's ambitious proposals to change health care in America are likely to alter the ground yet again.

Presidents and their administrations are constrained to some degree by the effect of economic policy decisions on the economies of other countries. Foreign governments have an intense interest in U.S. macroeconomic policy. Friendly governments—the European Community, Japan, and Saudi Arabia—favor a dollar that is neither overvalued nor undervalued and a healthy U.S. economy with full employment and a low inflation rate. If the dollar is weak, the value of much of their international currency reserves declines, and their goods are less competitive in U.S. markets, a problem that arose during 2002–2003 and then grew worse. If the dollar is too strong, foreign investment capital migrates to the United States, and the high competitiveness of foreign products in U.S. markets threatens to provoke trade restrictions. When unemployment in the United States rises, the major market for their goods contracts. When interest rates are higher in the United States than in Europe or Japan, investment capital moves to the United States. Consequently, foreign governments press U.S. administrations to keep the exchange value of the dollar from fluctuating widely and to hold down interest rates.

Presidents do not respond to all interest group constituencies, and the constituencies whose support they do seek vary in importance to them. In no case, however, do presidents make macroeconomic policy decisions without regard to some interest groups, which are major factors in the politics of economic policymaking.

The Economic Subpresidency

In discharging the role of economic manager, chief executives seek to meet popular and elite expectations that their actions will result in a prosperous economy. Presidents must develop and implement policies and build support for them in the public and in the Washington community. President Obama traveled extensively during the first months of his presidency to highlight features of his recovery plans for housing (Phoenix), energy (Denver), and jobs (Ohio). His speeches, press conferences, White House summits, and Saturday addresses were designed to sell his program. To accomplish these complex and demanding tasks, presidents need information, advice, and administrative assistance to focus energy on major issues, integrate the policies of their administrations, take account of all-important interests, and maintain the administration's cohesion. This advice and assistance is provided by a set of specialized organizations located in the presidency and in the executive branch, organizations that have been called the "economic subpresidency." All those engaged in making, defining, communicating, and implementing economic policy decisions, "whether they act personally or as part of an institution," are part of this policy-making system.[46] How presidents use the economic subpresidency varies across administrations and with economic conditions, but the system is central to policymaking and presidential management of the economy. Staff members serve in one of four major administrative units—the CEA, OMB, the Treasury Department, or the Fed—or on various intragovernmental committees and councils. Leading members of these units since the early 1950s are listed in Tables 9-2 through 9-5.

Council of Economic Advisers

The Council of Economic Advisers has three members, appointed by the president and subject to Senate confirmation, plus a small staff of approximately thirty-five, divided between professional economists and support personnel. Traditionally, most CEA members and professional staffers have had extensive experience in business or government. The CEA's chair (see Table 9-2) is responsible for administering the council, hiring staff, representing the CEA on other government councils and committees, and reporting to the president. He or she establishes the council's orientation according to the president's overall objectives. The chair's relationship with the president largely determines the CEA's influence in shaping economic policy.

TABLE 9-2　Chairs of the Council of Economic Advisers, 1953–2009

President	Chair	Years
Eisenhower	Arthur F. Burns	1953–1956
	Raymond T. Saulnier	1956–1961
Kennedy	Walter W. Heller	1961–1963
Johnson	Walter W. Heller	1963–1964
	Gardner H. Ackley	1964–1968
	Arthur M. Okun	1968–1969
Nixon	Paul W. McCracken	1969–1971
	Herbert Stein	1972–1974
Ford	Herbert Stein	1974
	Alan Greenspan	1974–1977
Carter	Charles L. Schultze	1977–1981
Reagan	Murray L. Weidenbaum	1981–1982
	Martin Feldstein	1982–1984
	Beryl Sprinkel	1985–1989
G. H. W. Bush	Michael J. Boskin	1989–1993
Clinton	Laura D. Tyson	1993–1994
	Joseph E. Stiglitz	1995–1997
	Janet L. Yellen	1997–1999
	Martin Baily	1999–2001
G. W. Bush	R. Glenn Hubbard	2001–2003
	N. Gregory Mankiw	2003–2005
	Harvey S. Rosen	2005
	Ben S. Bernanke	2005–2006
	Edward P. Lazear	2006–2009
Obama	Christina Romer	2009–

SOURCE: www.whitehouse.gov/cea.

The CEA has no operational responsibility but serves entirely in a staff capacity. It gathers information, makes economic forecasts, analyzes economic issues, and prepares the annual *Economic Report of the President,* presented to Congress. It provides the president with expert economic advice, and the members occasionally act as public spokespersons for the president. The council usually does not broker agreements among conflicting parties or coordinate policymaking within the administration, although its members tend to reflect the theories and policy views of the president. In general, Democratic presidents have had Keynesian CEA members, and Republicans have selected classical conservative and monetarist economists. Reagan, for example, appointed a conservative economist to chair the CEA at the start of his presidency and added a monetarist and a supply-sider. All three were committed to free trade, reduced government spending, a balanced federal budget, and limited federal intervention in the economy.

If presidents believe they need economic expertise and share basic interests and values with CEA members, the council may significantly influence economic policy-making. The council's expertise enhances presidential policies, and its analyses and forecasts acquire political significance through association with the presidency. In the long run, however, the council can do only what the president asks and allows it to do.

The CEA played a more significant role with respect to the deficit in the G. H. W. Bush administration than under Reagan. Its chair, monetarist economist Michael J. Boskin (1989–1993), enjoyed Bush's confidence and often acted as a spokesperson for the administration. Clinton appointed Laura D'Andrea Tyson (1993–1994) of Stanford University, who was an expert on trade policy and not a professional macroeconomist, to chair his CEA. When Tyson became chair of another White House coordinating unit—the National Economic Council—in 1995, three others succeeded her as CEA chair: Joseph E. Stiglitz (1995–1997), Janet L. Yellen (1997–1999), and Martin Baily (1999–2001). The rapid turnover is one indicator that the CEA may not have influenced Clinton policymaking.

The council's forecasts help set the boundaries of the president's legislative program and budget proposals. It is to the president's advantage for the council to approach its advisory task deductively, fitting program pieces together within the framework of the president's overall objectives. The council's contribution to policymaking is primarily conceptual and not in the realm of implementation or coordination. This is the reality that confronted George W. Bush's first CEA chair, R. Glenn Hubbard (2001–2003), a professor of economics and business at Columbia University, who had served in the Treasury Department under Bush I and was a major architect of the administration's 2003 tax cut proposals.[47] He was succeeded by Harvard economist N. Gregory Mankiw.[48] He resigned in 2005 and was replaced briefly by Harvey S. Rosen, a Princeton economist, and Ben S. Bernanke, who went on to become chairman of the Federal Reserve Board (see below). Stanford economist Edward P. Lazear became the CEA chair in February 2006 after serving on the President's Advisory Panel on Tax Reform. Obama selected Christina Romer as his CEA chair. Known for her research on the Great Depression, Romer taught at UC-Berkeley and Princeton University and served as co-director of the Program in Monetary Economics at the National Bureau of Economic Research and vice president of the American Economic Association.[49]

Office of Management and Budget

Presidents receive economic advice of a different sort from the roughly five hundred employees in the Office of Management and Budget. Whereas the CEA's primary concern is controlling the business cycle and achieving sustained economic growth, OMB's major focus is allocating resources to federal administrative agencies and their programs through the annual preparation of the president's budget. Its institutional bias is toward holding down spending. It is the principal instrument through which the president fashions the expenditure component of fiscal policy. In addition, OMB provides economic forecasts to the president and acts as a "legislative and regulatory gatekeeper" by conducting detailed policy analysis of proposed bills and agency rules.[50]

The Office of Management and Budget was originally a presidential staff agency, the Bureau of the Budget, staffed by an elite group of government careerists devoted to serving the presidency, whoever the particular president might be. Since 1970, when Nixon reorganized it, OMB has been more actively involved in serving the president's political needs. Beginning in the Nixon administration, OMB directors (see Table 9-3) have participated in developing presidential policies and building support for them. The budget has become as much a political weapon as a managerial tool or an instrument of fiscal policy.

The politicization of OMB and the political use of the budget were never more apparent than during the Reagan administration and David Stockman's tenure as budget director (1981–1986). Stockman dominated federal budgeting in a manner previously unknown. He centralized the executive budget process in OMB and involved himself extensively in the congressional budget proceedings through direct negotiations and bargaining with congressional committees.

Under Stockman's successor, economist James C. Miller III (1986–1988), OMB continued to serve Reagan's political interests but much less visibly. During the Bush I presidency, OMB was a major player in the economic subpresidency. Its director, Richard G. Darman (1989–1993), and the White House chief of staff, John Sununu, were the principal negotiators with Congress concerning fiscal policy. (Darman dealt primarily with spending, and Sununu with taxes.) OMB also became the dominant agency for economic forecasting.

The budget remained the main instrument for achieving the president's policy goals during the Clinton administration. Clinton named Leon E. Panetta (1993–1994), chair of the House Budget Committee, as his first OMB director. Panetta was a "deficit hawk" (a strong advocate for deficit reduction) and a Democratic loyalist who possessed parliamentary acumen and budgetary expertise.[51] He was influential in shaping Clinton's 1993 economic plan and selling it to Congress. When Panetta became Clinton's chief of staff in June 1994, economist Alice Rivlin (1994–1996) became OMB's director. Rivlin had served previously as director of the

TABLE 9-3   Directors of the Budget Bureau/Office of Management and Budget, 1953–2009

President	Director	Years
Eisenhower	Joseph M. Dodge	1953–1954
	Rowland R. Hughes	1954–1956
	Percival F. Brundage	1956–1958
	Maurice Stans	1958–1961
Kennedy	David E. Bell	1961–1962
	Kermit Gordon	1962–1963
Johnson	Kermit Gordon	1963–1965
	Charles E. Schultze	1965–1968
	Charles J. Zwick	1968–1969
Nixon	Robert P. Mayo	1969–1970
	George P. Shultz	1971–1972
	Caspar Weinberger	1972–1973
	Roy L. Ash	1973–1974
Ford	Roy L. Ash	1974–1975
	James P. Lynn	1975–1976
Carter	Bert Lance	1977
	James T. McIntyre	1978–1981
Reagan	David Stockman	1981–1986
	James C. Miller III	1986–1988
G. H. W. Bush	Richard G. Darman	1989–1993
Clinton	Leon E. Panetta	1993–1994
	Alice Rivlin	1994–1996
	Franklin D. Raines	1996–1998
	Jacob J. Lew	1998–2001
G. W. Bush	Mitchell E. Daniels Jr.	2001–2003
	Joshua B. Bolten	2003–2006
	Rob Portman	2006–2007
	Jim Nussle	2007–2009
Obama	Peter R. Orszag	2009–

SOURCES: John H. Kessel, *Presidents, the Presidency, and the Political Environment* (Washington, D.C.: CQ Press, 2001), chap. 5; "The Decision Makers," *National Journal*, June 23, 2001; and www.whitehouse.gov/omb.

Congressional Budget Office and was even more hawkish on the deficit than Panetta. Their presence "ensured that deficit reduction would command considerable attention" as the administration shaped economic policy.[52] Rivlin was succeeded by Franklin D. Raines (1996–1998), and Raines by Jacob J. Lew (1998–2001). George W. Bush chose as OMB director Mitchell E. Daniels Jr. (2001–2003), a lawyer with political experience on Capitol Hill and in the Reagan White House but not in budget-related positions.[53] Joshua B. Bolten, a lawyer and investment banker, was named as Daniels's successor in May 2003. He brought to the position Capitol Hill and previous White House experience in the Bush I administration. He had impressed George W. Bush as policy director for his presidential campaign in 2000 and as White House deputy chief of staff for policy during Bush's first two years in office. When Chief of Staff Andrew Card resigned in 2006, Bush appointed Bolten to the post. The new OMB director was Rob Portman, a former House member with experience on the Budget Committee and Ways and Means Committee. Portman had served as the U.S. trade representative before moving to OMB. After one year, Portman left, and former representative Jim Nussle, the unsuccessful 2006 Republican candidate for governor of Iowa, took the post. Nussle's credentials rested on his six years as chair of the House Budget Committee where he established a reputation as a highly partisan defender of Republican priorities, a style he brought to the White House. Peter Orszag became Obama's first OMB director after completing nearly two years as director of the Congressional Budget Office, serving on the Clinton administration's CEA staff, and spending an extended period at the Brookings Institution, a liberal Washington think tank.[54]

Treasury Department

The third institutional participant in the economic subpresidency is the Treasury Department, which is responsible for collecting taxes, managing the national debt, controlling the currency, collecting customs, and handling international monetary affairs, including management of the balance of payments and the value of the dollar in relation to other currencies. With more than 100,000 employees, it is the primary government source of information on revenues, the tax system, and financial markets. It also takes the lead in developing tax bills and steering them through Congress.[55]

Traditionally, the Treasury Department has been concerned about the adequacy of revenues, the soundness of the dollar, and the cost of financing the debt. To finance the debt, the department has advocated either low interest rates or a balanced budget. Before the Reagan administration, a situation in which high interest rates accompanied a large deficit was anathema to the institutional interests of the Treasury. Its position altered substantially under President Reagan and Secretary of the Treasury Donald T. Regan (1981–1985) (see Table 9-4). An avowed believer in supply-side economics, Regan argued that temporary deficits resulting from tax-cut incentives would ultimately lead to economic growth, expanded revenues, and balanced budgets. He opposed efforts to reduce the deficit by raising taxes. He was more concerned with the supply of money in the domestic economy than with the exchange value of the dollar. Regan's successor as secretary, James A. Baker III (1985–1988), concentrated heavily on exchange rate problems.

TABLE 9-4   Secretaries of the Treasury, 1953–2009

President	Secretary	Years
Eisenhower	George M. Humphrey	1953–1957
	Robert Anderson	1957–1961
Kennedy	C. Douglas Dillon	1961–1963
Johnson	C. Douglas Dillon	1964–1965
	Henry H. Fowler	1965–1968
	Joseph W. Barr	1968–1969
Nixon	David M. Kennedy	1969–1971
	John B. Connally	1971–1972
	George P. Shultz	1972–1974
	William E. Simon	1974
Ford	William E. Simon	1974–1977
Carter	W. Michael Blumenthal	1977–1979
	G. William Miller	1979–1981
Reagan	Donald T. Regan	1981–1985
	James A. Baker III	1985–1988
	Nicholas F. Brady	1988–1989
G. H. W. Bush	Nicholas F. Brady	1989–1993
Clinton	Lloyd M. Bentsen	1993–1994
	Robert E. Rubin	1995–1999
	Lawrence H. Summers	1999–2001
G. W. Bush	Paul H. O'Neill	2001–2002
	John W. Snow	2003–2006
	Henry M. Paulson	2006–2009
Obama	Timothy F. Geithner	2009–

SOURCES: John H. Kessel, *Presidents, the Presidency, and the Political Environment* (Washington, D.C.: CQ Press, 2001), chap. 5; "The Decision Makers," *National Journal*, June 23, 2001; and www.ustreas.gov.

Secretary of the Treasury Nicholas F. Brady played a marginal role in the economic subpresidency under President George H. W. Bush. One veteran White House observer and analyst suggests that the "patrician" Brady was no match for the "pit bull approach of his two economic policy colleagues," Darman and Sununu.[56]

President Clinton's first two secretaries of the Treasury, Lloyd M. Bentsen (1993–1994) and Robert E. Rubin (1995–1999), were central participants in the economic subpresidency. By appointing Bentsen, a moderate Democrat with business experience who chaired the Senate Finance Committee, Clinton sought to reassure the business community.[57] The appointment of Rubin, a Wall Street investment banker who had served as Clinton's chair of the National Economic Council (see discussion below), accomplished a similar purpose. Both men were deeply involved in shaping the 1993 economic program.[58] Lawrence H. Summers, a

Rubin protéegée as deputy secretary, served as secretary from 1999 to 2001. George W. Bush selected Paul H. O'Neill (2001–2002) as Treasury secretary. O'Neill was a ten-year veteran of OMB who later worked for International Paper before becoming CEO of Alcoa Aluminum.[59] But O'Neill proved to be an outspoken cabinet secretary. He sometimes questioned the administration's tax-cutting policies (he was not a supply-sider), frequently irked influential members of Congress, failed to calm investors in 2002 during the corporate scandals, and even upset international currency markets.[60] In short, he proved ineffective in the job and was the first member of the Bush cabinet to leave his position, replaced in January 2003 by John W. Snow. Snow had been CEO of CSX Corporation, a railroad freight company, and chair of the Business Roundtable, an elite corporate lobbying group. Snow left the administration in mid-2006 and was succeeded by Henry M. Paulson, former chair and CEO of Goldman Sachs, one of New York City's most successful investment banks. Timothy Geithner, Obama's choice to lead the Treasury Department, had worked there during three administrations. He also worked for the International Monetary Fund and was president and chief executive officer of the Federal Reserve Bank of New York before joining the administration.[61]

Organizationally, the Treasury Department is divided between large units with major line responsibilities, such as the Internal Revenue Service, and policy-related units, such as the office of the undersecretary for monetary affairs. The policy-related units, located in the office of the secretary, never have provided coordination of economic policy for an administration, although the potential exists for them to do so.[62] About 20 percent of the department's workforce, including the Secret Service, the Customs Service, and much of the Bureau of Alcohol, Tobacco, Firearms, and Explosives, was shifted to the new Department of Homeland Security.

Federal Reserve Board

The Federal Reserve Board is an independent agency charged with responsibility for regulating the money supply and the banking system. Its seven members are appointed by the president to fourteen-year terms with the consent of the Senate. The president designates one member of the board to act as its chair for a four-year term, but the chair, an important source of institutional influence, often serves beyond that limit, as shown in Table 9-5. The Fed has three traditional ways of controlling the money supply: the discount rate, reserve requirements, and open-market operations, the buying and selling of government securities that set the federal funds rate. In an effort to combat the recession of 2008–2009, the Fed developed new strategies to stimulate the economy.

TABLE 9-5   Chairs of the Federal Reserve Board, 1951–2009

President	Chair	Years
Eisenhower	William McC. Martin	1951–1961
Kennedy	William McC. Martin	1961–1963
Johnson	William McC. Martin	1963–1969
Nixon	William McC. Martin	1969–1970
Nixon	Arthur F. Burns	1970–1974
Ford	Arthur F. Burns	1974–1977
Carter	Arthur F. Burns	1977–1978
Carter	G. William Miller	1978–1979
	Paul A. Volcker	1979–1981
Reagan	Paul A. Volcker	1981–1987
Reagan	Alan Greenspan	1987–1989
G. H. W. Bush	Alan Greenspan	1989–1993
Clinton	Alan Greenspan	1993–2001
G. W. Bush	Alan Greenspan	2001–2005
	Ben S. Bernanke	2006–2009
Obama	Ben S. Bernanke	2009–

SOURCES: John H. Kessel, *Presidents, the Presidency, and the Political Environment* (Washington, D.C.: CQ Press, 2001), chap. 5; and "The Decision Makers," *National Journal*, June 23, 2001; www.whitehouse.gov/.

The discount rate is the interest rate charged commercial banks to borrow from the Federal Reserve. An increase in the discount rate tightens the availability of credit because it forces banks to charge more to their borrowers. Reserves are liquid assets banks hold to meet demands for ready cash from their depositors. The Federal Reserve requires commercial banks belonging to it to maintain a certain percentage (usually ranging from 10 percent to 20 percent) of their deposit liabilities in the form of cash in their vaults or on account with the regional reserve bank for this purpose. A reduction in the reserve requirement increases the amount of money banks may loan to their borrowers, and an increase in the reserve requirement decreases the availability of bank credit.

The Federal Open Market Committee (FOMC) approved thirteen consecutive reductions in the federal funds rate after Bush took office in January 2001. From a level of 6.5 percent, on January 1, 2001, the rate was progressively reduced to 1 percent, on June 25, 2003, producing the lowest consumer interest rates since 1958. These policy decisions were designed to encourage economic expansion. Unemployment had risen from an annual average of 4.0 percent in 2000 to 4.7 percent in 2001 and 5.8 percent in 2002; it then hit 6.4 percent in June 2003. Thereafter, the funds rate was steadily raised over four years to 5.25 percent, as economic growth accelerated and the Fed sought to slow inflationary pressures. The Fed reversed course in September 2007 and began reducing the federal funds rate and the discount rate in an effort to halt the global credit crisis that had emerged in the summer, eventually reaching zero in December 2008.

In 1995 the FOMC began releasing explicit statements of its short-term policy objectives.[63] It now issues a statement after each of its meetings, not just those in which a rate change has been approved. Since March 2002 it has also reported the positions of its twelve voting members, the seven members of the Federal Reserve Board and five of the twelve Federal Reserve Bank presidents.

Although neither the president nor Congress can tell the Fed how to conduct monetary policy, the board traditionally has been the target of political pressures, especially during adverse economic conditions. Depending on circumstances, the inflation resulting from expansionary monetary policy or the stagnation and unemployment caused by restrictive policy can draw fire. During the Clinton administration, members of Congress and Wall Street frequently criticized the Fed for raising interest rates at the first sign of inflation and reducing them too slowly, but relations were generally cordial between Clinton and Greenspan, the Fed chair.[64] Clinton twice reappointed Greenspan (1996 and 2000) to the post he first assumed in 1987, and George W. Bush reappointed him when his term expired in 2004. After serving an unprecedented five terms as Fed chairman, Greenspan retired in January 2006. Expressing popular sentiment, Mankiw wrote: "No aspect of U.S. policy in the 1990s is more widely hailed as a success than monetary policy. Fed Chairman Alan Greenspan is often viewed as a miracle worker."[65] That reputation dimmed after the severe recession's onset, and Greenspan acknowledged having made policy errors.

Greenspan generally worked well with the Clinton administration and admired the president's commitment to fiscal responsibility. His relations with George W. Bush were sometimes rocky. Although he had endorsed Bush's 2001 tax cuts, in February and July 2003, he warned Congress about the impact of ballooning deficits projected to flow from another round of cuts. By stressing the need for budget discipline, he weakened the case for even larger proposed tax cuts, and his memoir expressed strong disagreement with the Bush administration's policies. Greenspan was replaced by Ben Bernanke, former chair of the CEA, who was expected to provide a smooth transition to a post-Greenspan era. An expert on the Great Depression, Bernanke worked closely with Paulson and Geithner to fashion effective strategies to combat the recession.

Treasury Secretary Timothy Geithner and Federal Reserve Chair Ben Bernanke testified before Congress in March 2009 on the government's financial support for the failed insurance company, American Insurance Group (AIG). The severity of the economic crisis produced close cooperation among policymakers during both the Bush and Obama administrations.

Presidents and Economic Policy Coordination

The independence of the Fed, the operational needs and organizational interests of the Treasury Department, and the institutional perspectives of other departments and agencies have led presidents to seek various ways to coordinate economic policy. For reasons explained in chapter 6, the cabinet has not been a satisfactory vehicle for collective leadership. Instead, presidents have developed a variety of intragovernmental councils and committees designed to provide a cohesive macroeconomic policy and integrate it with other policy objectives. Most of these entities failed to survive the administrations of their creators because subsequent presidents sought mechanisms more compatible with their own operating styles. A brief review of these undertakings, however, reveals common patterns in their approaches and indicates the essential requirements for a minimal amount of coordination.

Probably the most significant development for macroeconomic policymaking occurred under President Kennedy with the creation of the "troika," an informal committee consisting of the chair of the CEA, the secretary of the Treasury, and the director of the budget. The troika's original purpose was to coordinate economic forecasting, but it quickly became a mechanism for developing cooperation within the economic subpresidency in formulating fiscal policy. This arrangement contrasted with President Eisenhower's sharply focused groups, which, although they met often, were too numerous to bring about effective coordination. When joined by the chair of the Fed to coordinate monetary policy, the group has been known as the "quadriad." The participants have a "mutual interest in cooperation, not in their legal independence from each other. For an administration's economic policy to succeed, the Fed should pursue a parallel monetary policy," and vice versa.[66]

Working with staff support from the CEA, the Treasury Department, OMB, and occasionally the Fed, the troika/quadriad has helped many presidents formulate macroeconomic policy in a rapid, adaptive manner with some measure of protection from political and bureaucratic pressures. Not all presidents have made extensive use of the troika, but it is a natural institutional grouping that continues to operate, with the Treasury Department assuming responsibility for revenue estimates, OMB generating estimates of federal expenditures, the CEA forecasting economic trends, and the Fed (when involved) projecting money supply requirements.

Under Lyndon Johnson, the troika operation became regularized, and it emerged as the principal mechanism for the development of fiscal policy advice and alternatives.[67] President Nixon was uncomfortable with attempts to make policy by cabinet-level committees, and in early 1971 he designated Secretary of the Treasury John B. Connally (1971–1972) as his economic "czar," with responsibility for making major decisions. Connally dominated the troika, but his successor as Treasury secretary, George P. Shultz (1972–1974), operated in a more collegial manner. At the start of his second term, in January 1973, Nixon made Shultz assistant to the president for economic affairs and named him to chair a new cabinet-level coordinating body, the Council on Economic Policy. Shultz, working through interdepartmental committees, became the dominant figure in making and expounding economic policy for the Nixon administration.

Shultz's more inclusive machinery ushered in a series of presidential experiments with coordinating councils or "troika plus" groups. Gerald Ford used the Economic Policy Board (EPB), which operated in a formal and structured way to coordinate domestic and foreign economic policies. The secretary of the Treasury chaired the EPB, which also included the secretaries of labor, commerce, and state, the chair of the CEA, the director of OMB, and the assistant to the president for economic affairs. The latter official also directed the small EPB staff, housed in the

Executive Office of the President. Departments and agencies provided information, analysis, and expertise.[68] President Carter replaced the EPB with the Economic Policy Group (EPG), cochaired by the secretary of the Treasury and the chair of the CEA. The EPG was a large, unwieldy body. It had no staff, was accessible to a wide range of interested officials, and was not organized as a formal advisory body to the president. Its operations remained so unstructured that it was unable to coordinate even minor policy initiatives.[69]

President Reagan replaced the EPG with the Cabinet Council on Economic Affairs (CCEA). Like its predecessor in the Nixon administration, the CCEA was a forum for discussion of issues and alternatives. Roger Porter, veteran of the Ford EPB, was its secretary and informally coordinated its operations. In addition to the council, the troika met regularly to coordinate economic forecasting. But coordination efforts did not ensure that struggles for influence would disappear. The major participants in these battles were Regan, Stockman, Baker, and Meese. The administration had clearly defined macroeconomic policy goals: to reduce the role of the federal government in the U.S. economy, thus reducing taxes and spending, and to increase productivity, savings, and investment, thus ensuring vigorous and sustained economic growth and full employment. There was, however, sharp disagreement over the means to the ends. The conflict reflected competition among classical conservative, monetarist, and supply-side theories and focused on the significance of federal budget deficits. The winners were Regan and Meese, the supply-side advocates, and Stockman was the principal loser.[70]

President George H. W. Bush continued the advisory group, renaming it the Economic Policy Council. Porter once again managed its activities, with the help of his staff in the Office of Policy Development, and served as assistant to the president for economic and domestic affairs.[71] But the council met irregularly and did not establish an effective roundtable process for preparing issues for presidential decisions. Nor did the troika, which had fallen into disuse during Reagan's second term, regain its importance. No single individual or group had responsibility for defining for the economic subpresidency how policies were to be integrated.

Given the high priority President Clinton placed on economic issues during the 1992 campaign, it is not surprising that he was deeply involved in making economic policy. One of his first acts was to establish the National Economic Council (NEC) to coordinate domestic and international economic policies in a way similar to the National Security Council's coordination of foreign and military policymaking.[72] Operating with a professional staff of about twenty, the NEC's first chair, Robert Rubin, established an open, collegial, and nonhierarchical process that incorporated a wide and balanced range of economic considerations into the issue recommendations sent to the president.[73] The NEC's effectiveness became apparent during the 1993 budget battles: cabinet members worked through the budget and refrained from the infighting and leaks that had plagued previous administrations.[74] But all was not well: Clinton's economic advisers frequently clashed with his political advisers, who had managed his campaign. These conflicts concerned the primary focus of the administration's economic program and were fought both within the presidency and publicly.[75] The economic advisers stressed the importance of deficit reduction and the impact of policy on financial markets. The political advisers wanted to emphasize the populist issues that had helped to elect Clinton.[76] Rubin emerged as the dominant economic adviser and continued in that role after becoming secretary of the Treasury. His successor at the NEC, Laura Tyson, was unable to parlay coordination into influence; Gene Sperling, the next director, proved more successful.[77]

Lawrence Lindsey, President George W. Bush's initial director of the NEC, brought an especially rich foundation of personal experience to the position. A former member of the Fed's Board of Governors, Lindsey served on the CEA's staff under Reagan and became a staunch defender of supply-side tax cuts; he also was a special White House assistant in the G. H. W. Bush administration. As the younger Bush's economic adviser during the 2000 presidential election and the architect of his tax-cut plan, Lindsey entered the White House amid widespread expectations that he would enjoy the president's confidence, but this became an issue during his two years of service.[78] Lindsey resigned his post in December 2002 at the same time Secretary O'Neill quit, a major shakeup in the administration's economic team that attracted much media attention.[79] Lindsey was succeeded by Stephen Friedman, a longtime partner in the Wall Street investment firm of Goldman Sachs, with extensive experience in public service.[80] Allan Hubbard, a classmate of the president's in the Harvard MBA program, assumed the director's job in 2005.

Most observers expected Lawrence Summers, the new NEC chair, to play a pivotal role in fashioning the Obama administration's economic policy. Summers, a former secretary of the Treasury and president of Harvard University, was a mentor to Secretary Geithner and comfortable playing a public role. When Geithner received negative marks in the media for his public announcements and appearances before Congress during the first months of the administration, Summers began to play a more visible role.

As in other areas of policy, the nation is heavily dependent on presidents' attitudes, values, and operating styles for economic leadership. Congressionally established advisory mechanisms, such as the CEA, are helpful, and presidents can take other measures to assist them in identifying issues and achieving policy coordination; but advisory staffs and coordinating mechanisms provide no guarantee that the president will adopt effective policies or achieve his objectives. There is also an important check on presidential economic policymaking—Congress's power over taxing, spending, and the monetary system.

Congress's Role in Macroeconomic Policy

Most of the executive branch agencies and processes involving macroeconomic policy and the president's economic role were established by statute: the Federal Reserve Act of 1914, the Budget and Accounting Act of 1921, and the Employment Act of 1946. Traditionally, Congress has dealt with economic policy through separate consideration of tax legislation and annual appropriations. Tax bills have entailed redistributive issues—that is, questions of who bears the burdens and which special interests will secure favorable provisions, or "loop-holes." The congressional tax-writing committees (House Ways and Means and Senate Finance) have jealously guarded their powers and have been unwilling to propose new tax legislation that does not accommodate special interests. Appropriations decision making, centered in the House and Senate Appropriations Committees, traditionally focuses on incremental changes in department and agency budget requests. The politics of the budget process is a highly stylized game in which the institutional participants play specific roles. The primary consideration in Congress is the amount of increase or decrease in each agency's base, which is the previous year's appropriation. The total level of expenditures is the sum of the twelve major appropriations bills passed annually.[81]

Congress does not attempt consciously to shape fiscal policy through its taxing or spending legislation. Rather, its money decisions are the product of its fragmented authority structure, as reflected in the multiplicity of powerful committees and subcommittees, the weakness of party organizations, and the strong constituency orientation of members because of their constant concern with reelection.

Although the Budget and Accounting Act of 1921 required the president to prepare an annual budget and a comprehensive plan for spending, and although the Employment Act of 1946 required an annual economic report projecting revenues and expenditures in light of economic forecasts, Congress imposed no such requirements on itself. Fiscal policy was whatever remained of the president's program after it emerged from "a piecemeal and haphazard legislative process."[82] The inability of Congress to participate rationally on an equal basis with the presidency in shaping fiscal policy led to conflict during the Nixon administration, when federal spending became a politically significant issue. Spending grew rapidly in response to previously enacted statutory "entitlements" that could not be disregarded without revising the original authorizing legislation. Entitlements include Social Security benefits, federal retirement, farm price support, welfare payments, and food stamps. Most entitlement payments to individuals increase automatically with the cost of living.[83] Runaway budget deficits burgeoned from 1971 to 1997 as spending on entitlements and other mandatory programs grew four times faster than did spending in discretionary areas.[84]

Nixon challenged Congress to curb spending; when it did not do so, he frequently vetoed spending bills and made extensive use of impoundment. The primary response of Congress to this controversy with Nixon and to frustration over its inability to shape policy was the Budget and Impoundment Control Act of 1974, which created a procedure for handling impoundments. More important, that statute established a congressional budget process, created House and Senate Budget Committees, and provided Congress with independent staff support for macroeconomic forecasting and budget analysis in the form of the **Congressional Budget Office.**

Central to the congressional budget process in its present form are the **budget resolution** and the **reconciliation legislation.**[85] The budget resolution must be approved by both the House and the Senate but does not require the president's signature. As such it does not have the force of law, but it serves as the vehicle for changes in budget policy, allocates available money to congressional appropriations committees, and may activate reconciliation legislation. Usually the budget resolution is merely the means by which Congress organizes its action, but it has also set in motion major changes in fiscal policy. Presidents Reagan (in 1981) and Clinton (in 1993), each with sharply different objectives, used the congressional budget process to change taxing and spending policy. In 1995 Republican congressional leaders used the budget process to impose far-reaching policy changes Clinton strongly opposed.

Each budget resolution contains totals for revenues, expenditures, the deficit or surplus, and the national debt for the next fiscal year. Congress must adhere to these totals as it makes taxing and spending decisions. The budget resolution also contains target totals for the next four fiscal years and allocations of new budget authority for the next year to the major areas of federal spending, for example, defense, agriculture, and interest on the national debt.[86] It may also include reconciliation instructions.

Reconciliation is the process Congress uses "to bring revenue and spending under existing law into conformity with the levels set in the budget resolution."[87] First, Congress incorporates in the budget resolution binding instructions to specific committees—those that have jurisdiction over revenues and mandatory spending programs—to recommend statutory changes that will achieve the spending and revenue levels set in the resolution. Next, the House and Senate enact the committees' recommendations in a reconciliation bill. Reconciliation is an optional process that has tended to be used when either the president or Congress seeks a multiyear deficit reduction agreement. Reconciliation legislation became the major means of reducing the deficit.

But the redesigned congressional budget process may be losing its potential to guide decisions. For a while, the increased centralization of budgetary decision making in Congress enhanced the legislative branch's ability to influence presidential budget policies while providing the president with greater leverage over congressional budget decisions. Congress and the president became, as Allen Schick put it, "more interdependent: each [was] more vulnerable than before to having its budget preferences blocked or modified by the other." [88] Budget resolutions, however, increasingly include unrealistic appropriations targets, and the budget committees have receded into the background.[89]

From 1981 onward, Congress was locked in protracted conflict with Presidents Reagan, Bush, and Clinton over fiscal policy and the deficit. After a brief respite, the same held true for George W. Bush. Reagan and Bush I resisted tax increases and attempted to control the deficit through spending cuts, while Congress fought to protect pork barrel projects benefiting its constituencies, entitlements, and other programs that enjoyed wide popular or strong interest group support. Clinton won congressional support for his five-year deficit reduction package in 1993 but then waged intense budget battles with a Republican-controlled Congress during his final six years in office. Although George W. Bush won congressional support for massive tax cuts during his first months in office, subsequent battles focused on the timed phase-in of those cuts and the administration's spending priorities. Cutting the budget deficit proved not to be a winning election issue in the 1990s, but cutting taxes and expanding the deficit proved successful for his reelection. Obama, presiding over the largest deficits in history, will no doubt blaze new paths in this evolving relationship.

Conclusion

Can the president bring order and cohesion to macroeconomic policy? Can the presidency serve as the instrument for effective management of the economy? Such questions have never had greater currency than with the advent of the Obama administration.

Three major obstacles confront presidents in the performance of their economic policy-making roles: expectations are inordinately and unrealistically high; they have only limited authority to meet those expectations; and the base of knowledge on which they act is often limited and unreliable. The problem of unrealistic expectations is not peculiar to macroeconomic policy. To be elected, modern presidents have tended to make sweeping promises, and the American people have developed a deep faith that a strong, capable president can provide solutions to their most pressing problems.

As presidents try to develop policies that meet popular expectations, they encounter all kinds of difficulties. George H. W. Bush discovered as the recession of 1991 dragged into 1992 that the public is impatient for tangible results and the pressure is great for actions that can provide a "quick fix." Approaching elections heighten the search for measures that can produce immediate results. Nor is it easy to sort through conflicting goals. Curbing inflation, for example, may lead to unwelcome consequences, such as increased unemployment and higher interest rates. The popular bias against inaction runs deep, but sometimes inaction may be the most prudent course to follow. In short, exaggerated popular expectations that the president will manage the economy effectively may limit his capacity to do so.

Presidents quickly discover that their authority to act is limited. In macroeconomic policy, three factors restrict the ability to act: congressional prerogatives, the independence of the Federal Reserve Board, and the absence of coordinating power within the executive branch. Presidents must collaborate with Congress in making fiscal policy. Their ability to increase or reduce taxes or spending depends on congressional responsiveness to their leadership, to their effectiveness as communicators and persuaders. In the face of the 2008–2009 crisis, Congress was persuaded to follow first President Bush and then President Obama in adopting a rescue plan for the financial sector and then a massive stimulus package. Without dire predictions, the debate would have been more protracted and more difficult.

Monetary policy is equally confining because of the Fed's independence. The only resources the president has available to influence the Fed are persuasion and the periodic opportunity to appoint new members to the board and to designate its chair. Although presidents have regularly tried to pressure the Fed, there is no assurance that monetary policy will be compatible with fiscal policy or that it will not impede the achievement of other policy objectives. As John Kessel concludes, "Presidents are in the position of having only partial control (shared power in fiscal policy, only power to persuade in monetary policy) over blunt instruments that only sometimes lead to the desired economic results."[90]

Economic forecasting is an inexact science subject to large margins of error. The validity of the projections provided by the Council of Economic Advisers, the Office of Management and Budget, the Treasury Department, and the Federal Reserve Board depends on the assumptions that underlie them and on the quality and quantity of information available. The assumptions vary with the institutional orientation of the agency making the forecast, the theories of the economists on the agency's staff, and political pressures affecting the agency. The Fed's assumptions, for example, reflect the influence of monetarism; OMB's, a traditional concern with budget balancing. Forecasters may feel pressured to resolve budget problems by adopting best-case scenarios of economic performance.[91] If the assumptions underlying a forecast prove wrong, then policies based on the forecast may lead to unanticipated outcomes. The record deficits incurred during his administration caught President Reagan by surprise because he enthusiastically accepted OMB's rosy scenario. As President Obama noted during his second prime-time press conference, a small difference in anticipated growth rates produced dramatically different projections of deficits for the coming decade. As he pointed out, however, many other decisions about the budget would be made during that time and would alter that picture.

The nation has moved from a conservative consensus on economic policy in the 1920s and early 1930s to a Keynesian consensus in the 1950s and 1960s to a lack of consensus from the 1980s to the present day. Policies have shifted from Nixon's imposition of wage and price controls to Reagan's embrace of supply-side theory, the older Bush's pragmatism, Clinton's emphasis on long-term growth and investment in human capital, the younger Bush's embrace of supply-side prescriptions for growth, to Obama's formulas for recovery and reform. Despite all these changes, presidents still lack the capacity to control the economy even though rapidly changing economic conditions, in the United States and elsewhere, would seem to require the maximum amount of adaptiveness. The president's ability to respond to new situations, such as a sudden, large increase in the price of oil, is limited. The factors that appear to affect economic policymaking most substantially are a president's ideology and ability to persuade other influential decision makers.

SUGGESTED READINGS

Fisher, Louis. *Presidential Spending Power.* Princeton: Princeton University Press, 1975.

Frankel, Jeffrey, and Peter Orszag. *American Economic Policy in the 1990s.* Cambridge: MIT Press, 2002.

Frendreis, John P., and Raymond Tatalovich. *The Modern Presidency and Economic Policy.* Itasca, Ill.: Peacock, 1994.

Greenspan, Alan. *The Age of Turbulence: An Adventure in a New World.* New York: Penguin Press, 2007.

Kessel, John H. *Presidents, the Presidency, and the Political Environment.* Washington, D.C.: CQ Press, 2001.

Kettl, Donald F. *Leadership at the Fed.* New Haven: Yale University Press, 1986.

Mills, Gregory B., and John L. Palmer, eds. *Federal Budget Policy in the 1980s.* Washington, D.C.: Urban Institute Press, 1984.

Niskanen, William A. *Reaganomics.* New York: Oxford University Press, 1988.

Palazzolo, Daniel J. *Done Deal? The Politics of the 1997 Budget Agreement.* Chatham, N.J.: Chatham House, 1999.

Porter, Roger B. *Presidential Decision Making: The Economic Policy Board.* New York: Cambridge University Press, 1980.

Schick, Allen. *The Federal Budget: Politics, Policy, Process.* 3rd ed. Washington, D.C.: Brookings, 2007.

Stein, Herbert. *Presidential Economics: The Making of Economic Policy from Roosevelt to Reagan and Beyond.* 3rd rev. ed. Washington, D.C.: AEI Press, 1994.

Stockman, David A. *The Triumph of Politics: Why the Reagan Revolution Failed.* New York: Harper and Row, 1986.

Tatalovich, Raymond, Chris J. Dolan, and John Frendreis. *The Presidency and Economic Policy.* Lanham, Md.: Rowman and Littlefield, 2008.

Tufte, Edward R. *Political Control of the Economy.* Princeton: Princeton University Press, 1980.

Wildavsky, Aaron, and Naomi Caiden. *The New Politics of the Budgetary Process.* 5th ed. New York: Longman, 2003.

Notes

1. Edmund L. Andrews, "Bad News Puts Political Glare on the Economy," *New York Times,* September 8, 2007, www.nytimes.com/2007/09/08/business/08policy.html?hp.

2. John P. Frendreis and Raymond Tatalovich, *The Modern Presidency and Economic Policy* (Itasca, Ill.: Peacock, 1994), 300.

3. "[T]he bounty of the 1990s resulted less from Clinton's personal stewardship of prosperity than from his willingness to follow the learned advice of others and, more fundamentally, from economic forces beyond his control." Raymond Tatalovich and John Frendreis, "Clinton, Class, and Economic Policy," in *The Postmodern Presidency: Bill Clinton's Legacy in U.S. Politics,* ed. Steven E. Schier (Pittsburgh: University of Pittsburgh Press, 2000), 41–42. Also see the review of Clinton's accomplishments by Paul J. Quirk and William Cunion, "Clinton's Domestic Policy: The Lessons of a 'New Democrat,'" in *The Clinton Legacy,* ed. Colin Campbell and Bert A. Rockman (Chatham, N.J.: Chatham House, 2001), 214–216.

4. Technically, the National Bureau of Economic Research sets the recession's beginning at March 2001; it lasted until November 2001, www.nber.org/cycles.html.

5. Edward R. Tufte, *Political Control of the Economy* (Princeton: Princeton University Press, 1978).

6. A. James Reichley, "A Change in Direction," in *Setting National Priorities: The 1982 Budget,* ed. Joseph A. Pechman (Washington, D.C.: Brookings, 1981), 236–240.

7. Bob Woodward, "Greenspan is Critical of Bush in Memoir," *Washington Post,* September 15, 2007, A1.

8. John H. Kessel, *Presidents, the Presidency, and the Political Environment* (Washington, D.C.: CQ Press, 2001), 150–151.

9. David M. Herszenhorn, "Bush and House in Accord for $150 Billion Stimulus," *New York Times*, January 25, 2008, http://www.nytimes.com/2008/01/25/washington/25fiscal.html?sq=2008.

10. "Sorting out the Bailouts," *CQ Weekly Online*, February 23, 2009, 394; "Federal Reserve: Opening the Flood Gates," *CQ Weekly Online*, February 23, 2009, 406–407, http://library.cqpress.com/cqweekly/weeklyreport111-000003058068.

11. Surveys have indicated that lump-sum payments to taxpayers, as used in 2008, are likely to result in recipients saving the money or using it to pay debts rather than using it for consumer purchases.

12. Michael Fletcher, "Obama Leaves D.C. to Sign Stimulus Bill," *Washington Post*, February 18, 2009, A5. "Economic Stimulus," Times Topics, *New York Times*, March 25, 2009, http://topics.nytimes.com/topics/reference/timestopics/subjects/u/united_states_economy/economic_stimulus/index.html.

13. "Sorting out the Bailouts."

14. Alan Stone, *Regulation and Its Alternatives* (Washington, D.C.: CQ Press, 1982), 262.

15. Lester M. Salamon and Alan J. Abramson, "Governance: The Politics of Retrenchment," in *The Reagan Record*, ed. John L. Palmer and Isabel V. Sawhill (Washington, D.C.: Urban Institute Press, 1984), 47.

16. Marshall R. Goodman, "A Kinder and Gentler Regulatory Reform: The Bush Regulatory Strategy and Its Impact" (paper presented at the annual meeting of the Midwest Political Science Association, Chicago, April 1991).

17. Robert W. Hahn and Robert N. Stavins, "National Environmental Policy during the Clinton Years," in *American Economic Policy in the 1990s*, ed. Jeffrey Frankel and Peter Orszag (Cambridge: MIT Press, 2002), 587.

18. David S. Cloud, "Industry, Politics Intertwined in Dole's Regulatory Bill," *Congressional Quarterly Weekly Report*, May 6, 1995, 1219–1224; and Bob Benenson, "GOP Sets the 104th Congress on New Regulatory Course," *Congressional Quarterly Weekly Report*, June 17, 1995, 1693–1697.

19. David S. Cloud, "Dole's Bill: An 'Aggressive' Position," *Congressional Quarterly Weekly Report*, May 6, 1995, 1221.

20. James A. Barnes, "Is Bush Poisoning His Well?" *National Journal*, April 14, 2001, 1120–1121; and Eric Pianin, "Administration Revisits Forest Lands Rules; Paper Industry, Western Governors Want Protective Regulation Scaled Back," *Washington Post*, July 7, 2001, A2.

21. Eric Pianin and Mike Allen, "Clinton Forest Rules to Stand," *Washington Post*, May 4, 2001, A1; Cindy Skrzycki, "OMB to Revisit Costs, Benefits of Rules," *Washington Post*, May 29, 2001, E1; Amy Goldstein, " 'Last-Minute' Spin on Regulatory Rite: Bush Review of Clinton Initiatives Is Bid to Reshape Rules," *Washington Post*, June 9, 2001, A1; Marilyn Geewax, "Bush Proving to be No Radical When It Comes to Regulation," Cox News Service, June 13, 2001; and Juliet Eilperin, "GOP Won't Try to Halt Last Rules by Clinton: Hill Power Shift Forces Retreat on Spring Plans," *Washington Post*, July 30, 2001, A1.

22. Shawn Zeller, "Free Market Crusaders," *National Journal*, January 11, 2003.

23. Paul Singer, "By the Horns," *National Journal*, March 25, 2005.

24. Benton Ives and Phil Mattingly, "Geithner Outlines Regulatory Overhaul," *CQ Weekly Online*, March 30, 2009, 728–730, http://library.cqpress.com/cqweekly/weeklyreport111-000003087459.

25. Walter W. Heller, *New Dimensions in Political Economy* (New York: Norton, 1966).

26. Jackie Calmes, "The Voracious National Debt," *Congressional Quarterly Weekly Report*, March 24, 1990, 896.

27. George Hager, "Deficit Shows No Gain from Pain of Spending Rules," *Congressional Quarterly Weekly Report*, July 20, 1991, 1963. Bush also encountered shortfalls in revenues arising from "technical reestimates" and higher projected spending for Medicaid.

28. Frendreis and Tatalovich, *The Modern Presidency*, 314.

29. Richard W. Stevenson, "The Wisdom to Let the Good Times Roll," *New York Times*, December 25, 2000, A1.

30. Clinton's term averages can be found in Tatalovich and Frendreis, "Clinton, Class, and Economic Policy," Table 1, 44. Unemployment data can be found in Harold W. Stanley and Richard G. Niemi, *Vital Statistics on American Politics 1999–2000* (Washington, D.C.: CQ Press, 2000), Table 11-10.

31. George Hager, "Time Is Ripe for Agreement but Gridlock Dies Hard," *Congressional Quarterly Weekly Report,* November 16, 1996, 3280–3281.

32. Daniel J. Palazzolo, *Done Deal? The Politics of the 1997 Budget Agreement* (Chatham, N.J.: Chatham House, 1999). Palazzolo contends that the process of moving toward a balanced budget was fifteen years in the making, stretching back to 1982.

33. Stevenson, "The Wisdom to Let the Good Times Roll," A12.

34. Glenn Kessler, "Bush Tax Cut Pares Government's Role," *Washington Post,* May 21, 2001, A1.

35. "Big Plans, Big Costs, Big Deficits," *CQ Weekly Online,* March 2, 2009, 472–481, http://library.cqpress.com/cqweekly/weeklyreport111-000003063696.

36. Schick, "Bush's Budget Problem," 4.

37. Testimony of Peter G. Peterson, president, the Concord Coalition, before the House Financial Services Committee, April 30, 2003, 3, www.concordcoalition.org/federal_budget/030430petersontestimonyexecsummary.htm. At the time of his testimony, Peterson was chair of the Federal Reserve Bank of New York; he had served as secretary of commerce in the Nixon administration.

38. See www.brillig.com/debt_clock.

39. Douglas W. Elmendorf, Jeffrey B. Liebman, and David W. Wilcox, "Fiscal Policy and Social Security Policy during the 1990s," in Frankel and Orszag, *American Economic Policy in the 1990s,* 117.

40. Amy Belasco, "The Cost of Iraq, Afghanistan, and Other Global War on Terror Operations Since 9/11," CRS Report for Congress RL33110, updated October 15, 2008, http://www.fas.org/sgp/crs/natsec/RL33110.pdf.

41. Paul E. Peterson and Mark Rom argue that presidents have little incentive to "manipulate the economy for either electoral or partisan reasons." In Peterson and Rom's view, presidents can best achieve their diverse objectives through economic policies that maintain a balance between inflation and steady economic growth with minimal rates of unemployment. See Peterson and Rom, "Macroeconomic Policymaking: Who Is in Control?" in *Can the Government Govern?,* ed. John E. Chubb and Paul E. Peterson (Washington, D.C.: Brookings, 1989), 149.

42. George Hager and David S. Cloud, "Democrats Tie Their Fate to Clinton's Budget Bill," *Congressional Quarterly Weekly Report,* August 7, 1993, 2122–2129.

43. Richard W. Stevenson, "Bush Signs Tax Cut Bill, Dismissing All Criticism," *New York Times,* May 29, 2003, www.nytimes.com/2003/05/29/politics/29TAX.html.

44. David R. Beam, "New Federalism, Old Realities: The Reagan Administration and Intergovernmental Reform," in *The Reagan Presidency and the Governing of America,* ed. Lester M. Salamon and Michael S. Lund (Washington, D.C.: Urban Institute, 1984), 440; and Paul E. Peterson, *The Price of Federation* (Washington, D.C.: Brookings, 1995), 69.

45. Peri Arnold, "Clinton and the Institutionalized Presidency," in Schier, *The Postmodern Presidency,* 26–28.

46. James E. Anderson and Jared E. Hazleton, *Managing Macroeconomic Policy: The Johnson Presidency* (Austin: University of Texas Press, 1986), 14.

47. For a brief profile, see "The Decision Makers," *National Journal,* June 23, 2001, 1896.

48. Jonathan Weisman, "Bush Tax-Cut Adviser Resigns: President Nominates Harvard Economist to Replace Hubbard," *Washington Post,* February 27, 2003, A9.

49. See http://www.whitehouse.gov/administration/eop/cea/members/.

50. Joseph A. Davis, "Policy and Regulatory Review: Growth in Legislative Role Sparks Concern in Congress," *Congressional Quarterly Weekly Report,* September 14, 1985, 1809.

51. M. Stephen Weatherford and Lorraine M. McDonnell, "Clinton and the Economy: The Paradox of Policy Success and Political Mishap" (paper presented at the annual meeting of the American Political Science Association, Chicago, August 31–September 3, 1995), 21.

52. Ibid., 28.

53. For a brief profile, see "The Decision Makers," 1905.

54. See http://www.whitehouse.gov/omb/organization_office/.

55. Anderson and Hazleton, *Managing Macroeconomic Policy*, 27.

56. Colin Campbell, "The White House and the Cabinet under the 'Let's Deal' President," in *The Bush Presidency: First Appraisals*, ed. Colin Campbell and Bert A. Rockman (Chatham, N.J.: Chatham House, 1991), 211.

57. Frendreis and Tatalovich, *The Modern Presidency*, 56.

58. Weatherford and McDonnell, "Clinton and the Economy," 20–21.

59. For a brief profile, see "The Decision Makers," 1987.

60. "Treasury: Blunt? Yes. Politically Savvy? No," *National Journal*, January 24, 2003, http://nationaljournal.com/members/news/2003/01/0124nj_oneill.htm.

61. See http://www.ustreas.gov/organization/bios/geithner-e.shtml.

62. Colin Campbell, *Managing the Presidency: Carter, Reagan, and the Search for Executive Harmony* (Pittsburgh: University of Pittsburgh Press, 1986), 123–135. Also see Kessel, *Presidents, the Presidency, and the Political Environment*, 127–129.

63. Cheryl L. Edwards, "Open Market Operations in the 1990s," *Federal Reserve Bulletin*, November 1997, 862, www.federalreserve.gov/pubs/bulletin/1997/199711lead.pdf.

64. For a brief biography of Greenspan, see http://www.biography.com/articles/Alan-Greenspan-9319769

65. N. Gregory Mankiw, "U.S. Monetary Policy during the 1990s," in Frankel and Orszag, *American Economic Policy in the 1990s*, 19.

66. Kessel, *Presidents, the Presidency, and the Political Environment*, 138.

67. Anderson and Hazleton, *Managing Macroeconomic Policy*, 83.

68. Roger B. Porter, *Presidential Decision Making: The Economic Policy Board* (New York: Cambridge University Press, 1980).

69. Campbell, *Managing the Presidency*, 138.

70. David A. Stockman, *The Triumph of Politics: Why the Reagan Revolution Failed* (New York: Harper and Row), 1986.

71. Campbell, "The White House and the Cabinet," 210.

72. Frendreis and Tatalovich, *The Modern Presidency*, 70.

73. Paul Starobin, "The Broker," *National Journal*, April 16, 1994, 878–883.

74. Weatherford and McDonnell, "Clinton and the Economy," 21.

75. Bob Woodward, *The Agenda: Inside the Clinton White House* (New York: Simon and Schuster, 1994).

76. Weatherford and McDonnell, "Clinton and the Economy," 39.

77. Kessel, *Presidents, the Presidency, and the Political Environment*, 143; Tatalovich and Frendreis, "Clinton, Class, and Economic Policy," 47; and Stevenson, "The Wisdom to Let the Good Times Roll," A13. For an overall evaluation of the Clinton economic policy-making system, see Jonathan M. Orszag, Peter R. Orszag, and Laura D. Tyson, "The Process of Economic Policy-Making during the Clinton Administration," in Frankel and Orszag, *American Economic Policy in the 1990s*, 983–1027.

78. For a brief profile, see "The Decision Makers," 1894–1895.

79. Still another major figure, Harvey Pitt, chairman of the Securities and Exchange Commission, had resigned a month earlier amid controversy over his role in selecting members to serve on a corporate accounting watchdog board.

80. See www.whitehouse.gov/news/releases/2002/12/20021212-9.html.

81. The appropriations do not include entitlement programs, such as Social Security, Medicare, and Medicaid, or interest on the national debt.

82. James L. Sundquist, *The Decline and Resurgence of Congress* (Washington, D.C.: Brookings, 1981), 199.

83. R. Kent Weaver, *Automatic Government: The Politics of Indexation* (Washington, D.C.: Brookings, 1988).

84. Palazzolo, *Done Deal?*, 20.

85. This discussion follows Allen Schick, *The Federal Budget: Politics, Policy, Process* (Washington, D.C.: Brookings, 1995), chap. 5.

86. Schick defines budget authority as "legislation that enables an agency to incur obligations. Obligations occur when agencies take any action . . . that commits the government to the payment of funds." Ibid., 19.

87. Ibid., 82.

88. Allen Schick, "The Evolution of Congressional Budgeting," in *Crisis in the Budget Process: Exercising Political Choice*, ed. Allen Schick (Washington, D.C.: American Enterprise Institute, 1986),15.

89. Stan Collender, "Happy New Year?" *National Journal*, July 1, 2003, www.nationaljournal.com/members/buzz/2003/budget/070103.htm.

90. Kessel, *Presidents, the Presidency, and the Political Environment*, 151.

91. Stockman, *The Triumph of Politics*, 97–98, 329–332.

CHAPTER 10

The Politics of National Security Policy

George W. Bush delivered extemporaneous remarks to relief workers during a September 14, 2001, visit to "Ground Zero" at the site of New York's World Trade Center, noting that their courageous efforts had served as an example for the entire nation.

National security policy ideally reflects long-term geopolitical conditions in the world. Examples are the long-standing alliance of the United States with the United Kingdom; the forty-five-year conflict between the United States and the Soviet Union following World War II; the intractability of religious and cultural differences in the Balkans, the Middle East, and Northern Ireland; and the vital role played by oil-producing states in the global economy. Seldom do single events serve as dramatic turning points that reshape the direction of policy, but millions of people were convinced that their lives and U.S. foreign policy were permanently altered by the events of September 11, 2001, when terrorist attacks fully or partially destroyed two symbols of American power in the world: the twin towers of the World Trade Center in New York City and the Pentagon, headquarters of the U.S. military, just across the Potomac River from Washington, D.C.

In a coordinated attack, three airliners carrying large fuel supplies were hijacked by small groups of men, who then sacrificed their own lives and those of the passengers by flying the planes directly into the targets. A fourth aircraft, presumably headed for Washington, D.C., crashed in Pennsylvania, the attack foiled by passengers aboard the plane. Millions witnessed the second attack on the World Trade Center on live television. The fireball and crumbling towers became horrific images in their collective memory. For days the nation's normal life seemed suspended as attention focused on stories of emergency evacuations, reports of heroic rescue efforts, the search for missing loved ones, and the expanding investigation. Approximately three thousand people died in the two incidents. In the aftermath, the economy was seriously disrupted with the stock exchanges closed for four days and the nation's air transportation system first shut down, and then resuming operation at severely reduced levels. The airlines entered a prolonged financial tailspin.

Only the surprise Japanese attack on Pearl Harbor, in December 1941, which led to U.S. involvement in World War II, had a similar galvanizing effect on the nation. Before the week was over, President George W. Bush had secured congressional approval of an emergency appropriation of $40 billion for disaster relief and increased preparedness. Congress also approved, by near unanimous votes (98-0 in the Senate; 420-1 in the House), a resolution authorizing the president to use "all necessary and appropriate force against those nations, organizations, or persons he determines planned, authorized, committed or aided the terrorist attacks . . . or harbored such organizations or persons."[1] National unity and patriotic fervor prevailed on Capitol Hill, where partisan conflict and recrimination had been building in the expected battle over budget priorities. In a vast outpouring of solidarity, people throughout the nation attended religious services and nondenominational ceremonies, gave blood, donated money, and flew the American flag in remembrance and support for those who had died or suffered losses. As the government prepared a response, Americans seemed almost reluctant to return to their daily routines, an unspoken acknowledgment, perhaps, that life in the United States had been irrevocably changed.

The administration clearly recognized how these events had altered its direction and focus. In a news conference held two days after the attacks, President Bush acknowledged that "this is now the focus of my administration. We will be very much engaged in domestic policy, of course. I look forward to working with Congress on a variety of issues. But now that war has been declared on us, we will lead the world to victory."[2]

Mobilizing public support for a war effort and fashioning an international response became the principal concerns of an administration that had been forced to scramble on the day of the attacks. On September 11, President Bush was in Florida at an event designed to build public support for his education program when he learned of the attacks. He returned to Washington by way of military installations in Louisiana and Nebraska only after the situation had stabilized and the danger of attempts on the White House and *Air Force One*, his plane, had been resolved. In his prime-time address to the nation that evening, Bush quietly reassured the American people that everything was being done to help the injured, continue the federal government's operations without interruption, and find those responsible for the attacks. In the following days, his rhetoric escalated to a virtual declaration of war against the enemies of civilization. The United States was about to launch a sustained assault against a very different kind of enemy in hopes of eradicating terrorism.

This effort began in Afghanistan with forces from the United States and other nations targeting the al Qaeda terrorist organization of Osama bin Laden and the fundamentalist Taliban regime that had provided it with sanctuary. Coordinated international efforts against other known terrorist organizations grew in the following months. But global unity diminished in 2002 when the United States expanded its focus to include the "rogue state" of Iraq, whose alleged ties to terrorism proved difficult to document.

The war on terrorism was a far cry from the national security challenges that prevailed during the last half of the twentieth century, which stemmed from the U.S.-Soviet rivalry. The dominant countries in world affairs following World War II, the United States and the Soviet Union, led two armed camps of nations—one democratically governed, the other ruled by Communist dictatorships. The industrial democracies and the Communist bloc coexisted in an uneasy peace, maintained in part by the threat of mutual nuclear annihilation. At the same time, each power grouping actively courted the support of the "uncommitted" developing countries, nations of the so-called third world. These countries, most facing enormous economic and social problems, varied in their orientations toward Washington and Moscow. Superimposed on the basic pattern of U.S.-Soviet competition was the twentieth-century technological revolution in communications, transportation, and weaponry, which had the effect of shrinking the world and making the risks of military confrontation greater than ever. In addition, the United States grew more economically interdependent with other countries, especially suppliers of basic raw materials, such as oil.

In an environment characterized by military precariousness and economic interdependence, no chief executive could focus primarily and indefinitely on domestic policy. Modern presidents from Franklin D. Roosevelt to George W. Bush were drawn almost irresistibly to concentrate instead on national security policy (foreign affairs and military policy). The reasons for this predictable emphasis across administrations are at least twofold: first, the crucial importance of the United States in the international community; and second, the political advantages presidents normally derive from devoting much of their energy to national security.[3]

Ronald Reagan came into office in 1981 committed to bringing about a conservative revolution in domestic and economic policy but found himself drawn toward national security issues. His successor, George H. W. Bush, was preoccupied with foreign and military policy from the start of his administration and only reluctantly turned his attention homeward when the economy faltered and his reelection campaign approached. In that campaign, Bill Clinton successfully attacked Bush for neglecting the health of the economy and other serious domestic problems and promised that, if elected, he would concentrate on them. Much to his dismay, Clinton discovered upon taking office that the end of the Cold War brought new conflicts and still greater uncertainty to international affairs. Clinton eventually involved himself extensively with foreign policy; in the last few months of his presidency, he seemed to be consumed by the desire to produce a long-evasive Middle East peace settlement.

During his first one hundred days in office, George W. Bush dealt primarily with domestic policy except for one incident when a U.S. plane collided with a Chinese jet fighter. The U.S. plane was forced to land on Chinese territory, a reminder that foreign policy can intrude unexpectedly on the national agenda. The attacks of September 2001 changed the administration's focus. The war on terrorism and the overthrow of Saddam Hussein's regime in Iraq became the defining features of Bush's presidency and will determine how he is remembered in history.

Barack Obama confronted an especially challenging set of problems when he entered the White House, as Thomas Ricks of the *Washington Post* explained: "President Obama has my sympathy. He has inherited the worst foreign policy situation that any new president has taken on. And what's really scary about that statement is, it's not even his number one problem."[4] With wars raging in Iraq and Afghanistan, instability in Pakistan, nuclear threats in Iran and North Korea, and anti-Americanism widespread even in NATO nations, Obama faced a daunting set of international issues that were still overshadowed by the economic problems at home. In short, the president did not have the luxury of choosing among problems; instead, he had to move forward on multiple fronts simultaneously. And with the recession spreading globally, the two sets of problems intersected.

This chapter examines the president's role in making and directing national security policy. It first reviews the major concepts and issues that have dominated that policy area since World War II. It then defines the essential paradox in national security policymaking as one in which the president is both the solution and the problem. Finally, the discussion turns to the relationship between the president and Congress with respect to national security and the problem of organizing an effective policymaking system for national security.

Issues in National Security Policy: Search for a New Consensus

For more than two decades, from the end of World War II until March 1968, America's principal national interest was clear-cut: military containment of communism. But when public reaction to the North Vietnamese Tet offensive precipitated Lyndon Johnson's decision to end the escalation of American involvement in the Vietnam War, the broad consensus undergirding U.S. national security policy began to disintegrate, a process that continued until Communist power collapsed in Eastern Europe in 1991. Until Tet, a succession of presidents from both political parties had consistently pursued the doctrine of **containment.** Bipartisan support for the consensus in Congress gave presidents a free hand in formulating and implementing foreign and military policies. The only effective constraints imposed on presidential actions were the boundaries of the consensus, which began to break up in 1968, when it became apparent that containment could be preserved only through an indefinite, limited war in Vietnam or greatly expanded U.S. involvement that carried risks of conflict with the Soviet Union.

Even after the United States failed to "contain" communism in Vietnam, presidents continued to employ single, overarching concepts to build domestic political support for their national security policies. They found that "selling programs to Congress and the American people in the postwar era was always made easier if they could be clothed in one garment."[5] Détente, human rights, the "evil empire," a "new world order," engagement, and enlargement emerged as successors to containment, but none proved to be the core of an enduring national consensus. The Bush administration's response to the threats of terrorism, tyrants, and weapons of mass destruction failed to provide the sustained political support missing for so long. A 2003 study from the Council on Foreign Relations eloquently made the case for the importance of having such a consensus:

From the fall of the Berlin Wall in 1989 to the fall of the Twin Towers in 2001, and even now after the Iraq War of 2003, the United States has not had a consistent national security strategy that enjoyed the support of the American people and our allies. This situation is markedly different from the Cold War era, when our nation had a clear, coherent, widely supported strategy that focused on containing and deterring Soviet Communist expansion. The tragic events of September 11, the increase in terrorism, and threats from countries such as North Korea and, until recently, Iraq create an imperative once again to fashion and implement a coherent national security strategy that will safeguard our national interests.[6]

Efforts to Rebuild Consensus, Nixon through Clinton

In 1972 and 1973 President Nixon told the American people that a policy of **détente** would ease, if not end, the U.S.-Soviet tensions of the Cold War. The government would implement détente through actions such as cultural exchanges, increased trade between the two countries, and negotiations to limit strategic nuclear weapons. Established attitudes and behavior patterns are not easy to change, however, and Nixon and his successor, Gerald Ford, found it convenient to seek support for their policies by citing threatening Soviet actions in various parts of the world, such as Africa, Latin America, and the Middle East.

Jimmy Carter effectively campaigned on the pledge, which he reaffirmed at the outset of his administration, that morality, manifested in universal commitment to the defense of **human rights,** would be the cornerstone of U.S. foreign policy. But the United States found it easier to protest and threaten to take action against human rights violations in countries not vital to its interests, such as the Soviet Union and its allies, than in those that were vital, such as South Korea and South Africa. The United States did not have the capacity to enforce the doctrine against powerful violators.

Reagan took office proclaiming belligerently that his administration's framework for national security policy was continued opposition to, and competition with, the Soviet Union, which he once called "the evil empire."[7] In practice, however, his anti-Soviet stance was less than doctrinaire—strong rhetoric was combined with restrained conduct. For example, Reagan's administration, intent on limiting nuclear weapons and curtailing the arms race, achieved the first arms reduction agreement of the Cold War, the Intermediate Range Nuclear Forces Treaty. It was a singular accomplishment, and it was realized not through belligerent opposition but through painstaking, lengthy give-and-take negotiations.

Reagan's ability to construct a new consensus with a strategic vision based on superpower conflict was undercut by the **Iran-contra affair.**[8] Journalists and political critics persisted in asking questions about explanations of the administration's actions and the president's knowledge of international events. Was it the president who set American foreign policy or his aides in the State Department, the Central Intelligence Agency (CIA), and the National Security Council (NSC)? These questions seemed fully justified when the administration acknowledged in November 1986 that it had sent a small number of obsolete weapons to Iran as a means of contacting and encouraging moderate political elements. Reagan vigorously denied that there had been any explicit exchange of arms for hostages, even though each hostage's release had been preceded by an arms shipment. In late November 1986 the president acknowledged that profits from the arms sales, between $10 million and $30 million, had been diverted to the Nicaraguan contras through a numbered Swiss bank account. This was a direct violation of the Boland amendment, adopted by Congress in 1984, which prohibited use of government funds to support covert operations against the government of Nicaragua. Reagan claimed he had not been fully informed about the matter. Selling arms to Iran in apparent exchange for American hostages called into question the commitment of the United States to resisting terrorism and isolating countries, such as Iran, that support terrorism. Rather than establishing a new consensus, Reagan's methods provided lessons in how not to manage foreign policy. His detached administrative style, which entailed extensive delegation and a disdain for factual details, allowed him to address "the big picture" but left many critical decisions to his subordinates. The operation of the foreign policy process, especially the independent role played by the NSC staff, contributed a great deal to Reagan's political difficulties and did little to protect him from foreign policy mistakes.

In contrast to Reagan, George H. W. Bush was a hands-on president deeply engaged in the formulation and implementation of national security policy. He concerned himself with its details and participated actively in negotiations with foreign leaders. In addition, he approached foreign policy with a pragmatic, rather than ideological, orientation. Critics complained, however, that his administration's foreign policy was purely tactical and lacked a strategic design.[9] The "new world order" Bush announced following the collapse of communism in Russia and throughout Eastern Europe was unable to sustain a national consensus, in part because its meaning remained unclear. Bush continued the policies of the late Reagan years but with greater flexibility and adaptiveness.[10] He provided "a kind of competent Reaganism" and "restore[d] professionalism to the conduct of foreign policy,"[11] highlighted by his skillful guidance of an international coalition against Sadam Hussein in the 1991 Persian Gulf War. Despite its success, Bush's foreign policy was essentially reactive. Its major initiatives—the invasion of Panama and the Gulf War—were responses to crises. The Bush administration was unable to develop a strategic design for the post–Cold War world or a replacement for the Soviet threat as the unifying force linking the United States with the NATO countries and Japan. From the start, the Clinton

TABLE 10-1   Presidential Use of Force Reported in Compliance with the War Powers Resolution, 1969–2009

President/term	*Times complied with War Powers Resolution*
Nixon (1969–1974)	0
Ford (1974–1977)	4
Carter (1977–1981)	1
Reagan (1981–1989)	14
G. H. W. Bush (1989–1993)	7
Clinton (1993–2001)	60
G. W. Bush (2001–2009)	39

SOURCES: Richard F. Grimmet, "War Powers Resolution: Presidential Compliance," original release March 2001 and updated version February 2, 2009. CRS Issue Brief for Congress, Congressional Research Service, Library of Congress, March 21, 2001, and February 2, 2009, http://assets.opencrs.com/rpts/RL33532_20090202.pdf. Also see CRS Report RL31185 "The War Powers Resolution: After Twenty-eight Years."

administration embraced numerous high-minded goals: expand democracy and human rights; alleviate disease, hunger, and poverty; encourage free markets within states and the growth of free trade between them; and control weapons of mass destruction.[12] Frequently, however, the administration found it difficult to translate these goals into workable policies in specific instances: nation building failed in Somalia, intervention failed to restore democracy in Haiti, indecision plagued Bosnia policy, and genocide was tolerated in Rwanda. Nor did the administration ever clearly resolve the question of when military power could appropriately be employed, despite using force in Bosnia, Haiti, Somalia, Iraq, Afghanistan, Sudan, and Kosovo. (See Table 10-1.) Clinton's administration also vacillated between multilateralism and unilateralism as means to achieve its ends, sometimes acting alone and at other times refusing to act unless allies joined in the effort.

The first extensive statement of the administration's strategy appeared in July 1994 and identified three central themes: domestic renewal, engagement abroad to enlarge market democracies, and multilateralism as a primary mode of operation.[13] Market democracies would be extended ("enlargement") and threats contained ("engagement") to achieve renewal at home.[14] Two of Clinton's biggest foreign policy successes—legislation implementing the North American Free Trade Agreement (NAFTA) and renewing and expanding the General Agreement on Tariffs and Trade (GATT)—were justified as improving the American economy. By 1998, however, official statements had shifted. Defending the nation from terrorism, drug trafficking, and crime, as well as from weapons of mass destruction, became more prominent goals than advancing market economies. The administration also recognized that managing the international financial markets was a critical task, an appropriate goal given the global impacts of financial crises in Mexico and Asia.[15] But the new statement of goals still lacked a unifying statement of purpose. Although Clinton was active on many fronts and willing to employ military force, he remained unable to articulate a clear strategy.

George W. Bush's National Security Strategy

On September 17, 2002, the Bush administration released a long-awaited statement on national security strategy, the first since 1999. Although Congress had mandated that such a report be issued within a president's first five months in office and annually thereafter, the Clinton administration had failed to issue one during its final year, and Bush's first report was twenty months late. In fact, Bush had ordered a wide-ranging strategic review in 2001 that was interrupted by the September terrorist attacks. Glimmers of the new strategy appeared in his 2002 State of the Union message and in two June speeches; internal documents, partially released in December 2002, also suggested the administration's thinking.[16] Together, these speeches and documents constituted a reformulation of American strategy praised by some observers as the boldest, most sweeping statement of grand strategy since the Marshall Plan was introduced in 1947.[17] Others reviled it as an attempt to create an "arrogant empire."[18]

Even before 9/11, the Bush administration adopted a different approach to the world by withdrawing from five international treaties, discontinuing major peace initiatives launched by the Clinton administration toward North Korea and the Middle East, and adopting an assertive tone that suggested a unilateral, rather than multilateral, mode of action. The terrorist attacks heightened these trends. "It [9/11] produced a mobilization of American power and yet a narrowing of American interests. Suddenly, Washington was more powerful and determined to act. But it would act only for its own core security and even preemptively when it needed to."[19]

In his State of the Union message of January 2002, President Bush warned three states to halt their pursuit of weapons of mass destruction and their sponsorship of terrorism. Iraq, Iran, and North Korea constituted what the president termed an "axis of evil."[20] In confronting the dangers posed by terrorist and rogue states, the interests of other states and their leaders were of secondary concern. Pakistan was pressured to support American efforts in Afghanistan, and Turkey to support the invasion of Iraq. Pakistan complied, but Turkey resisted. France, Germany, and Russia defied American pressure in the United Nations and opposed action against

Iraq, signaling a political division that seemed to threaten the foundations of NATO, the cornerstone of American foreign policy for a half-century.

Beyond the issue of alliance relations lay a more fundamental question: how should the United States wield its dominant, hegemonic power in the world? The administration's answer centered on three threats to American interests: terrorists, who use "premeditated, politically motivated violence" against innocents;[21] rogue states led by tyrants who sometimes support terrorists and aggressively seek weapons of mass destruction to further their own goals; and failing states, "countries in which the central government does not exert effective control over . . . significant parts of its own territory" and that are therefore susceptible to terrorist intimidation or become sources of regional instability.[22] Notably, Russia and China, great power competitors of the past and future, were portrayed as sharing values with the United States and engaging in peaceful competition.

The new strategy stimulated broad discussion and provoked enormous controversy.[23] Promoting democracy, free markets, and free trade throughout the world, particularly in Muslim nations, could be a means to enhance self-determination and human rights or a means to extend America's global control. Some observers doubted the administration's sincerity in endorsing institutions such as the United Nations, the World Trade Organization, and NATO and suspected a real preference for *"coalitions of the willing"*—temporary assemblages of supportive allies. How would the administration resolve the contradiction between promoting democracy and using undemocratic regimes to combat terrorism? Provoking the most public discussion were two controversial military strategies: "**preemption**—striking an enemy as it prepares an attack . . . [and] **prevention**—striking an enemy even in the absence of specific evidence of a coming attack."[24] After 9/11 the administration argued that action must be taken before the nation suffered another catastrophic attack. Unlike the leaders of major nations such as Russia and China, terrorists and tyrants are unlikely to be deterred from launching attacks by threats of retaliation because their behavior is irrational. The United States and its allies therefore must use intelligence to discover capabilities and then act appropriately even if an attack may not be imminent. This logic underlay the U.S. action against Iraq, whose leader, Saddam Hussein, resisted international inspection of his chemical, biological, and nuclear weapons programs, thereby providing a justification for preventive action.

When the Bush strategy was announced, the Council on Foreign Relations argued that it had not yet created a consensus. Three groups offered contending perspectives on the new global realities.[25] **Neoconservatives,** mostly in the Republican Party and including several notable figures in the Bush administration,[26] stressed the importance of maintaining U.S. military dominance and being willing to use force preemptively and alone, if necessary. **Moderates** in both the Republican and Democratic Parties identified the same three international threats but believed that alliance-based containment and deterrence, policy instruments of the past, could continue to provide national security. Finally, **liberals** (mostly Democrats) stressed the need for diplomatic and economic cooperation as the best way to address global poverty, weapons proliferation, and international resentment of U.S. power, the long-term dangers to American security. Rather than articulating a new national strategy, the Bush administration delivered the opening salvo on a major foreign policy debate that continued throughout Bush's time in office and was exacerbated by the frustrating experience in Iraq.

The message of President Bush's second inaugural address was clear: "The survival of liberty in our land increasingly depends on the success of liberty in other lands. The best hope for peace in our world is the expansion of freedom in all the world."[27] In this spirit, America would oppose tyrants and encourage democratic movements. Although this message harkened back to a traditional American mission of spreading democracy, it did not provide the foundation for a new consensus on foreign policy. Instead, the administration stubbornly proceeded to pursue its own policy. Even after the November 2006 elections rebuked the Republicans by returning control of Congress to the Democrats, the president spurned a bipartisan strategy on Iraq. The **Iraq Study Group,** co-chaired by former secretary of state James Baker (a Republican) and Lee Hamilton (a Democrat), former representative and deputy chair of the 9-11 Commission, proposed a way forward in Iraq that urged expanded regional diplomacy and expedited withdrawal of U.S. forces. Instead of adopting this widely endorsed strategy, the president proposed **the surge,** an increase of thirty thousand American troops in Iraq pursuing a strategy designed by the new commander, Gen. David Petraeus. The president had clearly decided to "go it alone" in this major military crisis, rejecting the election judgment, the results of national polls, and a Capitol Hill majority. Iraq clearly became "Bush's war." During his final months in office, Bush saw the surge strategy succeed and was able to negotiate a new agreement with Iraq on when American troops would withdraw (December 2011), but his final visit to Iraq in December 2008 was marred by an Iraqi journalist hurling his shoes at the president during a press conference, an insult in Iraqi society.

The Obama Era

If a national security consensus existed at the outset of the Obama presidency, it centered on "un-Bush," the desire to move beyond prominent elements of the

Bush-Cheney foreign policy. The main disagreement between the 2008 presidential candidates, Obama and Sen. John McCain, was on the centrality of Iraq in America's foreign policy. McCain saw it as the linchpin in the struggle with radical Islamic extremists and the key to fighting the war on terror. Unless U.S. troops and the Iraqi government prevailed, the country would become a sanctuary for terrorists. In contrast, Obama stressed the need to withdraw combat troops from Iraq within sixteen months, tolerate the imperfect conditions that would be left behind, and focus instead on the effort in Afghanistan where al Qaeda and the Taliban were clear targets. Stabilizing democracy in Pakistan figured prominently in Obama's plans but so did finding peace in the larger Middle East, halting the spread of nuclear weapons, rebuilding alliances, and closing Guantánamo Bay and discontinuing the use of torture. Obama was concerned with rebuilding America's soft power, particularly the respect and affection that international publics had traditionally held for the United States.[28]

The new administration wasted little time in pursuing many of these paths. After ordering a review of Iraq policy on his first day in office, the president announced his new policy on February 27, 2009, during a speech to U.S. Marines at Camp Lejeune, North Carolina. He said, "Let me say this as plainly as I can: by August 31, 2010, our combat mission in Iraq will end," a slight modification of his campaign promise of sixteen months. President Obama explained that progress in Iraq both on the battlefield and politically made this withdrawal possible, but he also made it clear that the transition would not be easy. Providing continued training and support for the Iraqis would require a commitment of between thirty-five thousand and fifty thousand service men and women. They would not be conducting combat missions and would be withdrawn by the end of 2011. To signal the nation's commitment to building regional stability and the shift to diplomatic rather than military means, he also announced the appointment of three experienced international negotiators to work in the region: George Mitchell, Dennis Ross, and Richard Holbrooke.[29]

By the end of March, a new strategy for Afghanistan had also emerged. President Obama increased American combat troops by seventeen thousand and explained that their goal would be "to disrupt, dismantle, and defeat al Qaeda in Pakistan and Afghanistan, and to prevent their return to either country in the future."[30] The press reported that the military requested still higher force levels, but after a vigorous debate, the president limited increases to another four thousand military trainers, bringing total strength to sixty thousand. This reflected a compromise between military and political advisers with Vice President Biden urging caution and clear goals. The president also committed additional funds to economic aid and training for both Afghanistan and Pakistan.[31] In related actions, the president used executive orders (see chapter 6) to end torture of suspected terrorists in U.S. custody and to dismantle the detention center at the Guantánamo Bay naval base, major concerns of world public opinion.

On other fronts, the administration sought to repair its relationship with Russia, describing the need to "reset or reboot the relationship," a phrase used in various ways by the president, the vice president, and Secretary of State Hillary Clinton. The clear implication was that things had gotten so bad during the Bush years that it was time for the two nations to start over. Obama's initial trip overseas (his first visit to a foreign nation was to Canada) was to attend a critical economic summit among the world's twenty largest economic powers, the so-called G-20, in London. He then traveled to NATO meetings that commemorated the sixtieth anniversary of the alliance. Obama struck a new, less arrogant posture and described his purpose as "to listen, not to lecture," a marked contrast to the image projected by the Bush administration. The shift was timely: the United States no longer dominated the global economy, and the message of unfettered free markets had been undermined by the global recession. In military terms, a severely stretched U.S. military was no longer singularly able to guarantee world peace.[32] Conditions were changing, and Obama seemed ready to adjust, but stitching these disparate actions together into a new foreign policy consensus would be a major challenge.

A Frustrating Search

Perhaps we should not be surprised that successive administrations have found it difficult to develop public support for a strategic consensus. Articulating a new foreign policy requires taking positions on scores, if not hundreds, of difficult issues, something politicians are reluctant to do.[33] Moreover, from an American perspective, the international environment is full of contradictory pressures and has become more and more unmanageable. With the disappearance in 1991 of the Soviet Union as one of the world's two superpowers, the number of regional and communal (ethnic, religious, tribal) conflicts proliferated. China aspires to become a global power, and other nations, such as Iran, hope to become regional powers. Numerous history-laden animosities have come to the surface, for example, between India and Pakistan, between Turks and Kurds, and in the Balkans, where the United States and its NATO allies intervened in Bosnia and Kosovo.

Iranian president Mahmoud Ahmadinejad addressed the UN General Assembly in September 2007 as tensions rose between Iran and the United States over American policy in Iraq and Iran's nuclear program.

"Security" has also taken on new meanings, with threats arising from uncontrolled immigration, international drug dealers, and most dramatically, international terrorists. The Bush administration believed that these threats are as pressing as those from ambitious nation-states. In marked contrast to the Cold War era, the new international agenda is heavily—some argue predominantly—economic, raising issues that intermingle with domestic social and macroeconomic policy matters and triggering lobbying efforts by a new range of interest groups. Recent presidents have not enjoyed the discretion or broad support in foreign and military policy accorded their predecessors at the height of the Cold War. The Bush strategy, weighed down by Iraq, was also unable to win such support, and Obama's ability to articulate a broad message in foreign policy was still untested.

The Problem with National Security Policymaking

Exercising effective international leadership is difficult for the United States; the government structure established in the Constitution—separate institutions sharing powers—creates continuing tension between the president and Congress over the control of national security policy. Edward S. Corwin observed that the Constitution "is an invitation to struggle" between the two branches "for the privilege of directing American foreign policy."[34] Although the struggle continues, and power over foreign policy is divided, the president has played the dominant role in shaping national security policy through most of the country's history. Presidential advantages of unity, secrecy, and dispatch are especially compelling during periods of crisis and potential conflict.

Dependence on presidential leadership carries risks, however. The idiosyncrasies of individual presidents' operating styles and personalities (see chapter 4) can be sources of uncertainty and noncohesiveness in policy and can exacerbate the institutional tensions between the legislature and the executive. The United States needs in its national security policy "institutions that provide continuity" and "structures and processes that promote coherence."[35] The problem is that if institutions, structures, and procedures respond to the short-term needs and whims of individual presidents, discontinuity in policy is likely to multiply. National security policymaking presents the United States with a circular and seemingly inescapable problem: the country depends on the president for central policy leadership, born of constitutional arrangements and operational imperatives, but this produces discontinuity in policy and a lack of cohesiveness that result from a policymaking system geared to presidential domination. The remainder of this chapter explores this paradox.

The President, Congress, and National Security

The powers of the federal government in international affairs are "inherent, plenary, and exclusive."[36] They are not granted expressly by the Constitution; rather, they derive from the nation's existence as a sovereign entity in the international community and cannot be exercised by the states or anyone else. The Constitution, however, is ambiguous in its assignment of the power to control foreign relations. Both the president and Congress have formal constitutional powers in this area, indicating that the founders intended control to be shared. In a 1793 debate with James Madison in the *Gazette of the United States*, Alexander Hamilton argued that direction of the nation's foreign policy is inherently an executive function.[37] Madison's position—that because the power to declare war is vested in Congress, presidential powers in this regard are merely instrumental—has not been borne out by subsequent events. Long-standing practice and necessity have combined to make the president the *sole organ* of the United States in the conduct of its external affairs. Presidents have monopolized negotiations and communications with other governments from the early years of the Republic.

Congress, however, has retained the ability to influence the substantive content of the foreign and defense policies the president implements. Major policies developed by the president cannot remain viable for long without congressional support in the form of implementing legislation and appropriations. Nevertheless, throughout most of U.S. history the president has been, and is today, the "most important single factor in the determination of American foreign policy." [38]

Powers of the President

In addition to the inherent powers derived from the country's involvement in the international community, the president has formal and delegated powers over national security. These stem, respectively, from specific constitutional provisions and Congress. The constitutional foundation is relatively modest: the power to receive ambassadors and ministers, the power to negotiate treaties, designation as commander in chief of the armed forces, the general grant of executive power, and the clause enjoining the president to "take care that the laws be faithfully executed." Operationally, these provisions result in four major areas of presidential authority— recognition and nonrecognition of other governments; making, implementing, and terminating international agreements; the appointment of personnel to conduct foreign and military policy; and the use of military force as a means of achieving policy goals.

Recognition and Nonrecognition of Foreign Governments. Article II, section 3, of the Constitution grants the president power to "receive Ambassadors and other public Ministers"—in essence, authority to recognize foreign governments. Because foreign diplomats are accredited to the president, the decision about whether to receive them and, in doing so, recognize their governments is exclusively the president's. By implication, the chief executive can also refuse to grant recognition or withdraw it.

Traditionally, under international law, governments grant recognition to other governments provided the latter are stable, have effectively established their authority, and are meeting their international obligations. Recognition allows the American government to express its approval or disapproval of foreign regimes, an effective weapon when exercised by a nation as powerful and influential as the United States. Other nations may alter their conduct at the prospect of U.S. recognition or the threat of its withdrawal. Once recognition is granted or relations are broken, this leverage is lost.

There are some well-known instances in American diplomatic history concerning the use of this power. After the Russian Revolution in 1917–1918, the United States refused to recognize the Communist government of the Soviet Union on the grounds that it had obtained power illegally, expropriated foreign-owned property without compensation, and oppressed its citizens. Yet in 1933 FDR established diplomatic relations with the Soviet Union when practical considerations made recognition advantageous to the United States. President Harry Truman, overcoming strong opposition in the State Department, granted recognition to the new state of Israel in 1948, making the United States the first nation to do so. U.S. support has been vital to the survival of Israel ever since.

When a Communist regime took power in China in 1949 after a revolutionary struggle, the United States refused to recognize it, instead regarding the Nationalist government on the island of Taiwan as the legitimate government of China. Not until 1979 did the United States establish diplomatic relations with the People's Republic of China (PRC) and withdraw recognition from Taiwan. At the same time, however, the United States did not recognize PRC sovereignty over Taiwan. Despite challenges in Congress, the Carter administration's policies toward the two Chinas were upheld. Similarly, reestablishing normal relations with Vietnam in July 1995 encountered opposition from those who viewed President Clinton's action as self-serving because he had avoided military service in the war (1965–1973). In its defense, the administration argued that it sought to achieve economic gain for both countries and an end to the internal debate that had divided America for thirty years.

Although presidents are legally free to exercise the recognition power on their own, political prudence dictates that they take congressional views and public opinion into consideration, effectively limiting the range of presidential discretion.

International Agreements. The Constitution also provides the president with authority to conduct negotiations with other nations that result in treaties or binding executive agreements. The constitutional basis for the treaty-making power is found in Article II, section 2, which declares that the president "shall have power, by and with the Advice and Consent of the Senate, to make Treaties, provided two thirds of the Senators present concur." The authority to make executive agreements is not mentioned explicitly, but its constitutionality is "universally conceded,"[39] perceived as arising from the president's role as the nation's official organ for the conduct of foreign relations and as a means for exercising powers in the commander in chief and "take care" clauses of the Constitution.[40] In addition, executive agreements may be concluded pursuant to provisions of valid treaties and of existing legislation.

Treaties require Senate approval, but executive agreements do not. The Senate's own members limited its role in the treaty-making process in 1789, when they set a precedent by refusing to advise George Washington on provisions of a treaty under negotiation. The Senate may, however, amend or attach reservations to treaties submitted for its approval. Amendments change the content of a treaty and therefore require additional negotiations with the foreign nation; reservations merely clarify the Senate's understanding of the treaty's provisions. The requirement of a two-thirds vote for approval gives the Senate substantial leverage over the executive in the treaty-making process, something presidents can sidestep by using executive agreements instead.[41]

Table 10-2 illustrates the dramatic change in the relative importance of executive agreements and treaties. By the late nineteenth century, agreements concluded in the previous fifty years slightly outnumbered treaties. That ratio widened over the next fifty-year period (1889–1939), then exploded during the period 1939–1989, when 11,698 new executive agreements were concluded as opposed to 702 treaties. The disparity narrowed only slightly from 1989 to 1999. Congress repeatedly has expressed its disapproval of the use of executive agreements in lieu of treaties, but the only limitation it has imposed, in the Case-Zablocki Act of 1972, is to require that the legislature be notified of all such agreements. Although Congress is free to take action against executive agreements to which it objects, it has been unable to impose effective limits on the president's power to make them.[42] As Table 10-3 shows, the ratio of executive agreements to treaties changed markedly under Clinton compared with his immediate predecessors, mainly because of the unusually large number of trade treaties concluded during his administration. The agreement/treaty ratio under George W. Bush moved closer to the historical pattern but revealed a striking decline in overall activity during the administration's first two years, probably reflecting both the emphasis on counterterrorism and the shift away from multilateralism.

Why use treaties at all? Presidents are compelled by domestic political considerations to submit international agreements for Senate approval as treaties. Approval by the Senate gives an international agreement a degree of legitimacy that it would

TABLE 10-2   Treaties and Executive Agreements Concluded by the United States, 1789–1999

Period	Treaties	Executive agreements
1789–1839	60	27
1839–1889	215	238
1889–1939	524	917
1939–1989	702	11,698
1990–1999	249	2,857
Total	1,750	15,737

SOURCE: *Treaties and Other International Agreements: The Role of the U.S. Senate,* Congressional Research Service, Library of Congress, January 2001, Table II-1. Report submitted to the Committee on Foreign Relations, U.S. Senate, 106:2, Senate print 106-71.

TABLE 10-3   International Agreements, 1969–2008

President/Term	Executive agreements	Treaties	Ratio
Nixon (1969–1974)	1,116	180	14.2:1
Ford (1974–1977)	677	99	25.6:1
Carter (1977–1981)	1,169	148	17.9:1
Reagan (1981–1989)	2,840	125	22.7:1
G. H. W. Bush (1989–1993)	1,350	67	20.2:1
Clinton (1993–2001)	2,058	209	9.9:1
G. W. Bush (2001–December 31, 2008)	1,822	131	13.9:1

SOURCES: *Treaties and Other International Agreements: The Role of the U.S. Senate,* Congressional Research Service, Library of Congress, January 2001. Data from Table II-2. Report submitted to the Committee on Foreign Relations, U.S. Senate, 106:2, Senate print 106-71. Data for 2000–2008 are from Office of Treaty Affairs, U.S. Department of State and Congressional Research Service and are not exact.

otherwise lack. President Carter submitted the agreement providing for gradual termination of U.S. control of the Panama Canal to the Senate as a treaty. He apparently calculated that such action would be difficult to defend publicly in any case and avoidance of Senate approval could impose unacceptable political costs on his administration. For similar reasons, Carter submitted the second Strategic Arms Limitation Talks (SALT II) agreement to the Senate as a treaty even though approval was unlikely.

On several occasions, however, modern presidents have taken important action through executive agreements, knowing that Congress was unlikely to support a treaty. In 1940 Franklin Roosevelt exchanged fifty "overage" destroyers for ninety-nine-year leases on bases in British possessions in the Western Hemisphere; in 1973 the United States and North Vietnam ended hostilities and exchanged prisoners of war through an executive agreement; and in 1981 the United States and Israel negotiated an agreement for strategic cooperation in the Middle East.

The decision to designate an international agreement as a treaty is the president's, based on political, rather than legal, grounds.[43] But few agreements are self-executing, forcing presidents to take note of congressional views because the administration will require legislation or an appropriation for implementation. During the Clinton administration, two important trade agreements, NAFTA and GATT, required legislation to become effective, allowing Congress to conduct an extensive debate over the merits and demerits of the agreements. Clinton needed the support of congressional Republicans because a majority of Democrats—fearing negative consequences for U.S. jobs—opposed both bills.

Although the president's power to negotiate international agreements is subject to political and constitutional limitations, the power to terminate such agreements is not. The Supreme Court ruled in 1979 that the president could unilaterally abrogate a defense treaty with Taiwan that was part of the agreements establishing diplomatic relations between the United States and the People's Republic of China.[44] Reinterpretation also gives presidents expanded power in the treaty area. The Reagan administration provides the best example: in 1985 it broadened the terms of the 1972 Anti-Ballistic Missile Treaty (ABM), over the objections of the Senate and the Soviet Union, to accommodate development of the strategic defense initiative.[45] George W. Bush announced in May 2001 that he would proceed with development and deployment of an antimissile defense system and hoped to establish a "new framework" with Russia that was likely to take the form of an executive agreement rather than a new or amended ABM treaty.[46] As one might expect, Russia's leaders did not respond well to this fundamental change in long-standing strategic policy.

Appointments. As noted in chapter 6, the power to appoint subordinates is an important part of presidential control over policy, but it is a power shared with the Senate. The most important appointments affecting national security are the positions of secretary of state, secretary of defense, director of national intelligence, and the president's assistant for national security affairs. With these appointments, presidents indicate the direction and orientation of the foreign and military policy of their administrations.

The choice of a well-known figure with definite policy views to serve as secretary of state—such as the selection of Gen. George C. Marshall by Truman, John Foster

Dulles by Eisenhower, and Gen. Alexander Haig by Reagan—reflects the intention to rely heavily on the secretary for advice and guidance. If presidents choose a relatively unknown individual—Kennedy's designation of Dean Rusk and Nixon's of William P. Rogers—it indicates that the executive intends to play the dominant role in foreign policy formulation and to relegate to the secretary management of the foreign affairs bureaucracy. Clinton selected Warren M. Christopher, a soft-spoken lawyer with a reputation as a shrewd negotiator, as a way to remain consistent with his campaign focus on domestic, rather than foreign, policy. Clinton signaled the reversal of policy emphasis at the beginning of his second term when he named Madeleine K. Albright, known for her strong policy views, to replace Christopher. George W. Bush's selection of Gen. Colin L. Powell communicated the president's intention to assemble an experienced and respected group of foreign policy advisers. Condoleezza Rice replaced Powell in the second term and was generally viewed as Bush's most trusted adviser on foreign policy. Hillary Clinton is a high-profile choice as secretary of state under Obama, evidence of his own self-confidence but also recognition that his former opponent for the presidential nomination would project to the world the kind of image he sought for the United States.

Similarly, the choice for the secretary of defense indicates the president's plans for that department. Kennedy's choice, Robert S. McNamara, president of Ford Motor Company, signified the president's determination to make the armed forces more efficient through application of modern management techniques. In 2001 Bush's selection of Donald Rumsfeld, a senior Republican with extensive Washington experience and a reputation as a hard-driving manager, made it clear that Bush would assemble a star-studded team of national security advisers. Only after Iraq had severely tarnished Rumsfeld's star did the president accept the secretary's resignation and replace him with Robert Gates, a former director of the CIA. Obama reassured many observers of his commitment to continuity as well as change when he retained Gates in the new cabinet.

The position of director of central intelligence involves managing the CIA and, until 2004, coordinating the activities of the intelligence community.[47] This position was often politically controversial during the Cold War because the CIA and other intelligence agencies had engaged in covert activities designed to assassinate foreign political leaders and overthrow foreign governments. Critics also charged the CIA with ineffective intelligence work, such as the failure to anticipate the Iranian revolution of 1978–1979, Iraq's invasion of Kuwait in 1990, the collapse of the Soviet Union in 1991, and the terrorist attacks of 2001. CIA directors have tended to be either intelligence professionals, such as William Colby and Gates, or experienced politicians, such as George H. W. Bush and William Casey, Reagan's first CIA director. George W. Bush retained Clinton's final CIA director, George J. Tenet, a move designed to enhance continuity, much as Kennedy had retained Dulles as CIA director and Richard Nixon had kept Richard Helms. After the 9/11 attacks, some members of Congress called for Tenet's dismissal, but Bush gave him a strong vote of confidence. In June 2004, however, Bush accepted Tenet's resignation. Tenet's role in advising the president on Saddam Hussein's weapons of mass destruction—the principal justification for invading Iraq—had become highly controversial. Following Tenet's departure, significant changes were made in the structure of national intelligence. Pursuant to recommendations of the 9-11 Commission, a new position, director of national intelligence, was created to coordinate intelligence gathering and analysis for the entire government. John Negroponte held this position from 2005 to 2007 and was replaced by John Michael McConnell.

The last members named to Obama's national security team were the intelligence leaders. Leon Panetta was a surprise choice as director of the CIA because his previous experience as a member of the House and White House chief of staff did not provide him with direct experience in intelligence. But Panetta was likely to help guide the agency through the political minefield of criticism and investigation expected to follow the Bush years. Retired admiral Dennis Blair was named director of national intelligence and brought experience in coordinating military intelligence with the CIA as well as four years at the Institute for Defense Analysis.

One of the most important national security appointments, that of assistant to the president for national security affairs, is not subject to Senate approval, even though these appointees often dominate foreign policy decision making. McGeorge Bundy, Henry Kissinger, Zbigniew Brzezinski, Colin Powell, and Condoleezza Rice have held this post. Rice coordinated administration deliberations and tried to mediate the reportedly opposing views of Rumsfeld and Powell on policy concerning Afghanistan and Iraq.[48] When Rice moved to the State Department, her deputy, Stephen J. Hadley, filled the National Security Council post. Obama chose retired general James L. Jones to fill this position. Jones is a skilled diplomat with experience as commander of NATO forces and an outspoken advocate of focusing on Afghanistan rather than Iraq. Jones is also knowledgeable about global energy issues.

The appointment power helps presidents control both the conduct and the content of foreign and defense policy. Presidents enjoy wide latitude in exercising the power, but they must be sensitive to the limits imposed by international and domestic politics reflected in the Senate.

The Use of Military Force. The Constitution states, "The President shall be Commander in Chief of the Army and Navy of the United States" and of the state militia when it is called into federal service (Article II, section 2). It does not, however, define the nature of the president's powers and duties as commander in chief. In fact, extensive powers pertaining to the use of military force are found in Article I, the legislative article. Most important, Congress is empowered to declare war. Constitutionally, then, the power to use military force is shared between Congress and the president. Historical practice, however, has resulted in a vast expansion of presidential authority to use force at the expense of the powers of Congress. The dominance of the president in this regard has been almost total in wartime; in times of peace, Congress has only partially reclaimed the ground it lost. The result has been the continual aggrandizement of presidential power, the rise of an "imperial presidency," as it was dubbed by Arthur M. Schlesinger Jr.[49]

Presidents have sweeping war powers based upon the Constitution, statutory delegations of authority by Congress, and judicial interpretations. The constitutional foundation of the president's war powers was established early in the Civil War when Abraham Lincoln linked the commander in chief clause to the take care clause.[50] As discussed in chapter 1, Lincoln used the resulting war powers to justify a wide range of actions to suppress the rebellion: activation of state militias, expenditure of appropriated funds for unauthorized purposes, suspension of the writ of habeas corpus in militarily insecure areas, and the imposition of a naval blockade of Confederate ports. The Supreme Court upheld the legality of the blockade in the *Prize Cases,* in which it declared that the president had a duty to defend the nation by appropriate means, including military action.[51] The refusal of the Court to overturn any of Lincoln's actions until after the war set a precedent of judicial deference during wartime.

Lincoln's actions demonstrated that the president's war powers extend far beyond mere military command. During World War II the president's powers as commander in chief expanded exponentially under FDR. Among other things, Roosevelt ordered the internment of all persons of Japanese ancestry, including naturalized and native-born U.S. citizens, who were residing in the Pacific Coast states. The Supreme Court acquiesced in this deprivation of basic civil liberties.[52] Roosevelt created emergency agencies with sweeping regulatory powers and demanded that Congress enhance his powers by repealing certain constraining sections of the Emergency Price Control Act.

Delegations by statute have further contributed to the development of the president's war powers. As discussed in chapter 1, during World War I Congress enacted laws that authorized the president to regulate, requisition, and purchase a wide range of materials and products, to prohibit exports, to license trade, to censor international communications, to regulate enemy aliens in the United States, and to seize and operate the railroads. These powers were expanded during World War II, and many delegations of power were open-ended and neither revised nor withdrawn until long after the conclusion of the war with passage of the National Emergencies Act of 1976.

In short, once war is declared, presidential powers are vast. To ensure national survival, presidential directives are followed without regard to constitutional considerations and with the acquiescence, if not full approval, of the Supreme Court and Congress. Some leading constitutional scholars have charged that the Constitution is suspended in wartime and the president becomes a de facto dictator.[53]

The president's power to use military force in peacetime, or even in periods of undeclared war, is less clear-cut. The Court has been reluctant to resolve questions in this area, but Congress at times attempts to assert its prerogatives. The president still has substantial responsibilities and concomitant powers to protect American lives and property abroad, discharge international obligations, and preserve national security. Constitutional language is vague, and statutory enactments are an incomplete guide to the exercise of this authority.

After World War II Congress and the president were united in the effort to contain communism, but the authority of the president to commit U.S. troops to fight abroad remained a sensitive issue. On several occasions between 1945 and 1965, presidents sent U.S. forces into combat or placed them in situations that could easily lead to combat.[54] These included the Korean War, the dispatch of four divisions to Western Europe as a permanent commitment to NATO, Eisenhower's responses to Chinese pressures on Taiwan and to increased tensions in the Middle East, the 1965 intervention in the Dominican Republic, and the Vietnam War.

Vietnam produced the most extensive and controversial instances of presidential war making in the post–World War II era, partly because it was America's longest conflict of the twentieth century (see Table 10-4). Beginning with Truman, presidents had made commitments of military aid and provided military advisers to the government of South Vietnam. By the end of 1963, more than sixteen thousand military advisers were in Vietnam, many of them actively participating in combat although not formally authorized to do so. In August 1964 the Johnson administration reported a confrontation between a North Vietnamese gunboat and a U.S. destroyer in the Gulf of Tonkin. At Johnson's request, Congress passed the Gulf of Tonkin Resolution, which authorized the president to "take all necessary

TABLE 10-4   Duration of U.S. Wars since 1900

War	Date war began	Length
World War I	April 6, 1917	1 year, 7 months, 5 days
World War II	Dec. 8, 1941	3 years, 8 months, 6 days
Korea	June 27, 1950	3 years, 1 month
Vietnam	Feb. 14, 1962	10 years, 11 months, 13 days
Persian Gulf	Jan. 17, 1991	1 month, 10 days
Kosovo	March 24, 1999	2 months, 27 days
Afghanistan	Oct. 7, 2001	7 years plus
Iraq	March 19, 2003	6 years plus

SOURCE: *USA Today,* March 26, 2003. Reported on History News Network, www.hnn.us/articles/1689.html; updated.

steps including use of armed force" to assist nations belonging to the Southeast Asia Treaty Organization (to which the United States was a signatory) in defense of their freedom. On the authority of the Constitution, the Southeast Asia Treaty, and the Gulf of Tonkin Resolution, Johnson ordered a vast increase in the strength of U.S. forces in Vietnam, which by late 1967 exceeded half a million. He also authorized military commanders to conduct air raids against military targets in North Vietnam.[55] President Nixon extended the scope of military operations even while trying to negotiate an end to U.S. involvement in the war. In 1970 he ordered a covert invasion of Cambodia and the bombing of Laos to destroy enemy supply and staging areas, and in December 1972 he authorized the bombing of the North Vietnamese capital city of Hanoi and the major port city of Haiphong. These actions were taken without consulting Congress.

Initially, Congress backed administration efforts to contain communism in Southeast Asia through the use of military force. As the war dragged on, however, popular support began to wane, a widespread domestic protest movement took shape, and opposition to U.S. policy rose abroad from the country's allies and from developing nations. Many members of Congress questioned the wisdom and the legality of placing the decision to use military force entirely in the president's hands. As long as presidential use of force appeared to be successful, congressional opposition was minimal. When the use of force appeared to be failing, or the risks increased and the costs in popular support became too great, Congress reasserted its constitutional authority to participate as an equal partner with the president in determining where and under what conditions the United States would wage war.

Although Americans remain sensitive to the experience with war powers during the Vietnam years, events can overtake caution. Congress overwhelmingly endorsed President Bush's request for authority to wage war on terrorism in September 2001, issuing what critics called a "blank check" to take whatever action he deemed necessary.[56] In October 2002 caution reemerged. Congress did not approve the original administration version of a resolution for the use of force in Iraq that was described as "the broadest request for military authority by any White House since President Lyndon B. Johnson won approval of the Gulf of Tonkin resolution in 1964."[57] Instead, Congress approved a version negotiated by the House International Relations Committee that placed modest restrictions on the president's actions.[58] As American casualties rose and the end of conflict was nowhere in sight, public and congressional opposition to the war grew stronger. The 2006 congressional elections that produced Democratic majorities in the House and Senate were widely viewed as a repudiation of the administration's policy in Iraq. Democrats launched several assaults on Bush's Iraq policy: they attempted to impose a timetable for withdrawing American troops, withdraw the 2002 authorization to use force, cut off funding for the war, and redefine the role of American forces. By the end of 2007, none of these efforts had succeeded. The president remained committed to success in Iraq and implemented the "surge" in force levels that triggered new tactics. Democrats were consistently thwarted by insufficient votes in the Senate where sixty votes were needed to prevent a filibuster. After reporting on the string of unsuccessful votes, *CQ Weekly* concluded: "In effect, the votes reaffirmed that the president, not Congress, is in charge of the war. Unless there is a significant shift on the battlefield in Iraq or in the dynamics on Capitol Hill, that's not expected to change."[59] As with Vietnam, Congress once again confronted a president relying on his own discretion in using military force.[60] And Schlesinger, among others, saw a return to the imperial presidency of the 1960s.[61]

Powers of Congress

Congress has substantial constitutional powers enabling it to claim parity with the president in shaping national security policy: the Senate's role in the appointment confirmation process and treaty approval; authorizations and appropriations needed to implement presidential decisions that are not self-executing; and the power to declare war. Congress, however, confronts steep hurdles in exercising those powers. During the Cold War a bipartisan foreign policy consensus produced presidential domination, with many arguing that executive control was required by operational realities: Congress could never match the president's superior capacity to guide national security coherently.

The failure of the Vietnam War—labeled by critics as a "presidential war"—ended, at least temporarily, Congress's deference to White House domination of national security policy. During the 1970s Congress limited presidents' ability to wage undeclared war, reduced unrestrained use of executive agreements, restored the treaty as the principal means of making international agreements, reassessed its sweeping delegations of authority to presidents in past wars and emergencies, and curbed secrecy and covert activities in the conduct of foreign and military affairs.

The most important congressional attempt to reclaim powers lost or given to the executive was the War Powers Resolution of 1973. Passed over Nixon's veto, House Joint Resolution 542 provided that the president might commit the armed forces to combat only in the event of a declaration of war, specific statutory authorization, or a national emergency created by an attack on the United States or its armed forces. The resolution urged the president to consult with Congress in "every possible instance" before committing forces to combat abroad, and it required consultation after such commitment. Specifically, it required a written report to Congress within forty-eight hours of a commitment and required ending the commitment within sixty days unless authorized by Congress. The commitment could be extended for thirty additional days if the president certified to Congress that military conditions required continued use of the forces to ensure their safety. Finally, it stated that, through use of a concurrent resolution that would not be subject to presidential veto, Congress might order the disengagement of U.S. forces before the end of the first sixty days. (A Supreme Court decision in an unrelated case would force Congress to substitute a joint resolution for the concurrent one, but joint resolutions are subject to a presidential veto.[62])

The War Powers Resolution now appears even less effective than before as a congressional means to control military actions initiated by presidents. Although presidents continue to meet the procedural requirements of the act and file the required reports (see Table 10-1), most of these involve routine updates of ongoing force commitments.[63] In only one instance since the act's adoption—the rescue of the *Mayaguez*, a merchant ship seized by Cambodian gunboats in 1975—did the president trigger the sixty-day clock. Every president subject to the War Powers Resolution has regarded it as an unconstitutional encroachment on presidential power and issued reports that carefully avoided any acknowledgment of its constitutionality. In addition, these presidents have circumvented the intent of the resolution by not activating the sixty-day clock and by stating that merely informing Congress meets the resolution's requirement of consultation. Congress has been unable to formulate a corresponding "unitary position or statement of institutional interest."[64] Nor has Congress challenged any president by starting the sixty-day clock on its own.[65]

President George H. W. Bush's actions during the Persian Gulf War of 1990–1991 are typical of how presidents deal with the War Powers Resolution.[66] Before sending U.S. armed forces to the gulf in response to Iraq's August 2, 1990, invasion of Kuwait, Bush on August 8 notified congressional leaders of the planned deployment. The next day, he sent the Speaker of the House and the president pro tempore of the Senate a letter stating that the report was "consistent with" the War Powers Resolution. During the next six months, a massive buildup of U.S. forces took place in the Persian Gulf area; the United States and Iraq exchanged bellicose threats; and the United Nations adopted a resolution imposing a deadline for Iraq to withdraw from Kuwait. At no point did either the president or Congress begin the sixty-day countdown. As he had from the beginning, the president continued to argue that he had the authority to force Iraq to leave Kuwait without congressional approval. Nevertheless, on January 8, 1991, one week before the UN deadline, Bush asked Congress to approve a joint resolution authorizing the use of force. Congress did so four days later by votes of 52 to 47 in the Senate and 250 to 183 in the House.[67] When Bush signed the resolution, he reasserted his position that the War Powers Resolution was unconstitutional. The resolution approved on January 12, 1991, has been recognized as the functional equivalent of a declaration of war. Whether Bush weakened his position—that he already had the authority to initiate hostilities—is an unanswered question.

At best, the War Powers Resolution provided Congress with a symbolic victory in the ongoing struggle between the president and Congress in making decisions about war and peace. It seemed to serve notice that sustained military commitments outside the country could no longer be made by presidential fiat but required congressional approval and, by implication, popular support. Presidents, however, have neither consulted Congress in "any meaningful manner" nor have they sought to make the law work by invoking its provisions.[68] Instead, they have sought to circumvent it. Ultimately, any expectation that the resolution's "procedures would actually lead to collective legislative-executive judgment in the war-making process was mistaken."[69] Presidential evasion, congressional acquiescence, and judicial deference have combined to bring about this result.[70] The war in Iraq adds further evidence. A costly American effort has been sustained despite widespread public disapproval, electoral repudiation, and active congressional opposition.

Despite its failings, the resolution persists because it suits congressional purposes. It "allows Congress the luxury of being politically comfortable with its decisions regarding a military action while providing a convenient forum for criticizing the President."[71] Congress can use the War Powers Resolution to force the president to end an unpopular military operation, or it can criticize presidential failure to comply with the procedural requirements of the resolution when public opinion is supportive or divided. Either way, Congress cannot lose.[72] The resolution reminds presidents that under the Constitution, they share with Congress the crucial decision to lead the nation into war. Thus far presidents have been no more willing than Congress to ask the Supreme Court to resolve the lingering ambiguities—an unwillingness that may stem on both sides from uncertainty about the outcome.[73]

Congress has not assumed added responsibility despite a desire and enhanced capacity to do so.[74] Even the traditional "power of the purse" that rests on congressional appropriation of funds has been eroded, with presidents supporting international projects by spending money from lump sum accounts and reprogramming funds from one purpose to another, effectively exercising "presidential spending power in national security."[75] Because of its internal fragmentation, Congress has difficulty asserting its prerogatives. Reforms during the 1970s, especially in the House, fragmented power even further with the addition of more subcommittees, making it still more difficult for Congress to speak authoritatively. These developments, along with additional pressures from interest groups and other domestic constituencies, made interbranch consensus more elusive. Although Republican majorities moved to consolidate legislative power in the 1990s (see chapter 5), the structural problems remain.

The constitutional "invitation to struggle" is still present. Four paths are possible for Congress: reversion to the pattern of acquiescence in presidential domination that prevailed from World War II until 1973; directing policy on its own because of popular pressures or distrust of the president's policies and capabilities; collaboration tempered by a sense of constitutional and political responsibility to be constructively critical; and all-out conflict, a pattern that nearly erupted during the Clinton impeachment. On the eve of the scheduled House vote on articles of impeachment, Clinton ordered an air attack on Iraq for its failure to cooperate with UN weapons inspectors responsible for overseeing Iraq's disarmament after the Persian Gulf War. The impeachment vote was delayed for several days. Congressional members questioned the president's motives in launching an attack that had been delayed numerous times in the past, including a month earlier. Republican leaders publicly spoke out against the action and expressed doubts about the president's credibility. Editorials wondered whether he was "risking lives to cling to power."[76] The impeachment imposed enormous strains on the delicate institutional relationships essential for effective foreign policy. The nation did not reach this level of distrust in 2007 when frustrated congressional Democrats confronted an uncompromising President Bush, but the level of institutional conflict was once again quite high.

Organizing and Managing National Security

Beyond dealing with the constitutional issues and political considerations involved in national security policy, the president also confronts a formidable administrative task: organizing the presidency and the executive branch to formulate and implement these policies. To do so may require establishing and changing structures and processes to enhance decision making and interagency coordination. As the Iran-contra investigation revealed, a lax approach to these tasks can be costly, but it is also possible to overemphasize them. One has to remember that "good organization does not insure successful policy, nor does poor organization preclude it."[77] Designing an effective system accomplishes three primary functions: it "creates capabilities" for performing tasks beyond the reach of individuals; it "vests and weighs particular interests and perspectives" by increasing or reducing the probability of their inclusion in decision making; and it "legitimates decisions" by ensuring that relevant parties are consulted and that decisions are made by proper authorities.[78]

Although national security organization does not have to conform to a specific model, whatever policymaking system is established must be capable of adapting to changing events and conditions, and it must be able to accommodate the operating style of the presidents, whose constitutional roles make them the focal point of the policymaking process. Congress has enacted legislation—the National Security Act of 1947 was the most far-reaching—establishing organizational units to aid presidents in the conduct of national security policy. The principal units are the National Security Council and its staff, the Departments of State and Defense, the Joint Chiefs of Staff, and until 2005 the CIA, now superseded by the National Intelligence Council headed by the director of national intelligence. Congress established these staffing units, but it cannot prescribe how presidents employ them. How presidents choose to work through staff, cabinet, and independent agencies is a matter totally at their discretion.

Presidential Management Styles

The NSC is the basic structure for the management of national security affairs. Since the council's creation in 1947, presidents have used it in various ways. Congress established the NSC in response to the pressures of the Cold War and in reaction, at least in part, to the administrative confusion that often characterized

Franklin Roosevelt's freewheeling approach to management. Chief executives, upon taking office, must define their roles in the national security policymaking system before they can design and manage the roles and relationships of other major participants in it.[79] According to conventional wisdom, the basic choice every president must make is whether to manage the system through the secretary of state and the State Department, as Truman did, or to centralize it in the White House, as Nixon did, with the national security assistant playing the major role. Failure to decide on a consistent approach is likely to result in confusion over policy goals and lack of cohesion in policy implementation, as was the case with Clinton.[80] Neither Clinton's national security assistant and the NSC staff, which nearly doubled in size to an all-time high of a hundred professionals,[81] nor Clinton's secretary of state and the State Department were clearly in charge. The result was a series of ad hoc reactions to crises, problems, and domestic pressures.

Within this range of possibilities, who exercises responsibility for foreign policymaking and implementation? One useful typology identifies four presidential management styles—department-centered, formalized, collegial, and palace guard—and features an accompanying role for the national security assistant—administrator, coordinator, counselor, and agent (see Figure 10-1).[82] Presidents with limited interest in the formation and implementation of foreign policy—Truman was one—deputize the secretary of state to act and speak for them and rely primarily on the State Department for analysis and implementation. In this *department-centered* style, the national security assistant (Truman's was Adm. Sidney Souers) plays the corresponding role of administrator and acts primarily as a high-level staff aide who supervises the advisory process and facilitates the presentation of views to the president but does not act independently or function as a primary policy adviser.

Dwight Eisenhower exemplified the *formalized* management style. He relied on the Departments of State and Defense as well as the intelligence community to develop a range of proposals and present them for his review and decision. His national security assistant, Robert Cutler, coordinated the flow of ideas and information to the president and secretary of state whose joint decisions were final. Reagan and George W. Bush came the closest to following Eisenhower's management example, but scholars disagree over its desirability.[83]

In the *collegial* management style, typified by Kennedy and Johnson, the president deals with ad hoc working groups in an informal national security process. Decision making is centralized in the White House, with the NSC staff performing independent analysis and policy review functions. National security assistants serve as counselors,

FIGURE 10-1   Presidential Management Styles and the National Security Assistant's Roles

Implementation Responsibility

		Low	High
Policymaking Responsibility	Low	Department-centered administrator	Formalized coordinator
	High	Collegial counselor	Palace guard agent

SOURCE: Cecil V. Crabb Jr. and Kevin V. Mulcahy, *American National Security: A Presidential Perspective* (Pacific Grove, Calif.: Brooks/Cole, 1991), 189.

providing advice designed to safeguard the president's interests, a role exemplified by McGeorge Bundy under Kennedy and Walt Rostow in the Johnson administration. Brent Scowcroft played such a role in George H. W. Bush's administration,[84] and Clinton's management of national security policy evolved to approximate the collegial style, with Sandy Berger serving as a counselor.[85] George W. Bush made similar use of Condoleeza Rice and Stephen J. Hadley, blending features of the formal and collegial styles.[86] The *palace guard* management style, associated with Richard Nixon, centralizes policymaking in the White House and maintains a tight rein on implementation.[87] Nixon's national security assistant, Henry Kissinger, acted as the president's agent, directing the policymaking process, serving as the president's closest policy adviser, and on occasion actively implementing policy by conducting negotiations with foreign governments.

Experience since 1947 suggests the administrator role is likely to be ineffective unless the president and the secretary of state are capable, hands-on decision makers. The agent role carries the risk that national security assistants may go into business for themselves, acting without presidential knowledge or approval, as Reagan's defenders claimed was the case with Adm. John Poindexter and his assistant, Lt. Col. Oliver North, in the Iran-contra affair. Whether presidents choose the coordinator or counselor role for a national security assistant should be determined by their management style. In either case, the national security assistant's personality must be compatible with the designated role.[88] Carter's system suffered because Zbigniew Brzezinski was an ambitious, assertive individual more suited to the role of agent than administrator, which Carter apparently wished him to play.

Not all presidents create a clearly articulated policymaking system. Reagan, who had six different national security assistants, failed to create a consistent approach. This instability became most evident during Reagan's second term, when turmoil prevailed in the relationship between Secretary of State George Shultz and the NSC staff. One national security assistant, Robert McFarlane, acted as a policy advocate rather than as an honest broker and carried out special missions for the president.[89]

National Security Organization and Management under George W. Bush

President George W. Bush's first-term challenge was to harmonize many powerful voices. With high-visibility, assertive personalities in cabinet positions and a highly experienced vice president, observers wondered what kind of role Condoleezza Rice, the national security assistant, would assume. The president gave Rice a vote of confidence at the outset of the administration by designating her rather than Cheney to chair, in the absence of the president, meetings of the principals committee, "the senior interagency forum for consideration of policy issues affecting national security."[90] The committee included the secretaries of defense, state, and Treasury as well as the White House chief of staff, the director of national intelligence, and the chairman of the Joint Chiefs of Staff.[91] Other members of the administration attended such meetings when matters touched their areas of responsibility; the vice president was free to attend all meetings, and his chief of staff and national security adviser attended as well. Rice was a steadying force during the period following September 11, 2001, when the administration fashioned a response to terrorism and launched the military action in Afghanistan. Clashes between Secretaries Rumsfeld and Powell, veterans of many bureaucratic battles, were just as bitter as observers had predicted. Rice helped to manage the policymaking system and ensure that the president's options were preserved.[92] She also emerged as a forceful defender of the administration's policies on television talk shows and through newspaper interviews. Rice, a veteran of the NSC system operated by Scowcroft, seemed to fill a counselor's role.[93]

Bush initially reduced the size of the NSC staff by 30 percent, to about seventy, but the total crept upward again to about eighty-five members by mid-2003.[94] Interagency cooperation was sought through a set of NSC policy coordination committees, seventeen of which were created in February 2001.[95] Each was staffed by a professional from the NSC; some were under the direction of the secretary of state and others under the national security assistant. What the administration created was a variation of Eisenhower's formalized system, which accommodates strong cabinet secretaries within a White House–centered staff system. This system is also consistent with the president's preference for reserving final judgment for himself. As in all other administrations, the product is a combination of the president's personal style, the qualities of the principal advisers assembled to help him, and the president's confidence in their advice.

The Bush team functioned smoothly during its first real test, the terrorist attacks on the World Trade Center and the Pentagon. Both President Bush and Secretary of State Powell were out of town at the time of the attack, but they returned to Washington to become central figures in fashioning the national response. Vice President Cheney and national security adviser Rice coordinated initial responses from the Presidential Emergency Operations Center, a nuclear attack shelter in the basement of the White House. This twenty-first-century attack was met with twenty-first-century government organization: the president remained in contact with the White House team throughout the crisis by secure telephone and even convened a teleconference meeting of the National Security Council. Upon his return to Washington, the president met regularly with the NSC and coordinated action with the FBI and the Transportation Department as well. In short, the system worked smoothly, producing several critical decisions about both tactics and strategy and projecting an image of calm determination after a jittery first day.[96]

Far more controversial was the administration's performance prior to and following the March 2003 invasion of Iraq. It appears that a powerful alliance of Vice President Cheney, Secretary Rumsfeld, and his principal deputy, Paul Wolfowitz, pressed aggressively for action against the regime of Saddam Hussein. These members of the administration were convinced that Hussein was actively developing weapons of mass destruction and was threatening to use them, something he had already done during the war with Iran and against his own Kurdish population. A debate ensued over whether the United States should take unilateral action against this "outlaw regime" or work through the United Nations. Initially, Secretary Powell won the internal policy battle. In a dramatic speech delivered at the UN on September 12, 2002, the president challenged that organization to enforce its sixteen previous resolutions on Iraq. He agreed to delay action until UN inspectors were once again dispatched to Iraq, supported by a unanimous November vote in the Security Council. When the inspectors reported that Hussein's regime refused to disclose and destroy its weapons, the United States prepared for military action, warned Hussein of the intent to act, and sought to build both national and international support. For a time it appeared that only British prime minister Tony Blair would join the effort, as both traditional (France, Germany) and new (China, Russia) allies on the Security Council opposed military action. Ultimately, Spain, Italy, Poland,

Australia, Japan, and forty-four smaller nations joined the truncated "coalition of the willing," calling into question U.S. relations with reluctant NATO partners and the other great powers. (Many of the original allies later withdrew their forces as the conflict dragged on and political pressures at home forced a change in policy.)

Launched on March 19, 2003, the military action in Iraq proved remarkably successful. Following a massive air assault, American and British ground forces made rapid progress from the invasion launch point in Kuwait. Audiences around the world experienced the rapid advance and intense fire fights with the help of "embedded journalists" traveling with the attacking forces. Despite being badly outgunned, the Iraqi forces used neither biological nor chemical weapons against the invaders; in fact, coalition forces were unable to find evidence that such weapons existed, the prime justification for the war. After the president announced the end of combat operations in a triumphal speech aboard the USS *Abraham Lincoln* on May 1, criticism mounted in both Britain and the United States that the respective administrations had used misleading intelligence to sell the military action to skeptical publics. American media particularly focused on the following sentence from the 2003 State of the Union message:

The British government has learned that Saddam Hussein recently sought significant quantities of uranium from Africa.[97]

In the run-up to the State of the Union speech, several administration spokespersons had claimed that Iraq was reestablishing a nuclear weapons program, but each time the claim was rebutted either within the government or by UN specialists, and Powell did not repeat it in his February 2003 presentation at the United Nations.[98] Nevertheless, the president used the nuclear threat as part of his justification for war. Without evidence of an imminent threat—a questionable nuclear argument and no evidence of chemical and biological weapons—the president's motivation, war rationale, and credibility were called into question.[99] In early July 2003 the White House acknowledged that Bush's charge against Hussein rested on faulty intelligence, a report that CIA and State Department intelligence officials had questioned for months. A succession of administration figures then stepped up to shoulder the blame for the speech error: Tenet, Rice, Hadley, and Michael Gerson, director of presidential speechwriting. Finally, hoping to bring the media furor to a halt, the president stated in late July that he took full responsibility for the erroneous statement.

The postwar peace went far less smoothly than the war. The administration had focused so intently on winning the military battle that it had ignored what to do once Saddam Hussein's regime had fallen. As many critics had predicted, nation building, led by the Christian, Western, pro-Israeli United States, proved enormously difficult in a confused political setting with warring religious and ethnic factions. Two factors began to erode public support: isolated but steady attacks on American forces produced continued casualties, and the cost of maintaining American military forces in Iraq rose to about $4 billion a month.[100] As the 2004 elections loomed, Democrats made faulty intelligence about weapons of mass destruction into a campaign issue.[101]

Scholars will dissect Iraq policymaking for decades. John P. Burke's early assessment, based on a review of the available information, is an unflattering portrait of seriously defective processes.[102] The prewar decision making was "ineffective in vetting information, exploring a full range of analysis, and considering competing views."[103] Dissenting views in the intelligence community were not debated in the NSC's principals committee, nor were the views of those less optimistic about the chances for establishing democracy in postwar Iraq. Instead of encouraging dissenting views, some of the president's advisers suppressed them and chose to maintain a disciplined administration message rather than reach high-quality decisions. Rice was unable to control the secretary of defense and vice president who ran roughshod over her efforts to coordinate policy and serve as an "honest broker" among the president's senior advisers. Powell consistently came out on the short end of the stick. This happened on an interpersonal level and carried over to lower-level committees where Rumsfeld's and Cheney's staffs dominated postwar planning, openly challenging the NSC's ability to coordinate policymaking. Jon Western, however, argues that the administration had one overriding success: convincing the American public that the threat from Iraq was real and that the United States "could effectively do something about it." In Western's account, Bush, like other presidents before him, "deliberately and selectively used its [the presidency's] executive advantages of intelligence collection and analysis to frame a particular version of the threat in order to influence public opinion."[104] The Bush administration was wildly successful in maintaining a unified front.

Conclusion

National security is the president's most important policy responsibility, presenting complex problems of leadership and management. For the nation, preserving and protecting its sovereignty and independence is of paramount interest. To a great extent, success depends on every president's personal performance. Presidents must interpret and exercise their powers within constitutional and statutory limits. To succeed, they must have congressional cooperation, which requires consultation. Yet operational realities require that presidents be accorded ample latitude to act independently and often secretly. Tensions inevitably arise between Congress and the president over national security policy.[105] But the tasks involved are primarily executive in nature, and executive control of foreign and military policy persists in spite of Congress's major constitutional role.[106] The Constitution and political prudence require "shared power and balanced institutional participation" as norms in national security decision making.[107]

Perhaps the most important lesson in this regard is that since 1945 most of the nation's successful foreign policies—the Truman Doctrine, the Marshall Plan, NATO, the Panama Canal treaty, arms control, and the Persian Gulf War—were "adopted by Congress and the people after meaningful debate."[108] For the most part, the major failures—FDR's Yalta agreements with Stalin, the Bay of Pigs invasion, the Vietnam War, and the Iran-contra affair—were initiated and implemented unilaterally by presidents. In the case of the Iraq War, Congress approved action, but it seems likely that Bush's legacy will be a controversial if not a failed adventure.

In the emerging international system, the United States remains the world's dominant power both militarily and economically, but its dominance does not mean America can always assert its will unilaterally. Finding the means to exercise power responsibly remains both the nation's and the president's major challenge.

Suggested Readings

Berman, Larry. *Planning a Tragedy: The Americanization of the War in Vietnam.* New York: Norton, 1983.

Burke, John P., and Fred I. Greenstein. *How Presidents Test Reality: Decisions on Vietnam, 1954 and 1965.* New York: Russell Sage Foundation, 1991.

Draper, Theodore. *A Very Thin Line: The Iran-Contra Affairs.* New York: Hill and Wang, 1991.

Fisher, Louis. *Presidential War Power.* Lawrence: University Press of Kansas, 1995.

———. *Congressional Abdication on War and Spending.* College Station: Texas A&M University Press, 2000.

George, Alexander L. *Presidential Decisionmaking in Foreign Policy: The Effective Use of Information and Advice.* Boulder: Westview, 1980.

Glennon, Michael J., and J. William Fulbright. *Constitutional Diplomacy.* Princeton: Princeton University Press, 1990.

Henderson, Philip G. *Managing the Presidency: The Eisenhower Legacy—From Kennedy to Reagan.* Boulder: Westview, 1988.

Henkin, Louis. *Constitutionalism, Democracy, and Foreign Affairs.* New York: Columbia University Press, 1992.

———. *Foreign Affairs and the United States Constitution.* 2nd ed. Oxford: Oxford University Press, 1997.

Hinckley, Barbara. *Less than Meets the Eye: Foreign Policymaking and the Myth of the Assertive Congress.* Chicago: University of Chicago Press, 1994.

Johnson, Loch K. *Bombs, Bugs, Drugs, and Thugs: Intelligence and America's Quest for Security.* New York: New York University Press, 2000.

Koh, Harold Hongju. *The National Security Constitution: Sharing Power after the Iran-Contra Affair.* New Haven: Yale University Press, 1990.

Korb, Lawrence J. *A New National Security Strategy in an Age of Terrorists, Tyrants, and Weapons of Mass Destruction.* New York: Council on Foreign Relations, 2003.

Mann, Thomas E., ed. *A Question of Balance: The President, the Congress, and Foreign Policy.* Washington, D.C.: Brookings, 1990.

Peterson, Paul E., ed. *The President, the Congress, and the Making of Foreign Policy.* Norman: University of Oklahoma Press, 1994.

Pious, Richard M. *Why Presidents Fail: White House Decision Making from Eisenhower to Bush II.* Lanham, Md.: Rowman and Littlefield, 2008.

President's Special Review Board (Tower Commission). *Report of the President's Special Review Board.* Washington, D.C.: Government Printing Office, 1987.

Savage, Charlie. *Takeover: The Return of the Imperial Presidency and the Subversion of American Democracy.* New York: Little, Brown, 2007.

Schlesinger, Arthur M., Jr. *The Imperial Presidency.* Rev. ed. Boston: Houghton Mifflin, 1989.

———. *War and the American Presidency.* New York: W. W. Norton, 2005.

Western, Jon. *Selling Intervention and War: The Presidency, the Media, and the American Public.* Baltimore: Johns Hopkins University Press, 2005.

Woodward, Bob. *Bush at War.* New York: Simon and Schuster, 2002.

———. *State of Denial.* New York: Simon and Schuster, 2006.

Notes

1. "Authorization for Use of Military Force," joint resolution adopted September 14, 2001, in *Washington Post*, September 15, 2001, A4.

2. Remarks of George W. Bush in a news conference September 13, 2001, as reported by eMediaMillWorks, www.washingtonpost.com.

3. The "two presidencies" thesis holds that presidents enjoy relatively greater success with Congress in foreign policy than in domestic policy. According to Terry Sullivan, modern Republican and Democratic presidents have had approximately equal success with foreign policy proposals, but Democratic administrations have done better with domestic policy because of their party's longtime domination of Congress. See Sullivan, "A Matter of Fact: The 'Two Presidencies' Thesis Revitalized," in *The Two Presidencies: A Quarter Century Assessment*, ed. Steven A. Shull (Chicago: Nelson Hall, 1991), 143–157. On the rise of partisan and ideological bickering over foreign policy issues in Congress during the 1990s, see James M. McCormick, Eugene R. Wittkopf, and David M. Dana, "Politics and Bipartisanship at the Water's Edge: A Note on Bush and Clinton," *Polity* 30 (Fall 1997): 133–149.

4. Interview with Tom Ricks broadcast on National Public Radio's *Morning Edition*, March 4, 2009, http://www.npr.org/templates/story/story.php?storyId=101395478.

5. James Chace, "Is a Foreign Policy Consensus Possible?" *Foreign Affairs* 57 (Fall 1978): 30.

6. Lawrence J. Korb, *A New National Security Strategy in an Age of Terrorists, Tyrants, and Weapons of Mass Destruction* (New York: Council on Foreign Relations, 2003), 1.

7. Strobe Talbott, *The Russians and Reagan* (New York: Vintage Books, 1984).

8. The most comprehensive and informative account of the Iran-contra affair is by Theodore Draper, *A Very Thin Line: The Iran-Contra Affairs* (New York: Hill and Wang, 1991). For the perspective of two participants in the congressional hearings, see William S. Cohen and George J. Mitchell, *Men of Zeal* (New York: Viking, 1988). The role of the CIA and Director William Casey receive careful attention from Bob Woodward in *Veil: The Secret Wars of the CIA, 1981–1987* (New York: Simon and Schuster, 1987). Also essential to a full understanding of Iran-contra is the report of the Tower Commission (John Tower, Edmund Muskie, and Brent Scowcroft): President's Special Review Board, *Report of the President's Special Review Board* (Washington, D.C.: Government Printing Office, 1987).

9. Terry L. Deibel, "Bush's Foreign Policy: Mastery and Inaction," *Foreign Policy* 84 (Fall 1991): 20–22; Steven V. Roberts, "The Second Sin of George Bush," *New Leader*, March 11–15, 1991, 3.

10. Daniel P. Franklin and Robert Shepard, "Analyzing the Bush Foreign Policy" (paper presented at the annual meeting of the American Political Science Association, Washington, D.C., August 29–September 1, 1991), 2–3.

11. Deibel, "Bush's Foreign Policy," 3–4.

12. David C. Hendrickson, "The Recovery of Internationalism," *Foreign Affairs* 73 (September-October 1994): 26–43. For similar criticisms, see Richard N. Haas, "Paradigm Lost," *Foreign Affairs* 74 (January-February 1995): 43–58; and Larry Berman and Emily O. Goldman, "Clinton's Foreign Policy at Midterm," in *The Clinton Presidency: First Appraisals*, ed. Colin Campbell and Bert A. Rockman (Chatham, N.J.: Chatham House, 1995), 290–324.

13. William J. Clinton, *A National Security Strategy of Engagement and Enlargement* (Washington, D.C.: Government Printing Office, 1994).

14. Berman and Goldman, "Clinton's Foreign Policy," 302–303.

15. William J. Clinton, *A National Security Strategy for a New Century* (Washington, D.C.: The White House, October 1998). For commentary, see Emily O. Goldman and Larry Berman, "Engaging the World: First Impressions of the Clinton Foreign Policy Legacy," in *The Clinton Legacy*, ed. Colin Campbell and Bert A. Rockman (New York: Chatham House, 2000); and James M. McCormick, "Clinton and Foreign Policy: Some Legacies for a New Century," in *The Postmodern Presidency: Bill Clinton's Legacy in U.S. Politics*, ed. Steven E. Schier (Pittsburgh: University of Pittsburgh Press, 2000).

16. These documents were National Security Policy Directive 17 and Homeland Security Policy Directive 4, released on December 12, 2002. See Korb, *A New National Security Strategy*, Appendix B.

17. John Lewis Gaddis, "A Grand Strategy of Transformation," *Foreign Policy* (November-December 2002), www.foreignpolicy.com/issue_novdec_2002/gaddis.html.

18. Fareed Zakaria, "The Arrogant Empire," *Newsweek*, March 24, 2003, 18ff.

19. Ibid.

20. George W. Bush, State of the Union message, January 29, 2002, http://www.cfr.org/publication/12473/.

21. Korb, *A New National Security Strategy*, Appendix B, 107.

22. Susan E. Rice, "The New National Security Strategy: Focus on Failed States," Brookings Policy Brief #116-2003, February 2003, 1, www.brookings.edu/search.aspx?doQuery=1&q=%22The+New+National+Security+Strategy%3a+Focus+on+Failed+States%22&start=0&num=10.

23. See, for example, three Brookings Institution policy briefs: Ivo Daalder, James M. Lindsay, and James B. Steinberg, "The Bush National Security Strategy: An Evaluation," Policy Brief #109-2002, www.brookings.edu/papers/2002/10defense_daalder.aspx; Michael E. O'Hanlon, Susan E. Rice, and James B. Steinberg, "The New National Security Strategy and Preemption," Policy Brief #113-2003,

www.brookings.edu/papers/2002/12terrorism_ohanlon.aspx; and Rice, "The New National Security Strategy."

24. O'Hanlon, Rice, and Steinberg, "The New National Security Strategy and Preemption," 2.

25. These three options are discussed in depth and presented as alternative drafts of presidential speeches in Korb, *A New National Security Strategy*, 1–96.

26. Prominently mentioned in many accounts are Vice President Dick Cheney, Secretary of Defense Donald Rumsfeld, and Deputy Secretary of Defense Paul Wolfowitz.

27. George W. Bush, Second Inaugural Address, http://www.vlib.us/amdocs/texts/bush012005.html.

28. Robert McMahon, "The Campaign and Foreign Policy," *Daily Analysis*, Council on Foreign Relations, October 31, 2008, http://www.cfr.org/publication/17655/.

29. Transcript of remarks by President Obama, February 27, 2009, Camp Lejeune, North Carolina, http://www.cfr.org/publication/18657/obamas_remarks_on_responsibly_ending_the_war_in_iraq .html?breadcrumb=%2Fregion%2F405%2Firaq.

30. Helene Cooper and Eric Schmitt, "White House Debate Led to Plan to Widen Afghan Effort," *New York Times*, March 27, 2009, http://www.nytimes.com/2009/03/28/us/politics/28prexy.html?_r=1.

31. Leslie H. Gelb, "The Holes in Obama's Afghanistan Plan," op. ed., *The Daily Beast*, March 27, 2009, http://www.cfr.org/publication/19007/holes_in_obamas_afghanistan_plan.html.

32. Roger Cohen, "America Agonistes," *New York Times*, April 1, 2009, http://www.nytimes.com/ 2009/04/02/opinion/02iht-edcohen.html.

33. See the comments of former representative Lee Hamilton, D-Ind., as reported by Charlie Cook, "China Crisis Halts Slide of Bush's Poll Ratings," *National Journal*, April 21, 2001, 1186.

34. Edward S. Corwin, *The President: Office and Powers*, 4th ed. (New York: New York University Press, 1957), 171.

35. Ibid.

36. Joseph E. Kallenbach, *The American Chief Executive* (New York: Harper and Row, 1966), 485.

37. Corwin, *The President*, 179.

38. Ibid., 185.

39. Ibid., 213.

40. Ibid.; Kallenbach, *The American Chief Executive*, 502.

41. The treaty-making process entails three distinct stages: negotiation, Senate approval, and ratification by the president. Contrary to popular understanding, the Senate does not ratify a treaty—it *approves* the treaty negotiated by the president. The president may refuse to sign, that is, to ratify, a treaty approved by the Senate, either because of amendments or reservations or because it was negotiated by a previous administration.

42. Cecil V. Crabb Jr. and Pat M. Holt, *Invitation to Struggle: Congress, the President, and Foreign Policy*, 4th ed. (Washington, D.C.: CQ Press, 1992), 6.

43. Harold Hongju Koh argues, however, that Congress should create by statute its own procedures for determining when international agreements should be submitted to the Senate for approval. See Koh, *The National Security Constitution: Sharing Power after the Iran-Contra Affair* (New Haven: Yale University Press, 1990), 195.

44. *Goldwater v. Carter*, 444 U.S. 996 (1979). Although the Court based its decision on the recognition of foreign governments, the case has been interpreted as authorizing unilateral presidential breaking of treaties in accordance with their terms.

45. Koh, *The National Security Constitution*, 43.

46. David E. Sanger and Steven Lee Myers, "Bush Seeks Missile Shield Along with Nuclear Cuts; Calls '72 Treaty Outdated," *New York Times*, May 2, 2001, A1. It was later revealed that the Bush administration was considering a radical departure from the past—abandoning all strategic weapons treaties to maximize

flexibility in making nuclear force decisions. Michael R. Gordon, "U.S. Weighing Future of Strategic Arms Pacts," *New York Times*, May 9, 2001, A1.

47. The intelligence community throughout most of the post–World War II period consisted of the Central Intelligence Agency; the National Security Agency; the Bureau of Intelligence and Research in the Department of State; the Defense Intelligence Agency; the intelligence offices of the Army, Navy, Air Force, and Marine Corps; the FBI; and the intelligence offices in the Departments of Energy and Treasury. Over time, the community grew to include units in the Coast Guard, the Department of Homeland Security, the Drug Enforcement Administration, and two specialized units in Defense, the National Geospatial Intelligence Agency and the National Reconnaissance Office, www.intelligence.gov/1-members.shtml.

48. Bob Woodward, *Bush at War* (New York: Simon and Schuster, 2002).

49. Corwin, *The President*, chap. 6; Arthur M. Schlesinger Jr., *The Imperial Presidency* (Boston: Houghton Mifflin, 1989), chaps. 1–7.

50. Corwin, *The President*, 229.

51. *Prize Cases*, 67 U.S. (2 Black) 635 (1863).

52. *Korematsu v. United States*, 323 U.S. 214 (1944).

53. Clinton Rossiter, *Constitutional Dictatorship: Crisis Government in Modern Democracies* (New York: Harcourt, Brace, 1963).

54. Such actions have numerous precedents, including Jefferson's dispatch of the Navy to stop the Barbary pirates from seizing U.S. merchant ships and holding their crews for ransom, and Theodore Roosevelt's contribution of U.S. Marines to the international expeditionary force that put down the Boxer Rebellion in China in 1904.

55. Larry Berman, *Planning a Tragedy: The Americanization of the War in Vietnam* (New York: Norton, 1982). For a comparative analysis of how Eisenhower and Johnson dealt with pressures to intervene militarily in Vietnam, see John P. Burke and Fred I. Greenstein, *How Presidents Test Reality: Decisions on Vietnam, 1954 and 1965* (New York: Russell Sage Foundation, 1989).

56. Ivo H. Daalder and James M. Lindsay, "The Bush Revolution: The Remaking of America's Foreign Policy" (paper delivered at the conference on "The George W. Bush Presidency: An Early Assessment," Woodrow Wilson School, Princeton University, April 25–26, 2003), 28.

57. Mike Allen and Charles Lane, "Resolution Likened to '64 Vietnam Measure," *Washington Post*, September 20, 2002, A20.

58. The House vote was 296-133, with all but 6 Republicans approving and Democrats dividing 81 yes and 126 no. The Senate vote was 77-23, with all but 1 Republican approving and 21 Democrats voting no; the independent also voted no.

59. John M. Donnelly, "Hard-Line Anti-War Votes Fail," *CQ Weekly Online*, September 24, 2007, 2760–2762, http://library.cqpress.com/cqweekly/weeklyreport110-000002591148.

60. In his well-known concurring opinion in *Youngstown Sheet and Tube Co. v. Sawyer* (1952), Justice Robert H. Jackson identified three scenarios for presidential use of force: presidents can act with the express or implied authority of Congress; presidents can act in direct opposition to the will of Congress; or presidents may act in the absence of express or denied authority, a "twilight zone." Louis Fisher, *Presidential War Power* (Lawrence: University Press of Kansas, 1995), 190.

61. Arthur M. Schlesinger Jr., *War and the American Presidency* (New York: Norton, 2005). Also see Charlie Savage. *Takeover: The Return of the Imperial Presidency and the Subversion of American Democracy* (New York: Little, Brown, 2007).

62. The Supreme Court's decision in *Immigration and Naturalization Service v. Chadha*, 462 U.S. 919 (1983), which held that the legislative veto was unconstitutional, made this provision inoperative.

63. Richard F. Grimmett, "War Powers Resolution: Presidential Compliance," *CRS Issue Brief for Congress*, Congressional Research Service, Library of Congress, Washington, D.C., March 21, 2001; updated June 9, 2003.

64. Robert A. Katzmann, "War Powers: Toward a New Accommodation," in *A Question of Balance: The President, Congress, and Foreign Policy*, ed. Thomas E. Mann (Washington, D.C.: Brookings, 1990), 55.

65. Congress considered triggering the clock in 1983, in legislation involving the multinational force in Lebanon, but ultimately authorized U.S. participation for eighteen months after reaching an agreement with the White House.

66. Joshua Lee Prober, "Congress, the War Powers Resolution, and the Secret Political Life of 'a Dead Letter,'" *Journal of Law and Politics* 7 (1990): 177–229.

67. Carroll J. Doherty, "Bush Is Given Authorization to Use Force Against Iraq," *Congressional Quarterly Weekly Report*, January 12, 1991, 65–70.

68. John M. Hillebrecht, "Ensuring Affirmative Congressional Control over the Use of Force: Two Proposals for Collective Decision Making," *Stanford Journal of International Law* 26 (1990): 511.

69. Michael J. Glennon, *Constitutional Diplomacy* (Princeton: Princeton University Press, 1990), 102–103.

70. Koh, *The National Security Constitution*.

71. Prober, "Congress, the War Powers Resolution," 229.

72. Ibid., 223–226, 229.

73. Citing as precedent the history of presidential war making, the Court could sustain the resolution. Or the Court might choose to overturn it, noting that because the resolution was forced on the presidency at a time of institutional weakness, it "undercuts the legitimacy of the executive branch." I. M. Destler, "The Constitution and Foreign Affairs," *News for Teachers of Political Science* (Spring 1985): 15.

74. James L. Sundquist, *The Decline and Resurgence of Congress* (Washington, D.C.: Brookings, 1981), 270.

75. William C. Banks and Jeffrey D. Straussman, "A New Imperial Presidency? Insights from U.S. Involvement in Bosnia," *Political Science Quarterly* 114 (Summer 1999): 200.

76. William Safire, "On Impeachment Eve," *New York Times*, December 17, 1998, A31. On the comments of Senate majority leader Trent Lott and House whip Tom DeLay, see R. W. Apple Jr., "No Reservoir of Credibility," *New York Times*, December 17, 1998, A1, A15. On the air attacks more generally, see Francis X. Clines and Steven Lee Myers, "Biggest Attack Since '91 War—Britain Gives Support," *New York Times*, December 17, 1998, A1, A15.

77. *Report of the U. S. Commission on the Organization of the Government for the Conduct of Foreign Policy* (Washington, D.C.: Government Printing Office, 1975), 1. Also see Burke and Greenstein, *How Presidents Test Reality*, esp. chap. 13.

78. Graham T. Allison and Peter Szanton, "Organizing for the Decade Ahead," in *Setting National Priorities: The Next Ten Years*, ed. Henry Owen and Charles Schultze (Washington, D.C.: Brookings, 1976), 232–233.

79. Alexander L. George, *Presidential Decisionmaking in Foreign Policy: The Effective Use of Information and Advice* (Boulder: Westview, 1980), 146. For a history of the NSC, see David Rothkopf, *Running the World: The Inside Story of the National Security Council and the Architects of American Power* (New York: Public Affairs, 2005).

80. Burt Solomon, "When It Comes to Geopolitics . . . Who's Painting the Big Picture?" *National Journal*, March 5, 1995, 550–551.

81. Ivo H. Daalder and I. M. Destler, "A New NSC for a New Administration," Policy Brief #68-2000, Brookings Institution, November 2000, www.brookings.edu/papers/2000/11governance_daalder.aspx.

82. Cecil V. Crabb Jr. and Kevin V. Mulcahy, *American National Security: A Presidential Perspective* (Pacific Grove, Calif.: Brooks-Cole, 1991), chap. 9. The discussion relies on Crabb and Mulcahy. For a similar typology related to "control" and "coordination," see Margaret G. Hermann and Thomas Preston, "Presidents, Advisers, and Foreign Policy: The Effect of Leadership Style on Executive Arrangements," *Political Psychology* 15, no. 1, 1994): 75–96.

83. For opposing views, see Fred I. Greenstein and Richard H. Immerman, "Effective National Security Advising: Recovering the Eisenhower Legacy," and Arthur Schlesinger Jr., "Effective National Security Advising: A Most Dubious Precedent," *Political Science Quarterly* 115 (Fall 2000): 335–351.

84. Larry Berman and Bruce W. Jentelson, "Bush and the Post–Cold War World: New Challenges for American Leadership," in *The Bush Presidency: First Appraisals,* ed. Colin Campbell and Bert A. Rockman (Chatham, N.J.: Chatham House, 1991), 99–103. Also see Burt Solomon, "Making Foreign Policy in Secret May Be Easy, but It Carries Risks," *National Journal,* January 12, 1991, 90–91.

85. Anthony Lake, who held the position before Berger, is best thought of as a coordinator, according to a written communication from Kevin Mulcahy.

86. John P. Burke, "From Success to Failure? Iraq and the Organization of George W. Bush's Decision Making," in George C. Edwards and Desmond King, eds. *The Polarized Presidency of George W. Bush* (Oxford: Oxford University Press, 2007), 176.

87. Crabb and Mulcahy, *American National Security,* 189–190.

88. Ibid.

89. Kevin V. Mulcahy, "The Secretary of State: Foreign Policymaking in the Carter and Reagan Administrations," *Presidential Studies Quarterly* (Spring 1986): 296.

90. To view the text of the National Security Presidential Directive that established the Bush system, see www.fas.org/irp/offdocs/nspd/nspd-1.htm.

91. Jane Perlez, "Directive Says Rice, Bush Aide, Won't Be Upstaged by Cheney," *New York Times,* February 16, 2001, www.nytimes.com/2001/02/16/politics/16SECU.html. In the intelligence reforms adopted in 2004, the director of national intelligence replaced the director of the CIA.

92. For a fascinating account, see Woodward, *Bush at War.*

93. Written communication from Kevin Mulcahy.

94. Ivo Daalder and I. M. Destler, "How Operational and Visible an NSC?" Brookings Institution, February 23, 2001, www.brookings.edu/opinions/2001/0223nationalsecuritycouncil_daalder.aspx.

95. The original NSC coordination committees were in the following areas: (a) regional committees for Europe and Eurasia, Western Hemisphere, East Asia, South Asia, Near East and North Africa, and Africa; and (b) functional committees for democracy, human rights, and international operations; international development and humanitarian assistance; global environment; international finance; transnational economic issues; counterterrorism and national preparedness; defense strategy, force structure, and planning; arms control; proliferation, counterproliferation, and homeland defense; intelligence and counterintelligence; records access and information security; and trade policy review group. National Security Presidential Directive 1, www.fas.org/irp/offdocs/nspd/nspd-1.htm.

96. David E. Sanger and Don Van Natta Jr., "In Four Days, a National Crisis Changes Bush's Presidency," *New York Times,* September 16, 2001, A1.

97. Full text of the speech is available at http://www.vlib.us/amdocs/texts/bush012003.html.

98. Walter Pincus, "Bush Faced Dwindling Data on Iraq Nuclear Bid," *Washington Post,* July 16, 2003, A1; Walter Pincus, "White House Backs Off Claim on Iraqi Buy," *Washington Post,* July 8, 2003, A1; Walter Pincus, "CIA Asked Britain to Drop Iraq Claim; Advice on Alleged Uranium Buy Was Refused," *Washington Post,* July 11, 2003, A1.

99. Dana Milbank, "Bush Remarks Confirm Shift in Justifying War; Standard of Proof for Weapons Drops," *Washington Post,* June 1, 2003, A18.

100. Richard Morin and Claudia Deane, "Support for Bush Declines as Casualties Mount in Iraq," *Washington Post,* July 12, 2003, A1.

101. Jim VandeHei and Helen Dewar, "Democrats Sharpen Attack on Bush over Iraq," *Washington Post,* July 16, 2003, A17.

102. Burke, "From Success to Failure?"

103. Ibid., 178.

104. Jon Western, *Selling Intervention and War: The Presidency, the Media, and the American Public* (Baltimore: Johns Hopkins University Press, 2005), 180, 217.

105. Barbara Hinckley suggests that the conflict between presidents and Congress is largely symbolic, staged to convince the public that both institutions are alert and active and that policymaking is democratic. Barbara Hinckley, *Less than Meets the Eye: Foreign Policymaking and the Myth of the Assertive Congress* (Chicago: University of Chicago Press, 1994), 175, 193.

106. Paul E. Peterson, "The International System and Foreign Policy," in *The President, the Congress, and the Making of Foreign Policy*, ed. Paul E. Peterson (Norman: University of Oklahoma Press, 1994), 12–14.

107. Koh, *The National Security Constitution*, 207.

108. Stephen E. Ambrose, "The Presidency and Foreign Policy," *Foreign Affairs* (Winter 1991/1992): 136.

CHAPTER 11

Barack Obama: Transition to Power and the First Hundred Days

Chief Justice John G. Roberts Jr. administers the oath of office to Barack Obama, as Michelle Obama holds the Lincoln Bible.

B y almost any standard, the 2008 presidential election was historic. It was the longest and most expensive presidential election in U.S. history. It resulted in the election of Barack Obama, the first African American president, and Joseph Biden, the first Catholic vice president. Had the Republican ticket won, Sarah Palin would have become the first female vice president, and John McCain the oldest newly elected president. In addition, Obama's chief rival for the Democratic nomination was Hillary Clinton, the first woman to come close to winning the top place on a major political party ticket. (Women have run as nominees of minor political parties since 1872, although they did not have a constitutional right to vote until 1920.)

The times surrounding the 2008 election were also historic. In the midst of the election cycle the United States suddenly confronted the worst economic crisis since the Great Depression of the 1930s. The primary focus of the election turned from the wars in Iraq and Afghanistan to salvaging the economy, and it became clear that whoever was elected would be forced to grapple with exceptionally daunting issues both at home and abroad.

The enormity of the economic crisis, coupled with two ongoing wars and serious national security threats in the post–9/11 world, made the transition to power after the election especially complicated. Even under ordinary circumstances, the presidential transition is a formidable challenge, with just three months to move from full-time campaigning to full-time governing. As Stephen Hess puts it, this shift involves a focus on the "three P's": personnel, process, and policy.[1]

The Transition

One of the first orders of business for a newly elected president is to select *personnel*. This step involves picking not only his most trusted advisers, including his White House staff, but also nominees to fill the top cabinet positions. In addition to the fifteen cabinet posts are more than one thousand other positions that require Senate confirmation.[2] Some eight thousand jobs in the executive branch are listed and described in the so-called Plum Book, which the Government Printing Office publishes every four years.[3] The new administration has to fill all of these positions. Selecting personnel involves thorough vetting. Applicants seeking high-ranking posts in the Obama administration had to fill out a seven-page questionnaire that included sixty-three specific questions concerning personal and professional information. It requested everything from personal financial information to links to the applicant's Facebook page and answers to questions such as "Do you or any immediate members of your family own a gun?" and "If you keep or have ever kept a diary that contains anything that could suggest a conflict of interest or be a possible source of embarrassment to you, your family, or the President-Elect if it were made public, please describe."[4] The *New York Times* called the questionnaire one of the most extensive and invasive of its kind.[5]

Selecting personnel gets a great deal of media attention, but *process* is just as important. Process refers to decisions about how the incoming president will organize his White House. Does he want a highly centralized staff structure with a chief of staff who acts as a gatekeeper or a more decentralized staff? Are there existing White House units he wants to abolish or new entities he wants to create? How will his staff relate to the cabinet? Such decisions may not get much publicity, but they can profoundly influence the effectiveness of the decision-making process in the new administration.[6]

Finally, the president-elect and his team must begin to craft a *policy* agenda for the new administration. Given the complexity of modern-day government and the magnitude of the issues it confronts, this task is very complicated. Moreover, establishing a policy agenda is only half of the puzzle. The transition team must also be thinking about how to implement it, which brings the discussion back to process. How will Congress, interest groups, and the public react to the policy proposals? In what order should they be introduced? How should they be promoted?

To deal with all of these issues, a transition team must be poised and ready to spring into action as soon as the election is over. Creating an effective transition team is itself a complicated and expensive process. The president-elect's political party used to pay for the transition, but that changed when Congress passed the Presidential Transition Act of 1963, which provided for federal funding of presidential transitions and for office space, information technology, furniture, equipment, and other logistical support. In 2008 the government allocated $8.5 million for the transition and provided approximately 120,000 square feet of fully furnished and equipped office space in Washington, D.C.[7] The Obama team set a goal to raise an additional $3.5 million from private donations to provide supplemental funding for the transition, and it opened an additional transition office in Obama's home town of Chicago. Private donations are limited by law to $5,000 each, and Obama banned donations from corporations, unions, political action committees, registered federal lobbyists, and registered foreign agents. Even with such limits, Obama raised $1.1 million in just the first ten days after the election.[8]

Both Obama and his Republican rival, John McCain, had been quietly organizing a transition team long before election day. McCain set up his transition operation at his campaign headquarters in Arlington, Virginia, and Obama, whose campaign headquarters were in Chicago, ran a separate transition operation in Washington.[9] President-elect Obama unveiled his transition operation—complete with a Web site (change.gov)—the day after the election, and he moved quickly to name his White House staff and cabinet nominees. Obama was also determined to have a highly disciplined and focused transition. This stood in stark contrast to the last newly elected Democratic president, Bill Clinton, whose transition was marked by delay, disorganization, and discord.

John Burke, who has written extensively about presidential transitions, points to Clinton in 1992 as an example of a transition that hurt the president-elect's "ability to take office smoothly, make decisions soundly, and govern effectively."[10] Clinton did not introduce his transition team until nine days after his election. He did not name a White House chief of staff until mid-December or unveil the rest of his senior White House staff until six days before the inauguration. He was also slow to nominate cabinet members (the first nomination came on December 10, 1992). Burke argued that Clinton also placed too much emphasis on people and too little on process: he focused a great deal on the personal characteristics of cabinet nominees and his personal comfort level with them, but gave little thought to how they would function as a group and how they would interact with the White House staff, which he had not yet chosen. And although developing a policy agenda was a major priority for Clinton, Burke argues that the Clinton transition "moved on too many policy fronts" and found it difficult to reconcile approaches to policy among competing factions within the team. The transition also became distracted by the tremendous controversy surrounding Clinton's early promise to allow gays in the military and by the poor vetting of some of his nominees that led to stormy confirmation battles with the Senate.[11]

Obama sought to avoid these mistakes. He looked to Ronald Reagan's 1980 transition, considered by many to be among the most effective in modern times, as a model. As former U.S. attorney general Edwin Meese III, who was Reagan's transition director, put it: "I think they read our book. They've almost followed the same pattern."[12] Obama announced his choice of Rahm Emanuel to be White House chief of staff on November 6, just two days after the election, and quickly convened an economic advisory board. He announced his choice of senior economic advisers on November 24, followed by the national security advisers on December 1, and energy and environment nominees on December 15. Nominating individuals in these policy clusters also helped to signal the order of his priorities and reassured the public that he was approaching national problems systematically.

Moving quickly and avoiding missteps are important. Political scientist James P. Pfiffner has emphasized that presidents must "hit the ground running" after they take the oath of office. As Pfiffner explains, presidents "want to take advantage of the 'mandate' from the voters and create a 'honeymoon' with Congress." Early victories in implementing their policy goals may provide momentum for additional victories. "This desire to move fast is driven by the awareness that power is fleeting."[13] As discussed in chapter 8, one of the president's most important resources for securing legislative victories is political capital, but that capital decreases over time. As political capital is expended, a president's influence and the ability to accomplish goals are diminished. That is why presidents are so eager to move quickly to implement their policy goals. This eagerness, however, comes at a time when they and their staffs are new to their jobs and relatively inexperienced. Pfiffner notes that a president's "greatest opportunity to work his will comes when he has the least ability to do it effectively; this is what makes planning an effective transition so critical."[14]

National security considerations made an effective transition especially important in 2008. This presidential transition was the first since the 9/11 terrorist attacks, and it took place during ongoing wars in Iraq and Afghanistan. Concerned that a disorganized transition might invite terrorist threats, President Bush began taking steps long before the election: the White House began meeting with the Obama and McCain campaigns in summer 2008, and on October 9 Bush signed an executive order creating the Presidential Transition Coordinating Council to help ensure an orderly transition.[15] To make sure that vital posts would not be vacant on inauguration day, the administration coordinated expedited security clearances for Obama nominees. Bush was acutely aware that on September 11, 2001, only 30 percent of his national security appointees were in place.[16] The Bush administration also provided daily national security briefings for the president-elect, and it even created a simulation of a terrorist attack to help the new administration prepare for such an emergency. As White House chief of staff Josh Bolton put it: "If a crisis hits on January 21, they're the ones that are going to have to deal with it. We need to make sure they're as well prepared as possible."[17]

President Bush reached out to Obama on election night, pledging his full cooperation to make the transition a smooth one. He repeated the pledge publicly the next day and invited the Obamas to visit the White House as quickly as possible. That visit took place a few days later, on November 10. In his weekly radio address on November 8, Bush said, "Ensuring that the transition is seamless is a top priority for the rest of my time in office." He continued, "My administration will work hard to ensure that the next president will hit the ground running."[18] Obama's transition team was highly disciplined and effective, but it also benefited from the cooperation it received from the outgoing Bush administration. If it takes two to transition, both partners in this quick-step dance were committed to getting it right.

On the policy front Obama also wasted little time. He announced on November 12 the creation of a team to review the policies and budgets of the federal agencies, and he created individual transition teams for the various cabinet departments, starting with the Treasury, State, and Defense Departments.[19] He also instructed his economic advisers to start working with Congress to create an economic stimulus package that he hoped to sign early in his administration.

Obama repeated on numerous occasions that there was "only one president at a time," and he steadfastly deferred to the Bush administration on foreign policy issues during the transition. But he was more willing to interject his views on economic issues.[20] For example, Obama lobbied the lame-duck Congress to release the second half of the Treasury Department's $700 billion bailout fund, which Congress did in January 2009—shortly before the inauguration. In so doing, the president-elect reached out to Republicans. The *New York Times* said, Obama "wooed enough Republican senators to release the bailout money. Even some he did not convince muted their opposition."[21] As we shall see, however, Republican support evaporated once Obama became president.

Some months before the election, Obama made it clear that he planned to follow Abraham Lincoln's example and appoint a "team of rivals."[22] Once elected, he followed through on that plan.[23] Most notably, he chose Hillary Clinton to be his secretary of state. He also nominated Bill Richardson, another former rival for the nomination, to head the Commerce Department. Obama asked Robert Gates, a Bush appointee, to stay on at the Department of Defense. His vice president, Joseph Biden, was yet another rival for the Democratic nomination. As David Axelrod, a senior adviser to Obama, put it: Obama's cabinet members would not be "potted plants." The president-elect "is someone who invites strong opinions," Axelrod explained. "He enjoys that. He thinks that's an important element of leadership."[24]

Despite the speed with which Obama chose his cabinet nominees, Senate confirmation came relatively slowly. Ten days after the inauguration, four of Obama's cabinet nominees were yet to be confirmed. That was the worst record since George H. W. Bush in 1989. In comparison, all of Jimmy Carter's cabinet nominees were confirmed by the end of January 1977, and even George W. Bush, whose transition was delayed by the contested outcome of the 2000 election, had only one unconfirmed cabinet nominee by the end of January 2001. (See Figure 11-1). The delay had several causes: some committees responsible for confirmation hearings were sidetracked by their work on an economic stimulus package; Republicans held up some of the nominations, including Hilda Solis to be labor secretary; and, on January 6, Richardson withdrew his nomination after a federal "pay to play" investigation of activities in New Mexico included him as part of its probe. Richardson vowed that he would be cleared, but the nomination would have been held up for at least six weeks. "Given the gravity of the economic situation the nation is facing, I could not in good conscience ask the president-elect and his administration to delay for one day the important work that needs to be done," Richardson said upon withdrawing.[25]

Despite these delays, the transition was largely hailed as a success. In the midst of a worsening economic crisis, Obama exuded confidence. He held frequent press conferences, gave weekly Saturday radio addresses, and positioned himself as a

FIGURE 11-1   Cabinet Appointments by Recent Administrations

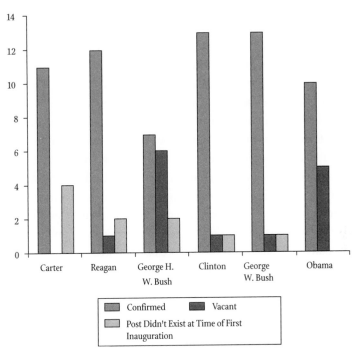

SOURCE: Jonathan Weisman, "Delays in Cabinet Nominations Demonstrate GOP Resolve," *Wall Street Journal*, January 24, 2009, http://online.wsj.com/article/SB123275672929711875.html#articleTabs%3Darticle.

pragmatic centrist. A Gallup poll conducted January 9–11, 2009, showed that he had a remarkable favorability rating of 78 percent (with only 18 percent unfavorable).[26] The transition was also good for Michelle Obama. The more the public got to know her, the more they liked her. During the campaign she had been a somewhat polarizing figure. A Gallup poll conducted May 30–June 1, 2008, showed that she had only a 43 percent favorability rating (30 percent unfavorable), and even as late as September 5–7, her favorability rating stood at 54 percent (30 percent unfavorable). By January 9–11, 2009, her favorability rating had risen to 68 percent (18 percent unfavorable).[27] As the inauguration loomed, excitement rose around the country, and Washington, D.C., braced for record-breaking crowds.

The Inauguration

Almost none of the ceremony associated with modern-day inaugurations is formally required, but it has become an important ritual that helps to unite the nation behind its new leader. The only constitutional requirement for the new president is to take the oath of office. Virtually everything else—taking the oath outdoors in front of a crowd, the use of a Bible during the swearing-in, giving an inaugural address, parades, balls—has emerged by way of tradition. George Washington took his first oath of office on a balcony of Federal Hall in New York in front of a huge crowd, but subsequent oaths were taken indoors until 1817. The chief justice of the New York state judiciary, Robert R. Livingston, administered the oath to Washington (members of the U.S. Supreme Court had not yet been appointed) and Livingston thought that taking the oath on a Bible would add legitimacy to the ceremony. Washington added the words "so help me God" to the end of the oath. Both traditions stuck, as did Washington's decision to give a speech after being sworn in. He moved indoors to the Senate chamber for the speech, and the practice of giving the speech to a joint session of Congress endured until 1817, when James Monroe broke tradition and gave the inaugural address outdoors to the general public.[28]

The ceremony took on special significance in 2009 because it marked the inauguration of the first African American president. The timing was propitious, as 2009 was the two hundredth anniversary of Abraham Lincoln's birth. Lincoln was the first president elected on an antislavery platform. As president, he signed the Emancipation Proclamation, which freed slaves in the Confederate states. In the end, he preserved national unity by winning the Civil War, which led to the Thirteenth Amendment to the Constitution in 1865, abolishing slavery throughout the United States. As we saw in chapter 3, Obama invoked the memory of Lincoln throughout the 2008 election. He announced his candidacy for president in the same place Lincoln had in 1858. He modeled his "team of rivals" on Lincoln's cabinet. He traveled from Philadelphia to Washington by way of the same train route Lincoln had taken to get to his inauguration in 1861. The Saturday before his inauguration, Obama spoke in front of the Lincoln Memorial—the site of two landmark events in the history of civil rights: Marian Anderson's 1939 concert (performed there after the Daughters of the American Revolution refused to give her permission to sing at Constitution Hall) and Martin Luther King's "I Have a Dream" speech in 1963. Obama took the oath of office on the same Bible Lincoln used during his first inaugural. The menu for the postinaugural luncheon was modeled on food prepared for Lincoln's, and it was served on replicas of Lincoln's White House china. Even the inaugural theme, "A New Birth of Freedom," was taken from Lincoln's Gettysburg Address.

In remarks delivered the day after Obama's victory, President Bush had spoken of the history made by the election of the nation's first African American president.

"No matter how they cast their ballots, all Americans can be proud of the history that was made yesterday," Bush said. "Many of our citizens thought they would never live to see that day. This moment is especially uplifting for a generation of Americans who witnessed the struggle for civil rights with their own eyes and four decades later see a dream fulfilled."[29] To see the dream fulfilled, an unprecedented number of people attended the inauguration. Despite frigid temperatures, the District of Columbia estimated that the crowd that filled the National Mall, the two-mile stretch between the Capitol and the Lincoln Memorial, was roughly 1.8 million, the largest gathering ever held on the mall.[30]

The inauguration was also the most expensive in American history, a fitting match to the nation's most expensive election. Obama's inaugural committee raised more than $53 million in private funds, which exceeded its goal of $45 million and topped the previous record of $42.3 million raised by Bush in 2005.[31] But such costs do not include the expense of security, cleanup, and other services provided by the District of Columbia and the federal government. It is hard to measure those costs, but some media reports estimated that the total tab could approach $160 million (the total cost of Bush's 2005 inauguration has been estimated at $157 million).[32] Offsetting the cost was the revenue generated by the influx of tourists to the nation's capital.

The historic nature of Obama's presidency, coupled with the magnitude of the economic crisis facing the country, created high expectations for his inaugural address. Obama was known for his oratory, and it was said that he was studying Lincoln's writings. Less soaring than some had anticipated, the speech acknowledged the nation's challenges and vowed to meet them.

That we are in the midst of a crisis is now well understood. Our nation is at war. . . . Our economy is badly weakened. . . . Homes have been lost; jobs shed; businesses shuttered. Our health care is too costly; our schools fail too many; and each day brings further evidence that the ways we use energy strengthen our adversaries and threaten our planet. . . . Less measurable but no less profound is a sapping of confidence across our land—a nagging fear that America's decline is inevitable, and that the next generation must lower its sights. Today I say to you that the challenges we face are real. They are serious and they are many. They will not be met easily or in a short span of time. But know this, America, they will be met. On this day, we gather because we have chosen hope over fear, unity of purpose over conflict and discord.

The president then called on people to pick themselves up and "begin again the work of remaking America." He also called for action "bold and swift" to stabilize the economy and "lay a foundation for new growth."[33] The scale of his ambitions echoed the New Deal of Franklin Roosevelt and signaled the course for his first hundred days and beyond.

The First Hundred Days

The practice of rating a president on the basis of his first one hundred days in office originated with Franklin Roosevelt. When FDR was sworn in during the midst of the Great Depression on March 4, 1933, some wondered if the nation would survive. The stock market had collapsed, banks had failed, unemployment had reached 25 percent, confidence was shattered, and the fear of public unrest was such that machine guns guarded government buildings.[34] The situation was so grave that Roosevelt spoke in his inaugural address of the possibility of imposing emergency powers that would temporarily suspend the normal legislative process, and the nation applauded.[35]

But FDR embraced optimism, called for action, and rallied the spirit of a down-trodden people. "This great Nation will endure as it has endured, will revive and will prosper," he confidently intoned. "So, first of all, let me assert my firm belief that the only thing we have to fear is fear itself—nameless, unreasoning, unjustified terror which paralyzes needed efforts to convert retreat into advance." He then called Congress into a special emergency session and promised "to recommend the measures that a stricken nation in the midst of a stricken world may require." The special session lasted three months, and people referred to it as the "Hundred Days."

Those hundred days produced an unprecedented amount of important legislation: fifteen major bills that greatly expanded the size of government through the creation of, among other things, the Federal Deposit Insurance Corporation to protect bank accounts, the Public Works Administration to provide jobs, and the National Industrial Recovery Administration to regulate industry and stimulate the economy. Ever since then, incoming presidents have been judged—perhaps unfairly—by the arbitrary benchmark of the first one hundred days.

What is striking about this time period is just how short it is. The snapshot taken at its end is incomplete and can be downright misleading. For example, our impression of what George W. Bush's presidency would focus on at the end of his first hundred days bears little resemblance to the political landscape after 9/11. Nevertheless, from the president's initial interactions with Congress and the people, the tone and the temperament he sets, and his first steps as a leader, much can be gleaned. As with the transition, during the first hundred days, personnel, process, and policy remain paramount, and, at the same time, politics colors everything.

TABLE 11-1   Status of Appointments Requiring Senate Confirmation at the End of the First Hundred Days, G. W. Bush and Obama Administrations

Appointments	G. W. Bush	Obama
Announced	201	222
Received by Senate	87	189
Confirmed by Senate	33	75

SOURCE: The White House Transition Project, http://whitehousetransitionproject.org/#HDay.

Personnel

Even when presidents are lucky enough to have all their cabinet members in place soon after taking the oath of office, hundreds of subcabinet and thousands of executive branch appointments remain to be filled. This is an essential task for a president to complete in order to move from campaigning mode to governing, and it was especially urgent for Obama given the challenges the administration faced. These appointees fill what are called "PAS positions," shorthand for presidential appointments requiring Senate confirmation. By the end of his hundredth day in office, Obama had set a record for selecting and nominating people to fill these positions: 222 names had been sent to the Senate for its advice and consent, but only 75 were confirmed, 8 short of Ronald Reagan's record of 83. Obama also fell 25 short of an unofficial goal of securing 100 confirmations in 100 days. In comparison, George W. Bush finished his first 100 days with only 33 positions confirmed.[36] (See Table 11-1.)

Table 11-2 shows the number of PAS appointments within the cabinet departments made during the first hundred days. It also shows a variance across departments in terms of how quickly nominees were sent to the Senate and then confirmed. Not surprisingly, given the ongoing wars in Afghanistan and Iraq, the State and Defense Departments had the best record of confirmed PAS appointments in 2009, although Homeland Security had a poor record. One department that was particularly slow to have its nominees confirmed was Health and Human Services (HHS).

Obama's first nominee to become HHS secretary was former senator Tom Daschle, who withdrew on February 3 after embarrassing revelations about his failure to pay some $140,000 in back taxes. Daschle, an expert on health policy, was widely viewed as an important player in fulfilling Obama's promise to reform

TABLE 11-2 Comparison of Number of Appointees Confirmed by the Senate in the G. W. Bush and Obama Administrations after the First Hundred Days

Cabinet departments	Posts needing Senate confirmation (N)[a]	Sent to Senate (by Obama)[b]	Confirmed Bush	Confirmed Obama
Agriculture	16	10	1	4
Commerce	23	9	1	3
Defense	53	21	2	11
Education	17	6	1	1
Energy	22	10	1	2
HHS	20	6	1	1
Homeland Security	20	8	1	2
Housing and Urban Dev.	15	7	1	1
Interior	17	8	1	1
Justice	37	12	1	9
Labor	19	7	2	1
State	55	22	9	11
Trans.	23	9	1	6
Treasury	33	8	3	2
Veterans	15	7	2	3
Total	385	150	28	58

a. Number excludes nominations for federal attorneys and marshals in Justice and most ambassadorial posts in State.
b. Number includes holdovers previously confirmed but not those nominated to Senate but then withdrawn.

health care, so his withdrawal was more than just an embarrassment; it imperiled one of the centerpieces of the president's policy agenda. Obama was initially reluctant to lose Daschle, but when he dropped out, Obama refreshingly admitted that he handled the situation poorly. "I think I screwed up," he told CNN's Anderson Cooper.[37] On March 2 the president nominated Kathleen Sebelius to the HHS post, but pro-life advocates in the Senate delayed her confirmation, and no subcabinet posts in the department were being filled either. Sebelius also faced embarrassing tax revelations of her own, admitting "unintentional errors" in her tax returns and paying some $8,000 in back taxes. The lack of leadership in the Health and Human Services Department became a matter of concern as the threat of a swine flu pandemic emerged. It was on Obama's ninety-ninth day in office when the Senate voted 65-31 to approve Sebelius, the last cabinet nominee to win confirmation.

Process

While Obama was filling cabinet and other executive branch positions, some observers noted that he was concentrating power in the White House by establishing a highly centralized decision-making process. That trend had been set during the transition, when Obama announced the creation of new offices in the White House to coordinate energy, climate change, health care, and urban policy initiatives. The *New York Times* noted that the creation of these offices signaled that Obama intended "to keep real power over domestic issues close at hand" and served to "shift the political center of gravity farther away from the cabinet."[38] In so doing, Obama chose powerful figures to serve as policy "czars" outside of the formal cabinet structure (see chapter 6). These included, among others, Carol Browner, whom Obama picked to be his assistant to the president for energy and climate change, and Paul Volcker on the economy. There was further evidence of centralizing power in the White House: the full cabinet met only once during Obama's first one hundred days in office. But in truth, Obama was following in the footsteps of all presidents since Richard Nixon; despite a proclaimed commitment to cabinet government, each of these presidents concentrated decision making in the White House.

Unlike cabinet secretaries, policy czars do not require Senate confirmation. As a result, Obama was able to choose some highly qualified individuals who might have provoked confirmation battles, notably Larry Summers as director of the National Economic Council and John Brennan as homeland security adviser. Had he not been forced to withdraw as the president's nominee for HHS secretary, Daschle would have served as both a cabinet secretary and a policy czar responsible for running the White House health care initiative. Indeed, as Obama's designated health reform czar, Daschle already had a prime first floor office in the West Wing of the White House when he withdrew his nomination.[39] Instead, Obama selected Nancy-Ann DeParle to advise him on health policy.

Some were concerned that Obama was centralizing too much power in the White House. Sen. Robert Byrd, D-W.Va., a long-time critic of the expansion of executive power, wrote a letter to the president that questioned the practice of creating czars to oversee policy. "The rapid and easy accumulation of power by White House staff can threaten the system of checks and balances," Byrd warned. "At the worst, White House staff have taken direction and control of programmatic areas that are the statutory responsibility of Senate-confirmed officials."[40]

Policy czars get lots of attention, but much of the work of communicating and implementing administration policies belongs to those who staff important posts in offices such as Congressional Liaison. Some administrations have filled those posts with inexperienced outsiders—Carter, for example, stands out. But when Obama chose Rahm Emanuel, a Washington insider and former aide to Bill Clinton to be his White House chief of staff, he signaled that he placed a premium on experience.

Given the scope and magnitude of the legislative agenda that Obama hoped to enact, the staffing of his Congressional Liaison Office was especially important. Recent administrations have tended to staff that office with lobbyists, but Obama appointed fourteen veterans of Capitol Hill, led by Phil Schiliro, who had served as a congressional aide for more than twenty-five years.[41] As chief of staff to Rep. Henry Waxman, D-Calif., and a top aide to former Senate majority leader Daschle, he had gained valuable inside knowledge of both the House and the Senate. Schiliro had also worked on important issues such as the environment that Obama wanted to showcase. David Marin, who worked opposite Schiliro as a top Republican aide to Rep. Thomas M. Davis III, R-Va., said: "Putting Phil Schiliro in charge of the White House legislative shop was a master stroke by President Obama," adding that his former adversary was "as knowledgeable on the issues of the day as any member of Congress."[42] This familiarity with policy allowed Schiliro to be more that just a tactician. Intent on maintaining a low profile—even refusing most interview requests—Schiliro helped to secure Obama's early legislative victories.

Policy

When it came to enacting legislation, Obama got to work even before he took the oath of office. He began lobbying for passage of an $800 million economic stimulus package in the final days of the Bush administration and then employed a full-court press on Congress once he took power. The result was passage of a sweeping economic rescue program after just twenty-four days in office. It was, as the *Washington Post* noted, "a legislative victory of the sort that few of his predecessors achieved at any point in their tenure."[43] But the victory was not bipartisan; it came without a single Republican vote of support in the House, and only three Republican votes in the Senate. Democrats did, however, maintain the support of centrist senators in their own party, and they accepted Republican amendments and proposals from senators such as Charles Grassley who, as *Politico* put it, "did not vote for the bill, but will remember the courtesy."[44]

Obama quickly put to rest speculation that he would jettison some parts of his domestic agenda in order to focus exclusively on the economy. Instead, he proceeded on many fronts, establishing a record described by *The Economist* as "a hundred days of hyperactivity."[45] For example, the president set a goal of enacting health care reform by the end of 2009, and he secured the inclusion of $19 billion in the stimulus package to help improve health information technology and to fund research assessing the effectiveness of various medical treatments. He also promised to push forward on legislation dealing with energy and the environment

President Obama signs the historic $787 billion economic stimulus package into law in Denver, Colorado. Vice President Biden looks on.

(including a controversial cap-and-trade bill), immigration reform, and education, important parts of his FY2010 record-setting $3.6 trillion budget proposed to Congress. Unlike the 1980s and 1990s when economic problems had prevented presidents from taking action on pressing domestic problems, Obama sold these major initiatives as part of his package to restore long-term economic health to the nation. Each day seemed to bring a new initiative, leading some observers to fear that the administration might lose its focus on solving the economic crisis. No less a figure than Warren Buffett, probably the most celebrated investor in the United States and an Obama supporter, publicly reminded the president that "job 1 is to win the war, the economic war. Job 2 is to win the economic war—and job 3."[46]

Obama's foreign policy agenda was equally full. He inherited wars in Iraq and Afghanistan, the threat of nuclear proliferation in Iran and North Korea, and tensions between Israel and the Palestinians, just for starters. He confronted an unexpected challenge from pirates off the coast of Somalia who kidnapped an American ship captain in April. Obama authorized a dramatic and successful rescue operation by Navy SEALs that was deemed an "early military victory" for the president.[47]

The president proved to be pragmatic when it came to foreign policy. He was cautious with regard to the pace of U.S. withdrawal from Iraq, sent seventeen thousand additional U.S. troops to Afghanistan, and called for arms reduction talks with Russia. The administration moved away from some of its most impassioned campaign rhetoric about the need to protect American jobs as it sought to strengthen trade relations with Canada, China, Colombia, Mexico, and South Korea.[48] During his first one hundred days in office, the president visited nine foreign nations and had one-on-one sit-down meetings with thirty-four heads of state.[49] As with his domestic policy, however, Obama signaled a clear break from the Bush administration on many fronts. He made this clear in speeches and town hall meetings around the world.

Obama also attempted to bolster America's reputation around the world. It was no accident that he granted his first formal television interview of his presidency to Al-Arabiya, the Arabic language news channel.[50] Later, in a speech in Strasbourg, France, Obama admitted that in the past the United States had "shown arrogance and been dismissive, even derisive" toward its allies, but he added that in Europe "there is an anti-Americanism that is at once casual, but can also be insidious. Instead of recognizing the good that America so often does in the world, there have been times where Europeans choose to blame America for much of what is bad." He said, "America is changing but it cannot be America alone that changes."[51]

Some conservatives complained that Obama was too apologetic for U.S. policy and too critical of the Bush administration in public remarks such as these. Asked about that by CNN's Fareed Zakaria, Defense Secretary Gates defended Obama. "I have not seen it as an apology tour at all, but rather a change of tone—a more humble America," Gates said. He added that the acknowledgement of mistakes was "not only factually accurate" but "unusual because so few other governments in the world are willing to admit that, although they make them all the time. And some of them make catastrophic mistakes."[52]

Obama also promised a return to "the moral high ground" in the war on terrorism, and he signed an executive order requiring the closure of the Guantánamo Bay detention center within one year. More controversially, he declassified and released Bush administration memos that authorized harsh interrogation techniques (considered torture by Bush's critics) such as waterboarding, and pointed to the memos as examples that America had lost its "moral bearings."[53] After first dismissing the idea of prosecuting those who had used or authorized such methods, the president seemed to backtrack, and Republicans, including former vice president Dick Cheney, slammed the president for undermining national security with the release of the memos.

Cheney had already been publicly critical of the president—an unusual position for a former vice president to take, at least so early in a new administration. In a March television interview with John King on CNN, Cheney criticized Obama for using the recession as an excuse to justify "one of the biggest expansions of federal authority over the private economy in the history of the Republic."[54] Asked about whether he thought the decisions to close Guantánamo Bay and to stop the enhanced interrogation techniques made Americans "less safe," Cheney responded, "I do. I think those programs were absolutely essential to the success we enjoyed of being able to collect intelligence that let us defeat all further attempts to launch attacks against the United States since 9/11." Now, he said, Obama "is making choices that, in my mind, will, in fact, raise the risk to the American people of another attack."[55] If Congress and the media got caught up in the controversy about Bush interrogation practices, the administration's ambitious legislative agenda could be derailed. Obama's congressional allies sought to contain both Republican demands for the release of intelligence gleaned through illegal methods as well as Democratic demands for a full, public investigation.

Politics

Despite the criticisms and controversies, Obama remained popular. His Gallup poll job approval rating at the end of the first hundred days stood at 65 percent.[56] Most significantly, Obama inspired confidence. An AP-GfK poll conducted April 16–20, 2009, showed that more Americans—48 percent—thought that things in the United States were "heading in the right direction" than those—44 percent—who thought they were "heading in the wrong direction." The "right direction" score was eight points higher than a month earlier, and a remarkable 31 points higher than October 16–20, 2008, when a similar AP-GfK poll found that only 17 percent thought that the country was heading in the right direction, and 78 percent thought it was heading in the wrong direction.[57]

Obama demonstrated a mastery of communicating with the public in his first hundred days, holding three prime-time news conferences, visiting eleven states, and making innovative uses of the new media (as discussed in chapter 3). Then, on the ninety-ninth day Obama was in office, Republican senator Arlen Specter of Pennsylvania announced that he was switching parties and would become a Democrat. Democrats looked forward to a filibuster-proof majority, assuming Al Franken, the Democrat in the contested Senate election in Minnesota, would be seated. The timing was perfect. Three days later, Supreme Court justice David Souter announced he would retire at the end of the term. Not only would a filibuster-proof majority make it easier to confirm Supreme Court nominees, but also it would facilitate passage of other legislation, such as health care reform, by depriving Republican opponents of their best tactic to block administration action or force policy concessions.

In a press conference marking his hundredth day, Obama noted the unusually wide array of crises and challenges facing his administration. "I would love a nice, lean portfolio to deal with," he said. "But that's not the hand that's been dealt us. . . . We happen to have gotten a big set of challenges, but we're not the first generation that's happened to. And I'm confident that we're going to meet those challenges just like our grandparents and forebears met them before."[58] The dizzying array of challenges also had a benefit of sorts. Stories that in a slower news cycle might have festered and hurt the administration, such as the torture memos, were quickly swept aside. Likewise, the media's focus on the crisis of the day allowed the president to proceed on some policy issues without as much scrutiny as he would have gotten under more normal circumstances.

As President Obama moved into the next hundred days—filling a seat on the Supreme Court, confronting a possible swine flu pandemic, weighing how to respond to failing banks and the faltering auto industry, waging two wars, pushing for health care reform, immigration reform, education reform, and reminding Americans, "yes we can"—it was evident that leadership style is an important element of success, one that had so far served this president well. But it is also important to remember that even the most charismatic president cannot govern single-handedly. That much, at least, the framers intended; that much remains a constant of the otherwise changing and changeable presidency; and that much, we hope, you have learned from this book.

NOTES

1. Stephen Hess, "A Checklist for New Presidents," *eJournal USA*, Vol. 14, No. 1, January 2009, 3, http://www.america.gov/publications/ejournalusa/0109.html.

2. Robert Pear, "Behind the Scenes, Teams for Both Candidates Plan for a Presidential Transition," *New York Times*, September 21, 2008, A22.

3. Lyndsey Layton and Lois Romano, "'Plum Book' Is Obama's Big Help-Wanted Ad," *Washington Post*, November 13, 2008, A1. A copy of the Plum Book can be found at http://www.gpoaccess.gov/plumbook/2008/index.html.

4. A full copy of the questionnaire can be viewed at http://graphics8.nytimes.com/packages/pdf/national/13apply_questionnaire.pdf.

5. Jackie Calmes, "For a Washington Job, Be Prepared to Tell All," *New York Times*, November 13, 2008, A1.

6. Hess, "A Checklist for New Presidents," 5; John P. Burke, *Presidential Transitions: From Politics to Practice* (Boulder: Lynne Rienner, 2000), 12.

7. General Services Administration, "GSA Turns Over Transition HQ to New Administration," News Release # 10556, November 5, 2008.

8. Alec MacGillis, "Obama Lists $1 Million-Plus in Donations for Transition," *Washington Post*, December 2, 2008, A6.

9. Pear, "Behind the Scenes," A22.

10. Burke, *Presidential Transitions*, 283.

11. Ibid., 293, 295, 317, 303–305.

12. Quoted in Craig Gilbert, "Obama Winning Praise for Transition Strategy," *Milwaukee Journal Sentinel*, December 21, 2008, A1.

13. James P. Pfiffner, *The Strategic Presidency: Hitting the Ground Running*, 2nd ed., rev. (Lawrence: University Press of Kansas, 1996), 6.

14. Ibid., 7.

15. Dan Eggen, "Bush Creates Council for Transition," *Washington Post*, October 10, 2008, A2.

16. Pear, "Behind the Scenes," A22.

17. Robert Barnes, Dan Eggen, and Anne E. Kornblut, "Preparing for the Obama Era; Bush Officials and President-Elect Working Together on Pressing Issues," *Washington Post*, November 9, 2008, A1.

18. Quoted in ibid.

19. Anne E. Kornblut and Michael Abramowitz, "Officials Guiding the Process are Named," *Washington Post*, November 13, 2008, A21.

20. Michael D. Shear, "President's 'One President' Gambit; Democrat Defers to Bush on Foreign Policy but Not on Economy," *Washington Post*, December 31, 2008, A2.

21. Peter Baker, "On Eve of History, Obama Follows Low-Key Path," *New York Times*, January 20, 2009, A1.

22. ABC News, "Obama Proposes 'Team of Rivals' Cabinet," May 22, 2008, http://blogs.abcnews.com/politicalpunch/2008/05/obama-proposes.html.

23. Christi Parsons, "Obama Hopes to Appoint a 'Team of Rivals,'" *Chicago Tribune*, November 15, 2008, http://archives.chicagotribune.com/2008/nov/15/nation/chi-team-of-rivalsnov15.

24. ABC News, "Will Obama's Team of Rivals Fare Better than Lincoln's?" November 23, 2008, http://blogs.abcnews.com/politicalpunch/2008/11/will-obamas-tea.html.

25. NBC News, "Richardson Withdrawal Leaves Cabinet Gap," January 6, 2009, http://www.msnbc.msn.com/id/28493919/.

26. All of Obama's favorability ratings can be found at www.pollingreport.com.

27. See http://www.pollingreport.com/o.htm.

28. For more about the early history of presidential inaugurations and the traditions that emerged around them, see: Charles C. Euchner and John Anthony Maltese, *Selecting the President* (Washington, D.C.: CQ Press, 1992), 191–198.

29. Transcript, "Bush Remarks on President-Elect Obama," *Washington Post*, November 5, 2008, http://www.washingtonpost.com/wp-dyn/content/article/2008/11/05/AR2008110502624.html.

30. Michael E. Ruane and Aaron C. Davis, "D.C.'s Inauguration Head Count: 1.8 million," *Washington Post*, January 20, 2009, B1.

31. David D. Kirkpatrick, "Obama's Inaugural Fundraising Topped $53 Million," *New York Times*, April 20, 2009, http://thecaucus.blogs.nytimes.com/2009/04/20/obamas-inaugural-fund-raising-topped-53-million/.

32. Eric Boehlert, "The Media Myth About the Cost of Obama's Inauguration," *Media Matters for America*, January 17, 2009, http://mediamatters.org/columns/200901170003.

33. For the full transcript of Obama's inaugural address can be found at http://abcnews.go.com/Politics/Inauguration/Story?id=6689022&page=1.

34. Kenneth T. Walsh, "The First 100 Days: Franklin Roosevelt Pioneered the 100-Day Concept," *U.S. News & World Report*, February 12, 2009, http://www.usnews.com/articles/news/history/2009/02/12/the-first-100-days-franklin-roosevelt-pioneered-the-100-day-concept.html.

35. "It is to be hoped that the normal balance of executive and legislative authority may be wholly adequate to meet the unprecedented task before us. But it may be that an unprecedented demand and need for undelayed action may call for temporary departure from that normal balance of public procedure." For the full text of Roosevelt's first inaugural address, see http://www.bartleby.com/124/pres49.html.

36. "Appointment Summary for Day 100," http://whitehousetransitionproject.org/#HDay.

37. "Daschle Withdraws as HHS Nominee," *CNN Politics.com* February 3, 2009, http://www.cnn.com/2009/POLITICS/02/03/daschle/.

38. Peter Baker, "Obama Reshapes White House for Domestic Focus," *New York Times*, December 20, 2008, A13.

39. CBS News, "West Wing on Steroids in Obama White House: President Surrounding Himself with Powerful Staff of Counselors, Envoys, and Policy 'Czars,'" January 25, 2009, http://www.cbsnews.com/stories/2009/01/25/politics/politico/main4751737.shtml.

40. Noelle Straub, "Sen. Byrd Questions Obama's Use of Policy 'Czars,'" *New York Times*, February 25, 2009, http://www.nytimes.com/gwire/2009/02/25/25greenwire-byrd-questions-obamas-use-of-policy-czars-9865.html.

41. Anna Palmer, "Legislative Affairs Team Gets to Work; Full Plate Awaits Hill Vets Staffing Office," *Roll Call*, January 21, 2009.

42. Quoted in: Jonathan Martin, "Big W. H. Role for Low-Profile Schiliro," *Politico*, February 22, 2009, http://www.politico.com/news/stories/0209/19139.html.

43. Michael D. Shear and Alec MacGillis, "Obama Scores Early Victory of Historic Proportions," *Washington Post*, February 14, 2009, A9.

44. John Aloysius Farrell, "7 Reasons Why Obama Bipartisanship Lives," *U.S. News & World Report*, February 17, 2009, http://www.usnews.com/blogs/john-farrell/2009/2/17/7-reasons-why-obama-bipartisanship-lives.html.

45. "A Hundred Days of Hyperactivity," *The Economist*, May 2, 2009, 27–28.

46. Warren Buffett as quoted in David Von Drehle and Michael Schirer, "Obama's Reform Agenda: Is He Trying To Do Too Much?" *Time* magazine, March 13, 2009, http://www.time.com/time/politics/article/0,8599,1884630,00.html.

47. Michael D. Shear, "An Early Military Victory for Obama," *Washington Post*, April 13, 2009, A9.

48. "Low Expectations Exceeded," *The Economist*, May 2, 2009, 28–29.

49. Mark Knoller, "Obama's First Hundred Days: By the Numbers," *CBS News*, April 29, 2009, http://www.cbsnews.com/blogs/2009/04/29/politics/politicalhotsheet/entry4977321.shtml.

50. Michael D. Shear and Glenn Kessler, "Obama Voices Hope for Mideast Peace in Talk with Al-Arabiya TV," *Washington Post*, January 27, 2009, A3.

51. Toby Harndon, "Barack Obama: 'arrogant US has been dismissive' to Allies," *Telegraph*, April 3, 2009, http://www.telegraph.co.uk/news/worldnews/northamerica/usa/barackobama/5100338/Barack-Obama-arrogant-US-has-been-dismissive-to-allies.html.

52. Josh Gerstein, "Gates: No 'apology tour,'" *Politico*, May 3, 2009, http://www.politico.com/politico44/perm/0409/gates_no_apology_tour_87d5dcd1-3187-4a91-831c-4d5b2cf2262f.html.

53. Ben Feller, "U.S. lost 'moral bearings': Obama," *Toronto Sun*, April 22, 2009, http://www.torontosun.com/news/world/2009/04/22/9198071-sun.html.

54. Mike Allen, "Cheney: Obama Wants 'massive expansion,'" *Politico*, March 16, 2009, http://www.politico.com/news/stories/0309/20013.html.

55. Douglass K. Daniel, "Cheney: Obama Detainee Policies Make America Less Safe," *USA Today,* March 15,2009, http://www.usatoday.com/news/nation/states/wyoming/2009-03-15-1905366589_x.htm.

56. See www.pollingreport.com.

57. Ron Fournier and Trevor Tompson, "AP Poll: After Obama's 100 days, US on Right Track," *Associated Press,* April 23, 2009. See www.pollingreport.com for the complete results of the poll and earlier results of similar polls.

58. "Transcript of Obama's 100th Day Press Conference," *Wall Street Journal,* April 30, 2009, http://blogs.wsj.com/washwire/2009/04/30/transcript-of-obamas-100th-day-press-conference/.

RESULT OF PRESIDENTIAL CONTESTS, 1912–2008

Year	Republican nominee (in italics) and other major candidates	Democratic nominee (in italics) and other major candidates	Election winner	Division of popular vote[a] (percent)	Division of electoral vote[b]
1912	*William Howard Taft* (incumbent president)	*Woodrow Wilson* (governor of New Jersey)	Wilson (D)	42-23	435-8
	Theodore Roosevelt[c] (former president)	James Champ Clark (representative from Missouri and Speaker of the House)			
1916	*Charles Evans Hughes* (justice, U.S. Supreme Court)	*Woodrow Wilson* (incumbent president)	Wilson (D)	49-46	277-254
	Elihu Root (former secretary of state)	None			
1920	*Warren G. Harding* (senator from Ohio)	*James Cox* (governor of Ohio)	Harding (R)	60-34	404-127
	Leonard Wood (general)	William McAdoo (former secretary of the Treasury)			
	Frank Lowden (governor of Illinois)	A. Mitchell Palmer (attorney general)			
	Hiram Johnson (senator from California)				
1924	*Calvin Coolidge* (incumbent president)	*John W. Davis* (former solicitor general)	Coolidge (R)	54-29	382-136
	Hiram Johnson (senator from California)	Alfred Smith (governor of New York)			
		William McAdoo (former secretary of the Treasury)			
1928	*Herbert Hoover* (former secretary of commerce)	*Alfred Smith* (governor of New York)	Hoover (R)	58-41	444-87
	Frank Lowden (governor of Illinois)	James Reed (senator from Missouri)			
		Cordell Hull (representative from Tennessee)			
1932	*Herbert Hoover* (incumbent president)	*Franklin D. Roosevelt* (governor of New York)	Roosevelt (D)	57-40	472-59
	Joseph France (former senator from Maryland)	Alfred Smith (former governor of New York)			
		John Garner (representative from Texas and Speaker of the House)			

Results of Presidential Contests, 1912–2008 *(Continued)*

Year	Republican nominee (in italics) and other major candidates	Democratic nominee (in italics) and other major candidates	Election winner	Division of popular vote[a] (percent)	Division of electoral vote[b]
1936	*Alfred Landon* (governor of Kansas)	*Franklin D. Roosevelt* (incumbent president)	Roosevelt (D)	61-37	523-8
	William Borah (senator from Idaho)	None			
1940	*Wendell Willkie* (Indiana lawyer and public utility executive)	*Franklin D. Roosevelt* (incumbent president)	Roosevelt (D)	55-45	449-82
	Thomas E. Dewey (U.S. district attorney for New York)	None			
	Robert Taft (senator from Ohio)				
1944	*Thomas E. Dewey* (governor of New York)	*Franklin D. Roosevelt* (incumbent president)	Roosevelt (D)	53-46	432-99
	Wendell Willkie (previous Republican presidential nominee)	Harry Byrd (senator from Virginia)			
1948	*Thomas E. Dewey* (governor of New York)	*Harry S. Truman* (incumbent president)	Truman (D)	50-45	303-189
	Harold Stassen (former governor of Minnesota)	Richard Russell (senator from Georgia)			
	Robert Taft (senator from Ohio)				
1952	*Dwight D. Eisenhower* (general)	*Adlai Stevenson* (governor of Illinois)	Eisenhower (R)	55-44	442-89
	Robert Taft (senator from Ohio)	Estes Kefauver (senator from Tennessee)			
		Richard Russell (senator from Georgia)			
1956	*Dwight D. Eisenhower* (incumbent president)	*Adlai Stevenson* (previous Democratic presidential nominee)	Eisenhower (R)	57-42	457-73
	None	Averell Harriman (governor of New York)			
1960	*Richard Nixon* (vice president)	*John F. Kennedy* (senator from Massachusetts)	Kennedy (D)	49.7-49.5	303-219
	None	Hubert Humphrey (senator from Minnesota) Lyndon B. Johnson (senator from Texas)			
1964	*Barry Goldwater* (senator from Arizona)	*Lyndon B. Johnson* (incumbent president)	Johnson (D)	61-39	586-52
	Nelson Rockefeller (governor of New York)	None			

Results of Presidential Contests, 1912–2008 *(Continued)*

Year	Republican nominee (in italics) and other major candidates	Democratic nominee (in italics) and other major candidates	Election winner	Division of popular vote[a] (percent)	Division of electoral vote[b]
1968	*Richard Nixon* (former Republican presidential nominee)	*Hubert Humphrey* (incumbent vice president)	Nixon (R)	43.4-42.7	301-191
	Ronald Reagan (governor of California)	Robert F. Kennedy (senator from New York)			
		Eugene McCarthy (senator from Minnesota)			
1972	*Richard Nixon* (incumbent president)	*George McGovern* (senator from South Dakota)	Nixon (R)	61-38	520-17
	None	Hubert Humphrey (senator from Minnesota)			
		George Wallace (governor of Alabama)			
1976	*Gerald R. Ford* (incumbent president)	*Jimmy Carter* (former governor of Georgia)	Carter (D)	50-48	297-240
	Ronald Reagan (former governor of California)	Edmund Brown Jr. (governor of California)			
		George Wallace (governor of Alabama)			
1980	*Ronald Reagan* (former governor of California)	*Jimmy Carter* (incumbent president)	Reagan (R)	51-41	489-49
	George Bush (former director of Central Intelligence Agency)	Edward M. Kennedy (senator from Massachusetts)			
	John Anderson (representative from Illinois)				
1984	*Ronald Reagan* (incumbent president)	*Walter F. Mondale* (former vice president)	Reagan (R)	59-41	525-13
	None	Gary Hart (senator from Colorado)			
1988	*George H. W. Bush* (vice president)	*Michael Dukakis* (governor of Massachusetts)	Bush (R)	53-46	426-111[d]
	Robert Dole (senator from Kansas)	Jesse Jackson (civil rights activist)			
1992	*George H. W. Bush* (incumbent president)	*Bill Clinton* (governor of Arkansas)	Clinton (D)	43-37	370-168
	Patrick Buchanan (journalist)	Paul Tsongas (former senator)			
1996	*Robert Dole* (senator from Kansas)	*Bill Clinton* (incumbent president)	Clinton (D)	49-41	379-159
	Patrick Buchanan (journalist)	None			

Results of Presidential Contests, 1912–2008 *(Continued)*

Year	Republican nominee (in italics) and other major candidates	Democratic nominee (in italics) and other major candidates	Election winner	Division of popular vote[a] (percent)	Division of electoral vote[b]
2000	*George W. Bush* (governor of Texas) John McCain (senator from Arizona)	*Al Gore* (incumbent vice president) Bill Bradley (former senator)	Bush (R)	47.9-48.4	271-266[e]
2004	*George W. Bush* (incumbent president) None	*John Kerry* (senator from Massachusetts) John Edwards (senator from North Carolina)	Bush (R)	50.7-48.3	286-251[f]
2008	*John McCain* (senator from Arizona) Mitt Romney (former governor from Massachusetts)	*Barack Obama* (senator from Illinois) Hillary Clinton (senator from New York)	Obama (D)	52.9-45.6	365-173

Note: The table begins with the year 1912 because presidential primaries were first held that year.

a. Division of popular vote is between the Republican and Democratic nominees.

b. Division of electoral vote is between the Republican and Democratic nominees.

c. When the Republican convention failed to choose him as its nominee (selecting instead the incumbent president, William Howard Taft), former president Theodore Roosevelt withdrew from the party and created the Progressive Party. As the Progressive Party nominee, Roosevelt received 27 percent of the popular vote and 88 electoral votes.

d. One Democratic elector from West Virginia reversed the vote for president and vice president.

e. One Democratic elector from the District of Columbia cast a blank ballot in protest.

f. One Democratic elector from Minnesota cast ballots listing John Edwards for both president and vice president, presumably in error.

PERSONAL BACKGROUNDS OF U.S. PRESIDENTS

President	Age at first political office	First political office / Last political office[a]	Age at becoming president	State of residence[b]	Father's occupation	Higher education[c]	Occupation
1. Washington (1789–1797)	17	County surveyor / Commander in chief	57	Va.	Farmer	None	Farmer, surveyor
2. Adams, J. (1797–1801)	39	Surveyor of highways / Vice president	61	Mass.	Farmer	Harvard	Farmer, lawyer
3. Jefferson (1801–1809)	26	State legislator / Vice president	58	Va.	Farmer	William and Mary	Farmer, lawyer
4. Madison (1809–1817)	25	State legislator / Secretary of state	58	Va.	Farmer	Princeton	Farmer
5. Monroe (1817–1825)	24	State legislator / Secretary of state	59	Va.	Farmer	William and Mary	Lawyer, farmer
6. Adams, J. Q. (1825–1829)	27	Minister to Netherlands / Secretary of state	58	Mass.	Farmer, lawyer	Harvard	Lawyer
7. Jackson (1829–1837)	21	Prosecuting attorney / U.S. Senate	62	Tenn.	Farmer	None	Lawyer
8. Van Buren (1837–1841)	30	Surrogate of county / Vice president	55	N.Y.	Tavern keeper	None	Lawyer
9. Harrison, W. H. (1841)	26	Territorial delegate to Congress / Minister to Colombia	68	Ind.	Farmer	Hampden-Sydney	Military
10. Tyler (1841–1845)	21	State legislator / Vice president	51	Va.	Planter, lawyer	William and Mary	Lawyer
11. Polk (1845–1849)	28	State legislator / Governor	50	Tenn.	Surveyor	U. of North Carolina	Lawyer
12. Taylor (1849–1850)	–	None [a]	65	Ky.	Collector of internal revenue	None	Military
13. Fillmore (1850–1853)	28	Stale legislator / Vice president	50	N.Y.	Farmer	None	Lawyer
14. Pierce (1853–1857)	25	State legislator / U.S. district attorney	48	N.H.	General	Bowdoin	Lawyer
15. Buchanan (1857–1861)	22	Assistant county prosecutor / Minister to Great Britain	65	Pa.	Farmer	Dickinson	Lawyer
16. Lincoln (1861–1865)	25	State legislator / U.S. House of Representatives	52	Ill.	Farmer, carpenter	None	Lawyer
17. Johnson, A. (1865–1869)	20	City alderman / Vice president	57	Tenn.	Janitor, porter	None	Tailor
18. Grant (1869–1877)	–	None [a]	47	Ohio	Tanner	West Point	Military
19. Hayes (1877–1881)	36	City solicitor / Governor	55	Ohio	Farmer	Kenyon	Lawyer
20. Garfield (1881)	28	State legislator / U.S. Senate	50	Ohio	Canal worker	Williams	Educator, lawyer

Personal Backgrounds of U.S. Presidents *(Continued)*

President	Age at first political office	First political office / Last political office[a]	Age at becoming president	State of residence[b]	Father's occupation	Higher education[c]	Occupation
21. Arthur (1881–1885)	31	State engineer / Vice president	51	N.Y.	Minister	Union	Lawyer
22. Cleveland (1885–1889)	26	Assistant district attorney / Governor	48	N.Y.	Minister	None	Lawyer
24. (1893–1897)							
23. Harrison, B. (1889–1893)	24	City attorney / U.S. Senate	56	Ind.	Military	Miami of Ohio	Lawyer
25. McKinley (1897–1901)	26	Prosecuting attorney / Governor	54	Ohio	Ironmonger	Allegheny	Lawyer
26. Roosevelt, T. (1901–1909)	24	State legislator / Vice president	43	N.Y.	Businessman	Harvard	Lawyer, author
27. Taft (1909–1913)	24	Assistant prosecuting attorney / Secretary of war	52	Ohio	Lawyer	Yale	Lawyer
28. Wilson (1913–1921)	54	Governor / Governor	56	N.J.	Minister	Princeton	Educator
29. Harding (1921–1923)	35	State legislator / U.S. Senate	56	Ohio	Physician, editor	Ohio Central	Newspaper editor
30. Coolidge (1923–1929)	26	City councilman / Vice president	51	Mass.	Storekeeper	Amherst	Lawyer
31. Hoover (1929–1933)	43	Relief and food administrator / Secretary of commerce	55	Calif.	Blacksmith	Stanford	Mining engineer
32. Roosevelt, F. (1933–1945)	28	State legislator / Governor	49	N.Y.	Businessman, landowner	Harvard	Lawyer
33. Truman (1945–1953)	38	County judge (commissioner) / Vice president	61	Mo.	Farmer, livestock	None	Clerk, store owner
34. Eisenhower (1953–1961)	–	None [a]	63	Kan.	Mechanic	West Point	Military
35. Kennedy (1961–1963)	29	U.S. House of Representatives / U.S. Senate	43	Mass.	Businessman	Harvard	Newspaper reporter
36. Johnson, L. (1963–1969)	28	U.S. House of Representatives / Vice president	55	Texas	Farmer, real estate	Southwest Texas State Teacher's College	Educator
37. Nixon (1969–1974)	34	U.S. House of Representatives / Vice president	56	Calif.	Streetcar conductor	Whittier	Lawyer
38. Ford (1974–1977)	36	U.S. House of Representatives / Vice president	61	Mich.	Businessman	U. of Michigan	Lawyer
39. Carter (1977–1981)	38	County Board of Education / Governor	52	Ga.	Farmer, businessman	U.S. Naval Academy	Farmer, businessman

Personal Backgrounds of U.S. Presidents *(Continued)*

President	*Age at first political office*	*First political office* / *Last political office*[a]	*Age at becoming president*	*State of residence*[b]	*Father's occupation*	*Higher education*[c]	*Occupation*
40. Reagan (1981–1989)	55	Governor / Governor	69	Calif.	Shoe salesman	Eureka	Entertainer
41. Bush, G. H. W. (1989–1993)	42	U.S. House of Representatives / Vice president	64	Texas	Businessman, U.S. senator	Yale	Businessman
42. Clinton (1993–2001)	30	State attorney general / Governor	46	Ark.	Car dealer	Georgetown	Lawyer
43. Bush, G. W. (2001–2009)	48	Governor / Governor	54	Texas	U.S. President	Yale	Businessman
44. Obama (2009–)	36	State legislator / U.S. senator	47	Illinois	Economist	Columbia	Lawyer

a. This category refers to the last civilian office held before the presidency. Taylor, Grant, and Eisenhower had served as generals before becoming president.
b. The state is where the president spent his important adult years, not necessarily where he was born.
c. Refers to undergraduate education.

THE CONSTITUTION
ON THE PRESIDENCY

ARTICLE I

Section 3. ... The Vice President of the United States shall be President of the Senate, but shall have no Vote, unless they be equally divided.

The Senate shall chuse their other officers, and also a President pro tempore, in the Absence of the Vice President, or when he shall exercise the Office of President of the United States.

The Senate shall have the sole Power to try all Impeachments. When sitting for that Purpose, they shall be on Oath or Affirmation. When the President of the United States is tried the Chief Justice shall preside: And no Person shall be convicted without the Concurrence of two thirds of the Members present.

Judgment in Cases of Impeachment shall not extend further than to removal from Office, and disqualification to hold and enjoy any Office of honor, Trust or Profit under the United States: but the Party convicted shall nevertheless be liable and subject to Indictment, Trial, Judgment and Punishment, according to Law.

Section 7. ... Every Bill which shall have passed the House of Representatives and the Senate, shall, before it become a Law, be presented to the President of the United States; If he approve he shall sign it, but if not he shall return it, with his Objections to that House in which it shall have originated, who shall enter the Objections at large on their Journal, and proceed to reconsider it. If after such Reconsideration two thirds of that House shall agree to pass the Bill, it shall be sent, together with the Objections, to the other House, by which it shall likewise be reconsidered, and if approved by two thirds of that House, it shall become a Law. But in all such Cases the Votes of both Houses shall be determined by yeas and Nays, and the Names of the Persons voting for and against the Bill shall be entered on the Journal of each House respectively. If any Bill shall not be returned by the President within ten Days (Sundays excepted) after it shall have been presented to him, the Same shall be a Law, in like Manner as if he had signed it, unless the Congress by their Adjournment prevent its Return, in which Case it shall not be a Law.

Every Order, Resolution, or Vote to which the Concurrence of the Senate and House of Representatives may be necessary (except on a question of Adjournment) shall be presented to the President of the United States; and before the Same shall take Effect, shall be approved by him, or being disapproved by him, shall be repassed by two thirds of the Senate and House of Representatives, according to the Rules and Limitations prescribed in the Case of a Bill.

ARTICLE II

Section 1. The executive Power shall be vested in a President of the United States of America. He shall hold his Office during the Term of four Years, and, together with the Vice President, chosen for the same Term, be elected, as follows. Each State shall appoint, in such Manner as the Legislature thereof may direct, a Number of Electors, equal to the whole Number of Senators and Representatives to which the State may be entitled in the Congress: but no Senator or Representative, or Person holding an Office of Trust or Profit under the United States, shall be appointed an Elector.

[The Electors shall meet in their respective States, and vote by Ballot for two Persons, of whom one at least shall not be an Inhabitant of the same State with themselves. And they shall make a List of all the Persons voted for, and of the Number of Votes for each; which List they shall sign and certify, and transmit sealed to the Seat of the Government of the United States, directed to the President of the Senate. The President of the Senate shall, in the Presence of the Senate and House of Representatives, open all the Certificates, and the Votes shall then be counted. The Person having the greatest Number of Votes shall be the President, if such Number be a Majority of the whole Number of Electors appointed; and if there be more than one who have such Majority, and have an equal Number of Votes, then the House of Representatives shall immediately chuse by Ballot one of them for President; and if no Person have a Majority, then from the five highest on the list the said House shall in like Manner chuse the President. But in chusing the President, the Votes shall be taken by States, the Representation from each State having one Vote; a quorum for this Purpose shall consist of a Member or Members from two thirds of the States, and a Majority of all the States shall be necessary to a Choice. In every Case, after the Choice of the President, the Person having the greatest Number of Votes of the Electors shall be the Vice President. But if there should remain two or more who have equal Votes, the Senate shall chuse from them by Ballot the Vice President.] [1]

The Congress may determine the Time of chusing the Electors, and the Day on which they shall give their Votes; which Day shall be the same throughout the United States.

No Person except a natural born Citizen, or a Citizen of the United States, at the time of the Adoption of this Constitution, shall be eligible to the Office of President; neither shall any Person be eligible to that Office who shall not have attained to the Age of thirty five Years, and been fourteen Years a Resident within the United States.

In Case of the Removal of the President from office, or of his Death, Resignation, or Inability to discharge the Powers and Duties of the said Office,[2] the Same shall devolve on the Vice President, and the Congress may by Law provide for the Case of Removal, Death, Resignation or Inability, both of the President and Vice President, declaring what officer shall then act as President, and such Officer shall act accordingly, until the Disability be removed, or a President shall be elected.

The President shall, at stated Times, receive for his Services, a Compensation, which shall neither be increased nor diminished during the Period for which he shall have been elected, and he shall not receive within that Period any other Emolument from the United States, or any of them.

Before he enter on the Execution of his Office, he shall take the following Oath or Affirmation: — "I do solemnly swear (or affirm) that I will faithfully execute the Office of President of the United States, and will to the best of my Ability, preserve, protect and defend the Constitution of the United States."

Section 2. The President shall be Commander in Chief of the Army and Navy of the United States, and of the Militia of the several States, when called into the actual Service of the United States; he may require the Opinion, in writing, of the principal Officer in each of the executive Departments, upon any Subject relating to the Duties of their respective Offices, and he shall have Power to grant Reprieves and Pardons for Offenses against the United States, except in Cases of Impeachment.

He shall have Power, by and with the Advice and Consent of the Senate, to make Treaties, provided two thirds of the Senators present concur; and he shall nominate, and by and with the Advice and Consent of the Senate, shall appoint Ambassadors, other public Ministers and Consuls, Judges of the supreme Court, and all other officers of the United States, whose Appointments are not herein otherwise provided for, and which shall be established by Law: but the Congress may by Law vest the Appointment of such inferior Officers, as they think proper, in the President alone, in the Courts of Law, or in the Heads of Departments.

The President shall have Power to fill up all Vacancies that may happen during the Recess of the Senate, by granting Commissions which shall expire at the End of their next Session.

Section 3. He shall from time to time give to the Congress Information of the State of the Union, and recommend to their Consideration such Measures as he shall judge necessary and expedient; he may, on extraordinary Occasions, convene both Houses, or either of them, and in Case of Disagreement between them, with Respect to the Time of Adjournment, he may adjourn them to such Time as he shall think proper; he shall receive Ambassadors and other public Ministers; he shall take Care that the Laws be faithfully executed, and shall Commission all the officers of the United States.

Section 4. The President, Vice President and all Civil Officers of the United States, shall be removed from office on Impeachment for, and Conviction of, Treason, Bribery, or other high Crimes and Misdemeanors.

ARTICLE VI

... This Constitution, and the Laws of the United States which shall be made in Pursuance thereof, and all Treaties made, or which shall be made, under the Authority of the United States, shall be the supreme Law of the Land; and the Judges in every State shall be bound thereby, any Thing in the Constitution or Laws of any State to the Contrary notwithstanding.

The Senators and Representatives before mentioned, and the Members of the several State Legislatures, and all executive and judicial Officers, both of the United States and of the several States, shall be bound by Oath or Affirmation, to support this Constitution; but no religious Test shall ever be required as a Qualification to any Office or public Trust under the United States.

AMENDMENT XII *(Ratified June 15, 1804)*

The Electors shall meet in their respective states and vote by ballot for President and Vice-President, one of whom, at least, shall not be an inhabitant of the same state with themselves; they shall name in their ballots the person voted for as President, and in distinct ballots the person voted for as Vice-President, and they shall make distinct lists of all persons voted for as President, and of all persons voted for as Vice-President, and of the number of votes for each, which lists they shall sign and certify, and transmit sealed to the seat of the government of the United States, directed to the President of the Senate; — The President of the Senate shall, in the presence of the Senate and House of Representatives, open all the certificates and the votes shall then be counted; — The person having the greatest number of votes for President, shall be the President, if such number be a majority of the whole number of Electors appointed; and if no person have such majority, then from the persons having the highest numbers not exceeding three on the list of those voted for as President, the House of Representatives shall choose immediately, by ballot, the President. But in choosing the President, the votes shall be taken by states, the representation from each state having one vote; a quorum for this purpose shall consist of a member or members from two-thirds of the states, and a majority of all the states shall be necessary to a choice. [And if the House of Representatives shall not choose a President whenever the right of choice shall devolve upon them, before the fourth day of March next following, then the Vice-President shall act as President, as in the case of the death or other constitutional disability of the President—][3] The person having the greatest number of votes as Vice-President, shall be the Vice-President, if such number be a majority of the whole number of Electors appointed, and if no person have a majority, then from the two highest numbers on the list, the Senate shall choose the Vice-President; a quorum for the purpose shall consist of two-thirds of the whole number of Senators, and a majority of the whole number shall be necessary to a choice. But no person constitutionally ineligible to the office of President shall be eligible to that of Vice-President of the United States.

AMENDMENT XX *(Ratified Jan. 23, 1933)*

Section 1. The terms of the President and Vice President shall end at noon on the 20th day of January, and the terms of Senators and Representatives at noon on the 3d day of January, of the years in which such terms would have ended if this article had not been ratified; and the terms of their successors shall then begin.

Section 2. The Congress shall assemble at least once in every year, and such meeting shall begin at noon on the 3d day of January, unless they shall by law appoint a different day.

Section 3.[4] If, at the time fixed for the beginning of the term of the President, the President elect shall have died, the Vice President elect shall become President.

If a President shall not have been chosen before the time fixed for the beginning of his term, or if the President elect shall have failed to qualify, then the Vice President elect shall act as President until a President shall have qualified; and the Congress may by law provide for the case wherein neither a President elect nor a Vice President elect shall have qualified, declaring who shall then act as President, or the manner in which one who is to act shall be selected, and such person shall act accordingly until a President or Vice President shall have qualified.

Section 4. The Congress may by law provide for the case of the death of any of the persons from whom the House of Representatives may choose a President whenever the right of choice shall have devolved upon them, and for the case of the death of any of the persons from whom the Senate may choose a Vice President whenever the right of choice shall have devolved upon them.

Section 5. Sections 1 and 2 shall take effect on the 15th day of October following the ratification of this article.

Section 6. This article shall be inoperative unless it shall have been ratified as an amendment to the Constitution by the legislatures of three-fourths of the several States within seven years from the date of its submission.

AMENDMENT XXII *(Ratified Feb. 27, 1951)*

Section 1. No person shall be elected to the office of the President more than twice, and no person who has held the office of President, or acted as President, for more than two years of a term to which some other person was elected President shall be elected to the office of the President more than once. But this Article shall not apply to any person holding the office of President when this Article was proposed by the Congress, and shall not prevent any person who may be holding the office of President, or acting as President, during the term within which this Article become operative from holdingthe office of President or acting as President during the remainder of such term.

Section 2. This Article shall be inoperative unless it shall have been ratified as an amendment to the Constitution by the legislatures of three-fourths of the several States within seven years from the date of its submission to the States by the Congress.

AMENDMENT XXIII *(Ratified March 29, 1961)*

Section 1. The District constituting the seat of Government of the United States shall appoint in such manner as the Congress may direct:

A number of electors of President and Vice President equal to the whole number of Senators and Representatives in Congress to which the District would be entitled if it were a State, but in no event more than the least populous State; they shall be in addition to those appointed by the States, but they shall be considered, for the purposes of the election of President and Vice President, to be electors appointed by a State; and they shall meet in the District and perform such duties as provided by the twelfth article of amendment.

Section 2. The Congress shall have power to enforce this article by appropriate legislation.

AMENDMENT XXV *(Ratified Feb. 10, 1967)*

Section 1. In case of the removal of the President from office or of his death or resignation, the Vice President shall become President.

Section 2. Whenever there is a vacancy in the office of the Vice President, the President shall nominate a Vice President who shall take office upon confirmation by a majority vote of both Houses of Congress.

Section 3. Whenever the President transmits to the President pro tempore of the Senate and the Speaker of the House of Representatives his written declaration that he is unable to discharge the powers and duties of his office, and until he transmits to them a written declaration to the contrary, such powers and duties shall be discharged by the Vice President as Acting President.

Section 4. Whenever the Vice President and a majority of either the principal officers of the executive departments or of such other body as Congress may by law provide, transmit to the President pro tempore of the Senate and the Speaker of the House of Representatives their written declaration that the President is unable to discharge the powers and duties of his office, the Vice President shall immediately assume the powers and duties of the office as Acting President.

Thereafter, when the President transmits to the President pro tempore of the Senate and the Speaker of the House of Representatives his written declaration that no inability exists, he shall resume the powers and duties of his office unless the Vice President and a majority of either the principal officers of the executive department or of such other body as Congress may by law provide, transmit within four days to the President pro tempore of the Senate and the Speaker of the House of Representatives their written declaration that the President is unable to discharge the powers and duties of his office. Thereupon Congress shall decide the issue, assembling within forty-eight hours for that purpose if not in session. If the Congress, within twenty-one days after receipt of the latter written declaration, or, if Congress is not in session, within twenty-one days after Congress is required to assemble, determines by two-thirds vote of both houses that the President is unable to discharge the powers and duties of his office, the Vice President shall continue to discharge the same as Acting President; otherwise, the President shall resume the powers and duties of his office.

NOTES

1. The material in brackets has been superseded by the Twelfth Amendment.
2. This provision has been affected by the Twenty-fifth Amendment.
3. The part in brackets has been superseded by Section 3 of the Twentieth Amendment.
4. See the Twenty-fifth Amendment.

Index

References in italics indicate illustrations and photographs.

AARP, 338
ABA. *See* American Bar Association
ABC News Survey, 90*n*84
Aberbach, Joel D., 240*n*33, 291*n*36, 294*n*97, 296*n*145
ABM (Anti-Ballistic Missile Treaty), 436
Abortion, 293*n*81, 318, 323
Abraham, Henry J., 192*n*14
Abramoff, Jack, 117
Abramowitz, Alan I., 139*n*111
Abramowitz, Michael, 330*n*35, 366*n*52, 479*n*19
Abramson, Alan J., 297*n*154, 413*n*15
Abramson, Paul R., 75, 79, 89*n*72, 90*nn*89–90, 90*n*92, 90*n*96, 90*n*101, 240*n*37, 240*n*39, 243*n*98
Active-negative presidents, 162, 163, 164
Active-positive presidents, 161–162, 164
Adams, John, 37, 152, 154, 321
Adams, John Quincy, 39, 80, 152, 154
Adams, Rebecca, 365*n*33
AFDC (Aid to Families with Dependent Children), 392
Afghanistan
    macroeconomic policymaking and, 387
    military operations in, 424, 428, 438
    national security and, 419
    Pakistan and, 425
AFL-CIO, 390
Age group voting patterns, 69–71
Agencies, 260–261
Agenda setting
    political capital and, 101–102
    as presidential power, 217–218
Agnew, Spiro, 112
Agricultural Adjustment Act of 1933, 206
Agricultural interest groups, 391
Agricultural policy, 335

Ahmadinejad, Mahmoud, *430*
Aid to Families with Dependent Children (AFDC), 392
Ainsworth, Scott H., 331*n*52, 366*n*35
Air traffic controllers, 272
Akerson, George, 123
Albright, Madeleine K., 437
Aldrich, John H., 75, 79, 85*n*14, 89*n*72, 90*nn*89–90, 90*n*92, 90*n*96, 90*n*101, 240*n*37, 240*n*39, 243*n*98
Alexander, Brad, 139*n*111
Alexander, Herbert E., 88*n*57
Alito, Samuel A., 311, 312, 318
Allbaugh, Joseph, 198*n*139
Allen, Claude A., 360
Allen, Mike, 240*n*31, 242*n*73, 413*n*21, 457*n*57, 480*n*54
Aller, Frank, 196*n*110
Allison, Graham T., 458*n*78
Al Qaeda, 16, 419, 428
Altschuler, Bruce E., 85*n*11
Alvarez, Lizette, 292*n*66
Amalgamated Meat Cutters v. Connally (1971), 294*n*94
Ambassadors
    nominations, 11, 18–19
    receiving, 18–19
Ambrose, Stephen E., 460*n*108
American Association of Retired Persons (AARP), 338
American Bar Association (ABA)
    ratings, 20, 303, 305, 311, 313
    Task Force on Signing Statements, 34*n*58, 34*n*61, 325, 333*nn*85–98
American Farm Bureau Federation, 391
American Federation of Labor, 316
American Gas Association, 390

Credits

12 Joseph E. Kallenbach, *The American Chief Executive: The Presidency and the Governorship* (New York: Harper and Row, 1966), chap. 2. **68** Data drawn from National Election Studies, Center for Political Studies at the University of Michigan's Institute for Social Research; Table 2a.1, http://www.umich.edu/~nes/nesguide/toptable/tab2a_1.htm. Responses to Question: "Generally speaking, do you usually think of yourself as a Republican, a Democrat, an Independent, or what?" **70** Excerpted from *Gallup Report*, November 1988, 6, 7; *The Gallup Poll Monthly*, November 1992, 9. Used by permission. 1996 data provided by Gallup Organization from poll conducted November 3 to November 4, 1996; 2000 data released Nov. 6, 2000, and posted on Web site, www.gallup.com.2004 data appear in *The Gallup Poll Tuesday Briefing*, November 5, 2004, 42–44. 2008 data from Gallup.com. http://proxy.nss.udel.edu:7410/poll/112132/Election-Polls-Vote-Groups-2008.aspx. **104** Michael Nelson, ed., *The Guide to the Presidency*, 2d ed., pp. 1698–1703. © 1996 by CQ Press. Reprinted by permission of the publisher. January 1996 to present from Gallup Web site www.gallup.com. **108 and 109** Samuel Kernell and Gary C. Jacobson, *The Logic of American Politics*, pp. 241 and 243. © 2000 by CQ Press. Reprinted by permission of the publisher. **118** Harold W. Stanley and Richard G. Niemi, *Vital Statistics on American Politics, 2003–2004* © 2003 by CQ Press. Reprinted by permission of the publisher. **146** Reprinted by permission of Greenwood Publishing Group, Inc. Westport, Conn., from *The Leadership Question* by Bert A. Rockman. © 1984 by Praeger Publishers; Fred I. Greenstein, *Personality and Politics*, p. 27. © 1975 by W.W. Norton. Used by permission of the author. **149** Harold W. Stanley and Richard G. Niemi, *Vital Statistics on American Politics, 1999–2000*, Table 6-2, 244–245. © 2000 by CQ Press. Reprinted by permission of the publisher. **153** Edward Pessen, *The Log Cabin Myth: The Social Backgrounds of the Presidents*, p. 68. © 1984 by Yale University Press, New Haven, Conn. Used by permission of the publisher. **162** James David Barber, *The Presidential Character: Predicting Performance in the White House*, 4th ed. (Englewood Cliffs, N.J.: Prentice Hall, 1992). **164** James David Barber, *The Presidential Character: Predicting Performance in the White House*, 4th ed. (Englewood Cliffs, N.J.: Prentice Hall,

1992). For Barber's views on Clinton, see the *News & Observer* (Raleigh, N.C.), January 17, 1993. **214** Adapted from Barbara Sinclair, "Hostile Partners: The President, Congress, and Lawmaking in the Partisan 1990s," in *Polarized Politics: Congress and the President in a Partisan Era*, Jon R. Bond and Richard Fleisher, eds. (Washington, D.C.: CQ Press, 2000), 145. **307** Drawn from tables 2 and 4 in Sheldon Goldman et al., "Picking Judges in a Time of Turmoil: W. Bush's Judiciary During the 109th Congress," Judicature 90 (May-June 2007), 272 and 282; and from table 6.1 (for Ford and Nixon) from Sheldon Goldman, *Picking Federal Judges: Lower Court Selection from Roosevelt through Reagan* (New Haven: Yale University Press, 1997), 227–229. Figures for George W. Bush courtesy of Sheldon Goldman. **315** Adapted from John Anthony Maltese, *The Selling of Supreme Court Nominees* (Baltimore: Johns Hopkins University Press, 1995), 3. Table 1. © 1995. **397, 399, and 401** John H. Kessel, *Presidents, the Presidency, and the Political Environment,* chap. 5. © 2001 by CQ Press. Reprinted by permission of the publisher. **424** Richard F. Grimmet, "War Powers Resolution: Presidential Compliance."*CRS Issue Brief for Congress,* Congressional Research Service, Library of Congress, September 20, 2001, http://www.house.gov/markgreen/crs.htm. **448** Cecil V. Crabb Jr. and Kevin V. Mulcahy, *American National Security: A Presidential Perspective,* p. 189. © 1991 by Thomson Learning. Used by permission of the publisher. **467** Jonathan Weisman, "Delays in Cabinet Nominations Demonstrate GOP Resolve," *Wall Street Journal,* January 24, 2009, http://online.wsj.com/article/SB123275672929711875.html#articleTabs%3Darticle. Used by permission.

PHOTOGRAPHS

1 AP Wide World Photos; **4** Library of Congress; **10** Library of Congress; **36** AP Wide World Photos; **49** AP Wide World Photos; **76** AP Wide World Photos; **92** Library of Congress; **110** Getty Images; **127** Reuters; **143** Reuters; **185** AP Wide World Photos; **200** Getty Images; **226** Reuters; **245** Pete Souza/White House via Getty Images; **249** AP Wide World Photos; **273** AP Wide World Photos; **298** AP Wide World Photos; **319** AP Wide World Photos; **334** AP Wide World Photos; **346** Getty Images; **368** National Archives; **403** Getty Images; **417** Reuters; **430** Reuters; **461** Reuters; **475** Reuters